THE CURSE OF BERLIN

For Margaret Legum:

In gratitude and
for Africa's future.

Adekeye Adebajo
Cape Town
December 2010

ADEKEYE ADEBAJO

The Curse of Berlin

Africa After the Cold War

Columbia University Press
New York

Columbia University Press
Publishers Since 1893
New York   Chichester, West Sussex
Copyright © 2010 Adekeye Adebajo

Library of Congress Cataloging-in-Publication Data

Adebajo, Adekeye, 1966–
   The curse of Berlin : Africa after the Cold War / Adekeye Adebajo.
     p. cm.
   Includes bibliographical references.
   ISBN 978-0-231-70200-3 (alk. paper)
   1. Africa—Foreign relations—1960– 2. Africa—Politics and government—1960–
   3. Berlin West Africa Conference (1884–1885—Influence. 4. Politicians—Africa.
   5. National security—Africa. 6. Hegemony. 7. African Union. 8. World politics—
   1989– Library 9. International relations—20th century. 10. International relations—21st
   century. I. Title.

   DT30.5.A334 2010
   327.6—dc22

                              2010012037

∞

Columbia University Press books are printed on permanent and durable acid-free paper.
This book is printed on paper with recycled content.
Printed in India

c 10 9 8 7 6 5 4 3 2 1

References to Internet Web sites (URLs) were accurate at the time of writing.
Neither the author nor Columbia University Press is responsible for URLs that
may have expired or changed since the manuscript was prepared.

Dedication

This book is dedicated to *Mzee* Ali A. Mazrui, foremost Prophet of Pax Africana and the undisputed doyen of Africa's international relations.

'The ancestors of Africa are angry. For those who believe in the power of the ancestors, the proof of their anger is all around us. For those who do not believe in ancestors, the proof of their anger is given another name... But what is the proof of the curse of the ancestors? Things are not working in Africa. From Dakar to Dar es Salaam, from Marrakesh to Maputo, institutions are decaying, structures are rusting away. It is as if the ancestors had pronounced the curse of cultural sabotage.'

Ali A. Mazrui, *The Africans*, 1986.

CONTENTS

PREFACE

BLACK BERLIN AND THE CURSE
OF FRAGMENTATION
FROM BISMARCK TO BARACK[1]

Ali A. Mazrui

It is one of the ironies of the great German leader Otto von Bismarck that he helped to unify Germany in the nineteenth century and initiated the division of Africa soon after. The unification of Germany led to the emergence of one of the most powerful Western countries in the twentieth century. The partition of Africa, on the other hand, resulted in some of the most vulnerable societies in modern world history.

In the second half of the twentieth century, Germany was divided again—but this time ideologically between communist East Germany and the capitalist Federal Republic of Germany.

German unification at the end of the twentieth century was almost a celebration of the centenary of Bismarck's final years as effective leader of the German Empire. Three European wars in the nineteenth century had helped unify the empire: Germany's war with Denmark in 1864, with Austria in 1866, and with France in 1871. Bismarck led the Germans in war and peace in this period—and he was made prince on 21 March 1871. He was appointed chancellor of the German Empire also in 1871 and proceeded to govern the Germans from that year until 1890. He became the most influential Western statesman of his day (see chapter 1).

Today, the most influential statesman of the Western world is Barack Obama—more by virtue of the power of the United States than as a result of his own sustained personal performance in world affairs for the time being. Out of the juxtaposition of Bismarck with Obama, a number of historical dialectics emerge, a number of political paradoxes. Obama is partly a descendant of the Africa that Bismarck had helped to partition.

Many Marxist-Leninist analysts have sought to establish an almost irrevocable link between colonialism and capitalism. And yet the histories of Germany and the United States have posed problems for that analytical perspective. In terms of performance as *capitalist* powers, Germany and the United States have been the most dazzling Western successes in the past century of capitalist history (for our purposes, Japan is not a Western power). But the latest global economic crisis, that began in 2007, has raised questions about the future of the West as a whole.

Dazzling as Germany and the United States have been in the *capitalist* game for a century, they have been relatively marginal as old-style *colonial* powers. Neither country built a large territorial colonial empire. The United States limited itself to the Philippines and a few islands as colonial possessions. Germany had a larger territorial appetite than the United States, but did not succeed in keeping its colonies for long.

In the history of territorial imperialism in the hundred years since the age of Bismarck, Germany and the United States have been dwarfs as colonial powers. Nevertheless, within the same period, Germany and the United States have often approximated the status of capitalist giants. That the two countries could be giants as capitalists and dwarfs as colonialists casts at least partial doubt on too easy a co-relation between capitalism and colonialism within the old Leninist paradigm.

The second dialectic concerning Germany and the United States is connected with the fact that Bismarck hosted a conference that officially launched the partition of Africa. The United States, on the other hand, produced citizens who launched the ideology of the unity of Africa. That conference that Bismarck hosted, in Berlin in 1884–1885, brought together some fourteen European powers. (Turkey was the sole non-Western representative). These states negotiated the ground rules for the European 'Scramble for Africa'. The United States was present at the Berlin conference, but did not compete for African territory.

On the other hand, US racial policies at home began to produce a cadre of African Americans who supported unification of the black world as a whole.

PREFACE

W.E.B. DuBois was born in February 1869 in Massachusetts. Before the end of the nineteenth century, he was active in the organisation of what became the first Pan-African Congress in 1900 (see chapter 12). Bismarck had played midwife to the partition of Africa. DuBois was to play midwife to the ideology of African unification. Yet divided Africa nevertheless managed to father a black president of the United States, Barack Obama, with potential credentials for helping Africa to transcend its fragmentation.

A related paradox concerned Bismarck himself, the man who unified Germany and helped to divide Africa. Even in the unification of Germany, he himself paid a price. As Ralph Haswell Lutz once put it: 'The tragedy of Bismarck's career was that he himself created in United Germany the monarcho-military power which first overthrew him and then, in the fateful years of 1914–1918, destroyed his empire.'[2]

Germany later had another fateful period under Adolf Hitler—eventually losing the Second World War (1939–1945) and being divided into East and West Germany for forty years. A new generation of German leaders in both East and West later attempted the Bismarckian task of another unification.

On the African front, Bismarck had declared a hundred years earlier, in 1889: 'I am not a colonial man.' And yet for a while, he succeeded in bringing Germany closer to the role of a colonial power in Africa than had any other figure in history. In the 1880s, Bismarck managed to gain control of Cameroon, Tanganyika (now Tanzania, following the incorporation of Zanzibar), Rwanda, Burundi, part of New Guinea, as well as South West Africa (now Namibia).

Bismarck had helped to set the stage for the West's penetration of Africa. His conference in Berlin in 1884–1885 had helped to define the rules of the annexation of the continent. For a while, Germany gained a share of the African spoils. Much later, Germany and the United States lived to become colonially peripheral powers but capitalistically central actors. The two countries built relatively small territorial empires, but against a background of considerable domestic capitalist development.

Both Germany and the United States touched the destiny of the black world. The United States was a major factor in the history of slavery. Germany was a major factor in the history of European imperialism as a whole—in spite of its own more modest colonial empire.

It just so happened that the last remaining colony in continental Africa in the 1980s was, in a sense, Bismarck's colony. This was Namibia in South West Africa. Once a German colony following the Conference of Berlin, it became a mandate of the League of Nations after the First World War (1914–1918)—and was then administrated by South Africa for seven decades.

South Africa was for a long time unenthusiastic about granting Namibia independence—least of all under the prospective rule of the South West African People's Organisation (SWAPO). Ronald Reagan's election as president of the United States in 1980 raised South Africa's hopes. Pretoria continued to drag its feet on the issue of Namibia's independence, urging Reagan to order his Western allies to cool their pressures on the apartheid regime.

Reagan's assistant secretary of state, Chester Crocker, disappointed South Africa in the end—and lent his weight to speedy independence for Namibia, mainly in order to facilitate a Cuban withdrawal from neighbouring and beleaguered Angola.

If it is indeed true that the Reagan administration became one of the architects of Namibia's independence by 1990, history had indulged its ironic sense of humour again. The last European colony on the African continent in the twentieth century was among the first of Bismarck's colonies in the nineteenth. And the United States was cast by history in the 1980s to recognise the claims of the Namibian people—and to put pressure on South Africa to relinquish Bismarck's last surviving black 'dependency'. It was a costly struggle. SWAPO fought hard and relentlessly. The logic of its heroism was at last recognised by both Washington and South Africa's Afrikaner successors to Bismarck.

By 1994, after 110 years of European penetration of the continent, Africa was trying to close the last chapter of partition with an election to abolish political apartheid in South Africa. Let us now look more closely at the wider ramifications of Bismarck's momentous Conference of Berlin.

Fragmentation and the Paradox of Racial Deficit

The partition of the continent unleashed unprecedented changes in African societies: political, economic, cultural, and psychological. This overview of those changes pays particular attention to their implications for problems of security and governance over that period of 110 years. It concludes with a search for solutions in the era of Nelson Mandela and Barack Obama.

As the new millennium unfolds, Africa consists of some fifty-four countries. Partly because of this fragmentation, at least a third of independent Africa has experienced large-scale political violence or war.[3] This does not include those countries that had relatively bloodless military coups d'état or occasional assassinations. After all, even the United States has had presidential assassinations.

Most of the political violence in Africa concerns ethnic, racial, religious, national, or ideological boundaries.

Countries differ in violence even when they are next-door neighbours. Barack Obama's father hailed from Kenya, which shares borders with five other countries. Four of those countries have experienced civil wars: Ethiopia, Somalia, Sudan, and Uganda. The fifth is Tanzania, which was partly born out of a revolution—the Zanzibar revolution of 1964. By comparison with its neighbours, Kenya has been spared large-scale civil conflict, except for a short but particularly violent upheaval in the aftermath of its 2007 election.

Let us now explore the subject of conflict in fragmented Africa in terms of a series of dialectical propositions—sometimes ironies, sometimes paradoxes, sometimes outright contradictions. At stake quite often are boundaries of identity, engulfed within frontiers of conflict.

Since the middle of the twentieth century, more people have died in Africa as a result of conflict between black and black than because of conflict between black and white. The 'tribal' divide has often been more deadly than the racial boundary. While anticolonial wars did cost a lot of lives (especially in places like Algeria, where more than a million people perished at the hands of the French), postcolonial wars have been even more ruthless.[4] The Algerian war was about the boundaries of France. Was Algeria part of France?

And yet the seeds of the postcolonial wars themselves lie in the sociological mess that the post-Berlin partition created in Africa by destroying ancient boundaries of identity and old methods of conflict resolution without creating effective substitutes in their place.

The Paradox of Fatal Borders

While most African conflicts are partly caused by borders, those conflicts are not necessarily *about* borders. The conflicts are partly caused by Bismarckian borders, because those were created by colonial powers to enclose groups with no traditions of shared authority or shared systems of settling disputes. The human chemistry between those groups has not necessarily had time to become congenial.[5]

On the other hand, African governments have tended to be possessive about colonial borders and have discouraged challenging them. The borders generate conflicts within them, but have not normally generated conflict across them. The border war between Ethiopia and Eritrea between 1998 and 2000 is more an exceptional interstate conflict than the rule.[6]

Between Religion and Ethnicity

While the worst conflicts in Arab Africa are at least partly religious, the worst conflicts in black Africa are ethnic (so-called 'tribal' conflicts). Algeria from 1991 had the worst conflict in Arab Africa proper, and the boundary was between Islamists and militant secularists. It was one of the ugliest wars in the world,[7] and spawned 100,000 deaths.[8] Egypt in Arab Africa has also had recurrent religious conflicts.[9] Again, the boundary has been between the sacred and the secular. The worst conflict in black Africa in the 1990s was between the Hutu and the Tutsi, especially the genocides in Rwanda and Burundi.[10] These recurrent explosions have been ethnic in the 'tribal' sense.

Sudan is caught in-between. Was the conflict between North and South primarily ethnic or primarily religious?[11] What about the Darfur chaos? Choose your own diagnosis. In Somalia, the conflict is often subethnic: between clans rather than between 'tribes'.[12]

Between Identities and Resources

While black against white in Africa is a clash over resources, black against black is more often a clash of identities. The thesis here is that racial conflicts in Africa are ultimately economic, whereas tribal wars are ultimately cultural. White folks and black folks fight about *who owns what*. Black folks and black folks fight about *who is who*. Apartheid in South Africa was ultimately an economic war. But Hutu against Tutsi is a cultural conflict. The demarcation of property may be less deadly than the clash of identities.

Modern Weapons, Premodern Armies

While African wars are fought with modern weapons, African armies are not yet modern armies. This is the boundary between the modern and the pre-modern. One of the destabilising forces that Bismarckian colonialism bequeathed to independent Africa was a standing army with Western weapons. One of the few African countries to consider whether to do without a standing army was Tanzania. In 1964, Julius Nyerere even had the opportunity to disband his entire army and not build an alternative one. He did disband the old one, but he did not follow Costa Rica's example and do without a military force.

At independence, the weapons were less modern but the armies more disciplined and professional. Now the weapons are more modern and the armies less disciplined and less professional. In Africa's armed forces, the boundary between the modern and the premodern is ominous. The weapons are of advanced technology; the disciplines are rustic and loose.

Between Dual and Plural Societies

While there are many more plural societies than dual societies in post-Bismarckian Africa, dual societies may be more dangerous in per capita terms. The distinction that this overview makes is between a plural society and a dual society.[13] A plural society is one that has multiple groups defined ethnically, racially, religiously, culturally, or by other parameters.

A dual society is one in which two groups account for over 80 per cent of the population. The United States is a plural society, but Belgium is a dual society of Flemish and francophone identities.[14] Dual societies run the following high risks:

Prolonged stalemate between the two groups, as in Cyprus between the Greeks and the Turks.[15]

Prolonged culture of polarised ethnic distrust, as in Belgium, Guyana, and perhaps Trinidad.

Prolonged period of tension and violence between the two groups, as in Northern Ireland and potentially between Berbers and Arabs in Algeria.

Separatism and secessionism either accomplished or imminent, as in Czechoslovakia (now split between Czechs and Slovaks)[16] or Sri Lanka (torn, for long, by a Tamil bid to secede from a Sinhalese-dominated polity).[17] Is there a risk in the future between the Shona and Ndebele in Zimbabwe?

Genocide and potential genocidal reprisal, as in the Hutu and Tutsi confrontations in Rwanda in 1994 and the fear of more genocidal eruptions in both Rwanda and Burundi.[18]

Between Regional and Ethnic Dualism

While ethnic dual societies should indeed be carefully watched, regional dual societies can be at least as dangerous. Regional dual societies include the following:

Sudan: North vs. South (civil wars 1955–1972 and 1983–2005).[19]
Nigeria: North vs. South (civil war 1967–1970).[20]
Uganda: North vs. South (civil conflicts since 1980).

United States: North vs. South (civil war 1861–1865)
Germany: East vs. West (post–Second World War).
Vietnam: North vs. South (post–Second World War).
Korea: North vs. South (post–Second World War).

On the evidence so far, dualism in society and politics may conceivably be even more dangerous than pluralism. A dual society often has a single divide that is potentially explosive. A plural society is better endowed with potential checks and balances.

Between Civil and Interstate Wars

While postcolonial Africa should indeed celebrate that it has relatively few conflicts between states today, should Africa also lament that it did not have more such interstate wars in the past? In fragmented Africa, has the balance between external conflict and internal conflict tilted too far to the internal side? And as human history has repeated time and time again, civil wars often leave deeper scars, and are often more indiscriminate and more ruthless than interstate conflicts, short of either a world war or a nuclear war. The United States, for example, lost more people in its own civil war in the 1860s than in any other single war in its 200–year history, including Vietnam and the two world wars.

Both before and after Bismarck, the history of the nation-state in Europe reveals a persistent tendency of the European state to externalise conflict and thus help promote greater unity at home. A sense of nationhood within each European country was partly fostered by a sense of rivalry and occasional conflict across the border with neighbours. And the consolidation of the European state as a sovereign state was also partly forged in the fire of inter-European conflicts. The Peace of Westphalia of 1648, which has often been credited as being the original formal launching of the nation-state system, was signed after thirty years of yet further interstate European conflicts.[21] The boundaries were sometimes national and sometimes religious—especially soon after the Reformation.

However, war has become too dangerous to be a reliable instrument of nation building and state formation in the future. If pluralism is to be diverted away from divisiveness towards more creative formations, certain positive values would need to be more clearly identified, cultivated, and institutionally consolidated. Borders need to be pacified, as in the case of the frontier between Ethiopia and Eritrea.

This is what brings constructive pluralism into relevance. On what values and principles does it need to rest? How can a constructive plural order be built?

Respecting Boundaries of Difference

Tolerance is measured by the moral and attitudinal yardstick of *acceptance of boundaries of difference*.[22] But we need to learn that victims of intolerance do not necessarily become paragons of toleration. The Christianity which suffered the tortures of Roman gladiators, became a religion of the Roman Inquisition of the sixteenth century. The Jews, who suffered under Hitler and the Nazis, became an occupying power in Palestine with thousands of political prisoners. The Muslims, whose entire calendar is a celebration of the Hijrah as asylum, are bombing each other's mosques across the sectarian divide in Southern Asia. The Tutsi in Rwanda as victims of yesterday have become the oppressors of today; and the Hutu as victims of today are destined to become oppressors of tomorrow. The price of toleration is eternal vigilance—cultivated and institutionally enforced. Boundaries of difference often need to be respected, in spite of the stresses of fragmentation.

Does constructive pluralism also involve maximisation of *choice*? One-party states restrict plurality of political organisation. Is proportional representation a better respecter of electoral choice and political pluralism than an electoral system that encourages a two-party state?[23] Is proportional representation a better respecter of ideological boundaries?

Let us now turn to the moral frontier both before and since Bismarck and since the partition of Africa. What about the clash between female circumcision and anti–female circumcision in relations between Africa and the West? Is pluralism endangered by the ferocity of the confrontation? What about polygamy in Africa? Is matrimonial pluralism constructive if undertaken entirely by consent? These are ethical boundaries that sometimes result in confrontations.

Concentration of power is, by definition, anti–pluralistic. Therefore, constructive pluralism needs conditions that enforce pluralization of power. Even in the new era of Barack Obama, is some degree of capitalism a precondition of constructive pluralism? All liberal democratic countries are capitalist, but not all capitalist countries are liberal democratic. ('All liberal democratic donkeys are capitalist animals, but not all capitalist animals are liberal democratic donkeys.')[24]

We referred earlier to how Bismarck laid the foundations of German preeminence in capitalism. Capitalism is a *necessary but not sufficient condition* for constructive pluralism, but Obama would insist that this capitalism must be regulated. Postcolonial Africa also needs to enhance and strengthen civil society at large.[25]

What about the primordial boundary between genders? Certainly, the empowerment of women requires special actions beyond capitalism. India is trying to secure reservation of seats in its legislature for women. I, too, have been consistently recommending the reservation of seats for women in African postcolonial legislatures, entailing three phases:

Phase I: Women candidates, women voters for the reserved seats.
Phase II: Women candidates, but voters will be both men and women in elections for the reserved seats.
Phase III: Abolish gender reservation of seats.

Throughout the three phases, women would still be free to compete with men for the remaining (nonreserved) seats of the legislature. The boundary between genders in postcolonial politics needs new rules of engagement.

Boundaries Between Civilisations

In discussing the 'Clash of Civilisations'[26] in the new millennium, there is a risk of mistaking symptoms of the postcolonial cultural disease for the disease itself. The deadly conflict in 2000 between Muslims and Christians in the northern Nigerian city of Kaduna was a symptom of the disease. The genocide perpetrated by the Hutu against the Tutsi in Rwanda in 1994 was a symptom of the disease. The rival African armies shooting at each other in the Democratic Republic of the Congo (DRC) in the new millennium are symptoms of the disease.

The 'Curse of Berlin' upon Africa relegates the continent to the bottom of the global heap, with the Western world at the top (see chapter 3). Africa has the largest percentage of poor people, the largest number of low-income countries, the least-developed economies, the lowest life expectancy, the most fragile political systems, and the most vulnerability to HIV and AIDS (whatever relationship there might be between HIV and the collapse of immunity systems in Africa). Berlin continues to cast its ominous shadow on a fragmented population.

The Western world, on the other hand, is triumphant at the top of the global caste system. What is more, the post-Bismarck Western world created the international caste system that reduced Africans to the 'Untouchables' or Harijans of global injustice. Borders can thus be hierarchical and not just horizontal.

Africa, since its partition, has seen its mineral wealth exploited for the benefit of others, its fertile land left undercultivated, its rich cultures destroyed, and its brain-power 'drained' to other parts of the world.

At the centre of this calamity is the role of the West in creating an international system that reduced proud Africans to the lowest caste of the twentieth century. How will postcolonial Africans overcome this condition in the twenty-first century?

In Search of Pan-African Solutions

Conflict prevention requires greater and greater sophistication in diagnosing conflict-prone situations. Unfortunately, Africa is full of contradictions— conflict generated by too much government versus conflict generated by too little, and conflict generated by too many ethnic groups, as distinct from conflict ignited by too few ethnic groups. It is dark outside. Africa is waiting for its real dawn. Hopefully, the wait will not be too long.

What is the solution in situations of acute state failure or political collapse? The state before total collapse may be the equivalent of a political refugee— desperate, bewildered, sometimes destructive, but fundamentally moaning to be rescued from a nightmare that may in part be of its own making. Are post-Berlin national borders in Africa to remain sacrosanct? We offer eight pan-African solutions to lifting this curse of fragmentation.

The first option is *unilateral intervention by a single neighbouring power* in order to restore order (see chapters 2, 5, and 6). There is the precedent of Tanzania's invasion of Uganda in 1979, with troops marching all the way to Kampala.[27] Tanzania then put Uganda virtually under military occupation for a brief period. The Ugandan state was temporarily a refugee camp. Tanzania's intervention was very similar to Vietnam's intervention in Cambodia in 1978 to overthrow Pol Pot—except that the Vietnamese remained in Cambodia much longer. The question arises whether Yoweri Museveni's Uganda[28] should have intervened more directly in Rwanda in April 1994 in a manner similar to which Julius Nyerere's Tanzania had intervened in Uganda fifteen years earlier.[29] Have Uganda and Rwanda also intervened in Zaire/Congo?[30]

The second cross-border scenario is *intervention by a single power but with the blessing of a regional organisation*. For a while, there was no real African precedent, but there was an Arab one—Syria's intervention in the Lebanese civil war in 1976 with the blessing of the League of Arab States. De facto, the Lebanese state was a refugee camp, with Syria as a sentry. Later, Nigeria's interventions in Sierra Leone and Liberia in the 1990s had wider blessing from the Economic Community of West African States (ECOWAS) (see chapter 6). The third scenario of cross-border intervention is *inter-African colonisation and annexation*. In a sense, this is a kind of *self-colonisation*. One precedent is Tanganyika's annexation of Zanzibar in 1964, partly under pressure from US president Lyndon B. Johnson and British premier Alec Douglas-Home. The West wanted to avert the danger of a Marxist Cuba on the clove island off the East African coast. Nyerere was persuaded that an unstable or subversive Zanzibar would be a threat to the mainland. He convinced the dictator of Zanzibar at the time, Abeid Karume, to agree to a treaty of union—using methods very much like those the British used to convince African chiefs to 'accept' treaties through which they ceased to be sovereign. Nobody held a referendum in Zanzibar to check if the people in the country wanted to cease being a separate, independent nation. But the annexation of Zanzibar was the most daring case of what became, de facto, Pax Tanzaniana. Ironically, Tanganyika had once been Bismarck's proudest African possession.

The fourth cross-border scenario as a solution to political collapse is *regional integration*. This is when the state as a political refugee is integrated with its host country. In the longer run, one solution to Rwanda and Burundi may well be a federation with Tanzania so that Hutu and Tutsi no longer have de facto ethnic armies of their own, but rather retrain their soldiers as part of the federal army of the United Republic of Tanzania. German colonialism before the First World War had leaned towards treating Tanganyika and Rwanda-Urundi as one single area of jurisdiction. All three countries had once been Bismarck's legacy to German imperialism.

Union with Tanzania for Rwanda and Burundi would, in the short run, be safer than union with the Democratic Republic of the Congo (formerly Zaire), in spite of both countries' shared post–First World War Belgian connection with the DRC and the link with the French language. Tanzania is a less vulnerable society than the Congo, and a safer haven for Hutu and Tutsi. It is indeed significant that, given a choice, Hutu and Tutsi on the run are more likely to flee to Tanzania than to the DRC, in spite of ethnic ties across the border with the Congo. Moreover, Hutu and Tutsi are becoming partially 'Swahilised' (speaking the Swahili language) and should be able to get along well with 'fellow' Tanzanian citizens. As citizens, they would be assimilated in due course; their former refugee state would be integrated. It would be a remarkable way of reversing the Bismarckian partition.

The fifth cross-border scenario for conflict resolution is the establishment of an *African Security Council*, complete with permanent members in the style of the fifteen-member United Nations Security Council. The current fifteen-member rotating Peace and Security Council of the African Union (AU) needs reconceptualisation. The permanent members could be Egypt or Libya from northern Africa, Nigeria from western Africa, Ethiopia or Uganda from eastern Africa, and the Republic of South Africa from Southern Africa (see chapter 2). There should be some nonpermanent members, ranging from three to five. The principle of permanent members would be reviewed every thirty years. For example, in another three decades, it may be necessary to add the DRC as a permanent member to represent Central Africa. In times of crisis, should the African Security Council meet at the level of African heads of state? Should each permanent member have a veto, as practised in the UN Security Council, or not? These issues would also need to be addressed.

The sixth cross-border scenario of conflict resolution in times of political collapse is *establishment of a pan-African emergency force*—a brigade to put out fires from one collapsed state or civil war before they spread to another, and to teach Africans the art of a Pax Africana (see chapter 2). Should this pan-African emergency force be independently recruited and trained in a specialised manner? Or should it be drawn from units of the armed forces of member states? And how are the training, maintenance, and deployment of the emergency force to be paid for? How can Western friends of Africa like the United States and the European Union help? Certainly the successes and failures of the Nigerian-led ECOWAS Ceasefire Monitoring Group (ECO-MOG) in Liberia in the 1990s should be studied carefully in preparation for this new venture.[31] There are times when renegade states are basically refugee states. Brutal villains in power are also pathetic casualties of history. The emergency force should be trained to use minimum violence. The US government under Barack Obama has now fortunately joined the search for answers (see chapter 13).

The seventh cross-border proposal is a *High Commissioner for Refugees and Displaced Africans under the African Union*. Since Africa has become one of the biggest concentrations of displaced persons in the world (generating one-third of all refugees on a continent containing only one-tenth of the world's population), it is increasingly imperative that Africans assume responsibility for at least some of the functions of refugee relief. What is demanded is not merely Africa's participation in refugee relief, but also Africa's *leadership*. An AU High Commissioner for Refugees and Displaced Africans, equipped with the necessary resources to coordinate with the Office of the UN High Commissioner for Refugees (UNHCR), would be a start.

Finally, the eighth cross-border scenario of conflict management would consist of *ad hoc solutions* from crisis to crisis—more in the tradition of mediation and a search for solutions than in the tradition of the use of force. Such ad hoc efforts are definitely much better than nothing, and could constitute a major part of Africa's search for Pax Africana: an African peace established and maintained by Africans themselves.

In this more modest tradition of intervention is the African Union's revised version of the Organisation of African Unity's (OAU) 1993 *Mechanism on Conflict Prevention, Management, and Resolution*, which for the first time gave the continental intergovernmental organisation a more active role in resolving internal civil conflicts (see chapter 12). Modest as the mechanism was, it signified a qualitative shift in the orientation of African heads of state. All these pan-African strategies would be partial attempts to reverse the post-Berlin partition of the continent.

The United Nations and Fragmented Cultures

But behind all the scenarios and all the search for solutions, behind the pain and the anguish, is the paramount question: Are we facing birth-pangs or death-pangs in the present crisis of boundaries of identity? Are we witnessing the real bloody forces of decolonisation—as the colonial structures within arbitrary borders are decaying or collapsing? Is the post-Berlin colonial slate being washed clean with the blood of victims, villains, and martyrs? Are the refugees victims of a dying order, or are they traumatised witnesses to an epoch-making rebirth? Civilisational, national, ethnic, religious, ideological, and other boundaries have been taking their toll.

Is this blood from the womb of history giving painful birth to a new order? And where does the rest of the world fit in? Africa overlaps with the Muslim world, and both are affected by the United Nations.

But we cannot talk about war and peace under the umbrella of the United Nations without discussing the UN's role in matters affecting Africa (see chapters 3 and 4).[32] The conclusion that has already been drawn from experience is that the universalism of states ostensibly achieved by the United

Nations is still a creature of the Western world—and the West still views the world partly through the tripartite lenses of medieval Islam duly adapted by the West.

What to medieval Muslim jurists was Dar el Islam, the Abode of Islam, has now become Dar el Gharb, the Abode of the West. Westerners are the preeminent pioneers. Until the 1990s, the Abode of War to Westerners was the communist world. Has the Abode of War now become the Muslim world, in all its complexity? Indirect warfare by the West included sanctions against Iraq before the US invasion of the country in 2003, sanctions that killed hundreds of thousands of children prematurely. Western-led sanctions against Libya in the 1990s also caused great suffering.

To some medieval Islamists there was the Abode of Ahd and/or Sulh—the home of contractual coexistence in exchange for tribute. Tribute is what the Western world has been receiving from most of the Third World in profits, interest on the crushing debt burden, and the returns on other forms of exploitation. And the United Nations has sometimes unwittingly provided an umbrella for this tripartite division of the world.

But when all is said and done, are there circumstances when the United Nations can be considered an *ally* of Africa and the Muslim world?

First, the UN is an ally in the *humanitarian role* of the world body and its agencies—such as responding to refugee crises or famine, drought, and other catastrophes. In such roles, it does not matter whether the immediate beneficiaries are Muslims, as in Somalia and Bangladesh, or non-Muslims, as in Rwanda. The UN is supportive of all such efforts.

Second, the United Nations is an ally when it provides an umbrella for mediation for some of the quarrels *between* Muslims or Africans—as in the effort to resolve the destiny of Western Sahara. In such instances, the UN helps Africa and the Ummah (the universalism of people) more directly. The UN helped in the quest for peace between Iran and Iraq in their 1980–1988 conflict. The UN has also helped Mozambique, Liberia, and Sierra Leone build peace in the 1990s and early twentieth century.

Third, the United Nations is an ally to Muslims when the world body provides peacekeeping troops and peacekeeping auspices in conflicts between Muslims and *non-Muslims* within or outside Africa. Over the years, United Nations troops have often been involved in the often thankless task of trying to keep the peace between the Arabs and the Israelis, especially prior to the Oslo peace process in 1993. Egypt, before its peace treaty with Israel in 1979, needed UN troops at times. The UN's long role in Cyprus since 1964 is another example of attempted mediation between Muslims and non-Muslims.

Fourth, the United Nations is allied to Muslims when the Western world has been divided! Africa and the Muslim world have sometimes propelled the UN to move decisively as an ally in such situations—as during the Suez war of 1956 when, in spite of the veto by Britain and France in the Security Council, the mood of the world body was opposed to the invasion of Egypt by Britain, France, and Israel. The US and the Soviet Union sometimes voted on the same side against Britain, France, and Israel.[33]

When the Western world was divided, the United Nations was also able to play a major *decolonizing role*. This is the fifth positive role of the UN. The United States was historically opposed to some of the older varieties of European imperialism. By the second half of the twentieth century, Washington was often on the same side as Moscow among the critics of old-style European colonialism.

Under these conditions it was indeed easier for the United Nations to become increasingly one of the great arenas for the anticolonial struggle waged by the peoples of Asia, Africa, and the scattered islands of the seas. The anticolonial role of the United Nations encompassed not only its Trusteeship Council but also its General Assembly, especially from the late 1950s onwards. This anticolonial role was often a great service to Africa and the Muslim world (see chapter 3).

Sixth, the United Nations can be an ally of the Muslim world when it takes seriously the idea of prosecuting war criminals and those who have committed crimes against humanity. Especially relevant for the Muslim world would be the prosecution of war criminals in Bosnia, some Serbs in Serbia, and many Serbs in Bosnia who committed crimes against humanity. The recent proceedings at The Hague have involved war crimes committed in Bosnia in the 1990s. The UN tribunal in Arusha, Tanzania; genocide in Rwanda; and 'ethnic cleansing' in Sudan's Darfur region are also relevant here. The United Nations has done well to appoint the relevant tribunals for these tasks, but has fallen far short of providing the resources for these complicated tasks.

Seventh, the United Nations has been an ally when Africa and the Muslim world were united. It has at times been possible to pass, through the UN General Assembly, highly contentious points of principle. The state of Israel is based on an ideology saying that a Russian who claims to be descended from Jews, and whose family has had no connection with the Middle East for the past two millennia, has more right to settle in Israel than a Palestinian who fled from Israel during the 1948 war. Was such discrimination racist? When Africans and Muslims were united in 1975, they managed to persuade the UN General Assembly to pass a resolution affirming that Zionism was a form of racism. But when Africans and Muslims were divided in 1991, that resolution was repealed by an overwhelming majority.

When Africans and Muslims were united, they could persuade the UN General Assembly not only to defy the United States, but also to move the Assembly itself out of New York in further defiance. Thus, when in 1988 the United States refused to grant a visa to Yasser Arafat, thereby preventing him from coming to New York to address the UN General Assembly on his recent declaration of an independent Palestinian state, the General Assembly denounced Washington's action as a violation of the host country's legal obligations under the 1947 Headquarters Agreement. The Assembly then shifted this December session to Geneva, Switzerland, to make it possible for the international diplomatic community to listen to Chairman Arafat. It was the first and only such move in the history of the United Nations. The unity of the African and Muslim members of the UN helped to persuade others to join their ranks.

Finally, is the UN an ally or an adversary of either African or Islamic values when the world body promotes such mega-conferences as the one in Beijing, China, in 1995 on the issue of women; the one in Copenhagen, Denmark, in 1995 on the issues of poverty and development; the one in Cairo, Egypt, in 1994 on the issue of population; and the one in Copenhagen in 2009 on the issue of climate change? Africans and Muslims themselves are divided as to whether these UN mega-conferences lead to the erosion of their values or help Islamic and African values find a new historical setting in the twentieth and twenty-first centuries. For example, are African and Muslim women being helped by the new global standards of gender equity being promoted at these conferences?

These mega-conferences have of course been global and have been part of the UN's universalism of nation-states. Some tension has at times been created with Islam's universalism of faith. But it is a tension that can itself be creative; it is a dialectic that can have a human face. At the very minimum, Africa, Islam, and the UN have one paramount interest in common: to ensure that Dar el Harb, the Abode of War, shrinks further and further into the oblivion of history, so that Planet Earth becomes a House of Peace at long last.

But we have to save the United Nations from being an extension of the US State Department in Washington, D.C., or being the diplomatic face of the

Brussels-based North Atlantic Treaty Organisation (NATO). We must save the United Nations from being manipulated by the five veto-wielding permanent members of the Security Council (the United States, Russia, China, Britain, and France), for reasons that have little to do with either world peace or the welfare of humankind (see chapter 3).

We must save the United Nations, with all its imperfections. And if Libya's Muammar Qaddafi is correct about the impending end of the nation-state, the United Nations organisation will one day become the United *Peoples* organisation, based on new principles of representation. Peace and the quest for conflict resolution will remain paramount imperatives.

Concluding Reflections: From Mandela's Legacy to Obama's Vision

A conference opened in Berlin in 1884 in order to inaugurate the era of competitive white imperialism in Africa. An election occurred in South Africa in 1994 to end the era of white minority rule on the continent. One hundred and ten years had elapsed since Otto von Bismarck launched the European 'Scramble for Africa'. What is the balance sheet of this chapter of African history—from Bismarck playing host to the Berlin conference to Nelson Mandela's election as president of post-apartheid South Africa?

There are at least two standards of evaluation. One is the depth or shallowness of the impact of European colonisation on Africa. How fundamental are the changes that were triggered across the decades by Europe's penetration of African societies? Were these 110 years the equivalent of a mere episode in millennia of Africa's experience? This is the *episodic* paradigm. Or did the era of European colonisation of Africa inaugurate the most far-reaching changes in Africa's recorded history? This is the *epic* paradigm.

The other standard of measuring the 110 years is on the basis of cost-benefit. What repercussions of European colonialism were beneficial for Africa and which ones were detrimental to African interests?

Let us first return to the standard of depth or shallowness of Europe's impact on Africa before evaluating whether the impact was helpful or harmful. According to the *epic* interpretation, the years 1884 to 1994 were not an ordinary century in Africa's experience. Those years unleashed unprecedented and wide-ranging changes in Africa—changes of immense implications for the peoples of the continent. Never before had the continent been subjected to such fundamental political, economic, cultural, and psychological influences as those transmitted during this period.

PREFACE

In this overview of the extended century since Bismarck, we have paid special attention to what went wrong in Africa in the aftermath of the European scramble for the continent. We have indeed implied that the colonial changes were both negative and deep. However, on the issues of security and governance, we have argued that some of the adverse repercussions of European penetration can indeed be reversed or corrected.

The continent that Bismarck's conference partitioned and racialized has eventually produced historical figures comparable to Bismarck in stature, but more positive in their impact on the human condition. One such figure is Nelson Mandela, who has contributed to the deracialization of the African continent (see chapter 10). The other is Barack Obama, who is redefining the racial history of the world (see chapter 13).

But in what ways have Nelson Mandela and Barack Obama—both Nobel peace laureates—been cast by history to help not only reverse the partition of the African continent, but also heal the division of the black world? Nelson Mandela is the most distinguished of the citizens of the African continent. Barack Obama has become the most elevated of the citizens of the African diaspora. While in prison for twenty-seven years, from 1963 to 1990, Mandela united the black world through his *martyrdom*. While campaigning for the US presidency in 2008, Obama united the black world through his *ambition*. Mandela became globally famous because of nearly three decades of heroic suffering. Obama became globally famous by the rapidity of his political triumphs. Mandela made history by refusing to be *vanquished*. Obama made history by insisting on being *victorious*. Mandela was part of the vanguard of the struggle against apartheid in South Africa. Obama was the ultimate beneficiary of the civil rights movement of the 1950s and 1960s in the United States.

For twenty-seven years while he was in detention, Nelson Mandela was a role model for the black world as a whole because he stuck to his principles in the face of adversity. Mandela has been a role model for Barack Obama, as well as for many others. There are signs that, like Mandela, Obama has learnt to stick to his principles in the face of massive adversity.

In the context of 'global Africa' as a whole, the torch has indeed been passed from an African warrior in his nineties to a black campaigner in his forties, from a former president in Africa to a new president in America, from an old voice of unity still reverberating from Southern Africa to a younger voice of redemption echoing in the African diaspora.

Mandela is one of the architects of a *post-racism* age. Obama is helping to foster a *post-racial* condition. A world without racism is not necessarily a world without race consciousness. Mandela is an abolitionist to end racism as prejudice; Obama seeks to realise a world without race-consciousness as a demographic category.

These are major steps towards reversing the global repercussions of the Berlin conference of 1884–1885. But other ghosts of Bismarck's conference will continue to haunt Africa for a few more generations to come. The struggle against the legacy of Berlin continues.

Ali Mazrui is director of Binghamton's Institute of Global Cultural Studies at the State University of New York. He was head of the Political Science Department and dean of the Faculty of Social Sciences at Makerere University in Uganda; and director of the University of Michigan's Centre for Afro-American and African Studies. Mazrui is one of the world's most prolific and controversial writers on Africa, having authored more than thirty books and hundreds of essays. In 1986, he wrote and hosted the influential nine-part documentary *The Africans: A Triple Heritage*, which established his global reputation. Mazrui obtained his doctorate from Oxford University, and has served in an advisory capacity to numerous organisations, including the United Nations.

ACKNOWLEDGEMENTS

Between 1986 and 1987, I spent a year studying at the Friedrich Schiller University in the East German town of Jena, and discovered one of my favourite cities in the world: Berlin. Two years later, after I had completed my bachelor's degree in German at the University of Ibadan in my native Nigeria—which included, as subsidiary subjects, precolonial African history taught by members of the famous 'Ibadan School of History', as well as the study of German historical figures such as Otto von Bismarck and literary figures such as Bertolt Brecht—the Berlin Wall fell, symbolising the end of the Cold War. This was the same year in which I won a Rhodes Scholarship to study international relations at Oxford University. In the town of 'the dreaming spires' a year later, I encountered the legacy of Cecil Rhodes, whose indelible imprint on the city included the towering Rhodes House and a statue on Oxford's high street. Before arriving at Oxford, I had spent the summer at the Alliance Française in the sleepy French town of Rouen in Normandy, where I was exposed to the rural charm and cultural arrogance of a country that had pursued the most neocolonial policies in post-independence Africa, while skilfully doing the most to promote European economic integration after the Second World War.

The Cold War came to an end in Africa, resulting in the independence of Namibia in 1990, the launching of a Nigerian-led peacekeeping mission to halt Liberia's civil war in the same year, the disappearance of the Soviet Union from the map of the world in 1991, and the first democratic election in South Africa in 1994: events that defined the start of the continent's post-apartheid era. I personally witnessed apartheid's funeral and the saintly Nelson Mandela's inauguration as president while serving as a United Nations electoral observer in South Africa in May 1994. Further studies took me to the United States to deepen my understanding of the post–Cold War era: the Fletcher

School of Law and Diplomacy in Massachusetts, the Brookings Institution in Washington, D.C., and Stanford University's Centre for International Security and Cooperation in California. In between, I served a year with the United Nations mission in Western Sahara—Africa's 'last colony'—where I witnessed a visit by the first African UN Secretary-General: Egypt's Boutros Boutros-Ghali. I also spent six months on a UN humanitarian mission traversing Iraq's eighteen governorates.

In the second post–Cold War decade, five more years were spent at the International Peace Academy (IPA)—now the International Peace Institute—in New York, where I worked to support and produce knowledge on Africa's fledgling regional organisations. Here, I had a front-row seat to the 'sacred drama' and the 'play within a play' that is the United Nations, at a time when the organisation was headed by its second African Secretary-General: Ghana's Kofi Annan, whom I encountered at annual board dinners of IPA, an institution of which he was the honourary Patron. In the big, rotten apple, I also taught a course for three years as an adjunct professor on conflict resolution in Africa at Columbia University's School of International and Public Affairs, seeking to combine theory and praxis. The next five years saw the 'return of the native', with my arrival at the southernmost tip of Africa to head the Cape Town–based Centre for Conflict Resolution (CCR), where I witnessed the last five years of the presidency of Thabo Mbeki, who oversaw the transformation of the Organisation of African Unity into the African Union in the South African port city of Durban in 2002. Throughout this period, I had travelled widely from the Cape to Cairo, visiting twenty-six African countries mostly during trips based around my work on strengthening Africa's security architecture. It was, for example, during one of these trips to Accra, that I directly encountered the legacy that Kwame Nkrumah had left on Ghana, memorialised by a magnificent bronze statue in the capital's main square.

Discussions at a conference in Singapore in 2005 to commemorate fifty years of the Afro-Asian Bandung Conference reminded me of the legacy of Mohandas Gandhi for both continents. I would later deliver the Gandhi memorial lecture at the Gandhi settlement (where the Mahatma had lived during some of his twenty-one years in South Africa) in Durban in 2008. Both events gave me an opportunity to research the increasing economic role of China in Africa. During a talk in Cape Town in 2006, I provocatively challenged a visiting African American freshman senator to explain why the Congressional Black Caucus, which had so heroically fought apartheid South

Africa, was now so weak on African issues. Two years later, the same senator—Barack Obama—whose father was Kenyan, was elected the first black president of the United States. Thus the past two decades (1989–2009), as covered in this book, have seen tremendous changes in global affairs in general and Africa's international relations in particular, with the end of the Cold War and the beginning of the post-apartheid era. These events have also represented something of a personal intellectual odyssey for this author, who entered the field at the dawn of the post–Cold War era. I have thus tried to reflect these personal and professional experiences in *The Curse of Berlin*.

I have attempted here to write the sort of book that I would like to have read while starting out in this field twenty years ago. While studying international relations in England and the United States during the first post–Cold War decade, much of the literature was extremely Eurocentric, and Africa was very marginal to Western concerns. The theories and concepts we learned related almost entirely to the West, the authors we read were disproportionately Western, and European history in the twentieth century masqueraded as world history! It was during this period that I stumbled upon a Kenyan author called Ali A. Mazrui while looking for literature that was not written by dead white men or Eurocentric thinkers! Few have thought as profoundly, or written and spoken as eloquently, about Africa as this committed Pan-African Prophet. I was immediately amazed at the master wordsmith's elegant and unconventional style, unflinching commitment to pan-Africanism, tremendous intellectual honesty, and fierce independence of thought. From this moment, I have often mined the vast treasure trove of what is now termed 'Mazruiana'. On topics ranging from African security, the United Nations, Afro-Asian cooperation, hegemonic leadership, external intervention in Africa, and pan-Africanism, to the significance for Africa of towering figures like Mahatma Gandhi, Kwame Nkrumah, Gamal Abdel Nasser, Muammar Qaddafi, Nelson Mandela, Thabo Mbeki, and Barack Obama, this Kenyan scholar has been writing insightfully about many of these issues for over four decades. On some of these subjects, Mazrui's was often the only solid literature available. I have thus dedicated this book to the 'Global African' to whom I personally owe an immense intellectual debt, as will be evident in these pages. It is my good fortune and particularly appropriate that Ali Mazrui generously agreed to contribute a substantial preface to introduce the book, one that masterfully draws together the threads of its main themes.

Many other debts have been accumulated over the past generation. First, I wish to acknowledge the unflinching support of my family—'Auntie', Tilewa,

ACKNOWLEDGEMENTS

Kemi, and Femi—who have encouraged me enormously and consistently throughout my twenty-year exile from the ancestral home. I would also like to thank my teachers at Oxford: my supervisor, Gavin Williams; and A.H.M. Kirk-Greene and Geoffrey Best, who taught me 'Africa's International Relations' and 'The Politics of the UN and Its Agencies' respectively. David Keen has been a mentor and friend since I first arrived at Oxford. Chris Landsberg arrived in the 'city of lost causes' a year after me to study international relations and stimulated my interest in South Africa, becoming a close academic and policy collaborator over the next two decades. In the US, my teachers and mentors on African politics and public policy included Martin Kilson, W. Scott Thompson, Pearl Robinson, Ibrahim Gambari, Margaret Vogt, Francis Deng, Michael O'Hanlon, and Stephen Stedman. I also thank the members of the soccer teams at St. Antony's College, Oxford, and the Fletcher School, for ensuring that, in pouring rain or glorious sunshine, the 'Beautiful Game' was always prioritised ahead of research!

James Mayall, who had earlier examined my doctoral thesis, was kind enough to review this entire manuscript and to offer extremely helpful comments. Roger Southall also read an earlier version of the manuscript and offered invaluable comments for which I am grateful. I thank a final anonymous reviewer for his or her comments. I must also thank all the other mentors, friends, teachers, and colleagues who generously read parts of this document, offered insightful suggestions, and hopefully helped me to avoid errors of fact and judgement: Amitav Acharya, Adebayo Adedeji, Kweku Ampiah, James Barber, Mwesiga Baregu, Mats Berdal, Simon Chesterman, Christopher Clapham, Devon Curtis, Sam Daws, Mette Eilstrop-Sangiovanni, Dianna Games, Keith Gottschalk, Chris Hill, John Hirsch, John Iliffe, Maureen Isaacson, James Jonah, Darren Kew, Gilbert Khadiagala, A.H.M. Kirk-Greene, Francis Kornegay, Chris Landsberg, Daniel Large, Garth Le Pere, Elisabeth Lindenmayer, David M. Malone, Khabele Matlosa, Hartmut Mayer, Paul Maylam, Raufu Mustapha, Musifiky Mwanasali, Bill Nasson, Angela Ndinga-Muvumba, Mike Pugh, Sarah Rowland-Jones, Chris Saunders, Tor Sellström, Ricardo Soares de Oliveira, See Seng Tan, Martin Uhomoibhi, Margaret Vogt, Kaye Whiteman, Gavin Williams, Douglas Yates, and Dominik Zaum.

In addition to the other institutions mentioned earlier, I would like to acknowledge the support of Devon Curtis, Megan Vaughan, and the staff of the Centre of African Studies at Cambridge University, where I spent a five-month sabbatical as a visiting fellow completing this book in a majestic and

ACKNOWLEDGEMENTS

idyllic setting. Eight of these chapters have been published in an earlier form, but have mostly been revised and updated here. Six new unpublished chapters (including the introduction) have also been added. I thank the institutions that allowed me the opportunity to test out many of these ideas during my time in England: the universities of Cambridge, Oxford, East London, Cranfield, Reading, Kent, Leeds, King's College London, and Chatham House in London.

In completing the book, I was fortunate to have been able to renew my collaboration with Jason Cook, a talented copy-editor with whom I had worked on three earlier books on West Africa's international relations. I'd like to thank him for responding with such professionalism and skill, and for meeting what looked like an impossible deadline! I'd also like to thank Michael Dwyer and his team at Hurst Publishers, as well as Glenn Cowley (who strongly believed in, and supported, this project from the very start), his successor Debra Primo, and their team at University of Kwazulu-Natal Press.

Finally, at the Centre for Conflict Resolution, Cape Town—my current employer—I would like to thank the board—particularly the dedicated chair until December 2009, Leon Levy—and staff, for the support that allowed me to complete this project. I must especially acknowledge the tremendous research support of CCR researcher Dawn Nagar, and the tireless efforts of CCR librarian Margie Struthers, who always responded with friendly efficiency to what must have seemed like endless requests to find literature and source photographs. She managed to track down every source I needed, for which I am most grateful. Finally, I wish to thank the main funders of CCR's Africa Programme: the governments of the Netherlands, Denmark, Sweden, Switzerland and Finland.

Adekeye Adebajo, Cape Town, April 2010

INTRODUCTION

BISMARCK'S SORCERY AND AFRICA'S THREE MAGIC KINGDOMS[1]

'[M]y map of Africa lies in Europe. Here is Russia, and here ... is France, and we are in the middle; that is my map of Africa.'[2]

Otto von Bismarck, chancellor of Germany, 1871–1890

Africa. A breathtaking continent of spectacular beauty conjures up extreme images of paradisiacal Eden as the birthplace of humankind and home to some of the greatest early civilizations. In stark contrast, for Afro-pessimists, Africa is a conflict-ridden, disease-afflicted 'Dark Continent' that offers a glimpse of apocalyptic Armageddon. For prophets of Afrophilia, the continent represents the probable beginning; for apostles of Afrophobia, it represents the possible end. However, for many Africans, it was the plague of European locusts in the form of European colonialism and imperialism that brought a 'Hundred Years of Pestilence' to their continent after the 1884–1885 Conference of Berlin, hosted by Germany's 'Iron Chancellor', Otto von Bismarck. European Pharaohs placed Africa in bondage, and the continent became entrapped between what Kenyan scholar Ali Mazrui described as the 'Legacy of Westphalia' (the cage of the nation-state) and the 'Protestant Ethic' (the prison-house of the capitalist system).[3]

The deleterious impact of the European presence distorted African politics, economics, and society; damaged indigenous cultures; and retarded socioeconomic development. Though Africa also benefitted from Western technology and education, this was done in a destructive and authoritarian manner that damaged rather than complemented indigenous systems. Africa's post-independence leaders have largely lacked the vision and resources, and sometimes the ingenuity and discipline, to reverse this legacy in the fifty post-independence years. In his Reith lectures of 1979, Ali Mazrui described Africa as a 'Garden of Eden in decay', lamenting how the most ancient of continents had squandered its bountiful inheritance. Paradise was lost, as European imperialists—led by Bismarck—committed the geopolitical version of the 'original sin'. As Mazrui poetically put it:

The Garden of Eden is in disrepair. Much of the natural beauty is still there, some of it lush, some of it rugged. The White Nile finds its way from Lake Victoria towards the Mediterranean, against the background of the Mountains of the Moon of Uganda. The rugged savanna country extends over hundreds of miles elsewhere. The torrents of Victoria Falls pound their way down to eternity. The sand dunes of the Sahara and Kalahari have their own story of majestic barrenness. Yes, man's first home is still beautiful—but the scars of the original sin are in evidence.[4]

November 2009 marked the twentieth anniversary of the fall of the Berlin Wall as well as the 125th anniversary of the start of the Conference of Berlin: both were significant events for Africa. The main argument here is that Africa suffers from a curse invoked in Berlin. The Berlin conference of 1884–1885, which was overseen by Otto von Bismarck, dealt with the issues of free trade in the Congo and the Niger as well as the status of protectorates, effectively setting the rules for the partition of Africa as the 'Scramble' for the continent's riches began. Berlin represented the compromises of avaricious European imperialists—Britain, France, Germany, Portugal, Belgium, Italy, and Spain—rather than the political and economic interests of Africa. The European curse of artificial nation-states has thus caused untold suffering in postcolonial Africa, resulting in unviable, dependent economies, artificially imported political systems, weak and Balkanised states, and insecure borders. In fifty years of independence, Africans have not done enough to reverse this blighted legacy. However, in order to understand contemporary African events and craft a better future, one must inevitably first understand the past. As the old adage goes, you have to understand where you are coming from in order to know where you are going.

As the Cold War was coming to an end, events in Berlin would once again have an enormous impact on Africa. The fall of the Berlin Wall in 1989 marked the end of the division of Germany and Europe, as well as the end of communist rule in Eastern Europe. But the earlier curse of Berlin remained to haunt Africa's future. Conflicts and disputes, some resulting from the colonial legacy of Berlin, continued between countries such as Ethiopia and Eritrea, Somalia and Ethiopia, Libya and Chad, and Nigeria and Cameroon. Other conflicts had more immediate internal roots. Where Africa had once feared intervention during the Cold War, marginalisation had now become a greater concern in the post-apartheid era. Attention, aid, and investment shifted to the emerging democracies of Eastern Europe, and resources were later diverted from African conflicts to reconstruction efforts in Afghanistan and Iraq by 2003. Africans had failed to overcome the colonial legacy of Berlin, as economic and political systems were still tied to those bequeathed by imperial statesmen in Berlin. African leaders had also failed to create effective regional integration schemes to overcome the bondage of the boundaries inherited from the era of the Berlin conference. Berlin is thus a metaphor to describe Africa's colonial and postcolonial experiences, as well as its continuing challenges of breaking the bonds of the political, economic, and cultural chains inherited from the colonial state.

We must briefly explain the title of this book: *The Curse of Berlin*. In the Christian tradition, the curse is as old as the Garden of Eden, which is believed to have been located in Africa. According to the Bible, God invoked the first curse for the 'original sin' after Adam and Eve—tempted by the Devil in the form of a serpent—had eaten the forbidden apple from the Tree of the Knowledge of Good and Evil. As a result of God's triple curse, Man had to work hard to harvest the land, Woman suffered pain in childbirth, and the Serpent crawled on its belly, being an enemy of humankind (Genesis 1–3). A curse is also a fundamentally African phenomenon in which much of the continent's population still believes. Senegalese filmmaker and writer Ousmane Sembène's brilliant 1974 movie *Xala* deals with a curse that rendered its businessman-victim impotent: an impotence that symbolized that of the post-independence African state. The more recent phenomenon of 'Nollywood' (the thriving Nigerian film industry) is also rife with stories of curses, reflecting widespread societal beliefs on the continent.[5]

As our title, *The Curse of Berlin* reminds us, historical and structural events continue to affect and shape Africa's contemporary international relations. This book adopts a historical approach even though its main focus is on contemporary issues. Part 1 focuses on Africa's quest for security. Its three chapters examine Africa's security institutions, which emerged largely from efforts at regional integration; the political, peacekeeping, and socioeconomic roles of the United Nations in Africa; and Africa's two UN Secretaries-General:

Egypt's Boutros Boutros-Ghali and Ghana's Kofi Annan. Part 2 assesses Africa's quest for leadership. Its five chapters examine the hegemonic roles of South Africa, Nigeria, China, France, and the United States on the continent. Part 3 examines Africa's quest for unity. Its five chapters assess the roles and significance for Africa of six historical figures—Nelson Mandela, Cecil Rhodes, Thabo Mbeki, Kwame Nkrumah, Barack Obama, and Mahatma Gandhi—and also analyse the African Union (AU) and European Union (EU) in comparative perspective.

If we are to understand Africa's current international relations properly, we cannot avoid examining the deleterious impact of the colonial era on Africa's development; the effects of the Cold War and the pernicious ideological battles of the superpowers—the United States and the Soviet Union—as well as France, on the continent; and the damaging effect of often externally backed autocratic misrule and economic corruption. France's arrogant postcolonial declaration of francophone Africa as a *chasse gardée* (a private hunting-ground) from which outsiders were excluded, must be understood by the need to restore some national honour and glory after humiliating defeats by Otto von Bismarck in 1871 and Adolf Hitler in 1940. China's current building of railways and roads to secure Africa's raw materials and minerals follow the same pattern established by European imperial powers over a century ago, with the important difference that Beijing is not setting up administrations and armies to control these countries. The current widespread fears of Washington, London, and Paris, as well as mostly white South African businessmen, that Beijing could exclude their own firms from these territories, are in some ways reminiscent of the fears that drove Bismarck to call the Conference of Berlin in 1884, effectively to set the rules for Africa's peaceful partition. Will contemporary Great Powers contemplate another peaceful economic partition of the continent, or will Africa's leaders muster the political will to craft regional economic and political arrangements to forestall such a ghastly outcome?

The UN's current role in Africa cannot be explained without providing a background of the role of the world body in Africa's decolonization efforts, and its significance as a protector of the sovereignty of African states and their aspirations to achieve rapid socioeconomic development. South Africa's contemporary role in Africa cannot be assessed without reference to the incredible psychological and cultural damage inflicted on the population by the country's racist leaders, the destructive military destabilization of the continent by the apartheid army, and the mercantilist actions of white South African entrepreneurs. The allure of Africa's most industrialised state can be explained by its status as Africa's 'El Dorado', with the Johannesburg gold rush of the 1880s (and Kimberly diamond rush of the 1870s) attracting buccaneers like Cecil Rhodes, tens of thousands more white settlers, as well as large financial capital from Western banks and governments. Similarly, Nigeria's current foreign policy role can only be properly understood through knowledge of the country's perception by its leaders as a 'Giant of Africa' playing a leadership role in the continent's decolonization and anti–apartheid efforts and seeking to provide peacekeeping leadership in Chad, Liberia, and Sierra Leone. The current role of the US, France, and China in Africa is inseparable from the destabilizing role that Washington and Paris played on the continent during the Cold War; as well as from Beijing's efforts to promote solidarity with African states as part of the 'global South' while opportunistically seeking to gain political advantages in its ideological struggle with Moscow.

Understanding Africa's contemporary leaders also requires a historical approach, and two of the continent's most prominent recent leaders—Nelson Mandela and Thabo Mbeki—are assessed respectively in comparison to the historical legacies of Cecil Rhodes and Kwame Nkrumah. The examination of US president Barack Obama's background and potential contributions to his country's policy towards Africa must necessarily be considered in the historical background of the pernicious US policies towards the continent during the Cold War. To understand the African Union, a historical background of the Organisation of African Unity (OAU) and the pan-African movement is essential. Also useful are potential comparative lessons from the European Union. Finally, contemporary Afro-Asian relations are assessed here within the historical background of the contributions of India's Mahatma Gandhi— surely the most important liberation leader of the twentieth century—as well as the cooperation that emerged between both continents after the 1955 Bandung conference, which culminated in the decolonization struggles waged largely through the Non-Aligned Movement (NAM) and the United Nations. This book thus assesses contemporary issues focusing centrally on how the past has shaped the present.

Despite the focus of the book on the 'Curse of Berlin', and on Africa being carved up by avaricious imperialists, we do not in any way wish to suggest that Africa and Africans have no agency in contemporary international relations. This story is still one of the continent trying to transform itself from a 'pawn' to a 'player' on the global geostrategic chessboard.[6] As Nigerian novelist Chinua Achebe wisely noted: 'Until the lions produce their own historian, the story of the hunt will glorify only the hunter.[7] The leadership roles of states such as South Africa and Nigeria are thus highlighted here; the visions and strategies of African statesmen—Kwame Nkrumah, Gamal Abdel Nasser, Nelson Mandela, Thabo Mbeki, Olusegun Obasanjo, Muammar Qaddafi, Boutros Boutros-Ghali, Kofi Annan, Adebayo Adedeji, and Alpha Konaré— are also given prominence. The contributions of African institutions such as the OAU, the AU, the Economic Community of West African States (ECOWAS), the Southern African Development Community (SADC), the Intergovernmental Authority on Development (IGAD), the Economic Community of Central African States (ECCAS), and the Arab Maghreb Union (AMU) in contributing to decolonization, regional integration, and peace-making efforts on the continent are recognized. Africa's potential to craft mutually beneficial political and economic alliances with external actors such as the UN, the EU, the US, and Asia is also investigated. The continent and its 800 million citizens are thus portrayed not merely as helpless victims of colonialism, but as actors on the poorest continent in the world seeking often courageously, despite incredible odds and constraints, to chart their own way forward to promote political unity and economic development in a difficult global environment.

We also do not wish to place the blame for all of Africa's contemporary problems on the European-inherited borders and European imperialism. But it is important to note that one cannot properly assess Africa's current situation without considering its colonial inheritance, which for better or worse—mostly for worse!—has largely determined Africa's contemporary international situation. The political and economic impact on Africa of the Berlin conference will therefore be examined, focusing on the damage to African political institutions and efforts to build sustainable economies. In the area of cultural imperialism, journalistic 'Afro-pessimist' writing by Western analysts has often followed in the notorious footsteps of authors such as Joseph Conrad and Graham Greene. This writing—which we have termed here as representing a form of 'Afrophobia'—still insists on stereotyping the continent with an apocalyptic brush. In response, scholars like Chinua Achebe, Ngugi wa Thiong'o, Frantz Fanon, and Edward Said have sought to 'deconstruct' these examples of 'Afrophobia'. Said, in particular, has noted the importance of culturally dehumanizing analyses of 'natives', and the simultaneous promotion of Western superiority, to the broader political imperial agenda. Analysts like Niall Ferguson and Michael Ignatieff, after the now discredited US invasion of Iraq in 2003, also seemed to want to revive the

'New Imperialism' of the nineteenth century at the dawn of the twenty-first.[8] The flippant insensitivity of such writing requires one to remind such prejudiced Western authors of the tremendous political, socioeconomic, and cultural damage that imperialism inflicted on Africa, Asia, the Caribbean, and Latin America.

This book mainly covers the twenty years of the post–Cold War era in Africa's international relations (1989–2009), with this introduction providing a background of the main impact on the continent of the hundred-year period after the Berlin conference, from 1884 to 1989. Africa's history has often tended to move in generations of roughly twenty to thirty-year periods: 1880–1910 saw the 'Scramble for Africa' when the colonization of the continent was largely completed; 1936 (Italy's colonization of Ethiopia) to 1957 (Ghana's independence) saw the growth of the nationalist struggle that resulted in the independence of the continent; and a 'Thirty Years War' was waged largely between 1960 and 1990, to free the rest of the continent from colonial and apartheid rule.

Our current twenty-year period in this volume (1989–2009) has seen monumental changes in Africa's international relations: the redefinition of pan-Africanism from political decolonization to socioeconomic decolonization with the death of the Organisation of African Unity and the birth of the African Union in 2002; the liberation of South Africa, the continent's richest and most industrialized country, which produced visionary leaders in Nelson Mandela and Thabo Mbeki between 1994 and 2008; the hegemonic peacekeeping role of Nigeria in Liberia and Sierra Leone between 1990 and 2003 in a quest for Pax Nigeriana; China's staging of a spectacular return to the continent, becoming its third largest external investor and ruffling Western economic feathers in the process; the declining of Africa's membership at the United Nations from a third during the Cold War to a quarter after the Cold War; the election of two Africans, Boutros Boutros-Ghali and Kofi Annan, as UN Secretaries-General during the critical post–Cold War period of 1992–2006; the historic election of Barack Obama, an African American with a Kenyan father, as US president in 2008 amidst a global financial crisis; the creation by the EU of the world's most far-reaching effort to integrate a continent; and Afro-Asian cooperation that saw China and other countries like India, Pakistan, Japan, and Malaysia investing in and keeping peace in Africa in a bid to revive the legacy of Mahatma Gandhi that had proved so instrumental in the political liberation of both continents. These are the trends we wish to understand in order to explain the most salient features of Africa's international relations over the past two decades. But first we must examine the political, socioeconomic, and cultural legacy of the Conference of Berlin of 1884–1885.

Bismarck and Africa's Century of Pestilence

Europe's Geostrategic Grandmaster

In talking of Otto von Bismarck's sorcery in the title of this introduction, it is important to note that sorcerers use supernatural power over others through evil spirits and witchcraft. Bismarck was undoubtedly the Grand Wizard of the Berlin conference. The effect of his colonial policies was that the German sorcerer and his European apprentices (Britain, France, Belgium, Portugal, Italy, and Spain) employed the Western wizardry of the technology of the industrial revolution of the Victorian age—scientific and technological advances; mass production of goods; improvements in health; global finance; expansion of railways and roads; the telegraph; and the maxim gun—to set the rules for the 'Scramble for Africa'. Europeans had even sometimes resorted to fireworks, electric batteries, and musical boxes as part of their repertoire of magic tricks to dazzle the 'natives'.[9] Bismarck used his political magic wand to cast a spell on Africa, having earlier done the same in Europe. The result of the damaging legacy of the German chancellor's sorcery was to force postcolonial Africa to pursue the three magic kingdoms of security, hegemony, and unity, in a bid to break the Bismarckian curse. This quest has, so far, proved as elusive as the earlier quest of greedy Europeans to find an African El Dorado (countries flowing with gold). In order to ensure peace in Europe through an intricate system of continental alliances, the German chancellor was the evil genius whose system also ensured the diversion of European quarrels and energies to dividing up Africa. As Ali Mazrui put it: 'One of the great paradoxes about Otto von Bismarck was that he united the Germans and helped to divide Africa.'[10]

Though they could not save their continent from colonial enslavement, the gods of Africa would invoke their own curse on Europe: exactly thirty years after the Berlin conference had set the rules for the partition of Africa, Europe's technological wizardry and industrial might was turned on itself as the First World War devoured the cream of European youth. A devastating conflict that resulted in over 9 million deaths marked the inexorable decline of the continent as the centre of the world's geopolitics. Russia's revolutionary leader Vladimir Lenin had famously described the First World War as the final 'imperialist war' that had its roots in the capitalist system.[11] The global conflict also marked the end of Germany's African 'Empire', as Cameroon, Tanganyika (now Tanzania), Togo, Rwanda, Burundi, and South West Africa (now Namibia)—territories five times larger than Bismarck's Reich—were parcelled out among Britain, France, Belgium, and South Africa. After the Second World War, Africa's ancestors invoked another curse in which Germany and Europe were themselves divided for nearly five decades, in the same way that Africa itself had been divided by Bismarck and his fellow imperialists. It is to the tale of Germany's Iron Chancellor and the significance of the Berlin conference for Africa that we must now turn our attention.

Otto von Bismarck became chancellor of Germany in 1871, the same year that he united the plethora of princely Germanic kingdoms through means of 'iron and blood'. This followed three decisive wars with Denmark (1864), Austria (1866), and France (1870–1871). Bismarck was a vain and arrogant man with boundless energy and a ravishing appetite for food and drink. A descendant of a Junker family of Prussian officers, he became known as the Iron Chancellor and an 'honest broker' who established an intricate network of political alliances that would largely preserve peace on continental Europe for four decades. He was a Colossus who bestrode the German Reich unchallenged for two decades, a political genius of realpolitik, and a supreme strategist. Under his guidance, Germany had become the leading industrial and military power on continental Europe. His biographer A.J.P. Taylor described Bismarck as 'the greatest master of diplomacy in modern history',[12] while H.L. Wesseling noted:

Bismarck's diplomatic talents were legendary. He had an exceptional intelligence, an amazing gift for languages, and great familiarity with Europe. He was hard to outdo in cynicism or misanthropy, be it by word of mouth or in writing. His diplomacy was consistent but opportunistic. Its foundations were patience and caution, but these qualities went hand in hand with resolution and quickness of action, for Bismarck believed firmly that chances did not come twice.[13]

Bismarck was the ultimate pragmatic strategist who understood well the uses and limits of power, and the need for military restraint and diplomatic skill to achieve a finely balanced diplomacy in order to maintain his complex set of alliances. These qualities were as present in his European diplomacy as they would be in his approach towards acquiring colonies in Africa. As the German chancellor himself noted: 'Politics are not a science based on logic;

they are the capacity of always choosing at each instant, in constantly changing situations, the least harmful, the most useful.'[14]

Bismarck had previously been known to oppose colonies in Africa, noting that 'I was not born to be a colonialist', and that Germany was 'not yet rich enough to afford the luxury of colonies'.[15] He felt that colonies were a wasteful venture that would drain resources, requiring expenditure on administration and defence, particularly since Germany, unlike Britain, lacked the commercial companies to exploit resources in the colonies and a large navy to patrol these territories. Bismarck changed his mind for three main reasons. First and most important, as the quotation at the beginning of this introduction suggests, Bismarck regarded Africa as an extension of the geopolitical struggle for leadership in Europe. As long as he could divert France's attention away from the painful loss of Alsace Lorraine in 1871, and exploit the rivalry between London and Paris over Egypt, West Africa, and the Horn of Africa; the Iron Chancellor could safeguard his intricate web of European alliances through acting as an 'honest broker' over Africa. As William Roger Louis noted: 'Europe, not Africa or the Pacific, continued to govern Bismarck's policy.'[16]

Bismarck secured the League of Three Emperors among Germany, Austria-Hungary, and Russia in 1873 to prevent a Russian attack on Austria-Hungary. He crafted the Triple Alliance between Germany, Austria-Hungary, and Italy in 1882 (after Rome was frustrated by Paris over colonial claims in Tunisia) to contain Austria's Italian rival. Bismarck felt that the credibility of this role in the end necessitated that he acquire an African empire, and possess territory that could, if necessary, be traded off with Britain and France to maintain much more important strategic relations in Europe. For example, in discussing his support of Belgian King Leopold's annexation of the Congo in August 1884 against French claims and British and Portuguese manoeuvring, Bismarck did not think the territory would be viable, but felt that it would 'always be useful for diverting troublesome rivalries ... that we could handle less easily ourselves'.[17]

The Iron Chancellor often offered to support France against Britain in Egypt, exploited differences with the British over Zanzibar, and created mischief by cosying up to the Boer Republics in South Africa to annoy the British. France believed that Egypt belonged to it, having 'owned' it under Napoleon Bonaparte, who had made his famous expedition to the land of the Pharaohs in 1798. Britain perceived Egypt as a valuable possession and key strategic route to India. London was also keen to settle British colonists in South Africa, particularly with the discovery of diamonds and gold by the

1880s. In order to secure French rapprochement, Bismarck picked quarrels with England. He would later settle his quarrel with Britain over Zanzibar in an attempt to secure British support for Austria against Russia. Africa was thus a pawn on a European strategic chessboard with the German chancellor as the Grandmaster, inviting European powers to settle their disputes over Africa in Berlin. Germany also wished to avoid a Franco-Russian alliance, while Britain sought German support against Russia.[18] As A.J.P. Taylor has noted: 'The German colonies were the accidental by-product of an abortive Franco-German entente.'[19]

Bismarck regarded the relationship between his country and England as resembling that of 'a wolf and a shark, both dangerous animals, but unable to get at each other'.[20] He never hid his irritation at British imperial greed in wanting to declare a 'Monroe Doctrine for Africa', claiming large tracts of territory—also in areas of German interest like South West Africa and Cameroon—without any effective occupation.[21] As the German chancellor graphically noted: 'The Englishman is like the dog in the fable... The dog who cannot bear that another dog should have a few bones, although the overfed brute is sitting below a bowl full to the brim.'[22] Bismarck often accused British officials of *Deutschfeindlichkeit* (hostility to Germany). But importantly, his quarrels with London were also a way of Berlin getting closer to Paris.

The second reason for Bismarck's change of mind over colonies related to powerful interest groups and German agriculture and industry seeking expansion and protection. Groups like the Gesellschaft für Deutsche Kolonisation (Society for German Colonisation) and the Kolonial Verein (Colonial Association) were pushing strongly for a German empire in Africa, describing the issue as a *Daseinsfrage:* a matter of life and death. These groups believed that colonies were a source of British industrial might and commercial enterprise,[23] and argued in favour of colonies due to the profits from new markets, particularly as the industrial heartland in the Ruhr had been blighted by a decade-long global Great Depression.[24] German commercial groups like the Hamburg Chamber of Commerce and Bremen tobacco merchants were warning Bismarck that their firms would be excluded from large parts of Africa, as the British were looking to annex Cameroon, Togo, and parts of South West Africa; the French were looking to seize Gabon; and the Portuguese and Belgians were looking to corner the Congo.[25] These groups also advocated a German empire in Africa as a means for Germany to relocate its surplus population abroad, in an early incarnation of Adolf Hitler's *Lebensraum* (living space) argument for the conquest of Eastern Europe. (In the British context, Cecil Rhodes had also championed the idea of acquiring colonies to settle surplus British populations and to create new markets for British goods.)[26] German business and other groups were thus gripped by a *Torschlusspanik* (door-closing panic), in which they felt that they would be excluded from the African El Dorado that British and French explorers were constantly evoking.[27] If German unification had been a question of 'blood and iron', the partition of Africa would be one of 'blood and treasure'.

The final reason that Bismarck sought an African empire was to derive short-term electoral advantage and, in the longer term, to gain prestige. Germany's public, press, and parliament (*Reichstag*) were calling loudly for colonies, and Bismarck ultimately felt that it was better to ride than resist the tide. As he noted: 'All this colonial business is a sham [*Schwindel*], but we need it for elections.'[28] The Iron Chancellor also recognised the prestige involved in an African empire, while Europe's most prominent historical figure of the age also feared the harsh judgment of history. As Bismarck told the German Diet in January 1889: 'I must remember that in twenty or thirty years' time I might be reproached for having been that timid chancellor who lacked the courage to secure for us what has turned out to be so valuable a possession.'[29] With an African empire based eventually on a quest for a *Mittelafrika* sphere of influence linking Tanganyika to South West Africa across the Zambezi river, the German chancellor launched his country into the era of *Weltpolitik*.

The Conference of Berlin

The 'New Imperialism' that erupted into the 'Scramble for Africa' by the 1880s was often described in terms of a game that frequently appeared to be played by petulant and pampered public schoolboys in the English tradition. Bismarck often talked derisively of the *Kolonialtummel* (the colonial whirl), while the French talked of *le grand jeu* (the great game). By the time the gun was fired before the dawn of the 'Naughty Nineties', avaricious *fin de siècle* European imperialists were pursuing the 'race to Fashoda', 'blind man's bluff' (often having no detailed ideas of the territories to which they were laying claim), the colonial 'steeplechase', and the 'gambler's kick'. They sought their own 'place in the sun', a sun, we were told, would never set on the British Empire. But thankfully the sun did set on the British and other European empires, and the greatest imperialist power—England—would eventually become the 'legatee of a declining estate', suffering one of the most spectacular declines of a contemporary Great Power after the Second World War, as another curse of Africa's ancestors was invoked. This imperial drama involved squabbling colonial governments; devious explorers of Africa's four great river systems—the Niger, the Zambezi, the Nile, and the Congo—like Heinrich Barth, David Livingstone, Henry Stanley, and Pierre Savorgnan de Brazza; vicious capitalist-politicians like Cecil Rhodes and King Leopold; and sanctimonious Christian missionaries too numerous to name. As has often been noted, Africa was conquered by the white man carrying the Bible in one hand, and the gun in the other.

Africa was often described in culinary terms as food to be devoured by greedy imperialists in juicy morsels at the avaricious imperial banquet in Berlin. The continent was frequently compared to a big fruitcake to be shared out: Tunis was described as a 'ripe pear', and terms like 'plums' and 'cherries' were bandied around to describe the compromises struck by European imperialists over African territories. Bismarck had rather appropriately described European imperialists as greedy dogs collecting more and more bones. Africa was notoriously declared a *res nullius*—a no-man's land—by European imperialists. Since the continent was inhabited by 'uncivilised natives' who were considered subhuman by many European leaders and scholars, the land could simply be seized and exploited by white colonialists. British explorer David Livingstone had described colonialism in the apparently benign terms of the 'three Cs': Commerce, Christianity, and Civilisation. The more malign 'three Ps' may, in fact, have been more accurate: Profit, Plunder, and Prestige. As English poet Hilaire Belloc so memorably put it: 'Whatever happens, we have got the Maxim gun, and they have not.'[30]

As late as 1880, very few African territories had come under direct European rule, and 80 per cent of the continent was still ruled by its own leaders. In 1880, the French colonized Algeria, while coastal stretches of Angola and Mozambique were under Portuguese rule.[31] Several historians have dated the beginning of the 'Scramble for Africa' to the British occupation of Egypt in 1882. A year earlier, France had declared a 'protectorate' over Tunisia. The breakdown of the Anglo-French-Egyptian conference of June 1884 clearly showed the depth of antagonism between London and Paris, as the two European imperial robber barons continued to squabble over stolen territories.[32] France declared a protectorate over Porto-Novo in Dahomey (now Benin) in January 1883, transferring its acrimony with Britain from North to West Africa.[33] Even before sending out invitations to the Berlin conference in October 1884, Bismarck himself had extended the *Reichsschutz* (the protection of the Reich) to South West Africa (now Namibia) and acquired that territory along with Cameroon and Togo by August 1884, as well as New Guinea in December 1884. A day after the end of the Berlin conference in February 1885, he acquired German East Africa: clear evidence, if any were needed, that the Berlin conference was indeed about how to ensure an orderly partition of Africa.

That conference began in snow-filled Berlin on Saturday, 15 November 1884. Fourteen largely Western powers (Germany, France, Britain, Portugal, Belgium, Spain, Italy, Russia, Austria-Hungary, the United States, Denmark, Sweden/Norway, the Netherlands, and Turkey) attended the meeting. This conference at which Africa's fate was effectively sealed was held in a music room with a large chandelier, red curtains, and grey marble pillars—the site of the famous Congress of Berlin that had settled European continental quarrels six years earlier—at Bismarck's official residence in Wilhelmstrasse. Significantly, no African representatives were present around the horseshoe table, even as delegates discussed a continent's future with a map of Africa in the background of the room.[34] European princes, barons, counts, and lords met in Berlin to set the rules for a continent's partition without even considering any indigenous African presence necessary. This was despite the legal fiction of treaties having earlier been agreed with many African leaders.

Germany's Iron Chancellor started the conference with a speech in French that championed Livingstone's 'three Cs': Commerce, Christianity, and Civilization. Bismarck disingenuously argued that the conference aimed to promote the 'civilisation' of the 'natives' by opening up Africa's interior to commerce and Christianity. He outlined the three main goals of the meeting: promote free trade in the Congo, ensure free navigation on the Congo and the Niger, and agree on rules for future annexation of African territories. The chancellor ended by hoping the meeting would serve the cause of peace and humanity.

Anglo-French rivalries lay at the heart of this conference, with Bismarck throwing his weight behind Paris and then London to ensure that both powers continued to remain rivals, and that Berlin could keep diverting their attention away from European disputes. Bismarck had opposed earlier British attempts to 'give' Portugal the mouth of the Congo, and the Anglo-Portuguese treaty was rendered a dead letter when Bismarck refused to recognise it in June 1884. France, which was less industrialized than Britain and Germany at the time, was also the world's leading protectionist nation (Portugal was another leading protectionist power). The German chancellor was particularly keen to ensure international control of the Congo river similar to that of the

Rhine and the Danube, and he described the Congo as 'the Danube of Africa'.[35] In Berlin, Britain regarded France as 'the enemy' and was prepared to make concessions to Bismarck on everything but the Niger. London, in fact, refused to discuss the Niger at the same level as the Congo, in an area in which it regarded commercial interests to be critical. In Whitehall and among British public opinion, the Niger was regarded, without any apparent sense of irony or arrogance, as an 'English river', since British explorers and traders had opened it up, and since it was under the protection of the Union Jack.[36] In the end, Bismarck backed London on the Niger in order to achieve free trade in the Congo.[37]

One of the most significant outcomes of the Berlin conference was Bismarck's successful support of Belgian King Leopold's annexation of the Congo: the continent's second largest country, covering a tenth of Tropical Africa. This triggered the start of one of the most sordid episodes in European imperialism, with widespread atrocities and forced labour on rubber plantations overseen by Belgian colonial authorities resulting in perhaps 10 million African deaths.[38] Leopold deceitfully sought to portray himself as a philanthropist through his International Association of the Congo, whose agents had signed 'treaties' with illiterate Congolese chiefs granting the association an exclusive commercial monopoly. The monarch even managed to secure US political support for his Central African empire, promising philanthropy and free trade in order to woo Washington. Leopold did not personally attend the meeting, but had intermediaries present in Berlin. Fearing that the Congo would be sold to Britain; France (which allied with Portugal in Berlin over the Congo) had agreed a treaty with King Leopold in April 1884.

During the Berlin conference, Bismarck also pushed London to sign a treaty recognizing Leopold's claims to the Congo in December 1884, with the veiled threat that Berlin would support Paris over disputes on the Niger if the British did not play ball. The delegates in Berlin thus effectively acted as midwives of the monstrosity that came to be known as the Congo Free State (Belgium would later formally annex the territory in 1908). Even though the meeting had agreed—at France's request—not to discuss sovereignty in Berlin, agreements such as these made it clear that informal negotiations in the corridors of the conference did address such issues, even if they were not discussed in the plenary sessions. Horse-trading over boundaries, flags, and territories often occurred away from the horseshoe table in Berlin. Leopold's representatives went to Paris in the middle of the Berlin conference in December 1884 to negotiate with the French government, thus effectively securing recognition of the Gallic position in Equatorial Africa. Bismarck also pressured the Portuguese to recognize Leopold's fiefdom in the Congo, before a final deal was struck in a rainy Berlin in February 1885.

On the final issue of setting rules for 'effective occupation' of African territories, the conferees in Berlin agreed that this term should apply only to coastal areas and exclude established protectorates. This suited Britain and France in particular, since they were laying claim to the largest territories on the continent. In the final agreement, any country setting up a protectorate in coastal areas would have to inform other signatories and would also have to exercise effective authority over the area. This agreement made possible the signing of the General Act of Berlin in February 1885. In his final speech to the conference, Bismarck summarized the meeting's achievements: free access for all Western nations to Africa's interior, free trade in the Congo basin, and consideration for the welfare of the 'native races' in providing them with the benefits of 'civilization'. This landmark conference in Berlin would prove to be a watershed in African history: it had set the rules for trade, navigation, and control of Africa to avoid conflicts among European nations. The deal for the peaceful partition of the 'Dark Continent' was sealed. A day after Berlin ended, Bismarck declared a protectorate over modern-day Tanzania, again exposing the hollowness of the humanitarian rhetoric that sought to mask the territorial ambitions that dominated the meeting. Berlin had fired the starting gun for the imperial partition, and in the next two and a half decades, almost the entire landmass of Africa would be parcelled out among European powers. As British premier Lord Salisbury later noted about the Scramble: 'We have been giving away mountains and rivers and lakes to each other, only hindered by the small impediment that we never knew exactly where they were.'[39]

Berlin represented an avaricious banquet at which gluttonous, corpulent European imperialists feasted on territories that clearly did not belong to them. They sought in the process to cloak the fraudulent scheme under patronizing and paternalistic moral platitudes of a *mission civilisatrice* (civilizing mission) that Africa's 'noble savages' had never agreed to. Berlin and its aftermath were akin to armed robbers forcibly breaking into a house and sharing out its possessions while the owners of the house—who had been tied up with thick ropes—were wide awake, but were powerless to prevent the burglary. It would be hard to find examples in world history in which a single meeting had had such devastating political, socioeconomic, and cultural consequences for an entire continent. As the *Lagos Observer* noted at the conclusion of the conference on 19 February 1885: 'The world has, perhaps never witnessed until now such highhanded a robbery on so large a scale. Africa is helpless to prevent it... It is on the cards that this "Christian" business can only end, at no distant date, in the annihilation of the natives.'[40] In similar vein, Nigerian nationalist leader Herbert Macaulay noted in 1905 about the European partition of Africa: 'The dimensions of the "true interests of the natives at heart" are algebraically equal to the length, breath and depth of the whiteman's pocket.'[41]

Political and Economic Impact of the Partition

Western scholars like Ronald Robinson and John Gallagher have often sought to explain imperialism by talking of the need for colonial powers like Britain to acquire African colonies in order to protect sea-lanes to India, frequently stressing strategy over conquest. Such analysts, however, engage in sophistry of the worst form.[42] It is almost as if Britain had some God-given right to conquer, rule, and exploit India as the 'greatest jewel in its imperial crown': an arrogance that Mahatma Gandhi heroically exposed as bankrupt in shattering the edifice of British imperialism. Surely, one cannot justify two wrongs to make a right by ignoring the moral bankruptcy and greed involved in colonizing India in the first place. An initial theft of territory on one continent surely cannot be used to justify further thefts on another continent! India was widely believed to have provided the capital for Britain's industrial revolution,[43] and the subcontinent was importing 40–45 per cent of British cotton by the end of the nineteenth century, helping the imperial power's international balance of payments: as clear a sign, if any more were needed, of the economic value of many colonies.[44] As British historian Eric Hobsbawn noted about the many Western scholars who reject economic explanations of imperialism: 'much of this literature amounts to denying facts which were obvious enough at the time and still are ... the division of the globe had an economic dimension ... the scramble for West Africa and the Congo was primarily economic.'[45] Much of this literature in the West has also tended to rely on one-sided sources in European government archives, as if history can simply be told objectively from information produced by self-justifying imperial politicians and administrators.

Modern scientific techniques were introduced into African colonial territories that led to the production of minerals and cash crops including cocoa, coffee, palm oil, rubber, cotton, phosphates, diamonds, gold, and tobacco. African economies were structured to produce crops to meet European consumer needs, a trend that accelerated during the Second World War between 1939 and 1945. This both increased the dependence of African economies on metropolitan economies, and in many cases negatively impacted the ability of African economies to produce their own food. Africans imbibed Western consumption patterns without Western production methods. The profits from African mines were spectacular enough for European imperial powers and their financial institutions to invest large sums of money in building railways on the continent. A driving motive for the Anglo-Boer war of 1899–1902 had clearly been the need by the British to protect gold mines. The search for new markets amidst a global Great Depression in the early 1880s was another widespread concern that spurred on imperialism.[46] Trade and missionaries had clearly followed the British flag, heeding their prime minister Lord Palmerston's credo: 'It is the business of Government to open and secure the roads for the merchant.'[47] Tens of thousands of British emigrants (50,000 in a single year) had sailed for South Africa's goldfields to make their fortunes in the 1880s in a venture backed financially by the City of London. In the process, the metropolis of Johannesburg was created, dominated by ruthless Randlords. Cecil Rhodes—one of the greatest beneficiaries of this 'gold rush'—had memorably noted that the British flag was his greatest commercial asset.[48] The gold from South Africa massively increased the Bank of England's own reserves[49], much to the gratitude of the 'Old Lady of Threadneedle Street'.

European imperialists also employed policies of *divide et impera* (divide and rule) to sow the seeds for many of Africa's post-independence problems by hastily transplanting institutions from the West without adapting them to fit African conditions. The British preservation of the Emirates of Northern Nigeria, the Kabakaship of Buganda, and the Sultanate of Zanzibar—which all resembled English monarchical institutions—would later lead to instability in post-independence Nigeria, Uganda, and Tanzania.[50] As Sudanese scholar Francis Deng perceptively noted:

African countries have yet to achieve clarity on what political framework will best manage their rich diversities of people, achieve good governance, and draw upon indigenous African cultures, values, and institutions as sources of strength and legitimacy... [T]he legacy of constitutions and political frameworks left behind by colonial powers has proven largely ineffective... [I]f an African nation's constitution and its attendant governing framework are to embody the *soul* of that nation, as they are expected to do, they must reflect the essential cultural values and norms of all of the nation's people and build on *their* worldview as the starting point for constitutionalism.[51]

Colonialism also had a devastating effect on African institutions by often allying itself to the most conservative leadership, concerned more with preserving the status quo than encouraging social reform or political change.[52] Colonial rule often represented 'imperialism on a shoestring' with a 'thin white line' of administrators.[53] By the mid-1930s, a mere 1,200 British administrators ruled over 43 million people in Tropical Africa; French West Africa's 15 million people were administered by 385 colonial officials; while 728 Belgian administrators ran the huge territory of the Congo.[54] Colonial administrators often regarded the Western-educated African elite as competitors for their positions and privileges, and often dismissed them as 'trousered natives' (complementing earlier colonial stereotypes of the 'lazy native' and the 'backward native'). British soldier-administrator Frederick Lugard, who was the architect of the policy of 'indirect rule' through traditional rulers and also created modern Nigeria in 1914, despised the 'Europeanised Africans' of Southern Nigeria in the same way that he had loathed the 'politically-minded Indians' while serving on the Asian subcontinent.[55] Similar to Livingstone's 'three Cs', Lugard had argued that Britain had a 'dual mandate' in Africa: Europe benefitted from African products, while Africans received manufactured goods as well as a Lugardian 'substitution of law and order for ... barbarism.'[56]

As a former colonial officer in Northern Nigeria and prolific scholar, A.H.M. Kirk-Greene, put it: 'Politics for the average British colonial administrator was something of a dirty word, with "politician" not far removed from "trouble-maker."'[57] There was no serious long-term preparation of Africans for self-government,[58] and much of the constitutional engineering and leadership training in Africa occurred in the decade after the end of the Second World War. European colonial powers also tended to favour certain African groups and regions, thus creating political and socioeconomic disparities in development, as well as marginalized groups and areas in countries like Nigeria, Sudan, Côte d'Ivoire, Senegal, the Democratic Republic of the Congo (DRC), Rwanda, and Burundi, which later erupted into post-independence conflicts. As Ugandan scholar Mahmood Mamdani noted in explaining the historical background to the Rwandan genocide of 1994, in which 800,000 people perished: 'The great crime of colonialism went beyond expropriating the native... *The greater crime was to politicize indigeneity.'*[59]

Some positive developments did, however, occur during the colonial era, though such progress would clearly have been better delivered on African terms without European domination and authoritarian rule. European colonial powers did build roads, railways, harbours, telegraphs, and telephones, though this infrastructure was often of a limited nature and often planned to transport African resources to coastal cities for export to Europe. Christian missionaries provided Western education, but tended to destroy African cultural beliefs in the process.[60] African women were also marginalized in access to education and the professions, a trend that has continued into the post-independence era. The fact that university education and constitutional development were introduced to African territories after the Second World War was a clear sign of the lack of priority given to such critical sectors. Most independent African countries had very few trained personnel to run the administrative systems inherited from colonial rule.

The creation of small, unviable states and many landlocked territories further contributed to the difficulties of development after independence. Imperialism damaged inter-African trade as well as the ability of countries to feed themselves. Colonial rule, however, provided hospitals, piped water, and sanitation, but again, these were very unevenly spread and concentrated largely in urban areas. For example, in Nigeria by the 1930s, there were twelve modern hospitals for 4,000 Europeans, compared to fifty-two such facilities for 40 million Nigerians.[61] The situation was also exacerbated by the social segregation and apartheid that was practiced in African colonies by European administrations. As the late Ghanaian historian Adu Boahen noted in his poignant elegy to imperialism: 'the colonial era will go down in history as a period of wasted opportunities, of ruthless exploitation of the resources of Africa, and on balance of the underdevelopment and humiliation of the peoples of Africa.'[62] It is to this humiliation and cultural imperialism that we next turn our attention.

Afrophobia and Cultural Imperialism

The late Palestinian American intellectual Edward Said's 1994 book *Culture and Imperialism* showed how culture was historically used by Western authors in support of the imperial project and to denigrate other cultures. Said deconstructed the prejudiced writings of eminent authors such as Joseph Conrad, Graham Greene, and V.S. Naipaul, criticising 'the stereotypes about "the African [or Indian or Irish or Jamaican or Chinese] mind", the notions about bringing civilization to primitive or barbaric peoples, the disturbingly familiar ideas about flogging or death or extended punishment being required when "they" misbehaved or became rebellious, because "they" mainly understood force or violence best; "they" were not like "us", and for that reason deserved to be ruled.'[63] What I refer to here as 'Afrophobia' thus represents conscious or unconscious stereotyping that dehumanises Africans.

Joseph Conrad expressed cultural imperialism in his 1899 novella *Heart of Darkness*. Though himself a Polish émigré to Britain who was able to see through the corruption of imperial domination, as Said notes, Conrad was ultimately unable to accept that the African characters he portrayed in his book also had independent lives and cultures not controlled by Western imperialism. In a celebrated 1975 critique of *Heart of Darkness*, Chinua Achebe described Conrad as a 'purveyor of comforting myths' and a 'thoroughgoing racist' whose work is 'a story in which the very humanity of black people is called in question'. As the Nigerian author noted: 'Heart of Darkness projects the image of Africa as "the other world", the antithesis of Europe and therefore of civilization, a place where man's vaunted intelligence and refinement are finally mocked by triumphant bestiality... Conrad did not originate the image of Africa which we find in his book. It was and is the dominant image of Africa in the Western imagination.'[64] The Africans in the book are depicted as animals who do not speak but make 'a violent babble of uncouth sounds'. They are mere props on the stage of a grand European imperial narrative.

Another apostle of Afrophobia was British author Graham Greene. In his travels through Liberia and Sierra Leone in the 1935 novel *Journey Without Maps*, Africans are consistently dehumanised. Despite a recognition of the damaging impact of Western colonialism on Africa, there is the same Conradian stereotyping: constant talk of diseases and plagues, with the 'natives' being described as similar to 'devils', groaning madmen 'without a tongue', 'cows', 'grasshoppers', and 'flies', and depicted as alternatively lazy or happy.[65]

Such attitudes of Afrophobia were reflected in J. Smith's 1851 book *Trade and Travel in the Gulph of Guinea*, which had chapters such as: 'Human Sacrifice—Nailing Prisoners, Jack Ketch, Decapitation, cooking and eating human flesh. King Pepple eats King Amacree's heart.'[66] Eerily similar stereotypes were employed during Liberia's civil war between 1989 and 1997. Journalistic headlines of the conflict read: 'They Cooked My Brother's Heart and Ate It' (South African journalist Philip van Niekerk in *The Observer*) and 'Sharks and Alligators' (*The Economist*).[67] American journalist Robert Kaplan's depiction of Liberia and Sierra Leone—based on a whirlwind trip—as representing a 'Coming Anarchy' in which crime, overpopulation, 'tribalism', and disease would destroy the world's social fabric, also followed in this tired apocalyptic tradition.[68]

Self-proclaimed Western 'experts' who usually do not bother to learn any indigenous African languages, preferring instead to cite seemingly omniscient Western diplomats or World Bank officials, continue to view Africa through distorted Eurocentric lenses and are still unable to shake off the colonial legacy of the 'White Man's Burden'.

This stereotyping of Africa has the same effect as such views did during the colonial era: it helps to shift responsibility and blame for Africa's crises from external factors and focuses solely on the supposed social pathologies of culturally backward Africans. Edward Said often noted that the power to narrate or to block narratives was an important manifestation of cultural imperialism. Today, the hold that the cartel of still mostly white men has over the mainstream international media is a powerful tool in shaping how people view the world. Depicting Africa as a 'hopeless continent' of culturally backward people prone to perennial conflicts is scarcely going to convince Western public opinion to support interventions to end these tragic wars. Such Afrophobic misrepresentations must be deconstructed, and Africans must force their own alternative narratives onto the global agenda.

More positively, in director James Cameron's charmingly subversive 2009 science fiction movie *Avatar*, Hollywood—not usually renowned for nuance or subtlety—managed to produce an anti–imperial film that even managed to satirise the George W. Bush administration's 'war on terror' between 2001 and 2008. The 'bad guys' in the movie are not predictably the alien 'natives.' It is the insatiable greed and unspeakable savagery of the neo-imperial wielders of Western technology that this clever slice of American popular culture condemns, telling a story about an alien world of Pandora that could easily represent Western colonial and neo-imperial history in Africa, Asia, the Caribbean, Latin America or even the US's own genocide against its indigenous population at the founding of the country.

Pax Africana: From Independence to Cold War

Turning now to Africa's independence struggle, Ghana's founding president, Kwame Nkrumah, famously urged his fellow Africans in the 1950s to 'seek ye first the political kingdom and all things will be added to it'. African nationalism, which gathered great pace from about 1935, even as colonial powers sought to incorporate new ruling elites into ruling structures, would finally lead to the independence of thirty-eight African states by 1968. In Africa's five post-independence decades since 1960, however, continental leaders and their

800 million citizens discovered that 'all things' have not been added to Nkrumah's political kingdom. Africa remains the world's poorest and most conflict-ridden continent; about 70 per cent of Africa's population lives below the poverty line; the continent is crippled by a $290 billion external debt; and Africa accounts for less than 2 per cent of world trade.

Amidst the backdrop of these difficult colonial and postcolonial eras, this book seeks to examine Africa's continued quest for three 'magic' kingdoms: security (involving efforts to create viable regional conflict resolution mechanisms), hegemony (involving regional leadership and external interventions), and unity (involving individual leadership and alliances with the American diaspora, comparative integration lessons from Europe, and coalitions with Asia and the broader Third World). Though set largely in the post-apartheid era, these fourteen chapters are necessarily grounded in the history of colonial Africa and the Cold War between 1884 and 1989. Without understanding this historical context in what I have described as Africa's 'Century of Pestilence', one cannot properly analyse and grasp the international relations of the two decades of Africa's post-apartheid era.

The use of the term *post-apartheid* situates this book in the context of Africa's own geostrategic changes, which are of course inextricably linked to larger global developments: the end of the Cold War and the ideological divisions between East and West in which Africa had been a major theatre. The end of apartheid in South Africa and the election of the revered Nelson Mandela as its president in 1994 effectively marked the attainment of Nkrumah's political kingdom. But to reach the socioeconomic kingdom, Africa still has to pursue three further quests for security, hegemony, and unity. This book seeks to provide an assessment of Africa's continuing efforts at achieving security and development; at providing regional leadership for regional integration and development; at transforming external influences—that were often malign during the Cold War—into more mutually beneficial relationships; at providing visionary continental leadership; at promoting viable regional integration; at benefitting from African diaspora communities; and at building political coalitions with Asian, Latin American, and other Third World allies in order to restructure the international political, economic, and legal systems in ways that are more advantageous to Africa.

Many African leaders and scholars continue to recognize the need to reverse the 'Curse of Berlin'. Following a genocide in which 800,000 of his citizens were killed by their fellow countrymen and -women in 1994, former Rwandan president Pasteur Bizimungu continually called, in 1995 and 1996, for the convening of a second Berlin conference in Africa.[69] During a lecture at Cambridge University in England in March 2009, which I attended, Ramtane Lamamra, the African Union's Peace and Security Commissioner, was asked to identify the most important security challenge for contemporary Africa. Without hesitation, the Algerian diplomat noted the risk of fragmentation of three of Africa's largest states: Sudan, the Democratic Republic of the Congo, and Nigeria. All three states are classic examples of the social engineering and political shenanigans that resulted from the Conference of Berlin. Lamamra also noted, in the same talk, that fewer than a quarter of Africa's colonially inherited borders had been delimited, suggesting that the colonial boundaries could still be a cause for future strife.[70]

Kenyan scholar Ali Mazrui has noted that at least 2 million Africans have died in a bid to defend colonial boundaries in Nigeria, the DRC, Sudan, and Ethiopia/Eritrea. In order to stabilize Africa's weak states, he called for Africa's neighbours (like Tanzania) to federate with weaker states (like Rwanda and Burundi), and for the UN to establish 'trusteeships' over other territories, which would be run largely by Africans and Asians.[71] Though it is clearly unrealistic to expect sovereign governments to accept federations led by larger states, the post–Cold War role of the UN in Mozambique, Liberia, Sierra Leone, and the DRC has indeed often resembled the establishment of 'trusteeships'. Nigerian Nobel laureate Wole Soyinka implored Africans in 1996: '[We] should sit down with square-rule and compass and re-design the boundaries of African nations.'[72] Prominent Nigerian historian A.I. Asiwaju, however, has convincingly argued against proposals such as these as being impractical, noting that African boundaries are remarkably durable, and that even the postcolonial exception of the creation of Eritrea from Ethiopia in 1993 was a reversion to an earlier colonial boundary. Asiwaju further argued that poor governance and inequitable socioeconomic development are often more fundamental challenges to postcolonial Africa that boundary revisions will not resolve. He therefore sensibly suggested instead that Africans pursue more effective regional economic integration schemes.[73] Most African governments clearly have many pressing internal issues—keeping soldiers in barracks, paying civil servants, providing social services—that could threaten their survival. Changing colonial boundaries thus often seems more like an exercise for academics in ivory towers that politicians in statehouses.

Former Ghanaian UN Secretary-General Kofi Annan noted in his 1998 report *The Causes of Conflict and the Promotion of Durable Peace and Sustainable Development in Africa* that the causes of African conflicts are multifaceted and include both internal and external factors.[74] He stressed the profound effect of colonialism and the Cold War in shaping the African state system. Colonialism created the conditions for many of the ethnic grievances of the post-independence era through arbitrarily drawn colonial boundaries. The Cold War affected the African state system by prolonging destabilising liberation wars and by creating military instability in countries like Somalia, Ethiopia, Liberia, Angola, and Mozambique. As the Cold War ended by 1989, the two superpower blocs—led by the United States and the Soviet Union—abandoned autocrats like Zaire's Mobutu Sese Seko, Somalia's Siad Barre, and Liberia's Samuel Doe who had served as reliable Cold War clients. Even as the foreign aid that sustained Cold War proxies in power was cut off, their trading networks came under increasing challenges from armed rebellions, which frequently replaced military coups as the main method for replacing sitting regimes.[75] Economic reforms mandated by the World Bank and the International Monetary Fund (IMF) further eroded the control of African autocrats, as urban riots and social instability accompanied enforced cuts in health and education and the removal of government subsidies on food and fuel. In an increasing number of states, African governments could no longer exercise normal state functions of providing security, order, and social services to their citizens, and lost control over the monopoly on violence and state bureaucracies.

Beside these external sources of conflict, Africa's post-independence leaders also contributed to conflicts on their own continent. Crafting of federations and concession of autonomy to 'minority' groups were rejected by many nation-builders who argued instead that one-party states were the only means to avoid destabilising ethnic wars and to preserve the unity they needed. Ghana, Guinea, Tanzania, and Kenya were some of the early pioneers of monopoly politics in the form of one-party states. No ruling party lost power in Africa between 1960 and 1990. Ethno-regional differences were also exacerbated by nepotism and favouritism in appointments to military, political, and bureaucratic positions. The state became a cash cow to be milked for political patronage. Many national armies in countries like Liberia, Côte d'Ivoire, Nigeria, and Sudan were turned into ethnic warrior enclaves in which the core consisted of kinsmen of the head of state. Urban bias in development policies further created an aggrieved countryside full of a ready army of unemployed youth who have today become the cannon fodder of Africa's warlords in countries like Liberia, the DRC, and Sierra Leone.[76] As Basil Davidson observed about post-independence Africa: 'This nation-statism looked like a liberation. In practice, it was not a restoration of Africa to Africa's own history, but the onset of a new period of indirect subjection to the history of Europe.'[77]

In seeking to promote effective peacebuilding in Africa, it is important to examine inherited Western political and socioeconomic structures, and to note that military solutions can only be short-term band-aids to more complex and deep-rooted social, economic, and political problems that armed peacekeepers can freeze but not resolve. External military power can only provide peaceful conditions to work out differences between parties. Viable indigenous institutions for managing conflicts and preventing them from becoming violent will still need to be built. Africa's civil society actors—women's groups, religious leaders, journalists, the business community, and academics—have therefore become more directly involved in efforts in post–Cold War Africa at promoting local justice and national reconciliation, socioeconomic reconstruction, reintegrating soldiers into society, and collecting information for early warning systems. They could provide a rich resource for what Ali Mazrui described as Pax Africana: a peace created, consolidated, and kept by Africans.[78]

This study seeks to fill a gap in the literature by providing a comprehensive volume that assesses the most important issues in Africa's international relations after the Cold War, focusing on the new institutions and main actors that are shaping diplomacy, security, and development in post-apartheid Africa. Though many studies have covered Africa's security, political, and socioeconomic challenges during the Cold War,[79] few comprehensive efforts exist on Africa's international relations after the end of the Cold War.[80] We focus on the quest of African actors to achieve greater autonomy within the international system in order to be able to promote security and development more effectively through regional organisations such as the AU, ECOWAS, SADC, and the New Partnership for Africa's Development (NEPAD), and to achieve a stronger African voice within international institutions such as the UN, the World Bank, the IMF, and the World Trade Organisation (WTO). Africa's quest for security is evident in post–Cold War efforts to improve the effectiveness of the African Union and subregional organisations, as well as in the establishment of new governance structures such as the African Peer Review Mechanism (APRM) of 2003.[81] But these institutions have often proved to be weak, and in the security field, the UN—the most legitimate institution in this crucial field due to its nearly universal membership of 192 states—has often had to play a leading role.

INTRODUCTION

The quest for hegemony by African actors like South Africa and Nigeria is also linked to a search for more autonomy, as regional actors have sought to build peace in the DRC, Burundi, Liberia, and Sierra Leone while increasing Africa's leverage over the international system through socioeconomic initiatives like NEPAD. These efforts have so far had only limited success. The role of China on the continent could reduce Africa's dependence on Western powers like the US, France, Britain, Portugal, and Belgium, while increasing the continent's diplomatic and economic leverage. However, it is far from certain that African governments will be able to craft a multilateral approach to engaging China for the mutual benefit of both parties, and South Africa could in the future find itself in an economic competition with the Asian giant that could create negative perceptions about both countries on the continent. Africa's quest for unity has seen leaders such as Kwame Nkrumah, Thabo Mbeki, and Nelson Mandela seeking to strengthen African military and political structures, but like many other continental efforts, a lack of capacity and unity has often frustrated Africa's quest for autonomy within the international system. The African Union must carefully examine whether there are lessons to be learned from the European Union that can be adapted to African circumstances, while Africa must continue to seek ways of using its diaspora to influence US policy towards their ancestral continent in more positive ways, with the election in 2008 of Barack Obama, an American president with African roots. Finally, the Afro-Asian coalition that was born at the Bandung conference of 1955 has been largely frustrated in its efforts to shape global institutions such as the UN, the World Bank, the IMF, and the WTO in ways that could increase the autonomy of the Third World against powerful Western actors. To complete this post–Cold War quest for the three magic kingdoms—security, hegemony, and unity—Africa must first reverse the Bismarckian 'Curse of Berlin'.

PART 1

THE QUEST FOR SECURITY

2

PROPHETS OF PAX AFRICANA

AFRICA'S SECURITY ARCHITECTURE[1]

'And across the parapet, I see the mother of African unity and independence, her body besmeared with the blood of her sons and daughters in their struggle to set her free from the shackles of imperialism.'[2]

Kwame Nkrumah, Ghanaian leader, 1957–1966

This chapter borrows its title from Kenyan scholar Ali Mazrui's seminal work of 1967, *Towards a Pax Africana*. The concept of Pax Africana suggests that Africans themselves should muster the will to resolve disputes that arise on their continent. The idea also asserts a willingness by Africans emerging from a century of colonialism not only to cast off their chains of bondage, but also to break away from the colonial midwives that delivered them to independent statehood. As Mazrui put it: '*Pax Africana* asserts that the peace of *Africa* is to be assured by the exertions of Africans themselves. The idea of a "Pax Africana" is the specifically military aspect of the principle of continental jurisdiction.'[3] Mazrui's idea of 'continental jusrisdiction' was a sort of Monroe Doctrine suggesting that outsiders should keep out of African disputes and let continental actors settle their own disputes. This call was made at a time when external intervention was becoming rampant as the Cold War's proxy wars threatened to tear apart countries like the Democratic Republic of the Congo (DRC) between 1960 and 1964. In his related idea of 'racial sovereignty', Mazrui argued that inter-African intervention by black states in the affairs of other brotherly states was more legitimate than intervention by outsiders.[4]

As noted in chapter 1, Africa continues to suffer from a curse inflicted in one of Europe's most famous and cosmopolitan cities: Berlin. The 1884–1885 Conference of Berlin, under the supervision of Germany's 'Iron Chancellor', Otto von Bismarck, effectively set the rules for Africa's partition. The European curse of artificial borders has caused untold suffering in postcolonial Africa. Just as Berlin marked the division of Africa, the gods of Africa wrought their revenge on Europe seventy-six years after Bismarck's conference. Many African states gained their independence just as the Berlin Wall was being erected in 1961. A city that had thus symbolised the division of Africa, now symbolised the division of Germany and Europe. As Ali Mazrui noted: 'Europe was ... sentenced to the same fate to which Europe had previously condemned Africa—partition and artificial frontiers.'[5]

Post-independence Africa has suffered from dozens of conflicts, with the curse of Berlin playing a role in border disputes between Morocco and Algeria, Ghana and Togo, Burkina Faso and Mali, Somalia and Ethiopia, Libya and Chad, and Nigeria and Cameroon. Wars were also fuelled by the superpower rivalries of the Cold War, as well as internal governance deficiencies on the part of autocratic African leaders. Since 1960, over forty wars have killed over 10 million Africans and spawned 10 million refugees. In the post–Cold War era, United Nations debacles in Somalia (1993) and Rwanda (1994) led to powerful Western actors abandoning Africa to its own fate (see chapter 3). The neglect of the continent forced regional actors like the Organisation of African Unity (OAU) (now the African Union [AU]), the Economic Community of West African States (ECOWAS), the Southern African Development Community (SADC), the Economic Community of Central African States (ECCAS), the Intergovernmental Authority on Development (IGAD), and the Arab Maghreb Union (AMU)—most of them primarily economic organisations—to adopt security roles. However, these institutions remain weak, lacking financial and logistical means.

This chapter examines Africa's peacekeeping travails, starting with an analysis of the African Union, before assessing the efforts of the principal regional security institutions on the continent: ECOWAS in the West, SADC in the South, ECCAS in Central Africa, IGAD in the East, and the AMU in the North. We focus particularly on five important themes: the financial and logistical weaknesses of regional organisations; the lack of political consensus among African leaders on collective security norms and practices; the controversial peacekeeping role of regional hegemons; the centrality of the UN's peacekeeping role in Africa; and the need to establish a clear division of labour among Africa's security actors.

The African Union: Konaré's Alchemy?

According to ancient folklore, Europe's alchemists sought to turn lead into gold and in the process discovered the scientific method. Africa's current alchemists, who are seeking to transform the OAU into an effective AU, must avoid the frustrations of their European counterparts and not pursue an elusive quest in search of an illusory El Dorado. Despite the creation of the OAU security mechanism in 1993, the organisation's deployment of small military observer missions (mostly fewer than a hundred personnel) to Rwanda, Burundi, and Comoros failed to stem instability in these countries and exposed its logistical and financial weaknesses. 75 per cent of funding for these missions was provided by external donors. The African Union, under the leadership of former Malian president Alpha Konaré between 2003 and 2008, did not define a proper division of labour between itself and Africa's security mechanisms and actors. Unlike the OAU Charter of 1963, however, the AU's Constitutive Act of 2000 allows for interference in the internal affairs of its members in cases of unconstitutional changes of governments, egregious human rights abuses and genocide, and conflicts that threaten regional stability. This is potentially revolutionary in light of the OAU's rigid, noninterventionist posture in the first three decades of its existence (see chapter 12). As Konaré noted: 'the African Union is not the former OAU, they are completely different. The AU will provide the potential leadership and take appropriate action without which conflicts cannot be resolved.'[6]

AU leaders established a fifteen-member Peace and Security Council (PSC) in July 2004 to make decisions on conflict prevention and peacebuilding (the council had met over a hundred times by August 2009), with its centrepiece project being the establishment of the African Standby Force (ASF) by 2010. The ASF, which can be deployed within thirty to ninety days, is being built around five subregional pillars and will undertake peace support operations on the continent.[7] A committee of military officers from AU member states, modelled on the UN system, is to provide the PSC with advice on deployment and security requirements. The AU has sought to promote an integrated standby system involving logistics, common doctrines, and unified training standards. Each subregion is to establish its own brigade headquarters, and the AU force is expected to be linked to the UN's standby system. About ten workshops were held between 2005 and 2007 involving the AU and the regional economic communities to discuss issues such as operating procedures, the civilian dimension of the standby force, rapid deployment capacity, and European Union (EU) support to the AU and the regional economic communities, though progress has so far been halting. The December 2007 report of the Audit of the African Union—chaired by Adebayo Adedeji, the former executive director of the UN's Economic Commission for Africa (ECA)—also noted that the research capacity of the Peace and Security Council must be strengthened, and that the resources devoted to the AU Peace Fund must be massively increased (the fund is only 6 per cent of the regular AU budget). The report further urged the PSC to seek greater participation of African civil society groups in its work.[8]

As the scaffolding for the AU's security structures was being erected, a heated debate erupted about regional hegemons Nigeria and South Africa (among others) being allowed permanent seats and veto power on the Peace and Security Council.[9] In the end, neither permanent seats nor veto power was permitted. However, Nigeria and South Africa, which closely coordinate their diplomatic positions, have been extremely influential in shaping the new AU, and both were instrumental in appointing Konaré as chair of the AU Commission (see chapters 5, 6 and 7).[10] Voting on substantive issues in the PSC is by a two-thirds majority, unlike the OAU's insistence on consensus.[11] The Panel of the Wise, established in 2007, should provide additional mediation support to the AU Commission, and should be linked to the UN's Mediation Support Unit (MSU) in New York.[12]

The AU has been explicitly mandated to coordinate the activities of Africa's subregional mechanisms. But organisations like ECOWAS and SADC, which established security mechanisms before the AU was born in 2002—and in the case of ECOWAS, have solid peacekeeping experience—often feel that the AU has more to learn from them than vice versa. A draft memorandum of understanding between the AU and the regional economic communities underwent at least five drafts between 2003 and 2007 before being finalised. The AU's peace and security protocols envisage the establishment of a continental early warning system, with the AU coordinating Africa's subregional early warning systems and linking the continent to the UN's early warning system. But experience so far has not been encouraging. Though both the AU's and IGAD's early warning systems are based in Addis Ababa, there has been only limited contact between the two institutions. The AU also suffers from many financial and personnel deficiencies that could hamper its conflict management ambitions. Its Peace and Security Commissioner, Algerian technocrat Said Djinnit (who held the position until 2008), was the most experienced of the AU's commissioners. However, tensions were reported within his department following efforts to recruit more staff, which met with some internal resistance.[13] Highly qualified staff members who served in the department often complained about an anti–intellectual culture. Differences were also reported between the Peace and Security Department and the office of the chair of the commission, and collaboration with the Political Affairs Department—headed by Gambian Julia Joyner—as well as with civil society actors, was not as far-reaching as expected. Another source of tension was between Konaré and the plenipotentiaries on the AU's Permanent Representatives Committee (PRC), with the ambassadors accusing the Malian of preferring to deal directly with his former colleagues (see chapter 12).[14]

Former Ghanaian UN Secretary-General Kofi Annan, in his March 2005 report to the General Assembly, titled *In Larger Freedom*, built on the UN high-level panel report of December 2004, calling on donors to devise a ten-year capacity-building plan with the AU. Both reports envisaged UN financial support for Africa's regional organisations in exceptional circumstances. This is a sensible recommendation that should go further in supporting Africa's regional organisations.[15] South Africa also sought to use its two-year stint on the UN Security Council (2007–2008) to strengthen the relationship between the UN and Africa's regional organisations. The UN Charter of 1945 allows regional organisations to undertake enforcement action under the authorisation of the fifteen-member UN Security Council. But the five veto-wielding members of the Council (the United States, China, Russia, France, and Britain) have maintained an ambiguous attitude towards regional organisations, refusing to fund, or sometimes even to recognise, their efforts, while insisting on maintaining political control over these missions. This led to tensions during the ECOWAS peacekeeping missions in Liberia and Sierra Leone in the 1990s (discussed later) when the UN deployed military observers alongside much larger ECOWAS forces, but refused to provide the financial and logistical muscle to strengthen the regional peacekeepers.

The OAU's cooperation with the UN further underlined the politicised nature of this relationship. Before the world body deployed peacekeepers to Rwanda in 1994, the OAU had about 340 military observers on the ground and had negotiated the Arusha Accord the previous year. Similarly, the OAU negotiated the Lusaka Accord for the DRC in 1999. In both cases, the UN was asked to deploy troops due to the OAU's military and financial deficiencies, but the world body simply brushed aside several of the OAU's recommendations on the disarming of militias and the size of forces to be deployed. In taking over the AU force in Burundi in 2004, the UN deployed a 5,650–

strong force that was double the size of the AU mission, while the world body annually spent three times as much on the UN force as the budget of the AU mission, having previously refused to support the African force directly. In order to avoid the UN Security Council blocking necessary peacekeeping interventions to save lives and restore order, both the AU and ECOWAS have set up security mechanisms that controversially do not require prior UN authorisation for action. The regional bodies simply *inform* the UN after they have taken action. This could result in an African subsystem of international law that ignores the global level, and could erode the UN's legitimacy as the body with primary responsibility for international peace and security.

In 2003, the European Union announced the creation of the African Peace Support Facility (APSF) with financing of about $250–300 million. But the dangers for the AU of relying excessively on external donors for such an important task as security could prove unsustainable in the long run. Pax Africana is as elusive as it was in the 1960s. In 2004, the AU budget was increased from $43 million to $158 million, with $62.2 million expected to go towards the regular budget and $95.2 million towards peace and security efforts on the continent. However, member states have failed to keep their accounts current even when the AU had a smaller budget of $40 million. In 2007, the AU's annual budget stood at $132 million. In the same year, donors were expected to contribute $142 million to the AU Peace Fund (more than its entire annual budget), while member states were assessed at $2.9 million. In addition to receiving regular contributions, the AU must improve its internal financial processes and recruit more able staff, as it is increasingly doing, before it can absorb such large funds. Operationalising the AU's new security mechanism under the leadership of the Gabonese chair of its commission, Jean Ping, will also require a level of political will and commitment that African leaders have not always demonstrated in the past.

The difficult experiences of the 7,000–strong AU peacekeeping mission in Sudan's volatile Darfur region, the AU Mission in Sudan (AMIS), between 2003 and 2007, were particularly instructive.[16] They resulted in the creation of the UN-AU Hybrid Mission in Darfur (UNAMID), with a mandate to oversee the implementation of the Darfur peace agreement of 2006 and to protect civilians.[17] Though there was agreement that the force should have a 'predominantly African character', there are serious doubts whether Africa's overstretched armies have sufficient military capacity to undertake such a mission successfully. Critics like Ugandan scholar Mahmood Mamdani employed the same argument as Sudanese leader Omar al-Bashir in depicting a humanitarian intervention as a 'civilising mission' that would be 'imperial'.[18] This, however, is a bizarre depiction for a force led by the UN—the most legitimate global intervener, with six other missions in Africa in 2009—and consisting mostly of African troops.

In trying to prove to the world that it had become a transformed organisation, the AU clearly bit off more than it could chew in Darfur. Konaré oversold the peacekeeping capacity of the AU to international actors, and both he and Said Djinnit often made a fetish of 'African ownership' (rather than recognizing the AU's limitations and seeking genuine burden-sharing with international actors). The organisation must be careful in future to avoid acting as an experimental guinea pig in failing to learn lessons from its financial and logistical difficulties in Burundi, Rwanda, Comoros, and Darfur.

ECOWAS: Nkrumah's Heirs

At the time of the creation of the OAU in 1963, Ghana's founding president, Kwame Nkrumah, was in a minority of one in calling for the establishment of an African High Command. The idea was to establish a supranational standing army involving all independent African states pooling their resources to advance the liberation of the continent and protect Africa from external intervention (see Chapter 12). Newly independent African leaders distrusted Nkrumah's intentions, and many placed more faith in defence agreements with external powers, most notably France, whose interventionist role earned it the sobriquet *gendarme d'Afrique* (see chapter 8).[19] Africa's leaders sought to freeze the colonial map of Africa inherited from the Berlin conference, stressing the inviolability of borders and seeking to entrench their own positions behind the shield of sovereignty. Today, Nkrumah's West African heirs are seeking to establish a common security institution short of the one that the visionary Ghanaian leader advocated over four decades ago. West African leaders have gone further than any other African subregion in devising a security mechanism.

Three civil conflicts of the 1990s—in Liberia, Sierra Leone, and Guinea-Bissau—claimed over 250,000 lives and spawned more than 1.2 million refugees.[20] All three countries remain fragile today. In response to these crises, ECOWAS[21] dispatched five peacekeeping missions—to Liberia (1990 and 2003), Sierra Leone (1997), Guinea-Bissau (1998), and Côte d'Ivoire (2003)—which eventually helped stem the conflicts, though almost all the conflicts eventually required UN peacekeeping assistance. ECOWAS's sacrifices of over a thousand fatalities were rare and noteworthy in the annals of international peacekeeping. West African leaders have also established, as part of a security mechanism, three key organs to implement their decisions: the ten-member Mediation and Security Council, the Defence and Security Commission, and the Council of Elders. An observation centre has been set up within the ECOWAS secretariat—which since 2007 has been called a 'commission' along bureaucratic lines similar to those of the AU—in Abuja, Nigeria, to analyse early warning information. About forty full-time personnel staffed ECOWAS's security institutions in 2007.

Encouragingly, civil society actors in West Africa have been consulted by ECOWAS to determine how they can best contribute to its early warning system. The ECOWAS mechanism also reflects some of the lessons learned from the peacekeeping experiences of the ECOWAS Ceasefire Monitoring Group (ECOMOG) between 1990 and 2003.[22] The Mediation and Security Council was inspired by the ECOWAS Committee of Nine on Liberia, which coordinated subregional peacemaking efforts in the 1990s. The Defence and Security Commission advises ECOWAS's Mediation and Security Council on mandates, terms of reference, and the appointment of force commanders for peacekeeping missions.

But three major flaws in ECOMOG's interventions in Liberia, Sierra Leone, and Guinea-Bissau must be corrected to ensure the smooth functioning of the ECOWAS mechanism. First, ECOMOG peacekeepers were deployed to all three countries before detailed logistical and financial arrangements had been made. The peacekeepers were ill-equipped and ill-prepared, and not all ECOWAS members were informed before full-scale deployment occurred. Second, the ECOMOG forces in Liberia and Sierra Leone were dominated by Nigeria, resulting in a lack of subregional unity and depriving the force of important legitimacy in fulfilling its tasks.[23] Third, the ECO-MOG missions in Liberia and Sierra Leone were under the operational control of ECOMOG commanders in the field, rather than the ECOWAS secretariat in Abuja. Since these commanders were all Nigerian—with the brief exception of Ghana's General Arnold Quainoo in Liberia in 1990—as were the bulk of the troops, Nigeria's military leaders were kept closely informed of military operations on the ground. This information, however, did not always filter speedily, if at all, to other ECOWAS members and the secretariat.

The ECOWAS mechanism further proposed that the powers of the organisation's executive secretary (and president of the commission after 2007) between 1999 and 2009—Ghanaian diplomat Mohamed Ibn Chambas—be broadened, giving him the authority to take initiatives for the prevention and management of conflicts, including fact-finding, mediation, facilitation, negotiation, and reconciliation. A deputy executive secretary for political affairs, defence, and security was appointed to manage field operations in support of ceasefires and peace agreements. This role is important in coordinating activities between the ECOWAS secretariat and field missions.

Based largely on the experiences of ECOMOG, the ECOWAS protocol of 1999 called for the establishment of a standby force of brigade size, consisting of specially trained and equipped units of national armies ready to be deployed at short notice. All fifteen ECOWAS states pledged one battalion each to the proposed force. It now remains to be seen whether this pledge can be translated into reality. The proposed subregional force will embark on periodic training exercises to enhance the cohesion of its troops and compatibility of equipment. ECOMOG's soldiers will undertake training exchange programmes in West African military training institutions, as well as external training involving the UN and the AU. ECOWAS is also establishing a standby force—as part of the AU-coordinated standby force—of 7,000 troops who can be deployed within ninety days (as well as a rapid reaction force of 2,773 troops who can be deployed within thirty days).

Many of the institutions proposed by the 1999 protocol represent an important step to improving ECOWAS's ability to manage conflicts, but they will also be expensive to staff. And ECOWAS, like the AU, has experienced funding problems, with member states failing to pay their dues consistently to maintain existing institutions (unpaid arrears stood at $38.1 million as the mechanism was being established in 1999). This will require greater commitment from member states, and more detailed financial arrangements must be made to ensure continued funding both from within and outside the subregion. The ECOWAS protocol of 1999 foresees troop-contributing countries bearing financial costs for the first three months of military operations before the ECOWAS commission takes over the costs of the mission. The initial agreement for the ECOMOG mission in Liberia was for each contingent to fund its own troops for the first month of the mission, after which all ECOWAS members were to assume responsibility for the force. But Nigeria ended up footing about 90 per cent of the costs. Similarly in Sierra Leone, Nigeria shouldered much of the financial burden for the mission. In Guinea-Bissau, France underwrote the financial costs of the peacekeepers, providing stipends, transportation, and some communication equipment. France, Britain, Belgium, the Netherlands, and the United States largely financed the ECOWAS force in Côte d'Ivoire. The ECOWAS community levy that was implemented in 2004 yielded some positive results: Nigeria alone provided $20 million from this levy.

The recent burden-sharing between ECOWAS and the UN is therefore welcome. However, while lightening ECOWAS's burden, the UN's recent peacekeeping roles in Liberia, Sierra Leone, and Côte d'Ivoire have somewhat overshadowed ECOWAS's efforts.[24] The presence of UN peacekeepers led to UN Security Council oversight of all three missions. ECOWAS's Mediation and Security Council, however, still has an important role to play in harmonising subregional policies to avoid damaging political divisions, as well as in mobilising international support for postconflict reconstruction efforts.

Nigeria's ability to continue to bankroll ECOWAS and subregional peacekeeping has come under enormous strain. Under the civilian regime of Olusegun Obasanjo, the country withdrew 8,500 peacekeepers from Sierra Leone in 1999–2000 (subsuming 3,500 under a UN mission), and insisted, before agreeing to deploy, that the UN take over a Nigerian-led ECOWAS peacekeeping mission into Liberia, after three months, in August 2003. Governance challenges also continue to bedevil West Africa's Gulliver. Elections that brought President Umaru Yar'Adua to power in April 2007 were marred by widespread allegations of fraud. The president's own ill health has also prevented dynamic leadership at home and abroad. It is thus unclear whether Nigeria can continue to play an effective security role in West Africa and whether the country might not itself become a source of subregional instability if its domestic challenges are not urgently addressed (see chapter 6).[25]

SADC: Mbeki as Pied Piper

An analysis of security in Southern Africa must necessarily begin with the centrality of South Africa's role in the subregion. Apartheid South Africa used its military strength aggressively to subdue its neighbours through a destructive policy of military destabilisation that resulted in about a million deaths and cost Southern Africa an estimated $60 billion in damages between 1980 and 1988.[26] South Africa currently accounts for about 80 per cent of the subregion's economic strength.[27] A democratic South Africa joined SADC in 1994.[28] During Nelson Mandela's presidency between 1994 and 1999, South Africa largely shunned a military role in the subregion out of fear of arousing charges of hegemonic domination. As SADC chair, however, Mandela became embroiled in a spat with Zimbabwe's Robert Mugabe over the structure of SADC's Organ on Politics, Defence, and Security (OPDS), which Mugabe chaired.[29] South Africa's first major peacekeeping mission was also marred by controversy. The legitimacy of the intervention as a SADC-sanctioned action was widely questioned. The leadership of the peacekeeping force by white South African officers from the apartheid army further fuelled passions.[30] The fact that South African soldiers shot their way into the Highlands Water Project (killing several Basotho guards)—which supplies South Africa's Gauteng industrial heartland with water—also raised issues about the strategic motives of the intervention.

Chastened by Mandela's bitter foreign policy experiences over Lesotho and a bruising diplomatic battle with General Sani Abacha's Nigeria in 1995, his successor, Thabo Mbeki, consistently sought multilateral solutions to resolving regional conflicts (see chapter 5 and 7). Mbeki was more prepared than Mandela to send peacekeepers abroad,[31] deploying about 3,000 troops to Burundi and the DRC. He acted as a 'Pied Piper of Pretoria' in playing the diplomatic tunes to which warlords, rebels, and politicians danced in the Congo, Burundi, and Côte d'Ivoire. It seems that all diplomatic roads during the Mbeki era led to Tshwane (Pretoria). In a short decade and a half, South Africa went from being the most destabilising force in Africa to being its most active peacemaker.[32]

Southern Africa's Fledgling Security Architecture

Like ECOWAS, SADC is currently attempting to create a security mechanism with clearly articulated structures to promote more predictable decisionmaking. A protocol on politics, defence, and security cooperation was signed in 2001. The protocol called for SADC states to coordinate their security policy through a troika of members under a one-year rotating chair supported administratively by the SADC secretariat in Gaborone, Botswana. The SADC protocol seeks to harmonise its members' foreign policy, and calls for initiatives ranging from conflict prevention to peace enforcement. The protocol places far more emphasis on prior approval from the UN Security Council than does the ECOWAS security mechanism. ECOWAS's difficult experiences with lacklustre UN support in Liberia and Sierra Leone in the 1990s meant that the organisation sought to retain as much autonomy as possible, so as not to let the UN block necessary humanitarian interventions while simultaneously failing to provide sufficient support. However, there is greater emphasis in the SADC protocol on external aggression due to Southern Africa's history of liberation wars and the specific situation in the DRC.

After a winding journey that stretched from Blantyre to Maputo to Harare to Dar-es-Salaam to Maseru, the SADC security locomotive finally reached Gaborone in 2003. By 2004, the organisation had unveiled its Strategic Indicative Plan for the Organ (SIPO) as a five-year project to implement its security protocol. SIPO outlined plans for work in four broad sectors: politics, defence, state security, and public security. The plan also sought to work more explicitly than ECOWAS with civil society actors and think-tanks in the subregion, and even aspired, unlike ECOWAS, to coordinate the participation of its members in UN peacekeeping missions. But the plan has often been rightly criticised for being too vague and general in its goals. This is, according to critics, more a long laundry list of desirable actions than an actionable, focused implementation plan.

SADC's amended treaty did not increase the powers of its former executive secretary, Prega Ramsamy, a low-key economist from Mauritius, who finished his term of office in August 2005. Mozambican technocrat and former cabinet minister Tomaz Salomao took over the position and has been more dynamic, while struggling to win over the support of his senior officials. There is a widespread feeling in the subregion that the SADC secretariat is weak because its leaders do not want an interventionist bureaucracy in such a sensitive field as security. The fact that Namibian technocrat Kaire Mbuende was dismissed as executive secretary by SADC leaders in 2000 due to what some regarded as an independent streak, somewhat bolsters this impression. Ramsamy was widely seen as cautious and unwilling to offend member states with politically sensitive activities. During his tenure, the SADC secretariat kept something of a distance from civil society groups, with the ironic result that a subregion with world-class security institutions did not reap the full benefits of this knowledge.

Though SADC has a department for politics, defence, and security within its secretariat in Gaborone, with directorates for politics and diplomacy, and defence and security, as well as a strategic analysis unit with a situation room, fewer than ten full-time staff members were working in these areas in 2009. Indeed, the OPDS directorate and secretariat have often operated independently from each other.[33] Despite SADC not yet having established as extensive a security structure within its secretariat as ECOWAS's, a remarkable feature of this subregion is an impressive core of world-class nongovernmental organisations centred largely but not exclusively around South Africa (in a recent global survey, seven of the top ten think-tanks in sub-Saharan Africa were based in South Africa).[34] One of the most impressive security bodies in Africa is the Southern African Defence and Security Management (SADSEM) network, consisting of security institutions in South Africa, Botswana, the DRC, Mozambique, Namibia, Tanzania, Zambia, and Zimbabwe. SADSEM trained over 1,000 senior officials, military officers, and civil society leaders between 2000 and 2008, and the network involves one of the closest collaborations between civil society groups and military officers on the continent. SADSEM, which seeks to interact closely with SADC military institutions, has tremendous potential to impact the long-term military leadership within Southern Africa, though it has not always been able to gain access to the top echelons of state houses and the SADC secretariat.

SADC states are also seeking to build their own standby peacekeeping brigade (SADCBRIG) as part of the AU force to be established by 2010. They have embarked on joint peace support exercises such as Blue Hungwe, Blue Crane, Tanzanite, and Airborne Africa. Also, the Regional Peacekeeping Training Centre (RPTC), in Harare, Zimbabwe, trained over 3,000 military officers from six subregional states, but political differences led to a withdrawal of its funds by the Danish government in 2000. The RPTC has since restarted its activities following a decision to bring the centre under the umbrella of the SADC secretariat in Gaborone. It remains to be seen whether the centre can attract sufficient funding to maintain its activities. SADC has also reported some progress in developing an early warning system, though this system lags behind the mechanisms developed by ECOWAS and IGAD.

Like ECOWAS, SADC has experienced financial problems, with many of its members failing to keep their accounts current, resulting in a debt of $9 million in July 2001. The organisation still remains largely financed by external donors, with $23.7 million out of a $40.4 million 2006–2007 budget (60 per cent) earmarked for foreign donors.[35] The SADC standby force—part of the African standby system—envisages a planning cell within the SADC secretariat in Botswana, and member states are expected to sustain the mission for three to six months, until the AU or the UN takes over funding. But South Africa's experience in Burundi (discussed later) should give members pause for thought over such an uncertain arrangement. SADC announced the establishment of the standby peacekeeping brigade at its Lusaka summit in August 2007, and made provisions for appointing a special representative and force commander. The crises in Zimbabwe and the DRC, however, have often dominated security discussions within SADC. By March 2009, some progress had been made in both cases. However, with the ousting of Thabo Mbeki from power in South Africa in September 2008, it is unclear whether his successors will have the will and dexterity to continue his activist peacemaking role on the continent. (See chapter 5 and 11).

ECCAS: Mobutu's Troubled Legacy

The Great Lakes region, encompassing Burundi, Rwanda, Tanzania, and Uganda, contains some of Africa's most spectacular landscape: rolling hills, dense forests, rising mountains, and lush valleys. But recent events have turned a natural paradise into a human-made disaster. The Great Lakes have become infested with ethnic crocodiles of the genocidal species. Rwanda and Burundi are tragic twins seemingly fated to repeat cycles of bloody massacres in a struggle between a Hutu majority and a Tutsi minority with deep roots in a pernicious process of Belgian colonial social engineering. The conflict in the DRC has involved seven foreign armies and a myriad of militias and mercenaries in a state the size of Western Europe that was destroyed by the thirty-one-year autocratic misrule of Western-backed Mobutu Sese Seko.[36] Military clashes between former allies Uganda and Rwanda, and their looting of the Congo's mineral resources, further exacerbated the conflict.

An estimated 2.5 million people have died in the Congo since August 1998, and the war has spawned more than 600,000 refugees. The withdrawal of most of the foreign armies from the country by 2002 offered an opportunity for the 16,700–strong (about 20,000 in January 2010) UN Organization Mission in the Democratic Republic of the Congo (MONUC) to oversee peace efforts. However, instability continued in Ituri and Kivu provinces, and the UN force was clearly insufficient to keep the peace throughout the country. In December 2002, the Global and All-Inclusive Agreement on the Transition in the DRC was signed in Tshwane (Pretoria) by all of the Congo's main parties. The accord called for a two-year transition period, during which Joseph Kabila would run the country with four vice presidents selected by all parties. The corrupt, fractious coalition of warlords often worked at cross-purposes with each other. The DRC held historic elections in 2006, overseen by MONUC. The incumbent president, Joseph Kabila, won the election after a runoff in October 2006. However, fighting between Kabila's troops and those of his closest rival, Jean-Pierre Bemba (who later fled into exile in Portugal and was subsequently arrested for war crimes allegedly committed by his troops in the Central African Republic) in Kinshasa in August 2006, rendered the security situation unstable. Instability also continued in the country's Ituri, Kivu, and Bas-Congo provinces, and it was clear that a premature withdrawal of the billion dollar a year UN mission could result in full-scale fighting.

Three of the major challenges of conflict management in the Great Lakes region are the reluctance of the UN Security Council to play a substantial peacekeeping role, the lack of effective security institutions in the subregion, and the absence of a regional hegemon. The UN mission in the Congo struggled to keep the peace amidst logistical and other difficulties. The Great Lakes region itself does not have an established institutionalised framework for managing conflicts. The Economic Community of the Great Lakes States (CEPGL), involving Rwanda, Burundi, and the DRC, has long since become moribund. The potential of the Congo—based on its size, strategic location, and natural resources—to play a lead role in the Great Lakes, as Nigeria has done in West Africa, and South Africa in Burundi and the DRC, has been diminished by the state's decay into a carcass on which neighbouring birds of prey like Uganda and Rwanda feasted.

The Economic Community of Central African States was created in 1983 to promote regional integration. ECCAS brought together eleven subregional states.[37] At a meeting in Gabon in 1997, Central African leaders proposed the creation of a security mechanism for the prevention and management of conflicts. The aim of the mechanism was to establish a legal and institutional framework to promote and strengthen peace and security in Central Africa. The Council for Peace and Security in Central Africa (COPAX) was established under the auspices of the UN Standing Committee for Security Questions in Central Africa.[38] In 1999, ECCAS's mandate was broadened to stress conflict prevention and peacebuilding, and the Central African Early Warning System (MARAC) was established at its secretariat in Libreville, Gabon. Establishment of the Defence and Security Commission (CDS), consisting of subregional defence chiefs, was also ambitiously announced to coordinate future peace support operations and to plan for the establishment of the Central African Multinational Force (FOMAC).[39]

However, technical problems with creating ECCAS's structures, as well as the pursuit of parochial national interests by member states, have frustrated the effective operation of this security mechanism. Only six professional staff worked in the ECCAS secretariat in October 2007, although there were plans to recruit more personnel. ECCAS's members have struggled to agree on the relationship between ECCAS, COPAX, and MARAC. Moreover, Central African states have responded to the failure to create an institutional framework for managing conflicts by seeking membership in alternative subregional organisations: the DRC joined SADC in 1997, while Burundi and Rwanda joined the East African Community (EAC), consisting of Kenya, Tanzania, and Uganda, in 2006. More optimistically, senior ECCAS officials met six times between July 2003 and December 2004, and are establishing a 2,177-strong regional brigade as their contribution to the African standby force, though there is no expectation that such a force would be able to stem instability in this subregion.

The civil war that erupted in Burundi in 1993 lasted for a decade and resulted in over 200,000 deaths. Beginning in April 2003, under the auspices of the African Union, the South African–led AU Mission in Burundi (AMIB), a 2,366–strong force bolstered by Ethiopian and Mozambican troops, attempted to implement a fragile peace accord. The small peacekeeping mission struggled to maintain security and was largely bankrolled by South Africa, which eventually convinced the UN to take over the force by November 2004. A small South African protection force guarding Burundian political leaders continued to operate under the AU umbrella. The UN had earlier established an office in Burundi in 1993 to support peace efforts. In March 2004, Kofi Annan proposed the establishment of the UN Mission in Burundi (MINUB) with an authorised strength of 5,650 peacekeepers. Though 7,329 Burundian combatants were demobilized between December 2004 and April 2005, internal political divisions among the fractious transitional government continued. The country's constitution was finally adopted in February 2005 following a referendum, and a presidential election in August 2005 saw Pierre Nkurunziza become president. However, political and security tensions continue in this tiny Central African country.[40]

IGAD: Nyerere's Triple Legacy

Turning from Central to Eastern Africa, we find Julius Nyerere, Tanzania's founding president, who left an enduring legacy on three of Africa's subregions. Nyerere was an ardent supporter of the liberation struggle in Southern Africa who hosted the OAU's Liberation Committee. He ordered his troops into the Eastern African state of Uganda in 1979 to end the tyrannical reign of Idi Amin, whose soldiers had earlier launched incursions into Tanzanian territory. The revered 'Mwalimu' (Teacher) was also a patient and skilful mediator who dedicated the last years of his life—until 1999—to trying to find a solution to the conflict in Burundi. He thus left a legacy on security issues in Southern, Eastern, and Central Africa.

Nyerere's heirs in the Eastern African states of Djibouti, Ethiopia, Eritrea, Kenya, Somalia, Sudan, and Uganda are members of IGAD, a subregional body originally created in 1986 to combat drought and to promote development. In 1996, the organisation's charter was revised to include a focus on peace and security. Six years later, IGAD developed its intricate Conflict Early Warning System (CEWARN), based in Ethiopia, with strong assistance from civil society groups. CEWARN focuses on cattle rustling, small arms trafficking, and refugee flows, and has national focal points in each IGAD member state that work with civil society groups.[41] Critics have noted, however, that the mechanism does not address the root causes of conflicts based on problems of governance and interstate disputes.[42] Like Africa's other subregional organisations, IGAD remains poorly staffed, poorly funded, and poorly equipped. Only four professional staff worked in IGAD's Division of Peace and Security in 2007, while the organisation's early warning system had six professional staff.

Despite these problems, the organisation is coordinating the East African Standby Force (EASBRIG), part of the African Standby Force, which involves IGAD members as well as Comoros, Madagascar, Mauritius, Seychelles, and Rwanda. In a 'Great Leap Forward', East African states established their own security mechanism in 2005, and called for a brigade and logistical headquarters in Addis Ababa as well as a planning cell in Nairobi. Like SADC, but unlike ECOWAS, the EASBRIG force is to come under an AU or UN umbrella.

Security on the Horn of Africa is complicated by this subregion's involvement in an Afro-Arab security complex that has seen an alliance between Sudan, Ethiopia, and Yemen; the influence of Saudi Arabia's Wahabi movement in Ethiopia and Eritrea; a jihad movement in Uganda; and alleged terrorist cells in Somalia.[43] These concerns led the United States to establish a military base of 1,700 soldiers in Djibouti in 2002 as part of its global 'war on terror' (see chapter 8). IGAD members also remain deeply divided: Ethiopia and Eritrea fought a bloody border war between 1998 and 2000; Uganda and Sudan have supported each other's rebels; Eritrea has clashed with Djibouti and Sudan; and Ethiopia and Somalia have lingering historical animosity from Somalia's failed irredentist bid to claim Ethiopia's Ogaden region in the war of 1977–1978.[44] Somalia itself currently remains an anarchic state after a botched UN peacekeeping mission was withdrawn from the country in 1995. Ethiopia and Sudan were historically the imperial powers on the Horn of Africa, with their emperors and *khalifas* (kings-in-waiting) embarking on expansionist conquests.[45] Ethiopia's military strength, intelligence-sharing with the US, and hosting of the AU Commission, however, continue to confer on it the status of a leading power and potential hegemon in Eastern Africa. Oil-rich Sudan could also have been a hegemonic rival to Ethiopia in Eastern Africa, but risks internal fragmentation after five decades of intermittent civil wars.[46] The jihadist ideology of the rulers in Khartoum has also alienated African opinion across the continent.

The 1,000–strong Ugandan contingent that deployed in Somalia under an AU flag in 2007, alongside Ethiopian troops who were propping up a weak transitional federal government, represented, to many in Africa, a misguided mission that was utterly unable to stem the reckless bloodbath in Mogadishu, and more of an auxiliary of Pax Americana's erratic 'war on terror' than a mission to promote sustainable peace on the Horn of Africa. In what appeared to be a carefully coordinated military operation, a US gunship bombed a Somali village, and its special forces were reported to be operating on the ground in Somalia. Ethiopia, which had launched several incursions into acephalous Somalia since 1992, deployed troops to Mogadishu in December 2006, seeking to protect its southern flank and to prevent a hostile government in Mogadishu from forging an alliance with Eritrea.[47] Ethiopia failed to stem instability in Somalia and suffered hundreds of fatalities before withdrawing its troops from the country by December 2008, though there have been reports of further incursions back into Somali territory.

Given its divisions, IGAD has failed to coordinate its peacemaking efforts effectively. Significantly, under the chairmanship of Algerian leader Abdelaziz Bouteflika, it was the OAU, and not IGAD, that devised the peace plan for ending the Ethiopia-Eritrea War in 2000. It was also the UN, and not IGAD, that deployed 36,000 troops to oversee two peace processes in Sudan. However, despite its deficiencies, IGAD has devoted much time and resources to peacemaking initiatives in Sudan and Somalia, often with the financial support of the US and the EU.

The Arab Maghreb Union: Qaddafi's Mischief

The Maghreb region has been compared to a bird, with Algeria, Mauritania, and Tunisia constituting the body and Morocco and Libya the necessary wings for the bird to fly. But this is a bird that has been so incapacitated by conflict between its various body parts that it has had difficulty lifting off. Morocco and Algeria have used Western Sahara as a stage to play out their rivalry over leadership of Northwest Africa for the past three decades. The Sahara conflict has been relegated to the background of the world's concerns. The failure, since UN peacekeepers and OAU observers arrived in 1991, to implement a peace agreement to hold a referendum in Western Sahara, has been due to three factors. First, both Morocco, which has illegally occupied the territory since 1975, and the Popular Front for the Liberation of Saguia el-Hamra and Rio de Oro (POLISARIO), transferred the military conflict that was waged for fifteen years to the diplomatic battlefield, and efforts at identifying voters for the referendum effectively became a proxy for waging war by other means. Second, the main external implementing agents of the peace agreement, the UN and the OAU, were distrusted by both parties. Third, two of the five permanent members of the UN Security Council—the US and France—are traditional allies of Morocco and have desisted from applying pressure on the kingdom for fear of triggering domestic instability. It is tragic that the long-suffering Saharan refugees who have inhabited the barren, inhospitable Algerian desert for the past three decades may never be offered a free and fair referendum through which to express their right to determine their own political future[48] and finally resolve the status of Africa's last colony.

Neighboring oil and gas-rich Algeria has been prevented from assuming its role as the natural hegemon of the Maghreb due to a bloody civil war after its military brass hats annulled democratic elections that Islamists were poised to win in 1991, resulting in 100,000 deaths and $20 billion in damages.[49] Abdelaziz Bouteflika, like Nigeria's Umaru Yar' Adua, has been dogged by reports of ill health and fraudulent elections, but has been more active in African diplomacy. In power since 1999, he extended his rule for another five years in April 2009. He has relied on iron-fisted military brass hats to rule, and a 'state of emergency' was still in place in 2009.[50] The Arab Maghreb Union, created in 1989 to promote economic cooperation between its members as a first step towards 'complete integration', became dormant due to the continuing friction in bilateral relations between Algiers and Rabat. With the conflicts in Western Sahara and Algeria, as well as devastating terrorist attacks in Algeria and Morocco, the Maghreb could yet become a boiling cauldron whose eruption into further violence could engulf the entire subregion. No regional peacekeeping has occurred in Northwest Africa, and a subregional brigade for an African standby force appears to be a long way off.

Concerns continue to be raised by many in sub-Saharan Africa that the states in the Maghreb have their bodies in Africa and their heads and hearts in the Middle East. Egypt, another potential North African hegemon, remains the political and cultural centre of the Arab world; between 1958 and 1961 it created, under Gamal Abdel Nasser's leadership, the United Arab Republic—a political union with Syria. Morocco left the OAU in 1984 over the Western Sahara dispute after the organisation recognised POLISARIO's Saharan Arab Democratic Republic (SADR) as one of its members. However, the leaders of Algeria and Libya, in particular, continue to play an important role within the AU, while Libya, Algeria, and Egypt (along with South Africa and Nigeria) contribute 75 per cent of the AU's assessed operating budget. In some ways, the heir of Nkrumah's pan-African political and military vision is Libya's mercurial Muammar Qaddafi, the moving force behind the transformation of the OAU into an AU. But the eccentric 'Brother Leader's' vision for a federalist United States of Africa, an all-African army, and a common monetary union, like Nkrumah's vision, was rejected by most African leaders at the AU summit in Accra, Ghana, in July 2007. Qaddafi used his oil wealth to buy influence within the AU by hosting several important meetings and provided $4.5 million to pay off the arrears to the OAU of Comoros, Guinea-Bissau, Equatorial Guinea, Liberia, Niger, São Tomé and Príncipe, and Seychelles in 1999. He also sought to serve as peacemaker in Ethiopia/Eritrea and Guinea-Bissau.[51] With strong leaders like Mbeki and Obasanjo having left the political stage and unable to block his ascension, Qaddafi finally became chair of the AU for the first time in January 2009 (see chapter 12).

In the politics of the Maghreb, Qaddafi's role has been important. Just before his country took over the presidency of the AMU from Algeria in 2003, the Libyan leader said: 'It's time to put the union in the freezer.'[52] In December 2004, Tripoli announced that it was leaving the AMU. Only pleas from Rabat and Tunis prevented Qaddafi from carrying out his threat. But the fact that, up until December 2009, the subregional body had held only one summit in 1994, suggests that the AMU is more virtual than real. Regional tensions were also heightened by Mauritania's allegations that Libya was funding plots to overthrow Maaouiya Ould Sid Ahmed Taya. Mauritania's president was eventually overthrown in an apparently 'homegrown' putsch in August 2005.

Amidst sporadic rumours of a rapprochement between Algiers and Rabat, the Sahara dispute remains stalemated. One potentially encouraging development in calming the tensions of the Maghreb is the free trade agreement that the US signed with Morocco in 2004. Washington, which designated Rabat as a major non–North Atlantic Treaty Organisation (NATO) ally in 2004, is now arguing for Algeria, Morocco, and Tunisia to create a single market. France has also called for closer Maghrebi integration into the EU, with

French president Nicolas Sarkozy championing a Mediterranean Union encompassing key players in North Africa, Europe, and the Middle East.[53] The AMU has made the least progress of Africa's five subregions in establishing a brigade for the African standby force, though NATO offered rapid reaction training to subregional states in 2004. It was this offer that provoked Qaddafi's threat to abandon the AMU. But officials from Libya, Algeria, Tunisia, Egypt, and POLISARIO held four meetings of experts between 2005 and 2007 (not all countries attended all the meetings) to discuss the establishment of the AU-coordinated North African Standby Brigade, which was expected to be based in Egypt and have a planning cell in Algeria. These plans, however, remain on paper, and Morocco (not a member of the AU) continues to absent itself from these discussions.

Concluding Reflections: Towards A New Berlin Conference in Africa

We conclude with four policy recommendations. First, it is critical that African leaders increase their commitment to providing more financial support to peace and security initiatives as well as to strengthening the capacity of the AU and the regional economic communities. While continuing to expect some external financial support, Africans must show a determination to take the lead to resolve their own problems in order to avoid being caught up in external agendas and priorities. Second, there remains an urgent need for Western donors to demonstrate a similar generosity to Africa, as they have done in Bosnia, Kosovo, East Timor, and Afghanistan. For example, in 2000, while $2 billion was pledged for the reconstruction of the Balkans, barely $150 million was pledged for Sierra Leone. Thirty thousand NATO troops were deployed to tiny Kosovo, in contrast to 20,000 UN peacekeepers to the gigantic Congo. The AU mission in Darfur was grossly underfunded, with a $200 million shortfall announced in July 2005. Third, there is a pressing need to establish a proper division of labour between the UN and Africa's fledgling security organisations. In Sierra Leone, Liberia, Côte d'Ivoire, and Burundi, the UN took over peacekeeping duties from African regional institutions. The willingness of Western peacekeepers, those that have both the equipment and resources, to continue to contribute to UN missions in Africa, remains important. (See chapter 3). Finally, the missions in Sierra Leone, Liberia, Burundi, and the Congo could signify an innovative approach to UN peacekeeping in Africa based on regional pillars supported by local hegemons like Nigeria and South Africa whose political dominance is diluted by multinational peacekeepers from outside their subregions. By placing regional forces under the UN flag, the hope is that the peacekeepers will enjoy the legitimacy and impartiality that the UN's universal membership often provides, while some of the financial and logistical problems of regional peacekeepers can be alleviated through greater burden-sharing.

In concluding this journey that has stretched from Cotonou in the West to Casablanca in the North, it is important that we return to Berlin, where we started the voyage. After the Cold War ended in 1989, events in Berlin would once again have an enormous impact on Africa. The fall of the Berlin Wall appeared to lift the curse of Africa's ancestors over the division of Germany and Europe, marking the end of communist rule on the continent. As Nigerian Nobel laureate Wole Soyinka noted in 1990: 'Such is the poetic mischief of which history often proves itself capable. A century to the partitioning of the African continent at the Berlin Conference, Berlin itself is liberated and reunited.'[54] But the earlier Bismarckian curse of the past still remains to haunt Africa's future: a bloody brother's war was fought over the colonial border of Ethiopia and Eritrea, while Nigeria and Cameroon continued their squabble over the Bakassi peninsula, which was largely decided in favour of Cameroon by the International Court of Justice (ICJ) in 2002.

African leaders must now organise a new Berlin Conference on their own continent. While the decision to freeze the map of Africa in the 1960s may have been wise in a sovereignty-obsessed era of insecure, unconsolidated nation-states,[55] Africans must now muster the ingenuity to craft new arrangements that better reflect their own current realities. Federations and regional trade blocs must be negotiated and territorial boundaries agreed in the long term that reflect the political, socioeconomic, and cultural realities of a vast continent and help to avoid future conflicts. After detailed planning, African leaders must proceed to the ancient empire of Ethiopia—the seat of African diplomacy—and reverse the scandalous act of cartographic mischief inflicted on the continent by European statesmen in Berlin over a century ago. African leaders should invite the ancestors to this continental diplomatic feast, so that Nkrumah can pass on the torch of pan-Africanism to Mbeki, and the curse of Berlin over Africa can finally be lifted.

3

FROM GLOBAL APARTHEID
TO GLOBAL VILLAGE

AFRICA AND THE UNITED NATIONS[1]

'The question that arises is whether the triumph of those market ideologies is polarizing the globe along racial lines more deeply than ever, with black people almost everywhere at the bottom, white people in control of global wealth, and Asian people in intermediate levels of stratification. Is this the global apartheid that is emerging, at its sharpest between white and black?'[2]

Ali A. Mazrui, professor of international relations

During his welcome address to the UN's World Summit on Sustainable Development in South Africa's industrial heartland of Johannesburg in August 2002, then–South African president Thabo Mbeki noted: 'We have converged at the Cradle of Humanity to confront the social behaviour that has pity neither for beautiful nature nor for living human beings. This social behaviour has produced and entrenched a global system of apartheid. The suffering of the billions who are the victims of this system calls for the same response that drew the peoples of the world into the struggle for the defeat of apartheid in this country.'[3]

This chapter seeks to address the concept of 'global apartheid'—used above by both the scholar Mazrui and the statesman Mbeki—which describes the political and socioeconomic inequalities that exist between the rich countries of the industrialised North and the poor countries of the global South. These inequalities are deeply embedded in the world's first truly universal organisation: the United Nations. The paradox of the 192–member world body is that while it embodies ideals of justice and equality, the power politics embodied in its structures—particularly the powerful fifteen-member Security Council— often mean that the Brahmins of international society (the 'Great Powers') can manipulate the system to the disadvantage of the Dalits (the wretched 'Untouchables'). The tale of Africa and the United Nations is thus a 'sacred drama'[4] in which Africa has sought to transform itself from a pawn on the chessboard of the Great Powers to an influential player in global geopolitics.[5]

The apartheid system that we describe here is of course different from the legalised racism in South Africa or the pre–civil rights United States, and focuses more on the fact that the majority of populations in much of the Third World live in widespread poverty as a result partly of the global structures of political and economic power. Like domestic structures in racist societies in South Africa and the United States of the past, however, the consequences of apartheid are similar in terms of darker populations in the Third World suffering the worst forms of an oppressive, unjust system. We must, however, also acknowledge that some former Dalits, such as Singapore, South Korea, and more recently China and India, are joining the ranks of the nouveaux riches in the international caste system, and their interests increasingly converge more with the rich and diverge more with the poor. In this chapter, global apartheid is examined in three important areas: politics (focusing particularly on the UN Security Council, which has yet to allow Africa and South America permanent seats alongside every other region of the world); peacekeeping (focusing particularly on UN peace operations, which have been marred by the tragedies in Somalia in 1993 and Rwanda in 1994); and socioeconomic development (focusing particularly on the challenges of aid, trade, and debt, which continue to bedevil Africa's development despite the efforts of UN specialised agencies, programmes, and funds).

The need to strengthen the UN's role in keeping Africa's peace and promoting economic development on the continent is clear. Between 1948 and 2007, about 40 per cent of the UN's peacekeeping and observer missions (twenty-six out of sixty-three) took place in Africa, with the continent hosting nearly half of the UN peacekeeping missions in the world (seven out of seventeen) in 2009; Africa has produced two UN Secretaries-General, Egyptian Boutros Boutros-Ghali and Ghanaian Kofi Annan, who both held office during the critical post–Cold War period of 1992–2006 (see chapter 4); much of the UN's socioeconomic and humanitarian efforts are located in Africa; and the world body has established subregional offices in West Africa, the Great Lakes region, and Central Africa, as well as peacebuilding offices in Liberia, Guinea-Bissau, the Central African Republic, Angola, Sierra Leone, and Burundi. The UN Environment Programme (UNEP) has its headquarters in Nairobi, Kenya—now one of the UN's biggest hubs—and the UN Economic Commission for Africa (ECA) is based in Addis Ababa, Ethiopia.

Ending Political Apartheid

The United Nations emerged like the mythical Egyptian phoenix from the ashes of the Second World War in 1945. The organisation was born in the US city of San Francisco with the lofty aspirations to 'save succeeding generations from the scourge of war ... to reaffirm faith in fundamental human rights, in the dignity and worth of the human person, in the equal rights of men and women and of nations large and small ... to promote social progress and better standards of life in larger freedom'.[6] Only four African states were present at this grand diplomatic banquet: Liberia, Ethiopia, Egypt, and South Africa—whose racist white minority regime denied the most fundamental rights to its black majority. The National Party would institutionalise the racist policy of apartheid in South Africa three years after the creation of the UN.

Africa played an important role, along with allies from Asia, Latin America, and the Soviet bloc, in the now 130–member Group of 77 (G77) and China—sometimes with the Nordic countries and Canada[7] in support—on issues such as decolonisation, sanctioning apartheid, and promoting socioeconomic development. African states at the UN, with their Southern allies, also established new concepts in international law in areas related to self-determination (Western Sahara); decolonisation and the right to use force in wars of national liberation (Algeria, Angola, Mozambique, and Zimbabwe); racial discrimination (particularly in declaring apartheid in South Africa to be a 'crime against humanity'); permanent sovereignty over natural resources; and the recognition of the international seabed as a 'common heritage of mankind'.[8]

The death knell was finally sounded on the notorious European legal concept of declaring colonial territory *res nullius:* the argument that, since these territories were inhabited by 'native savages' in an era of the Western *mission civilisatrice*, they could be seized by, and carved out among, European colonial powers in the gluttonous imperial feast that took place in Berlin in 1884–1885 (see chapter 1).[9] As Kenyan scholar Ali Mazrui, one of Africa's keenest longtime observers of the UN, has noted: 'For several centuries, rules of European statecraft and diplomatic history had made it perfectly legitimate for a European power to colonise and subjugate a non-Western society. Millions of people in Africa, Asia, and indeed the Americas, fell under European "sovereignty"... It has taken the joint struggles of people of African and Asian ancestry to challenge some of the arrogant and ethnocentric assumptions of international law... The West has been encouraged to re-humanise itself.'[10]

The landmark UN General Assembly Resolution 1514 of 1960—the Declaration on the Granting of Independence to Colonial Countries and Peoples—laid the foundations for the UN's decolonisation efforts. Much to the horror of the UN's largely Western founders, African members and their allies sought to transform an organisation fashioned for peace into one that supported 'just wars' of liberation from colonial oppression. Between 1945 and 1960, forty African and Asian countries, with combined populations of 800 million—over a quarter of the global population at the time—won their independence. During the height of the Cold War in 1980, Africa provided a third of the General Assembly's members (fifty-one out of 154 members). Today, it provides a quarter (fifty-three out of 192 members).

The Group of 77 developing countries (consisting of 130 members) continues to dominate the UN General Assembly's agenda. The 118 states of the Non-Aligned Movement (NAM)—most of which belong to the G77—led the expansion of the UN Security Council from eleven to fifteen members in 1965, and of the Economic and Social Council (ECOSOC) from eighteen to fifty-four members by 1973 (from twenty-seven members in 1965). The African Group at the UN was created in 1958, and soon made its presence felt (often as the Afro-Asian group) on decolonisation and anti–apartheid issues, eventually ostracising South Africa. Simeon Adebo, Nigeria's permanent representative to the UN between 1962 and 1967, noted: 'After the OAU [Organisation of African Unity] came into existence; it spoke with one voice more often than any other group except the Soviet.'[11] The General Assembly also kept up pressure for the liberation of colonial territories.[12] But African members were by no means always united, and many of the francophone African states backed France, even on controversial issues such as its colonial occupation of, and brutal civil war in, Algeria between 1954 and 1962 (which killed over one million Algerians), as well as its atomic tests in the Sahara in the early 1960s.[13]

After the emergence of a Third World majority in the General Assembly by the 1960s, a committee on decolonisation was established in 1962. A special committee against apartheid was created in the same year, and the Convention on the Elimination of Racial Discrimination was agreed upon in 1966. Members of the Palestine Liberation Organisation (PLO) were invited to address the General Assembly's Special Political Committee from 1965 onwards. The unspoken Afro-Arab pact of this era involved African members agreeing to support the Palestinian struggle against Israel, in exchange for Arab members backing the struggle against apartheid in South Africa. Due to pressure from a determined Southern majority—led by Salim Ahmed Salim, Tanzania's formidable permanent representative to the UN at the time—the People's Republic of China took its permanent seat at the UN in 1971 (which had previously been held by US ally Taiwan), in the face of vociferous US opposition. Washington was later instrumental in denying Salim the opportunity to become UN Secretary-General in 1981, describing him as a 'dangerous radical' for his efforts on behalf of communist China.

The African states and their allies also played a decisive role in ending apartheid in South Africa itself. From 1952 onwards, the issue was taken up increasingly forcefully by India (which was particularly concerned about the plight of South African Indians) and African states. By the 1960s, apartheid was being described by the General Assembly as a 'threat to international peace and security'. The UN Special Committee Against Apartheid was established in 1962, and set up the South African Trust Fund to support the oppressed black majority, as well as bodies calling for a sports boycott and an oil embargo. South Africa was suspended from the General Assembly in September 1974, and the African National Congress (ANC) and the Pan-Africanist Congress (PAC)—the country's two leading liberation movements—were invited to participate in debates held by relevant UN bodies on the evils of the apartheid minority regime. In November 1977, the Security Council imposed a mandatory arms embargo on Pretoria—the first time in the UN's history that this measure had ever been employed. The Security Council continued to call for amnesty for political prisoners in South Africa; an end to indiscriminate and often lethal violence against peaceful demonstrators; and from 1985, a lifting of the draconian 'state of emergency' that gave the apartheid military and police special powers of repression.[14] Following a negotiated transition in South Africa between 1990 and 1994, the 3,000–strong UN Observer Mission in South Africa (UNOMSA) was dispatched in September 1992 to monitor political rallies and to support local mediation committees. Under Algerian UN Special Representative Lakhdar Brahimi, the mission observed South Africa's first democratic elections, which brought Nelson Mandela's ANC to power in May 1994.[15]

The Failed Reform of the UN Security Council, 2004–2005

In December 2004, the UN's High-Level Panel on Threats, Challenges, and Change submitted the report *A More Secure World: Our Shared Responsibility* to then–Secretary-General Kofi Annan.[16] Two months later, the African Union's (AU) committee of fifteen foreign ministers met in Mbabane, Swaziland, to craft a common African response to the report. Their response became known as the 'Ezulwini Consensus'. This comprehensive document—the only common response by any region of the world to the High-Level Panel report—called for an expansion of the Security Council from fifteen to twenty-six members, with two permanent seats holding veto power for Africa, as well as two additional rotating seats to add to Africa's existing three rotating seats. Ezulwini also called for a strengthening of the UN General Assembly to make it more democratic, and advocated that the UN's Economic and Social Council be empowered to play a major role in implementing the Millennium Development Goals' aim of halving poverty by 2015. At this meeting, AU foreign ministers also called for strengthened peacekeeping in Africa, including the financing of African regional organisations by the UN. They further supported the idea of establishing a UN Peacebuilding Commission (which was created in December 2005 to mobilise international support for postconflict countries); rejected the proposal for a Human Rights Council with universal membership (this body was established in December 2005 with forty-seven members and can now expel members by a two-thirds majority); and backed the idea of a 'responsibility to protect' doctrine, and a common definition of terrorism. Ezulwini also advocated increased access to, and support for, HIV/AIDS treatment and research as well as healthcare systems. The ministers further called for a plan to manage the sustainability of Africa's debt burden of $290 billion, and for greater transparency in negotiations at the World Trade Organisation (WTO).[17]

Having provided a general background to some African perspectives on the UN reform process of 2004–2005, we now focus on the specific issue of the failed effort to reform the Security Council. This reform effort—the most discussed proposal in the UN reform agenda—died an ignominious death amidst the horse-trading between African foreign ministers and the Group of Four (G4) (Japan, Germany, Brazil, and India); Chinese intransigence; US and Russian ambivalence; and the anti–permanent membership 'spoilers' of Pakistan, Italy, Canada, and Mexico in the 'Uniting for Consensus' group. It was hard to discern a clear direction during this surreal process of smoke and mirrors. Some background is important to understanding this arcane debate.[18]

In the past four decades, every effort at reforming the Security Council—the UN's most powerful decisionmaking body—has failed. The effort in 2005 was no exception. The UN's Open-Ended Working Group on Council Reform, established in December 1993, has long been dismissed as the 'Never-Ending Working Group'. The five veto-wielding permanent members of this anachronistic Council—the United States, Russia, China, Britain, and France—still reflect the alliance of victors dating from the end of the Second World War in 1945. While the formal use of the veto by the Permanent Five (P5) has declined, the veto is still effectively exercised in the closed-door consultations of the Council, which is where much of its serious business occurs. Many of the archaic procedures and policies of the Council are well known to the five permanent members, which also have privileged access to UN documents through secretariat staff. Decisions are often based on complex and not always visible trade-offs between P5 members spanning many years. Since no written records of the closed-door consultations are kept, the five permanent members represent the Council's institutional memory, which gives them a huge advantage over the ten rotating members—sometimes dismissed as 'tourists' by P5 members—which only serve two-year terms.[19] As Dumisani Kumalo, South Africa's permanent representative to the UN between 1999 and 2009, observed: 'To this day, no structure deemed "strategic" can be created in the UN without the automatic participation and membership of the P5. The permanent members also enjoy a stranglehold over key positions within the UN Secretariat.'[20]

A reconstituted Security Council would almost certainly give Africa an enhanced presence at the top table of global diplomacy, helping to ensure that, with consistently strong representation, the continent could seek to check the excesses of the P5, and that Africa's security concerns are taken more seriously. This is particularly important given that about 60 per cent of the Council's deliberations focus on the continent, and that in 2009 about 70 per cent of UN peacekeepers were deployed in Africa. The UN Security Council must thus still undergo democratisation so that it includes a more consistently strong African presence in particular and more members of the global South in general. Africa should also build a peacekeeping coalition at the UN with Asia and other regions that have contributed to UN peacekeeping efforts in Africa, to ensure that the world body does not ignore future genocides, as occurred in Rwanda in 1994, resulting in 800,000 deaths.

The UN High-Level Panel of 2004 had suggested an increase in Council membership from fifteen to twenty-four members: the creation of six new permanent members without veto power, and three more rotating two-year nonpermanent seats, in addition to the five veto-wielding permanent members. According to the terms of this proposal, Africa would gain two permanent seats and an additional rotating seat to add to the three it already holds. An acrimonious meeting of AU leaders in Addis Ababa in August 2005 exposed the continent's deep divisions over this issue, with countries like Egypt, Libya, Algeria, and Zimbabwe reportedly opposing the pragmatic approach of Nigeria and South Africa, which were willing to drop the unrealistic insistence on a veto for new Council members (Germany and Japan, as well as their Brazilian and Indian allies, were also prepared to drop the veto). This lack of African consensus—with China, which was determined mainly to exclude Japan from the Council, reportedly influencing several countries in a bid to stall Security Council reform—contributed significantly to the failure to achieve Security Council reform at the September 2005 summit. The African bloc of fifty-three states—representing about a quarter of the 192–strong General Assembly membership—was thus unable to play the bridging role required to reach the 128 votes needed to obtain a two-thirds majority, and put pressure on veto-wielding Washington and Beijing to agree to the expansion of the Security Council.

Disputes also emerged in Africa as to which countries would fill the two permanent African seats. Egypt, Nigeria, and South Africa all declared their candidacies. Kenya, Libya, and Senegal also expressed interest. It is important, since the issue of UN Security Council reform will surely reemerge in future, to assess the current strengths and weaknesses of Africa's three leading candidates in this contest: Nigeria, South Africa, and Egypt. Cynics dismissed Nigeria as too 'anarchic', Egypt as too 'Arab', and South Africa as too 'albinocratic'.

In its favour, Nigeria—Africa's most populous state, with about 140 million residents, and the sixth largest oil producer in the Organisation of the Petroleum Exporting Countries (OPEC)—has an impressive peacekeeping record, dating from the UN's protracted Congo crisis in the 1960s until more recent peacekeeping missions in Liberia and Sierra Leone in the 1990s (see chapter 6). Nigeria hosted a UN anti–apartheid conference in 1977 and chaired its anti–apartheid committee for much of the latter's existence. It has produced impressive UN technocrats such as Simeon Adebo (former executive director of the UN Training and Research Institute), Adebayo Adedeji (former executive secretary of the UN Economic Commission for Africa), and Ibrahim Gambari (UN Special Representative in Sudan's Darfur region and a former

Undersecretary-General for Political Affairs). But Nigeria is in the throes of a difficult transition from fifteen years of military misrule, and continues to suffer from the excesses of a profligate political class and communal strife that have resulted in over 10,000 deaths since 1999. The country also conducted a deeply flawed election in 2007 that saw the accession of Umaru Yar'Adua to the presidency. It is therefore unclear whether Nigeria will be a force for stability or instability in Africa.[21] However, Nigeria convincingly won a non-permanent seat on the Security Council in 2010–2011.

South Africa, which also won a two-year nonpermanent seat on the UN Security Council by an overwhelming majority in 2007–2008, has several advantages: as Africa's richest country—albeit with massive inequalities—its constitutional democracy is widely admired; it has produced four Nobel peace laureates—Albert Luthuli, Desmond Tutu, Nelson Mandela, and F.W. de Klerk;[22] and former president Thabo Mbeki won much praise for his peace-making efforts in the Congo, Côte d'Ivoire, and Burundi (see chapters 5 and 11). South Africa, a respected member of the global South, also has wide-ranging trade interests in Asia, Europe, and the Americas, and under Mbeki's presidency between 1999 and 2008, established a strategic partnership with Brazil and India. The country also organised two high-profile UN summits on race and sustainable development. On the negative side, South Africa's military, academic, and economic institutions are still widely viewed as white-dominated, and memories of the country's destructive destabilisation of the region in the 1980s still linger amidst concerns over whether many South Africans have truly embraced an African identity (see chapter 5).[23] Xenophobic attacks by South African mobs against their fellow Africans from neighbouring countries and beyond in May 2008, and an abysmal response to the brutality on the part of the country's leadership, further damaged South Africa's pan-African credentials.

Egypt, the final leading candidate for a future African Security Council seat, has a proud history of international peacekeeping, and produced a UN Secretary-General, Boutros Boutros-Ghali, and two Nobel peace laureates, President Anwar Sadat (1970-1981) and Mohamed El-Baradei, who was director-general of the International Atomic Energy Agency (IAEA) from 1998 to 2009. But the country has been accused of having its body in Africa and its heart and head in the Middle East. The apparent Arab League support for Cairo's candidacy as an African permanent member of a reformed UN Security Council at a meeting in Algiers in 2005 reinforced this perception. As early as the 1950s, Egypt's legendary leader Gamal Abdel Nasser had annoyed black Africans by speaking patronisingly of 'diffusing the light of civilisation into the furthest parts of the virgin jungle'.[24] The country's leader, Hosni Mubarak, was seen, until the battle for a Security Council seat in 2005, as largely detached from African affairs, as he rarely attended continental diplomatic meetings. Questions also continue to be raised about Egypt's democratic and human rights record, with the septuagenarian Mubarak extending his twenty-four-year rule in flawed elections in 2005.

Ending Peacekeeping Apartheid

Between 1948 and 1978, the UN deployed only thirteen peacekeeping missions around the globe. But since 1990 and the end of the Cold War, over forty-seven such missions have been deployed.[25] The UN peacekeeping budget was $5 billion in 2005 (equal to US expenditures in Iraq for one month in the same year).[26] In July 2009, seven of the UN's seventeen peacekeeping missions were in Africa (Western Sahara, Liberia, Côte d'Ivoire, Democratic Republic of the Congo, South Sudan, Sudan's Darfur region, and the Central African Republic/Chad), while about 70 per cent of its personnel were deployed on the continent. But despite the importance of the UN to Africa, there is still a paucity of knowledge among many African practitioners and policymakers about the organisation, and about how best to access it to serve the continent's peacekeeping needs.[27]

The Brahimi Report of August 2000 had sought to strengthen the UN's peacekeeping capacity, and suggested innovations such as preapproving funds for peacekeeping missions; improving the rapid deployment of civilian personnel to UN missions, as well as strengthening communication between headquarters and the field; and increasing the size of the UN's Department of Peacekeeping Operations (DPKO) from 400 to 600 personnel.[28] However, this report, named after the man who chaired it, Algeria's Lakhdar Brahimi,[29] was disappointingly short on details on how to improve relations between the UN and Africa's regional organisations—the continent's main peacekeeping preoccupation. The report's constant warnings that the UN should not undertake those missions where it could not guarantee success was seen by many in Africa as code for avoiding African conflicts, following UN debacles in Somalia in 1993 and Rwanda in 1994. A report named after one of Africa's most illustrious public servants had thus ironically ignored the continent's most urgent peacekeeping needs.

Unlike the August 2000 Brahimi Report, the December 2004 High-Level Panel report seemed at first to give priority to relations between the UN and

Africa's regional organisations. This approach was championed by a prominent African on the panel, Salim Ahmed Salim, former OAU Secretary-General, who for twelve years in Addis Ababa (1989–2001) had experienced the frustrations of seeking assistance from the UN Security Council in many African conflicts, such as those in Burundi, Liberia, and Sierra Leone.[30] David Hannay, another panel member and former British permanent representative to the UN, was also a strong advocate of strengthening ties between the UN and Africa's regional organisations, having worked closely with Ibrahim Gambari, Nigeria's former permanent representative to the UN (1990–1999), on these issues between 1994 and 1995.[31] The UN High-Level Panel held one of its meetings in Addis Ababa in April 2004, and met with senior African Union officials and African civil society actors to gain their perspectives on relations with the UN. At the time, it was felt that this was a clear sign of the panel's desire to focus on the UN's ties with African actors and institutions. But in the end, the panel's report devoted about five paragraphs out of 302 to Africa's most important peacekeeping challenges. Like the Brahimi Report before it, another high-level group had failed to grasp the UN-regional cooperation nettle, despite assurances from representatives during their meetings (one of which this author attended) that this was a key area of high priority.

Kofi Annan's March 2005 report to the General Assembly, *In Larger Freedom*, called on donors to devise a ten-year capacity-building plan together with the African Union, which is developing an African standby force, to be deployable by 2010. The pan-continental force is based on five subregional brigades built around members of the Southern African Development Community (SADC), the Economic Community of West African States (ECOWAS), the Economic Community of Central African States (ECCAS), the Intergovernmental Authority on Development (IGAD), and the Arab Maghreb Union (AMU) (see chapter 2). Both Annan's 2005 report and the UN High-Level Panel report of 2004 advocated UN financial support for Africa's regional organisations. Although there is still resistance to this idea, particularly among the P5 and within the UN secretariat, the world body must learn lessons from ECOWAS's difficult experiences in Liberia and Sierra Leone (1990–2003), and from the AU's difficult peacekeeping experience in Burundi (2003–2004) and Sudan's Darfur region (2003–2007) (see chapter 2). These challenges effectively forced both organisations to hand all four missions over to the UN. Africa must ensure that the UN assumes its proper peacekeeping responsibilities, supporting and taking over regional peacekeeping missions to ensure sufficient legitimacy and resources. The continent must be vigilant to ensure that the proposed UN-AU ten-year capacity-building plan is implemented, given the tendency, since 2002, of donors such as the Group of Eight (G8) industrialised countries to make similar yet unfulfilled promises.

In the first four and a half decades of the UN's existence, there was only one UN peacekeeping operation in Africa—the controversial Congo intervention (1960–1964).[32] The UN only returned to Africa as a peacekeeper twenty-five years later, in 1989, when it administered apartheid South Africa's military withdrawal from Namibia, and supervised that country's first democratic election in 1990. During the next decade, seventeen peacekeeping operations were undertaken by the UN in Africa. There were relative successes in Namibia and Mozambique, but also catastrophic failures in Angola, Somalia, and Rwanda.[33] The cooperation between the UN and the Nigerian-led ECOWAS peacekeeping missions in Liberia and Sierra Leone between 1993 and 2000 yielded some positive results. However, this relationship was also characterised by serious challenges, including tensions between the ECOWAS Ceasefire Monitoring Group (ECOMOG) and the UN over strategy, division of labour, and the sharing of scarce resources, as well as conditions of service and remuneration. In addition, there was often poor communication and a lack of trust between the two organisations.[34] There still remains a pressing need to establish a proper division of labour between the UN and Africa's fledgling security organisations, which need to be greatly strengthened.[35] As Salim Ahmed Salim, former Tanzanian permanent representative at the UN and the country's former foreign minister, insightfully noted: 'combining the principle of neighbourhood with the principle of distant impartiality ... is critical because at times keeping neighbours out of each other's problems carries the risk of fomenting suspicion and resentment'.[36]

Ending Socioeconomic Apartheid

Turning from peacekeeping to socioeconomic apartheid, the influence of Western countries was critical to the UN's socioeconomic work from the time that these organisations were created. Just as the world body had been a product of the Western political and legal system, so too were the UN's socioeconomic institutions set up to promote development. Many of these organisations had been established on the basis of socioeconomic challenges that had faced Western Europe in the nineteenth and early twentieth centuries. The UN Educational, Scientific, and Cultural Organisation (UNESCO), for example, emerged from a British-led conference of education ministers in London in 1942.[37] Specialised agencies, including the UN Relief and Rehabilitation Administration (forerunner of the current Office of the UN High Commissioner for Refugees [UNHCR]), the Food and Agriculture Organisation (FAO), the International Bank for Reconstruction and Development (IBRD) (now the World Bank), and the General Agreement on Tariffs and Trade (GATT) (now the World Trade Organisation) were established between 1943 and 1945, with the United States hosting many of their preliminary meetings.

At the time of their creation, many of these specialised agencies were staffed largely by idealistic Western liberals in a cosy club of mostly Euro-American citizens.[38] From the 1960s onwards, African states and their Asian and other allies expanded on these institutions, leading the creation of the UN Conference on Trade and Development (UNCTAD) in 1964[39] and the UN Development Programme (UNDP)[40] in 1965. These governments sought to use these institutions to promote their own socioeconomic development. The global South thus forced the UN to move away from focusing exclusively on the peace and security issues that preoccupied its Great Powers, towards the socioeconomic development needs of its poorest members. In the politicised environment of decolonisation and the Cold War, Africa and its Third World allies ignored the original intentions of the UN's predominantly Euro-American founders for the specialised agencies—that they would focus on purely technical issues, and leave political issues to the Security Council and General Assembly. Instead, the Afro-Asians brought ideological struggles into many of these organisations.[41]

This was during an era, from 1974 onwards, in which the South was confrontationally demanding a fundamental restructuring of the international system through a New International Economic Order (NIEO) that would result in the transfer of resources and technology from the rich North to the poor South. This shift also reflected the euphoric possibility of increasing Southern leverage that followed OPEC's tripling of world oil prices in 1973. Meanwhile, at the First UN Conference on Women, in 1975, the Third World majority passed a resolution equating Zionism with racism (which was later rescinded in 1991). The Southern 'barbarians'—in the form of what Martiniquan scholar Frantz Fanon had described as the 'wretched of the earth'[42]— were finally at the gates of the hallowed mansions and manicured lawns of the exclusive Northern 'gentlemen's club' to challenge the rules of global apartheid that they had had no say in setting. The UN currently has about thirty specialised agencies, funds, and programmes; it was always going to be difficult for UN headquarters in New York to coordinate them all. Many of these bodies had autonomous budgets, and together they had more staff than the UN secretariat. In 1995, 14,000 staff worked in the UN secretariat, while 39,000 people staffed the UN's agencies, programmes, and funds.[43] These bodies soon developed into fiefdoms controlled by powerful cabals.

The Rise and Fall of UN Socioeconomic Reforms, 2004–2005

Perhaps the most disappointing outcome of the UN reform process of 2004–2005 was the failure to make substantive progress on issues relating to development, aid, and trade. Since Africa is the continent most negatively affected by this situation, there remains an urgent need for its governments and civil society activists to continue to push (together with their Third World, Chinese, and Western allies) for the development of a fair international trading and financial system. UNCTAD's suggestion, in September 2004, that the international donor community annul Africa's debilitating debt of $290 billion must be strongly supported. It is significant to note, as does a 2004 UNCTAD report, that between 1970 and 2002, Africa borrowed $540 billion and paid back about $550 billion in principal and interest.[44]

The West must also open its markets to freer and fairer trade with Africa. Development assistance urgently needs to be increased to 0.7 per cent of the national incomes of rich countries: a target set at the UN as far back as 1970, and met consistently since then largely by only a few donors, notably the Nordic countries and the Netherlands. Donors need to coordinate their efforts better, and richer countries from Asia, the Middle East, and Africa must join the current group of largely Western donors to contribute more to global development efforts.

Only a few African countries have so far seen an effective alleviation of their debt burden under the World Bank's Heavily Indebted Poor Countries (HIPC) initiative. Even many of the countries that have reached the HIPC's completion point could not sustain their debt levels, both because growth and export levels had been overestimated, and because the cost of importing oil rose astronomically during the 2004–2007 period (reaching $100 a barrel in December 2007). Africa's debts were largely accumulated by corrupt, monstrous autocrats like Zaire's Mobutu Sese Seko, Somalia's Siad Barre, and Liberia's Samuel Doe, many of whom were fed with Western or Soviet grants and loans during the Cold War era. Faced with raging conflicts, grinding poverty, and an AIDS epidemic that threatens to wipe out large populations in Africa,[45] the governments that have inherited these debts cannot morally continue to be forced to use a quarter or more of their export earnings to service loans that everyone knows can never be repaid. Scarce resources that should be going towards health and education are being used to service unpayable debts, a form of socioeconomic apartheid that must be halted forthwith if Africa is to recover from its three-decade economic crisis since 1980.

Africa's share of global trade declined from about 6 per cent in the early 1980s to only 2 per cent in 2006.[46] The global trading system, as represented by the inequities of the WTO and the two Bretton Woods institutions—the World Bank and the International Monetary Fund (IMF)—must also be reformed as soon as possible in ways that give Africa a greater voice. African and other Southern representation in the highest decisionmaking organs of these organisations must be urgently increased. Unfair trade practices by rich countries also make it harder for African countries to lift their economies out of poverty. Most industrialised countries impose high tariffs on agricultural and manufactured goods—the areas of comparative advantage for African states. This has led to grotesque distortions between North and South: the agricultural subsidies of rich countries, at $311 billion, exceeded the total national income of sub-Saharan Africa, at $301 billion, by 2001.[47]

There are, however, also divisions between members of the global South. At World Trade Organisation negotiations, countries such as Brazil, India, South Africa, and China made concerted efforts with other members of the Group of 20+ (G20+) in the Doha negotiations to promote world trade and present a bloc that could more effectively defend Southern interests from the protectionist excesses of the rich North.[48] There were, however, accusations from some members of the seventy-nine-strong African, Caribbean, and Pacific (ACP) group that Southern countries like South Africa, India, and Brazil were engaging in nontransparent negotiations in smoke-filled 'green rooms', cutting deals with powerful, rich countries that could benefit them as big agricultural producers. These ACP members complained that such deals contradicted the interests of weaker countries, which were insisting on concrete trade concessions from richer countries. South Africa was particularly criticised by other African delegates for acting as a self-appointed African spokesperson without necessarily promoting the continent's interests.[49]

In recognition of the pernicious effect of the rich world's agricultural subsidies, the WTO's Doha trade round agreed in 2001 to eliminate these subsidies, although significantly, no timetable was set for this process. By 2009, not much progress had been made. These subsidies must be urgently eliminated, with a clear plan for the extent of the reductions needed each year. Meanwhile, as subsidies and tariffs (as well as poor domestic governance, as evidenced by deeply flawed elections in Nigeria and Kenya in 2007, and Zimbabwe in 2008) continue to cripple Africa's economic prospects, the rich world has become less generous with development assistance. Between 1990 and 2001, official development assistance (ODA) fell from 0.33 to 0.22 per cent of the gross national income of donors. It was established that in order to meet the Millennium Development Goals' aim of halving poverty by 2015 in Africa and elsewhere in the developing world, a minimum of $100 billion a year would need to be provided by the industrialised world. This figure would still represent only 0.43 per cent of the national income of Organisation for Economic Cooperation and Development (OECD) countries. By 2010, no African country was on track to meet even the limited aspirations of the Millennium Development Goals.

During the 2005 Group of Eight meeting in Gleneagles, Scotland, there was euphoric talk—spurred on by well-meaning but naive Irish rock stars Bob Geldof and Bono—about 'Making Poverty History' and unveiling a 'Marshall Plan' for Africa. The Gleneagles accord promised to begin lifting Western export subsidies that harmed African agricultural products; to double aid to Africa to $50 billion by 2010; and to write off $55 billion of debt involving fourteen African countries. There were also promises to support African peacekeeping and the battle against AIDS, as well as infrastructure projects. But as often occurs in these cases, the devil was in the details: there was no timetable for eliminating farm subsidies; only about a third of the promised aid was new money; and, based on recent experiences, future fiscally conscious Western governments are unlikely to honour these pledges, particularly with over $3 trillion being devoted to stemming the global financial meltdown between 2007 and 2009. By 2010, none of these targets were on track to be met, and there was deep disillusionment in Africa with the growing practice of donors to make pledges that they had no intention of honouring in the first place.

Aside from Bono and Geldof, some Africans have themselves offered dangerous and simplistic recipes for resolving Africa's economic crisis. Dambisa Moyo, a Zambian analyst and former employee of the World Bank and Goldman Sachs, in her 2009 book *Dead Aid*, called for an end to aid in Africa in five years, while correctly acknowledging the pernicious impact of Western agricultural subsidies on African economies.[50] Without providing much convincing evidence, she blamed aid for corruption and conflict in Africa, as well as for preventing the building of social capital and attracting foreign investment. Moyo called instead for the use of private capital markets, remittances from African diasporas, microfinance, and Chinese investment: impractical solutions that have surely been overtaken by the global financial crisis of 2007 to 2009. In a simplistic work that ignores the thinking of leading African scholars such as Adebayo Adedeji, Thandika Mkandawire, Mbaya Kankwenda, Bade Onimode and Adebayo Olukoshi, she consistently placed the blame for Africa's socioeconomic ills disproportionately on Africans, while drawing fatuous comparisons with China and India. In a March 2009 interview with Richard Dowden—the director of the Royal African Society—Moyo made the astonishing comment that 'South Africa and Botswana ... don't rely on aid and guess what? For some reason they have lower poverty levels.'[51] To describe a country like South Africa—the world's most unequal society, with unofficial unemployment estimated by some at 40 per cent and with some of the most widespread poverty in the world—in such terms, would usually be enough to cast doubt on any author's opinions.[52] As Madeleine Bunting rightly noted in reviewing Moyo's book: 'The result is an erratic, breathless sweep through history and current policy options for Africa, sprinkled with the odd statistic. There are so many generalisations skidding over decades of history, such frequent pre-emptory glib conclusions ... her grasp of the political economy of Africa is lamentable.'[53]

Offering another perspective to Moyo is Kenyan Nobel peace laureate and environmental activist Wangari Maathai.[54] She cited positive examples of 'millennium villages' in Kenya's Nyanza province in which health, education, and farming improved dramatically as a result of carefully targeted aid and the involvement of citizens in socioeconomic development. Maathai also noted how aid became politicised during the Cold War and, in contrast to Moyo's ahistorical approach, showed how aid often undermined its stated objectives of poverty alleviation and socioeconomic development. Aid was diverted, in many cases, with the conscious knowledge of donors who were supporting strategic allies during the Cold War. Maathai, who co-chaired the Jubilee 2000 campaign for debt cancellation in Kenya, noted the heavy-handed 'conditionalities' on African governments to slash health and education budgets and to liberalise their markets before obtaining debt relief. Like late South African economist Margaret Legum,[55] Maathai criticised the irresponsibility of creditors who lent billions of dollars to corrupt and often unaccountable governments without a proper assessment of whether these debts could be repaid. The Kenyan Nobel laureate further noted that, despite the cancellation of $88 billion of African debt by 2008, poor countries were still returning an average of $5 in debt service for every $1 in aid that they received. As Maathai put it: 'It makes no sense for African governments to receive aid on the one hand, while on the other paying back debts acquired in the past by discredited regimes for projects that in the main did not benefit the African people.'[56] She went on to criticise the continuing unfair trade practices of the United States, European countries, and some East Asian countries that continue to protect cotton, wheat, sugar, and other products through subsidies and tariffs. This analysis, unlike Moyo's, clearly demonstrates the continuing structural problems that Africa faces in confronting socioeconomic apartheid.

The UN System vs. the Bretton Woods Institutions

The Bretton Woods institutions—the World Bank and the IMF—had been set up by the United States in 1944–1945 specifically to prevent or circumvent some of the economic crises of the 1930s Depression era that were thought to have contributed to the Second World War. Though both organisations are formally UN specialised agencies, they enjoy total autonomy from the world body. Powerful Western actors thus maintain a strong grip on these bodies, with voting weighted according to each country's contributions. An apartheid system was established in which an American always occupied the head of the World Bank in exchange for a European heading the IMF. ECOSOC was thus marginalised, and the UN's economic development bodies simply lacked the enormous funds of the Bretton Woods institutions and bilateral aid donors.

As early as 1963, Alex Quaison-Sackey, Ghana's permanent representative to the UN between 1959 and 1965, had noted: 'The World Bank tends to be parsimonious; it does not lend money without the fulfilment of rigorous conditions—and it does not do so, even then, without protracted negotiations.'[57] He called instead for a UN development fund to assist African countries. The views of a fellow Ghanaian, Kenneth Dadzie, who was secretary-general of UNCTAD between 1986 and 1992, are also worth considering in this regard. Dadzie noted that the World Bank and the IMF had been pursuing their own path since the early 1960s, increasingly making access to their funds by African governments conditional on adopting domestic measures that they had recommended. He further noted that agencies such as the

UNDP tried to provide technical assistance to African governments from 1965 onwards, but did not have the resources of the two Bretton Woods institutions. However, the latter are renowned for their 'one size fits all' prescriptions for countries with very diverse needs and problems.

Dadzie also pointed to the reduced Western interest in negotiating development cooperation during the 1980s. This was an era of neoliberal Reaganomics and Thatcherite economic policies that obsessively stressed the role of the private sector and the market, promoted the deregulation of the financial sector (which eventually contributed to the global financial crisis from 2007 onward), and frowned on active government intervention in the economy. While conceding that UN development bodies were prone to duplication and a lack of coordination, Dadzie noted that in 1986, about 75 per cent of Overseas Development Assistance was provided by bilateral donors, 15 per cent by the World Bank and other financial institutions, and only 6 per cent by the UN. He observed that this aid was often politicised, particularly if coming from the United States, France, and Japan.[58] As Dadzie bluntly put it: 'The critical issue has been the unwillingness of the great industrial powers to ... share with their developing country partners the management of the global economic commons that the world's trading, monetary, and financial systems represent.'[59] Adebayo Adedeji, one of the most eloquent and strident critics of the pernicious impact of the Bretton Woods institutions' structural adjustment programmes on Africa's socioeconomic development,[60] used his position as executive secretary of the UN Economic Commission for Africa between 1975 and 1991 to push for alternatives that stressed solutions developed by Africans and adapted to their own specific circumstances—solutions that involved African self-reliance, regional integration, and popular participation in the development process. As Adedeji sadly noted in 2009 about the organisation he had so courageously led:

[T]he ECA has abandoned ship, leaving behind the theoreticians, prophets and marabouts of development, who, together with the Bretton Woods institutions, constitute the Development Merchant System (DMS). These actors constitute the 'sellers' of the DMS, while African political regimes are the 'buyers'. Both have profited and are profiting from this trade, while the mass of African people constitute the permanent underdogs and losers of this system.[61]

By 2002, the UN still accounted for only 8 per cent of ODA, the EU for 10 per cent, international development associations and banks for 8 per cent, while 69 per cent of total ODA of $58.3 billion came from bilateral donors. By this time, the UN was focusing largely on humanitarian assistance and technical cooperation rather than on providing capital to African countries. ECOSOC, which was created to oversee many of the UN's specialised agencies, has not been able to coordinate them effectively. During the UN reform process of 2004–2005, Southern efforts to convert ECOSOC into a more effective coordinating body failed spectacularly. Powerful Western governments continue to prefer to exert their influence through the Bretton Woods institutions and the WTO which they control rather than through the UN.[62] As former UN Secretary-General Boutros Boutros-Ghali put it in 2009: 'Development is as important as peace to the United Nations. But, unfortunately, development has become an ugly word in the post–Cold War era... [M]any states prefer to provide aid bilaterally, rather than multilaterally; they are willing to be generous in emergency humanitarian cases, but not in meeting long-term development needs.'[63] Boutros-Ghali further observed about the Bretton Woods institutions and the WTO: 'These are organisations in which democratic values do not count for much in decision and policy-making. The underlying objective of these institutions is to support the status quo, not to be critical of it.'[64] In 2008, Washington and its European allies still had 53 per cent of voting shares in the IMF, while sub-Saharan Africa had only two executive directors on a twenty-four-member IMF and World Bank board of governors.[65]

But things may be starting to change, with the pernicious effects of the global financial crisis of 2007 to 2009 on the West and the expansion of the G8 to twenty countries by 2009. Before the Group of 20 (G20) meeting in London in April 2009, Brazilian president Luiz Inácio Lula—a man from a poor, working-class background—caused a storm by saying that the global financial crisis had been caused by blue-eyed white men with blonde hair who had arrogantly seen themselves, he implied, as masters of the universe. Across the Third World, the three-quarters of the world's nonwhite population perfectly understood Lula's words, but much of the Western media was aghast at the lack of political correctness from a global statesman. The fact that the most powerful man at the G20 summit was Barack Obama, an 'Afro-Saxon' US president with a Kenyan father, seemed, however, to vindicate Lula (see chapter 13). Obama himself noted that, a few years ago, anyone predicting a meeting with rich countries and emerging economies hosting a US president called 'Obama' would have been dismissed out of hand. The fact that China—the new 'workshop of the world'—is in 2010 the world's second largest economy (after the US), and that three of the five largest banks in the world are Chinese, was further proof of the shifting global balance of power (see chapters 8 and 9). With China stumping up $40 billion to help refinance the International Monetary Fund, the London summit was forced to agree to discuss an end to the sixty-five-year system of 'global apartheid' in which an American always heads the World Bank and a European the IMF. The weighted voting that allows mostly rich Western countries to dominate both Bretton Woods institutions should also come to a speedy end with emerging heavy-hitting G20 countries like China (and surely others like India, Indonesia, Brazil, and South Korea) increasing their influence within these institutions.[66]

Reflecting on the impact of the global financial crisis on African countries, which for decades obediently followed the often misguided economic advice of the two Bretton Woods institutions, Adebayo Adedeji noted scathingly: 'the meltdown of the global financial architecture represents a judgment on the corrupt and evil world that has been overly concerned with the free market ideology at the expense of economic rationality.'[67] The Nigerian economist noted the deleterious effects of financial deregulation across Africa on productivity-oriented entrepreneurs, decrying the rise of unscrupulous currency speculators. Adedeji further observed that, due to volatile macroeconomic conditions, banking and financial sectors in Africa performed dismally in supporting productive investments that could have promoted domestic agriculture, manufacturing, and infrastructure development. He therefore called for the establishment of strong, independent institutions to monitor African central banks in order to ensure that 'financialisation becomes a true instrument for development'.[68] It is worth taking heed of the wise words of this former UN insider and his consistent critique of the Bretton Woods–inspired structural adjustment programmes that have done so much harm to African societies since the 1980s.

Concluding Reflections: Towards a Global Village

The United Nations has grown from an organisation of only fifty-one members in 1945 to 192 today. In the process, it has become the first truly universal organisation in world history. The UN has helped keep the peace around the world; advance socioeconomic development; feed the hungry; promote human rights; preserve historical monuments; protect workers, refugees, and the environment; and raise consciousness of the rights of women and children. But despite its lofty rhetoric, the world body has often failed to live up to its aspirations, and the global apartheid between the rich North and the global

South persists. Perhaps we should take heed of the words of the Swedish former UN Secretary-General Dag Hammarskjöld (1953–1961) that 'the UN was not created to take humanity to heaven, but to save it from hell'.[69]

More optimistically, Kwesi Armah, Ghana's high commissioner to Britain in the early 1960s, noted: 'there would be neither a world moral opinion nor the means of expressing it if the United Nations did not exist. It is a battleground of ideas, a sounding-board of political, social, and economic theories.'[70] In relation to Africa's contributions to the UN, it is appropriate again to quote the profound words of Alex Quaison-Sackey, Ghana's former permanent representative to the UN, who noted in 1963: 'Africa has helped to make the United Nations more truly itself.'[71] In the past six decades, through its decolonisation and anti–apartheid struggles waged with its Third World, Soviet, and Western allies, as well as through its diplomats, international civil servants, and two UN Secretaries-General, Africa has—through what former Ghanaian president Kwame Nkrumah described as 'the African Personality in world affairs'[72]—helped to humanise the world body, transforming it from an organisation focused largely on the destructive power politics of the Great Powers, to one that has been forced to promote the socioeconomic needs of the world's poorest inhabitants.

As Ali Mazrui has pointed out, Africa—which had once believed that its village was the world—is helping to shape the idea that the world must become a more humane global village. Socioeconomic development, human dignity, and peace must be the hallmarks of this village. But Mazrui has also noted the limits of the influence of Africa and its allies within the UN: 'The most powerful of its members are not prepared to let it assert greater control over the destiny of this shared planet. The world may be in the process of becoming a village, but this particular village council has yet to become authoritative. The numerals of power can only work effectively when not only the council but also the population of the village has accepted democracy in both intention and its implementation.'[73] Ending global apartheid in the spheres of politics, peacekeeping, and socioeconomic development is the surest way to ensure the survival and success of the world body for another six decades. Africa stands ready to play its part in these noble efforts.

In this vein, it is perhaps appropriate to conclude this chapter with the words of one of the greatest Africans ever, Nelson Mandela. (see chapter 10). In a speech to commemorate the UN's fiftieth anniversary at the General Assembly in October 1995, he said: 'We come from Africa and South Africa on this historic occasion to pay tribute to that founding ideal, and to thank the United Nations for challenging, with us, a system that defined fellow humans as lesser beings... The youth ... are ... bound to wonder why it should be that poverty still pervades the greater part of the globe; that wars continue to rage; and that many in positions of power and privilege pursue cold-hearted philosophies which terrifyingly proclaim: I am not your brother's keeper! For no one, in the North or the South, can escape the cold fact that we are a single humanity.'[74] Africa's enduring legacy to the UN, as embodied by its most revered global statesman, could well be the concept of *ubuntu:* the gift of discovering our shared humanity.

4

THE PHARAOH AND THE PROPHET

BOUTROS BOUTROS-GHALI AND KOFI ANNAN[1]

'We all come "out of Africa." Africa is the mother of us all, and Egypt is the oldest daughter of Africa. This is why I have loved Africa and tried so hard throughout my life to help her. This is why the horrors inflicted in and on Africa cause such pain. But anyone who knows Africa knows that its people will endure and ultimately succeed.'[2]

Boutros Boutros-Ghali, United Nations Secretary-General, 1992–1996

This chapter examines the role of the Secretary-General as the 'face' of the United Nations, focusing specifically on the two African Secretaries-General: Boutros Boutros-Ghali (1992–1996) and Kofi Annan (1997–2006). Though we characterise Boutros-Ghali and Annan respectively as 'Pharaoh' and 'Prophet', every Secretary-General has exhibited such traits, as well as those of a third and more common metaphor, a sort of 'Pope'. Through these three lenses, the chapter examines the major achievements and failures of Boutros-Ghali and Annan, as well as the reaction of key actors at the United Nations to the efforts of both men to achieve their objectives in the areas of peace and security, socioeconomic development, and 'humanitarian intervention'.

The Secretary-General has frequently either sought or been driven to play the role of Secular Pope in leading debates and pushing the United Nations to act in support of its Charter principles. In addition, however, the different incumbents have, to varying degrees, sought to play the role of Stubborn Pharaoh by asserting the independence of the office and the secretariat—sometimes leading to clashes with powerful member states. Third, since the

UN has a Third World majority and North-South issues have come to fill the void left by East-West politics at the organisation, every Secretary-General since the age of decolonization has had to portray himself as a kind of 'Southern Prophet', championing the development and security interests of the weak against the powerful.[3] These different roles have complicated the lives and the legacies of each Secretary-General, though most obviously in the two African post–Cold War incumbents.

Boutros-Ghali and Annan

Egyptian scholar-diplomat Boutros Boutros-Ghali served as UN Secretary-General between 1992 and 1996. Having obtained a doctorate in international law from the Sorbonne in Paris, taught at Cairo University for twenty-eight years, and published widely in law and politics journals, Boutros-Ghali was the most intellectually accomplished Secretary-General in the history of the post. As Chinmaya Gharekhan, the former permanent representative of India to the United Nations and Boutros-Ghali's representative to the UN Security Council, noted: 'Boutros-Ghali is an intellectual giant... He provoked us into thinking along new, creative lines. He frequently liked to act as the devil's advocate. His own contributions were original and unorthodox.'[4] David Hannay, the permanent representative of Britain to the UN between 1990 and 1995, who regarded the Egyptian scholar-diplomat as the most assertive holder of the post since Dag Hammarksjöld, similarly noted: 'Boutros-Ghali ... was a man of charm and erudition. He had an encyclopaedic knowledge of international, and in particular of African, affairs... He was forceful and decisive, perhaps sometimes too much so for his own good.'[5]

Before becoming UN Secretary-General, Boutros-Ghali had served on the International Law Commission and the International Commission on Jurists, which gave him insights into the workings of the world body. A Coptic Christian from a rich and politically connected family, Boutros-Ghali acquired a deep sense of *noblesse oblige* and a commitment to public service. His grandfather Boutros Ghali Pasha had served as prime minister of Egypt under the British protectorate before being assassinated, and two of his uncles had served as foreign minister. Like Dag Hammarskjöld, the Swedish administrator who occupied the office between 1953 and 1961,[6] Boutros-Ghali was aloof and often impatient with people who were less intelligent than him. UN staff came to refer to their Egyptian boss as 'the Pharaoh,' due to his authoritarian leadership style. Boutros-Ghali did not endear himself to staff for publicly criticising his own secretariat and for tactlessly telling the *New York Times* that the only way to run a bureaucracy was the way he had treated the Egyptian civil service: 'by stealth and sudden violence'.[7] As Marrack Goulding, an insightful British diplomat who served as the Egyptian scholar-diplomat's Undersecretary-General for Peacekeeping between 1992 and 1996, noted: 'Boutros-Ghali has charm, gracious manners, and an agreeable wit, but he can become assertive in argument, speaking directly and not always resisting the temptation of the *bon mot* that will raise a laugh but may also cause offense.'[8]

Kofi Annan, a citizen of Ghana, was appointed Secretary-General in 1996 under controversial circumstances. The United States stood alone among the fifteen Security Council members in vetoing Boutros-Ghali's reappointment. Washington and London then launched a manipulative campaign on behalf of Annan, arguing that continued support for Boutros-Ghali suggested to the world that there was no qualified black African candidate. Paris assumed a typically Gallic cultural arrogance, posturing about Annan's lack of fluency in French. Eventually everyone agreed to Boutros-Ghali's departure and Annan became the first Secretary-General from sub-Saharan Africa.[9]

Boutros-Ghali later talked of betrayal by his 'closest collaborator', and some of the American officials involved in ousting Boutros-Ghali, like Bob Orr and Michael Sheehan, later joined Annan's UN.[10] Many of the respected intellectuals whom Annan relied on in office were North American, and he sought the advice of American universities rather than Southern ones. But he did also have key policy advisers from the global South: Iqbal Riza (Pakistan), Shashi Tharoor (India), and Lakhdar Brahimi (Algeria).

At the time of his appointment, Annan was widely regarded as a competent administrator who had climbed up the UN system after a thirty-year career spanning the fields of finance, personnel, health, refugees, and peacekeeping. He was charming and affable, and, like the Burmese Secretary-General between 1961 and 1971, U Thant, unflappably calm. Annan seemed, at first, to be like Hammarskjöld, painfully shy and somewhat uncomfortable in the glare of the media cameras. He appeared to be better suited to the discreet role of a faceless bureaucrat than the high-profile role of a prophetic statesman. But Annan's mild-mannered side masked a tough interior and a quiet determination to achieve his goals. Where Boutros-Ghali was arrogant and cerebral, Annan was affable and charming. Where Boutros-Ghali was seen by his staff as an aloof, pompous Pharaoh, Annan was regarded at the

United Nations as an accessible, personable Prophet. But while even Boutros-Ghali's worst enemies conceded that he was an intellectual, even Annan's best friends did not sell him as a scholar. Annan and his Swedish wife Nane soon became regular New York socialites. The introverted Boutros-Ghali avoided the social limelight.

Before becoming UN Secretary-General, Annan had been promoted by Boutros-Ghali to the post of Undersecretary-General for Peacekeeping in 1993. Despite some of the myths around Annan's outstanding performance in this role, his tenure saw monumental blunders in Bosnia and Rwanda that did great damage to the UN's reputation. Independent reports later commissioned by the UN and released in 1999 criticised Annan and his officials who had adopted a bureaucratic posture of undue caution and overrestrictive interpretations of UN mandates[11], although the Security Council's powerful veto-wielding permanent members (particularly the US, Britain, and France) also share a great deal of the blame for these two debacles. About three months before the start of the Rwandan genocide in 1994, during which 800,000 people were killed, the senior officials in the 2,500–strong UN peacekeeping force in Rwanda had warned Annan's office of the impending slaughter. They had received instructions to avoid a Somalia-like UN fiasco and to avoid the use of force at all costs.[12]

In Bosnia, in July 1995, UN peacekeepers—who had been warned by Annan's officials against the use of air strikes except if the UN mission was directly threatened—had failed to act, as 7,400 Muslims were slaughtered by Serbs in a UN-declared 'safe haven'.[13] In both cases, the responsibility for acting lay largely with the UN's powerful states, but the independent inquiries into both incidents noted that Annan's staff had not fulfilled their own responsibility to report transparently and courageously to the UN Security Council. In the face of mass murder, a pedantic insistence on neutrality had trumped an impartial duty to call murder by its name and to press the Security Council to act. As UN Secretary-General at the time, Boutros-Ghali must also share some of the blame for these failures.

After his appointment, Annan received universally positive press from a fickle Western media, many of which slavishly reflected their governments' views. But very little was known about this enigmatic figure outside UN circles, where he had acquired an almost unblemished reputation for being a competent civil servant with an impressive grasp of complex details. Since he spent much of his career in the UN bureaucracy, Annan was seen by many as a creature of the system. He started off cautiously and his reforms were methodical rather than revolutionary, continuing the reduction of staff begun under his predecessor and initiating efforts at better coordination among UN departments.

In the Byzantine world of UN politics, various informal interest groups battle each other for plum posts. Annan appeared to have little patience for this kind of intrigue, believing instead in a charmingly antiquated version of meritocracy and 'equitable geographical distribution' in this world of egocentric godfathers. He also seemed to have made few political enemies during his ascent to the top: a truly impressive feat in the often ruthless political environment of jostling chiefs who jealously guard their bureaucratic fiefdoms. A further quality that characterised Annan's career was loyalty: he moved some of his closest and most competent advisers from his days as Undersecretary-General for Peacekeeping—including Iqbal Riza, Shashi Tharoor, and Elisabeth Lindenmayer—to senior positions in his new office.

The Secular Pope

It was Soviet leader Joseph Stalin who famously asked: 'How many battalions does the Pope have?' What is true of the pontiff in the Vatican is also true of the 'Pope on the East River'. With no standing army, the UN Secretary-General must depend entirely on member states to provide the troops and resources needed to fulfil the mandates entrusted to him. It is the moral authority and skills at stitching together 'coalitions of the willing' and building consensus among the Great Powers that often gets the job done. Every Secretary-General has few other resources in his armoury than the moral authority of the position.[14]

Boutros-Ghali played the Secular Pope in bluntly condemning the double standards of powerful Western powers in selectively authorising UN interventions in 'rich men's wars' in Europe while ignoring Africa's 'orphan conflicts'. His enduring legacy to the United Nations will be *An Agenda for Peace*, a landmark document published in 1992 on the tools and techniques of peace-making, peacekeeping, and peacebuilding for a post–Cold War era. The Security Council had asked the Egyptian scholar-diplomat to present it with such a text in January 1992. In true professorial style, Boutros-Ghali spent forty hours meticulously polishing countless drafts of the text. His *Agenda* called for 'preventive deployment', a rapid reaction UN force to enable action without the need to seek new troops for each mission, heavily armed peace enforcers for dangerous missions, and the strengthening of regional peacekeeping bodies to lighten the burden on the United Nations.[15] As well as advancing theory, Boutros-Ghali's tenure also witnessed the rise and fall in the practice of UN peacekeeping in Bosnia, Cambodia, Haiti, Rwanda, and Somalia. At its peak in 1994, the United Nations deployed 75,000 peacekeepers to seventeen trouble spots at an annual cost of $3.6 billion. During the previous four decades, the United Nations had deployed only thirteen peacekeeping missions.[16] But Boutros-Ghali was a pragmatist who recognised the limits of the secular pope-hood in a system dominated by Great Powers. As he put it: 'I do not claim to elevate the vision of the Utopian city called for by the Islamic thinker Al-Farabi to that of a Utopian world, for I cannot promise to go beyond what is feasible and what is possible. Despite the close ties that bind me to optimism, my ties to realism are even closer.'[17]

Amidst fierce opposition from within the UN system and some senior aides who found *An Agenda for Peace* 'pontificating and paternalistic', Boutros-Ghali published *An Agenda for Democratization* in 1996 (having also published *An Agenda for Development* in 1993). Boutros-Ghali, as a citizen of the Third World and experienced in the inequities of the system of 'global apartheid'[18] through which Great Powers manipulated the UN to serve their parochial interests (see chapter 3), noted nonetheless that '[h]uman rights are, by definition, the ultimate norm of all politics'.[19] He argued in *An Agenda for Democratization* that democracy was critical for achieving peace and development and that both must be pursued simultaneously. But he argued for democratization not just at the domestic level *within* states, but also at the international level *between* states: a key theme throughout Boutros-Ghali's tenure based on three decades of theory and praxis of international law. He further pushed for international criminal tribunals (though he felt the obsessive pursuit of justice could sometimes compromise reconciliation) to achieve greater international democratization, and called for greater civil society participation in UN bodies like the Economic and Social Council (ECOSOC).[20]

Similar to the Peruvian Secretary-General between 1982 and 1991, Javier Pérez de Cuéllar, with his focus on human rights, Kofi Annan has perhaps been the most moralistic and proselytizing UN Secretary-General: an irony for a self-declared 'pragmatist' Christian. Annan often spoke out forcefully on human rights issues. In East Timor in 1999, he pushed strongly for an international force to stop the abuses of militias against civilians who had voted for independence from Indonesia. At the UN General Assembly session in 1999, following the controversial US-led intervention in Kosovo (carried out without a UN Security Council mandate), Annan presented himself as the champion of 'humanitarian intervention' in noting: 'the core challenge to the Security Council and the United Nations as a whole in the next century is to forge unity behind the principle that massive and systematic violations of human rights—wherever they take place—cannot be allowed to stand.'[21]

Leader after leader from the global South lined up in the General Assembly after Annan's 1999 speech to condemn an idea that they saw as a threat to their sovereignty and their own hold on power. Algerian leader Abdelaziz Bouteflika criticised the concept of 'humanitarian intervention' for its potential to legitimise abuses by powerful states against weaker ones—a fear that seemed to have been confirmed by the US-led invasion of Iraq without UN Security Council authorisation four years later, which was partly justified on humanitarian grounds. Theo Ben-Gurirab, Namibia's foreign minister and president of the General Assembly at the time, publicly criticised Annan's views at a diplomatic reception. At the African Union (AU) summit in Addis Ababa in July 2004, Annan also called for an end to dictatorships in Africa in full glare of all the assembled continental leaders. He often advocated for African countries to cut their military expenditure and to adopt economic reforms. Annan spoke out frequently on the need for an interdependent world to tackle 'problems without borders': AIDS, refugees, poverty, terrorism, and weapons of mass destruction. The Ghanaian is the only living Secretary-General to have been awarded the Nobel Peace Prize, which he shared with the organisation in 2001 (Hammarskjöld was awarded the prize posthumously in 1961).

Annan's promotion of 'humanitarian intervention' in cases of gross human rights abuses and his publishing of reports on Rwanda and the Balkans critical of the United Nations cannot be separated from some sense of responsibility that he felt at the lacklustre reaction of the UN Secretariat in New York and its member states to these tragedies. Though he has not publicly admitted it, the fact that he has championed the issue of 'humanitarian intervention', together with the political risks he incurred to place it on the international agenda, suggest that these experiences at least left some emotional scars that the painfully private and usually unruffled diplomat would probably never openly admit to. Some members of Annan's staff argued that these failures were some of the worst experiences in Annan's life, and that he felt to some extent personally responsible for them.[22]

The Stubborn Pharaoh

Attempts by a Secretary-General to play the role of 'Stubborn Pharaoh' have occasionally met with fatal resistance from powerful members of the Security Council. Both the hapless Norwegian Secretary-General from 1946 to 1953, Trygve Lie, and the heroic Dag Hammarskjöld, were damaged by Russia. China cast sixteen vetoes to prevent Austrian Kurt Waldheim's bid for a third term in 1981. The United States vetoed Boutros-Ghali's reappointment in 1996, while its Congress fatally wounded Kofi Annan in 2005. The permanent five veto-wielding Security Council members—the US, Russia, China, Britain, and France—have often appeared to prefer office-holders that are more 'Secretary' than 'General'. As Brian Urquhart, the long-serving Undersecretary-General for Peacekeeping and a preeminent British scholar on the UN, once put it: 'political differences dictate a search for a candidate who will not exert any troubling degree of leadership, commitment, originality, or independence.'[23]

Of the two African Secretaries-General, Boutros-Ghali was seen as a pompous Pharaoh. He broke tradition by appointing an Indian diplomat, Chinmaya Gharekhan, as his 'personal representative' to the Security Council, thus failing to attend himself the informal meetings of the UN's most powerful body, which he found tedious and some of whose permanent representatives he found mediocre. Boutros-Ghali therefore incurred the wrath of many of the powerful permanent representatives at the UN, and neglected to give a personal stamp to the most important relationship in his job.[24] The appointment of Gharekhan also alienated officials in Kofi Annan's Department of Peacekeeping, who tried to undermine him, thus contributing to the debacle in Rwanda. Boutros-Ghali often annoyed permanent representatives during meetings with him by cutting them off in mid-sentence to inform them that he had previously talked to their foreign ministers or presidents.[25] The Egyptian also frequently scolded African ambassadors in New York for not keeping properly abreast of matters concerning their continent.[26] He often said he was more of a politician than a diplomat. American journalist Stanley Meisler described the Egyptian scholar-diplomat as 'the most stubbornly independent secretary-general in the half-century history of the United Nations.'[27]

Senior American political figures like Jeane Kirkpatrick and Richard Armitage accused Boutros-Ghali of trying to become 'chief executive officer of the world' and 'the world's commander-in-chief'.[28] John Bolton, the acerbic US permanent representative to the UN between 2005 and 2006, accused Boutros-Ghali of behaving like 'the commander in chief of the World Federalist Army'.[29] These attacks were ironic considering that Boutros-Ghali was, at first, regarded as an American favourite by a sceptical Third World at the UN. Irresponsible American politicians eventually turned him into a bogeyman, blaming Boutros-Ghali for everything from the death of US soldiers in Somalia, to the failure to protect 'safe havens' in Bosnia, to obstruction of reform within his own bureaucracy. The Egyptian thus became a pawn in a political chess game that resulted in the end of his reign. He was particularly scapegoated for the Somali debacle in 1993, a fiasco that had been entirely planned and directed from the Pentagon. Bosnia's failures were largely due to European realpolitik and US policy vacillations. Anglo-French pressure prevented Boutros-Ghali from ordering air strikes against the Serbs, as London and Paris argued that this would have put their own troops in harm's way. But the pugnacious US permanent representative to the UN, Madeline Albright, accused the United Nations of 'betrayal', and when Boutros-Ghali complained about the 'vulgarity' of the language of the US delegation, it was clear that relations between these two strong personalities had reached a head: the time was fast approaching when an irresistible force would confront an immovable object.

Contrary to claims by his critics, Boutros-Ghali's tenure witnessed one of the most far-reaching reforms in the history of the organisation. The Washington-backed American Joseph Connor was made Undersecretary-General for Management in 1994 and cut the UN bureaucracy from 12,000 to 9,000 while freezing the UN budget, saving $100 million a year. Departments were slashed by a third, new performance criteria were introduced, and increased computerisation cut down on the organisation's notorious paper-load. Boutros-Ghali also appointed more American nationals to top positions than any of his predecessors. But fact became irrelevant in a silly season of populist electioneering. The Bill Clinton administration (1993–2000)—notorious for a reactive foreign policy and led by a president obsessed with short-term polls—failed to defend the United Nations but instead joined the criticisms of UN profligacy. Boutros-Ghali complained prophetically that he felt like a man condemned to execution.[30] Madeline Albright boosted her own chances of winning bipartisan support for her successful bid to become the first female US secretary of state in 1997 by acting as Clinton's willing executioner: she personally put Boutros-Ghali's head to the guillotine and administered the fatal blow. She then presented the bodiless head to a bloodthirsty US Congress in a modern version of King Herod's gift of John the Baptist's head to his sanguinary wife's daughter, Salome. In her 2003 memoirs, *Madam Secretary*,

Albright noted that her nemesis was 'hyper status-conscious and seemed to believe that administrative tasks were beneath him'.[31]

During his tenure in office, Boutros-Ghali displayed a fierce and often courageous independence, insisting, for example, on maintaining a veto over air strikes in Bosnia, and complaining that the North Atlantic Treaty Organisation (NATO) was trying to manipulate the UN. To Washington's annoyance, he refused to approve a UN deployment in Haiti in 1994 until the troop contributors and time frames had been properly resolved.[32] During the Rwandan Genocide in the same year, he dared call 'genocide' by its name, again annoying the Clinton administration, which did not want to describe the massacre for what is was for fear that it might be asked to intervene to stop it. As Boutros-Ghali noted in a not too subtle jab at his successor, Kofi Annan, in one of his final statements as UN Secretary-General in 1996: 'If one word above all is to characterize the role of the Secretary-General, it is independence. The holder of the office must never be seen as acting out of fear of, or in an attempt to curry favour with one state or group of states.'[33] Like a curse of the ancestors, these words would later come back to haunt Annan.

Boutros-Ghali demonstrated his independence by consistently complaining about the undemocratic nature of the Security Council. He chastised his political masters on the Council for turning the United Nations into an instrument of parochial national interest over Iraq and Libya, and he berated them for their lack of political will in dumping impossible tasks in Bosnia and Rwanda on the United Nations without providing the organisation with the resources to do the job. Boutros-Ghali also criticised Washington relentlessly for refusing to pay its $1.3 billion debt to the United Nations while domineeringly seeking to set its agenda. In his bitter 1999 memoir, *Unvanquished*, the Egyptian's indictment of the United States in blocking UN action to halt the genocide in Rwanda in 1994 is devastating.[34]

However, though Boutros-Ghali focused much of his venom on the United States, he often failed to point out in similar detail some of the shortcomings of other powerful members of the United Nations. For example, France, the closest ally of this Sorbonne-educated intellectual who headed the French-led Francophonie after 1996, gets off particularly lightly for its training and arming of Hutu death squads before Rwanda's 1994 genocide. Boutros-Ghali in fact not only supported the controversial French postgenocide military intervention in Rwanda, Opération Turquoise, in 1994, but actively lobbied for it in the Security Council.[35]

Despite some of Boutros-Ghali's arrogance and tactlessness (not uncommon at this level of responsibility among many senior Western officials in similar positions), some of the visceral reactions to Boutros-Ghali were reminiscent of the treatment of another outspoken senior African at the UN: Amadou-Mahtar M'Bow. The Senegalese was director-general of the UN Educational, Scientific, and Cultural Organisation (UNESCO) between 1974 and 1987 and was eventually hounded out of office following a sustained disinformation campaign orchestrated by powerful Western governments and media organs.[36] Like the Shakespearean Iago's hatred for the black Othello, the venom of the attacks on both African officials was often irrational and incomprehensible. Though Boutros-Ghali often 'spoke truth to power', his utterances were sometimes treated as those of an 'uppity native': the Egyptian himself complained that the British media were unhappy with him over the Bosnia crisis 'because I am a WOG'.[37] The American stereotype of the 'angry black man' appeared to be revived in some of the dismissive outbursts against the Egyptian scholar-diplomat. Like M'Bow, many Western governments and scholars reacted strongly against an intelligent, articulate, outspoken African who did not look like nor sound like them, and who dared to act as their equal or even superior.

One of his critics, Mats Berdal, a respected Norwegian scholar of the UN, argued that 'Boutros-Ghali lacked the key qualities of political judgment and tact', noting further that temperament was more important to the job of UN Secretary-General than intellect.[38] While one can agree on Boutros-Ghali's personal tactlessness, his political judgement was almost always correct and he had a sound political antenna. Indeed, as Marrack Goulding noted about his former boss: 'he knew where power lay and he knew that power could not be ignored, even if what the powerful demanded was sometimes unpleasant or unfair.'[39] The fact that, in the first vote for Boutros-Ghali's reelection in 1996, fourteen out of fifteen members of the Security Council agreed to keeping the Secretary-General (leaving the US diplomatically isolated as the sole dissenting voice), suggests that the vast majority of governments were angrier at the tactlessness of America's heavy-handed efforts to remove Boutros-Ghali than they were about the undoubted arrogance of the 'Pharaoh'. As to Berdal's idea of temperament trumping intellect in this job, this is of course more soundbite than solid social science. The better temperament of Kofi Annan and predecessors like U Thant did not make them any more successful in the job once they had incurred the wrath of the Americans. This suggests that understanding the rather limited powers of this office is more important to sound analysis than the temperament or intelligence of office-holders.

The Southern Prophet

Every UN Secretary-General must pay careful attention to the 'global South' and its economic and security priorities in order to maintain the support of the vocal majority in the 192–member General Assembly. The 118–member Non-Aligned Movement (NAM) was founded in 1961 (see chapter 14) and most of its members are part of the 130–member Group of 77 (G77), set up in 1964 in the context of the first UN Conference on Trade and Development (UNCTAD). The G77 continues to dominate the General Assembly agenda. The African Group at the United Nations was created in 1958 and soon made its presence felt on decolonization and anti–apartheid issues.[40]

Both Boutros-Ghali and Annan were in a sense Prophets of Pax Africana,[41] expanding peacekeeping on their own continent. Ironically, it was the North African Boutros-Ghali—whose country is usually accused by black Africans of having its body in Africa and heart and head in the Middle East—who was seen as the more genuinely committed to African issues. This was despite the fact that Annan came from Ghana, a country led by Kwame Nkrumah that had carried the torch of pan-Africanism and blazed the independence trail in black Africa in 1957 (see chapter 11). Many senior Africans at the United Nations (both in the secretariat and in permanent missions) distrusted Annan and doubted his conviction on African issues.[42]

Boutros-Ghali was steeped in the intricacies of Third World diplomacy, having served as Egypt's minister of state for foreign affairs for fourteen years, between 1977 and 1991, under the autocratic regimes of Anwar Sadat and Hosni Mubarak. He had a profound and intuitive grasp of the global South and was deeply involved in both the Arab-Israeli dispute and the politics of the Organisation of African Unity (OAU).[43] Boutros-Ghali was thus more cautious than Annan in pushing a human rights agenda that he knew many sovereignty-obsessed governments in the South would oppose. However, he did not always agree with Southern governments on issues like democratisation and human rights. Annan, in contrast, spent more than thirty years in the UN system before becoming Secretary-General, serving mostly in Western capitals like New York and Geneva. He returned to Ghana for two years in 1974 to head the Ghana Tourist Development Company, but left in frustration over heavy state control and the corruption of the profligate regime of General Kutu Acheampong. Annan's feel for African politics was thus less sure than Boutros-Ghali's.

As Secretary-General, Boutros-Ghali often expressed the Southern criticism that the rich North was too focused on peace and security issues and did not pay enough attention to socioeconomic development.[44] He often decried the lack of democratization in the decisionmaking structures of the World Bank and the International Monetary Fund (IMF) (see chapter 3). Boutros-Ghali frequently voiced the Southern concern that the anachronistic UN Security Council was in urgent need of democratisation to ensure the presence of permanent members from other regions of the world in a body that did not have any such membership from Africa and South America. But he was astute enough to understand the UN's power dynamics. As Kenyan scholar Ali Mazrui perceptively noted: 'Even with the best intentions in the world, Boutros Boutros-Ghali has felt that it is more important that the United Nations should exercise more power in Africa than that Africa should exercise more influence in the United Nations. Quite understandably, the Secretary-General has felt that Africa needed the United Nations' help more than the United Nations needed Africa's help.'[45]

Each year before the annual Group of Seven (G7) (later Group of Eight [G8]) summits of industrialised countries, Boutros-Ghali wrote to the G7 leaders to ask them to address Africa's plight so that the continent could benefit from the fruits of globalisation. Each year, he received only perfunctory responses. In reaction to the criticisms of his *An Agenda for Peace* from the Southern majority in the General Assembly, he produced *An Agenda for Development* a year later. The Egyptian scholar-diplomat also organised a series of UN conferences that focused on social and economic issues such as the Rio Conference on Environment and Development in 1992, and the World Summit for Social Development in Copenhagen in 1995.

A common myth about Kofi Annan was that he was a great reformer. On assuming office in 1997, he sought to reduce staff within the organisation by 10 per cent; asked the UN General Assembly to stop 'micro-managing' the UN budget; and requested a freer hand in making high-level appointments. The Assembly—many of whose members came to believe that Annan's tenure ironically led to Western domination of strategic positions in the UN secretariat and the marginalisation of African staff—duly ignored his suggestions. Critics in the South further accused Kofi Annan of not standing up to the United States when it used the United Nations to spy on Iraq and rained down bombs on Kosovo, Sudan, Afghanistan, and Iraq without the approval of the Security Council. James Jonah, the Sierra Leonean former Undersecretary-General for Political Affairs between 1992 and 1994, once summed up the difference between Africa's two Secretaries-General thus: 'If the Security Council tells Boutros-Ghali to jump, he will ask "Why?" If the Council asks Annan to jump, he will ask "How high?"'[46]

But as Ibrahim Gambari, Nigeria's permanent representative to the United Nations between 1990 and 1999 and later Undersecretary-General for Political Affairs under Annan, noted: 'It would be very unwise for any Secretary-General to antagonize the only superpower left in the world.'[47] Annan's supporters have argued that the enduring lesson of Boutros-Ghali's departure was not to confront directly the world's sole superpower. Trained in the United States at the elite Massachusetts Institute of Technology and Macalester College, Annan never quite shook off the impression of being totally indebted to Washington, which almost single-handedly ensured his ascent to the top UN job. Unlike Boutros-Ghali, whose appointment was based on support from the OAU, the choice of Annan was built on a solid Anglo-Saxon foundation.

Some Africans have criticised Annan for not being 'African' enough, for not identifying enough with the continent, and for not promoting African candidates to top UN posts in the way senior officials from other regions promote their own candidates. Boutros-Ghali, in contrast, was sometimes accused of practising favouritism through packing the United Nations with Egyptian nationals. It has often been said that Annan's transitional team did not contain a single African. Annan was said to be reluctant to attend African diplomatic summits and to meet regularly with African ambassadors for informal lunches at the United Nations.[48] His apparent discomfort with an African identity suggests a certain insecurity: even as he tries to distance himself from his roots through what sometimes appears to be an affected English accent, his Ghanaian intonations come through strongly as if to remind him that he cannot escape his ancestry. Annan has often shown a superficial understanding of Africa, describing a traditional society where people sit under a tree and talk, and referring nebulously to Africa's 'spirit of forgiveness and reconciliation.'[49] He has often employed similar stereotypes of Africa as an undifferentiated continent of conflicts with views that one might find in many parts of the often Afro-pessimistic Western media. As Annan said: 'If you mention Africa today, people see it as a continent in crisis ... nobody wants to invest in a bad neighbourhood.'[50]

Annan annoyed African diplomats during the Rwandan Genocide of 1994 by casually telling *Le Monde* that the reason African countries were not contributing troops was because they 'probably need their armies to intimidate their own populations'.[51] (African troops were, in fact, offered by Ghana, Tanzania, and Nigeria,[52] but the West, particularly the United States, dragged its feet on providing the promised logistics to transport them to Rwanda.) When

Annan ran into trouble with his American critics in 2005, it was mostly Western loyalists, rather than senior Africans at the UN, whom he turned to for help, as during a famous 'secret' dinner in the home of former US ambassador to the UN Richard Holbrooke.

One lingering accusation that Annan has not quite been able to shake off is that, while serving as Undersecretary-General for Peacekeeping in 1994, he did not respond appropriately to a cable warning of an impending genocide in Rwanda. Much controversy still remains over Annan's failure to report the contents of this cable, sent in January 1994 from Canadian UN force commander General Roméo Dallaire, who asked for authorisation to take military action to forestall the impending genocide, to both Boutros-Ghali and the Security Council. A subsequent UN inquiry report published in December 1999 criticised Annan and his deputy, Iqbal Riza, for this shortcoming.[53] As the genocide began, Boutros-Ghali was on a tour of Europe; not only was he slow in returning to New York, but he also dithered before belatedly calling for a stronger UN force. Boutros-Ghali later admitted that he felt personally responsible not for his failure to respond timeously, but for failing to convince the Great Powers to do so.[54] The refusal to act was also due, importantly, to the powerful members of the Security Council—particularly the United States—that erroneously viewed Rwanda through a tainted Somali prism.

But Annan has rarely taken direct individual responsibility for his role in this tragedy. Instead, he has often hidden behind formulations of collective responsibility by citing the culpability of 'the international community' and 'the world'. On a visit to Kigali in May 1998, Annan insensitively noted about the 1994 genocide: 'It was a horror that came from within.'[55] He dismissed criticisms of his role during the genocide as 'an old story which is being rehashed', before adding: 'I have no regrets.'[56] Annan faced a hostile reception from Rwanda's leaders, who openly denounced him and shunned an official reception in his honour.

Annan has, however, shown a consciousness of the need to maintain African support: UN Special Representatives to Angola, the Central African Republic, the Democratic Republic of the Congo (DRC), and Sierra Leone were African; Gambari was appointed as Annan's Special Adviser on African Conflicts in 1999, and as Undersecretary-General for Political Affairs in 2005; Olara Otunnu served as his Special Representative for Children and Armed Conflict between 1998 and 2005; and Patrick Hayford, Ghana's former High Commissioner to South Africa, served as a director in Annan's office. Annan also commissioned special reports on peace and development in

Africa in 1998 and pushed forcefully for new UN peacekeeping missions in the DRC, Liberia, Sierra Leone, South Sudan, and Darfur. He focused international attention on neglected conflicts in Western Sahara and Algeria, and consulted regularly with, and sought the advice and guidance of, African leaders.

African Prophet or American Poodle?

Kofi Annan's first trip on assuming office was to Washington, D.C., in March 1997. Though this was the start of a bid to collect a US debt to the United Nations of $1.6 billion—being withheld in order to secure internal UN management reforms and reduced American contributions to the organisation—the symbolism of the visit confirmed to many the great debt that the Ghanaian himself owed to the superpower for his election. Annan acted as a travelling salesman, going above the head of cantankerous and sometimes ignorant US legislators, to champion the UN cause at college campuses, business forums, and town halls. His diplomatic tact and assiduous courting of key American constituencies yielded some fruit: Washington started to repay its long-over-due debt to the United Nations, while tycoons Ted Turner and Bill Gates contributed generously to the funding of various UN programmes.

Though the US had played a central role in creating the UN in 1945 and the American public largely supported the organisation, powerful interests within the US Congress led by Jesse Helms, the prejudiced, conservative chairman of the Senate Foreign Relations Committee at the time, together with the conservative majority of Republican congressman Newt Gingrich, consistently attacked the UN. The Clinton administration was often unwilling to expend much political capital defending the world body from often outlandish and ill-informed attacks in perverse acts of infanticide. Some Americans complained that black UN helicopters were flying around the country in a bid to create a 'world government', while UN-declared 'World Heritage sites' in the US (of which there are about 878 around the world) were seen as a sign of the violation of American sovereignty.

The US wielded tremendous influence on Annan, persuading him to appoint UN special representatives to Afghanistan, Iraq, and the DRC. He often stayed close to Washington, establishing a particularly close relationship with its dynamic ambassador to the UN between 1999 and 2000, Richard Holbrooke, with whom he courted the US Congress to repay the country's debt to the world body. Holbrooke described the Ghanaian Secretary-General as 'the international rock star of diplomacy'.[57] However, Annan's relations with Washington were eventually badly affected by his refusal to give carte blanche to US policies in Iraq. Seen at first as a 'made in America' UN Secretary-General, Annan eventually acquired American critics in government and media circles.

These critics accused Annan of being naive and idealistic. He embarked on a visit to Baghdad in February 1998 to negotiate the reentry of UN weapons inspectors against the express wishes of then–US secretary of state Madeleine Albright, who was said to browbeat Annan and even screamed at him.[58] Albright had done the most to remove Boutros-Ghali and in effect secure Annan's appointment: for her, this was now payback time. During the trip to Baghdad in 1998, Annan smoked cigars with Saddam Hussein and said that he could do business with the Iraqi dictator if it meant preventing a war. This statement was treated by Annan's critics as almost analogous to Neville Chamberlain's visit to Munich in 1938 to appease Hitler. The Ghanaian demonstrated uncharacteristic hubris after UN staffers applauded him into the building following this Baghdad trip, and he seemed to start believing in the propaganda of the ultra-loyalists around him who worshipped their saintly leader. The agreement with Hussein however soon unravelled, and Annan lost his halo among his former devotees in the US government and media.[59]

Many of Annan's staff eventually felt that he was endangering the lives of UN personnel in Iraq by not closing the office there in order to placate Washington, after the US invasion of the country in 2003 without UN Security Council authorisation. Many UN employees also saw his proposals to reform the UN as an effort to curry favour with the George W. Bush administration. After Annan's failure to take action against powerful staff members accused of sexual harassment, nepotism, and corruption, a demoralised UN Staff Council—already enraged by the death of twenty-two of their colleagues in a Baghdad bombing in August 2003—passed an unprecedented vote of no confidence in Annan's leadership in November 2004.

Things got worse when Annan began an ambitious reform agenda in the wake of acrimonious disputes over the US-led invasion of Iraq in 2003. He convened a High-Level Panel to propose reforms for more effective management of collective security threats by the United Nations, which submitted its report in December 2004. Annan also offered his own proposals in a March 2005 report, *In Larger Freedom*.[60] More than 150 heads of state met in New York in September 2005 to recite obsequies for the ill-fated effort at change. The event left Annan's legacy—already badly tarnished by Iraq's Oil-for-Food scandal (discussed later)—in disarray. Spectacular failures in the process included an inability to reform the anachronistic fifteen-member Security Council, no substantive measures being taken to improve the UN's peacekeeping capacity, and little more than rhetoric on issues of aid, trade, and debt (see chapter 3).[61] The 101 recommendations of Annan's High-Level Panel report were derided as '101 Dalmatians'.

Annan was seen by many in the global South to have sought to use the reform effort in 2005 to repair his damaged relationship with Washington, and there is ample evidence that the reform process and Annan's 2005 *In Larger Freedom* report (drafted largely by two Americans, Bob Orr and Stephen Stedman) were crafted explicitly to gain Washington's support.[62] Even some of Annan's senior aides, like the British Undersecretary-General for Political Affairs, Karin Pendergast, complained that, as important as the US was, one could not focus disproportionately on one country to the detriment of the interests of the other 191 states. During the 2005 reform process, there were disappointments for the global South's 'development agenda', with the combative US ambassador to the UN, John Bolton—the only one of America's permanent representatives with whom Annan had a difficult relationship—seeking (despite Annan's efforts to tailor the reforms in ways that were acceptable to Washington) to reverse many of America's earlier commitments on aid and the Millennium Development Goals. Bolton was eventually overruled by US secretary of state Condoleezza Rice.[63]

Annan's relationship with the George W. Bush administration was badly affected by two issues in 2004. First, having annoyed the global South by not openly condemning the US invasion of Iraq in 2003, he clumsily and belatedly declared the invasion to be 'illegal' during a television interview. Second, Annan wrote a letter to Bush warning of the negative consequences of attacking the Iraqi city of Falluja. While the Ghanaian was correct on the merits of both incidents, the hawkish Bush administration regarded his interventions as an attempt to influence the 2004 US election campaign—dominated by the controversial invasion of Iraq—in favour of Democratic Party candidate John Kerry. The Falluja letter had been sent two days before the election, and was regarded as a treacherous act by the unforgiving Bush administration.

These incidents added fuel to the fire, as US senator Norm Coleman and conservative *New York Times* columnist William Safire both called for Annan's resignation. Bush refused to offer his support to the beleaguered Secretary-General, and senior American officials refused to meet with Annan on a proposed trip to Washington, D.C., in December 2004. Karma seemed finally to have caught up with Annan: he almost appeared to be suffering the curse of Africa's ancestors, having cooperated in the betrayal of the continent's first UN Secretary-General and his own boss, Boutros Boutros-Ghali, who had promoted him to Undersecretary-General of Peacekeeping in 1993. The Oil-for-Food scandal would provide Washington with the opportunity to carry out the political crucifixion of Annan. In a programme run by UN officials to provide humanitarian relief to the sanctions-hit regime of Saddam Hussein in Iraq, the Cypriot head of the programme, Benon Sevan, was accused during an independent investigation of having received kickbacks of about $150,000 from the Iraqi government. Annan was also accused of serious management failures for not having reported financial irregularities to the Security Council and for not implementing a system of effective oversight for the programme. Five separate US congressional investigations into the Oil-for-Food scandal were opened, with great attention focused on allegations that Annan's son, Kojo, had acted improperly in his financially beneficial relations with Cotecna, a Swiss company later hired by the United Nations.[64] It was also discovered that Kofi Annan had met with Cotecna executives three times.

Compounding the failure of UN reform was the release of three reports by Paul Volcker, former chairman of the US Federal Reserve, on the Oil-for-Food scandal in Iraq. These revealed corruption and mismanagement within the UN secretariat, though they stopped short of calling for the Secretary-General's head. Two of Volcker's investigators resigned in protest at what they saw as the gentle treatment of Annan. When reports of the Secretary-General's son's connections with Cotecna first broke in 1999, the United Nations launched a lackadaisical internal investigation that cleared Annan of any wrongdoing in a single day, again underlining the lack of accountability and culture of rarely accepting responsibility for failures within the UN secretariat. Annan astonishingly would later seek to blame Kojo's behaviour not on his own failings as a parent, but on 'the environment in Lagos', again reinforcing negative stereotypes about Africa. The Ghanaian's obsession with loyalty and wishing to please everyone and to be liked—impossible at such a high level of responsibility—had finally caused him tremendous personal and political damage. As with Rwanda and Srebrenica, though the companies of powerful UN member states like Russia and France benefitted disproportionately from the Iraq programme, and both Washington and London were aware of many of the flaws in the programme, the failure of the secretariat to act transparently would again damage Annan politically. The pugnacious US permanent representative to the UN, John Bolton, later noted: 'Annan was simply not up to the job, but neither [Colin] Powell nor [Condoleezza] Rice was prepared to push to remove him, despite his manifest inadequacies and the Oil for Food scandal.'[65]

These events effectively turned the Secretary-General into a lame duck two years before the end of his term. Amidst his tribulations, Annan figuratively and literally lost his voice; his hands visibly trembled in meetings; his shoulders slumped; he seriously considered early resignation; and he was reportedly on the verge of a nervous breakdown. Annan had become a deer caught in the headlights of a US 'juggernaut' that threatened to flatten him. The sense of siege on Turtle Bay was palpable. As the battle clarion was sounded, the General lacked the backbone to rally his troops. He lost his nerve, and declared himself a conscientious objector. John Darnforth, the US ambassador to the UN, was eventually instructed to call off the 'mad dogs' that had been unleashed on Annan, belatedly pledging support for the UN Secretary-General. But the damage had already been done. A melancholy Annan naively lamented the strange disappearance of once loyal 'friends'.[66]

Annan's shameful treatment and dismissal of Iqbal Riza and Elizabeth Lindenmeyer—*chef de cabinet* and Riza's deputy respectively, and two of his closest and most loyal lieutenants whom he had known and worked with for over two decades—revealed the shocking sense of panic and desperation that had taken over the thirty-eighth floor of the UN secretariat. Following a meal with powerful, largely North American friends in Richard Holbrooke's home in December 2004—during which Annan had been dutifully taking notes— the Secretary-General effectively followed promptings that he fire some of his closest lieutenants and appoint as his deputy Mark Malloch-Brown, a South African–British former World Bank official and longtime friend of Annan who was the administrator of the UN Development Programme (UNDP). It is widely said that Malloch-Brown (the British minister for Africa under Gordon Brown's premiership) ran the UN for the last two years of Annan's tenure. Even the Ghanaian's initially sympathetic American biographer, James Traub, notes that the Americans reduced him to their 'puppet' through Malloch-Brown.[67]

Concluding Reflections

What, then, is the legacy of Africa's two UN Secretaries-General? Boutros-Ghali combined the roles of Secular Pope, Stubborn Pharaoh, and Southern Prophet in a sort of holy trinity. Despite his pompous arrogance, his tenure as Secretary-General was not without achievements: peacekeeping successes in

Cambodia, El Salvador, and Mozambique were achieved under his watch, and he forcefully defended the organisation against its critics. His landmark 1992 report, *An Agenda for Peace*, remains an indispensable guide to the tools and techniques employed by the United Nations. But he also made serious errors. In both Somalia and Western Sahara, Boutros-Ghali was regarded as less than neutral, having previously supported incumbent regimes while serving as Egypt's minister of state for foreign affairs. His decision to appoint US admiral Jonathan Howe as his Special Representative to Somalia, his support for Howe's recklessly aggressive actions against supporters of Mohammed Farah Aideed, and his bruising confrontation with Madeleine Albright were, in retrospect, costly errors. For all his undoubted achievements, Boutros-Ghali eventually earned himself the unenviable distinction of being the only UN Secretary-General to have been denied a second term in office.

In his own ten-year tenure, Kofi Annan courageously, but perhaps naively, championed the cause of 'humanitarian intervention'. After a steep decline in the mid-1990s, peacekeeping increased again by 2005 to around 80,000 troops with a budget of $3.2 billion. African countries like Sudan, the Congo, Liberia, Ethiopia/Eritrea, and Côte d'Ivoire were the main beneficiaries. Annan also moved the UN bureaucracy from its creative inertia to embrace views and actors from outside the system. He reached out for advice from civil society groups, organising seminars with policy institutes and encouraging the United Nations to work more with these actors in the field. He also promoted the cause of women in UN institutions, appointing Canada's Louise Fréchette as his deputy, and Ireland's Mary Robinson as his High Commissioner for Human Rights.

Right-wing British politician Enoch Powell once famously noted that all political careers end in failure. This appeared to be particularly apt as one observed the tragic twilight of Annan's tenure as Secretary-General. In retrospect, the 2001 Nobel citation that praised him for being 'pre-eminent in bringing new life to the organisation'[68] sounded anachronistic by 2006 in light of Rwanda, the Oil-for-Food scandal, and the failure of UN reform in 2005. Annan's troubled exit from the post could yet transform him, in the hands of future historians, into a prophet without honour, embroiled in scandal during his final years and rendered a lame duck by the country that did the most to anoint him Secretary-General in 1996. Annan finally and painfully discovered the ancient wisdom: one needs a long spoon to sup with the devil.

PART 2

THE QUEST FOR HEGEMONY

5

MESSIAH OR MERCANTILIST?

SOUTH AFRICA IN AFRICA[1]

'We look upon ourselves as indispensable to the White World... We are the link. We are white, but we are in Africa. We link them both, and that lays on us a special duty.'[2]

Hendrik Verwoerd, prime minister of South Africa, 1958–1966

At a meeting in Cape Town in January 2004, Adebayo Adedeji, the eminent Nigerian economist and chair of South Africa's peer review process, ended a talk on South Africa's role in Africa by asking the question that John the Baptist had famously put to Jesus: 'Are you the messiah we have been waiting for or should we wait for someone else?' Adedeji has also been among the few analysts who have clearly understood the damaging effects on South Africa's current continental leadership ambitions of the 'beggar thy neighbour' mercantilist trade policies, economic sabotage, and dislocation, as well as the destructive military policies of successive apartheid regimes.[3] Mercantilist states have historically believed in pursuing policies such as maintaining favourable trade balances with their neighbours, establishing colonies, developing mining and industry, and accumulating gold reserves: an accurate reflection of South Africa and its historical role in Africa. South Africa's past military destabilisation of Southern Africa and the domineering mercantilist economic role of its white entrepreneurs have left profound scars on its neighbours and a distrust that even a black-led African National Congress (ANC) government will need decades to overcome. In a real sense, apartheid South Africa was a regional *tsotsi* that threw its weight around like a township bully.

This chapter historicises South Africa's foreign policy on the premise that one cannot explain the country's current foreign policy without properly understanding how the past has shaped the present. We examine key events during four important historical periods: 1945–1980, 1980–1994, 1994–1999, and 1999–2008. Many Southern Africans still fear today that contemporary institutions such as the Southern African Development Community (SADC) and the Southern African Customs Union (SACU) could be used as instruments by a black-led government to fulfil the historical aims of South Africa's white leaders and big business to incorporate neighbouring vassals into a South African-dominated 'constellation of states'. These sentiments are often greatly underestimated by many ahistorical scholars of South African foreign policy, though the South African government itself tends to be more sensitive about its past.[4]

In a sense, post-apartheid South Africa is still haunted by past domestic, regional, and external structures that continue to disturb its present. Domestically, South Africa's economy and the senior levels of key institutions such as universities, nongovernmental organisations and the military continue to be controlled by its white minority, who were the key beneficiaries of apartheid. Regionally, South Africa's control of about 80 per cent of the subregional economy and a 9:1 trade balance with its neighbours continue to spread fears of a mercantilist ogre dominating Southern Africa; and externally, much of South Africa's trade remains with Western Europe, the United States, and Asia in ties established largely when apartheid's architects believed that the country was a Western bulwark against communist infiltration into Africa. South Africa's leaders effectively established a Pax Pretoriana in Southern Africa through administering Namibia between 1919 and 1989; creating institutions such as SACU through which Pretoria exerted economic influence over Botswana, Swaziland, and Lesotho; and through military destabilisation policies of awesome destructiveness in countries such as Angola, Mozambique, Lesotho, Zambia, and Zimbabwe.

The rather arcane and often esoteric academic debates about whether South Africa is a 'hegemon', 'pivot', or 'middle power' can be sensibly settled by clearly defining the terms.[5] 'Constructive' hegemons are able not only to articulate the rules and norms for respective regions, but also to convince other states to follow such rules.[6] A pivotal state is an *important* rather than a *dominant* state, and South Africa is a pivot in global terms and a hegemon in regional terms. The middle-power robes are also ones that are made to be worn by South Africa, since the country does seek, through multilateral organisations, to play a leadership role in security, trade, and economic issues as a respected voice of the global South.

But even hegemony may be insufficient to describe the preponderance of power that South Africa enjoys over its neighbours. Another emotive term—imperialism—may in fact be more appropriate to describe apartheid South Africa's role in Africa. American scholar Tony Smith notes that '[i]mperialism may be defined as the effective domination by a relatively strong state over a weaker people whom it does not control as it does its home population, or as the efforts to secure such domination'.[7] Smith reminds us that it was the 'fragility or malleability' of the social and political systems of states in Africa, Asia, and Latin America and the narrow definitions of their security interests by London and Washington that made Pax Britannica and Pax Americana possible. This was certainly the perception of Southern African states that were economically dependent on South Africa. Apartheid's rulers also tied their security to the economic control and military dominance of their neighbours. As Mexicans have noted about the United States, so too have Batswana, Swazis, Basotho, and Namibians certainly had many reasons to complain that they are so close to South Africa and so far from God!

Each time imperial Britain and America contradicted their 'liberal' political principles, they justified it by the need to restore order in the light of local anarchy or to ward off the interests of rival powers. South Africa's apartheid leaders simultaneously justified their incursions into, and occupation of, Angolan territory in the 1980s by the need to ward off the 'red peril' posed by a Russian-backed Cuban army. Post-apartheid South Africa's military intervention into Lesotho in 1998 was also justified as a bid to restore order after fears of a military coup d'état. The tiny mountain kingdom, however, through its Highlands Water Project, supplies water to South Africa's industrial heartland of Gauteng: a strategic factor in the intervention.

Western imperialism involved God, gold, and glory[8], with missionaries seeking to convert Africans from their 'pagan' ancestor worship; with private business interests seeking mineral and agricultural resources; and with empire-builders justifying the whole enterprise as a *mission civilisatrice* of 'savage barbarians'.[9] In the South African case, could the expansion of mostly white-led businessmen and civil society activists across the continent represent a modern-day equivalent of a bygone era? Nineteenth-century Cambridge historian John Seeley noted that the British seemed to 'have conquered and peopled half the world in a fit of absence of mind'.[10] Trade followed the flag and the British military and government provided support to the activities of firms like the British South Africa Company and the East India Company. In the South African context, this equation may have been reversed, with the flag following trade. Could a post-apartheid South Africa be forced to protect the activities of its own trade pioneers, such as De Beers in the Democratic Republic of the Congo (DRC) and Randgold in Côte d'Ivoire? Could South Africa's peacemaking efforts become linked to interventions in strategically important countries such as the Congo in which it dominates the telecommunications market, in which its companies control mines, and in which its leaders have backed state electricity utility Eskom's plans to establish a hydropower project by the 2020s centred around Congo's Grand Inga Falls, to supply electricity to the entire continent?

South Africa in Africa: Within or Apart?

The Heirs of Cecil Rhodes, 1945–1980

Cecil Rhodes, the greatest individual historical symbol of imperialism until his death in 1902, dreamed of building a railway from the Cape to Cairo.[11] This ruthless diamond and gold magnate fought to spread what he saw as 'enlightened' British culture, values, and institutions to as much of Africa as possible. Rhodes had described Africa north of the Limpopo as South Africa's 'natural hinterland' (see chapter 10). Interest groups such as the South African Federated Chamber of Industries and the South African Foreign Trade Organisation saw the potential for business opportunities north of the Limpopo. The country's post-1945 leaders were in a genuine sense the heirs of Cecil Rhodes. South African premier between 1948 and 1954, D.F. Malan, spoke of 'preserving Africa for white Christian civilization',[12] and believed that Euro-Christians needed to establish a trusteeship over Africans.[13] Apartheid governments thus saw themselves as very much part of the West. The country had been a member of the 'white dominions' (along with Australia, Canada, and New Zealand) sharing Western culture, economic systems, and security concerns.[14] South Africa's largest trading partners were, and still largely remain, countries such as Britain, the US, Germany, France, and Japan.

During the Cold War era, apartheid's leaders sought to manipulate American support by playing up the threat of a 'total onslaught' by a communist bogeyman. They also presented themselves as a bridge between Africa and the West. Hendrik Verwoerd, the Grand Wizard of apartheid and South African premier between 1958 to 1966, claimed that whites had brought civilisation, economic development, order, and education to Africa, and that South Africa would determine the continent's destiny.[15] Even before Thabo Mbeki, these were the 'Renaissance men', seeking to spread enlightenment to a 'Dark Continent'. Such patronising thinking was very much a feature of South African political thought from Cecil Rhodes to F.W. De Klerk.

After the Second World War ended in 1945, South Africa assumed that it would form a partnership with European empires to bring development to the rest of Africa.[16] Pax Pretoriana established a security bloc with other albinocracies in the region: Rhodesia and the Portuguese 'empire' in Angola and Mozambique. Both Verwoerd and John Vorster (the apartheid leader between 1966 and 1979) had visions of a South African–led Southern African common market and a political Commonwealth. Foreign policy was effectively geared towards ensuring the security of white rule over a black majority. Shortly after the founding of the United Nations in 1945, the supposedly 'liberal' South African premier Jan Smuts sought to incorporate Namibia into South Africa, as he had earlier sought to annex Botswana, Swaziland, and Lesotho—an aim also pursued by his successors until 1955. Smuts, the author of some of the declaration of aims in the preamble to the UN Charter that stressed fundamental human rights, denied that racial discrimination violated the human rights of blacks, since he saw such policies as necessary to protect 'the more backward sections of our multiplex society'.[17] Like Rhodes, Smuts supported a united Africa within the British Empire and Commonwealth, a vision also backed by South African big business, which sought a continued supply of cheap foreign labour and access to African mines and markets.

South Africa's leaders worked hard to prevent European imperial powers from granting independence to their African colonies for fear that the example might influence the country's own black population. Apartheid's founding premier in 1948, D.F. Malan, outlined an 'African Charter' in a bizarre and quixotic bid to promote 'pan-African' regional cooperation. Malan's successor in 1954, J.G. Strijdom, was also a champion of white supremacist (*baasskap*) and anti–communist policies. Strijdom was the first to congratulate Sudan on gaining its independence in 1956, and Pretoria sent a representative to Ghana's independence celebration a year later. But due to the opposition of African governments to apartheid and domestic racist sensitivities about black African diplomats working in Pretoria, South Africa could not capitalise on these early contacts.[18]

The apartheid regime faced widespread international condemnation for its racist policies and the Sharpeville killings of 1960, shortly after which the country left the Commonwealth. African diplomats at the UN urged member states to sever diplomatic relations with Pretoria. (see chapter 3). The Organisation of African Unity (OAU), created in 1963, ostracised South Africa. With the independence by 1980 of Angola, Mozambique, and Zimbabwe as a result of a Portuguese coup and determined African guerrillas, South Africa's albinocratic rulers feared that the fall of these regional dominoes had left them vulnerable. They thus stepped up military activities to protect white rule. The dreams of apartheid's leaders of their country becoming '*n Afrika-horende volk*' (a nation that belongs to Africa) had morphed into a tragic nightmare, as the country was instead treated as an international leper by most of the world.

The Southern African Customs Union, established in 1910 between South Africa, Botswana, Lesotho, and Swaziland, perfectly symbolised Pretoria's mercantilist approach towards its neighbours. Through SACU, Pretoria pursued one-sided trade deals while restricting access to its own markets. SACU set out to create a common market with free movement of goods and services—but significantly, not of people. This was, however, a market that distributed its rewards unevenly. Agricultural products, vital for other SACU members, were excluded from tariff-free trade. South Africa unilaterally determined the union's tariffs and was responsible for administering all duties, which were paid directly into a fund in Pretoria. Far from promoting industrial development within SACU, South Africa blocked the industrialisation efforts of other members.[19] The 'rand zone' was also created, in 1974, pegging South Africa's currency to those of Namibia, Swaziland, and Lesotho.[20] South Africa's mines, farms, and industry attracted hundreds of thousands of workers from neighbouring countries, becoming a major source of revenue for Mozambique, Malawi, and Lesotho. South Africa's Industrial Development Corporation also provided millions of rand in loans to South African firms to set up businesses in Southern Africa.

With no change in the policy of apartheid at home, African states ratcheted up the pressure by pushing the UN to impose an arms embargo on the apartheid state in 1977. South Africa suffered a decline of economic growth from 5.5 per cent between 1960 and 1974 to 1.9 per cent between 1974 and 1984.[21] But by 1984, South Africa had become a nuclear power, underlining the strong technological base and sophistication of its economy.

The Limits of Pax Pretoriana, 1980–1994

The Southern African Development Coordination Conference (SADCC) was established in 1980 to reduce the subregion's economic dependence on

South Africa. By the end of 1989, the government of the hard-line P.W. Botha had built up an external debt of $20 billion, and the rand was in freefall.[22] Abroad, the regime sought an implausible 'constellation' of Southern African states with its 'domestic' homelands of Transkei, Bophuthatswana, Venda, and Ciskei, as well as 'regional homelands' such as Lesotho, Swaziland, and Botswana, which all declined to join such a monstrous body. This period also saw an increase in military destabilisation policies, which rained death and destruction on neighbouring countries.[23] Apartheid's leaders effectively tried to reduce Southern Africa to a region of 'broken-back' states that would come under Pretoria's heavy hammer. An estimated 1 million people died as a result of these policies, while South Africa's economic sabotage cost the region an estimated $60.5 billion between 1980 and 1988 alone.[24] The collective memory of these actions is still fresh in the minds of regional states. In 1988, the reckless South African gendarme finally got its comeuppance, as Cuban troops in Angola shattered the myth of white military invincibility by giving the South African Defence Force (SADF) a bloody nose in the famous battle of Cuito Cuanavale. This incident, more than any other, probably did more to hasten the negotiations that resulted in the withdrawal of foreign troops from Angola, the independence of Namibia, and the end of apartheid in South Africa. As Cuban leader Fidel Castro noted: 'From now on the history of Africa will have to be written before and after Cuito Cuanavale.'[25]

Though South West Africa, as Namibia was formerly known, had been granted to South Africa under a League of Nations mandate as a reward for Pretoria's assistance to the Allies in the First World War of 1914 to 1918, the people in the territory had never been consulted. With the demise of the League and the birth of the United Nations in 1945, pressure mounted from Afro-Asian states for Pretoria to repeal apartheid laws and to hand over the territory to the UN's Trusteeship Council. An obstinate South Africa instead sought to create facts on the ground, killing protestors who were resisting forcible removals and extending apartheid laws to what it saw as its 'fifth province'. South African parastatals Soekor and the Industrial Development Corporation were large investors in the territory. With the South West African People's Organisation (SWAPO) launching a guerrilla war of independence in 1966, an advisory opinion of the International Court of Justice confirmed five years later that South Africa's continued administration of the territory was illegal. Following the start of the withdrawal of Cuban troops from Angola in 1989 (completed in 1991), a UN mission was subsequently established in Namibia that steered the country to independence in March 1990.

South Africa's seven-decade imperial presence in Namibia had finally ended. Internal changes in South Africa itself, fuelled by the 'mass action' and international sanctions of the 1980s, would eventually see F.W. de Klerk hand power to a black-led government under the saintly Nelson Mandela (released from twenty-seven years in jail) following a 'negotiated revolution' between 1990 and 1994. Apartheid was formally dead and the world witnessed its funeral, though its burial would clearly still take several decades to occur.

The Mandela Era, 1994–1999

In the post–Cold War era, the reluctance of Western countries to intervene militarily in African conflicts led many observers to question whether potential African hegemons such as South Africa and Nigeria could fill the security vacuum (see chapter 7). During Mandela's inauguration in May 1994, US vice president Al Gore urged Mandela to send peacekeepers to Rwanda.[26] Based on its history, post-apartheid South Africa still struggles to shake off an identity as a Western Trojan horse in Africa. Some of its leaders continually assert their African identity and acknowledge debts from the liberation struggle, though many South Africans, still suffering from the psychological effects of apartheid leaders' denigration of black Africa, remain ambivalent towards the continent. Immigration policies in post-apartheid South Africa have thus tended to be skewed against black Africans.[27] Between 1994 and 2000, the South African police forcibly deported 600,000 migrants[28] amidst growing hysteria about a 'flood' of illegal aliens. Many Africans are also pejoratively derided as *amakwerekwere* in a new version of the apartheid-era *swart gevaar* (black peril).

Xenophobia is still rife throughout South African society, as incidents such as the killing of two Senegalese and a Mozambican—who were flung to their deaths from a moving train in September 1998—graphically illustrated. Data from 2001 showed that 85 per cent of South Africans felt that undocumented migrants should be denied their freedom of speech, while 60 to 65 per cent of South Africans thought that migrants should be denied police protection or access to social services.[29] Only with the realisation of a skills shortage in the country have there been conscious efforts since 2001 to attract talent from the rest of the continent. South Africa's failure to gain the support of most African states to host the Olympics in 2004 was an early sign of lingering suspicions of the country's leadership ambitions on the continent.[30]

Under Mandela's rule, between 1994 and 1999, South Africa had a globally revered statesman, one of the most representative political systems on the continent, arguably its best army, and Africa's largest economy. In 1993, Mandela had set out the six cardinal principles of his country's foreign policy: the centrality of human rights; promotion of democracy worldwide; promotion of justice and respect for international law; peaceful resolution of disputes; the centrality of Africa; and regional and international cooperation.[31] It is important, however, to note from the outset some of the constraints on post-apartheid South Africa's ability to act as a regional hegemon.[32] While South Africa has by far the most developed economy in Africa, its society remains deeply divided and its government faces huge socioeconomic challenges in reversing the massive inequalities resulting from four decades of apartheid social engineering and a century of British colonial rule. Unemployment is estimated at 40 per cent, and South Africa's former president Thabo Mbeki himself talked of a 'South Africa of two nations': one comprising a disproportionately white population with a standard of living similar to that of Spain, the other comprising the mainly black, chronically underdeveloped three-quarters of the population with a standard of living similar to that of Congo-Brazzaville. As Kenyan scholar Ali Mazrui succinctly put it: 'the Whites said to the Blacks: "You take the Crown and we will keep the Jewels."'[33] South Africa's economy experienced jobless growth and shed about 1 million jobs between 1994 and 1999. The country still has a serious lack of administrative capacity. The economy remains largely controlled by a white minority, while about 60 per cent of the senior echelons of South Africa's military are still dominated by white apartheid-era officers.[34] All these factors have hampered South Africa's diplomacy in Africa.

A democratic South Africa joined the reformed SADCC, the Southern African Development Community, in 1994. The country led peacemaking efforts in Burundi, the DRC, and Lesotho. Perhaps the most significant event in South Africa's post-apartheid Africa policy, however, was the bruising battle with Nigeria. After the brutal hanging by the regime of General Sani Abacha of activist Ken Saro-Wiwa and eight of his Ogoni campaigners during the Commonwealth summit in Auckland in November 1995, a deeply betrayed Mandela called for the imposition of oil sanctions on Abacha and called on a SADC summit to take collective action against Nigeria. However, even Mandela's iconic status failed to rally a single Southern African state to take action against Nigeria. Instead, it was South Africa that was being accused by many African leaders of sowing seeds of division in Africa and undermining African solidarity (see chapter 7).

During Mandela's presidency, South Africa largely shunned a military role out of fear of arousing allegations of hegemonic domination. But the country's first major peacekeeping mission was marred by controversy. After a constitutional crisis in Lesotho, its prime minister, Pakalitha Mosisili, invited SADC to send troops to the country to help restore order. South Africa undertook the intervention with Botswana in September 1998, but faced stiff opposition from sections of Lesotho's army and parts of the population, resulting in widespread disorder before the situation was eventually brought under control. The legitimacy of the intervention as a SADC-sanctioned action was widely questioned. The leadership of the peacekeeping force by white South African officers from the apartheid army (the force commander had been part of South Africa's destructive forces in Angola) further fuelled passions,[35] as did the historical memory of forty-two people commemorated on a plaque in Maseru who had been killed by South African commandos in 1982.[36]

The Mbeki Era, 1999–2008

Under Thabo Mbeki's presidency, between 1999 and 2008, South Africa established solid credentials to become Africa's leading power. (see chapter 11). At a foreign policy retreat in February 2001, Mbeki identified five key priorities for South Africa's external relations: restructuring the OAU/African Union (AU) and SADC; reforming regional and international organisations such as the United Nations, the World Trade Organisation (WTO), the World Bank, and the International Monetary Fund (IMF); hosting major international conferences; promoting peace and security in Africa and the Middle East; and fostering ties with the Group of Eight (G8) industrialised countries while devising a strategy for the global South.[37] Chastened by Mandela's bitter foreign policy experiences over Nigeria and Lesotho, Mbeki consistently sought multilateral solutions to resolving regional conflicts, and skilfully used both a strategic partnership with Nigeria and his chairmanship of the AU between 2002 and 2003 to pursue his goals.

Mbeki was more prepared than Mandela to send peacekeepers abroad,[38] which increased South Africa's credibility as a major geostrategic player in Africa. The South African leader was also the chief mediator in Côte d'Ivoire and the DRC. There was a clear sense under Mbeki that foreign policy was made at the presidency by a man who was the long-serving head of the ANC's international relations department in exile. Mbeki was the first chairman of the AU and chairman of the Non-Aligned Movement (NAM); he was the intellectual architect of the New Partnership for Africa's Development (NEPAD); and under his leadership, South Africa hosted two high-profile

UN conferences on racism and sustainable development. The country was also president of the influential Group of 77 (G77) developing countries at the UN during critical debates on reforming the organisation in 2005–2006, while South Africa won a two-year seat on the UN Security Council in 2007–2008. South Africa further played an important role through 'sports diplomacy' under both Mandela and Mbeki in promoting itself as an African power. The country hosted the African Cup of Nations in 1996; helped to finance Mali's hosting of the event in 1998; and hosted the All-Africa Games in 2003. It promoted 'cultural diplomacy' by financing the restoration of Mali's famous library in Timbuktu, and through Mbeki's championing of the idea of an African Renaissance. The need to add more flesh to the skeletal bones of the African Renaissance was satisfied, to some degree, by the creation of NEPAD and the AU by 2002.

During its stint on the UN Security Council in 2007–2008[39], South Africa should have focused largely on African issues and not become embroiled in unnecessary spats with Western powers over Iran and Myanmar. At the UN, South Africa sometimes cut the figure of a fifteen-year-old juvenile trying to change the world, with Western emperors having to tell the kid that he was wearing no clothes! Tshwane (Pretoria) should simply have abstained and hidden behind Russian and Chinese vetoes. The hypocrisy of countries like the US, which invaded Iraq in 2003 without UN approval, must naturally be exposed. But post-apartheid South Africa should clearly not have been making the same arguments over Myanmar as the apartheid government was making over punishing Pretoria's own behaviour.[40]

Despite Mbeki's efforts to integrate South Africa into the rest of Africa, it is unclear how deeply entrenched these efforts are within South Africa's population and its political and business elite. Many in Africa question whether Mbeki's heirs will maintain the same level of commitment to the continent that he has demonstrated. South Africa's cultural schizophrenia is evident in the fact that its new rulers continue to refer to its black population using the apartheid-era term 'African', leaving one wondering whether the country's 'coloureds', Asians, and whites are also not African. Many black South Africans still talk about the rest of Africa as if they were not part of it.[41] The fact that so many symbols of apartheid still litter South Africa's political landscape a decade and a half after the end of apartheid astonishes many African visitors. Street names still bear the names of apartheid stalwarts like Verwoerd and Botha. Statues of imperial rogues such as Cecil Rhodes are ubiquitous in Cape Town. Military monuments in Tshwane celebrate white supremacy in wars of dispossession of the black majority.[42] Most astonishing, outside South Africa's parliament—the deliberative body of Africa's greatest hope—stands a statue of Louis Botha, a white military conqueror on horseback! Nothing could better symbolise South Africa's cultural limbo, caught between a shameful past of arrogant European racism and struggling to arrive at a future as the midwife of Africa's Renaissance.

Many African governments and people have expressed unease about what they perceive to be South Africa's protectionist trade and xenophobic immigration policies. They have accused its leaders of ingratitude after three decades of support for the ANC, at enormous cost to their countries. (The ANC, though also faced harsh treatment from governments in Zimbabwe and Mozambique in the 1980s). Thirty-one Somalis, many of them shopkeepers outcompeting locals, were murdered in Cape Town in 2006.[43] Furthermore, senior South African Home Affairs officials have called for the declaration of a 'war' on 'illegal immigration', which they described as one of the country's 'major social and economic plagues'. As with preludes to mass killings, African migrants have been dehumanised as parasitic 'cockroaches', making it easier to justify their annihilation. Immigration policies have tended to be skewed against black Africans. An estimated 177,000 Zimbabweans were deported between 2005 and 2006. In 2000, Operation Crackdown continued apartheid-era practices through the arrest of people in areas with black immigrant populations, in an incident that saw the destruction of valid documents and other illegal actions by the police. People were also sent to the notorious Lindela detention centre, and *Human Rights Watch* reported that undocumented migrants died in detention. The South African Human Rights Commission (SAHRC) condemned the nature of the arrests.

Sections of the South African media, through inflammatory and stereotypical coverage of immigration issues, have also contributed to the creation of a xenophobic environment. Even legal migrants and genuine asylumseekers are sometimes demonised as a lecherous, impoverished 'flood' threatening to overwhelm the country. Words like 'hordes', 'waves', 'flocking', and 'streaming' are ubiquitous in this reporting. Nigerians are condemned as drug-traffickers, Congolese as diamond-smugglers, Basotho as smugglers of copper wire, Mozambicans as carjackers, and Zimbabwean women as prostitutes. Citizens of countries in North America and Western Europe who are also involved in crimes are rarely reported on, however. The Africanisation of crime clearly makes it easier to perpetuate xenophobic violence against these migrants.

The traumatic xenophobic attacks in South Africa in May 2008—an issue that a complacent government had been warned about in the 2007 African Peer Review Mechanism (APRM) report[44]—demanded a critical reflection on their implications for the country's much-vaunted African Renaissance project. South African mobs in xenophobic acts of almost unimaginable savagery slaughtered about two dozen of their fellow Africans from neighbouring countries (mostly Mozambicans and Zimbabweans).[45] The embarrassment of the images beamed across the world, drenching the rainbow flag in a deathly red, was felt throughout the continent. There was much poignant symbolism in this situation. Even as Mbeki, the prophet of Africa's Renaissance—and himself once an exile in several African countries—stumbled wearily to a visibly tragic *fin de régime*, the xenophobic attacks could well have represented the smouldering ashes of the death of his project.

Many Africans have also complained about the aggressive drive by South Africa's mostly white-dominated corporations in search of new markets north of the Limpopo. South African business interests have not helped their cause in Africa by talking as if they were determined to follow in the colossal footsteps of Cecil Rhodes. Graeme Bell of Standard Bank talked of a 'sense of pioneering'; the managing director of Shoprite Checkers spoke of 'an army on the move';[46] while others have talked of conquest as if Africa were a helpless virgin waiting to be deflowered by rampaging white industrialists.

South African firms have established interests in mining, banking, retail, communications, arms, and insurance, often with the active support of host governments. By 2003, South African companies were operating Cameroon's national railroad and Tanzania's national electricity company, and managing the airports of seven African countries. In the same period, Shoprite's seventy-two outlets in the rest of Africa were sourcing South African products worth 429 million rand rather than buying some of these products—including basic items such as eggs—in their host countries.[47] Local resentment was swelling in places like Kenya, Tanzania, and Nigeria to what some saw as efforts to export apartheid labour practices and destroy infant industries. These criticisms, however, should be balanced by the creation of jobs and improvements in infrastructure and services in these countries. In 2000, South Africa was the largest single foreign investor in the rest of Africa. A year later, South Africa's foreign investment in the rest of the continent had increased by a staggering 300 per cent since 1996, to 26.8 billion rand, as the excess capital built up under the era of international sanctions found profitable havens on the continent. By 2002, the rest of Africa accounted for 16.74 per cent of South African exports, while its imports from the rest of Africa represented an anaemic 3.62 per cent (see chapter 9).[48]

In 2006, South Africa remained the largest single investor in the rest of Africa, at 80 billion rand, and almost all of its companies on the continent were reporting high returns, with South Africa accounting for 35 per cent of Africa's gross domestic product. One important but often underreported aspect of this trade is that migrants from the rest of Africa have set up restaurants, spaza shops, fast-food restaurants, barbershops, craft stalls, and Internet cafes in many South African cities. The tens of thousands of mostly Southern Africans who buy goods in South Africa to resell in their home markets also contribute an estimated 20 billion rand annually to the local economy (an estimated 450,000 shoppers travelled by road and 90,000 by air to Johannesburg in 2005 alone).[49] These figures certainly contradict the depiction of African migrants as parasitic leeches who are exploiting South Africa's riches, and render the horrific xenophobic violence in May–June 2008 even more tragic.

In reaction to these concerns, Mbeki consistently stressed that South Africa has 'no great power pretensions' on the continent.[50] In February 2000, South Africa established a $30 million African Renaissance and International Cooperation Fund to promote democracy, development, and security on the continent. The Mbeki administration also initiated efforts in 2005 to ensure that South African firms developed broad-based economic empowerment through strategic partnerships that promoted development in African countries. South Africa now has embassies in all fourteen SADC countries as well as in eighteen other African countries: more than in any other region in the world.[51]

Despite these positive developments, in the minds of many people in Southern Africa there remain uncomfortable parallels between the foreign policy goals of apartheid's leaders and Mbeki's leadership role in Africa. Apartheid leaders sought to secure the white state, promote economic and technical links with their neighbours, and establish the country as a leading continental power.[52] Mbeki shared the latter two goals, but rather than securing the white state for apartheid, he tried to create a state that lifted his country's black majority out of poverty. In both cases, the principal goal was to pursue the national interest to benefit specific groups *within* South Africa. Whereas political factors were obstacles to apartheid leaders playing a leadership role in Africa, the economic activities of South African firms may eventually become a major obstacle to the country's current political leadership ambitions.[53]

Foreign Policy in the Post-Mbeki Era

Kgalema Motlanthe took over the South African presidency in September 2008, seven months before the end of Mbeki's term. Mbeki had been 'recalled' by the ANC, having earlier lost the presidency of the party to Jacob Zuma in December 2007. Motlanthe, in his seven-month stint, pursued a cautious foreign policy that demonstrated more continuity than change from the Mbeki administration. In Zimbabwe, South Africa continued to work through SADC to seek a power-sharing deal for the country, which was finally achieved in February 2009. After elections in April 2009, South African president Jacob Zuma—who had won plaudits for his past peacemaking role in Burundi as deputy president—was determined to focus more attention on domestic socioeconomic challenges, but could not completely ignore continental diplomacy.[54]

Kgalema Motlanthe's appearance at the Group of 20 (G20) summit in London in April 2009 was quiet. Former president Thabo Mbeki's intellect, vision, and energy had earned the widespread respect of world leaders, and Mbeki would have thrived at this summit, which, had he not been prematurely removed from office, would have been his swansong on the international stage. At a press conference after the summit, Motlanthe reportedly told journalists that South Africa was not representing Africa at the meeting, but was in London as a result of being an emerging market. This reflected the continuing schizophrenia in South Africa's continental role: the country wants to occupy an African permanent seat on a reformed UN Security Council (see chapter 3), but does not seem to want to represent African interests in international financial forums.

The one issue that had dominated global headlines before the G20 summit was South Africa's denial of a visa to Tibet's spiritual leader, the Dalai Lama, in March 2009 for a meeting with his fellow Nobel peace laureates in South Africa, which the government was involved in as part of the campaign for hosting the football World Cup in 2010. This decision was apparently taken after political pressure from Beijing. Despite South Africa being China's second largest trading partner in Africa after Angola (see chapter 9), this action would have been more befitting a dependent, resource-poor 'banana republic' than one of Africa's powerhouses. South Africa should have, as Nigeria—China's fourth largest trading partner in Africa—did in 2008, let the Dalai Lama visit,[55] and simply distanced itself from the formal meeting.

Jacob Zuma who assumed the presidency after democratic elections in April 2009 has wide-ranging peacemaking experience in South Africa's Kwazulu-

Natal province as well as in Burundi. But he noted that he would strike a balance between foreign and domestic policy, signalling that he would neither travel as extensively as Thabo Mbeki nor take such a hands-on approach to foreign policy. Zuma appointed Maite Nkoana-Mashabane, South Africa's former High Commissioner to India and Malaysia, as his foreign minister in May 2009. Ebrahim Ebrahim, Zuma's former cellmate on Robben Island and a senior adviser to Zuma in the deputy presidency, was appointed as deputy foreign minister. Ebrahim confirmed that Zuma would leave the running of the ministry to the minister.[56] The Department of Foreign Affairs was renamed the Department of International Relations and Cooperation, to reflect South Africa's new desire to become an aid donor. In explaining the change of name, Nkoana-Mashabane quipped: 'A colleague of mine said affairs do not last, relations do.'[57] The minister stressed the continuity of Mbeki's multilateral approach to Africa. As she put it: 'The approach of this leadership would be to work with partners ... so that it does not become a South African thing; so it does not become us talking down to neighbours and African brothers and sisters. That's what Africans hate, they don't want to be told, or talked down to... That reminds them of our colonial past.'[58]

The most important possible shift in South Africa's early foreign policy under a new administration was the naming of Angola as a strategic ally on the continent, thus ending the frosty relationship between Mbeki and Angolan president Eduardo Dos Santos. Zuma had visited Luanda as deputy president in August 2004 and as president of the ANC in March 2008. By this time, Angola had become South Africa's second largest trading partner in Africa after Nigeria. In August 2009, in a bid to thaw the frosty relationship between Tshwane and Luanda under Mbeki, Zuma went to Angola as his first state visit, taking with him a large business and high-powered ministerial delegation in August 2009. The strategic partnership between the two strongest powers in Southern Africa (Angola has oil and diamonds as well as a battle-hardened army) could revive SADC and provide a powerful ally in both subregional and continental diplomacy. Ebrahim Ebrahim also expressed a determination to build strong ties with former liberation movements in Angola, Mozambique, Namibia and Zimbabwe, and to expand relations with Tanzania and Uganda, suggesting a primarily SADC focus.[59] Whereas Mbeki sought leadership at the continental AU level, which he was often unable to translate into leverage at subregional level, Zuma, if his strategy succeeds in securing strong subregional diplomacy, could give South Africa even greater influence at the continental level.

Policy Recommendations: The Bicycle Strategy of South Africa's Bilateral Ties in Africa[60]

If South Africa is to consolidate its strategic bilateral relations developed in Africa since 1994, it must choose five key strategic partners and 'hubs' (regional powers), one in each of Africa's five subregions. In addition, South Africa should pick two additional 'spokes' (influential actors) in each subregion that are important enough to increase the country's strategic engagement in the areas of diplomacy, conflict management, and trade relations. Tshwane's bilateral relations would thus resemble a gigantic bicycle, with five hubs and ten spokes: a necessary vehicle to get a handle on a strategic approach to promoting peace and prosperity in Africa. At the head of this bicycle would be the presidency, with its hands firmly on the handlebars, controlling the speed at which the vehicle travels. The other four wheels would consist of the Department of International Relations and Cooperation; the Department of Trade and Industry; government parastatals and institutions like the Industrial Development Corporation and the Development Bank of Southern Africa; and South Africa's business sector with its investments in Africa. Each of these four sets of actors would have bells on their handlebars to warn the presidency of any impending bumps on the road. As is often said about the integration process in the European Union (EU), South Africa's political and economic leaders will have to keep pedalling to avoid falling off this contraption.

The five hubs are Angola in Southern Africa, Nigeria in West Africa, the Democratic Republic of the Congo in the Great Lakes region, Ethiopia in Eastern Africa, and Algeria in North Africa. In Southern Africa, the two spokes would be Mozambique and Zimbabwe. In the Great Lakes region, the two spokes would be Burundi and Rwanda; in West Africa, Ghana and Côte d'Ivoire; in Eastern Africa, Sudan and Tanzania; in North Africa, Egypt and Libya. It is around these five hubs and ten spokes—a total of about a quarter of the African Union's membership—that South Africa can build solid strategic bilateral relationships in Africa. This list is by no means static, and may change in the future based on new geopolitical and economic shifts on the continent. For example, the demise of Muammar Qaddafi in Libya could eliminate the country as a North African spoke. Countries like Zambia and Kenya could also become more strategic actors for South Africa in the future, and be promoted to spokes.

Five of these strategic countries—Nigeria, Angola, Algeria, Libya, and Sudan—produce 80 per cent of Africa's oil and possess 90 per cent of the continent's petroleum reserves.[61] Four other important countries included here—Nigeria, Algeria, Libya, and Egypt—contribute, along with South Africa, 75 per cent of the African Union's annual assessed budget. Based on history, population, subregional political clout, trade, and the importance of bilateral ties developed over the past decade and a half, these are the key actors for promoting South Africa's bilateral interests in Africa.

Concluding Reflections: From Pax Pretoriana to Pax South Africana

Despite its ignominious past, post-apartheid South Africa, under Thabo Mbeki's leadership between 1999 and 2008, transformed itself in a short decade and a half from being Africa's most destabilising power to being its most energetic peacemaker. The country has become an African power and could aspire to global middle-power status through its policy of building strong continental institutions and working through its African allies, as well as countries such as Brazil and India, in international political and trade forums where its voice is widely respected. Despite the likely focus on domestic priorities, South Africa's future lies in Africa, and its ambitions to play a role on the global stage can only be achieved by being accepted as a leader on its own continent. The country has many elements of 'soft power'[62] that it can use to promote its interests and win friends in Africa. The supreme irony is that while South Africans may be the most ignorant people about the rest of Africa, much of Africa's elite probably know more about South Africa than any other country on the continent.

Pax South Africana, as opposed to the discredited Pax Pretoriana, can use the South African Broadcasting Corporation's (SABC) twenty-four-hour news channel—the first in Africa—to reach elites in about forty African countries. The channel could be used to expose Africans further to South Africa, while simultaneously improving the knowledge of South Africans about the rest of the continent. (In June 2009, however, the SABC was experiencing serious financial problems as well as turmoil within its leadership, after its entire board was forced to resign.) Many of Africa's academics and students can also be found at top South African universities such as Witwatersrand and Cape Town. Several South African think-tanks and policy institutes such as the Cape Town–based Centre for Conflict Resolution and Johannesburg's Electoral Institute of Southern Africa are led and staffed by Africans from the rest of the continent. These are rich resources of 'soft power' that South Africa can use to create both a pan-African 'brain trust' capable of ensuring substantive contributions to knowledge production and policy debates about Africa, as well as a South African population who are more accepting of their African identity.

Cape Town is rapidly becoming an attractive site for the global film and advertising industries. South Africa could use this advantage to tell African stories through African eyes and provide a better image of the continent than the brutal savagery of wars that has become the staple diet for Western audiences. The South African film *Tsotsi*, which in 2006 won Hollywood's Oscar for best foreign language film, is a prime example of this approach. The film showed not only that an African language can carry a movie and attract global attention, but also that it is possible to tell authentic African stories that have universal appeal and real characters, rather than the more stereotypical Hollywood fare of dehumanised or brutally evil characters in films such as *Rise and Fall of Idi Amin* (in stark contrast to the excellent *The Last King of Scotland*), *Black Hawk Down*, and *Lord of War*. South African mobile giants Mobile Telephone Networks (MTN) and Vodacom could connect the entire continent with their mobile phone network, while South African technology and capital, if applied in a developmental manner, could help build the roads, railways, and ports that Africa badly needs for its industrial takeoff. South Africa leads the Southern Africa Power Pool, alongside Angola, Botswana, the DRC, and Namibia. South African Airways is by far the most reliable airline on the continent.

Paradoxically, South Africa is both the most pan-African and the least pan-African country in Africa. Its national anthem starts with the words 'God bless Africa'; its ruling party is called the *African* National Congress; its other main black liberation movement is called the *Pan-Africanist* Congress; and many of the leaders of its liberation movement grew up in exile in Lusaka, Gaborone, Harare, and Dar-es-Salaam. But as we have also noted, many of South Africa's white leaders viewed the country as a European outpost, a kind of Australia in Africa, and many South Africans still hold the image of Africa as a 'Dark Continent' of conflicts and diseases that they exist apart from rather than within.

Post-apartheid South Africa is neither a messiah nor a mercantilist power. It is simply an aspiring middle power seeking to punch above its weight in global politics. Through an effective foreign policy, Mandela, Mbeki, and their heirs have sought to reverse the country's massive domestic problems inherited from the inequities of apartheid. But South Africa cannot be Africa's messiah because the country simply lacks the economic and military muscle and political legitimacy to impose its preferences on its own Southern African subregion, let alone on the continent. Mbeki grasped one basic reality: only by working through other regional states can South Africa promote its diplomatic interests within Africa. His successors must take this lesson to heart.

South Africa is also no longer the mercantilist power it once was under apartheid. The country is gradually loosening its protectionist policies in Southern Africa. South Africa agreed to restructure SACU to render greater benefits to its other members, whose share of revenues increased from 2.6 per cent in 1969–1970 to 31.8 per cent in 1991–1992.[63] In October 2002, a new SACU agreement was signed in Gaborone, Botswana, that sought to democratise the institution and introduced decisionmaking by consensus. To avoid unilateral trade deals such as the controversial one that South Africa negotiated with the European Union in 2000 (which excluded other SACU members), a clause was introduced into the 2002 accord that requires all SACU members to be involved in future trade negotiations with third parties.[64] By April 2004, SACU's headquarters had been moved from South Africa's Department of Trade and Industry to an independent secretariat in Namibia. Policymakers in Tshwane are now increasingly conscious of the need to promote investment and industrialisation policies that benefit their neighbours. South Africa thus pushed SADC to establish a free trade area by 2008 (a missed deadline), a customs union by 2010 (another missed deadline), and a common market by 2015. But a serious rift erupted within SACU by June 2009 that threatened the very existence of the organisation. Against South Africa's wishes and in contradiction of the 2002 SACU accord on external trade agreements, Botswana, Swaziland, and Lesotho signed interim economic partnership agreements with the EU to maintain the access of their goods to this important market. South Africa, Namibia, Nigeria, and many African states opposed these agreements on grounds that they locked Africa into a structural relationship of dependence on the European market, and refused to sign. With South Africa threatening to tighten customs controls to avoid transhipment of EU goods from its three SACU partner countries, the prospects for regional integration in Southern Africa were looking dim in December 2009.[65]

In order for South Africa to atone for the military and economic sins of the past, it must establish more equitable trade relations with its neighbours and actively promote their economic development. In October 1994, regional states such as Namibia were still complaining about the destruction of their local industries by unfair pricing and competition from South African firms.

They also argued that SACU regulations prevented them from protecting their infant industries from such actions. There were widespread complaints of dumping of cheaper South African goods to the detriment of local producers.[66] South Africa, in contrast, was still protecting its own infant industries through import substitution strategies. Zimbabwe has also often complained about South Africa's protectionism of its textile industry. In order to promote regional integration, Tshwane must reduce the imbalance of regional trade, increase access to its markets for these states, transform the migrant labour system into a more mutually beneficial labour market, build a transport infrastructure that benefits the entire subregion, and increase joint infrastructure projects that can provide jobs and investment for its neighbours.[67]

Pax South Africana must thus adopt an enlightened policy of developing the continent to enhance the country's security, create viable markets for its goods, and prevent poorer neighbouring populations from arriving at its own doorstep. The discovery of mass graves in Namibia near a former South African military base in 2005 was a clear sign that the past has not been completely buried. South Africa—the land of truth and reconciliation—should perhaps consider paying reparations to its neighbours for the military and economic destruction wrought by successive apartheid regimes. This seemingly controversial idea actually has a solid historical foundation. Successive German governments that took no part in the Nazi Holocaust paid reparations to Israel and Jewish victims after 1945. Japan paid reparations (often in the form of grants) to some of its Asian neighbours for its destructive imperial policies in the 1920s and 1930s, and invested heavily in those neighbours. Countries have often been held accountable for the sins of the past, not just governments. Post-apartheid South Africa can surely provide grants, investments, and special trade concessions to its SADC neighbours to atone for the sins of an inglorious mercantilist past in pursuit of a messianic mission in Africa.

6

GULLIVER'S TROUBLES

NIGERIA IN AFRICA[1]

'No country that is confronted with a long period of political instability, economic stagnation, and regression, and is reputed to be one of the most corrupt societies in the world, has a moral basis to lead others. If it tries to, it will be resisted.'[2]

Adebayo Adedeji, Nigeria's minister of economic development
and reconstruction, 1972–1975

The above statement by one of Nigeria's most respected public servants, Adebayo Adedeji—the country's minister of economic development and reconstruction between 1972 and 1975, author of a landmark report on reviewing Nigeria's foreign policy in 1976,[3] and executive secretary of the UN's Economic Commission for Africa (ECA) between 1975 and 1991—sums up succinctly the challenges that could prevent Nigeria from playing a leadership role in the post–Cold War era. Following one civil war, seven military regimes, and three failed democratic experiments, many observers—drawing inspiration from Nigeria's foremost contemporary *griot*, Chinua Achebe—have noted that the country, from the ravaged mangrove swamps of the oil-producing Niger Delta to the religious ferment of the powerful North, through the conflict-ridden Middle Belt to the bustling cities of the volatile South, is 'no longer at ease', and have wondered whether things could 'fall apart'.[4]

Anglo-Irish author and clergyman Jonathan Swift wrote his classic *Gulliver's Travels*—from which this chapter borrows its title—in 1726, as a satire of human frailty as well as his own age, in which Whig politicians were persecuting their Tory opponents. As part of Gulliver's travels, he encounters tiny creatures in the land of Lilliput who end up behaving in a treacherous and cruel manner and tying up Gulliver, who appears to be a giant in comparison to them.[5] While Nigeria, as the most populous country and one of the most powerful states in Africa, can be likened to Gulliver, the metaphor of Lilliputian can equally be applied to many of its leaders whose petty ambitions and often inhumane greed—like the creatures in Swift's tale—have prevented a country of enormous potential from fulfilling its leadership aspirations and development potential. As Kenyan scholar Ali Mazrui noted in 2001: 'The giant of Africa was in danger of becoming the midget of the world. Africa's Gulliver faced the threat of becoming the Lilliput of the globe.'[6]

In its five decades of independence, Nigeria has been reduced to a giant with clay feet, a colossal collection of impoverished masses, a crumbling Tower of Babel built on the rickety foundations of oil rent that its leaders have simply collected and squandered.[7] Despite its enormous oil wealth as the world's sixth largest producer, Nigeria remains a largely poor country, with over 70 per cent of its population still living on less than $1 a day, life expectancy at an abysmal forty-seven years, and a ranking of 159 out of 177 states on the UN Human Development Index in 2006.[8] Nigeria's crumbling infrastructure and many of its corrupt and visionless leaders have failed spectacularly to diversify its economy to reduce its huge dependence on oil, which still accounts for over 90 per cent of the country's foreign exchange earnings.

Aside from poor and badly maintained infrastructure (roads, railways, and port facilities), the country also suffers from a neglect of its agriculture and manufacturing sectors, skilled-labour shortages, limited access to long-term investment capital, and unpredictable and often corrupt bureaucratic rules that have rendered the investment climate inhospitable. As Chukwuma Soludo, the governor of Nigeria's Central Bank between 2004 and 2009, put it: 'Nigeria's railways ... have been virtually dormant for decades; its roads and highways remain in a state of massive disrepair. Water and electricity are way below the minimum needs of the country's expanding population... Although succeeding governments have committed significant resources to the needs of the infrastructure sector, many such schemes have fallen victim to corruption and rent-seeking behaviour.'[9]

The country's leaders have clearly lacked a sense of *noblesse oblige* (the obligations of rank). An estimated $380 billion of the country's oil wealth was stolen by its post-independence leaders: about two-thirds of all economic aid given to Africa during this period.[10] The government of General Ibrahim

Babangida (1985–1993) was unable to account for $12.4 billion of missing oil revenues that were part of a windfall from the Gulf War of 1991.[11] The family of General Sani Abacha (1993–1998) had to return $700 million (out of a reported $3 billion) in looted money after his death in June 1998. Despite allegedly spending more than $2 billion in reconstructing roads and $16 billion on the power sector,[12] the civilian regime of Olusegun Obasanjo (1999–2007) failed to revive the country's dilapidated infrastructure and electricity sector, and the country's oil refineries were producing less when he left office in 2007 than when he was first elected in 1999.[13]

The parlous state of electricity generation had a particularly deleterious effect on the country's manufacturing sector, as well as on private households. The state-owned National Electric Power Authority (NEPA)—often derided as 'Never Expect Power Always'—could only supply electricity to about 40 per cent of the country's population, forcing many companies and homes to run their own private generators. Transmission and distribution equipment were badly maintained due to inadequate funding and corruption, while revenue collection was abysmal: about 30–40 per cent of power supplies are never even billed, let alone collected! The power sector was thus losing $2 million a month, with government subsidies running at $400 million a year: larger than the country's health budget.[14]

The Obasanjo regime announced that it had lost $4 billion in potential oil revenues in 2006 to insecurity and the damage of pipelines by armed militants in Nigeria's volatile southeast Niger Delta region.[15] As Adigun Agbaje, Adeolu Akande, and Jide Ojo eloquently noted: 'Nigeria is a resource-rich country of poor people in which pathological substance often triumphs over sanitised form; institutional recession masquerades as institution building; endless new constitutions parade as substitutes for constitutionalism; and ... performance is often in direct contrast to fervent declarations of intent and achievement.'[16]

This chapter assesses the legacy of president Olusegun Obasanjo, and briefly examines the idea of Pax Nigeriana as a way of understanding Nigeria's historical leadership ambitions in Africa. The concept of 'concentric circles' is thereafter used to assess the domestic, regional, and external influences on Nigeria's foreign policy. We also briefly examine the role of culture in Nigeria's foreign policy.

Obasanjo's Legacy: Deux Ex Machina?

In April 2007, Nigeria staged what was widely believed to be the most flawed and fraudulent elections in its forty-seven-year history. The country's own

50,000–strong independent election observers, the Transition Monitoring Group (TMG), described the process as a 'sham' and a 'charade', while Nigeria's *This Day* newspaper labelled the poll a 'rigging and killing extravaganza'.[17] Groups like the Nigerian Bar Association, the Nigerian Labour Congress, the Nigerian Union of Journalists, and the Academic Staff Union of Universities also criticised the elections. Ballot boxes were stuffed and stolen, voters were intimidated, and results appeared out of thin air in areas where voting had clearly not taken place, particularly in the Niger Delta. In May 2007, the septuagenarian ruler of the People's Democratic Party (PDP), Olusegun Obasanjo, handed over a poisoned presidential chalice to Umaru Yar'Adua—the governor of the northern Katsina state and the first university graduate to rule the country—after an overwhelming 70 per cent victory (and the award to the PDP of twenty-eight out of thirty-six state governorships) that many believed to have been achieved through fraudulent means.

Yar'Adua, describing himself to Nigerians as a 'servant-leader', promised to make electoral reform a priority and to avoid a repeat in the elections of 2011. Election tribunals also overturned the results of six governors and more than a dozen senators by January 2008.[18] The country's foreign policy voice has been surprisingly muted during the presidency of Yar'Adua (slowed by illness and less experienced in this area than Obasanjo), as complaints have continued about the lack of adequate funding of the country's embassies abroad.[19]

Despite his flawed *fin de régime*, Obasanjo's tenure was not without some achievements. He correctly identified early in his rule that Nigeria's debt issue would be an obstacle to sustainable development. He therefore travelled tirelessly to Western capitals in pursuit of the annulment of the country's $30 billion external debt, and along with his able and forceful finance minister between 2003 and 2006, Ngozi Okonjo-Iweala, he was able to negotiate a deal that effectively wiped out Nigeria's entire external debt by paying $12.4 billion and having $17.6 billion annulled: the largest such financial deal in sub-Saharan Africa.[20] Obasanjo's regime stemmed inflation at 10.9 per cent in 2006, achieved 5–6 per cent growth rates, stabilised the naira (the national currency), improved the country's credit rating to increase investment, built up foreign exchange reserves, which stood at $48 billion in April 2007, and introduced competitive tendering in procurement that saved the country a reported $750 million by 2008.[21] Widely praised bank reforms by Chukwuma Soludo, the energetic governor of Nigeria's Central Bank, brought some stability to the sector, reducing the number of banks from eighty-nine in June 2004 to twenty-five by January 2006.[22]

Obasanjo's Economic and Financial Crimes Commission (EFCC), led by the fearless Nuhu Ribadu, recovered over $5 billion in stolen assets and prosecuted eighty-two corrupt businessmen and policemen.[23] In unprecedented moves in 2005, Tofa Balogun, Nigeria's inspector-general of police, was convicted of corruption and jailed; Fabian Osuji, education minister, and Mobolaji Osomo, housing and urban development minister, were also fired for respectively bribing legislators to pass a budget and selling government properties (including to close relatives of Obasanjo's wife).[24] Investment banks like JPMorgan, Citibank, Deutsche Bank, and Standard Bank also increased their presence in Nigeria, while $1 billion of portfolio inflows entered Nigeria in the first half of 2006 alone.[25] Obasanjo's regime was credited with improving the telecommunication sector, reportedly increasing telephone lines from 400,000 to 40 million in six years.[26] This period also saw the establishment of a parastatal for diaspora affairs to enable a group of Nigerians estimated at 17 million to contribute to the country's development.[27] According to Nigeria's government, in the first six months of 2007, Nigerians in the diaspora sent home an estimated $8 billion in remittances.[28]

But Okonjo-Iweala was dismissed by Obasanjo as finance minister (and resigned after a brief stint as foreign minister) in 2006, and the EFCC was accused of manipulation by Obasanjo to target his political opponents selectively. Obasanjo's unsuccessful and undignified attempt to change the Nigerian constitution in April 2006 to allow himself to run for a third presidential term badly damaged his democratic credentials: he reportedly offered bribes of $400,000 to senators and representatives; had armed police break up a meeting in Abuja of legislators and governors opposed to the third-term; and threatened impeachment of state governors who failed to support the bid.[29] Obasanjo's anticorruption drive was often undermined by accusations of bribing legislators. The former military general who had previously carved out a role as an elder statesman after relinquishing power in 1979, had already revealed his antidemocratic colours in 1989 when he said: 'My present suggestion that we adopt a one-party system is very much in consonance with a possible and logical outcome of our political development.'[30] Obasanjo's legacy was also tarnished by an ugly spat with his vice president, Atiku Abubakar, which saw both men accusing each other of corruption relating to the government's Petroleum Technology Trust,[31] while Obasanjo attempted unsuccessfully to exclude Atiku from contesting presidential elections in 2007 through dubious means.

Obasanjo's legacy must be assessed against the background of the serious socioeconomic difficulties inherited from four years of Nigeria's profligate

Second Republic, from 1979 to 1983, followed by sixteen years of military misrule under Generals Muhammed Buhari, Ibrahim Babangida, and Sani Abacha, from 1983 to 1999.[32] Obasanjo, a former military leader and respected international statesman who had handed power back to civilians in 1979, had seemingly emerged from jail as a deus ex machina. He was to be a bridge between the military and civilians, between the North and the South, a new broom to sweep out the corruption and abuses of military brass hats who had lost any sense of purpose beyond plundering the national treasury and pummelling innocent citizens into brutal submission. At the beginning of his presidential term in 1999, Obasanjo inherited a plethora of conflicts: Ogonis against Andonis, Ijaws against Itsekiris, Tivs against Jukuns, Chambas against Kutebs, Katafs against Hausas, Yorubas against Hausas, and Hausas against Igbos.[33] Some of these conflicts continued under Obasanjo's rule, leading to an estimated 12,000 deaths from violence related to religious and ethnic feuds. Nigeria's 'imagined communities'[34] developed their own differing interpretations of the same history and proceeded to defend these interpretations on the basis of birthright and blood. Though these conflicts over land, religion, resources, and chieftaincy titles mostly had local roots, opportunistic political leaders exploited them for their own parochial ends, realising how easy it was to light a fuse under simmering local brushfires.

Nigeria's economic problems also forced many of its citizens to turn to religion for succour. The popularity of both Islamic and Christian fundamentalist groups increased, even as wealthy and ostentatious preachers played on the gullibility of their desperate flock. As Nigerian businessman-politician Pat Utomi put it: 'In Nigeria, attitudes vary across a spectrum of fatalistic disposition, in which all is literally left in God's hand by fundamentalist Muslims and prosperity preaching Pentecostals alike.'[35] Under Obasanjo's rule, religion was turned into a political weapon, particularly as prominent members of an insecure Northern Nigerian political class (including former heads of state Shehu Shagari and Muhammed Buhari), whose members had long ruled the country, reacted to the election of a Southern president in 1999 by supporting calls for sharia criminal law in the North. During Obasanjo's first term in office, from 1999 to 2003, a dozen states in Northern Nigeria (containing about a third of Nigeria's population) declared the constitutionally questionable application of shar'ia criminal law. In a situation repeated sporadically between 1999 and 2007, communal riots between Muslims and Christians in Kaduna in 2000 led to hundreds of fatalities, while Plateau state also experienced similar clashes in 2004.[36] An attack by a radical Muslim sect, Boko Haran, led to hundreds of deaths in Bauchi state in July 2009, in violence that also spread to Borno and Yobe states.

Both Northern and Southern politicians often failed to condemn the destructive acts of ethnic mafias in violence that resulted from religious riots. Obasanjo, as a self-described born-again Christian Southerner with a need to maintain the political support of the largely Muslim North, had to walk a political tightrope. His regime drifted uneasily between anarchy and tyranny.[37] It used either too little or too much force to manage religious, resource, and ethnic conflicts. In Kaduna and Aba, Obasanjo was slow to control rampaging mobs. In Odi and Gbeji in 2000 and 2001 respectively, his soldiers employed disproportionate force to 'pacify' the area in a military campaign of awesome destructiveness totally unworthy of a democratic government.

Obasanjo's rule proved to be a bundle of contradictions. Considered as an indispensable force for stability, he instead oversaw one of Nigeria's worst periods of instability. Considered a force for unity, he presided uneasily over a country that perhaps became more divided than at any time in its history since the civil war of 1967 to 1970. Considered a force for national salvation, he instead watched helplessly as the country was nearly torn apart by sectarian violence. One must concede that much of this rot had set in under successive inept administrations since 1979, but these divisions were exacerbated under Obasanjo's rule. In his 2006 memoirs, Nigeria's Nobel laureate, Wole Soyinka, best described the flaws in the former Nigerian president's character: 'Obasanjo is a man of restless energies... A bullish personality, calculating and devious, yet capable of a disarming spontaneity, affecting an exaggerated country yokel act to cover up the interior actuality of the same, occasionally self-deprecatory yet intolerant of criticism, this general remains a study in the outer limits of compulsive rivalry, even where the fields of competence or striving are miles apart.'[38] Suffering from what many critics have described as a 'messiah complex', Obasanjo seemed to suffer from delusions of grandeur in which he viewed himself in the same light as Nelson Mandela, South Africa's saintly post-apartheid leader and Nobel peace laureate (see chapter 10). Some of Obasanjo's supporters described him as 'the founder of modern Nigeria', a sort of African Ataturk (founder of modern Turkey). But it is clear that Obasanjo lacked the stature of Mandela, one of the greatest moral figures of the twentieth century. The South African leader's graceful exit from power in 1999 after a single presidential term was in stark contract to Obasanjo's tawdry efforts to seek an unconstitutional third presidential term in 2006.

Obasanjo, who acted as his own oil minister throughout the eight years of his rule, further tarnished his historical legacy through an arrogant penchant for omniscient and omnipotent behaviour. In a survey by *Afrobarometre*, his approval rating had plummeted from 84 per cent in 2000 to 32 per cent by 2005, as Nigerians became increasingly disenchanted with his autocratic leadership style.[39] While in office he did not neglect his business affairs: Obasanjo Holdings, claiming to be Nigeria's leading agricultural company, also had wide-ranging interests in banking, as well as food and packaging; the former president gained stakes in oil and gas company Sahara Energy, and in Dangote Holdings; and he reportedly had substantial property in Abuja and Lagos.[40] Seemingly claiming a divine mandate, during the debates on a third presidential term in April 2006, Obasanjo made the notorious comment to the *Washington Post*: 'I believe that God is not a God of abandoned projects. If God has a project he will not abandon it.'[41] Thankfully, Nigeria's legislators and civil society actors did not agree that the Almighty had a role to play in changing the country's Constitution to give Obasanjo a third presidential term.

Between 2007 and 2009, the regime of Umaru Yar'Adua was dogged by accusations of slow delivery on development promises, and the president himself faced constant speculation about his health. Unlike during the Obasanjo era, Nigeria's voice also became less audible in continental diplomatic forums under the more low-key Yar'Adua. By March 2009, world oil prices had dropped from over $100 a barrel to $40, even as Nigeria faced the negative effects of the global financial crisis that started in 2007. A property boom in Nigeria finally went bust, and the previously dynamic Nigerian Stock Exchange fell by about 40 per cent, with reports that the country's banks were also experiencing liquidity problems amidst a string of bad loans. The continuing problems in the oil-rich Niger Delta meant that Angola overtook Nigeria as Africa's largest oil producer in 2008. With declining foreign capital and investment, Nigeria's electricity sector and infrastructure still remained in a parlous state, as Gulliver's troubles continued.[42]

Pax Nigeriana: Understanding the Context of Nigeria's Post–Cold War Foreign Policy[43]

Nigeria has often been described as a regional hegemon and 'Giant of Africa', on account of its population of 140 million, geographical size, and relatively large economic and human resources. The country is the world's sixth largest oil producer, as well a large exporter of oil to the United States (supplying 12 per cent of US oil by 2007); possesses gas reserves that could supply Western Europe for a decade; and accounts for 75 per cent of West Africa's economic strength and about 60 per cent of its population. The aspiration to continental leadership, manifest since independence in 1960, is central to understanding some principal features of Nigeria's foreign policy, such as the breaking of diplomatic relations with France in 1961 over the issue of nuclear testing in the Sahara; the creation of the Economic Community of West African States (ECOWAS) in 1975; membership in the 'Frontline States' of Southern Africa in the struggle against Rhodesia-Zimbabwe and apartheid South Africa from the 1970s; the country's long-term chairmanship of the UN Special Committee Against Apartheid; and its leadership of peacekeeping missions in Chad (1979–1982), Liberia (1990–1998 and 2003), and Sierra Leone (1997–2000).

Pax Nigeriana[44] represents Nigeria's ambition to play a political, economic, and military leadership role in Africa or on issues related to the continent. Politically, Nigeria sought to exert its leadership at the UN, in the Organisation of African Unity (OAU), and in the Non-Aligned Movement (NAM), and to speak loudest for African concerns. Militarily, the country has sent peacekeepers to the Congo, Chad, Liberia, Sierra Leone, and Somalia; and provided military assistance to Tanzania and Gambia, as well as to liberation struggles in Southern Africa in the 1970s and 1980s. Economically, Nigeria has tried to exert its leadership through ECOWAS as well as through its 'oil diplomacy', by providing economic assistance to its poorer neighbours.

Pax Nigeriana is reflected in the utterances of Nigeria's soldiers, diplomats, politicians, journalists, and students who share a common belief in Nigeria's 'manifest destiny' with special responsibilities to be a regional 'big brother'. The metaphor of a benevolent older brother who is more experienced and thus responsible for protecting his younger siblings has often been employed in Nigeria's diplomatic and popular parlance. This 'big brother syndrome', which has afflicted Nigeria's leaders since independence, smacks of a paternalism that has often irritated its neighbours. Nigeria's leaders almost gave the impression that all the country had to do was simply appear on the African stage in 1960 and all other countries would bow in deference at the splendour of the African colossus that the gods had sent to fulfil their messianic mission on the continent. The country's leadership role is widely seen as inevitable, but its unilateral, arrogant style has often been questioned by its neighbours.

Nigeria must thus learn to treat its neighbours with respect and consult more closely with them if its leadership aspirations for Pax Nigeriana in West Africa are to be realised. Most of these countries do not question the need

131

for Nigeria's leadership, but rather its penchant for a unilateral diplomatic style that offends the sensibilities of smaller, poorer, and weaker states. There still remains much unease in the subregion about Nigeria's domination of the ECOWAS Ceasefire Monitoring Group (ECOMOG) military commands in Liberia and Sierra Leone.[45] Sule Lamido, Nigeria's foreign minister under Obasanjo's first term, between 1999 and 2003, recognised these fears in noting: 'It is important that while you are playing the role of Big Brother, you have to recognise that the countries you are dealing with are sovereign nations. You have to know this and recognise that psychological feeling of independence.'[46]

Pax Nigeriana, unlike Pax Britannica or Pax Americana in an earlier age, has not involved militarily expansionist imperialism or a quest for a 'Greater Nigeria'. That is not to suggest, however, that Pax Nigeriana is purely altruistic. Since its civil war of 1967 to 1970, Nigeria has sought to loosen France's neocolonial ties in West Africa (see chapter 8) and to gain more security and larger markets for itself. But one can explain Nigeria's military interventions in Liberia and Sierra Leone in the 1990s not through *military* aggrandizement for political control of Liberia and Sierra Leone, but rather through *political* aggrandizement for long-term military and economic influence in West Africa.

The ECOMOG interventions were consistent, for example, with actions like the creation of ECOWAS in 1975, and Nigeria's military intervention in Chad between 1979 and 1982. Over 200,000 Nigerian soldiers have been deployed to peacekeeping missions around the globe, and the country has contributed troops to nearly forty major UN and regional peacekeeping missions in Africa, Asia, Europe, and the Middle East.[47] ECOMOG was a Pax Nigeriana, but was also an exercise in 'hegemony on a shoestring'. Nigeria lacked the military and economic resources as well as the international political support to act as an effective hegemon. Hegemony essentially requires both the *capacity and legitimacy* and also the *ability* to provide leadership to convince other states to follow one willingly.[48] Nigeria was unable to impose its will on Liberia and Sierra Leone, and is an *aspiring* rather than an effective hegemon.

Nigeria's foreign policy—based on the fact the country is the largest black nation in the world and that one in every five Africans is a Nigerian—has exhibited a 'missionary zeal' that has claimed a special responsibility to protect, or at least speak on behalf of, black people in apartheid South Africa, pre–civil rights America, and contemporary Brazil. As Nigerian leader between 1966 and 1975 General Yakubu Gowon noted: 'Peoples of African descent throughout the world see in a strong Nigeria a banner of hope, and an instrument for achieving self-respect for the black man, so long degraded everywhere.'[49]

But there were some contradictions in Nigeria's leadership aspirations: between 1983 and 1985, the country expelled 3 million mostly West African immigrants, amidst a deepening domestic economic crisis in Nigeria. This dealt a severe blow to the credibility of Pax Nigeriana. Not only did these populist actions contradict the commitment of a Nigeria-led ECOWAS to the free movement of persons across West Africa, but they also violated the norms and principles of protecting fellow Africans that had guided Nigeria's foreign policy since its independence in 1960.[50]

The 'Concentric Circles': Domestic, Regional, and External Influences on Nigeria's Foreign Policy

Since Nigerian public opinion has tended to exert more influence over foreign policy under civilian governments (which have to be more accountable to parliament, the public, and the press) than under military regimes (which have often been able to ignore such influences), it is important to explain the diverse sources of Nigeria's foreign policy. Between 1960 and 2009, the country was under military rule for twenty-nine of its forty-nine years of independence—about 60 per cent of this period. Costly and ultimately domestically unpopular military interventions in Liberia and Sierra Leone in the 1990s could probably only have been sustained by military brass hats who were unaccountable to the Nigerian electorate. Significantly, the civilian administration of Olusegun Obasanjo withdrew the bulk of Nigeria's 12,000 peacekeepers from Sierra Leone in 1999–2000.

It is thus important to understand the domestic, regional, and external constraints and influences on Nigeria's foreign policy. Nigerian diplomats and scholars have often explained the country's foreign policy in terms of four 'concentric circles' of national interest, as eloquently described by Nigerian scholar-diplomat Ibrahim Gambari, foreign minister between 1984 and 1985.[51] The innermost circle represents Nigeria's own security, independence, and prosperity and is centred on its immediate neighbours—Benin, Cameroon, Chad, and Niger[52]; the second circle revolves around Nigeria's relations with its ECOWAS neighbours; the third circle focuses on continental African issues of peace, development, and democratisation; while the fourth circle involves Nigeria's relations with organisations, institutions, and states outside Africa.[53] This concept still guides Nigeria's foreign policy priorities.

Domestic

We begin our examination of the 'concentric circles' with the innermost domestic circle. Nigeria, on account of its human and natural resources, is one of Africa's most strategic countries. Yet the country's potential is limited by its enormous domestic problems, which continue to raise serious doubts about its ability to fulfil its stated hegemonic ambitions. As earlier noted, Nigeria has been wracked by violence related to disputes over religion, resources, land, and ethnicity that resulted in over 12,000 deaths in the first decade of the return to civilian rule between 1999 and 2009. The country's 85,000–strong military is also desperately in need of reform after over two decades of decay and politicisation that have adversely affected its professionalism.

Internal threats to national security have further emerged from radical religious groups, as well as ethnic militias such as the Niger Delta People's Volunteer Forces (NDPVF) and the Oodua People's Congress (OPC). Nigeria's oil-producing areas have remained volatile, a situation that was dramatically symbolised by the strong campaign waged against foreign oil companies and the Nigerian government by international nongovernmental organisations following the hanging of Ken Saro-Wiwa and eight Ogoni environmental activists in November 1995. This was perhaps the greatest foreign policy debacle in Nigeria's history: the hanging of the 'Ogoni Nine' by General Sani Abacha during a Commonwealth summit in Auckland, New Zealand. Nigeria was subsequently suspended from the Commonwealth and branded an international pariah. Foreign oil companies, led by Shell, have justly been accused of decimating Nigeria's oil-producing areas and of neglecting the social needs of the people in the region. Shell's use of substandard and environmentally unfriendly equipment and methods resulted in a reported 40 per cent of its oil spills occurring in Nigeria despite operating in about a hundred countries. The livelihood of the people in these areas has been destroyed by polluted rivers and forests and oil-strewn fields. Shell also reportedly provided funds for a brutal military campaign in the Niger Delta that resulted in dozens of deaths and the destruction of hundreds of homes in the 1990s.[54] In February 2007, the Movement for the Emancipation of the Niger Delta (MEND), whose leaders had been accused of disrupting the flow of oil and kidnapping foreign oil workers in pursuit of a greater share of oil revenues to develop their region, threatened a war that could eventually lead to the disintegration of Nigeria, if not carefully managed.[55] Shell paid compensation of $15.5 million to the Ogoni community in June 2009 just before a court case charging the company of complicity in the murder of the 'Ogoni Nine'.

Regional

While Nigeria's hegemonic ambitions in Africa are not in doubt, the results of its numerous economic and diplomatic initiatives over the past five decades cannot be described as an unqualified success. For example, despite its enormous oil wealth, Nigeria did not completely succeed in its goal of using ECOWAS as an instrument to reduce the dependence of francophone West African states on France. Three decades after ECOWAS sought to establish a customs union, informal trade (smuggling) within West Africa far outstrips formal trade, even as the subregion's resourceful traders continue to exploit porous borders and largely inconvertible currencies to their advantage.[56] Despite plans to create a common West African currency, the continued existence of a francophone currency zone tied to the euro (formerly the French franc) is perhaps the clearest sign of the divisions from the 'Curse of Berlin' that still frustrate regional integration within ECOWAS, as well as hamper the achievement of Pax Nigeriana. Nigeria's unstable macroeconomic environment and inflationary fiscal deficits have also further reduced the prospects for a successful monetary zone.[57]

ECOWAS still contains some of the poorest countries in the world, and many of these countries have little or no industry, energy, cash crops, or minerals. They have thus relied heavily on customs duties for much of their government revenues. There remain no less than ten mostly inconvertible currencies within ECOWAS, making intracommunity trade and inward investment difficult. Subregional exports also remain competitive rather than complementary, and colonial trading patterns with the West inherited from the Conference of Berlin era in the late nineteenth century have largely remained intact. Furthermore, there are serious infrastructural difficulties in transportation and communication. ECOWAS has thus become more of a political forum attempting to forge subregional political consensus, than an economic union providing tangible benefits for increased trade.

Nigeria's trade with the rest of the world is also still mostly outside its own region. In the last quarter of 2005, 53 per cent of Nigeria's exports went to the US, 21.8 per cent to Asia, 18.5 per cent to Europe, and only 7 per cent to

Africa. Nigeria's imports in the same period followed the same pattern: 36.8 per cent from Europe, 30 per cent from Asia, 24 per cent from the US, and 9 per cent from Africa. In numerical terms, however, Nigeria's exports to West Africa for the whole of 2005 totalled $3.4 billion, including oil, cement, cotton, sugar molasses, and cosmetics. A joint development zone has been established with São Tomé and Príncipe to manage common maritime resources, while a West African gas pipeline project runs from Nigeria through Benin, Togo, and Ghana.[58]

In terms of regional stability, West Africa remains at the epicentre of many of Africa's conflicts and is one of the world's most unstable subregions. Nigerian-led peacekeeping interventions into Liberia and Sierra Leone in the 1990s lasted a total of eleven years, resulted in over 1,500 Nigerian fatalities, and cost the country's treasury billions of dollars. Though embroiled in political, financial, and military difficulties (as well as challenges of HIV/AIDS), these interventions were the first in the post–Cold War era to be launched by a subregional organisation—ECOWAS.[59] The ECOMOG interventions succeeded in defusing civil conflicts in Liberia and Sierra Leone, though instability later returned to Liberia. These interventions—launched by Generals Babangida and Abacha—were consistent with Nigeria's historical pursuit of grandeur and leadership on the continent.[60] Nigeria also restored the elected leader of São Tomé and Príncipe, Fradique De Menezes, to power following an attempted coup in July 2003, and led peacemaking efforts in Togo in 2005. Nigeria sent peacekeepers to Sudan's Darfur region in 2004 under an African Union (AU) mission; former Nigerian foreign minister Babagana Kingibe was AU special envoy in Darfur, while Nigeria's chief of defence staff, General Martin Agwai, was force commander of the UN-AU hybrid mission in Darfur between 2007 and 2009.[61] Ibrahim Gambari was appointed UN Special Representative to Darfur in December 2009.

As earlier noted, General Olusegun Obasanjo's civilian administration, between 1999 and 2007, faced pressure from parliament, the press, and public opinion that Generals Babangida and Abacha were more easily able to ignore or did not have to face (in the case of parliament).[62] It was thus significant that Obasanjo withdrew 8,500 Nigerian troops from Sierra Leone and insisted that the UN take over the mission, to which he then contributed 3,500 Nigerian peacekeepers. In August 2003, Obasanjo also insisted that a UN mission take over a Nigerian-led peacekeeping mission in Liberia three months after its deployment in order to share the costs more equitably. It is likely that Nigeria will continue to seek UN legitimacy and burden-sharing in future peacekeeping missions under civilian regimes, though its participation in the ill-equipped and poorly resourced 7,000–strong AU peacekeeping mission in Sudan's Darfur region between 2004 and 2007 suggests that some lessons of the ECOMOG missions of the 1990s remain to be learned. (see chapter 2).

External

Nigeria's most important multilateral ties are with the UN, where it is aspiring to become a permanent member of a reformed Security Council; the Commonwealth (headed by a Nigerian diplomat Emeka Anyaoku between 1990 and 2000), from which the country was suspended between 1995 and 1999, largely under the regime of General Sani Abacha; and the EU, its largest external trade partner. Nigeria has participated actively in UN peacekeeping, was the longtime chair of the UN's Special Committee Against Apartheid, and supported decolonization and anti–apartheid efforts within the UN and the Commonwealth.[63] EU sanctions were also imposed on Nigeria under the regime of General Abacha; while development issues within the UN, the Commonwealth, and the EU have been vigorously pursued by Nigeria's diplomats.[64]

Nigeria's relations with four of the five veto-wielding permanent members of the UN Security Council—France, Britain, the US, and China—have also been important. After 1960, France undertook over twenty-one military interventions in Africa to prop up or to change out-of-favour regimes.[65] (see chapter 8). The Gallic nation was the major obstacle to the realisation of Nigeria's hegemonic ambitions in West Africa. But relations between the two countries have improved in the post–Cold War era, and some policymakers and business interests in France have started to regard Nigeria—an important trading partner—as less of a rival and more of an ally in managing local conflicts. The ECOMOG interventions in Liberia and Sierra Leone seemed to mark Nigeria's opportunity to dominate its subregion free of the constraint of the interventionist French gendarme. Paris, however, still retains strong ties and a military base in Côte d'Ivoire. Since 2003, France has contributed 4,600 troops to serve alongside a UN peacekeeping mission in its former colony.

Britain was, of course, Nigeria's former colonial power, and ties between Abuja and London have often involved profitable economic relationships and occasionally political tensions over domestic and foreign policy issues.[66] British prime minister Margaret Thatcher's (1979–1990) reactionary stance towards Rhodesia-Zimbabwe and apartheid South Africa led to serious tensions between Lagos and London, including the nationalization of the assets of British Petroleum in Nigeria in 1979. A British intervention into Sierra Leone in 2000 to shore up the collapsing UN peacekeeping mission (UNAMSIL) went against London's traditional post-Suez military noninterventionist stance in Africa[67], and also sparked Anglo-Nigerian rivalry for influence in this former British colony. This was an extremely rare military intervention in Africa by the 'Mother Country', however, and Britain often avoided the direct military adventurism of France in the postcolonial era.

Another important bilateral relationship involves Nigeria's ties with the world's sole superpower: the United States. Nigeria has been a major exporter of oil to the US since the 1970s, and currently accounts for about 12 per cent of total American oil imports. But this strong trade relationship has not always translated into smooth political relations, and there were tensions between the two countries over US policies in Southern Africa in the 1970s and 1980s. In the 1990s, the relationship between Washington and successive military regimes in Nigeria became strained, and only belatedly did the US provide some military assistance to support Nigeria's peacekeeping efforts in Liberia and Sierra Leone. After 1999, Washington provided support to Nigeria's civilian government for democratic and security sector reform, and identified Nigeria and South Africa as Africa's 'pivotal states'.[68]

Finally, China has been increasingly assisting Nigeria in the area of infrastructure and investing in the country's oil sector. The regime of General Sani Abacha had initiated Nigeria's 'Look East' policy—involving mainly Chinese railway construction and purchase of Nigerian oil—in a bid to break out of a Western-imposed diplomatic isolation. Under Obasanjo's regime, $10 billion worth of contracts were signed for further railway reconstruction and the Chinese presence in the Nigerian oil sector increased massively. Nigeria has subsequently been identified as one of China's special economic zones in Africa, and plans are under way to create a manufacturing and assembly zone for Chinese firms to invest in. But there have also been complaints about the dumping of cheap Chinese goods of dubious quality and the destruction of Nigeria's textile industry. However, the fact that Nigeria had by 2008 become China's fourth largest trading partner in Africa (after Angola, South Africa, and Sudan) provides Abuja with a potential source of increased leverage in its dealings with its Western partners (see chapter 8).[69]

Culture and Foreign Policy

We next turn to the issue of culture, described by American scholar Joseph Nye as part of 'soft power': nonmilitary resources that countries can deploy to influence others to follow their lead and to desire what they themselves want.[70] Within the Nigerian context, we focus briefly here on Nigeria's hosting of the pan-African Festival of Arts and Culture (FESTAC) in 1977, and the phenomenal rise of 'Nollywood', Nigeria's prolific indigenous film industry, which has attracted devotees from all across the continent and from within the African diaspora.

Nigeria's Festival of Arts and Culture in 1977 was a redefinition of pan-Africanism by an increasingly self-confident nation that had long defined itself to be the 'Giant of Africa'. The festival involved 70,000 artists and delegates from fifty-nine countries across Africa as well as members of the diaspora from the Caribbean, South America, North America, and Australasia. As American academic Andrew Apter noted: 'Nigeria emerged as the unequivocal leader of the new black world. Spending lavishly on its global citizens, the Nigerian state accrued political capital as master of ceremonies while recasting the nation in indigenous terms as the *fons et origo* of virtually all black cultural traditions.'[71]

FESTAC involved events like durbars, regattas (with war canoes), and traditional dances, as well as elaborate works of art and the construction of a stunning thirty-one-metre-high national theatre and sprawling festival village. Apter placed the festival in the context of imperial spectacles such as London's Crystal Palace Exhibition (1851) and America's Columbian Exposition (1893), noting that such 'cultural productions' revealed connections between empire and knowledge. FESTAC represented a national showpiece by a self-confident elite to mark the arrival into the ranks of the nouveaux riches of the world's largest black nation and to promote African culture as a sign of equality with a West that had often denigrated the continent's traditions. This event marked the celebration of a party that Nigerians assumed would never end. The decision to build a brand-new capital in Abuja by 1991, with spectacular highways, conference centres, and religious buildings—as well as the impressive ECOWAS secretariat, which is a potent symbol of Nigeria's regional leadership—was also taken during the euphoric days of the oil boom. Abuja's street-names reflect a pan African identity, and the Nigerian capital has served as the centre of many continental peacemaking initiatives on conflicts such as those in Liberia, Sudan, and Togo.[72]

But it is the phenomenon of Nigeria's prolific film industry—Nollywood—that has attracted the most recent positive international attention to the country. Nollywood makes over 2,000 films a year, more than America's Hollywood or India's Bollywood.[73] The industry is thought to employ about 1 million people, including production and distribution, making it the second largest employer in the country with annual sales estimated at $250–350 million.[74] The films are widely available to both rich and poor, not just in Nigeria but also across West, East, and Southern Africa. Nollywood may in fact be leading the way to the first authentic African cinema to have wide appeal across the African continent and its diaspora.[75]

Concluding Reflections: Four Pillars of Support

We offer here two key policy recommendations to guide Nigeria's future foreign policy. First, Nigeria will need to improve bilateral relations and form strategic partnerships with four important pillar states—South Africa, France, Ghana, and Côte d'Ivoire—in order to promote and support its foreign policy objectives in Africa.[76] Second, Nigeria must put its own house in order before its leadership ambitions can be taken seriously. The relationship between Nigeria and South Africa (discussed in detail in chapter 7), under the leadership of Olusegun Obasanjo and South African president Thabo Mbeki, between 1999 and 2007, was the most strategic partnership in Africa. Abuja must also maintain and strengthen its military relationship with Ghana, which proved so critical to the success of ECOMOG's efforts in Liberia and Sierra Leone between 1990 and 2003. Nigeria must further continue to improve its relations with France. Despite past suspicions of French intentions in Africa, Nigerian policymakers must stop their knee-jerk response to every action by francophone states as containing a hidden agenda by a French puppeteer, and take cognisance of the changing French role in Africa. It is time for political cooperation between the two countries to catch up with their lucrative economic relationship.

Nigeria must also continue to improve ties with Côte d'Ivoire, still potentially—despite its civil war since 2002 and the delusional pretensions of Senegal—the richest and most important francophone state in West Africa. Nigeria and Côte d'Ivoire have historically been both the financial backbone of ECOWAS and the leaders of the anglophone and francophone blocs in West Africa. A strategic partnership between Abuja and Abidjan could help bridge the anglophone-francophone dichotomy inherited from the legacy of

Berlin, which has hampered regional economic and military cooperation in West Africa for the past five decades. Nigeria should also continue to play a supportive role within ECOWAS in efforts to end the Ivorian crisis. Both governments should also meet more regularly to promote trade and political cooperation.

Finally, a truly democratic Nigeria will be important for building subregional and international support for the country's foreign policy objectives and guaranteeing the international legitimacy and securing the external support for any future military interventions, while avoiding the charges of hypocrisy faced by General Abacha in restoring democracy to Liberia and Sierra Leone while denying it to Nigerians at home. An arrogant unilateralism has sometimes been evident in Nigerian diplomacy, particularly during the era of General Abacha's abrasive foreign minister, Tom Ikimi, between 1995 and 1998. Ikimi's brusque style was subsequently dubbed 'area boy diplomacy'[77] by his Nigerian critics. Abuja will have to be careful not to arouse the fears of its neighbours through unilateral military interventions and other actions that make it appear to be pursuing parochial policies in an effort to dominate its subregion. In order to fulfil its leadership ambitions in West Africa, Nigeria must be able to provide not just the military muscle for subregional peacekeeping, but also the vibrant domestic market that can sustain economic integration, provide economic assistance to its neighbours, and ease the acceptance of its leadership role in West Africa. Only by being strong at home can Nigeria effectively contribute to resolving problems abroad. Gulliver must learn to speak softly, even as he carries a big stick.

7

AN AXIS OF VIRTUE?

SOUTH AFRICA AND NIGERIA IN AFRICA[1]

'Our location [Nigeria and South Africa], our destiny and the contemporary forces of globalisation have thrust upon us the burden of turning around the fortunes of our continent. We must not and cannot shy away from this responsibility.'

Olusegun Obasanjo, Nigerian president, 1999–2007

In the next chapter in this volume, we examine US president George W. Bush's depiction of Iran, Iraq, and North Korea as forming an 'axis of evil', and investigate whether a similar caricature can be applied to the roles of China, the United States, and France in Africa. In the inter-African context, it is perhaps worth speculating whether a phrase that has taken on negative connotations can be inverted for more positive ends. One important issue that has generated much debate within and outside Africa is whether potential hegemons South Africa and Nigeria can form an 'axis of virtue' to play a leadership role in managing Africa's conflicts through the African Union (AU), the Southern African Development Community (SADC), and the Economic Community of West African States (ECOWAS); drive economic integration and development through the New Partnership for Africa's Development (NEPAD); and promote democratic governance on a troubled continent.

General Abdulsalaam Abubakar, Nigeria's military leader between 1998 and 1999, called for South Africa and Nigeria to establish an 'axis of power' to promote peace and stability on the continent.[2] In the post–Cold War era, the reluctance of Western countries to intervene militarily in African countries after debacles in Somalia (1993) and Rwanda (1994) led many observers to ask whether South Africa and Nigeria—the latter of which was at that time leading a peacekeeping mission in Liberia under the auspices of the ECOWAS Ceasefire Monitoring Group (ECOMOG)—could fill this security vacuum. Though South Africa, accounting for about a third of Africa's economic strength, is wealthier than Nigeria, it faces even more powerful military challengers and political rivals in Southern Africa. The apartheid-era army's destabilisation of its neighbours has left a profound distrust of South African military interventionism, which remains strong today. During the 1990s, Nigeria was willing but unable to carry out swift and decisive military interventions in West Africa. South Africa was arguably more able but largely unwilling to undertake such military actions in its own subregion. South Africa has military and economic capacity but lacks the legitimacy to play a hegemonic role. Nigeria has more legitimacy in its own subregion, but lacks the military and economic capacity to act as an effective hegemon. While South Africa and Nigeria are militarily and politically powerful relative to other regional states, they must still develop the capacity and legitimacy to influence their respective regions and they have often failed to convince other states to follow their lead on vital political, security, and economic issues. Pax South Africana must contend with 'bargainers' like Zimbabwe, Angola, and Namibia, while Pax Nigeriana faces 'bargainers' like Côte d'Ivoire, Senegal, and Burkina Faso. These states have the capability to increase significantly the costs for the aspiring hegemons when attempting to impose their will on their respective regions.

This chapter focuses on the potential of South Africa and Nigeria to play a continental leadership role during three periods: first, the apartheid era, from 1960 to 1993; second, the rule of Nigeria's General Sani Abacha and Nelson Mandela, from 1994 to 1998; and third, the presidencies of Thabo Mbeki and Olusegun Obasanjo, from 1999 to 2007. The first two years of the presidency of Nigeria's Umaru Yar'Adua (2007–2009) and the ousting of Thabo Mbeki from power in September 2008 have led both countries to adopt a less activist Africa policy, as well as to a lull in bilateral relations, despite Yar'Adua's visit to South Africa in June 2008. The chapter will thus not focus on this evolving period.

The Prophet and the Pariah, 1960–1993

The *annus mirabilis* of African independence in 1960 saw the birth of Nigeria amidst great hopes for a political and economic giant that was expected to take its preordained place in the African sun. In the same year as Nigeria's independence, South Africa was about to be expelled from the Commonwealth for the bloody killing of sixty-nine unarmed black civilians in Sharpeville during another ugly display of its policy of legally sanctioned racism. Many felt that the apartheid state was heading towards civil war. South Africa's foreign policy, like Nigeria's, was suffused with a missionary zeal, as apartheid's leaders talked patronisingly about their country having special responsibilities to spread Western values north of the Limpopo in a macabre *mission civilisatrice* (see chapter 5). In the three decades that followed, both African giants failed to achieve their leadership aspirations, but for very different reasons.[3]

In the case of Nigeria, its West African subregion was littered with francophone states that looked to France—the self-appointed *gendarme d'Afrique*—for protection against this potential neighbourhood bully. The Gallic power intervened in the region with reckless abandon, regularly landing its gendarmes in Africa and effortlessly shuffling regimes around its *pré carrée* (backyard) (see chapter 8).[4] Nigeria's attempts at seeking greater political influence in West Africa through economic means were consistently frustrated by France, which encouraged francophone states to create rival trade blocs.[5] In its three decades of existence, the Nigerian-led ECOWAS[6] did not even come close to its goals of establishing a common market. Threats to build a 'black bomb' to counter Pretoria's nuclear capability remained an empty boast.

South Africa, in contrast, was able effortlessly to subdue its neighbours both economically and militarily through a policy of destabilisation. Pretoria had nuclear capability, a flourishing arms industry, and some world-class manufacturers. South Africa dominated the Southern African Customs Union (SACU) and established, alongside Botswana, Swaziland, Lesotho, and Namibia, the common market that eluded ECOWAS.[7] However, this was a market that distributed its rewards unevenly. SACU was dominated by a South Africa that unilaterally determined how much to pay out to its neighbours and sometimes frustrated their efforts at industrialisation. Despite their attempts at reducing their dependence on Pretoria through the Southern African Development Coordination Conference (SADCC)[8], established in April 1980, many of the region's Lilliputian states still traded covertly with, and depended on, the South African Gulliver.

In spite of the external constraints on Nigeria playing a hegemonic role in Africa, the country provided leadership to the anti–apartheid and decolonisation struggles. Lagos gave liberation movements financial and material backing, and established the Southern African Relief Fund (SARF) in 1976, with chapters in all regions of Nigeria, to provide scholarships and relief materials to South African students and refugees. Nigeria's civil servants also had a 'Mandela Tax' deducted directly from their monthly salaries, while 400 black South African students arrived in the country during 1977 alone.[9] Nigeria's contributions to the liberation struggle were aptly recognised by its invitations to meetings of the Frontline States of Southern Africa, its long chairmanship of the UN Special Committee Against Apartheid, and its hosting of a UN anti–apartheid conference in 1977. The UN Conference Against Apartheid in Lagos in August 1977 recommended a mandatory arms embargo against Pretoria, which the UN General Assembly agreed to three months later. In his opening address to the conference in Lagos, Nigerian leader General Olusegun Obasanjo characterised the countries supplying the apartheid regime with arms as 'flies [that] have landed and are feeding in the full glare of the world. And when we move to destroy these flies no-one should complain'.[10]

Since South Africa was diplomatically isolated and forced to bear the brunt of many of the international community's sanctions, it was denied a global stage, and it was Nigeria that spoke loudest for African concerns: Nigeria was the prophet, South Africa the pariah. To announce its status as the leading state in Africa, Nigeria hosted the lavish Festival of Arts and Culture (FES-TAC) in 1977 (see chapter 6).[11] However, Nigeria's president, Shehu Shagari, cut off support to Southern African liberation movements in 1980, ostensibly as part of domestic austerity measures. This funding was resumed in 1983 and continued until South Africa's domestic transition, which began in 1989.[12] Nigeria led an African boycott of the Commonwealth Games in Edinburgh in 1986 to protest Britain's refusal to impose sanctions on the apartheid regime. Its head of state between 1976 and 1979, General Olusegun Obasanjo, also co-chaired a visit of the Commonwealth Eminent Persons Group to South Africa in 1986.

After Mandela's release from jail in February 1990, he visited Nigeria within three months to express his gratitude for the country's support during the liberation struggle. He also received a reported $10 million campaign contribution for the African National Congress (ANC) from Nigerian head of state General Ibrahim Babangida.[13] In April 1992, President F.W. De Klerk led a South African business delegation to Nigeria: a clear early recognition by South Africa's business community of the huge potential of Africa's largest market. The ANC was furious that Nigeria had not informed its leaders about De Klerk's visit, but Abuja brushed aside these complaints, saying that it needed no such authorisation.[14] Despite this minor spat, there were great expectations that the impending installation of an ANC-led government in South Africa would usher in the birth of a strong alliance between Africa's two economic powerhouses.

King Baabu and the Avuncular Saint, 1994–1998

These hopes were soon dashed by the unexpected souring of relations between Pretoria and Abuja. In order to understand South Africa's troubled relations with Nigeria during this second phase, from 1994 to 1998, it is important first to understand the two main protagonists in this tale: General Sani Abacha and Nelson Mandela. In his 2002 play *King Baabu*,[15] Nigerian Nobel literature laureate and political activist Wole Soyinka created one of the most grotesque and absurd figures in world drama. Baabu is a bumbling, brainless, brutish buffoon and greedily corrupt military general who exchanges his military attire for a monarchical robe and a gown. The play is a thinly disguised satire of General Abacha's debauched rule between September 1993 and his death—in the company of Indian prostitutes—in June 1998.

Abacha joined the Nigerian army at the age of nineteen and established himself as an infantryman with training in Nigerian and British military institutions. He was involved in his first coup d'état in 1966, fought bravely to keep Nigeria united during the country's civil war between 1967 and 1970, and was instrumentally involved in two further coups in 1983 and 1985, with the second eventually propelling him to the position of chief of defence staff and *khalifa* (king-in-waiting) to General Ibrahim Babangida.[16] He eventually took advantage of a weak, illegitimate interim government to seize full power following the annulment of elections in June 1993. The election was widely believed to have been won by Moshood Abiola, whom Abacha subsequently jailed when he tried to claim his mandate.

In power, Abacha was ruthless and reclusive, but hardly as inept as the caricature depicted by Soyinka and believed by many of Nigeria's political opposition, who greatly underestimated him. Depicting him as a semi–literate buffoon, Nigeria's civil society groups had assumed that Abacha would not last five weeks in power, let alone five years. But Abacha was a survivor who understood how to control Nigeria's powerful army and how to buy off the country's opportunistic political class. He was also able to ward off oil sanctions by the West by playing on the greed of its oil companies and governments, by employing lobbyists in the United States, and by tacitly threatening a withdrawal of Nigerian peacekeepers from Liberia and Sierra Leone in the full knowledge that Western countries were not keen to intervene in either country. By the time of his death in 1998, Abacha had managed to push all five government-created political parties to adopt him as their presidential candidate. When Abacha died, he was also four months away from achieving what no other military ruler in Nigeria had dared to do: metamorphosing from military dictator to civilian ruler.

Nelson Mandela (see chapter 10) is perhaps the starkest contrast that one can imagine to Abacha. An educated middle-class lawyer from a chiefly Xhosa family and a cosmopolitan anglophile, this 'father of the nation', who had spent twenty-seven years as a political prisoner for his beliefs, embodied his people's aspirations for a democratic future. Mandela, an iconic figure and winner of the Nobel Peace Prize in 1993, has been widely celebrated as a political saint and one of the greatest moral figures of the twentieth century. As president, he came to symbolise his country's racial reconciliation, and his charisma helped South Africa's young, democratic institutions to flower. He also gave the country an international stature that a former global pariah could never have dreamed of. Mandela served as a further contrast to Abacha by bowing out as president, as promised, after the end of his first term in 1999.[17]

Under Abacha's autocratic rule, by 1995, South Africa and Nigeria had traded places from the apartheid era: it was now Nigeria, and not South Africa, that was being considered for expulsion from the Commonwealth. It was Nigeria, under a repressive military regime, that was facing mounting criticism over its human rights record; it was Nigeria that was becoming increasingly isolated in international society; and it was Nigeria that was considered to be possibly heading towards civil war. Having abandoned its apartheid past, South Africa was widely acknowledged to be the most likely political and economic success story in Africa. South Africa seemed better positioned than Nigeria to become the continent's champion. While military leaders proliferated in West African countries like Nigeria, Sierra Leone, and Gambia, post-apartheid South Africa sought to provide a democratic model for its subregion, with its avant garde government of national unity between 1994 and 1996 and its support for the spread or restoration of democracy in neighbouring Mozambique, Lesotho, and Malawi. Mandela set up the Truth and Reconciliation Commission (TRC), to look into the injustices of an undemocratic past, while Abacha set up the Provisional Ruling Council (PRC), to bury the country's democratic future.

The nadir of relations between post-apartheid South Africa and Nigeria was undoubtedly reached after the brutal hanging by the Abacha regime of

Nigerian activist Ken Saro-Wiwa, and eight of his fellow Ogoni campaigners, during the Commonwealth summit in Auckland, New Zealand, in November 1995.[18] Before this incident, Mandela—under pressure from Nigerian pro-democracy activists as well as Western and a few African governments—had gone to Abuja to intercede with Abacha for the release of Moshood Abiola.[19] In the same year, Mandela sent Archbishop of Cape Town and Nobel peace laureate Desmond Tutu, and then Deputy President Thabo Mbeki, to Abuja to plead for the release of political prisoners, including Abiola and Olusegun Obasanjo, two close friends of many ANC stalwarts.

During the Commonwealth summit in Auckland, Mandela believed that he had received personal assurances from Abacha of clemency for the 'Ogoni nine'. Learning of the executions, Mandela felt deeply betrayed, having reassured his fellow Commonwealth leaders that the executions would not occur and having used his moral stature to assuage their anger against the Nigerian government.[20] A furious Mandela reacted impulsively, accusing Abacha of behaving like an 'insensitive, frightened dictator' who engaged in 'judicial murder' (echoing British premier John Major's phrase), and warning that Abacha 'is sitting on a volcano and I am going to explode it under him'.[21] South Africa's president called on Washington and London to impose oil sanctions on Abacha, and advocated Nigeria's expulsion from the Commonwealth. On his return home, Mandela recalled his high commissioner to Nigeria, George Nene, who had been somewhat unfairly criticised by South African civil society groups for not having made contact with Nigerian opposition leaders and gaining better access to a notoriously reclusive leadership.[22] Nigeria's leaders, in fact, felt that Nene had become too close to the opposition and had lost all leverage with the Abacha government.[23]

In December 1995, Mandela called a SADC summit to take collective action against Nigeria. In retaliation, Abacha refused to let Nigeria's footballers defend their African Cup of Nations crown in South Africa in 1996. The vituperative exchanges continued, as Nigeria's pugnacious minister of information, Walter Ofonagoro, accused Mandela of being a 'black head of a white country' who could not be trusted: a particularly hurtful and insensitive statement that hit at the most sensitive spot of a black-led government that had inherited a country in which whites still controlled the economy and key institutions. Ordinary South Africans would not easily forgive Nigeria for this personal slur on the country's saintly icon.

Mandela was about to learn the dismaying intricacies of African diplomacy. Even his iconic status failed to rally a single Southern African state to take action against Nigeria. The fuse of the volcano that 'Madiba' (Mandela's clan name) had threatened to explode under Abacha had spectacularly failed to ignite. Instead, it was South Africa that was being accused by many African leaders of becoming a Western Trojan horse, sowing seeds of division in Africa and undermining African solidarity. Egyptian UN Secretary-General at the time, Boutros Boutros-Ghali, reminded Mandela of Nigeria's peacekeeping sacrifices in Liberia and Sierra Leone.[24] South Africa's diplomats soon became concerned that Pretoria would become diplomatically isolated within Africa, adversely affecting its bid for a permanent seat on the UN Security Council. ANC stalwarts also reminded Mandela of the country's debt of gratitude to Nigeria during the anti–apartheid struggle, as well as Nigeria's continued campaign contributions to the party. These voices eventually drowned out the efforts of South African trade union, business, environmental, women's, and youth groups that were lobbying their government to take even stronger action against Nigeria.

The decisive intervention that changed South Africa's policy was that of Deputy President Thabo Mbeki. Having served as head of the ANC office in Lagos between 1977 and 1978 during the military regime of General Olusegun Obasanjo, Mbeki understood both the country and its main players. Concerned that the situation could precipitate the disintegration of Nigeria, he devised a strategy with South Africa's high commissioner, George Nene, to engage rather than confront the Nigerian regime. He embarked on diplomatic missions to Abuja and initiated contacts between the security agencies of both countries.[25] South Africa pulled out of the Commonwealth Action Group on Nigeria, which had been set up shortly after the Auckland summit; refused to sanction Nigeria at the UN Commission on Human Rights; and cancelled a major conference of Nigeria's once-welcomed pro-democracy groups scheduled to take place in Johannesburg.[26] The first Nigerian ambassador to South Africa, Alhaji Shehu Malami, presented his credentials to Mandela in August 1996.

Mbeki provided a detailed justification of South Africa's policy to his country's parliamentarians in May 1996, telling them: 'We should not humiliate ourselves by pretending that we have a strength which we do not have.'[27] Arguing that Pretoria did not have the leverage to dictate to Abuja, Mbeki urged South Africa instead to encourage efforts to support Nigeria's transition to democratic rule. He warned South Africa not to overestimate its strength in a fit of arrogance, and noted the failure of the West, which had the power to impose oil sanctions on Nigeria, to act. Instead, Mbeki observed that Mandela had been set up for failure and ridicule by Western countries that preferred to protect their oil profits, investments, and Nigerian assets.[28] Western governments, steeped in the art of realpolitik, had made critical noises to assuage domestic public opinion in their countries while quietly continuing to do business with Abacha's autocratic regime. It is probably not an exaggeration to note that this single incident would shape Mbeki's future policy of 'quiet diplomacy' towards Zimbabwe.[29] Having felt that Mandela had been set up for failure on Nigeria by the West, Mbeki was determined not to suffer the same fate over Zimbabwe. Unlike Mandela's reaction to Abacha, Mbeki pointedly ignored calls by Western leaders to sanction Robert Mugabe, judging that such actions would not only be ineffective but could also result in a loss of leverage within both Zimbabwe and the broader African context.

General Abacha's sudden, dramatic death in June 1998 greatly increased the chances of the tale of the prophet and the pariah becoming a tale of two prophets. Mbeki travelled to Abuja shortly after General Abdulsaalam Abubakar had assumed power, urging the Nigerian government to restore civil liberties and to release political prisoners. In August and September 1998, Abubakar travelled to South Africa. In yet another sign of restored cooperation between the two countries, Nigeria's new military ruler invited Mandela to attend the ECOWAS summit in Abuja. The mild-mannered Abubakar oversaw a transition to democratic rule in Nigeria by May 1999, bowing out gracefully after less than a year in power. The conservative F.W. De Klerk—who had previously been a staunch defender of apartheid—had also, under severe domestic and international pressure, similarly reformed the very apartheid system over which his National Party had presided for nearly fifty years. In the end, both Abubakar and De Klerk midwifed democratic transitions in Nigeria and South Africa.[30]

The Philosopher-King and the Soldier-Farmer, 1999–2008

Thabo Mbeki[31] and Olusegun Obasanjo[32] assumed the presidencies of their respective countries in 1999. They are very different personalities. Mbeki, a pipe-smoking, Sussex University–trained economist, often wrote his own speeches, fancied himself as a philosopher-king who developed the idea of an African renaissance, and was widely celebrated as the intellectual father of NEPAD (see chapter 11). Obasanjo, a career soldier and engineer who has reportedly ghostwritten several biographies but is not considered to be an intellectual, established one of Africa's largest farms, in his hometown of

Ota, upon retirement as military head of state in 1979. The two men had a close personal relationship, dating back to Obasanjo's 1976–1979 tenure as leader of Nigeria and Mbeki's 1977–1978 tenure as the ANC representative in Lagos.

From this firsthand experience, South Africa's future president developed a great admiration for Nigeria's sense of fierce independence. Mbeki attended Nigeria's lavish Festival of Arts and Culture in 1977; went to social weddings and funerals; devoured the vibrant press, educational excellence, and rich literature; marveled at the country's entrepreneurial spirit; admired radical anti–establishment Nigerian musician Fela Anikulapo-Kuti, whose 'African Shrine' he visited in Lagos; watched the popular television series *Village Headmaster;* and befriended key senior officials and radical intellectual Yusuf Bala Usman. Mbeki clearly recognised the huge importance of the country for Africa.[33] As he later noted about Nigeria: 'It's an extraordinary society, an African society. It doesn't have this big imprint of colonial oppression. It's something else. Very different from here [South Africa]. You get a sense that you are now really being exposed to the real Africa, not where *we* come from ... they do their own thing. [And] they are of such importance on the African continent that they could mislead lots of people.'[34]

But Mbeki often felt that Nigeria's lack of a white-settler experience made Lagos impatient of a need to accommodate South African whites, and the ANC was often irritated by the frustration of the Obasanjo military administration with what the latter saw as the lacklustre 'armed struggle' (a frustration many South Africans themselves later expressed about Zimbabwe's opposition movement to Robert Mugabe's regime) as well as with Lagos's insistence on backing a common front of the ANC, the Pan-Africanist Congress (PAC), and the Soweto Student Representatives Council (SSRC).[35] Obasanjo also met South Africa's future leaders during his visit to the apartheid enclave as co-chairman of the Commonwealth Eminent Persons Group in 1986. As head of state between 1976 and 1979, he developed a close working relationship with Southern African leaders like Robert Mugabe, Sam Nujoma, and Eduardo Dos Santos, at a time when Nigeria was considered a member of the Frontline States and a generous supporter of liberation movements in the subregion.[36] Upon becoming president, Obasanjo's first foreign trip abroad was to attend Mbeki's inauguration in June 1999.

Both Mbeki and Obasanjo were respected internationally, but faced enormous economic and political difficulties at home. Mbeki, though respected as a technocrat, inevitably struggled to fill the shoes of his saintly predecessor,

Nelson Mandela. Obasanjo, rejected by his own Yoruba people in Nigeria's 1999 presidential election, did not totally shake off his military image. Both faced severe criticism at home for embarking on frequent foreign trips and for not spending more time on alleviating pressing problems of poverty, unemployment, and crime at home. Mbeki was criticised for his domestic AIDS policies; Obasanjo was castigated for not preventing massacres of civilians by his army. Both leaders, however, worked closely at managing African conflicts through the AU, SADC, and ECOWAS (see chapter 2). They also attempted to promote norms of democratic government through the African Union, whose founding charter they were instrumental in shaping.[37]

The AU, NEPAD, and Pax Africana

Mbeki and Obasanjo challenged the Organisation of African Unity's (OAU) inflexible adherence to absolute sovereignty and noninterference in the internal affairs of member states.[38] At the OAU summit in Algiers, Algeria, in 1999, both were among the leaders who pushed for the ostracism of regimes that engaged in unconstitutional changes of government. The organisation subsequently barred the military regimes of Côte d'Ivoire and Comoros from attending its summit in Lomé, Togo, in 2000. The two leaders insisted that the OAU must recognise the right of other African states to intervene in the internal affairs of its members in egregious cases of gross human rights abuses and to stem regional instability.

Both Mbeki and Obasanjo stressed the importance of conflict resolution in Africa in a bid to achieve a Pax Africana.[39] Obasanjo hosted a Commonwealth meeting that discussed land reform in Zimbabwe in September 2001. He led peacemaking efforts in Liberia, Sierra Leone, and the Great Lakes region. Mbeki, with the help of Mandela and Deputy President Jacob Zuma, lent his country's weight and resources to peace efforts in Burundi. South Africa's president between 1999 and 2008 was also active in negotiations to restore constitutional rule to Côte d'Ivoire as the AU mediator to the country beginning in November 2004. Mbeki also helped to convince Charles Taylor to leave power for exile in Nigeria in August 2003, as a military rebellion from the countryside sought to force him out, threatening massive bloodshed in the capital of Monrovia. But Tshwane (the new name for Pretoria) and Abuja have felt the strain of peacekeeping burdens respectively in Burundi (under the AU) and Liberia (under ECOWAS) on their fragile economies. In the future, South African and Nigerian peacekeepers are likely to serve mainly under the UN, as the cases of Burundi and Liberia—where both South Africa and Nigeria, though continuing to contribute troops, insisted that the UN take over peacekeeping responsibilities from weak regional organisations—clearly demonstrate. This not only represents an attempt to legitimise such military actions, but is also a conscious effort to alleviate fears of aggressive regional hegemons pursuing their own parochial interests under the guise of keeping peace in Africa.

Both Mbeki and Obasanjo lobbied the rich world on behalf of Africa at annual Group of Eight (G8) meetings, though the results were often disappointing. Both drove the NEPAD process. This plan is based on a straightforward bargain between Africa and its largely Western donors: in exchange for support from external actors, African leaders agreed to take responsibility for, and commit themselves to, democratic governance. In October 2001, sixteen African leaders met in Abuja for NEPAD's first implementation meeting. Tunji Olagunju (who studied at Sussex with Mbeki and was Nigeria's influential high commissioner in South Africa between November 1999 and September 2005) and Dele Patrick-Cole (a former Nigerian ambassador to Brazil) were both involved in the process of drawing up the arrangements for NEPAD.[40] Obasanjo also hosted a meeting between NEPAD and the heads of Africa's regional economic communities in Abuja in October 2003, in an effort to encourage them to align their integration programmes with NEPAD's goals.[41] As key members of NEPAD's implementing committee, Mbeki and Obasanjo coaxed twenty-seven of their fellow leaders to sign up to its peer review mechanism, which critics still argue lacks the 'teeth' to bite autocratic offenders.

During the process to transform the OAU into the AU, Mbeki and Obasanjo ensured that the organisation adopted a gradualist approach to unity rather than the more federalist model championed by Libya's maverick leader, Muammar Qaddafi, who became chair of the AU in January 2009. Significantly, this event occurred after both Mbeki and Obasanjo had left power and were thus no longer able to block the erratic 'Brother Leader's' ambitions. The two leaders also successfully pushed for Mali's outgoing president, Alpha Konaré, to become the first chairperson of the AU Commission in 2003, in order to have a strong, visionary leader who could interact easily with other heads of state.[42]

Despite the domestic constraints of South Africa and Nigeria, the Tshwane-Abuja axis still has the most potential to drive Africa's renaissance. In October 1999, the two countries established a binational commission, thereby formalising the strong ties between them. This commission has five concrete objectives: provide a framework for joint efforts to bring Africa into the mainstream of global political, social, and economic developments; provide a basis for the governments and private sectors of both countries to promote bilateral trade and industry; improve bilateral relations in the fields of technology, education, health, culture, youth, and sports; maximise socioeconomic development through collaborative use of human and natural resources; and establish the mechanisms to promote peace, stability, and socioeconomic integration in Africa.[43]

Eight binational meetings were held during the period 1999–2009, with Nigeria and South Africa alternating as host. The fourth meeting, in 2002, initiated the idea of a South Africa–Nigeria free trade area, while the fifth meeting, in 2003, called for a joint business investment forum. By the time of the sixth meeting, the focus was on eight working groups: trade, industry, and finance; mineral and energy; agriculture, water resources, and environment; foreign affairs and cooperation; defence; immigration, justice, and crime; social and technical issues; and public enterprises and infrastructure. At the sixth meeting, held in Durban, South Africa, in 2004, officials discussed how to increase trade, with the Nigerians urging the South Africans to accelerate discussions with their Southern African Customs Union partners (Botswana, Swaziland, Lesotho, and Namibia) in order to establish the proposed free trade area. The meeting further urged the establishment of a special implementation committee to ensure an effective monitoring mechanism, as well as to develop a concrete programme of action with clear time frames. Continuity of officials was also encouraged, as well as participation of legislators and chief executives of South African provinces and Nigerian states in future binational sessions.[44] On the tenth anniversary of the creation of the BNC, an eighth meeting was held in Abuja in February 2009 which discussed the state of bilateral activities, how to strengthen BNC structures, as well as African and global issues. Activities were also held in South Africa and Nigeria in October and November 2009 to commemorate the tenth anniversary: business round tables, civil society and parliamentary meetings, and cultural events.

There have been some strains in relations between Tshwane and Abuja that the binational meetings have sought to address. In response to difficulties experienced by Nigerians in obtaining visas to South Africa, Abuja imposed stricter visa requirements on South African citizens visiting Nigeria by 2009. Nigerian diplomats have often complained about negative press reports and xenophobic stereotypes of Nigerians, as drug-traffickers and criminals, in the

South African media and popular imagination (The 2009 movie, *District Nine*, being an egregious example).[45] They have noted that local South Africans, as well as Mozambicans, Moroccans, Indians, Pakistanis, Chinese, Russians, and Italians, also engage in such criminal activities, but that the nationals of these countries in South Africa are not tarred with the same broad brush as are Nigerians. A Johannesburg radio station, 94.7 Highveld, was forced by South Africa's Broadcasting Complaints Commission to apologise after it claimed that Nigerian president Olusegun Obasanjo was carrying cocaine in his bag when he attended Mbeki's inauguration in June 2004.[46] Some Nigerian diplomats have attributed these caricatures of their nationals by sections of South Africa's press to the generous contribution that their country made to the anti–apartheid struggle.[47] Showing clear concern about the image of Nigerians in South Africa, the Nigerian consulate in Johannesburg took out advertisements in major South African newspapers to warn South Africans not to become involved in the scams of Nigerian fraudsters peddling get-rich-quick schemes.[48]

South African Corporates 'Invade' Africa's Largest Market

After 1994, South Africa's corporate community began to view Nigeria with great interest, helped by its long-serving and energetic high commissioner in Abuja, former trade unionist Bangumzi 'Sticks' Sifingo.[49] (He was replaced in 2008 by Kingsley Mamabolo, the former Special Representative to the Great Lakes region, who is one of South Africa's most experienced multilateralists.) The South African telecommunications giants Mobile Telephone Networks (MTN) and M-Net/SuperSport blazed the trail and listed on the Nigerian Stock Exchange. MTN spent $340 million launching its mobile telephone network in Nigeria in August 2001,[50] with plans to spend $1.4 billion in the country over a decade. In 2003–2004, MTN Nigeria's post-tax profit of 2.36 billion rand surpassed MTN South Africa's 2.24 billion rand profit.[51] By June 2004, MTN had 1.65 million subscribers in Nigeria,[52] which increased ten-fold to 16.5 million by December 2007, representing a staggering 29 per cent of all its African subscribers in sixteen countries, and more than its 14.8 million South African subscribers.[53] It was MTN's success that convinced many other South African firms that Nigeria was worth investing in. South Africa has only six big cities, compared to Nigeria's twenty-seven,[54] a figure underlining the sheer size of the latter's huge market of 140 million potential consumers. As a senior executive of South African beer and beverages multinational SABMiller—which belatedly entered the Nigerian market in 2008—noted, if South African firms do not have a Nigeria strategy, they do not really have an Africa strategy.[55]

Other South African 'blue chip' companies that followed MTN included Stanbic, Rand Merchant Bank (involved in equity funding deals), and more recently, retirement fund administrator Alexander Forbes. Within a year of operations, Stanbic's Nigerian affiliate was contributing 13 per cent of its Africa-wide revenues (1.26 billion rand). In 2008, Alexander Forbes bought a 40 per cent stake in Nigeria's pension sector, comprising 8 million potential state employees.[56] Sasol, the world's largest producer of petrol from coal, made a $1.2 billion investment in Nigeria to export natural gas. South Africa's government-funded Industrial Development Corporation invested in Nigerian oil, gas, infrastructure, tourism, and telecommunications. South Africa's Spoornet worked with the Nigerian Railway Corporation to revive Nigeria's railways. Protea had four hotels in Lagos in 2008, with another eight under construction.[57] Fast-food chains Chicken Licken and Debonairs Pizzas established franchises in Nigeria. Johncom opened Exclusive Books and Nu-Metro cinemas in Abuja and Lagos, as well as DVD and CD manufacturing plants. Shoprite Checkers opened an outlet in Lagos in 2006 that became profitable within a year. A Nigeria–South Africa chamber of commerce was also established in 2001, while a joint business investment forum met in South Africa three times between 2004 and 2008. By 2003, Nigeria had already become South Africa's third largest continental trading partner, after Zimbabwe and Mozambique, and its largest continental importer. Three years later, Nigeria became South Africa's largest trading partner on the continent, and bilateral trade stood at 11 billion rand (around $1.5 billion) in 2007, a figure that increased to 22.8 billion rand (about $3 billion) by 2008.[58] Businesspeople from South Africa and Nigeria now frequently cross each other's borders, with over a hundred South African firms working in Nigeria by September 2007, up from fifty-five in 2003.[59]

Of Nigeria's exports to South Africa in 2003, 98.3 per cent consisted of oil, though Nigeria's Union Bank and First Bank also had representative offices in South Africa. In 2005, Nigerian oil company Oando set up shop in Johannesburg.[60] Three years later, the Dangote Group, Nigeria's largest industrial conglomerate, bought 45 per cent of South Africa's Sephaka Cement, at a cost of 3 billion rand, in preparation for an expected construction boom for the 2010 football World Cup.[61] These latest investments could go some way to convincing Nigerians—who have often accused South Africans of predatory, mercantilist behaviour—that the South African market may be opening up to their own firms in reciprocation. Many Nigerian professionals also work in South Africa, in fields like academia, medicine, accounting, human resources, and property. In turn, South Africa sells Nigeria a more diverse range of goods, including machinery, electrical equipment, wood, paper, foodstuff, beverages, spirits, tobacco, sugar, plastics, and rubber.

Troubles in a Marriage of Necessity

An important obstacle to the hegemonic ambitions of South Africa and Nigeria is the fact that the relationship between both countries relied too heavily on the personal relationship between Thabo Mbeki and Olusegun Obasanjo. There were many calls to institutionalise the bilateral relationship between Tshwane and Abuja, so that it would survive the exit of one or both leaders from the national stage. The creation of a binational commission and growing commercial ties may eventually help to overcome this problem, but this is far from certain. It is also uncertain whether Mbeki's successors will maintain the same level of commitment to this relationship specifically, and to Africa in general (see chapter 5). By 2006, both Mbeki's dominance over the ANC, and Obasanjo's grip on the ruling People's Democratic Party (PDP) seemed to be weakening. Mbeki faced open challenges to his leadership after ousting his deputy, Jacob Zuma, in June 2005 (following corruption allegations), while Obasanjo lost a bid in Nigeria's parliament in May 2006 to amend the constitution to allow him to run for a third term in office (see chapter 6). Nigeria's instability continued, with militias in the oil-producing Niger Delta shutting down a third of the country's oil production in a bid to force the government to address the neglected area's socioeconomic grievances.[62] South Africa's socioeconomic challenges also continued, with the country remaining the most unequal society in the world. In the end, Obasanjo left power in May 2007, while Mbeki was 'recalled' from office by his own party in September 2008, having lost the leadership of the ANC to Jacob Zuma in December 2007.

The Tshwane-Abuja alliance was a marriage of necessity for Mbeki. Unable to assert leadership effectively in Southern Africa because of lingering suspicion from its neighbours—and because of further resistance from states like Angola and Zimbabwe seeing themselves as potential regional hegemons—he had to venture outside his own subregion to find the allies and additional legitimacy needed to bolster his continental leadership ambitions. South Africa reached out to Africa's most populous state—Nigeria—and worked closely with it in diplomatic forums in pursuit of continental initiatives like the AU and NEPAD. This sometimes created tensions, with Obasanjo's professional diplomats and policy advisers privately criticising him for his fondness for Mbeki and for ceding too much intellectual influence to Mbeki and South African mandarins who were less experienced than Nigeria's diplomats in the labyrinthine intricacies of African diplomacy.

There were also some tensions between South Africa and Nigeria over Zimbabwe during the Commonwealth summit in Abuja in 2003. Mbeki had sought to ensure Mugabe's invitation to the summit, but Obasanjo, under pressure from Britain, Canada, and Australia, did not want to disrupt the summit he was hosting by admitting the Zimbabwean president. In Abuja, Mbeki also clumsily tried to replace the Commonwealth Secretary-General, New Zealand's Don McKinnon, with former Sri Lankan foreign minister Lakshma Kadrigamar, but lost by forty votes to eleven, with Nigeria voting against the South African proposal.[63]

By 2005, more serious differences between South Africa and Nigeria emerged over three issues: proposals for a reformed UN Security Council; Côte d'Ivoire; and the AU chair. Both countries had consistently expressed an interest in occupying one of two permanent African seats on an expanded UN Security Council. Though this proposal failed to find enough support within the UN General Assembly in September 2005 (with most AU leaders having argued for Africa to insist on a veto, see chapter 3), the acrimonious contest saw some Nigerian officials privately questioning the authenticity of South Africa as a black African state, while the South Africans maneuvered behind the scenes to undermine Nigeria, for example by focusing attention on their greater financial muscle. Tensions were also evident in Côte d'Ivoire after the rebel Forces Nouvelles withdrew support from Mbeki's mediation efforts in 2005, accusing him of bias towards President Laurent Gbagbo. The rebels then urged the AU chairman, Obasanjo, to find an alternative way of resolving the impasse. At a meeting of the AU Peace and Security Council on the margins of the UN General Assembly in September 2005, ECOWAS was tasked with overcoming this impasse: a clear attempt to shift the locus of peacemaking from Southern to West Africa.[64]

The Nigerians increasingly faulted Mbeki for his role in Côte d'Ivoire, accusing him of seeking to claim all the glory from any peacemaking success and according to them failing to report back on his efforts to Obasanjo, the AU chair who had appointed him.[65] Though Mbeki and Obasanjo jointly visited Côte d'Ivoire in November and December 2005, it was clear to close observers that a rift had opened between them. Yet another area of discord between Mbeki and Obasanjo opened at the AU summit in Khartoum, Sudan, in January 2006, when Mbeki (supported by other African leaders) strongly opposed the suggestion that Obasanjo continue as AU chair for a third consecutive term. Obasanjo was not offered a third term, echoing his failure to secure a third term as Nigerian president. The incident apparently led to his early departure from the summit.[66]

The fact that binational meetings between South Africa and Nigeria failed to take place between 2005 and 2007, for the first time since their inception in 1999, was another source of concern for the state of Africa's most strategic bilateral relationship. The seventh binational meeting did not take place until May 2008, in Nigeria, following Obasanjo's departure from power and the election of President Umaru Yar'Adua the previous year. A month later, Yar'Adua led a 300–strong business delegation to South Africa for a meeting of the joint business investment forum. He also addressed the South African parliament in Cape Town a month after horrific xenophobic attacks against foreigners that had resulted in about two dozen deaths (see chapter 5). During a toast in honour of Yar'Adua, Mbeki noted: 'This is a matter that has deeply shamed many South Africans, who in response have rejected these completely unacceptable criminal activities and rallied support for the foreign nationals in our country.'[67] Mbeki went on to reiterate the importance of the 'strategic partnership' between both countries, and called for a further expansion of economic ties. In October 2008, Mohamed Marwa, a former military administrator turned politician, became Nigeria's High Commissioner to South Africa, replacing Olugbenga Ashiru, who had assumed office in October 2005.

Concluding Reflections

We conclude this chapter by briefly assessing the prospects for the future leadership role of South Africa and Nigeria in Africa. South Africa has embarked on 'cultural diplomacy' in helping to finance the restoration of numerous precolonial manuscripts and building an archive to house them in one of the world's oldest libraries, in Mali's famous city of Timbuktu,[68] and in championing the idea of an African renaissance . This concept could be translated into a pan-African cultural event—a South African FESTAC—that could at once establish the country's leadership role on the continent and help this culturally schizophrenic country to embrace an African identity and learn more about the African culture that apartheid's leaders long denied to the majority of its population. Today, only South Africa—the wealthiest and most industrialised country on the continent—could afford to host a lavish festival on the scale of Nigeria's FESTAC in 1977.

However, the idea of South Africa and Nigeria as continental leaders is far from universally accepted. The strategic alliance between both countries is seen by some as little more than a new breed of African imperialism.[69] South Africa's bid for the Olympic Games in 2004 failed, in part, due to a lack of African support. Nigeria failed to gain African support for its successful UN Security Council bids in 1977 and 1993, after breaking the rotation rules of the African Group. In the more recent debates about permanent seats for South Africa and Nigeria on the AU's fifteen-member Peace and Security Council in 2003–2004, other states refused to accept any special permanent status or veto power for both countries, and instead created five three-year renewable seats to complement the ten biannual rotational seats.[70] Neither country was able to carry its own subregion to support the dropping of a veto for potential UN Security Council members during discussions on UN reform in 2005 (see chapter 3). South Africa and Nigeria must consult with other African governments and ensure that their actions are not seen as attempts to dominate the continent in pursuit of their own parochial interests. Only by taking measures to alleviate such concerns can both countries become the beacons of democracy and engines of economic growth to which their leaders clearly aspire.

8

AN AXIS OF EVIL?

CHINA, THE UNITED STATES, AND FRANCE IN AFRICA[1]

'Why do I, for instance, believe that the present occupant of the White House in the United States of America [George W. Bush] is one of the most dangerous fanatics ever to bestride the destiny of the world? It is not because one loves whom he labels, enemies of humankind, it is simply because he is himself a fundamentalist of the most unmanageable kind. He sees himself as spokesman and protagonist of "The Chosen" against "All Others", and thus exempt from the laws which bind the organization that attempts to hold the world together [the United Nations].'[2]

Wole Soyinka, Nobel literature laureate, March 2003

In this post–9/11 'age of terror', one of the most infamous and inelegant political phrases that has been coined was US president George W. Bush's depiction of Iran, Iraq, and North Korea as forming an 'axis of evil'. This chapter examines whether a similar caricature can be applied to the roles of the three main external powers in post–Cold War Africa: China, the United States, and France. A historical approach is adopted and some of the political, military, and economic roles that all three countries have played and are currently playing on the continent are assessed. Carrying the Bushism further, these actors can also be depicted as three cowboys in a spaghetti Western of 'the Good, the Bad, and the Ugly', with France arrogating to itself the *mission civilisatrice* of spreading 'enlightenment' and culture to barbarous natives; with Western 'Orientalists' hypocritically seeking to convince us about how bad and evil rapacious Chinese 'mercantilists' are for Africa; and with 'ugly' Americans continuing to rampage through Africa in search of markets to conquer and 'mad mullahs' to vanquish. This chapter endeavours to shatter the 'Orientalist' myth that often describes China's role as that of a 'yellow peril' seeking to monopolise markets, coddle caudillos, and condone human rights abuses on the continent, while Western powers such as the United States and France are portrayed in contrast almost as knights in shining armour, seeking to assist Africa's economic recovery, spread democracy, and contribute to conflict management. By focusing comparatively on the historical and contemporary role of the United States and France in Africa, these ahistorical distortions are hopefully dispelled. China's own historical and contemporary role is likewise assessed without unrealistically romanticising or unfairly condemning it.

China and Africa: The Great Leap Forward

In examining China's role in Africa, it is important to place this relationship in a historical context of Afro-Asian cooperation during the age of decolonisation from the 1950s, before analysing Beijing's more contemporary role in the post–Cold War era. Most, but not all, 118 members of the Non-Aligned Movement (NAM) are part of the Group of 77 (G77) of the now 130 developing countries that have historically been aligned to China. The G77 was set up in June 1964 in the context of the first UN Conference on Trade and Development (UNCTAD), and continues to dominate the UN General Assembly's agenda. The African Group at the UN was created in 1958 and soon, along with Asian allies, made its presence felt on decolonisation and anti–apartheid issues, eventually ostracising South Africa at the UN and maintaining pressure for the liberation of Zimbabwe/Rhodesia and Namibia/South West Africa (see chapter 3).[3]

During this period, the Convention on the Elimination of Racial Discrimination was agreed upon, a committee on decolonisation was established, and a special committee against apartheid was created. As a result of the pressure of a determined Southern majority, including twenty-six African states and led by Tanzania's formidable permanent representative at the UN, Salim Ahmed Salim, the People's Republic of China (PRC) took its permanent seat on the UN Security Council in 1971, in the face of strong opposition from Washington. Solid African backing also helped China to secure the 2008 Olympic Games.

China's relations with Africa have thus historically been grounded in a shared history of political and economic dominance by Western colonial powers. Following his victory in 1949, Chinese leader Mao Zedong was determined to spread his revolution abroad against 'anti–imperialist' forces. Legendary Chinese premier Zhou Enlai had famously noted that 'revolutionary prospects' were 'excellent' in Africa. Consequently, on historic trips across the continent in 1963–1964, Zhou consistently stressed the shared history of colonial oppression. Beijing proved that this was not mere rhetoric by providing essential support and military training to liberation movements across the continent. China supported liberation movements in Southern Africa and used Kwame Nkrumah's Ghana as a conduit for support to opposition groups.[4] Beijing also channelled economic assistance to agriculture and light industries, contributing $2.5 billion to thirty-six African countries between the mid-1950s and mid-1970s. Algeria, Egypt, Somalia, Tanzania, and what was then Zaire—now the Democratic Republic of the Congo (DRC)—received the lion's share of Chinese assistance.

Between 1961 and 2006, 2,000 students from forty-eight African countries studied in China, while 15,000 Chinese technical experts were sent to the continent to grow rice and build factories, roads, bridges, and airports. Some of these projects, however, were criticised for not transferring technology to recipients and for not using sufficient local content. Despite such criticisms, the Chinese assistance included some grand projects such as the 2,000–kilometre, $484 million Tanzania-Zambia (TAZARA) Railway, completed in 1975. This was an impressive feat of engineering that took five years and needed more than 50,000 labourers to finish. Beijing had provided long-term, interest-free loans to complete the project after the World Bank, Washington, London, and Ottawa had turned down requests from Lusaka and Dar-es-Salaam to fund the project.[5] Under Chinese leader Deng Xiaoping's 'Open Door' policy from 1978, the PRC de-emphasised the 'export' of its revolution abroad and focused on a strategy of promoting trade and investment to strengthen its economy, adopting a policy of 'socialism with Chinese characteristics': a move towards a capitalist-market economy.

China's economy grew at an unprecedented average of 9 per cent between 1989 and 2009 and its gross domestic product tripled in the same period. The country has the world's largest population, at 1.3 billion people; it has lifted more people (400 million) out of poverty than any other nation in history and, by some estimates, is on course to overtake the United States as the world's largest economy by 2025, after having become the world's second largest economy by 2010. As a corollary, China's growing political, economic, and security ties in Africa since the end of the Cold War have attracted much attention as one of the most important developments in the geostrategy of this age. Beijing's 'peaceful rise' to Great Power status has been nothing short of breathtaking, and Africa must now devise strategies to engage the world's next superpower. China, unlike the West, is investing heavily in the infrastructure sectors—roads, railways, electricity—that Africa needs for its industrial takeoff. Beijing has helped to revive Zambia's copper mines and exported timber from Mozambique. It has also invested in the oil sectors of countries such as Nigeria, Angola, Sudan, Equatorial Guinea, Gabon, and Chad, ruffling Western feathers in the process, as American, French, and other European companies are also operating in most of these countries. By 2006, China was importing about a third of its energy from Africa.[6]

Such developments have caused concerns among China's Western competitors, some of which have often failed to note that India, Malaysia, Japan, as well as North and South Korea have also joined the quest for Africa's energy and other resources. As US congressman Christopher Smith ahistorically and hypocritically noted in July 2005: 'China is playing an increasingly influential role on the continent of Africa, and there is concern that the Chinese intend to aid and abet African dictators, gain a stranglehold on precious African natural resources, and undo much of the progress that has been made on democracy and governance in the last 15 years in African nations.'[7] But the view from Africa has often been quite different from this hysteria. As Garth le Pere aptly put it: 'The imperative for coherent policy responses towards China by Africans must ... not fall prey to lazy caricature and crude stereotyping lest we fall into a trap of moral relativitism where the West is held to one set of standards and China to another.'[8] Former Nigerian finance minister between 2003 and 2006, Ngozi Okonjo-Iweala, was equally blunt in noting: 'China should be left alone to forge its unique partnership with African countries, and the West must simply learn to compete.'[9]

Meanwhile, in policy terms, Beijing has increasingly stressed political non-interference and a need for countries to find their own paths, rather than adopting a Chinese model. High-level visits to Africa by the Chinese leadership and to Beijing by African leaders have confirmed the strong bonds between China and Africa. Former Chinese president Jiang Zhemin visited Africa in 1996; following that, President Hu Jintao visited the continent five times between 1999 and 2007, while over thirty African leaders visited China between 1997 and 2009. Beijing held the first Forum on China-Africa Cooperation (FOCAC) in October 2000, with forty-four African governments in attendance. At the summit, Western aid conditionalities were criticised, and

Beijing soon announced the annulment of $1.2 billion of African debt to thirty-one African countries. A second FOCAC summit was held in Addis Ababa, Ethiopia, in December 2003.

By 2004, Africa's exports to China had reached $11.4 billion; Sino-African trade had grown from $2 billion in 1999 to $55.5 billion in 2006. Beijing offered the continent $5 billion in loans and credit in the same year and had become the third largest foreign investor on the continent (at an estimated $6.6 billion) behind the United States and Europe, having set up over 1,000 enterprises in Africa. In November 2006, forty-three African leaders trekked to Beijing for a third FOCAC summit, where China promised to double aid to the continent, train 15,000 Africans, and provide 4,000 scholarships. More than 400 Chinese lecturers have been sent to Africa, while 15,000 of its medical experts have been dispatched to forty-two African countries.[10] In November 2009, a fourth FOCAC meeting was held in the Egyptian Red Sea resort of Sharm-el Sheikh. The summit agreed to expand high-level exchanges, promote regional stability, work to achieve the UN Millennium Development Goals' aim of halving poverty by 2015, and enhance collaboration on climate change and trade and financial issues. A three-year Action Plan was also agreed, with Beijing further undertaking to expand cooperation in the fields of agriculture, science and technology, and malaria treatment and prevention. Finally, the summit agreed to provide $10 billion in concessional loans to African governments between 2010 and 2012; increase tariff-free access for African goods into Chinese markets; assist African entrepreneurs to establish businesses in China; grant 5,500 scholarships for Africans to study in China; and continue to build schools across the continent.[11]

Though China's trade with Africa is only 2 per cent of its total global trade, its direct investment in Africa represents 16 per cent of its total global investment. What is significant about these growing ties is the diversity of Beijing's trade with Africa, ranging from oil in Nigeria, Angola, Sudan, and Congo-Brazzaville (an impressive 28 per cent of China's oil imports came from Africa in 2006); to tourism, construction, wholesale, retail, energy, transport, communications, and health across the continent; to education in Sierra Leone, Seychelles, Ethiopia, and Senegal; to manufacturing in Morocco and Zimbabwe; to fisheries in Gabon and Namibia; to building stadiums in Mali, Djibouti, and the Central African Republic; and to agriculture in Zambia and Tanzania. But some of Beijing's actions in Africa have not been without controversy: China became a large investor (40 per cent of the largest venture) and importer of oil from the Sudanese government of Omar al-Bashir, which has been accused of widespread human rights violations in South Sudan and more recently in Darfur. China also imported oil from the equally controversial autocratic and corrupt government of Equatorial Guinea, and sold arms to Ethiopia and Eritrea during their bloody 1998–2000 civil war, in violation of a UN Security Council resolution that China itself, as one of five permanent members of the Council, had agreed to.[12] Beijing's insistence on a policy of noninterference and close ties with autocratic and corrupt regimes in Africa have been criticised, as has its use of an estimated 80,000 Chinese labourers in its projects in Africa.[13] By the end of 2004, Chinese textile exports to South Africa had grown from 40 to 80 per cent, forcing an estimated 75,000 people out of jobs; in neighbouring Lesotho, 10,000 jobs were lost and ten clothing factories closed as a result of competition from cheaper Chinese imports. Nigeria's textile industries in Kano and Kaduna were said to have been similarly negatively affected.[14]

A critical area of interest to Africa in which China has played a supportive role is peacekeeping through the UN. After debacles in Somalia and Rwanda in 1993 and 1994, Western peacekeepers largely abandoned the continent for several years (discussed in more detail below). By May 2007, China had deployed 1,800 peacekeepers to UN missions in Sudan, the DRC, Liberia, Côte d'Ivoire, Ethiopia/Eritrea, and Western Sahara. Though this was not a large number considering the 80,000 UN peacekeepers deployed globally at the time, the symbolic value of these troops is greatly appreciated in many African quarters, particularly when contrasted with the more selective and often self-interested Western peacekeeping engagements on the continent. But China's sales of large arms to countries such as Zimbabwe, Ethiopia, and Sudan continue to cause some discomfort on the continent.

In August 2007, the powerful fifteen-member UN Security Council decided to deploy 26,000 'blue helmets' to Sudan's volatile Darfur province by the end of 2007. The UN–African Union (AU) hybrid operation in Darfur (UNAMID) was mandated to bolster the struggling 7,000–strong AU mission in Darfur that had been deployed by 2004 (see chapter 2). Diplomatic pressure exerted by China—one of five veto-wielding permanent members of the UN Security Council along with the United States, Russia, Britain, and France—appears to have been instrumental in twisting the arm of Sudanese leader Omar al-Bashir. Beijing thus reversed its traditional rhetorical policy of nonintervention in Africa to convince Khartoum—in whose oil sector China had a dominant position (see chapter 9)—to accept a UN force, apparently under threat of a boycott of China's showpiece $40 billion

Olympic Games in 2008: Beijing's 'coming-out' party as a superpower.[15] In another sign of Beijing's growing assertiveness, China has pushed for UN Security Council action in Somalia since 2007. Despite concerns about Beijing's self-interested role in Africa, however, China is clear about what its interests are in its relations with Africa. It is likewise incumbent on African governments to devise a coherent, collective approach to defining their own interests, using Beijing's presence on the continent to reduce their dependence on and increase their leverage with Western powers such as the United States and France.

The United States and Africa: In Search of Enemies[16]

After the Second World War ended in 1945, the United States at first portrayed itself as an anticolonial power, urging decolonisation in Africa and Asia. With the onset of the Cold War by the 1950s, Washington changed its anticolonial tune in Africa and talked instead of a global struggle for 'containment' and 'anti-communism'. The United States no longer urged its European allies—Britain, France, Portugal, and Spain—to surrender their African possessions acquired at the height of the 'Scramble for Africa'. Instead, Washington came to regard the ubiquitous presence of the French gendarme in Africa as a useful way of keeping the Soviet bear out of large parts of the continent. The US also provided military assistance to its North Atlantic Treaty Organisation (NATO) ally Portugal, which helped the Iberian power to maintain its colonial presence in Angola, Mozambique, and Guinea-Bissau, and delayed the independence of these countries until a military coup in Lisbon in 1974.

The Cold War's 'axis of evil' involved the two superpowers—the United States and the Soviet Union—and France. All three powers turned Africa into a strategic playground to conduct their ideological games, resulting in the deaths of millions of Africans. The continent was flooded with billions of dollars of weapons provided to local proxies in countries such as Angola, Ethiopia, Liberia, Mozambique, and Somalia. During the Cold War, Washington's policies in Africa frequently ignored principles as basic as democracy and development and focused parochially on containing the 'red peril' through protecting and providing military and financial assistance to often brutal and undemocratic clients, such as Liberia's Samuel Doe, Zaire's Mobutu Sese Seko, and Somalia's Siad Barre, in exchange for political support and military bases.[17]

The Clinton Administration, 1993–2000

After the end of the Cold War, Washington announced in the early 1990s that its Cold War–era obsession with 'containment' was to be replaced by what President Bill Clinton's national security adviser, Anthony Lake, described as a policy of 'enlargement', which envisaged the United States seeking to enlarge democracies worldwide, rather than keeping tyrants in power. Though Washington abandoned its former African clients on whom it had lavished billions of dollars in arms and aid during the Cold War, Clinton's democratisation record in Africa was abysmal. Policy often resembled the Cold War era, as strategic rationales were found to justify a failure to support multiparty democracy in various African countries.[18] Despite the efforts of courageous African civil society activists and democrats to replace autocratic regimes in countries such as Benin, Mali, Niger, Zambia, Sierra Leone, and Nigeria, 'enlargement' of democracies was soon replaced by American support for a cantankerous warlord's gallery that Clinton, during a diplomatic safari to Africa in 1998, arrogantly dubbed Africa's 'new leaders': Uganda's Yoweri Museveni, Ethiopia's Meles Zenawi, Eritrea's Isais Afwerki, and Rwanda's Paul Kagame. None of these leaders could be accurately described as operating anything like a genuine multiparty system, and most of them were thinly disguised autocrats. No sooner had Clinton anointed them as Africa's model rulers than these leaders went to war against each other: Ethiopia and Eritrea fought a bloody border war between 1998 and 2000, while Uganda and Rwanda, after invading the DRC in a bid to topple the regime of Laurent Kabila in 1998, soon fell out over strategy and the spoils of war in the mineral-rich country and turned their guns on each other, killing scores of Congolese civilians in clashes in Kisangani.

Undoubtedly, the worst failures of US policy towards Africa in recent times were Clinton's actions in Somalia and Rwanda. In a secret, botched mission to hunt down Somali warlord Mohammed Farah Aideed, planned entirely by the Pentagon without the UN's knowledge, eighteen American soldiers and about a thousand Somalis, including women and children, were killed in October 1993. In order to deflect the strong domestic backlash and to prevent the Republican Party from generating political capital from these events, Clinton inaccurately blamed the military fiasco on the UN and withdrew his troops from the Horn of Africa, effectively crippling the mission without achieving peace in Somalia.[19]

Six months after the Somali debacle, the Clinton administration led efforts in the UN Security Council to force the withdrawal of most of a 2,500–strong

UN peacekeeping mission (which had no American soldiers) from Rwanda. As Canadian UN force commander Roméo Dallaire has often noted, the UN peacekeepers could probably have prevented the worst excesses of the Rwandan genocide if their mandate had been strengthened to enforce peace.[20] Washington, however, blocked any effective UN response to the killing of 800,000 people. It is important to note that the United States was not being asked to provide peacekeepers in Rwanda, but merely to mandate the UN to take action to save helpless victims of genocide. But with congressional midterm elections approaching in the United States, cynical political calculations took precedence over an international moral and legal obligation to prevent genocide. Clinton's officials were ordered not to describe the massacres as 'genocide' in a bid to escape pressure for the UN Security Council to mandate a military intervention to stop the massacres.

In the area of development, 85 per cent of American trade and investment in Africa was concentrated during the Clinton era, as it still largely is today, in four countries: the oil-rich trio of Nigeria, Angola, and Gabon, as well as South Africa. The fact that $2 billion of American aid annually has typically gone to the autocratic regime of Egypt (Israel receives over $3 billion a year), while forty-eight sub-Saharan African states, comprising some of the poorest countries in the world, usually have to share less than $1 billion, is the clearest sign that political and strategic considerations, rather than poverty and democratic considerations, continues to drive Washington's policy towards the continent. The US Congress passed the African Growth and Opportunity Act (AGOA) in May 2000, granting more generous access to African goods in selected sectors of the American market. The controversial act called for African countries to fight corruption, respect intellectual property, and remove barriers to US trade and investment (some thirty-seven African countries were deemed eligible for the programme by 2007). AGOA did yield some dividends for Africa. In the first seven months of 2002, African apparel exports to the United States exceeded $100 million, while an estimated 200,000 new jobs were created in Africa between 2000 and 2002 as a result of increased exports from AGOA.[21] But despite some progress, AGOA has had very limited success: the act allows market access to a limited number of African goods in selected sectors of the American market in exchange for low tariffs and free access for US investors to a wide range of African industries.[22] Most of the benefits of AGOA were also from oil imports to the US, which grew by 53 per cent in 2005, while non-oil African exports fell by 16 per cent. Significantly, AGOA did not envisage opening up America's wasteful and heavily subsidised agricultural sector—at a cost of $108.7 billion in 2005—in which Africa has a comparative advantage, with about 70 per cent of its population working in this vital sector.[23] By 2006, 93 per cent of AGOA imports were petroleum products. The foreign textile companies set up in Lesotho, Namibia, Malawi, Mauritius, and Swaziland—largely by companies from China, Malaysia, and Singapore—to take advantage of AGOA, also largely faltered: 20,000 textile jobs were lost in Lesotho between 2005 and 2007, while a Malaysian-run factory in Namibia closed down after only five years of operation.[24]

The Bush Administration, 2001–2008

Under the administration of George W. Bush between 2001 and 2008, Washington's foreign policy was almost universally perceived to be arrogant and unilateral. In what most of the world regarded as the illegal invasion of Iraq in March 2003, the United States was widely seen as behaving like a rogue elephant, throwing its weight around and trampling allies and enemies like grass under its rampaging feet. Bush's invasion of Iraq—undertaken without the authorisation of the UN Security Council—was seen to have undermined the authority of the UN, an organisation historically viewed with great reverence by African states as the best guarantor of their security and sovereignty.

Drawing on a sanctimonious, muscular, born-again Christianity, Bush's arrogant and deeply insulting insistence—in the days following terrorist attacks on the US on 11 September 2001—that the whole world decide whether it was 'with America or with the terrorists' came right out of an atavistic Old Testament world where doctrines such as 'an eye for an eye' reigned supreme. In this absolutist 'new world order' there was no more room for nuance or subtlety. One could not at the same time condemn terrorism and caution America not to kill innocent civilians in Afghanistan and Iraq in a vainglorious attempt to 'impose' democracy around the world through the barrel of a gun. The frequent depiction by Bush and his senior officials of America as a 'liberator' was also repugnant in its hypocrisy and historical inaccuracy—at least as viewed by Africans, Asians, Caribbeans, Latin Americans, and Middle Easterners who have suffered and in some cases continue to suffer from the brutality of American-backed tyrants.

Prominent Africans added their voices to the widespread criticisms of American unilateralism under the Bush administration. Former South African president Nelson Mandela launched a scathing attack before the United States invasion of Iraq in 2003: 'What I am condemning is that one power, with a president who has no foresight, who cannot think properly, is now willing to plunge the world into a holocaust. Why does the United States behave so arrogantly? ... Who are they now to pretend that they are the policeman of the world?'[25] Nigerian Nobel literature laureate Wole Soyinka also noted in March 2003: 'The present occupant of the White House in the United States of America is one of the most dangerous fanatics ever to bestride the destiny of the world.'[26] Pallo Jordan, chair of South Africa's foreign affairs parliamentary committee at the time, noted: 'What is projected here is an international community living under a "Pax Americana", underwritten by that country's overwhelming military power. The Machiavellian principle of: "It is better to be feared than loved", seems to be the watchword in D.C.'[27] African leaders were almost unanimous in expressing opposition to an American military invasion of Iraq. There were antiwar demonstrations on the 'African street' from the Cape to Cairo.[28]

The profound concern in Africa about Bush's 'war on terror' was that new justifications would be found—as occurred under the Clinton administration—to back autocratic allies who supported the United States in its declared hunt for terrorists, rather than supporting democratic allies and principles. The establishment in 2002 of a US military base and a joint Horn of Africa command in Djibouti, with about 1,500 soldiers and the goal of tracking terrorists in the region, may yet come to mirror Washington's support of autocratic governments in Kenya, Somalia, and Sudan during the Cold War. The support of these three countries was justified at the time by the need to protect strategic sea-lanes used for transporting oil from the Middle East. In 2003, Washington launched its $100 million East Africa Counter-Terrorism Initiative (EACTI) to provide training and equipment to states in the region, particularly Kenya and Ethiopia. The United States also strengthened security ties with Eritrea, while continuing to maintain strong ties with Ethiopia, with the aim of benefitting from the intelligence network of the preeminent military power on the Horn of Africa.

Another American counter-terrorist effort, the Pan-Sahel Initiative (PSI), worked with autocratic regimes in Mauritania and Chad. The US European Command further collaborated with Senegal, Gabon, Mali, Ghana, Uganda, Namibia, and South Africa to upgrade ports and airfields and signed access agreements allowing Washington to deploy rapidly to counter terrorists in Africa. In 2005, the $500 million five-year Trans-Sahara Counter-Terrorism Initiative (TSCTI) was launched to build the capacities of African states such as Algeria, Chad, Ghana, Mali, Morocco, Niger, Nigeria, Mauritania, and Tunisia to patrol borders and intercept terrorist groups.[29] Some African regimes appeared to be taking advantage of American fears about the spread of terrorism on the continent to crack down on domestic dissent. In a striking replay of Washington's response to the attacks of 11 September, Morocco, with its autocratic political system and draconian press laws,[30] rushed anti–terrorism legislation through its rubber-stamp parliament, allowing capital punishment against terror suspects. This followed the deadly suicide attacks in Casablanca in May 2003.[31] The US Central Intelligence Agency has also reportedly used Moroccan territory to question suspected terrorists, conducting interrogations that have often disregarded due process.[32] Other countries, such as Tanzania, have drawn up anti–terrorism legislation that civil libertarians have criticised as giving the government too much power to clamp down on genuine domestic dissent.

During the US presidential campaign of 2000, Bush had reiterated his lack of interest in Africa and subsequently spoke about Africa as if it was a country, rather than a continent. As he noted in June 2001: 'Africa is a nation that suffers from incredible disease.'[33] By 2006, the US Congress had cut funds for Bush's Millennium Challenge Account (MCA), launched in 2002 to assist African states. The rhetorical commitment of the administration to democratic governance was not matched by funds to promote the principle in Africa. The programme was slow to disburse funds (only $1.75 billion by 2006 instead of the $5 billion target), and only Madagascar, Cape Verde, and Benin had signed a 'compact' to receive assistance.[34] Like AGOA, the MCA laid down strict but nebulous criteria for African governments to receive funding, such as 'encouraging economic freedom', 'investing in people', and 'ruling justly'. These conditions were less than transparent, as autocratic regimes such as Burkina Faso and Gambia qualified for funding. Though Washington provided Africa with $4 billion of 'aid' in 2005, as much as $1.2 billion of this figure (25 per cent) was emergency food aid, mostly bought from US producers, shipped by American vessels, and distributed by US non-governmental organisations (NGOs). Only $517 million of these funds went directly to development assistance.[35]

While the Bush administration was critical of the increasingly autocratic regime of Robert Mugabe in Zimbabwe, it closely embraced the autocratic regime of Hosni Mubarak (in power for twenty-nine years in 2010 having banned his main opposition, the Muslim Brotherhood, and been frequently accused of human rights abuses), which still receives $2 billion annually in

American aid. Two oil-rich political strongmen were also welcomed to Washington: Gabon's late Omar Bongo, who was in power from 1967 until his death in June 2009, met with President Bush in May 2004; and Equatorial Guinea's Teodoro Obiang Nguema, who took power through a military coup three decades ago, met with Secretary of State Condoleezza Rice in April 2006. Both Bongo and Nguema had been criticised in US State Department reports for flouting human rights and engaging in massive corruption.

The one area, however, that the Bush administration can be given some credit for was its substantive contribution to the global battle against AIDS, announced in January 2003.[36] The President's Emergency Plan for AIDS Relief (PEPFAR) involved a five-year commitment of $9 billion between 2004 and 2008 to fifteen of the most heavily affected countries, including twelve in Africa: Botswana, Côte d'Ivoire, Ethiopia, Kenya, Mozambique, Namibia, Nigeria, Rwanda, South Africa, Tanzania, Uganda, and Zambia. However, questions have been raised as to why heavily affected countries such as Malawi and Lesotho were not included in the programme,[37] and some of the anti–abortion and anti–condom conditions attached to funding weakened the programme's effectiveness. Nevertheless, the Bush administration's provision of resources in this vital area far exceeded the spending of the Clinton administration, which talked a good game but delivered little to Africa.

The American-encouraged Ethiopian military invasion of Somalia in 2007, later backed by a Ugandan contingent under an AU flag, propped up a weak interim government in Mogadishu. This mission represented, to many in Africa, a misguided attempt that was utterly unable to stem the reckless bloodbath in Somalia; Ethiopia later withdrew its troops from Somalia in December 2008 after having suffered dozens of fatalities. The intervention was more of an auxiliary of Pax Americana's erratic 'war on terror' than a mission to promote sustainable peace on the Horn of Africa. As Kenyan scholar Ali Mazrui noted: 'I am saddened by it, as an admirer of the Ethiopian people, that they allowed themselves to be more or less bought by the Americans, to be their mercenaries in Somalia.'[38]

Equally disturbing to many Africans was the American decision in February 2007 to establish a new Africa Command (AFRICOM) on the continent by September 2008. This plan, championed strongly by Donald Rumsfeld—the cashiered former US defence secretary and architect of the Iraq debacle—was ostensibly meant to strengthen Washington's military cooperation with Africa. The details remained vague, but it seemed that the Pentagon was seeking to consolidate three commands covering Africa into one, in order to be able to intervene more effectively on the continent to fight terrorism, stem conflicts, and provide humanitarian assistance. This approach could further increase America's prioritising of militaristic anti–terrorist approaches towards engaging Africa. Although Africans were often assured by American planners that AFRICOM would not result in a large US military footprint on the continent and that Washington could deploy troops from bases elsewhere, Africa would be wise to reject such a close embrace with Uncle Sam and the dangers that such intimacy could bring for its own long-term security. Based on the history of US policy on the continent narrated here, Africa should be wary of a self-appointed American policeman offering to patrol the continent in search of enemies.[39] The election of Barack Obama—who had a Kenyan father—as the first black US president in November 2008, offered an opportunity for Washington to change the style and substance of its often pernicious policy towards Africa (see chapter 13).

France and Africa: Folie de Grandeur[40]

For nearly four decades after 1960, France's relations with its former African colonies smacked of a paternalistic neocolonialism.[41] Brazzaville had been the seat of General Charles de Gaulle's government-in-exile during the Second World War, and military victories in Africa had helped restore some French honour. As former French president François Mitterrand remarked in 1957: 'Without Africa, France will no longer have a history in the twenty-first century.'[42] Gabonese autocrat Omar Bongo reflected the other side of this clientelistic relationship: 'Africa without France is like a car without a driver. France without Africa is like a car without fuel.'[43] An intricate network of political, military, economic, and cultural ties have been used to promote what French leaders since de Gaulle have regarded as a *politique de grandeur*. France has attempted to use Africa to raise its status from a middle-ranking to a great power. With the end of the Cold War, the idea of an exclusive French sphere of influence in Africa has been increasingly challenged, leading to policy reversals in Rwanda and Zaire (now the DRC) that have left France's Africa policy in disarray.

France's policy in Africa has historically been one of *folie de grandeur:* a chronic delusion of greatness. Following Hitler's blitzkrieg in 1940 and military defeat in Vietnam's Dien Bien Phu in 1954 and Algeria in 1962, postwar France was a nation in deep psychological trauma. The Suez debacle of 1956 (when American and UN pressure led to a humiliating withdrawal of French,

British, and Israeli troops from Egypt) was a further blow to the already fragile national psyche. Britain drew the lesson from Suez that the world had changed from the 'gunboat diplomacy' of old to the superpower diplomacy of the nuclear age. France, however, attempted to cling to the illusion of remaining a great power by creating its own sphere of influence in Africa.[44] Paris had also sought an African empire after a humiliating defeat by Germany's Otto von Bismarck in 1871 (see chapter 1). After 1960, France lost an empire, but found a new role as an African power. In the process, as Ali Mazrui put it: 'De Gaulle succeeded in creating the impression that France in imperial decline was, at the same time, France in international ascendancy. French-speaking Africans continued to follow with awe.'[45]

La Gloire de Notre Père et l'Enfant Terrible

Charles de Gaulle created the 'imperial presidency' of the Fifth Republic in 1958 and attempted to reestablish France's grandeur through its African colonies. This was a form of diplomacy that entailed an emphasis on style over substance, as de Gaulle withdrew from NATO's military command in 1966, established an independent nuclear *force de frappe*, and railed against American 'economic imperialism' in Europe. In reality, France's economic recovery and military security still depended largely on the United States.

The Gallic quest for grandeur and glory demanded that in the 1950s, African leaders such as Léopold Senghor, Félix Houphouet-Boigny, Modibo Keita, and Sékou Touré were carted off to the National Assembly in Paris, where they served as *députés*. De Gaulle encouraged a paternalistic relationship, with some African leaders referring to him as 'Papa': they were his children, and as inexperienced infants they had to do as they were told. Under French rule, in countries such as Algeria—which was claimed as a French *département* despite the geographical absurdity of such a notion—Arabic was not allowed to be taught in schools, and students had to learn in French. France's relations with Africa were entrusted to one man in the Elysée Palace's shady Cellule Africiane (African Unit): Jacques Foccart. This *éminence grise* and *l'homme de l'ombre* ('the man of the shadows') was a master of the *secret du roi*, establishing his infamous *réseaux africains:* clandestine networks of spooks and soldiers, murderers and mercenaries, priests and policemen.

In a 1958 referendum, de Gaulle offered France's African colonies a choice between a Communauté Française, in which Paris would still retain control over their foreign and defence policy, or independence, in which France would sever all financial and economic ties. Only *l'enfant terrible*, Guinea's Sékou Touré, urged his people to vote *'oui'* to independence. Despite a 96 per cent vote in favour of independence, de Gaulle's riposte was that of a ruthless and vindictive father: all economic aid was stopped, Guinea was expelled from the franc zone, and telephones, archives, and civil service files were all carted back to France. *Liberté, égalité,* and *fraternité* were never principles to be applied to Africans. This was a clear lesson to other *enfants terribles:* there were enormous costs in disobeying Père de Gaulle. Though all francophone African countries were eventually granted nominal independence by 1963, all signed neocolonial cooperation agreements: economic and military pacts that gave France continued influence over their sovereign affairs.

Gendarme d'Afrique

There are three pillars to French policy in Africa: military, financial, and politico-cultural. By adroitly creating an intricate network of dependency around these areas, Paris was able to retain influence over its former African colonies. This was the patron-client system that came to be known as *Françafrique*.[46] The most sensitive areas of sovereignty (defence, foreign, and monetary policies) were circumscribed by post-independence agreements with all of France's former possessions.[47] Paris also maintained military bases in Djibouti, the Central African Republic, Côte d'Ivoire, Gabon, and Senegal.

Since 1960, the French gendarme has acted like a 'pyromaniac fireman', intervening about forty times in countries such as Cameroon, the Central African Republic, Chad, Congo-Brazzaville, Côte d'Ivoire, Djibouti, Gabon, Mauritania, Niger, Rwanda, Senegal, Togo, and Zaire, often to prop up dictators in trouble. As former French foreign minister Louis de Guiringaud arrogantly put it: 'Africa is the only continent ... where [France] can still with 300 men, change the course of history.'[48] In the most extraordinary incident, Paris flew David Dacko to the Central African Republic in 1979 to replace tyrannical leader Jean-Bédél Bokassa. Bokassa had squandered a third of his country's national income on staging a Napoleonic coronation, crowning himself Emperor Bokassa I in 1977. His killing of schoolchildren and the revelation of a gift of diamonds to President Valéry Giscard d'Estaing finally proved too embarrassing, even for France. Giscard thus toppled a hunting companion he had once described as France's best friend in Africa. The French argument that the country's military agreements in Africa ensured political stability was clearly bogus: between 1963 and 1966, there were thirteen coup attempts in francophone Africa. French interventions also often kept despotic dinosaurs such as Zaire's Mobutu Sese Seko, Togo's Gnassingbé Eyadéma, and Gabon's Omar Bongo in power long after their sell-by dates.

La Chasse Gardée

The franc zone saw thirteen francophone African states tying their CFA (Communauté Française Africaine) franc to the French franc, with Paris effectively controlling the zone's central banks and the French treasury holding all their foreign reserves. Eighty thousand French expatriates flooded into Africa *pour faire le* CFA. French industrial giants such as CFAO, SCOA, Elf-Aquitaine, and Bouyges continued to monopolise markets they had cornered in colonial days, in a clear sign of the continued 'Curse of Berlin'. France's cooperation agreements gave it priority access to Africa's strategic minerals: by 1995, Gabon and Niger provided Paris with 100 per cent of its uranium, Guinea 90 per cent of its bauxite, and Cameroon, Congo-Brazzaville, and Gabon 70 per cent of its oil.[49] In return, France channelled 80 per cent of its foreign aid to francophone Africa, although some of this was tied to compulsory purchases of French products at inflated prices.

For a while, the franc zone created a stable, convertible currency that helped economic growth and attracted foreign investment. But devaluations in Ghana and Nigeria led to smuggling and uncompetitive industries in the zone. The overvalued CFA franc also resulted in capital flight and distressed banks. An important aspect of French policy was to keep Nigeria and other trespassers out of its *pré carré* (backyard) or *chasse gardée* (private hunting-ground). De Gaulle therefore sent arms to Biafran secessionists during Nigeria's civil war of 1967 to 1970, while President Georges Pompidou encouraged francophone states to create their own economic community to counter Nigeria's strength in the Economic Community of West African States (ECOWAS), which was established in 1975 to promote economic integration (see chapter 6).

La Francophonie

Presidents Georges Pompidou (1969–1974), Valéry Giscard d'Estaing (1974–1981), François Mitterrand (1981–1995), and Jacques Chirac (1995–2007) all continued de Gaulle's activist Africa policy. France created its Rue Monsieur (Ministry of Cooperation) in 1961 to conduct its Africa policy. The

Quai d'Orsay (Ministry of Foreign Affairs) was simply bypassed, allowing the Elysée (presidency) to continue its peculiar form of personalised diplomacy with African autocrats. Pompidou extended French influence to the former Belgian colonies of Burundi, Rwanda, and Zaire, and established a biannual Franco-African summit in 1973. Mitterrand created a wider *francophonie* involving Canada, Vietnam, and the Levant in 1986, and set up a *ministère de la francophonie*. In 1996, France spent over $1 billion on promoting its language and culture abroad. Since 1969, Paris has also sponsored a film festival in the Burkinabè capital of Ouagadougou which has contributed positively to the development of African cinema.

At international forums such as the UN and the Organisation of African Unity (OAU), twenty-two francophone African states often supported France, even on issues such as decolonisation, French arms sales to apartheid South Africa, and French nuclear testing in the Algerian Sahara. In Gabon, the French ambassador frequently attended cabinet meetings, while Gabonese officials submitted annual reports of imports from nonfrancophone countries for French approval.[50] French officers continued to serve in the Senegalese army and Côte d'Ivoire's civil service until the 1970s. French *coopérants* provided technical assistance to African ministries, sometimes overruling ministers and acting as powers behind the throne. *La francophonie*, though, is a somewhat hollow concept in Africa. Despite the aping of French culture by a few culturally assimilated elites, over 70 per cent of so-called francophone Africans do not, in fact, speak French. The often quoted statistic that the DRC is the world's second largest francophone country is a misguided illusion: most Congolese are illiterate farmers who are more concerned with basic survival than *haute couture*. France's preposterous *mission civilisatrice* was largely used to enslave the vast majority of its colonial subjects, while a tiny elite played at being black Frenchmen, carrying baguettes under their armpits in cities such as Abidjan, Ouagadougou, and Libreville.

La Fin d'Une Époque

By 1990, pro-democracy demonstrations in Benin, Côte d'Ivoire, Gabon, and Niger had forced many francophone states to adopt various forms of multiparty democracy. At the Franco-African summit in the French town of La Baule in 1990, Mitterrand announced a policy shift that was subsequently dubbed Paristroika: it sought to link continued aid to democratic reforms. But the French applied democracy inconsistently, sanctioning sham elections in Burkina Faso, Chad, Côte d'Ivoire, Cameroon, Gabon, Niger, and Togo between 1992 and 1996, and resuming aid to fraudulent, undemocratic regimes. Having periodically rigged elections in its African possessions during colonial times, it has been easy for France to condone undemocratic behaviour in Africa. Former president Chirac described democracy as a 'luxury' for Africa, demonstrating a paternalism that is all too typical of the French political class, many of whose members—including Chirac himself—have themselves often been embroiled in sleaze and scandals. Countries such as Côte d'Ivoire and Gabon funded the political campaign of Gaullist parties, which returned the favour upon assuming parliamentary power in 1993. Mitterrand's son, Jean-Christophe—nicknamed *Papa-m'a-dit* ('Daddy told me')— ran Africa policy from the Elysée in a Foccartiste manner, establishing close personal relations with African autocrats and eventually becoming embroiled in a corruption scandal. Gabon provided French oil giant Elf with a quarter of its oil in 1989 and close personalized relations were established with the autocratic and corrupt Omar Bongo until his death in June 2009. In Congo-Brazzaville, the equally corrupt and autocratic Denis Sassou Nguesso formed close personal ties with Elf-Congo, which controlled 75 per cent of the country's oil production and lent him $6 billion. Both African dictators also reportedly bought property in France.[51]

However, the deaths of Ivorian leader Félix Houphouet-Boigny in 1993 and Jacques Foccart in 1997 symbolised a definite *fin d'une époque* in Franco-African relations. These two figures were the most symbiotic of the personalised relationship between France and Africa: Houphouet-Boigny was the unrivalled doyen and sage of francophone African diplomacy, and the most respected interlocutor between France and Africa; Foccart was, for over two decades, the most influential French official in African affairs. In the post–Cold War era, modernisers eventually appeared within the French political establishment who favoured *l'ouverture:* a policy of ending the 'special relationship' with francophone Africa and focusing more on Eastern Europe and Asia. On entering the Hôtel Matignon in 1993, patrician premier Edouard Balladur enunciated the famous 'Balladur Doctrine'—sometimes also referred to as the 'Abidjan Doctrine'—of withholding future French assistance to African states until they had signed up to the strict dictates of the World Bank and the International Monetary Fund (IMF). Paris thus signalled an end to *la fin du mois:* payment of civil service salaries in francophone Africa by the French treasury.

The 50 per cent devaluation of the CFA franc in January 1994 dealt a devastating blow to the Franco-African relationship. For four decades, the CFA had been tied to the French franc at an exchange rate of one to fifty. Not surprisingly, African leaders regarded the *fait accompli* as treacherous; as some noted at the time, it was as if an umbilical cord had been broken. France's commitment to the *franc fort* and efforts to reduce its own budget deficit to qualify for the European Monetary Union (EMU) in 1999 were more pressing priorities (see chapter 12). France thus shifted its African burden to Bretton Woods institutions it had earlier castigated as being neoimperialist American creatures.

Events in Africa's Great Lakes region further revealed France's weakening grip on its former colonies and exposed the bankruptcy of its Africa policy. Having armed and given military support to the Hutu-dominated regime of Juvénal Habyarimana in Rwanda in its struggle against the Uganda-based, Tutsi–dominated Rwandan Patriotic Front (RPF), France's clients lost power to the RPF by June 1994.[52] The new Rwandan regime—seen as part of an 'Anglo-Saxon' plot due to its close ties to Uganda in what has been dubbed France's 'Fashoda syndrome', again underlining the legacy of Berlin—was excluded from the Franco-African summit in Biarritz in 1994. Paris also tried to prevent European Union (EU) funds going to Rwanda; its Opération Turquoise of July 1994 allowed Hutu *génocidaires* who had massacred 800,000 mainly Tutsi civilians to escape into Eastern Zaire, and human right groups implicated France in continued military assistance (including providing training, supplying arms, and engaging in diplomatic contacts) to its former genocidal Hutu allies.[53]

Events in the DRC in 1997 would further see Paris wrong-footed in its support for a sinking Mobutu Sese Seko. In May 1996, angry protestors burnt down the French cultural centre in the Central African Republic. (An angry crowd had similarly burned down the French consulate, resulting in the intervention of French legionnaires in 1991.) In the Central African Republic in January 1997, a bloody French reprisal in revenge for the killing of two French officers left a hundred civilians and fifty mutinous African soldiers dead.[54] This followed a pattern established in colonial times: in Madagascar in 1947, French soldiers massacred an estimated 86,000 Madagascans after a raid by independence fighters on a French military base; while over 1 million Algerians were killed in France's savage colonial war between 1954 and 1962. Proving further that old habits die hard, in October 1997, Paris helped Denis Sassou-Nguesso use military means to topple the elected government of Pascal Lissouba in Congo-Brazzaville.[55]

There were other important developments in Franco-African relations during this period. Under the socialist government of Lionel Jospin between

1997 and 2002, the administration pursued an Africa policy described as 'neither interference, nor indifference'.[56] The budget of the Rue Monsieur was slashed from 8.3 billion French francs in 1992 to 6.7 billion in 1997, and the ministry has since been absorbed into the Quai d'Orsay. Meanwhile, the French military presence in Africa was reduced from 8,000 to about 5,600, leading to the closure of two military bases in the Central African Republic in April 1998. France now seeks increasingly to intervene in African countries such as the DRC and Chad under the multilateral cover of the EU and/or the UN. But as long as France retains its historical quest for grandeur, as long as African despots continue to deliver votes in diplomatic forums and to fund French political campaigns, as long as French businesses continue to profit from cosy and sometimes corrupt African relationships, and as long as French national pride remains tied to an image of cultural superiority, France is unlikely to disengage totally from its African 'sphere of influence'.

Adieu, l'Afrique?

As France's xenophobic and draconian immigration laws are brutally applied to African citizens, leaders such as Mali's former president and chair of the AU Commission between 2003 and 2008, Alpha Konaré, openly criticised the excesses of the 'mother country'. The European Court of Human Rights and human rights NGOs have condemned France for the use of torture and other abuses. By 1990, nearly 5 million Muslims were living in France. During the 1991 Gulf War, French Muslims were openly suspected of being 'fifth columnists'. Populist politicians such as Interior Minister Charles Pasqua fanned the flames of populist xenophobia by suggestions in the late 1980s of stripping the citizenship of children born in France to immigrant parents. Muslim girls wearing *foulards* soon started being expelled from French public schools. By July 2009, French president Nicolas Sarkozy was seeking to ban their wearing in public. The infamous Debré law in 1997 was a throwback to the Nazi era: citizens were asked to report anyone harbouring foreigners to the authorities, as asylum rights were being effectively rescinded. In the 1990s, despite complaints that foreigners were stealing jobs from French citizens, 30 per cent of North African youths in France (most of them French citizens) were unemployed, and 50 per cent of black Africans in France were unemployed, compared to a national unemployment rate of 12 per cent. The environment was ripe for Jean-Marie Le Pen, a fascist, right-wing populist and former military parachutist, to spread fear and xenophobia. In the event, Le

Pen won 15 per cent of presidential votes in 1995, which he increased to 17 per cent seven years later, making it into a second-round runoff with President Chirac. That nearly one in five French citizens were prepared to vote for an openly racist politician was itself a disturbing sign of the Gallic loss of a national moral compass.[57] As British academic Theodore Zeldin perceptively noted about the myth of French cultural 'exceptionalism':

The real cause of dissatisfaction with foreigners in France comes not from the French feeling humiliated by borrowing from America or from other countries, but from an annoyance that foreigners are not borrowing much in return. It is the absence of exchange that is galling to the pride. But the more they insist that they are different from others, the more they discourage foreigners from borrowing.[58]

The changing relationship between France and Africa was further evidenced in Côte d'Ivoire, a country embroiled in civil war since 2002, in which 4,600 French troops are deployed alongside a UN peacekeeping force. In one of his typically arrogant moments during a visit to Senegal in February 2005, President Chirac complained that the peace process in Côte d'Ivoire was too slow because the South Africans did not understand 'the soul and psychology of West Africans'. Regional actors, not least the South African president at the time, Thabo Mbeki, were taken aback by the arrogance and insensitivity of this statement, which underlined the continuing paternalism with which many French politicians, demonstrating the lingering after-effects of the 'Curse of Berlin', still regard their former colonies. In November 2004, after government soldiers in search of rebels killed nine French soldiers in the northern city of Bouaké, French troops destroyed the entire Ivorian air force of nine planes, resulting in violent demonstrations against French interests and a mass evacuation of 10,000 mostly French citizens from Côte d'Ivoire. Jittery French troops killed at least fifty demonstrators outside Abidjan's Hôtel Ivoire. The distrust between the former colonial master and many Ivorians—fanned by a government that feared that Paris was bent on its removal—soon reached new heights. Ivorian leader Laurent Gbagbo's supporters accused France of trying to 'recolonise' the country by using 'agents' such as Burkina Faso. While Gbagbo talked of leaving the French-dominated CFA franc currency zone, his hard-line speaker of parliament, Mamadou Coulibaly, called for a complete break with the former colonial power.[59]

The election of President Nicolas Sarkozy in May 2007 saw the rise to power in France of a former right-wing interior minister (2002–2004; and 2005–2007) who had increased police harassment of immigrants. In 2005, Sarkozy had infamously dismissed the alienated and marginalised rioting

Maghrebi and black African youth in Paris's hopeless, impoverished *banlieues* (suburbs), calling them *'racaille'* (scum) who needed to be cleaned up with a water-hose. This was after French police had allegedly accidentally electrocuted two immigrant youths they had been chasing. Sarkozy had also earlier supported the US invasion of Iraq.[60] This acerbic, deeply prejudiced politician did not waste time in revealing his true colours on the global stage. During a speech in Dakar in July 2007, Sarkozy noted: 'One cannot blame everything on colonisation—the corruption, the dictators, the genocide, that is not colonisation.' He went on to note that France might have made 'mistakes', but believed in its 'civilising mission ... and did not exploit anybody'. The French pseudo-philosophical president then incredibly noted: 'Africans have never really entered history. They have never really launched themselves into the future. In a world where nature controls everything, man has remained immobile in the middle of an unshakable order where everything is determined. There is no room either for human endeavour, nor for the idea of progress.' This speech was widely condemned in West Africa, by the AU Commission chair at the time, Alpha Konaré, and in some French intellectual circles. Thabo Mbeki, who had earlier been insulted by Chirac, sent Sarkozy a bizarre letter published in *Le Monde*, praising parts of the same speech and noting: 'What you have said in Dakar, Mr President, has indicated to me that we are fortunate to count you as a citizen of Africa, as a partner in the long struggle for a true African renaissance in the context of a European renaissance.'[61]

Achille Mbembe's eloquent riposte perhaps best captures the surprise of many in Africa: 'That two years before he exits power, Mbeki would tie his impeccable pan-Africanist credentials to Sarkozy is but the latest paradox in the political journey of a man who has thrived on contradictions' (see chapter 11).[62] A few days later, Sarkozy returned the favour to Mbeki by calling for the Group of Eight (G8) industrialised countries to be expanded to a G13, with South Africa as the only African country in this proposed new club! (A Group of 20, with South African membership, eventually met in London in April 2009). Sarkozy subsequently made a state visit to South Africa in March 2008. Paris continued to back autocrats Didier Ratsiraka in Madagascar until 2002 and Gnassingbé Eyadéma in Togo until his death in 2005, again due partly to fears of their 'Anglo-Saxon'–influenced opponents: Marc Ravalomanana and Gilchrist Olympio. This paranoid attitude again underlined the continuing curse of the 'Fashoda syndrome'. France also provided military support to prop up the autocratic regimes of Chad's Idriss Déby and the Central African Republic's François Bozizé as late as 2006,[63] and saved the Déby regime from falling again in 2008. But these actions may well represent the last gasps of a dying French gendarme. This century will surely see the end of five decades of an often sordid and pernicious relationship between France and Africa. Paris will most likely retain interests in wealthier countries such as Cameroon, Congo-Brazzaville, and Gabon, and is already trading more profitably with South Africa, Nigeria, and Algeria, and involving nonfrancophone countries in its diplomatic summits and military training programmes. When France does decide to bid a final farewell to Africa, all those with a genuine concern for the future of the continent will heave a huge sigh of relief. In the post–Cold War era, French intervention has become a costly anachronism and a relic of a bygone age of neocolonial delusion. A fitting epitaph on the tombstone of the extinct gendarme could read: *'C'est magnifique, mais ce n'est pas la grandeur'* (It's magnificent, but it's not greatness).

Concluding Reflections

This chapter has assessed comparatively the roles of China, the United States, and France in Africa. Unlike Paris and Washington, Beijing was a member of the global South and acted with the Group of 77 developing countries at the UN, often portraying itself—even now—as an anticolonial power and a poor, developing country. China benefitted from Third World support to gain its seat on the UN Security Council in 1971 and used its powerful position in the world body to deflect criticisms of its policies on the UN Human Rights Commission (now the Human Rights Council) and other international bodies. In the current age, Beijing still employs the rhetoric of anticolonialism and noninterference in its dealings with Africa, but the country is in fact becoming a more status quo power and less revisionist Third World ally wanting to overturn an unjust international system dominated by Western great powers. As China grows richer and becomes tied ever deeper into a web of Western investments, trade, and global institutions, the country relies increasingly on the West to maintain its staggering growth rates. China—already one of five veto-wielding permanent members of the UN Security Council—was admitted into the World Trade Organisation (WTO) in 2001.

For all the talk about Africa and China, the West still remains far more important politically and economically to China than Africa. Beijing also seeks the West's acceptance far more than it does Africa's. China's sensitivity to Western criticisms over human rights issues in Tibet before its hosting of the 2008 Olympics clearly demonstrated this fact. Beijing's larger interests are likely to continue to coincide more with the West's than with Africa's, though Chinese economic rivalry is also likely to continue with the United States, France, and other countries in the quest for Africa's resources. Like American firms, French companies have lost contracts to Chinese firms in places such as Angola and Gabon. This will be a complex relationship of cooperation and competition. China has started to play a more assertive role on the UN Security Council, as evidenced by its taking the lead on UN action in Sudan and Somalia in 2007, and by its deployment of peacekeepers to six UN missions in Africa. The one advantage that Beijing has over its Western rivals is that most African leaders do not perceive it to be a neoimperial power.[64] This is indicated by the strong admiration expressed by most of the forty-three African leaders that made the trip to the FOCAC summit in Beijing in 2006.

Many African leaders seem to view China—in contrast to countries such as the United States and France—as representing an opportunity to increase their leverage towards the West. That Beijing is prepared to invest in the much-needed infrastructure that Africa badly needs for its industrial takeoff, and that China's purchase of Africa's raw materials has helped to increase global prices, have been widely seen as positive for the continent. But it should also be noted that many African countries are still politically, economically, and culturally tied more closely to the West than to China. Anglo-Saxon and French culture are far more pervasive in Africa than Chinese influence, though kung fu movies starring Bruce Lee and others have been a staple diet on the continent for decades. Africans still travel much more to the West than to China, and most Africans seeking education abroad still prefer Western institutions to Chinese ones. American, French and British universities and military institutions are thus still more likely to educate future African leaders than Chinese ones. Washington and Paris also still have much larger, often long-standing military and trade ties on the continent than does Beijing. One should therefore not exaggerate China's ability to dislodge Western interests from Africa in the short term. While China's trade with Africa was $50.5 billion in 2006, US trade with the continent was $71.1 billion.[65] It must also be noted that, though Washington has been critical of China's role in Sudan and Angola, contacts and cooperation between American and Chinese officials on Africa—through a China-US dialogue—are increasing, and appear to have been helpful in efforts to deploy the UN-AU peacekeeping force to Darfur in 2007.

The principal fear about US policy towards Africa remains that its 'anti–communist' support for autocratic regimes during the Cold War could be replaced by an 'anti–terrorist' support for similar regimes in the post–Cold

War era. As with China, African leaders must be strategic about seeking to support more positive aspects of US policy, such as the funding of HIV/AIDS programmes, while trying to improve initiatives such as AGOA (trade) through pro-Africa lobbies in the US Congress and through American NGOs. Pressure must also be put on Washington to use its clout in institutions like the WTO, the World Bank, and the IMF—where it plays a dominant role—to ensure a greater Southern voice, fairer trade for Africa, and an annulment of the continent's external debt of $290 billion. The United States must be urged to support democratisation, economic development, and integration efforts in Africa more effectively. France appears to be loosening its old neocolonial ties with Africa, not only because the anachronistic system of *Françafrique* has been widely discredited by embarrassing policy failures in Rwanda and the DRC, but also because it has become financially difficult for Paris to maintain extensive military bases and financial support for its twenty-two former colonies on its own. France has thus sought increasingly to share this burden with its allies through three key means. First, Paris has engaged key countries like South Africa and Nigeria, which it would previously have simplistically lumped into an 'Afro-Saxon' camp.[66]

Second, Paris has encouraged its former colonies to sign up to structural adjustment programmes with Bretton Woods institutions it had previously dismissed as instruments of Anglo-Saxon control. The third approach has been to multilateralise French initiatives by using the EU and the UN to lend cover to largely unilateral geostrategic military interventions in the DRC, Chad, and Côte d'Ivoire. There remain elements of change and continuity in France's Africa policy. Nicolas Sarkozy's rise to power, however, has failed to convince Africans that the French leopard is capable of changing its spots.

It is however not only China's post–Cold War relations with Western powers in Africa that could trigger controversy. Beijing's ties with key African actors could also ruffle feathers. Former South African president Thabo Mbeki warned in December 2006 that Africa risked entering into a 'colonial relationship' with China if the continent continued to export raw materials to the country while importing Chinese manufactured goods. But another danger is that both South Africa and China could come to be regarded as the new 'economic imperialists' in Africa. Tensions have been reported in the DRC, where Beijing provided a $5 billion loan for infrastructure projects in 2007 in one of South Africa's most strategically important countries. However, as with Western actors in Africa like the United States and France, both rivalry and cooperation are the more likely outcome of this growing relationship between Beijing and Tshwane (see chapter 9).

AN AXIS OF EVIL?

China, the United States, and France are all engaged in the epic game of Great Power rivalry, for which Africa is again—as in the era of the Conference of Berlin and the Cold War—providing a backdrop and a grand stage. All three powers are pursuing economic, military, and political strategies to augment their own interests, and they broadly (perhaps with the exception of France) seem to know what they want from Africa and how to pursue it as part of an overall global strategy. African leaders, however, do not seem to know what they collectively want from these three powers, and how to use their newfound leverage with China's increasing presence on the continent to pursue their own goals and produce more mutually beneficial relationships. Africa must act strategically to define its own interests and negotiate more skilfully and firmly to ensure that these three powers continue to provide infrastructure projects in ways that promote regional integration; that the United States and France remove agricultural subsidies that hurt African farmers; that the three powers contribute to peacemaking efforts in Africa in less self-interested ways; that Africans, and not citizens of these countries, lead projects on the continent; that infant industries on the continent not be destroyed and that investments be made in ways that allow Africa to grow; and that regimes abusing human rights and rattling sabres not be provided with arms and political support. Only then can a potential 'axis of evil' be transformed into an 'axis of virtue'.

9

THE SPRINGBOK AND THE DRAGON

SOUTH AFRICA VS. CHINA IN AFRICA[1]

'If we can take the Congo, we can have all of Africa.'[2]

Mao Zedong, leader of China, 1949–1976

This chapter examines the relationship between South Africa and China since 1994. We assess mercantilist perceptions of both countries on the continent, analyse their bilateral relationship, and examine relationships of potential and real competition in seven strategic countries (Angola, Zimbabwe, Zambia, the Democratic Republic of the Congo [DRC], Nigeria, Sudan, and Tanzania) across three African subregions. South Africa is depicted as a springbok based on the fact that many of its corporate investors in the rest of Africa are mostly white. There are about 5,000 white South African businessmen in Tanzania, most of whom are Afrikaners. The springbok is of course the animal that has symbolised the largely Afrikaner South African rugby team since 1912. Afrikaners saw rugby as a 'macho' sport requiring 'physical resilience and collective discipline' and, from the 1930s, the sport was used as part of the Afrikaner 'nationalist project'. Many have also described rugby as a second religion for Afrikaners. By the 1960s, many captains and coaches of the Springboks were members of the National Party and the Broederbond (a secret society of powerful individuals who wielded tremendous political clout), and nearly all the managers of the national rugby team belonged to the Broederbond.[3] This background makes Nelson Mandela's donning of the Springbok jersey in willing the team to victory during the 1995 rugby World Cup in South Africa (an event celebrated in Clint Eastwood's 2009 movie *Invictus*) all the more remarkable, and legitimises our own use of the term for South Africa. Regarding the depiction of China as a dragon, this is of course a common, widespread, and clichéd symbol that has often been used to suggest an image of fire-breathing, aggressive Chinese corporations rampaging through the continent (see chapter 8).

There are some similarities between South Africa and China historically. Both are economic and political giants in their regions that are feared as well as envied. Whereas the Frontline States established the Southern African Development Coordination Conference (SADCC)[4] in 1980—now the Southern African Development Community (SADC)—to counter and isolate apartheid South Africa, the Association of Southeast Asian Nations (ASEAN)[5] was established in part to counter China's military strength. Each country has its own larger-than-life 'Founding Father', Nelson Mandela and Mao Zedong. While Deng Xiaoping—with his 'Open Door' policy—was responsible for opening China up to the world in 1978, Thabo Mbeki—with his African Renaissance—was responsible for opening up Africa to South Africa after 1999. Just as the 2008 Olympic Games represented the 'coming-out' party of China as a Great Power, the 2010 football World Cup established South Africa, which hosted the event, as a regional power with global aspirations. Both countries are dominant-party states with ruling parties—the African National Congress (ANC) and the Chinese Communist Party (CCP)—that were once committed to economic policies of controlling the 'commanding heights' of their economies, which they pragmatically abandoned in pursuit of a market economy. The labour practices of firms from both countries on the continent have been questioned, with both South Africa and China being accused of mercantilist behaviour. South Africans and Chinese also periodically display signs of nationalism, with Chinese leaders and scholars touting their great ancient civilisation, and their South African counterparts touting their world-class infrastructure and democratic institutions. These nationalisms appear to be attempts to gain acceptance into the Western 'whiteman's club', despite the widespread grinding poverty in both countries.

But there are, of course, also substantial differences between South Africa and China. While South Africa has a functioning democratic system and a vibrant media, China's omnipotent Communist Party continues to block political and press freedoms. While South Africa is increasingly accepted as a regional power and aspires to a permanent seat on the UN's fifteen-member

Security Council (see chapter 5), China is increasingly becoming a global power and is one of only five veto-wielding members of the UN Security Council (along with the United States, Russia, Britain, and France). While South Africa, the continent's wealthiest country, is a medium-sized global economy, China had the world's second largest economy in 2010 (after the US). While South Africa has a population of about 48 million, China has 1.3 billion people, the largest population in the world and about one-fifth of the global total. While China topped the gold medal table at the Beijing Olympics in 2008, very few expected South Africa's Bafana Bafana (the national team) to qualify for the second round of the football World Cup in 2010.

Just as Coca-Cola and McDonalds have spread American 'cultural imperialism' around the globe, South African fast-food chains like Nando's, Steers, and Chicken Licken are becoming household names across Africa as a veritable example of the country's 'soft power of the belly'. Nando's has even gone global, with its chains rapidly increasing in London, Oxford, Leeds, Cambridge, and other British cities, in a startling example of cultural 'counter-penetration'[6] in which Western consumers have embraced a successful African fast-food export. South African Breweries' (SAB) purchase of Miller—making it amongst the largest beer manufacturers in the world—ensures that Africa will be able to compete as a super-heavyweight in the global 'beer wars'. Shoprite's seventy-two outlets in the rest of Africa could make it the continent's 'supermarket of choice'. NuMetro has also spread out continentally; its cinemas now connect African filmgoers to the latest Hollywood fare, and have turned South Africa into a Trojan horse for exporting American culture to the rest of Africa.

Culturally, Chinese movies and particularly kung fu movies like Bruce Lee's *Enter the Dragon* have been a staple diet for Africa's masses for fifty years. Chinese restaurants are also plentiful in all parts of Africa, as they are all over the world. Two generations of African students have been trained in Chinese institutions, while Beijing has facilitated and supported a franchise system of Confucius Institutes[7] to promote greater understanding of Chinese culture and the teaching of Mandarin to rival similar initiatives in Africa by the US Information Agency, Alliance Française, and the British Council. Chinese programmes appear increasingly on African satellite television. There is a Chinatown in Johannesburg, with Chinese citizens having controversially been granted access to South Africa's Black Economic Empowerment (BEE) programme, which benefits historically disadvantaged groups. Chinese traders and communities live in Lagos, Khartoum, and Windhoek. There have even been reports of members of the estimated 80,000 Chinese workers in Africa giving birth to mixed-race babies in remote parts of Ghana. At a higher level of society, Jean Ping, the former foreign minister of Gabon and chair of the African Union (AU) Commission since 2008, is half-Chinese, the offspring of a Chinese trader father and a Gabonese mother. The seed of China's social penetration is spreading throughout Africa as surely as its economic influence. But Western cultural influence and trade still far surpass Chinese penetration of Africa, and the continent's future leaders and coup-makers are still more likely to be trained in American, British, French, Belgian, and Portuguese institutions than in Chinese ones.

Both South Africa and China have worked together in global forums and groupings such as the Group of 77 (G77), the Non-Aligned Movement (NAM), the World Trade Organisation (WTO) and the Group of 20 (G20) to seek a fairer global trading system; collaborated within the UN Security Council between 2007 and 2008 to thwart Western policies on Iran and Zimbabwe; and pushed for a restructuring of the World Bank and the International Monetary Fund (IMF) to give greater voice to non-Western states. The two main questions that this chapter seeks to address, however, are whether South Africa and China will become collaborators or competitors in post–Cold War Africa; and whether their roles will come to be perceived negatively as those of 'economic imperialists' on the continent. Both countries, for example, secure much of their oil supplies from Nigeria and Angola, which are South Africa's top two continental trading partners respectively, while Angola and Nigeria are China's first and fourth largest trading partners in Africa respectively. Nigeria and Angola are also the only two countries in Africa with which South Africa has a negative trade balance, and are the fastest-growing markets for South African investments on the continent.[8]

Before assessing the role of South Africa and China in Africa, it is important to note that we categorically reject the hypocritical efforts of many Western 'Orientalists' to convince Africans how bad and evil the rapacious Chinese 'mercantilists' are for the continent (see chapter 8). While we do not condone Beijing's support for corrupt regimes in oil-rich Sudan and Angola, such actions must at least be examined in context to avoid the Orwellian-inspired approach of many Western analysts of some pigs being more equal than others.[9] China's approach to Africa at least appears to treat the continent in a dynamic manner as a market for consumer goods rather than just a dumping ground for humanitarian charity, as some Western governments seem to perceive the continent.[10]

Friends or Foes? The Sino–South African Relationship

Because apartheid South Africa had recognised Taiwan, and China had traded covertly with the racist regime in Pretoria (while also supporting South Africa's liberation struggle), as well as supported apartheid South African–backed anti–Soviet rebels in Angola, Mozambique, and Nigeria during these countries' civil wars, diplomatic relations between the 'new' South Africa and the People's Republic of China (PRC) were not established until January 1998. High-level visits have since occurred, with then–South African deputy president Thabo Mbeki visiting Beijing in April 1998, and president Nelson Mandela visiting China in May 1999. In April 2000, Chinese president Jiang Zemin visited South Africa, with both countries pledging to build South-South cooperation and to restructure Western dominance of the global economic architecture.[11] South Africa and China established a binational commission in 2001—the only one of its kind established with an African country at the time[12]—through which to coordinate their bilateral relations and to promote increased investment, trade, skills transfer, and cultural exchanges. Thabo Mbeki paid a state visit to China with a business delegation in December 2001 to practicalise these ideas. The binational commission met in both countries three times between 2001 and 2007, during which time a centre for Chinese studies was established at Stellenbosch University, a $5 billion China-Africa development fund was created, with its headquarters in Johannesburg, and a free trade agreement was planned between China and the countries of the Southern African Customs Union (SACU): South Africa, Botswana, Swaziland, Lesotho, and Namibia.

Trade between South Africa and China, enhanced by the establishment of the South Africa–China Business Association (SACBA), increased from $1.5 billion in 1997 to about $9 billion in 2006. Between 2006 and 2008, South Africa became Beijing's second largest trading partner in Africa after Angola, with 16 per cent of total continental trade in 2008.[13] While China exports manufactured and agricultural goods, electronics, and textiles to South Africa, it imports manganese, gold, copper, tobacco, aluminium, car parts, and chrome ore. This is the most diversified bilateral relationship that China has on the continent. Most of Beijing's other trade in Africa is based solely on importing raw materials and minerals. Beijing also exports electronic goods to ten other, mostly Southern African countries, using South Africa as a base. Another difference between the more economically advanced South Africa and other African countries is that South African brand-names such as SAB Miller, Anglo Gold Ashanti, Anglo American, Standard Bank, BHP Billiton, and Spur all have a presence in China. By 2007, South Africa had over 200 projects in China worth over $330 million.[14]

Tensions in this relationship have revolved around Chinese exports of garments, which led to an estimated 23,000–85,000 South African job losses, in response to which South African labour unions successfully lobbied their government for curbs on Chinese imports in 2006.[15] Former South African president Thabo Mbeki warned in December 2006 that Africa risked entering into a 'colonial relationship' with Beijing if the continent continued to export raw materials to China while importing Chinese manufactured goods. At the 2006 Forum on China-Africa Cooperation (FOCAC) summit in Beijing, Mbeki suggested strengthening Africa's role in this multilateral process by increasing African inputs through an expanded business dialogue linked especially to socio-economic development on the continent, technology transfer, and investment.[16] The South African president also argued for linking FOCAC more closely to the UN's Millennium Development Goals' aim of halving poverty by 2015 (see chapter 3), the Mbeki–initiated socio-economic plan, the New Partnership for Africa's Development (NEPAD) of 2001 (see chapter 7).

Like Mbeki, the Congress of South African Trade Unions (COSATU) also described the relationship with China as 'colonial', noting that these ties have increased Africa's dependence on mining and undermined its light industry sector.[17] There have been further complaints in South Africa about the quality of cheap Chinese products, derisively referred to as *'fong kong'*. But another danger in this relationship is that both South Africa and China could come to be regarded as the new 'economic imperialists' in Africa. While South African investments in the rest of Africa amounted to $5.6 billion in 2005, Chinese investments were estimated at $3 billion in 2006, though South Africa's tough labour laws could make it difficult for its companies to compete with China's more flexible state-sponsored companies on the continent. China's state-owned company Zhong Xing Telecommunication Equipment (ZTE) and its private multinational company Huawei are expected to give South African giants Vodacom and Mobile Telephone Networks (MTN) a run for their money in African markets.[18]

But amidst this rivalry, there has also been substantive Sino–South African cooperation. China's Export-Import (Exim) Bank has been consulting with South Africa's ABSA Capital for advice on future investment opportunities in Africa. One of the most important recent developments in bilateral relations was the 2007 purchase by China's Industrial and Commercial Bank

(ICBC) of 20 per cent of the shares of South Africa's Standard Bank at a cost of 36.7 billion rand ($5.5 billion). This represented the largest foreign direct investment in South Africa's history, and could establish a future partnership for the economic domination of the continent, though both rivalry and cooperation are the more likely outcome of this growing bilateral relationship. Having received $1 billion from its Chinese partner, Standard Bank's Africa Equity Fund was targeting investments in Egypt, Morocco, Nigeria, and Kenya by 2009.[19]

Southern African Case Studies: Angola, Zimbabwe, and Zambia[20]

Angola

Angola's future potential as a regional power is clear: this is a diamond- and oil-rich state (Africa's largest oil producer in 2008, with reserves of 4 billion barrels); a strong, battle-hardened army that has intervened successfully in the DRC and Congo-Brazzaville; and a country that has not been shy about projecting military power abroad. Angola could become a future rival to South Africa in Southern Africa. From 2000, contacts increased between the militaries of both countries, and in August 2004 then–South African deputy president Jacob Zuma visited Luanda, followed by Fernando de Piedade Dias Dos Santos, the Angolan prime minister's visit to South Africa in February 2005. Despite acrimonious diplomatic ties resulting from Luanda's expectations of stronger South African support against National Union for the Total Independence of Angola (UNITA) rebel leader Jonas Savimbi, bilateral trade increased from $97 million in 1995 to $460 million in 1998. By 2002, South Africa had become Angola's largest source of imports, accounting for 12 per cent of the total. A South Africa–Angola chamber of commerce was launched in 2003, and Angola entered the South Africa–initiated NEPAD African Peer Review Mechanism (APRM)—which twenty-nine African countries have joined—in July 2004. Angolan imports from South Africa increased by 500 per cent between 2007 and 2008 through companies such as Pep Stores and Nampak, as well as through several hundred South African exporters, even as Luanda became Tshwane's second largest oil supplier in Africa after Nigeria. By 2007, Angola was South Africa's second largest trading partner in Africa and bilateral trade stood at $14.3 billion.[21] Upon assuming the presidency of South Africa in May 2009, Jacob Zuma proved his determination to transform this relationship into a strategic one by embarking on his first state visit to Angola three months later, marking a thawing of the acrimonious relationship between Tshwane and Luanda that had existed during the presidency of Thabo Mbeki between 1999 and 2008 (see chapter 5). Thousands of Angolan students also study in South African secondary schools and universities: a potential source of producing pro–South African elites in future.[22]

After Angola had problems accessing loans from Western-dominated international financial institutions for its postwar reconstruction efforts in 2002—the IMF reported that $8.5 billion of public money was unaccounted for between 1997 and 2001—China stepped into the breach. Between 2004 and 2006, China's Exim Bank provided $4 billion in loans to the Angolan government (including for large-scale infrastructure projects involving roads, railways, and low-cost housing), making China the largest player in the country's reconstruction efforts after its devastating twenty-seven-year civil war, in which apartheid South Africa had played a destructive role in support of Jonas Savimbi's UNITA rebel group. Ironically, Beijing had also supported UNITA as part of its broader ideological battle with the Soviet Union. In May 2007, a $500 million Chinese loan was agreed to help with integrating infrastructure projects into the national economy. These loans were significant because the World Bank and IMF had been unwilling to provide credits to the Eduardo Dos Santos government.

But Beijing's loan to Luanda came with strings attached: 70 per cent of public tenders for construction and civil engineering contracts went to Chinese firms, while 50 per cent of procurement materials financed by Exim Bank loans had to be sourced from China. In March 2006, Angola, for a short time, became the largest source of oil imports to China. In the same period, 45 per cent of Angola's oil exports went to China, a figure equivalent to 15 per cent of global Chinese oil imports. Angola is one of the few African countries with a disproportionately favourable trade balance with China: in 2006, Angolan exports of $10.9 billion (almost all consisting of oil) accounted for the bulk of bilateral trade of $11.8 billion, though China was Angola's fourth largest importer. Angola remained China's largest trading partner in Africa between 2006 and 2008, accounting for 25 per cent of total continental trade in 2008.[23] Beijing also agreed to construct a justice palace and housing projects in Angola; aside from infrastructure, Chinese companies are also involved in telecommunications and the extractive industry. But there have also been tensions in this bilateral relationship, including the breakdown of talks in March 2007 over China's desire to build an oil refinery in Angola.[24] The government in Luanda has very consciously and cleverly diversified its dependence, and not allowed Chinese companies to dominate its oil market. Western firms like

Exxon, Mobil, British Petroleum, Eni, Agip, Total, and Chevron continue to operate in Angola, increasing Luanda's leverage on both Western and Chinese companies. In 2006, the US and South Korea imported more Angolan oil than did China.[25] Beijing has insisted on using Chinese workers in its projects in Angola, arguing that this approach is better for productivity, discipline, and morale. But this has also led to much resentment, and in contrast to Beijing, Western companies like Chevron employ 88 per cent local staff.[26]

Zimbabwe

In the case of Zimbabwe, many analysts tended to focus disproportionately on the dispute between South African president Nelson Mandela and Zimbabwean leader Robert Mugabe over the chairing and functions of the SADC security organ between 1994 and 1996. However, after Mandela came to power in 1994, there were trade tensions between Pretoria and Harare over South Africa's protectionism and heavy-handed use of its economic muscle in trade negotiations.[27] By 1998, trade disparities between both countries—at a time when South Africa was Zimbabwe's largest trading partner—had reached 13 billion rand against Zimbabwe, and Harare felt forced to impose a 100 per cent tariff to protect its domestic industries.[28] A proposed loan of $500 million from Thabo Mbeki's South Africa to Zimbabwe in 2005 reportedly included conditionalities of purchasing agricultural inputs and petroleum from South Africa, as well as demands for both political and economic liberalization.[29] Also attracting little comment is the fact that South African companies have used what some in Zimbabwe see as 'beggar-thy-neighbour' mercantilist policies to increase their market share in Zimbabwe's tourism, services, and exports industries. South African mining and industrial groups have obtained bargains even amidst Zimbabwe's political and economic crisis.[30] Several South African companies have thus profited handsomely from this situation: sugar giant Tongaat Huletts; Victoria Falls–based Tourvest; Impala Platinum; Metallon Group (gold); and at least twenty banks, insurance groups, and retailers.[31] Mugabe's electoral defeat at the 2008 polls, and the power-sharing deal through which opposition leader Morgan Tsvangirai became prime minister in February 2009, created an opportunity for the eventual departure of the long-ruling Zimbabwean leader. Socioeconomic reconstruction in Zimbabwe must be strongly supported and pushed by South Africa—which mediated the 2009 government of national unity under Thabo Mbeki—to ensure a reliable ally and stable neighbour. In 2007, Zimbabwe still remained South Africa's third largest trade partner in Africa, with imports and exports valued at $13.2 billion.[32]

As a result of sanctions imposed on Robert Mugabe's regime by powerful Western governments and international financial institutions in reaction to increasing domestic repression, he defiantly looked to China for support. As Mugabe memorably put it during the silver jubilee of Zimbabwe's independence celebrations in May 2005: 'We have turned East where the sun rises, and given our back to the West, where the sun sets.'[33] China extracted chrome, copper, nickel, and platinum from Zimbabwe, and processed iron and steel. In 2003, for example, Shanghai Baosteel Group invested $300 million in mining and metals, creating 2,000 jobs in the process. Zimbabwe also exported tobacco and cotton to China, with Beijing providing a credit line of $200 million. China has helped to rehabilitate the country's railway and invested in its telecommunication sector, becoming Zimbabwe's second largest trading partner (with $187 million in exports in the first half of 2007) after South Africa. Zimbabwe also bartered its tobacco and cotton to repay its loans to China, and was controversially supplied with military equipment by Beijing. This issue became an embarrassing diplomatic fiasco when Beijing sought to deliver military equipment to the Mugabe regime in Zimbabwe in May 2008. Trade unions in South Africa, Mozambique, Namibia, and Angola mobilised resistance to offloading the arms, which eventually may have been taken to the DRC and flown to Zimbabwe.[34] Such incidents could hurt China's reputation in Africa and complicate its relations with the West.

Chinese companies have also been accused of contributing to Zimbabwe's de-industrialisation through exports of textiles, toys, and buses, and the quality of some Chinese products (derogatorily termed 'zhing zhong') has been questioned by Zimbabweans. But Beijing has played a cautious game in not providing substantial backing for the unpopular Mugabe regime: a clear sign of China's traditional caution not to oppose Western foreign policy too overtly in Africa. As with Angola, Beijing insisted on 70 per cent of contracts in Zimbabwe being set aside for its companies, and similar to their dealings with Luanda, the Chinese were also pragmatic in their relations with Mugabe, refusing to extend a $2 billion loan to the internationally isolated regime in 2006.[35]

Zambia

In the case of Zambia, South African and Chinese firms have both profited from trade with this copper-rich country. South African multinational Anglo

American was involved in Zimbabwe's copper mines even before its independence in 1964, though it has subsequently withdrawn from the country. By 2006, South Africa became the country's largest investor, ploughing $373 million into manufacturing, agriculture, retail, tourism, and services, and creating an estimated 22,000 jobs in the process.[36] In 2007, Zambia was South Africa's fourth largest trading partner in Africa, with imports and exports valued at $11.5 billion.[37] Complaints in 2003 by workers at a Shoprite store in Zambia about maltreatment of local workers and the insensitivity of South African managers, however, highlighted some of challenges of the role and perceptions of South African business on the continent.[38]

Chinese firms are operating in diverse sectors of Zambia's economy: mining, textile, construction, banking, and services, in a relationship that stretches back four decades. Beijing is currently Zambia's third largest investor after South Africa and Britain. Bilateral trade of $20 million in the early 1990s had increased to $300 million by 2006. In November 2006, China signed an agreement to build prestige projects such as the Chambishi copper mine and Mulungushi textile factory. Beijing's purchase of the country's raw materials was also thought to have contributed to an average 9 per cent growth in Zambia's mining sector between 2002 and 2005. China's plan to create special economic zones in Africa—ironically replicating in China itself Western colonial enclaves like Hong Kong, Macao, and Shanghai[39]—centres on establishing such a zone in Chambishi, the heartland of the country's copper belt, which would also export other regional commodities like diamonds, cobalt, uranium, and tin. A $250 million copper smelter is also to be built that could create 60,000 jobs, while $800 million of credit is to be provided to Chinese firms.[40] Much of this planning, however, was undertaken before the more recent fall in the demand for copper amidst the global financial crisis of 2007–2009.[41]

As in other countries such as Nigeria and Zimbabwe, complaints have been heard in Zambia about the low wages paid by Chinese firms, low-quality goods, employment of Chinese workers instead of local Zambians, and poor working conditions. These complaints could potentially do great damage to China's reputation in Africa. A Chinese-run coal mine in Southern Zambia was closed after reports of workers being sent into shafts without proper protective clothing. In one of the worst mining accidents in Zambia's history, forty-six miners were killed in the Chinese-run Chambishi mine in 2006. (It should also be noted that mining accidents—including one in February 2009 that resulted in several fatalities—are not uncommon in China itself, where working conditions are often abysmal.) These incidents could hold lessons for South African–owned firms operating on the continent.[42] Strong anti–Chinese sentiments were voiced by politician Michael Sata during Zambia's 2006 presidential election (which he lost), with the Chinese astonishingly threatening to withdraw all assistance from the country should Sata have won: yet another detour from Beijing's professed noninterference posture.[43]

Central, Western, and Eastern African Case Studies: Democratic Republic of the Congo, Nigeria, Sudan, and Tanzania

Democratic Republic of the Congo

Situated in Central Africa, the Democratic Republic of the Congo, based on its size as Africa's second largest country—in terms of land mass—after Sudan, its strategic position at the heart of Africa, and its rich mineral resources, is the most important country for the stability of a large part of Africa: one of the key reasons why South Africa pushed for the Congo's inclusion in SADC in 1997. During the early part of the DRC conflict from 1997, differences between South Africa and its militarily interventionist neighbours—Zimbabwe, Angola, and Namibia—paralysed SADC, and the Organisation of African Unity (OAU) took over mediation efforts. The Inter-Congolese Dialogue, held in South Africa in 2002, resulted in a power-sharing agreement, with South Africa also sending 1,400 troops to a strengthened UN mission in the Congo (MONUC). Then South African president Thabo Mbeki brokered the Pretoria accord between Kinshasa and Kigali, and South Africa helped steer the peace process, which led to the country's first elections in forty years in 2006 (see chapters 5 and 11). It is thus important for South Africa to continue efforts to stabilize a country in which a decade-long war claimed an estimated 2.5 million lives, internally displaced 3.4 million people, involved seven foreign armies, and spanned three of Africa's subregions.[44]

A critical part of South Africa's role in the Congo, however, relates to its economic role. Some have questioned Tshwane's motives in playing such an active mediation role in the DRC, wondering about a link to its economic interests in the Congo, which have involved mining, agriculture, fishery, energy, construction, and communication. South African companies in the country include Ashanti Gold, De Beers, Anglo Vaal Mining, BHP Billiton, JIG Mining, Meorex, Kumba Resources, and Mwana Africa. BHP Billiton signed an agreement to invest $2.5 billion in an aluminium plant in Bas Congo in 2005. By 2007, the DRC was South Africa's seventh largest trading partner in Africa, with imports and exports valued at $4.1 billion.[45] But South African companies have been accused of using dubious means to pursue their business interests in the Congo, and twelve South African firms, including 'blue-chip' companies such as De Beers, Anglo American, Anglo Vaal Mining, and Iscor, were all cited in a 2002 UN report for allegedly being involved in illicit looting of the Congo's mineral resources.[46] Anglo Gold Ashanti CEO Bobby Godsell also admitted that the company had paid bribes of $9,000 to Nationalist and Integrationist Front (FNI) rebels in northeastern DRC.[47] More positively, Vodacom has provided scholarships to Congolese students to study in South Africa, and sponsored sports events in the DRC. South African retailers and fast-food franchises also opened shop in Kinshasa and Lubumbashi, with Shoprite announcing an $80 million investment in the Congo in 2007.[48]

The South African government has also signed a bilateral agreement with Kinshasa in areas of finance and infrastructure, and used government-linked organisations like the Industrial Development Corporation (IDC), the Council for Scientific and Industrial Research, and the South African Diamond Board to pursue its interests. The IDC, for example, acquired a 10 per cent stake in the $400 million Kolwezi copper and cobalt project. South Africa's most ambitious project in the Congo, however, is Eskom's fifteen-year effort to transform the Congo's Grand Inga Dam into a source of electricity for much of Africa. In a strategic move to gain regional support, the South African government worked with the governments of the DRC, Angola, Botswana, and Namibia to create a company, Westcorp, in order to fund the $5 billion third phase of the Inga project, which could eventually cost $50 billion.[49] South Africa's multilateral regional strategy employed here could be a way of limiting Chinese influence on the continent.

China's Mao Zedong is famously quoted to have said in 1964: 'If we can take the Congo, we can have all of Africa.'[50] But as legendary Argentinian guerrilla and freedom fighter Che Guevara discovered himself in the 1960s, the Congo was not as fertile a soil for fermenting socialist revolution as Mao had thought. In the more contemporary Congo, during the country's 1998–2002 civil war, some Chinese companies were implicated in illicit export of coltan also involving invading Rwandan and Ugandan armies. But, as earlier noted, South African companies were likewise accused of engaging in similar activities, as were many Western companies. Until 2007, the DRC was not among China's top ten African trading partners. In September of that year, however, came news that China had agreed an $8 billion deal with the Congo, in which $5 billion would go towards infrastructural development (including a 3,200–kilometre railway and a 3,200–kilometre road, as well as several hospitals). China also pledged to invest $3 billion in the country's mining sector: a direct challenge in an area of large South African investment.[51]

Nigeria

Situated in Western Africa, Nigeria is the continent's largest market, with 140 million consumers, and since 1994 has been viewed by South Africa's corporate community with great interest[52] (see chapters 6 and 7). South African telecommunications giants MTN and M-Net/SuperSport blazed the trail and became listed on the Nigerian Stock Exchange. MTN spent $340 million launching its mobile telephone network in Nigeria in August 2001,[53] with plans to spend $1.4 billion in the country over a decade. In 2003–2004, MTN Nigeria's post-tax profit of 2.36 billion rand surpassed MTN South Africa's 2.24 billion rand profit.[54] By June 2004, MTN had 1.65 million subscribers in Nigeria.[55] It was MTN's success that convinced many other South African firms that Nigeria was worth investing in.

Other South African companies that followed MTN included Stanbic, Rand Merchant Bank, and Protea Hotels. Sasol, the world's largest producer of petrol from coal, made a $1.2 billion investment in Nigeria to export natural gas. The South African government–funded Industrial Development Corporation invested in Nigerian oil, gas, infrastructure, tourism, and telecommunications. South Africa's Spoornet worked with the Nigerian Railway Corporation to revive Nigeria's railways. South Africa's Portnet agreed to rehabilitate port facilities in Lagos. Chicken Licken, Nando's, and Debonairs established franchises in Nigeria. A Nigeria–South Africa chamber of commerce was established in 2001. Nigeria became South Africa's largest trading partner on the continent, and bilateral trade stood at 22.8 billion rand in 2008.[56] Over a hundred South African firms worked in Nigeria by September 2007.[57]

Nigerians have accused South African firms of patronising behaviour and for operating apartheid-style enclaves for their staff. They have described South Africans as 'neocolonialist' mercantilists bent on dominating the huge Nigerian market and repatriating profits without opening the South African market to Nigerian goods. Other Nigerians, however, have praised the skill and professionalism of South African firms, which they say has improved competition and standards in Nigeria. Nigerians have also been the main beneficiaries of the jobs and goods provided by South African companies in their country.

China has a less diverse, but large and growing, role in Nigeria. In 2008, this was China's fourth largest trading relationship in Africa after Angola, South Africa, and Sudan;[58] and Beijing has entered the top ten global trading partners of Abuja. As former Nigerian president Olusegun Obasanjo put it during Chinese president Hu Jintao's state visit to Abuja in April 2006: 'The twenty-first century is the century for China to lead the world. And when you are leading the world, we want to be close behind you. When you are going to the moon, we don't want to be left behind.'[59] Between 2002 and 2005, Sino-Nigerian trade increased by $3 billion (it was only $178 million in 1996),[60] and by 2007, China had a trade surplus of $250 billion with the West African Gulliver during a period in which Beijing won lucrative oil blocks.

The autocratic regime of General Sani Abacha (1993–1998) had initiated Nigeria's 'Look East' policy. Like Zimbabwe's Robert Mugabe and Sudan's Omar al-Bashir, this represented a bid to break out of Western-imposed diplomatic isolation due to the human rights abuses of the regime. In December 1995—a month after the execution of human rights environmental campaigner and writer Ken Saro-Wiwa and eight fellow campaigners by the Abacha regime, an act that South Africa and many Western countries condemned (see chapter 7)—the China Civil Engineering Construction Corporation signed a $529 million contract to rehabilitate Nigeria's railways. Western countries like the US remained reluctant to provide arms to the Nigerian government, even under the elected government of Olusegun Obasanjo (1999–2007). From 2003, Beijing—in a move similar to its actions in Sudan (discussed later)—provided Abuja with patrol boats, combat-trainer aircraft, and MiG jet fighters. But as in Sudan, Chinese workers became vulnerable to their government's interventionist policies, and five Chinese oil workers were kidnapped by Nigerian militia groups (and later freed after a ransom was paid). The Movement for the Emancipation of the Niger Delta (MEND) militant group, warned China and its oil companies to leave the region.[61]

Under Obasanjo's regime, a $2 billion Chinese loan was extended to Nigeria for further work on Nigeria's railway, at a time when about a hundred Chinese companies were operating in the country. Like Angola, another African oil giant, Nigeria negotiated loans with China that would be managed by the Chinese to compensate for its own lack of governance capacity. In December 2004, the Great Wall Industry Corporation of China launched a Nigerian communications satellite at a cost of $200 million. A China Trade Exhibition, the largest in Africa, was organised by the China Council for the Promotion of International Trade (CCPIT) and held in Lagos in November 2001, with forty-eight Chinese firms attending. Two years later, China constructed the Abuja Sports Complex and has since become a major player in Nigeria's lucrative construction sector. In November 2006, the China Civil Engineering Construction Corporation won an $8.3 billion contract for railway construction expected to stretch from the southern port city of Lagos to the historic northern city of Kano. Beijing also sought to import more agricultural products from Nigeria, and had 400 agricultural experts in the country by 2007.

In the banking sector, the China Development Bank outlined plans to acquire a strategic equity stake in one of Nigeria's largest banks, the United Bank of Africa (UBA). This again underlined China's long-term and diverse strategic planning in Africa. The move was similar to the stake bought in South Africa's Standard Bank, as Beijing sought to use the market knowledge of two of Africa's largest economies to penetrate other regional markets. Nigeria has also been identified as one of China's special economic zones, with plans to create a manufacturing and assembly zone for Chinese firms to invest in. In 2007, a $500 million free trade zone was set up in Nigeria's western state of Ogun to host 100 Chinese companies, with joint funding from Chinese and Nigerian interests.[62] But as in Zimbabwe, there were complaints in Nigeria about the dumping of cheap Chinese goods of dubious quality, and the destruction of the country's textile industry—particularly in the northern states of Kano and Kaduna—by cheaper Chinese textiles. Nigeria's 175 textile plants (with 250,000 workers) in the 1980s had declined to only twenty-six (employing 24,000 people) by October 2007, again due in part to stiff competition from China. About 75 per cent of Kano's manufacturers were forced to close in the 1990s due apparently to competition from Chinese goods. As in South Africa, local resentment swelled up against Chinese firms amidst accusations of harsh labour practices, low wages, and poor corporate governance.[63] Nigeria's National Agency for Food and Drug Administration and Control (NAFDAC) also complained in 2007 that Chinese-made drugs and toothpaste were harmful to consumers.[64]

Sudan

Situated in Eastern Africa, Sudan is geographically Africa's largest country and its growing oil resources could make it one of the continent's leading countries, if it can stabilize long-running conflicts in South Sudan, Darfur, and the Blue Nile, and establish sound democratic governance.[65] South Africa was asked often by both sides to mediate the conflict in South Sudan, but declined in favour of regional actors within the Intergovernmental Authority on Development (IGAD). Tshwane, however, agreed to chair the African Union Committee on Post-Conflict Reconstruction in Sudan, and has provided capacity-building training to Khartoum and Juba through its foreign ministry and the University of South Africa (UNISA). Sudanese leader Omar al-Bashir first visited South Africa in August 1997, and a South African business delegation went to Sudan in July 2001. South Africa established an embassy in Khartoum in January 2004 and a consulate in Juba in March 2007, with Mbeki having visited both capitals.[66]

Like South Africa, China also has its own interests in Sudan. In 2008, Khartoum was Beijing's third largest trading partner in Africa after Angola and South Africa.[67] Between 2000 and 2004, China bought more than 80 per cent of Sudan's oil, a figure that dropped to 40 per cent by 2007 as the country's oil production expanded. In 2006, China accounted for 20.8 per cent ($1.6 billion) of Sudan's total imports, while accounting for 75 per cent ($4.2 billion) of its exports. This was up from 4.3 per cent of imports and 6.8 per cent of exports a decade earlier.[68] In 2004, Chinese firms agreed to undertake the $1.8 billion Merowe Dam (with China's Exim Bank providing a $530 million loan), which was followed by the El Galil power station, in a sector in which South Africa's Eskom has great interest on the continent. A year later, more Chinese foreign direct investment—$351.5 million—went to Sudan than to any other African country: the ninth largest investment destination for Chinese foreign direct investment around the world. In 2007, two Chinese firms were awarded a $1 billion contract to build a railway connecting Port Sudan to Khartoum.[69] These lucrative trade deals underline the importance of Khartoum to Beijing.

In July 2007, the powerful fifteen-member UN Security Council decided to deploy 26,000 'blue helmets' to Sudan's volatile Darfur province by the end of 2007. The UN-AU hybrid operation in Darfur (UNAMID) was mandated to bolster the struggling 7,000–strong AU mission in Darfur that had been deployed by 2004 (see chapter 2). Diplomatic pressure exerted by China appears to have been instrumental in twisting the arm of Sudanese leader Omar al-Bashir during a visit to Khartoum by Chinese president Hu Jintao in February 2007. Beijing thus reversed its traditional rhetorical policy of non-interference in African countries to convince al-Bashir to accept a UN force, apparently under threat of a boycott of China's showpiece Olympics in 2008.[70] This again underlined China's sensitivities to Western reactions in its dealings with Africa.

But one significant issue that has often been overlooked in the relationship between China and Sudan is that Khartoum actually appears to have initiated this courtship of the dragon. Following its military coup in June 1989, the jihadist regime of al-Bashir found itself financially bankrupt and diplomatically isolated. Within fifteen months of taking office, al-Bashir had visited Beijing. A $300 million arms deal with China emerged the following year, and during Sudan's civil war, Beijing provided Khartoum with military aircraft and other weapons. This was as interventionist a policy as one can imagine, and many Western scholars tend to take literally the rhetoric of Chinese 'noninterference'—a general principle entrenched in the charters of the UN, the AU, ASEAN, and other international organisations—rather than looking at the actual actions that Beijing takes. US oil giant Chevron had discovered Sudan's oil in 1978. But due to political pressure from Washington—which branded Khartoum, whose leaders had hosted Osama bin Laden in their country between 1991 and 1996, as a 'sponsor of state terrorism'—Chevron sold its concessions in 1992. It was the need for revenues from oil to prosecute its illconceived war in South Sudan and to run its administration, that had forced the al-Bashir government to 'Look East' to China. The Sudanese government is also one of the few in Africa that has ensured that Beijing gives priority to local labour: 93 per cent of workers in the Chinese oil sector in 2007 were locals.[71]

It was after another visit by al-Bashir to Beijing in September 1995 that China's Exim Bank became involved in developing Sudan's oil industry. The Chinese built a 1,600–kilometre oil pipeline and oil refinery in Sudan by 2000, committing human rights abuses in the process and receiving military protection from Khartoum that resulted in the depopulation of Dinka and Nuer groups in the oil-rich South.[72] African governments like Sudan are rarely granted any 'agency' by Western analysts. They are instead often portrayed merely as pawns on a Chinese chessboard rather than as proactive actors devising viable strategies and not just simply reacting to the advances of a firebreathing dragon. The malevolent guile and farsightedness of Sudanese diplomacy is one of the reasons why al-Bashir and his regime have been able to survive economically better than others like Zimbabwe's Robert Mugabe. But despite close government relations between Khartoum and Beijing, there have been complaints among Sudanese citizens about the dumping of cheap Chinese goods, and demands for their government to protect Sudanese industry and the craft sector from the pernicious effects of competition from China.[73] The attacks on Chinese oil workers in Kordofan in October 2007 by the Justice and Equality Movement (JEM) Darfuri rebel group represented another clear sign of the dangers of China's high-profile role in the country, and further proof that the 'noninterference' rhetoric is rather empty among most anti–Khartoum Sudanese actors.

Tanzania

Also situated in Eastern Africa, Tanzania, a SADC member with which South Africa has strong economic ties, could serve as a bridge between Eastern and Southern Africa in the same way that the DRC could bridge Southern and Central Africa. By 2007, Tanzania was South Africa's eighth largest trading partner in Africa, with imports and exports valued at $2.9 billion,[74] and Standard Bank (Stanbic) had its most profitable African market in Zambia and Nigeria.[75] In the same year, about 5,000 South African businesspeople— the largest presence on the continent—lived in Dar-es-Salaam and Arusha. Tanzania's capital came to be known as 'little Pretoria' by some, as a result of its large Afrikaner (referred to as *'Kuburu'* in the local vernacular) presence. They worked in sectors as diverse as banking, construction, mining, tourism, retail, and telecommunications, and created some resentment among locals for their apparently draconian labour practices at companies like the South African–run TanzaniteOne mine. The fatal shooting of alleged trespassers by a South African security firm that was guarding the mine led to much local criticism and may yet fuel more widespread anti–South African sentiment.[76]

China has also benefitted from its historical relationship with Tanzania, and used it to extend trade in an area of large South African economic interests. Beijing has invested in sectors as diverse as coal mining, farming, textiles, manufacturing, and fishing. By 2006, China had become the fourth largest foreign investor in Tanzania, with projects worth $833 million. By 2005, Chinese exports were worth $304 million, while Tanzanian exports to China had reached $170 million. As earlier noted, Beijing is also planning to invest in an ambitious special economic zone in Zambia's copper belt that is expected to link the Tanzania-Zambia railway to the Angola-bound Benguela railway, thus creating an unprecedented infrastructure corridor across the continent linking Southern and Eastern Africa. This could also result in the creation of a Chinese manufacturing and assembly hub for Eastern Africa and the rehabilitation of the Dar-es-Salaam port.[77] China has further exported vehicles, textiles, chemicals, electrical appliances, and steel to Tanzania, while Tanzania has exported dried seafood, copper, cotton, timber, iron, and steel to China.[78]

Concluding Reflections

The experiences from these seven case studies show that competition and col-laboration are likely to be key features of Sino–South African relations in future. But the actions of both South Africa and China could also result in accusations of 'economic imperialism' and widespread resentment. South African firms have been criticised in countries like Tanzania, Nigeria, Zambia, and Zimbabwe for what have been described as 'mercantilist' business prac-tices and 'draconian' labour practices. Chinese firms have also aroused similar resentment in Nigeria, South Africa, Zambia, and Sudan. Despite Beijing's often vacuous 'noninterference' rhetoric, its support of abusive or neglectful governments in Sudan and Nigeria (under General Sani Abacha) has exposed its workers to attacks and kidnappings from militant groups. These actions are likely to focus minds in China as the argument that business is separate from politics wears increasingly thin.

Beijing usually insists that Western companies that invest in China must hire local labour, but often does not practice what it preaches at home in its dealings with Africa. As a result, there have been anti–Chinese demonstra-tions in Zambia and Namibia, and resentment has been expressed in South Africa, Nigeria, Zimbabwe, and Sudan about the destruction of local busi-nesses and dumping of cheap, poor-quality goods from China. Some coun-tries, like Sudan and Egypt, have been able to insist that Chinese firms employ local labour. Other African governments must follow suit and insist that Bei-jing apply the same principles that it requires Western companies to follow in China. What is good for China is surely also good for Africa.

More positively, these cases demonstrate Beijing's ability to increase the leverage of African regimes with Western actors, which still dominate most African economies in a continuation of the 'Curse of Berlin' (see chapter 1). China's presence appeared to have inspired Britain, in conjunction with the World Bank, to announce a £1 billion infrastructure project, in February 2009, to rebuild the road and rail network of Zambia, Zimbabwe, Botswana, Malawi, Tanzania, South Africa, Mozambique, and the DRC.[79] Such initia-tives are welcome, and likely would not occur without Beijing's presence and focus on infrastructure projects in Africa. Regarding the leverage of African countries, only in Sudan does China dominate the oil market. In other coun-tries, like Nigeria, Angola, and Gabon, African governments have sought to balance China's role with those of Western companies, allowing neither side to dominate and thus forcing them to negotiate on a more competitive basis. This leverage can be used for positive ends to build infrastructure, promote regional integration, and advance socioeconomic development. But such leverage can also be used for less benign ends. Pariah regimes in Sudan, Nigeria, and Zimbabwe all adopted a 'Look East' policy to try to break out of their Western-imposed diplomatic isolation, and used Chinese weapons to commit human rights abuses and to entrench autocracy. Such actions are unlikely to be in Beijing's long-term interest on the continent.

Just as the United States has adopted South Africa and Nigeria as strategic partners through which it wants to engage with Africa, China appears to be adopting a similar approach with both countries, which are now among Beijing's top four trading partners in Africa. Tshwane and Abuja have clout in regional bodies like the AU, SADC, and the Economic Community of West African States (ECOWAS), and could also help mediate Beijing's role with Western powers in Africa. But although China supported South Africa and Nigeria in their unsuccessful bid to secure permanent seats on an expanded UN Security Council in 2005, Beijing also reportedly played a negative role, using countries like Zimbabwe to stall the reform effort, which both Tshwane and Abuja strongly supported (see chapter 3). South Africa and Nigeria must insist that China, in return for its lucrative African trade, genuinely support African interests and initiatives at the UN, the World Bank, the IMF, and the WTO. South Africa's membership with China in the Group of 20 could also help in promoting a mutually beneficial relationship for the global South.

In theory, South Africa should have a clear advantage over China on the continent, since it is a leading player in key regional bodies like the AU, SADC, and NEPAD in which Beijing has no presence. Tshwane could therefore shape African multilateral policies towards, and engagement with, China in ways that are consistent with its own interests. However, China may paradoxically be more accepted in parts of Africa than South Africa is. Beijing seems to have a more farsighted, strategic approach to Africa than Tshwane, and its infrastructure projects, investments, and loans have often had an immediate, concrete impact on many African economies. Perhaps South Africa's evolving economic assistance programme to African countries will help soften the hard edge of its aggressive, mostly white capitalists. Even though Beijing opportunistically backed rebels linked to apartheid South Africa in civil conflicts in places like Angola, Mozambique, and Nigeria as part of its ideological battle with the Soviet Union during the Cold War, China carries less baggage on the continent than apartheid South Africa, which aggressively bullied its neighbours, destroyed lives, and damaged infrastructure. Though South Africa is geographically part of Africa, its culturally schizophrenic citizens have not always regarded themselves, nor been accepted, across the continent, as Africans. Many white South African entre-preneurs are still viewed with deep suspicion throughout the continent, and questions are still asked as to whether they are apartheid wolves in African sheepskin (see chapter 5).

China's own dual personality in Africa is well expressed in German play-wright Bertolt Brecht's 1943 *The Good Person of Szechuan*. In this play, the gods come down to look for a good person on earth and find only a prostitute, Shen Te, who has to sell her body to survive. The gods compensate Shen Te for her hospitality to them and she buys a shop, but soon faces parasites who wish to sponge off her kindness. In order to survive, Shen Te has to turn to her ruthless, hard-nosed, alter-ego businessman, Shui Ta, who clears the shop of the spongers.[80] The China that seeks to spread prosperity and technology to Africa acts as Shen Te, but the ruthless hard-headed Shui Ta is never far behind, wanting to exploit raw materials and corner market share.

However, both Pax South Africana and Pax Sinica could come to represent a new breed of economic exploitation and political imperialism in Africa. Care must be taken to manage both countries' roles in Africa. Otherwise, as the springbok and the dragon make love or make war—to paraphrase the words of an old African proverb—it is the African grass under their heavy feet that is likely to suffer.

PART 3

THE QUEST FOR UNITY

10

MANDELA AND RHODES

A MONSTROUS MARRIAGE[1]

'[C]ombining our name with that of Cecil John Rhodes in this initiative is to signal the closing of the circle and the coming together of two strands in our history.'[2]

Nelson Mandela, president of South Africa, 1994–1999

This chapter explores the issue of reconciliation and the controversial co-joining of two historical figures under the Mandela Rhodes Foundation in 2002: nineteenth-century imperialist Cecil Rhodes, and twentieth-century liberation hero Nelson Mandela. Whereas Rhodes was an expansionist *empire*-builder (with modern-day Zambia and Zimbabwe—former Northern and Southern Rhodesia—once named after him), Mandela was a *nation*-builder par excellence who did the most to unite a South Africa divided for decades by colonialism and apartheid and on the brink of a potential civil war. Both men had strong Christian roots: while Rhodes's father was the vicar of the English town of Bishop's Stortford, Mandela attended two elite Methodist schools (Clarkebury and Healdtown), and at the University of Fort Hare joined the Student Christian Association, assisting in providing Sunday-school classes. Mandela also went to a school where one of his teachers changed his ancestral name of Rolihlahla ('troublemaker') to the Christian name Nelson. We thus examine the roles of both men in empire and nation-building, as well as assess their life missions: while Rhodes pursued a *mission civilisatrice* (civilizing mission) in which European churches had played a role in Africa during the age of imperialism in the nineteenth century, Mandela embodied a quasi–religious 'prophetic' leadership that eventually freed his people from the bondage of apartheid by 1994.

As Robert H. Jackson and Carl G. Rosberg noted in their classic 1982 study on African leadership typologies: 'The Prophet, political or religious, is a revolutionary—that is, one who prophesies a better future, whose attainment requires the radical transformation of the present... [T]he Prophet is a political agent, but is also a moral agent—a political-religious man.' The authors go on to note that both political and religious prophets must exercise power to serve a higher goal in search of a 'New Jerusalem'. Prophets must cultivate a team of disciples who believe fervently and have unwavering faith in the prophet's vision of a new utopia. Such prophets tend to flourish during evil and oppressive times.[3] Mandela's struggle for South Africa's liberation certainly embraced this definition of prophetic rule, as the charismatic icon of the African National Congress's (ANC) liberation movement was able to build up and maintain a devoted following even during almost three decades in jail. Mandela's presidency, from 1994 to 1999, could also be seen in prophetic terms, as he sought to reconcile a deeply divided society and to point his 48 million disciples to a better future. His rule represented prophetic nation-building.

Mandela and Rhodes: Good vs. Evil?

Before assessing the individual legacies of their nation- and empire-building endeavours, we must first examine Nelson Mandela and Cecil Rhodes comparatively as historical figures. My own personal association with the legacy of Cecil Rhodes began in 1990 on winning the single Rhodes Scholarship from Nigeria to study at Oxford University. An alarmed uncle exclaimed at the time: 'That thing is dripping with blood. Cecil Rhodes was a bloody imperialist!' My thoughts at the time were more practical: to get a good education at a world-class institution, and if the money of a robber-baron who had plundered Africa's wealth was paying for it, then at least a slice of the treasure was returning to the continent. I would accept even the crumbs from the great imperialist's gluttonous feast. Having won the golden fleece from the city of 'dreaming spires', I now have the opportunity to return to the legacy of the self-styled 'Colossus'. I remember my stomach churning at dinners at Rhodes House in Oxford when the assembled dignitaries would turn to a large portrait of the colonialist and raise their glasses to 'The Founder'. My own silent protest involved refusing to partake in this strange ritual of the most secret of societies.

MANDELA AND RHODES: A MONSTROUS MARRIAGE

Still struggling a decade later to come to terms with my own personal discomfort with this association, I was shocked to discover the creation of the Mandela Rhodes Foundation in South Africa in 2002. The Rhodes Trust in Oxford contributed £10 million over a decade to scholarships, child healthcare, and sporting facilities for disadvantaged communities. But despite the positive impact that these funds will doubtless have, I wondered whether this was not a tragic perversion of a genuine African hero. As Paul Maylam, a historian at South Africa's Rhodes University (named after our subject) in Grahamstown, and author of the excellent 2005 book *The Cult of Rhodes*, noted: 'The arch-imperialist colonizer of the nineteenth century was being conjoined with the great anti–imperialist freedom fighter of the twentieth century.'[4]

There are some similarities between Mandela and Rhodes: both are among the most well-known historical figures in African history; both have had countless books, documentaries, and monuments devoted to them; both have had universities and streets named after them; both were anglophiles, though in Rhodes's case he was actually born in England and moved to South Africa at the age of seventeen; both trained as lawyers, pursuing their degrees part-time; both were awarded honorary doctorates by the universities at which they studied—Witwatersrand (Mandela) and Oxford (Rhodes); both were pan-Africanists, with Rhodes seeking to use force and economic muscle to unite the continent[5], while Mandela sought more peaceful means of conflict resolution and regional cooperation and integration; and both spent much of their life in Cape Town, with Mandela mostly in jail there for a third of his life, while Rhodes lived in the opulence of the Groote Schuur, his grand estate at the foot of Table Mountain, which he bequeathed to the state and which became the South African head of state's official residence in Cape Town (until Mandela declined to live there after 1994). Very few black scholars have also published major works on either historical figure.

The contrasts between Rhodes and Mandela, however, are enormous. While Rhodes was one of the greatest imperialists of the nineteenth century, Mandela was one of the greatest liberators of the twentieth. While Mandela struggled financially as a lawyer and spent twenty-seven years of his life in jail protesting the evil injustices of the apartheid regime, Rhodes lived a wealthy life aggressively promoting the interests of the British Empire through often harsh and unjust means. While Rhodes visited unimaginable cruelty upon black populations in South Africa, Zambia, and Zimbabwe, Mandela was the very embodiment of reconciliation, promoting the idea of what his fellow

Nobel peace laureate, Archbishop Desmond Tutu, described as a 'rainbow people of God'.[6] While Rhodes is now widely despised across Africa as an aggressive racist, Mandela remains one of the greatest moral figures of the current age, as evidenced by his award of the Nobel Peace Prize in 1993. While Rhodes died a relatively early death at the age of forty-eight and drank excessively, the teetotal Mandela has lived a long life and turned ninety in 2008. While Mandela married three times and produced six children (three of them died), Rhodes never married, and there is scarcely any record of any relationships with women.

Cecil Rhodes: Colossal Imperialist

Given his destructive legacy of empire-building, Cecil Rhodes, who died in 1902, undoubtedly remains the greatest individual historical symbol of imperialism in the Victorian age.[7] Independent Zimbabwe removed statues of Rhodes from the streets of Harare and Bulawayo after 1980. Zambia toppled a statue of Rhodes upon achieving independence in 1964, and both countries—former Southern and Northern Rhodesia respectively—sought to remove the imperial stain by rebaptizing themselves. South Africa has not yet started a proper debate on the numerous Rhodes memorials that litter its post-apartheid landscape. An effort by academic Roger Southall to change the name of Rhodes University in August 1994 was soundly defeated in the university senate.[8]

With the support of the British government, which awarded his British South Africa Company a royal charter in 1889—significantly, four years after the Conference of Berlin and at the zenith of the 'Scramble for Africa' (see chapter1)—to seize, administer, and populate land with white settlers. Rhodes dispossessed black people of their ancestral lands in modern-day Zimbabwe and Zambia through aggressive and duplicitous means, stealing 3.5 million square miles of black real estate in one of the most ignominious 'land-grabs' in modern history.[9] Modern-day Malawi—then the protectorate of Nyasaland— was also run by one of Rhodes's lieutenants, and this powerful politician-plunderer secured British protection for Botswana and Lesotho. Rhodes also had unrealised designs on parts of Portuguese-ruled Mozambique and Belgian-administered Congo. He was an often unscrupulous businessman as well as a crude racist. Rhodes infamously said: 'I prefer land to niggers ... the natives are like children. They are just emerging from barbarism [and] one should kill as many niggers as possible.'[10] Even before apartheid was passed into law in 1948, as prime minister of Cape Colony between 1890 and 1895, Rhodes was its forerunner, helping to disenfranchise black people through introducing new property and educational criteria into what had hitherto been considered the relatively 'liberal' Cape Colony.[11] As Rhodes told the Cape Town parliament in 1887: 'the native is to be treated as a child and denied the franchise... We must adopt a system of despotism, such as works so well in India, in our relations with the barbarians of South Africa.'[12] He forcibly removed blacks to native reserves through the Glen Grey Act of 1894, which presaged apartheid's notorious Bantustan policies by half a century. Rhodes further pushed the Cape parliament to introduce hut and labour taxes on blacks to force them into the cash economy; packed over 11,000 black miners into inhumane, dog-patrolled, wire-protected barracks; and supported draconian labour laws (including the legal flogging of 'disobedient' black labourers through the notorious 'strop bill') that facilitated the continued supply of human fodder to his mines and impoverished the black population. As premier of Cape Colony, Rhodes also introduced social segregation (later called apartheid) for nonwhites in schools, hospitals, theatres, prisons, sports, and public transport; forced blacks to carry passes (a precursor of apartheid's 'dumb pass'); and removed thousands of members of these groups from the colony's electoral rolls.[13]

Paul Maylam described Rhodes as an 'aggressive imperial expansionist, a crude racist, a ruthless capitalist and a supreme exploiter and manipulator,'[14] noting also that 'Cecil Rhodes is still the most written about figure in Southern African history and in British imperial history'.[15] The 'cult' of Rhodes is represented by some twenty-six biographies, seven novels, six plays, and countless monuments, memorials, universities, films, and documentaries. Incredibly, Africans and Afrikaners, who suffered disproportionately from Rhodes' policies, have written the least about him. Rhodes is buried in Zimbabwe's Matopos Hills—venerated by his admirers as 'Rhodesia's Valhalla'. However, there have been calls by his detractors—including Robert Mugabe as recently as 2002—for his bones to be disinterred and returned to England.

It is important to demythologise the 'cult' of Rhodes that has been carefully cultivated by a legion of his supporters since his death in 1902. Such supporters seek to portray Rhodes as a selfless visionary with a sense of *noblesse oblige* (obligations of rank) who embarked on a civilizing mission to spread enlightened British values, culture, and institutions to noble African 'savages'. Rhodes's obsessive quest to achieve immortality saw his name and image memorialised in Cape Town (statues, street names, and a grandiose memorial above the main university); Kimberley (a statue on horseback); Grahamstown (Rhodes University); and Oxford (the Rhodes House and a statue on the high street). These were all efforts to deify Rhodes as a 'Colossus', whether looking down broodingly on shoppers on Oxford's busy high street, or on the inhabitants of the southernmost tip of Africa in Cape Town, or on conquered people in Zimbabwe's Matopos Hills. Rhodes dreamed of building a railway from the Cape to Cairo, and sought to paint as much as possible of the map of Africa in the imperial Union Jack of his native Britain. His scholarship scheme, which started after his death in 1902, sought to create a 'heaven's breed' of largely Anglo-American 'rulers of the world' from the British Commonwealth and Germany. Rhodes saw the English as '[God's] chosen instrument in carrying out the divine idea over the whole planet', arguing that 'the more of the world we inhabit the better it is for the human race'.[16]

This strange Englishman seemed to confirm Lenin's belief that imperialism was the highest form of capitalism,[17] with Rhodes harnessing political power, as prime minister of Cape Colony from 1890 to 1895, as well as economic power, as a diamond and gold magnate. Rhodes used his economic wealth (he controlled 90 per cent of the world's diamonds) to buy political power, and used political power to protect and extend his wealth. He perverted politics as he had business, using patronage—in the form of shares or land—to buy off politicians (as he had bought off diamond prospectors) in Britain and South Africa, including members of the Afrikaner Bond with whom he had established an alliance in the Cape parliament in order to pass harsh legislation against blacks and to protect white Afrikaner farmers.[18] Rhodes headed the De Beers mining firm and used his British South Africa Company (the Chartered Company) to dispossess black people of their ancestral lands.

One must unequivocally reject the argument of Rhodes's many apologists that he was a 'man of his times'. Many of the politician-plunderer's contemporaries criticised him, including writer Olive Schreiner, a friend who later turned against him and wrote a devastating critique of his ruthless imperial methods in 1897, *Trooper Peter Halket of Mashonaland*.[19] (There were, after all, abolitionists—including many church activists and individuals like Englishman William Wilberforce—who condemned slavery even when its practice was widely accepted.) Rhodes was an often ruthless and unscrupulous businessman and politician as well as a crude racist whose views would presage later Hitlerite and apartheid notions of racial supremacy. He bought off rival entrepreneurs, politicians, and journalists to further his expansionist aims.

Cecil Rhodes had described Africa north of the Limpopo as South Africa's 'natural hinterland', extending railways and telegraph poles northwards. Interest groups like the South African Federated Chamber of Industries and the South African Foreign Trade Organisation identified business opportunities north of the Limpopo very early, with South Africa's post–Second World War white leaders encouraging this expansion after 1945. These men were thus, in a genuine sense, the heirs of Cecil Rhodes. Even in the post-apartheid era, South African business interests have often talked as if they are determined to follow in Rhodes's colossal footsteps. Mostly white South African businesses have fanned out across the continent since 1994 in areas like mining, banking, retail, communications, armaments, and insurance, making references to a 'sense of pioneering' and describing themselves as 'an army on the move'. By 2000, South Africa had become the largest single foreign investor in the rest of Africa. These developments are linked to the legacy of Cecil Rhodes, who played such a vital role in opening up South Africa to Western investment and rapid industrialisation (see chapters 5 and 9).

Rhodes's premiership ended in disgrace in January 1896 when he was forced to resign after the ill-fated attack of his lieutenant, Leander Starr Jameson (after whom the main hall at the University of Cape Town is named), on Johannesburg, then part of the Afrikaner Transvaal republic. This incident ended Rhodes's enduring dream of uniting the 'white races' of South Africa, and many believe that it helped sow the seeds of the Anglo-Boer war of 1899–1902.[20] Bernard Magubane condemned Rhodes as 'a robber and a racist to the core who ruthlessly, cynically pursued his goals. No shortcut was too dishonourable for him to use to achieve his vision. He was possessed of imperial greed and insatiable rapaciousness.'[21] Maylam's epitaph to Rhodes's unscrupulous greed is equally devastating: 'In reflecting on the life and career of Rhodes I find little to redeem him. I have not come across a sentence spoken or written by him that is inspiring or uplifting; his utterances range from the ordinary to the abhorrent. His crude racist outbursts have been well documented. He possessed an authoritarian personality, and some of his ideas about empire were puerile. His methods were often dubious or despicable... Rhodes does not deserve to be rehabilitated.'[22] Robert Rotberg was a little less harsh in describing Rhodes as 'a rich capitalist, ruthless conqueror, corrupter of opponents, English and male chauvinist, bombastic buccaneer, successful politician, farming pioneer, supporter of education, instinctive globalizer, and amazing visionary'.[23] Rudyard Kipling, the great poet and champion of imperialism, wrote an eloquent ode to his friend in 1902 called 'The Burial', in which he noted:

It is his will that he look forth
Across the world he won—
The granite of the ancient North—
Great spaces washed with sun.
There shall he patient take his seat.[24]

More than 6,000 Rhodes scholars have studied at Oxford since 1903 in a scholarship scheme that excluded women until 1976 and had clearly been initially designed for white males, as evident from Rhodes's will.[25] The Rhodes trustees themselves today remain mainly white men and most of the scholarships still go disproportionately to white Americans, Canadians, Australians, and South Africans. Rhodes, not reputed to have been a particularly good student, had himself studied at Oxford (taking eight years to achieve a 'gentleman's pass')—which controversially awarded him an honorary doctorate in 1899. (It is often said that Rhodes himself could not have become a Rhodes scholar!) Without any apparent irony, Oxford established a Rhodes Chair in Race Relations in 1953.

The Rhodes Scholarship is the most enduring legacy of this arch-imperialist. The South African scholarships have been particularly controversial, since they have effectively served as a form of white 'affirmative action' for over a century. Students from schools listed in Rhodes's will—Diocesan College ('Bishops'), St. Andrew's College, the South African College Schools (SACS), and Stellenbosch high school for boys (Paul Roos Gymnasium)—none of which admitted either blacks or girls until the 1980s, continued to obtain four of the nine scholarships. The first Afrikaner scholar declined the scholarship in 1903, as the scheme was seen as privileging 'Anglo-liberal whites'. As apartheid South Africa became increasingly diplomatically isolated, American Rhodes scholars led petitions and protests to increase black representation on the scheme, and even to cut off scholarships to the country altogether. The pressure eventually led the Rhodes trustees belatedly to take to court, in 1985, the four 'whites only' schools for boys to force them to admit blacks and girls. Only in 1976 were the first black Rhodes scholar (Ramuchandran Govender) and the first woman Rhodes scholar (Sheila Niven) chosen—seventy-two years after the first South African scholars went up to Oxford.[26] Four black scholars were elected in the first eighty years of a scheme that still appears to be more albinocratic than meritocratic. Even today, there is no systematic plan in place to attract the 'best and brightest' black talent to the scholarships. Based on Rhodes's sordid historical legacy, a debate in South Africa on the wisdom of yoking the saintly Mandela to a colossal imperialist seems to be long overdue.

A visit by this author to the Bishop's Stortford Museum—Rhodes's original birthplace—in February 2009 provided another interesting dimension to his legacy through this small, sleepy English town in Hertfordshire with charming pubs and St. Michael's Church, where Rhodes's father had been Vicar between 1849 and 1876. In the museum, indigenous African music played in the background amidst African axes, shields, and other weapons forged by African blacksmiths. African drums and baskets were also on display. There were depictions of slavery and imperialism, and a recognition that Rhodes's legacy had been contested, even during his own lifetime. Numerous pictures of Rhodes littered the room: growing up as a child in Bishop's Stortford; as prime minister of Cape colony; and with Lord Kitchener during the Anglo-Boer war. I was told by museum staff that even though many schoolchildren visited, many English pupils did not learn about Cecil Rhodes in their education. Of far greater interest in the same building was the Rhodes Art complex, which offered theatre, comedies, and the music of the 'Rhodes Rocks' on Fridays. It is this entertainment that sustains the not very busy museum, and many in the town clearly think about Rhodes more in terms of entertainment than imperialism. The commercialisation and packaging of this ruthless businessman in his English hometown was perhaps the ultimate irony in the quest for immortality of a megalomaniac plunderer-politician.

Nelson Mandela: An African Avatar

Nelson Mandela, South Africa's first democratically elected president, has been the subject of at least four major biographies and numerous collected volumes written about him by authors like Fatima Meer, Anthony Sampson, Mary Benson, Martin Meredith, Tom Lodge, and Elleke Boehmer.[27] Twenty-six films and documentaries have also been made about Mandela's life, while coffee-table books continue to fill the shelves of bookshops in South Africa and around the world. It is important to shed more light, as Tom Lodge has done in his impressive 2006 book, on the importance of Mandela's childhood in shaping his leadership qualities; Mandela's role in 'leading from prison'; the mythical cult that was consciously developed around his iconic status; and Mandela's 'messianic' leadership of South Africa's democratic transition. In addition, we briefly assess Mandela's role as a prophetic leader in both the African and global settings.

Mandela grew up in a chiefly Xhosa household, attending elite Methodist schools modelled on the English education system. He developed great

223

respect for English democratic institutions and gentlemanly manners, becoming a lifelong anglophile. Mandela studied at the black elite Fort Hare University, where he read William Shakespeare, Alfred Tennyson, and Victorian poetry, and also met Oliver Tambo, the future head of the African National Congress. Moving to Johannesburg, he met another ANC stalwart who became his mentor and confidant, Walter Sisulu, with whom he spent most of his twenty-seven years in jail. Before prison, Mandela had married two women—Evelyn Mase and Winnie Madikizela (he later married Mozambican Graça Machel)—and became deeply involved in ANC politics. His participation in the political struggle in apartheid South Africa led to an absentee father role, which caused Madiba (Mandela's clan name) much personal anguish.

Mandela's intellectual thinking was particularly influenced by members of the Communist Party of South Africa (CPSA)—later the South African Communist Party (SACP)—like Nat Bregman, Joe Slovo, and Ruth First, and Madiba helped to found the ANC Youth League in 1944 (though he also called for curtailing communist influence in the ANC).[28] He gradually metamorphosed from a black nationalist who expressed concern that South African Indians were dominating the liberation struggle to a prophet of multi–racialism. He also read the writings of pan-Africanists like George Padmore and Kwame Nkrumah. At first inspired by Gandhian tactics of 'passive resistance' (see chapter 14), Mandela would eventually come to play a leadership role in the Defiance Campaign of 1952, before initiating the 'armed struggle' that led to a life sentence in 1964. As he memorably put it, quoting an African proverb: 'the attacks of the wild beast cannot be averted with only bare hands.'[29] Madiba's visit to Tanzania, Ethiopia, Zambia, Egypt, Tunisia, Morocco, Algeria, Ghana, Senegal, and Guinea in 1962 had given him great insights into continental diplomacy and the tactics of other liberation movements. He was particularly influenced by Algeria's Front de Libération Nationale, and had always adopted a much broader pan-African vision of his country's struggle, as the name of his party—whose members were sheltered during the apartheid struggle by many neighbouring countries, at huge costs to themselves—suggested.

Mandela spent twenty-seven difficult years in jail: his eyes, lungs, and prostate were badly affected by the squalid conditions on Robben Island. But this was also a forum in which the ideological struggles of the ANC were played out, as Mandela and Govan Mbeki (father of former president Thabo Mbeki) battled over the role of traditional chiefs, the prospects for revolutionary warfare, and the roles of Steve Biko's Black Consciousness Movement and the Communist Party in South Africa's liberation. Mandela read widely and wrote memoirs, which were smuggled out of jail.[30] He became a 'constant gardener', planting vegetables during his long captivity. Mandela's relationship with his second wife, Winnie, sadly ended when the relationship that had sustained him in jail for almost three decades disintegrated bitterly and in public within two years of his release from prison.

Madiba and his comrades stubbornly stuck to their principle of majority rule, and refused offers from successive apartheid regimes to renounce their armed struggle in exchange for their freedom. Despite being isolated in jail, Mandela instinctively appeared to know when to negotiate with apartheid's leaders, requesting a meeting with Minister of Justice Kobie Coetsee in 1985, and eventually meeting both President P.W. Botha and President F.W. De Klerk while still a prisoner. As Mandela noted: 'There are times when a leader must move out ahead of his flock.'[31] Like a good shepherd, he skilfully guided his followers to freedom. Mandela's prophetic leadership was clearly decisive in ending apartheid and in ushering democratic rule to South Africa. Acrimonious battles took place between Mandela and De Klerk during the country's democratic transition of 1990 to 1994, with Mandela angrily accusing De Klerk of acting in bad faith in not curbing the excesses of his security forces. During a cabinet meeting in January 1995 in the government of national unity, then-president Mandela chastised deputy president De Klerk so harshly that the latter considered resigning.[32] Mandela had been somewhat uneasy about sharing the Nobel Peace Prize with De Klerk in 1993, feeling that the longtime apartheid-supporting National Party stalwart was unworthy of the accolade.[33] As Tom Lodge noted: 'Mandela was a patriarchal personality conscious of his messianic stature: such leaders do not share moral authority easily.'[34]

Madiba personally embodied his people's aspirations for a democratic future, becoming the leading apostle of reconciliation. He emerged from prison without any apparent bitterness towards his former enemies, and tirelessly promoted national reconciliation. Mandela has been widely celebrated as a political saint and one of the greatest moral figures of the twentieth century. As president, he came to symbolise his country's racial reconciliation. The charisma of this 'Founding Father' helped South Africa's young, democratic institutions to flower between 1994 and 1999, and gave the country an international stature of which a former global pariah could never have dreamed. In contrast to Africa's other post-independence 'Founding Fathers', such as Ghana's Kwame Nkrumah, Zambia's Kenneth Kaunda, Kenya's Jomo Kenyatta, Senegal's Léopold Senghor, and Tanzania's Julius Nyerere, he bowed out gracefully at the end of his first presidential term in 1999, setting a standard for future African leaders aspiring to greatness. As Kenyan scholar Ali Mazrui has noted: 'If in the last half of the twentieth century there was one single statesman in the world who came closest to being *morally number one* among leaders of the human race, Nelson Mandela was probably such a person.'[35] In a similar vein, Kofi Annan, the Ghanaian Secretary-General of the United Nations between 1997 and 2006, wrote: 'To this day, Madiba remains probably the single most admired, most respected international figure in the entire world.'[36]

One of the most noticeable aspects of post-apartheid South African bookshops is the paucity of black authors on the shelves. Even the authoritative, excellent biography of the country's greatest icon—Nelson Mandela—is written by a white Englishman, Anthony Sampson. The publication, in 2006, of a collection of essays, *The Meaning of Mandela*, by three of the greatest living black intellectuals, was therefore particularly welcome.[37] The first essay in this book, by Henry Gates, an African American scholar at Harvard University, is a tribute to both Mandela and the 'Father of Pan-Africanism', W.E.B. Du Bois, who had unsuccessfully sought to produce an encyclopaedia of the African world. Such an encyclopaedia was finally completed by Gates in 1999, and dedicated to Du Bois and Mandela: two of the greatest prophets of pan-Africanism. The second essay, by Cornel West, also an African American scholar, at Princeton University, places Mandela in the context of a 'grand democratic legacy' stretching back to Socrates. West moves from the universal Greek philosopher to describing Mandela as an heir of pan-African prophets like Du Bois, George Padmore, Martin Luther King, Malcolm X, and Patrice Lumumba. Mandela is depicted as a secular prophet, an African Moses leading his people to the promised land from the oppression of white Pharaohs. He urged his people to be set free, and then performed the 'miracle' of the improbable democratic transition in South Africa's own version of the parting of the Red Sea.

West, however, warns against making Mandela 'some kind of icon on a pedestal belonging to a museum'. He calls for a 'culture of criticism ... dialogue and ... contestation' to protect post-apartheid South Africa's fledgling democracy. He also draws parallels between the shallow, conspicuous consumerism of the African American 'bourgeoisie' and South Africa's new suburban 'Wabenzi'.[38] A fiery proselytizer, West makes elegant references to both the

Bible and the blues tradition, describing Mandela as the 'jazzman of the freedom struggle'.[39] This essay is an exuberant celebration of the black experience in the motherland and the diaspora that places Mandela in the pantheon of other black political deities who came before him.

Nigerian Nobel literature laureate Wole Soyinka rounds off the collection of essays with a tribute to his fellow laureate and 'favourite Avatar' in typically fluent prose. Soyinka sees Mandela as the very expression of 'a humanistic will and political vision' and 'a symbol of the culture of dialogue backed by an unparalleled generosity of spirit'. Like West, he urges us to maintain a 'sense of proportion, and avoid further banalising a symbol that is already stretched to an almost inhuman dimension'.[40] For Soyinka, Mandela is an icon and globally recognised symbol of his country's freedom who has been constrained from defining his own identity beyond the mythical figure that his party and supporters have created for him. In Soyinka's 1988 collection of poems, *Mandela's Earth*, he had written:

> *Your bounty threatens me, Mandela, that taut*
> *Drumskin of your heart on which our millions Dance. I fear we latch, fat leeches*
> *On your veins ...*
> *What will be left of you, Mandela?*[41]

Returning to the 2006 collection of essays, Soyinka bemoans the 'soulless, truly horrendous sculpture that dominates Mandela Square in Sandton'.[42] The placing of Mandela's statue in a shopping complex in the heart of Johannesburg could be seen as the commercialisation of this icon, akin to the artworks with Mandela's signature that stirred such controversy in 2005 and 2006 between Madiba and his former lawyer, Ismail Ayob. These incidents, along with the creation of the Mandela Rhodes Foundation and the yoking of Mandela's image to that of Cecil Rhodes at Oxford University, could eventually dent Madiba's legacy.

One of the little-noticed aspects of Mandela is that he promoted an ecumenical approach and tolerance to religion. During his inauguration in May 1994, he ensured that prayers were offered by Jewish, Muslim, Christian, and Hindu ministers. Shortly after becoming president, he visited a mosque and a synagogue, and attended an interdenominational church service. As Archbishop Desmond Tutu noted: 'Madiba's own passion for equality and democracy as well as the enjoyment of inalienable rights for all must to a very considerable extent have been lit by the biblical teaching of the infinite worth of everyone because of being created in the image of God.'[43] Mandela demonstrated these qualities as president through spectacular acts of reconciliation:

he visited P.W. Botha, the hard-line South African leader between 1978 and 1989 who never repented for apartheid's sins; he had tea with the widow of the architect of apartheid, Hendrik Verwoerd, in the segregated all-white 'Republic' of Orania and accompanied her to lay a wreath at the grave of her late husband; he lunched with Percy Yutar, the prosecutor who had sent him to jail; he enthusiastically supported South Africa's Truth and Reconciliation Commission (TRC) process; and during the rugby World Cup in Johannesburg in 1995 he donned a Springbok jersey—a symbol of Afrikaner supremacy for many black South Africans—and willed a practically lily-white team to victory.[44] This gesture was later celebrated in Clint Eastwood's 2009 movie *Invictus*.

As president, despite Western pressure (especially from Washington), Mandela consistently upheld personal loyalty, as seen, for example, in his insistence on maintaining his close friendship with Libya's Muammar Qaddafi and Cuba's Fidel Castro, both of whom had strongly supported the ANC's liberation struggle. This loyalty was to serve Mandela well in brokering a deal in 1999 on the Lockerbie airline bombing of 1988 (blamed on Libya by the US and Britain), which eventually lifted United Nations sanctions on Tripoli (imposed in 1992) by 2003. Mandela was, as usual, ahead of his time: the West has now welcomed Qaddafi back into the international fold, visiting him, hosting him, and trading profitably with him. After 2000, however, Mandela did forego personal loyalty and a conscious post-retirement decision always to be supportive of his successor, when he began to criticise Thabo Mbeki's government and pushed for the provision of anti–retroviral drugs to HIV/AIDS sufferers in South Africa, where 5 million people are afflicted by the pandemic (see chapter 11). This was a battle that Mandela—much to his later regret—had neglected during his own tenure in office. Madiba also courageously sought to champion human rights in Africa, though he was politically hurt and diplomatically isolated on the continent by a bruising diplomatic battle after Nigeria's autocratic General Sani Abacha had brutally hanged Ken Saro-Wiwa and eight Ogoni activists in November 1995 (see chapter 7).[45]

As another prophet Jesus famously proclaimed twenty centuries ago during the Sermon on the Mount: 'Blessed are the peacemakers, for they shall be called children of God.'[46] One of Mandela's lasting legacies will be his efforts—not always successful—at promoting national and international peacemaking. He tirelessly reached out to his former enemies at home, and led peacemaking efforts in Burundi, the Democratic Republic of the Congo

(DRC), and Lesotho.[47] During his presidency between 1994 and 1999, South Africa largely shunned a military role for fear of arousing allegations of hegemonic domination, since the apartheid army had been particularly destructive in Southern Africa, causing an estimated 1 million deaths, as well as $60 billion in damages in the 1980s alone.[48] In what came to be known by some as the 'Mandela Doctrine', Mandela told his fellow leaders at the Organisation of African Unity (OAU) summit in Ouagadougou, Burkina Faso, in 1998: 'Africa has a right and a duty to intervene to root out tyranny... [W]e must all accept that we cannot abuse the concept of national sovereignty to deny the rest of the continent the right and duty to intervene when behind those sovereign boundaries, people are being slaughtered to protect tyranny.'[49]

Nelson Mandela did not just fight injustice in South Africa and Africa; he also fought for the rights of all oppressed and impoverished people around the globe. Even after retiring from office, South Africa's prophet employed his incredible moral stature to become one of the fiercest critics of American president George W. Bush's invasion of Iraq in 2003. As Madiba wondered: 'Why does the United States behave so arrogantly? ... Who are they now to pretend that they are the policeman of the world?'[50] Mandela also spoke for the majority of what Martiniquan intellectual Frantz Fanon described as the 'Wretched of the Earth'—an expression Mandela used in his Nobel Prize speech in 1993—in an address of profound humanity commemorating the UN's fiftieth anniversary in New York in October 1995: 'What challenges us, who define ourselves as statespersons, is the clarion call to dare to think that what we are about is people—the proverbial man and woman in the street. These, the poor, the hungry, the victims of petty tyrants, the objectives of policy, demand change.'[51]

But the prophetic Mandela did, of course, have some flaws: his lambasting of critical black journalists; his suggestion while he was president that Archbishop Desmond Tutu not criticise the ANC in public; his occasional intolerance of dissent, which led to the ousting in 1996 of Pallo Jordan as minister of telecommunications and of Bantu Holomisa as deputy minister of environment; and his obsessive loyalty to some politicians and businessmen, such as Allan Boesak, Stella Sigcau, and Sol Kerzner, who were accused of wrongdoing. Ahmed Kathrada, one of the most perceptive observers of Mandela—a close friend of fifty years who spent two and a half decades with him imprisoned on Robben Island—is typically insightful in this regard, echoing both West and Soyinka:

The Mandela mythology has often not done justice to the real Madiba. Yet it is his virtues more than any kind of imperiousness that has made it difficult for people to see him as anything less than a flawless hero. He has weaknesses and failings ... an uncommon amalgam of the peasant and the aristocrat; the quintessential democrat who nonetheless possesses something of the autocrat; the traditionalist who is an innovator; a man who is at once proud but also simple; soft and tenacious; determinedly obstinate and flexible; vain and shy; cool and impatient.[52]

In similar vein, Mandela's authorised biographer, Anthony Sampson, noted perceptively: 'No saint could have survived in the political jungle for fifty years, and achieved such a worldly transformation. Mandela has his share of human weaknesses, of stubbornness, pride, naiveté, impetuousness... [B]ehind his moral authority and leadership, he has always been a consummate politician.'[53] As a weary Mandela himself recognised: 'I am sorry if I am seen as a demi–god... I am a peg on which to hang all the aspirations of the African National Congress.'[54]

Critics have also noted that Mandela may have ended up doing more long-term damage as president by papering over racial differences and not forcing whites to show more contrition to their largely black victims of apartheid. They have also observed that many of South Africa's 5 million whites continue to enjoy their privileged lifestyles, while the national high priest, Madiba, appears to have absolved them of their sins without a proper confession and penance. Mandela's legacy in liberating his country is secure, but the success of his efforts at national reconciliation will only endure if rapid progress can be made to narrow the country's grotesque socioeconomic inequalities, which have made South Africa the most unequal society in the world. Mandela is, however, a prophet who was honoured in his own land. History will doubtless be much kinder to his nation-building than to Rhodes's empire-building.

Concluding Reflections

Let us return briefly to the significance of the Mandela Rhodes Foundation. The Warden of the Rhodes Trust at the time, John Rowett, pushed this idea strongly until the foundation was unveiled at the centenary celebrations of the Rhodes Trust in Cape Town in February 2003.[55] The South African president Thabo Mbeki adopted a pragmatic approach to the creation of this foundation when he noted in Cape Town in November 2004: 'To place the names of Mandela and Rhodes side-by-side in this manner is an innovative, unusual, and visionary thing to do... [T]hose aspects of Cecil Rhodes' otherwise contested legacy which can be put to work for the good of Africa, are being harnessed—in particular his legacy of excellence in education, and entrepreneurship... While Rhodes' continental vision opened up Africa to Europe, Mandela's vision restores Africa to itself.'[56] Undoubtedly, much good will come out of this foundation in terms of educating children and providing them with better healthcare. But one must also ask whether the possible damage to Mandela's historical legacy makes this monstrous marriage worth the candle. As Antony Thomas, a Rhodes biographer, noted: 'To link the Rhodes name with Mandela is blasphemy. It's unbelievable. It's linking the architect of apartheid with the exponent of its destruction. It shows terrible insensitivity.'[57] Similarly, David Beresford argued that 'the linkage of Mandela's name with that of Rhodes is not only historically inappropriate, but raises puzzling questions as to where the *quid pro quo* lies.'[58]

In stark contrast to these views, some prominent black South Africans have supported the idea of the Mandela Rhodes Foundation. Njabulo Ndebele, the former vice chancellor of the University of Cape Town and a trustee of the Mandela Rhodes Foundation, noted in 2003: 'Is it not remarkable that Rhodes' dream of inter-ethnic co-operation should, at this time in world history, combine with Mandela's dream of reconciliation, the latter encompassing a much more complex human environment?'[59] Jakes Gerwel, chair of the Mandela Rhodes Foundation and director-general in the presidency during Mandela's tenure, argued in 2005: '[Mandela's] agreement to the joining together of the names of Nelson Mandela and Cecil John Rhodes—two famous but historically very different and contrary South African figures— was another example of Mandela not allowing his focus to be distracted by arguments that divide and impede progress.'[60] Defining critics of this perverse scheme as divisive and reactionary, however, would appear to contradict the very principles of open debate that Mandela stands for and has spent his whole life defending. Since Mandela, in a sense, belongs to the whole world— and not just to South Africans—it is, in fact, critical that his prophetic legacy is preserved through open contestation and debate by his legions of admirers, like this humble author, who is himself also linked to the legacy of Cecil Rhodes through his Oxford scholarships.

With the creation of the Mandela Rhodes Foundation in 2002 and the establishment of a Mandela Rhodes building for the foundation in Cape Town in 2005 (donated by De Beers), Mandela—one of the greatest moral figures of the twentieth century—may have, in effect, rehabilitated a grotesque imperialist of the nineteenth century. Surely Madiba could have used the Rhodes Trust and its generous £10 million donation to pursue his good deeds without forever linking his name to that of Rhodes. The trust surely needed Mandela's legitimacy more than he needed its money. It is shocking to visit Rhodes House in Oxford today, and to see Mandela's picture with a white bust of Cecil Rhodes lurking behind him, as well as a painting of each hanging side by side. Surely, Jews would not create a Herzl (founder of the Zionist movement) Hitler Foundation—so why have Africans accepted this monstrosity? Has Mandela perhaps taken reconciliation too far, in rehabilitating an evil figure that Africans really should condemn to the pit-latrine of history?

11

THABO MBEKI

A NKRUMAHIST RENAISSANCE?[1]

'We were mere schoolboys when we saw the black star rise on our firmament, as the colonial Gold Coast crowned itself with the ancient African name of Ghana. We knew then that the promise we had inherited would be honoured. The African giant was awakening! But it came to pass that the march of African time snatched away that promise. Very little seemed to remain along its path except the footprints of despair.'[2]

Thabo Mbeki, president of South Africa, 1999–2008

'No Prophet is honoured in his own land.' The biblical saying epitomises the fate of two African philosopher-kings: Ghana's founding president, Kwame Nkrumah (1957–1966),[3] and South Africa's second post-apartheid president, Thabo Mbeki (1999–2008).[4] Mbeki can in some ways be regarded as this age's Nkrumah. Both believed in Africa's ancient glory and sought to build modern states that restored the continent's past. Both were renaissance men: visionary intellectuals committed to a pan-African vision. Both hosted pan-African conferences and were instrumental in the creation of the Organisation of African Unity (OAU) and the African Union (AU). Both were at core African nationalists who flirted with communism.[5] While Nkrumah championed the African Personality, Mbeki promoted the African Renaissance. Both the African Personality and the African Renaissance were widely used but nebulous concepts that lacked a clear definition and road-map of how to operationalise them in practice. Both leaders were peacemakers: Nkrumah sent 2,000 peacekeepers to the Congo in 1960 to assist a United Nations mission, and was on a peace mission to Vietnam when his regime was toppled in a coup d'état in February 1966; Mbeki sought to make peace in the Democratic Republic of the Congo (DRC), Burundi, and Côte d'Ivoire, and sent over 3,000 peacekeepers to the DRC, Burundi, and Sudan's Darfur region. Both leaders sought to speak on behalf of Africa in multilateral forums, often to the irritation of other regional governments. Both were accused of monarchical tendencies at home, and in the end were toppled in apparent acts of regicide: Nkrumah by the military, and Mbeki by his African National Congress (ANC) party.

But there were differences between the two leaders. Nkrumah was charismatic and, for a while, enjoyed the unparalleled adulation of the Ghanaian masses. Mbeki did not inherit the charisma of South Africa's first post-apartheid president, Nelson Mandela (see chapter 10), and relied more on political managerialism and visionary skills to rule. Nkrumah was able to mobilise and rally the masses; Mbeki relied on manoeuvring within his party. Nkrumah favoured a more federalist 'United States of Africa'; Mbeki's vision was more gradualist. Nkrumah adopted a personality cult, and 'Nkrumahism' was developed into an anti–imperial ideology of pan-Africanism. Mbeki avoided a personality cult, and no ideology bearing the name 'Mbekism' ever came into existence during his rule.

Mbeki's African National Congress and Nkrumah's Convention People's Party (CPP) were electorally dominant in South Africa and Ghana, and both leaders seemed to use their parties as Leninist vanguards, ruling in a top-down fashion and perceiving themselves as guardians of 'national revolutions'. Nkrumah deployed CPP cadres in a bid to transform the colonial civil service; Mbeki deployed ANC cadres in an attempt to transform the apartheid bureaucracy. Both leaders were masters of political intrigue and manipulation. Both could be indecisive with difficult decisions, and often left unpleasant tasks to lieutenants, avoiding direct confrontation with rivals. Both stressed party discipline and personal loyalty. Both bred a climate of fear within their parties. The ANC and the CPP not only came to be closely identified with the state, but also came under the control and manipulation of their leaders. Close supporters lacked an independent power base, were dependent on Nkrumah and Mbeki for support, and tended towards sycophancy and subservience. Both leaders doled out patronage through state agencies and controlled their parliamentary parties with an iron grip. Both railed against corruption, and were widely perceived as not being too personally ostentatious with regard to wealthy living (though seemingly condoning some instances of corruption, especially in favour of their parties, and not reining in lieutenants). Both Mbeki and Nkrumah were broadly seen to be more interested in power than wealth, and both sought to prevent the ascendancy of an organised 'left'.

Nkrumah and Mbeki both became increasingly paranoid, with Nkrumah being deeply affected by two assassination attempts. Both eventually spawned factionalised parties. Both were nocturnal workaholics who survived on only a few hours of sleep, with Mbeki famously surfing the Internet late at night. Both were pragmatic politicians who dispensed with ideology if they felt that it impeded the achievement of practical goals. Both regarded themselves as philosopher-kings who sought the company of intellectuals (Nkrumah had fourteen publications to his name, and Mbeki published three books of speeches, many of which he wrote himself),[6] though many members of their intelligentsia were ironically opposed to their rule. Both seemed to focus disproportionately on foreign policy as they tired of incessant party squabbles. Both tried to run foreign policy from well-staffed presidential units, and both are likely to be remembered more in the long term for their foreign policies than their domestic achievements.

But despite histrionic depictions of Mbeki as a dictator by an erratic South African commentariat, it was Nkrumah's rule that represented autocracy. Some might even argue that Mbeki and Nkrumah are too different to be compared with each other. Perhaps Zimbabwe's Robert Mugabe may be a closer contemporary comparison to Nkrumah's autocratic rule, and Libya's Muammar Qaddafi to his pan-African federalism. But we argue here that there are three key points that make the comparison between Nkrumah and Mbeki valid. First, both men were visionary intellectuals who had spent over a decade in exile, and both wrote books and/or speeches propounding important ideas about how Africa should promote development and economic integration. Second, both Nkrumah and Mbeki were clearly the dominant foreign policy figures on the African stage in their respective eras. This does not mean, of course, that their visions were realised, but it is sufficient that they promoted ideas and initiatives to which other African leaders and outsiders were forced to react. In the end, both leaders played a large part in the creation of the OAU and the AU. Finally, the leadership of the dominant parties in Ghana and South Africa—the CPP and the ANC—under Nkrumah and Mbeki, had several similarities in the way that both men wielded power. Both leaders had a ruthless streak, were intolerant of criticism, sought to ensure that their leadership was not challenged (even refusing to groom clear successors), suffered from a certain paranoia, micro-managed key appointments, and demanded absolute loyalty from their lieutenants. There is thus a solid basis for comparing the leadership styles and domestic and foreign policy achievements of Nkrumah and Mbeki.

We begin by assessing some of the concepts and typologies of leadership styles in Africa—demonstrated by Nkrumah and Mbeki—which are analysed under the general framework of monarchical and prophetic traditions in African politics. Next, we examine the performance of both leaders in three key spheres: politics, foreign policy (pan-Africanism), and socioeconomic development—their quest, in a sense, for three African magic kingdoms. We conclude with some retrospective thoughts on the legacies of both leaders within the contemporary context of Ghana, South Africa, and the broader African context. We however do not wish to present an exaggerated picture of the influence of individual leaders (even powerful ones) in shaping events solely through their own actions, nor do we wish to ignore the fact that other actors, institutions, and variables had an effect on the events described here.

Monarchical and Prophetic Traditions in African Politics

Kenyan scholar Ali Mazrui was one of the early pioneers of the study of personal rule and leadership styles in Africa. He noted that African leaders attempted to use monarchical styles 'to strengthen the legitimacy of the regimes with sacred symbols and romantic awe'.[7] Mazrui further identified monarchical tendencies in African political culture as part of the need of many African leaders to revive a splendid past in order to restore a sense of national dignity that had been damaged by the effects of slavery and European imperialism.[8] Nkrumah thus sought to ancientise and modernise his country, taking the name of the ancient African empire of 'Ghana' but embarking on an industrialisation project in a bid to replicate the success of Western societies. His concept of 'African Personality' sought to win recognition of the glory of Africa's cultural contributions to the world and gain some African self-respect that had been systematically eroded by Western imperialism.[9] Like Nkrumah, Thabo Mbeki similarly sought to modernise South Africa and to restore Africa's past glory through his promotion of an African Renaissance. He sought to build a modern African state, even sending his brother Moeletsi to study the British cabinet structure before assuming the presidency.[10]

In his most famous essay, written in 1966 shortly after Kwame Nkrumah fell from power, Ali Mazrui depicted the Ghanaian leader as a 'Leninist Czar': a royalist revolutionary.[11] The Kenyan scholar argued that Nkrumah had ruled in a monarchical fashion and thus lost the organisational effectiveness of a Leninist party structure. The Ghanaian leader had wanted 'Nkrumahism' to leave a historical and revolutionary mark similar to the impact of Leninism. As Mazrui noted: 'Nkrumah's tragedy was a tragedy of *excess*, rather than of contradiction. He tried to be too much of a revolutionary monarch.'[12] Mazrui concluded that Nkrumah would be celebrated more as a great pan-African than a great Ghanaian, an insight that has proved to be largely accurate. 'Nkrumahism' became the nebulous ideology that the Ghanaian admirer of Lenin sought to develop, and like Lenin, Nkrumah had requested, in an early will, that his body be embalmed and preserved after his death![13]

Robert Jackson and Carl Rosberg, in their innovative 1982 study *Personal Rule in Black Africa*, noted: 'The prophet, political or religious, is a revolutionary—that is, one who prophesies a better future, whose attainment requires the radical transformation of the present.'[14] A main feature of prophetic rule is that it has a religious side to it. At Africa's current socioeconomic stage of development, miracles have proved difficult to perform, as the stuff of which miracles are made has been in short supply. Economic development, after all, is a painstaking, gradual process that requires such things as decades of careful planning, adequate capital, and competent technocrats to bring about. The vision of paradise that once overwhelmed the disciples and guaranteed their adherence to the Faith is simply not within the African Prophet's capability to bring about rapidly, as the cases of Nkrumah and Mbeki proved. It is this failure to fortify the faith of the masses through signs of divine healing—socioeconomic development, elimination of poverty, and transformation of society—that cost prophets like Nkrumah and Mbeki their political lives.

Nkrumah and Mbeki can also be seen, in a sense, as tragic figures in African Shakespearean dramas. Where Nkrumah might be seen as a Julius Caesar, it is Coriolanus who best mirrors Mbeki's fate. Nkrumah's Sierra Leonean biographer, Bankole Timothy (who was later deported from Ghana by Nkrumah's security forces), observed that the Ghanaian leader was accused of trying to build 'a great African Empire with himself as Caesar'.[15] We will recall that in Shakespeare's play, the Roman Senate had made Caesar *dictator perpetuus* of Rome, as the Ghanaian parliament effectively made Nkrumah Ghana's dictator. As Caesar had been viewed as ruthless and accused of weakening the powers of the Senate, so too was Nkrumah viewed by his critics. The plot that killed Caesar was intended to prevent him turning Rome into a monarchy; Nkrumah had himself revealed his monarchical tendencies, which Ghana's military putschists in 1966 declared that they had intervened to end. Both Caesar and Nkrumah effectively fell after suspicions that they would turn republics into monarchies. Like Caesar's patricians, Nkrumah's political class lived lavish lifestyles and lacked a sense of *noblesse oblige*. While Caesar had a statue of himself installed in a Roman temple, Nkrumah had a statue of himself erected outside the Ghanaian parliament.[16] A new coinage appeared bearing the inscription 'Kwame Nkrumah, *civitatis Ghaniensis conditor*':[17] here was Ghana's answer to imperial Rome's Caesar! As Brutus had betrayed Caesar, so too did some of Nkrumah's closest lieutenants, like Alex Quaison-Sackey and Kofi Baako, who had been vocal apostles of Nkrumahism, also betray their leader after his fall from power, even if it was the soldiers—rather than the politicians—who plunged the knife into his back. Before the coup that toppled him, Nkrumah's Egyptian wife, Fathia Rizk, had warned him—after a bad dream—about a forthcoming tragedy, fearing the 'Ides of February'.

During his student days in Moscow, Mbeki's favourite play had been Shakespeare's *Coriolanus*. This was the tragedy of a heroic Roman soldier whose demise was brought about by obduracy and pride. Like *Julius Caesar*, it is a play about politics and betrayal. Coriolanus becomes a war hero, is banished from Rome, defects to the Volsces, and is subsequently killed. The flaw in Coriolanus's character contributes greatly to his downfall in a play that is widely considered to be Shakespeare's most political.[18] Coriolanus refuses to swagger, to celebrate his battlefield victory, and to show off his war wounds, arguing that 'I play the man I am'. Rather than the conventional perception of Coriolanus as a 'vainglorious proto-fascist' and a 'tyrant driven by hubris',[19] Mbeki instead regarded the Roman soldier as the model for a twentieth-century revolutionary, noting that Coriolanus was full of 'truthfulness, courage, self-sacrifice, absence of self-seeking, brotherliness, heroism, optimism'. Mbeki admired Coriolanus for being prepared to go to war against his own people, whom Mbeki described as 'rabble ... an unthinking mob, with its cowardice, its lying, its ordinary people-ness'.[20] The similarity of the fates of Coriolanus and Mbeki are eerie: both were seen as aloof and arrogant; both refused to kow-tow to popular perceptions of how a leader should behave; and both were ultimately brought down by character flaws of obduracy and arrogance.

The Political Kingdom

Kwame Nkrumah

Nkrumah had famously implored Africa's liberation fighters: 'Seek ye first the political kingdom and all things will be added to it.' He also argued that 'political power is the inescapable prerequisite to economic and social power'.[21] In the end, Nkrumah would be disappointed that the political kingdom did not necessarily lead to the socioeconomic kingdom of industrialisation and development. The Ghanaian leader had spent ten years in America, earning degrees from the Universities of Lincoln and Pennsylvania, before spending two years in England. He returned home by 1947 to become secretary-general of the United Gold Coast Convention (UGCC) before creating his own Convention People's Party two years later. Nkrumah was jailed in 1948 and again in 1950, before becoming 'Leader of Government Business' in 1951. When Ghana was delivered to independence by its British midwife in March 1957, this small state on Africa's West Coast instantly shot to international fame as the first self-defined black African state to win its independence.[22] (Sudan with a largely Arab leadership had won its independence in 1956). Though the CPP had won clear majorities in each of Ghana's three pre-independence elections, its vote had never exceeded 35 per cent of the enfranchised electorate.[23] Thus, even in the independence struggle, Nkrumah's party had been unable to mobilise half the eligible voters. There thus existed many disgruntled groups—the Ga Standfast Association, secessionists, trade unionists, cocoa growers, and market-women—whose support could be mobilised for parochial issues (which the opposition opportunistically, and sometimes irresponsibly, did).

The Ghanaian 'right' (comprising conservative professional and commercial elites of the old-style United Gold Coast Convention group) had never forgiven Nkrumah, its former secretary-general, for outmanoeuvring them by correctly reading the pulse of the radicalised Ghanaian populace in demanding 'self-government now' and creating his own breakaway CPP. This condescending elite regarded Nkrumah as an upstart, and patronisingly referred to the CPP stalwarts as the 'commoner's party' packed with 'standard six drop-outs' and 'verandah boys'. A great deal of personal animosity therefore developed between the CPP and the leaders of the National Liberation Movement (NLM)—and later the United Party—turning Ghanaian politics into a cutthroat 'zero-sum' game in which the winner would keep all the spoils from the battle.

Having secured power in March 1957, Nkrumah set about de-democratizing the Ghanaian political system, arguing disingenuously that opposition was alien to African society. He smashed civil society by replacing it with his own peculiar brand of one-party rule under a socialist ideology. The methods employed were varied, but a notable feature was Nkrumah's conscious efforts to cloak his actions behind a veneer of constitutional legality, even though it was clear that these were expedient acts in which laws were adapted to suit the leader's political goals.

Nkrumah began by virtually declaring the constitution a 'dead letter'—he outlawed the opposition NLM as a regionally and ethnically based party, disbanded regional assemblies, appointed CPP apparatchiks as regional commissioners, and replaced pro-NLM chiefs with compliant pro-CPP ones. With the Ghanaian 'right' safely out of the way, he turned his attention to preventing the ascendancy of an organised 'left'. The euphemistic-sounding Industrial Conciliation Act was enacted in 1957 to outlaw most labour action. The United Grand Farmers Council and the Trades Union Congress were brought under CPP control barely six months after independence, while the youth movements were co-opted through the establishment of the Young Pioneers as an ancillary of the CPP. The only opposition newspaper, the *Ashanti Pioneer*, was censored and converted into a pro-CPP organ. Academic freedom was stifled in Ghana's universities, and the judiciary's chief justice, Arku Korsah, was dismissed in 1963 for reaching a verdict that Nkrumah regarded as anti–government. By 1964, a de jure one-party state had been established under CPP hegemony.

Between 1958 and 1961, Nkrumah passed six draconian bills that completed the obliteration of civil society and further reduced the judiciary to an instrument of his coercive rule. The most infamous of these—the innocuous-sounding Preventive Detention Act of July 1958—allowed the government to hold persons suspected of constituting a threat to state security for five years without trial. In 1960, Nkrumah used a referendum to secure a strong presidency and de jure one-party rule. The massive 90 per cent majority for both these proposals reflected the increasing electoral fraud perpetrated by the CPP as it tightened its grip on the levers of state. Nkrumah had become increasingly intolerant of opposition and sought to subordinate all major interest groups under party control.

The CPP as a dominant political party came not only to be closely identified with the state, many of its parliamentarians were spectacularly corrupt, embezzling public funds. Through the system of bloated parastatals set up to control public and private enterprise, Nkrumah doled out patronage and played factions in parliament against each other to maintain his dominant position as the arbiter of the fate of party and state. As an Accra joke of the period so fittingly described this state of affairs, the first item on the agenda for party meetings chaired by Nkrumah was always 'Any Other Business'.[24] One aspect of Nkrumah's rule that many critics saw as evidence of the growing 'madness' of the Ghanaian 'King' was the development of a personality cult and hero-worshipping of a divine sort. There were a plethora of praise-names, like Redeemer (Osagyefo), Fount of Honour, Father of the Nation, Messiah, Teacher, Ideological Mentor, The Infallible, Man of Destiny, Star of Africa, Deliverer of Ghana, His High Dedication, Gandhi of Ghana, Show Boy, and Golden Boy of Africa.[25]

Nigerian Nobel literature laureate Wole Soyinka created one of the most memorable portraits of Nkrumah's autocratic rule in his satirical 1967 play *Kongi's Harvest*. Written and performed during Nkrumah's reign and published a year after his fall from power, the play was set in a fictional African state called Isma. Kongi is a 'repressive, ambitious' and messianically deluded tyrant who develops an ideology of 'Kongism' complete with 'algebraic quantums'. He is assisted by a fraternity of sycophantic Aweris and backed by a brutal Carpenter's Brigade. Some of Kongi's main opponents, like Oba Danlola, have been slammed into detention, but the autocrat has failed to quell the Oba's opposition. Danlola's nephew, Daodu, leader of a farming cooperative, and Kongi's ex–mistress Segi, also oppose his tyrannical rule. A plot is hatched to assassinate Kongi during the New Yam Festival, which Kongi narrowly survives.[26]

The parallels between Kongi's and Nkrumah's rule are unmistakable. Kongism ridicules Nkrumahism as well as the algebraic pretensions of Nkrumah's reportedly ghost-written 1964 treatise *Conscienscism*.[27] The Christ-like delusions of Kongi recall those of the Redeemer. The Aweris clearly represent the clique of sycophantic politicians around Nkrumah. The Carpenter's Brigade could represent the thuggish Worker's Brigade and the Youth Pioneers. Danlola's dignified presence recalls Ghana's patrician opposition politician J.B. Danquah, who died in Nkrumah's jail in February 1965. Danlola and Segi could represent the groups of farmers and market-women groups who increasingly opposed Nkrumah's rule. The failed plot to kill Kongi mirrors the two unsuccessful assassination attempts on Nkrumah's life.

In assessing the balance sheet of Nkrumah's rule, it is clear that the Ghanaian Prophet failed in his attempt to lead the faithful to a 'New Jerusalem'.

Nkrumah destroyed democracy in Ghana so decisively that, by 1960, out of thirty-two opposition leaders at independence in 1957, one was in detention, one was in exile, and twelve had crossed the floor of the House to the government side.[28] The two assassination attempts on Nkrumah's life in 1962 and 1964 appeared to be genuine grounds for concern, but also provided ample evidence of the dangers inherent in repressive policies with no outlet for dissent against the government. Nkrumah had tried to revitalise his party, but within two years the new revolutionaries turned out to be no more than opportunistic sycophants. Not only was Nkrumah attempting to carry out a revolution without genuine revolutionaries, the CPP also lacked competent, skilful cadres in the numbers needed to ensure the success of any revolution. The able and efficient Ghanaian civil servants to whom Nkrumah increasingly turned after 1961, like Michael Dei–Anang and A.L. Adu, were unable to fulfil his socialist dreams. After all, they were not revolutionaries but conservative-minded bureaucrats who strove for status quo and stability, rather than revisionism and revolution.

With no real opposition, the CPP was splintered by 1961. The assassination attempts on Nkrumah increased his paranoia and sense of insecurity, and in his latter years he isolated himself in Christianburg Castle (now Osu Castle) guarded by soldiers: the new 'Governor General' was now playing the authoritarian role that Her Majesty's colonial government had bequeathed to her West African 'jewel in the crown'. In the end, Nkrumah was trapped: he could neither retreat nor advance with confidence.[29] Having lived his last six years in exile in Guinea,[30] he died of cancer, a lonely and sad man, in a Romanian hospital in 1972.[31] His body was brought home to be buried in his ancestral home of Nkroful, before being moved to Accra in 1992 where he lies buried next to his Egyptian wife who died in 2007.

Thabo Mbeki

South Africa's president between 1999 and 2008, Thabo Mbeki remains an enigma to many. The saintly footsteps of founding president Nelson Mandela were clearly going to be hard for Mbeki to follow.[32] Mbeki built his support around a group of trusted loyalists, many of whom, but not all, had been in exile with him.[33] Even as deputy president, Mbeki sought to overcome the deficiency of living in Mandela's shadow through visionary leadership. He called for an African Renaissance—an expression used by earlier pan-Africanists like Nigeria's Nnamdi Azikiwe—as a doctrine for Africa's political, economic, and social renewal and the reintegration of Africa into the global economy. Mbeki urged Africans to adapt democracy to fit their own specific conditions without compromising its principles of representation and accountability. The foot-soldiers of Africa's Renaissance were urged to embrace the same revolutionary zeal that had freed the continent from the twin scourges of colonialism and apartheid.

Through this doctrine, Mbeki challenged Africans to discover a sense of their own self-confidence after centuries of slavery and colonialism, which had systematically denigrated their cultures and subjugated their institutions to alien rule.[34] The African Renaissance did not naively assume, as some critics asserted, that this renewal was already under way: it merely sought to set out an inspiring vision and prescribe the policy actions that could create the conditions for Africa's rebirth. With Mbeki as chief architect, the drafting of the New Partnership for Africa's Development (NEPAD) in 2001 and the birth of the African Union in 2002 were clearly attempts to add policy flesh to the skeletal bones of the Renaissance vision. There is some truth, however, to the criticism that the Renaissance was devoid of substantive policy content. In an insightful analysis in 2002, Peter Vale and Sipho Maseko noted: 'South Africa's idea of an African Renaissance is abstruse, puzzling, even perhaps mysterious, more promise than policy.'[35] The Renaissance project was also an effort by a self-confessedly 'disconnected' Mbeki to reconnect with his African roots.[36] As his excellent biographer Mark Gevisser noted: 'From a very young age, his response to this condition of disconnection had been to sublimate all emotions, all relationships, all desires, into the struggle for liberation.'[37] Mbeki's understanding of Africa often appeared similar to many African Americans longing for a return to a nostalgic, romanticised past. Gevisser captured well the ambiguities in Mbeki's engagement with Africa: 'Mbeki is not an "outside observer": he crossed over into "real Africa" as other South Africans have not. And yet his relationship to this "real Africa", of which he has been made a citizen is fraught with ambivalence, for with every example he presents, it becomes clearer that even though he is attracted to it, it is antithetical to everything he stands for.'[38]

Mbeki sought to use the Renaissance vision to convince fellow South Africans—who had for years been indoctrinated by racist white rulers to view Africa as a place of darkness and disease from which they existed apart (see chapter 5)—to embrace not just a new South African identity, but a new *African* identity as well. As Mbeki told his fellow South Africans in June 1999: 'No longer capable of being falsely defined as a European outpost in Africa, we are an African nation in the complex process simultaneously of formation and renewal... We will work to rediscover and claim the African heritage, for the benefit especially of our young generation.'[39] As has been noted by Ali Mazrui, no other African leader than a black South African president could have made Mbeki's famous May 1996 'I am an African' speech without being marched off to an asylum! In the speech, Mbeki set out an inclusive definition of South Africa that was a stirring attempt to encourage his compatriots to embrace and celebrate the African identity they had long been denied. In the lyrical speech, the then–South African deputy president stated: 'I am an African. I owe my being to the hills and the valleys, the mountains and the glades, the rivers, the deserts, the trees, the flowers, the seas and the ever-changing seasons that define the face of our native land.'[40]

Thabo Mbeki studied economics at Sussex University in England between 1962 and 1965. This prophet of the African Renaissance often paradoxically cuts the picture of a black Englishman with his stiff and formal demeanour, sports jacket, designer suits, Bay Rum tobacco and pipe (perhaps inspired by Labour leader Harold Wilson, whom Mbeki admired during his student days), and constant quoting of William Shakespeare and W.B. Yeats. As a child, Thabo had attended the black elite missionary school Lovedale and studied Shakespeare, Jane Austen, and Joseph Conrad. His political mentor was the ANC leader in exile, Oliver Tambo, from whom he learned the skills of compromising, winning over enemies, stitching disparate coalitions together, and avoiding direct confrontation. Mbeki was the leading ANC figure in the secret meetings with white politicians, businessmen, and intellectuals in the 1980s. He played an instrumental role in convincing Afrikaner general Constand Viljoen and his Freedom Front to take part in the first postapartheid elections in 1994.

During negotiations with Frederick De Klerk's National Party in 1991, the ANC replaced Mbeki as chief negotiator with the tougher trade unionist Cyril Ramaphosa, a rival for the leadership and Mandela's preferred successor, who later became a business tycoon. As Mandela noted about Mbeki: 'He would not confront problems directly as I have done. He is too diplomatic for that. He is sometimes criticized by our own people, who say he is indecisive when faced with a situation that requires firmness.'[41] On Mbeki's assumption of the ANC presidency in December 1997, Mandela praised Thabo's brilliance but warned ominously: 'One of the temptations of a leader who has been elected unopposed is that he may use his powerful position to settle scores with his detractors, marginalise them, and in certain cases, get rid of them and surround himself with yes-men and -women.'[42] Mbeki would gain his own revenge during a party in honour of Mandela's eightieth birthday in July 1998. In a generous but needling speech, Thabo compared his president to Shakespeare's King Lear, which some read as reference to an autocratic, senile leader retreating to retirement and old age.

Mbeki was considered by many of his critics to be aloof and arrogant, in contrast to his fiery rival Chris Hani, who was assassinated in Johannesburg in 1993. Allies describe this aloofness more as shyness than arrogance.[43] With his father, Govan Mbeki, having been jailed with Nelson Mandela on Robben Island, Mbeki was born into the liberation struggle and devoted fifty-two years of his life to serving the ANC. Though he spent a year in the Soviet Union undergoing military training, he let his membership in the South African Communist Party (SACP) lapse a year after the Berlin Wall fell in 1989, demonstrating deft pragmatism. Mbeki's critics saw him as a scheming, manipulative Machiavellian figure who brooked no dissent, surrounded himself with mediocre allies who would not challenge him, and ruthlessly co-opted or eliminated political rivals through smear campaigns. This was the 'Prince' to Nkrumah's 'King'. The reported discovery in 2001 of a 'plot' against Mbeki by three rivals—Cyril Ramaphosa, Mathews Phosa, and Tokyo Sexwale—was a paranoid carryover of liberation-style tactics into a democratic order. In cabinet, Mbeki's ministers often withheld their opinions because they feared that he might not agree with them.[44]

Mbeki's often trenchant backers, like Ronald Suresh Roberts and Christine Qunta, have sought to highlight the personal and ideological agendas of those who dominate the media in the interests of the status quo and are uncomfortable with an assertive, intelligent pan-African who is not afraid to force whites to confront sensitive issues of race and poverty.[45] Though seen as a good technocrat, the workaholic Mbeki was a micro-manager who as president insisted on appointing provincial premiers and top civil servants, and centralizing power in an executive with over 300 staff.

Another criticism of Mbeki's administration was that it did not clamp down on corruption and incompetence as severely as it should have done. By far the most serious and potentially damaging case for Mbeki's legacy was a controversial arms deal between 1997 and 1999 with European firms worth 30 billion rand (about $4 billion) at the time, but that subsequently rose to 43 billion rand (about $6 billion). As deputy president, Mbeki was in charge of the arms procurement programme, and was subsequently accused by the *Sunday Times* (South Africa) of benefitting personally from this deal. Promises that the arms purchases would create 64,000 jobs and bring 110 billion rand (about $16 billion) of investment into South Africa did not materialise. Despite reports that some of the funds went to ANC party coffers, other allegations of embezzlement were levelled at senior ANC figures.[46] Corruption was also evident at a broader level: in February 2008, a report by the Public Services Commission noted that cases of corruption in South Africa had doubled and that the costs of combating this scourge were increasing by 186 per cent every year.[47]

The intensely private Mbeki ruled as a self-styled philosopher-king whose tough exterior probably masked a vulnerability born of having effectively grown up in exile without his parents and having had a son from his young adulthood 'disappear' in apartheid South Africa. Mbeki was criticised for being too thin-skinned to media criticisms, and his relationship with the media deteriorated badly during his presidency. In 1998 as ANC president, he criticised South Africa's Truth and Reconciliation Commission (TRC) for its condemnation of the ANC for alleged torture and executions of dissidents in its camps in Angola, and unsuccessfully sought a court injunction to prevent publication of the TRC report. Four years later, Mbeki's supporters humiliated Mandela at an ANC meeting for speaking out against the government's controversial AIDS policies (discussed below) outside party structures. In 2004, Mbeki harshly criticised Archbishop Desmond Tutu's statements that South Africa was sitting on 'a powder keg of poverty', that only a tiny elite benefitted from the government's Black Economic Empowerment (BEE) programme (discussed later), and that sycophancy had replaced robust debate. Some of the media attacks against Mbeki, though, by critics like Xolela Mangcu, Mondli Makhanya, and Justice Malala, were of a personalised and emotional nature and often lacked both subtlety and substance.[48] The blacklisting of certain anti–government critics by the state-funded South African Broadcasting Corporation (SABC), however, will remain a blemish on Mbeki's record, even if this did not reach the depths of Nkrumah's press censorship or the actions of previous apartheid regimes.

Undoubtedly, the most controversial policy of Mbeki's presidency was what his critics dubbed his 'AIDS denialism'.[49] South Africa is estimated to have the largest number of people infected with HIV/AIDS—5 million—but its president said in 2003 that he did not know anyone who had died of the disease. Mbeki set up a presidential AIDS advisory council, half of whose members belonged to the 'dissident camp' of scholars who did not believe mainstream views that HIV necessarily caused AIDS. Though Mbeki has denied holding this view himself, he sent mixed messages on this key issue, through his advisory panel and his own utterances, that negatively affected public information campaigns. The ANC leadership eventually convinced Mbeki to withdraw from a public debate on the issue. In 2004 the government agreed to roll-out anti–retroviral drugs in earnest, after South Africa's Constitutional Court had ordered it to do so two years earlier, and under pressure from the medical community as well as civic groups, trade unions, and churches, as well as Nelson Mandela and Desmond Tutu. The decisive intervention apparently came from Mbeki's international investment council (including advice from figures like George Soros and Neil Fitzgerald), which cautioned Mbeki about the negative effect that South Africa's AIDS policies were having on foreign investment. While Mbeki's administration complained about the high costs, toxicity, and uncertain efficacy of anti–retrovirals, his critics noted that the government had spent billions of rand on a controversial arms deal and a presidential jet. The explanations offered for Mbeki's obstinate stance on this issue revolved around his strong rejection of claims that AIDS originated in Africa and is spread by what is sometimes stereotypically depicted as uncontrolled black sexuality. But this debacle will undoubtedly do great damage to Mbeki's historical legacy.

The Pan-African Kingdom

Kwame Nkrumah

In the foreign policy field, Kwame Nkrumah played a tremendous role in Africa's liberation struggle and provided a vision of pan-African unity. Though he was widely vilified in Ghana after his demise, Nkrumah remained a hero for many Africans, someone who gave them a sense of dignity and put the continent on the international map. More than any other individual, he ensured that a pan-African organisation was born, placing pan-Africanism on the international agenda when other states were still in the colonial womb.[50] Ali Mazrui has ranked Nkrumah as the most important pan-African figure of the twentieth century,[51] while in a poll in the London-based magazine *New African* in 2004, Nkrumah was rated the second greatest African of all time after Nelson Mandela.[52]

As Nkrumah famously noted: 'The independence of Ghana is meaningless unless it is linked up with the total liberation of the African continent.'[53] Nkrumah's pan-African vision was of a 'Union Government of African States' with a common currency, an African defence command, and a common foreign policy.[54] But the Ghanaian leader was widely distrusted by his fellow African leaders for backing armed dissidents, and even his union with Guinea and Mali of 1960 proved to be short-lived, becoming moribund by January 1962.[55] Foreign policy successes after 1957 proved to be few and far between. Nkrumah realised after independence that he would have to use his head-start of early independence to establish his small country as an important African state. He therefore tried to establish Accra as the centre of pan-African conferences, before large, potentially powerful states like Nigeria[56] and conservative francophone African states attained their independence. Nkrumah still regarded himself as a revolutionary who was yet to complete his revolution at home and abroad. But neither Ghana nor Africa were ripe for revolution, and there was more importantly a dearth of revolutionaries in both country and continent.

Nkrumah alienated many African leaders by his harbouring of rebel groups in Ghana, accusations of his alleged involvement in the assassination of Togo's President Sylvanus Olympio in January 1963, and his irredentist claims on part of that country. By the time that thirty-one African heads of state gathered in the Ethiopian capital of Addis Ababa in 1963 to sign the Charter of the Organisation of African Unity, Nkrumah was in a minority of one in pushing for an integrated African political and economic entity. The 'National Personality' had scored a stunning triumph over Nkrumah's 'African Personality.'[57]

But Nkrumah's energy, dedication, and contributions to African liberation and the cause of pan-Africanism were indisputable. He hosted the first Conference of Independent African States in Accra in April 1958, which aimed to forge closer unity between independent African states and to liberate the rest of the continent from colonial rule. Ten months later, Nkrumah hosted the All-African People's Conference in Accra, which involved delegates from sixty-two African nationalist organisations, including Martiniquan intellectual and Algerian freedom fighter Frantz Fanon, who argued forcefully in Accra for the use of violence as self-transforming for liberation movements in reaction to Nkrumah's own more Gandhian 'Positive Action' (see chapter 14).[58] In November 1959, Nkrumah hosted the All-African Trade Union Federation in Accra, involving unionists from across the continent. Five months later, Accra hosted a conference on 'Positive Action and Security' in Africa to discuss the liberation of Algeria and South Africa, and to prevent the continent from becoming a dumping ground for nuclear weapons from the West. Six years later, Ghana hosted the OAU summit.[59] Nkrumah also contributed troops to the UN's mission in the Congo between 1960 and 1964 to help keep the country united, and promoted the idea of an African High Command to deter external actors from waging proxy wars and to liberate the continent from alien rule. Nkrumah was undoubtedly the foremost political prophet of Pax Africana[60], even if his vision remained unfulfilled in his own lifetime.

Thabo Mbeki

As a student at Sussex university, Thabo Mbeki imbibed the ideas of Aimé Césaire, Léopold Senghor, W.E.B. Du Bois, and Frantz Fanon. His master's thesis focused on industrialisation in West Africa, as a strong pan-African awareness developed. Mbeki's African Renaissance vision was inspired by his shock at what he saw as the 'slave mentality' of black South Africans after his return home from exile in 1990. As he put it: 'The beginning of our rebirth as a Continent must be our own rediscovery of our soul... It was very clear that something had happened in South African society, something that didn't happen in any other African society. The repeated observation is that "These South Africans are not quite African, they're European."'[61] Mbeki also criticised the black intelligentsia, many of whose members he felt were timid and too deferential to their white colleagues. He was determined, through his African Renaissance, to reverse damaging stereotypes about the continent, noting in 1995: 'Many in our society genuinely believe that as black people we have no capacity to govern successfully, much less manage a modern and sophisticated economy. These are very quick to repeat the nauseating refrain— look what has happened in the rest of Africa!'[62]

Under Mbeki's foreign policy, South Africa established solid credentials to become Africa's leading power. He consistently sought multilateral solutions to resolving regional conflicts. This explains Mbeki's policy of 'quiet diplomacy' towards Zimbabwe's Robert Mugabe. He skilfully used both a strategic partnership with Nigeria and his chairmanship of the African Union between 2002 and 2003 to pursue his foreign policy goals on the continent. He was more prepared than Mandela to send peacekeepers abroad, which increased South Africa's credibility as a major geostrategic player in Africa. Mbeki also used his consensus-building skills to serve as chief mediator in Côte d'Ivoire and the DRC, though he was more successful in the latter than the former.[63] (See chapter 5 for more details of Mbeki's foreign policy.)

Mbeki was the first chair of the African Union at its birth in Durban, South Africa, in 2002, and chaired the Non-Aligned Movement (NAM); he was the intellectual architect of NEPAD; and under his leadership, South Africa hosted two high-profile United Nations conferences on racism and sustainable development. The country permanently hosts the AU's Pan-African Parliament, which was established in Midrand in 2004. South Africa was president of the influential Group of 77 (G77) developing countries at the UN during critical debates on reforming the organisation in 2005–2006, while the country won a two-year seat on the UN Security Council between 2007 and 2008. Assistance to NEPAD, however, failed to deliver the $64 billion a year that Mbeki and other African leaders had hoped, leading to a widespread questioning of the initiative by African civil society groups as being a 'top-down' plan by continental leaders who had failed to consult their citizens. South Africa was increasingly accused of seeking to dominate the initiative for its own parochial foreign policy interests.

Despite Mbeki's efforts at integrating South Africa into the rest of Africa, it is unclear how deeply entrenched these efforts are within South Africa's population and its political and business elite. Many in Africa question whether Mbeki's heirs, under a Jacob Zuma presidency and beyond, will maintain the same level of commitment to the continent that he has demonstrated. Many African governments and people have thus expressed unease about what they perceive to be South Africa's mercantilist trade and xenophobic immigration policies. They have accused its leaders of ingratitude after three decades of support for the ANC at enormous cost to their countries, though the ANC also suffered harsh treatment from governments in Zimbabwe and Mozambique in the 1980s.

But despite its ignominious past, post-apartheid South Africa has, in a short decade and a half largely under Mbeki's leadership, transformed itself from being Africa's most destabilising power to being its most energetic peacemaker. The country is becoming an African power and can aspire to global middle-power status through building strong continental institutions and working through its African allies, as well as countries like Brazil and India in international political and trade forums, where its voice is widely respected. This is the foreign policy legacy that Mbeki has bequeathed to his successors. As Ali Mazrui noted: 'Thabo Mbeki has been more active [than Mandela] in Pan-African affairs from Haiti to Harlem, from Kingston to Kinshasa, from Togo to Timbuktu. South Africa under Thabo Mbeki is among the leaders of the re-globalisation of Pan-Africanism.'[64]

The Socioeconomic Kingdom

Kwame Nkrumah

In the realm of economic policy, the prophetic Nkrumah failed to perform any miracles. It was clear from the start that Nkrumah was in a hurry: 'What other countries have taken over three hundred years to achieve, a once dependent territory must try to accomplish in a generation if it is to survive.'[65] In Nkrumah's Ghana, between 1950 and 1960, government expenditure increased by over 200 per cent, though the country's earning power had scarcely changed. The state's indebtedness was further increased by control of significant areas of marketing, purchasing, banking, and private trade.[66] To make matters worse, parastatals set up to control public and private enterprise in Ghana, like the important Cocoa Marketing Board, were 'extravagant, incompetent and nepotistic'.[67] Nkrumah's mono-crop economy was vulnerable to price fluctuations in the international commodity markets, which made fiscal policy and long-term planning difficult. With cocoa constituting 70 per cent of Ghana's exports in 1966,[68] the precipitous decline in world cocoa prices in 1961–1962 further weakened the economy and made socialistic wealth redistribution efforts impossible. An 'austerity' budget was introduced, triggering a strike by railwaymen and harbour workers in Sekondi–Takoradi, who protested against a compulsory savings scheme and centralisation of trade unions under CPP control. Nkrumah declared a 'state of emergency' and used the Industrial Relations Act of 1958 to force an end to the strike.

More positively, Nkrumah was able to complete the Volta River hydroelectric project at Akosombo, and a steelworks at Tema. The Volta project aimed to create an allied aluminium industry, but swallowed up much of Ghana's revenues and increased the country's indebtedness. Nkrumah's pragmatism was evident in his tapping the American Kaiser corporation to implement the project. The aluminium, however, was exported in ingots and not turned into the finished goods that might have earned Ghana more revenue. Nkrumah's obsession with the Volta project led to neglect and taxing of the cocoa sector to subsidise the initiative. He did not believe that Ghana would be able to build an indigenous entrepreneurial class and generate sufficient private capital, and so promoted state-led industrialisation largely based on foreign capital and technical expertise.[69] In the end, however, Nkrumah lacked both the capacity and the resources to transform his vision of an industrialised state into practice.

However, Nkrumah did make some progress in increasing the access of Ghanaians to primary and secondary education, built roads and harbours, expanded telecommunications and health services, and provided cheap electricity.[70] Between 1961 and 1963, in particular, he embarked on large government spending on roads, schools, hospitals, and other services. Despite his socialist rhetoric, Nkrumah acted pragmatically in his bid to secure foreign investment and development aid, often courting Western firms and governments. During a period of widespread nationalisation in the Third World, he guaranteed foreign firms that their assets would not be expropriated and that they could repatriate profits to their home countries.[71] But Nkrumah's ambitions were larger than his country's resources, and he failed to tailor his cloth according to Ghana's size. Positive reserves of £190 million in 1957 had been depleted into an external debt of £250 million by 1966.[72] One of the largest sources of discontent with Nkrumah's regime was his taxing of the price of cocoa in July 1965, which forced farmers to contribute compulsorily to national development, even as they complained about being short-changed by the CPP-controlled Ghana Farmers Cooperative Council.[73] Two days before the February 1966 coup, Nkrumah again reduced the prices paid to cocoa farmers in an unpopular budget pushed by the International Monetary Fund (IMF).[74] The Osagyefo had thus dangerously harmed the golden goose that laid his country's eggs. Not surprisingly, cocoa farmers were among the most jubilant group as the news of Nkrumah's demise reached the streets of Ghana.

Thabo Mbeki

Whereas Nkrumah had sought the political kingdom, Thabo Mbeki's approach could perhaps be descried as 'Seek ye first the *socioeconomic* kingdom, and all other things would be added to it.' Post-apartheid South Africa inherited a struggling economy that had been badly affected by international trade sanctions and built up a $16.7 billion external debt. Mbeki himself talked of 'two nations': a white population of about 5 million with a standard of living similar to that of Spain; and 35 million blacks with a standard of living similar to that of Congo-Brazzaville. By 2005, whites still controlled about 97 per cent of the Johannesburg Stock Exchange's wealth. Mbeki had in fact borrowed the concept of the 'two nations' from Benjamin Disraeli, the British prime minister of the late nineteenth century who had similarly argued that British citizens were becoming polarised between rich and poor groups, creating 'nations within the nation' that could result in social conflict.[75] Post-apartheid South Africa still remained deeply unequal, and one of Mbeki's nagging fears while in office was that the anger and frustrations of a seething black majority would boil over at the slow pace of socioeconomic transformation.[76] As Mbeki put it in 1998: 'We are faced with the danger of mounting rage to which we must respond seriously.'[77]

Mbeki was the chief architect of South Africa's controversial move from the state-led Reconstruction and Development Programme (RDP) in 1994—which prioritised jobs, welfare, housing, education, and health—to the market-led Growth, Employment, and Redistribution (GEAR) programme in 1996, as the country's currency—the rand—plummeted dangerously and faced collapse. Mandela's popularity was skilfully deployed to counter leftist critics of GEAR within the Congress of South African Trade Unions (COSATU) and the SACP. The ANC, its parliamentarians, and its coalition partners were effectively bypassed during one of the most radical policy shifts in the post-apartheid era. This approach was consistent with Mbeki's top-down, technocratic approach of a vanguard party led by policy intellectuals.[78] The ANC was determined to prove its competence in managing the economy and saw maintaining the confidence of the white business community at home as well as the confidence of foreign investors as critical to promoting the socio-economic transformation of the black majority. Taxes were cut by 72 billion rand (about $10 billion) between 1994 and 2004, even as unemployment reached an estimated 40 per cent. Fearing white capital flight and responding to the changed international climate after the collapse of the Soviet Union in 1991, the government soon abandoned the party's historical commitment to nationalisation of the 'commanding heights' of the economy amid much protests from the ANC's trade union and communist allies. Mbeki's arrogance and intolerance of criticism was evident when he addressed the ANC's SACP alliance partners in 1998, characterising opponents of GEAR of 'fake revolutionary posturing ... charlatans, who promise everything is good, while we all know that these confidence tricksters are telling the masses a lie.'[79]

With an $850 million loan from the International Monetary Fund in 1993 (which reportedly, as a condition, forced a cut in government deficit spending and a reduction of wages),[80] the influence of the Bretton Woods institutions—the World Bank and the IMF—grew in crafting the country's macroeconomic strategy. A World Bank official, Richard Ketley, helped to draft GEAR, and external donors insisted that Mandela retain apartheid-era Reserve Bank governor Chris Stals in his post. The ANC government seemed to lack confidence in its economic management skills and spent much time placating its white business community, raising questions about whether the party was really in power or merely in office. Mbeki—whom critics like Patrick Bond accused of 'talking left and walking right'[81]—later confirmed this sense of disempowerment at being forced to sign up to the 'Washington Consensus' (with its free markets and neoliberal macroeconomic policies) through GEAR.[82] He seemed to be relying on the 'magic of the market' to distribute wealth to the country's black masses, and only belatedly—with the promotion of a 'developmental state' beginning in 2005—realised that the market distributes its rewards unevenly. Half a million jobs were shed in South Africa in five years after 1994, and the expected flood of foreign investment turned out to be a cruel mirage.

Even as the ANC pushed for privatisation of state-owned industries, it faced widespread opposition from its trade union allies.[83] Mbeki was like a King Canute seeking in a courageous but ultimately futile effort to roll back the waves of globalisation and their pernicious effects on his economy. In the end, he placed too much faith in external actors to deliver on their aid, debt, and investment promises to Africa. While Mbeki consistently attended summits of the Group of Eight (G8) industrialised countries in various capitals, there was no substantive delivery on pledges made to Africa after these summits. But on the plus side, the country enjoyed fourteen consecutive years of economic growth, from 1994 to 2008; increased social welfare assistance from 2.5 million in 1995 to 12 million in 2007; built 2.3 million housing units between 1994 and 2008 (though the quality and durability of these houses have often been questioned); and expanded electricity to 80 per cent of households by 2007.[84]

The one policy that Mbeki consistently pushed, in contrast to Nkrumah, as part of his socioeconomic legacy, was Black Economic Empowerment, in a bid to build a black entrepreneurial and middle-class. BEE aimed to ensure that black managers occupied corporate positions, that black entrepreneurs benefitted from government contracts, and that wealth was transferred from white to black hands. State parastatals like Eskom thus set aside contracts for BEE groups. But this 'affirmative action' policy has been criticised for benefitting a tiny elite of ANC-connected individuals such as Saki Macozoma, Cyril Ramaphosa, Tokyo Sexwale, and Patrice Motsepe. Critics have also argued that whites often ran the management and operational functions of many 'empowerment' companies, while black non-executives fronted for them.[85] In response, defenders of BEE have pointed to the increase of black and women managers. They have also criticised the obsessive focus on the equity element of BEE and its simplistic depiction of the initiative as handing out shares to influential black individuals, rather than focusing on the other six aspects of BEE: management; employment equity; skills development; enterprise development; preferential procurement; and the residual element.[86]

The Thabo Mbeki–led ANC set out consciously to deracialise capital, which would effectively—though the ANC did not use the expression—create a black 'capitalist class' who would be both productive and patriotic, rather than comprador and parasitic. The Mbeki government embarked on a belated attempt to extend BEE to make it more 'broad-based' in 2001, with more projects crafted to benefit local communities, rural populations, and wider constituencies. A large part of the motivation of BEE was to prevent a social explosion (one of Mbeki's perennial fears) and to ensure political stability by building a black capitalist class which had a stake in the country's future.[87] South Africa's black middle-class is now said to number over 400,000 people,[88] and the Mbeki government also announced that it would use the first surplus in the country's history, in 2007, to provide 78 billion rand (about $10 billion) to the poor through a social security system by 2009–2010. Some have criticised this welfarist approach, which they caution could create a culture of dependency rather than stimulate entrepeneurship and wealth creation.

During his nine years in power, Mbeki provided South Africa with macroeconomic stability, and the country managed to promote socioeconomic reforms more rapidly than any other postcolonial African state. But this has neither created sufficient jobs, alleviated poverty quickly enough, nor created a large class of productive and socially conscious black entrepreneurs. The power-cuts and 'load-shedding' that occurred across South Africa in 2007 exposed some of the complacency at the heart of the Mbeki administration, since the government had been warned a decade before to build new power reactors. The aftermath of the divisions within the ANC that emerged after the Polokwane summit in December 2007, at which Mbeki lost the party presidency to Jacob Zuma, saw troubling threats to 'kill for Zuma' and criticisms of 'reactionary judges'. Horrific xenophobic attacks by rampaging South African mobs against foreigners from other African countries (mostly from Mozambique and Zimbabwe) in May 2008, and the slow and irresponsible response by South African leaders to these attacks, suggested that the country was 'no longer at ease' (see chapter 5). Following Mbeki's ousting in September 2008, a splinter party calling itself the Congress of the People (COPE), led by senior ANC figures Sam Shilowa and Mosiuoa Lekota, appeared within two months. South Africa's potent mix of populism, violence, poverty, and political instability has raised serious questions about the state that Mbeki was bequeathing his successors, as well as his own ultimate legacy in the area of socioeconomic transformation. As South African analyst Andile Mngxitama observed in 2009: 'The populism of Zuma emerged as a direct consequence of the failure of Mbeki's market populism to address the issues of poverty, land, housing and health care. The spinning stats and Irish poetry couldn't hide the ugly truth.'[89]

Concluding Reflections

Nkrumah in Retrospect

With economic failures at home and the tarnishing of Ghana's international image by domestic atrocities, cynicism reached a new peak in Nkrumah's Ghana. The prophetic vision had not been rewarded, and the sceptical masses began to remark that 'Nkrumahism [is] the highest stage of opportunism.'[90] Having worked so tenaciously to secure the political kingdom, the Prophet discovered that all other things were not automatically added unto it. But despite these failings, it can hardly be denied that Nkrumah's illustrious life was not without some achievements. In the educational sphere, for example, by 1964, primary school enrolment since 1950 had increased seven times, middle school enrolment had quadrupled, and secondary school enrolment had risen ten times.[91] In foreign policy, Nkrumah believed unflinchingly in his pan-African vision, investing much of his country's resources in hosting many conferences in support of African liberation.

Unlike other African potentates after their fall from power, Nkrumah did not pursue the comforts and wealth of a Swiss villa, but went back to Africa to live out his last days in a modest house in Guinea, writing about 'Dark Days in Ghana': the title of a book published in 1968. This book—a bitter apologia—showed Nkrumah to be a delusional Emperor without clothes, as he sought to order the soldiers to the barracks after the coup and seemed unaware of his own failings in power. Particularly disingenuous was Nkrumah's attempt to explain away the prisoners in his jails as largely 'criminal detainees', claiming against all evidence and logic that there were few 'political detainees' in Ghana under his rule.[92] Some estimates put the number of those detained by Nkrumah by 1966 at about a thousand people.[93] A sympathetic and insightful biographer and friend, Basil Davidson, a British journalist-historian, captured Nkrumah's tragedy succinctly when he wrote: 'Highly intelligent, he could be intellectually shallow; ruthlessly clear on many things, he could be quite the reverse on others. It was a very human situation, with pettiness and grandeur marching hand-in-hand.'[94]

Few can deny the tremendous economic problems that confronted Ghana's underdeveloped economy at independence in 1957. The general structural weaknesses of a colonial economy inherited from the 'Curse of Berlin' were abundantly clear, and Nkrumah's successors—both 'madmen' (civilians) and 'specialists' (soldiers)[95]—performed even worse than he did on the economic front (with the possible exception of Jerry Rawlings between 1981 and 2000). Richard Rathbone was therefore correct in noting that too much literature on Ghana has accorded undue autonomy to Ghanaian politics and relied on a 'Great Man tradition of political analysis'.[96] All that politicians and soldiers in Ghana have been able to do is to tinker with the economy. No leader has yet been able to restructure the country's economy with any recognizable effect on the lives of common Ghanaians after five decades of independence.

Mbeki in Retrospect

Thabo Mbeki and his deputy president, Jacob Zuma, fell out in 2001 when the latter was being touted as a possible successor at a time of mounting criticism of Mbeki's HIV/AIDS and Zimbabwe policies. By June 2005, Mbeki faced more open challenges to his leadership from within the ANC after ousting Zuma as the country's deputy president following corruption allegations. With Zuma avoiding conviction for both rape and corruption charges in 2006, Mbeki looked increasingly isolated. Many saw opposition to his leadership style, rather than pro-Zuma enthusiasm per se, as accounting for Zuma's ascendancy. New social movements like the Anti–Privatisation Forum, the Concerned Citizens Forum, and the Landless People's Movement were also springing up across the country to challenge the slow pace of socioeconomic transformation, in which only 3 per cent of a target of 30 per cent of land was distributed in a decade. Though Mbeki played an admirable peacemaking and diplomatic role in Africa and his government provided some housing, electricity, and social grants to impoverished South Africans, the AIDS debacle could well become his Achilles heel when future historians chronicle his legacy.

The story of Mbeki and Zuma was in fact akin to Wole Soyinka's 1963 play *The Lion and the Jewel*. The play is set in a pre-independence Western Nigerian village of Ilujinle, and centres on the courting of a beautiful young woman, Sidi, by Lakunle—a Westernised school teacher with little understanding of his own country and its customs—and Baroka, a traditional *bale* (chief) who is resisting modernisation and Western influences on his village. Both men desire Sidi, but in the end it is the wily sixty-two-year-old Baroka who wins the affection of the young woman by setting a devious trap in which he pretends to be sexually impotent in order to lure the 'jewel of Ilujinle' into the 'Lion's den'. Baroka consummates the courtship, and Sidi agrees to marry him.[97]

This author watched a performance of the play in South Africa in 2008, as the power struggle between Thabo Mbeki (South Africa's president) and Jacob Zuma (the ANC president) raged. Soyinka's play can, in a sense, be read as a parable of this power struggle, with Mbeki representing the Westernised, urbane Lakunle, who is out of touch with his own citizens; Zuma (who often wears Zulu traditional outfits and had taken three wives in traditional ceremonies by January 2010) representing Baroka; while Sidi, the jewel, represents the ANC presidency, for which both men fought such a bitter struggle in Polokwane. In the end, it was Zuma who took both the jewel and the crown. Like Baroka, Zuma relied on guile and a better understanding of the masses to mobilise support for his spectacular victory in December 2007.

In 2006, Cameroonian scholar Achille Mbembe linked Zuma's following to a millenarian form of politics, contrasting it vividly with Mbeki's modernism:

[T]here must emerge a false *maprofeti* (prophet), generally a person of very humble origins. Backed by a certain level of mass hysteria, the *maprofeti* then claims that a great resurrection is about to take place. Whenever questioned about the sources of his actions and authority, he invariably refers to the authority of his 'ancestors', his 'tradition' or his 'culture'... Although of a secular nature, the new millenarianism and nativist revivalism is using eschatological language of the 'revolution second coming' in order to paint as the epitome of the Antichrist one of the most worldly, cosmopolitan and urbane political leaders modern Africa has ever known.[98]

Nkrumah and Mbeki: La Fin de Régime

By the end of their respective reigns, both Nkrumah and Mbeki had become isolated figures surrounded by sycophantic advisers who told them what they wanted to hear. Both of these 'detribalised', urbane, and cosmopolitan leaders were accused of turning to their ethnic kinsmen towards the end of their rule: Nkrumah's bodyguards were fellow Nzimas and Fantis, while Nzimas were increasingly appointed into his cabinet;[99] Mbeki relied increasingly on a

'Xhosa Nostra'—members of his ethnic Xhosas—who were overrepresented in his cabinet. By 2004, eighteen out of forty-nine ministers and deputy ministers were Xhosa.[100] Both leaders attempted to carry out a socioeconomic revolution without genuine revolutionaries. They lacked competent cadres and administrators in the numbers needed to ensure the success of their revolutions. While Nkrumah led a poor, cocoa-based economy to punch above its weight, the limits of a mono-crop economy eventually contributed to his downfall. Mbeki led Africa's richest and most industrialised state, but the increasing inequalities inherited from the colonial and apartheid eras eventually increased support for a Jacob Zuma–led leftist coalition, and led to Mbeki's ouster. While Nkrumah redistributed poverty, Mbeki's economy grew, but many of South Africa's poor also grew poorer. Having worked so tenaciously to secure the political kingdom, both leaders discovered that all other things were not added unto it. Failure to deliver the economic kingdom in the end led to the political crucifixion of both prophets.

Kenyan scholar Ali Mazrui had famously argued in 1966 that Nkrumah was a great pan-African, but not a great Ghanaian. Will Mbeki come to be viewed in a similar vein as a great pan-African but not a great South African? When Nkrumah was ousted from power, an angry mob destroyed his statue, and streets named after him were changed. Within twenty-six years, Nkrumah's successors had so mismanaged the country that nostalgia for his memory had returned. A new statue and memorial park were built in his honour in 1992 in an impressive act of national restitution. Will South Africans also come to view Mbeki more favourably with the passage of time?

12

TOWERS OF BABEL?

THE AFRICAN UNION AND THE EUROPEAN UNION[1]

'[U]p till now the Berlin Conference has been the basis of our division, of this segregation.'[2]

Muammar Qaddafi, leader of Libya and African Union chair, 2009–2010

The biblical Tower of Babel is a story that can be read as a sign of the overweening ambition of humankind and the overcontrolling nature of God. English poet John Milton's classic *Paradise Lost* of 1667 had, after all, portrayed a vain God—wanting to be forever worshipped, for hymns to be sung to him, and demanding absolute obedience—being plunged into a Celestial civil war by a 'radical' Satan who instigated a third of the angels in rebellion against 'Heav'n's awful Monarch'. Lucifer reasoned that it was 'Better to reign in Hell than serve in Heav'n'. Though Milton sees God as just and loving and acknowledges his ultimate triumph over Satan, some critics have noted that his portrayal can be read as support for a revolt against tyrannical rule, particularly since God had banished Adam and Eve from the paradisiacal Garden of Eden for eating an apple—and thus introduced Death to the world—and then, according to them, taken satisfaction at his own son's crucifixion.[3] Whatever the merits of these biblical arguments, the end of the Tower of Babel tale is less sanguinary and more benign than the other story we have just retold. As some will recall the story of Babel, humankind took advantage of speaking a common language to build a city with a tower that would reach Heaven in order to 'make a name' for themselves. When God saw the tower, he noted that, if humankind could build such a tower speaking a common language, then there were no limits to what else it could do. The Almighty thus confused their languages, so that humankind would no longer be able to understand each other, and scattered them to all corners of the earth. Babel was where God invoked this curse.

In a sense, humankind has been attempting to come together to learn to speak a common language ever since God dismantled the Tower of Babel. We argue in this chapter that the African Union (AU)—and before it the Organisation of African Unity (OAU)—as well as the European Economic Community (EEC) and the European Union (EU), can be seen as efforts to create 'perfect unions'—modern Towers of Babel—by bringing together scattered African and European diasporas. This is, of course, not a perfect comparison: the AU—with some of the poorest countries in the world—was born in 2002, while the EU—with some of the world's wealthiest states—celebrated its fiftieth birthday in 2007.[4]

The AU has identified as a sixth subregion (in addition to North, West, Eastern, Central, and Southern Africa) the diaspora of Africans in the Americas, Brazil, and the West Indies, together with expatriate Africans largely in the West,[5] some of whom Kenyan scholar Ali Mazrui famously described as 'Afro-Saxons'.[6] The African Union is currently attempting to unite a continent of 800 million inhabitants in fifty-four countries from the Cape to Cairo; some of its leaders, like Libya's Muammar Qaddafi, talk of creating a 'United States of Africa'; and the organisation seeks to establish an African Economic Community (AEC) by 2028. African leaders have further sought to defy the 'Curse of Babel' by making Swahili the first official African language to fill the interpreting booths of the African Union in 2004. The European Union could also be said to be striving towards reversing the curse by bringing together 500 million people in twenty-seven countries from Sofia to Stockholm in order to create the world's largest market and its only supranational body. The EU accounted, in 2007, for about 30 per cent of the world's nominal gross domestic product, at about $16.8 trillion. Africa in contrast accounts for less than 2 per cent of world trade. But progress has been made by both unions, even though continuing frustrations would suggest that the 'Curse of Babel' will eventually prevent the AU and the EU from reaching the Nirvana of political, economic, cultural, and linguistic integration.

This chapter is divided into four key themes that assess experiences and actors in Africa and Europe comparatively. First, we analyse the quest for economic and political integration. In this section we adopt a historical approach that examines pan-African efforts to attain political freedom, from the first Pan-African Congress in 1900 up until the fifth Manchester conference in 1945. We then assess the struggle for African unity after decolonisation from the 1950s, culminating in the creation of the OAU by 1963, and the birth of the AU in 2002. The chapter proceeds to examine comparatively, in the same section, European efforts at integration after two bloody civil wars—more popularly known as the First and Second World Wars—and the expansion of the six–member EEC into the twenty-seven-member EU by 2007. The second section examines the roles and impact of four prophetic visionaries who championed African and European integration: two West Africans—Nigeria's Adebayo Adedeji and Mali's Alpha Konaré—and two Frenchmen—Jean Monnet and Jacques Delors. The third section briefly examines the two hegemonic engines on each continent that have acted as motors of integration efforts: Nigeria and South Africa in Africa, and Germany and France in Europe. Finally, we examine the roles and impact of two countries that some AU and EU members have regarded as regional 'spoilers' that have sometimes derailed integration efforts: Libya in Africa and Britain in Europe.

The Integrationists

From London to Addis Ababa: The Organisation of African Unity[7]

Fifteen years after the 1884–1885 Conference of Berlin (see chapter 1), the pan-African movement was born in 1900. Trinidadian lawyer Henry Sylvester-Williams organised the first Pan-African Conference in London. It was in the same year that William E. Du Bois—the 'Father of Pan-Africanism'—uttered the remarkably prescient prophecy: 'The problem of the twentieth century is the problem of the colour line.'[8] Between 1919 and 1945, five Pan-African Congresses took place, in Paris (1919), London (1921 and 1923), New York (1927), and Manchester (1945).[9] These congresses were at first dominated by African Americans like Du Bois. But in time, black Caribbeans in Europe, and Africans from countries like Sierra Leone, Ghana, Ethiopia, Liberia, and Nigeria increasingly participated in them.[10]

Initially, the demands of these early pan-Africanists were limited to education for Africans, economic development, and racial equality. Eventually, however, the doctrine of pan-Africanism not only came to emphasise the existence, worth, and strength of African cultures, but also called for African unity so that these cultures might flourish in freedom, unhampered by the denigrating influences of Western 'civilisation', which in Africa signified slavery and colonialism.[11] Pan-Africanism, therefore, represented the reaction by the black African diaspora to the indignities that blacks had suffered from Caucasian Euro-Americans. Some sought refuge in an idealised African past, free of slavery and xenophobia. In the francophone world, writers like Aimé Césaire, Antoine Diop, and Léopold Senghor also contributed to the movement, developing the idea of *négritude*, which glorified black culture, looked back nostalgically at a rich African past, and affirmed the worth and dignity of black people across the globe.[12] As Aimé Césaire noted: 'My Négritude is no tower and no cathedral / It delves into the deeper red flesh of the soil.'[13]

Nigerian Nobel literature laureate Wole Soyinka famously ridiculed the romanticisation of this apolitical, moderate approach to pan-Africanism in wryly noting: 'The tiger does not profess its tigritude, it pounces.'[14] By the time of the fifth Pan-African Congress, held in the English city of Manchester in 1945, not only had the Second World War of 1939–1945 shifted the global balance of power away from the imperial European powers, but the pan-African movement had also shifted its centre of influence to Africa itself. The conference was now dominated by indigenous Africans like Kwame Nkrumah, Nmamdi Azikiwe, Obafemi Awolowo, Jomo Kenyatta, and Hastings Banda, men who later led their countries to independence. William Du Bois, in fact, was the only African American at the 1945 congress. He passed the torch of pan-Africanism to Nkrumah and moved to Ghana, where he spent the last years of his life. Both Du Bois and George Padmore (who served in Nkrumah's government) were buried in Accra.

A historic battle was waged for the soul of pan-Africanism between a 'radical' Casablanca minority bloc led by Ghana's Kwame Nkrumah, and the majority of African leaders—under the Brazzaville and Monrovia blocs—who favoured a more gradualist approach to continental unity.[15] Nkrumah's rejected vision of a 'Union Government of African States' would have involved common economic planning (including a common currency and monetary zone), an African defence command, and a common foreign policy. The Ghanaian leader was widely distrusted by his fellow African leaders for backing armed dissidents, and even his union with Guinea and Mali of 1958 proved to be short-lived (see chapter 11).

The protracted Congo crisis of 1960–1964 further illustrated the divisions among African states, as the 'moderates' mostly backed President Joseph Kasavubu against Prime Minister Patrice Lumumba, who was supported by the 'radicals'.[16] The threat of further foreign intervention in the heart of Africa, this time as an extension of the Cold War, brought home anew the need for what Ali Mazrui in a classic 1967 study described as a Pax Africana[17]—a peace secured, kept, and consolidated by Africans themselves—which would allow African states to resolve their disputes independently. This would be a stark contrast to the militarily expansionist and culturally destructive Pax Europea of the previous century. Where Pax Africana sought to stabilise and unite a continent, Pax Europea had sought to divide and conquer a continent (see chapter 1).

In May 1963, thirty-one African leaders met in the ancient Ethiopian capital of Addis Ababa and signed the Charter of the Organisation of African Unity, effecting the disintegration of the rival African blocs of Casablanca, Brazzaville, and Monrovia. The OAU Charter clearly reflected the triumph of the gradualist, evolutionary path over the speedy, revolutionary course of the 'radicals'. Four of its seven principles were concerned with sovereign rights—an emphasis of the Monrovia group. The two concessions to the Casablanca group—non-alignment and support for Africa's emancipation—had already been adopted by almost all African states as part of their foreign policy objectives. There is no reference in the charter to pan-Africanism or political union. There are two noteworthy institutional flaws in the OAU Charter that plagued the organisation during its three decades of existence. First, the charter rendered the OAU's executive and administrative branches ineffective by according them only limited powers. Resolutions of the OAU Assembly (consisting of all member states) were not legally binding, rendering the Assembly little more than a deliberative forum at best, or a 'talking shop' with no implementation mechanisms at worst. Second, the OAU's Commission of Mediation, Conciliation, and Arbitration, set up as the organisation's diplomatic machinery for conflict resolution, was not a judicial organ and did not have any powers of sanction. Along with the Economic and Social Commission, the Educational, Cultural, Scientific and Health Commission, and the Defence Commission, the conflict resolution machinery of the OAU remained largely moribund after its creation in 1963.[18]

Africa's 'Thirty Years War' refers to the Cold War struggle of the OAU between 1963 to 1993 to achieve a Pax Africana in which Africans themselves would resolve their own conflicts. Ironically, the seat of the OAU secretariat, Ethiopia, itself experienced a thirty-year civil war, with the federal government fighting Eritrean and Tigrayan rebel groups.[19] The backdrop of the OAU's debates and attempts to maintain peace throughout Africa was thus a bloody civil war in its host country. It would be difficult to imagine diplomats at the United Nations (UN) trying to resolve global disputes while civil war raged in the United States. This, though, was the very situation confronting African multilateral diplomacy.[20] But despite its shortcomings, the OAU deserves credit for its firm commitment to decolonisation and the anti–apartheid struggle in South Africa. The continental body displayed pragmatism and flexibility on an issue over which most of its members were not prepared to compromise. The organisation furnished ideological and diplomatic support to African liberation movements through multilateral forums in which it was well-represented, such as the UN, the Group of 77 (G77) developing countries, and the Non-Alignment Movement (NAM). With admirable tenacity and diplomatic skills, African governments sponsored resolutions in the UN condemning Rhodesian and South African excesses,[21] leading to the imposition of economic sanctions against the two pariah states—the first in UN history (see chapter 3).

From Durban to Accra: The African Union and the New Interventionists

In creating the African Union in the South African port city of Durban in 2002, it seemed at first that African leaders had finally realised that grandiose plans, ad hoc committees, and numerous high-sounding resolutions could not bring about the continent's economic and political integration. African governments were forced to recognise that economic development and integration could not simply be legislated into existence. The glue that had held the OAU together for three decades—the liberation of Southern Africa and the elimination of apartheid—had come unstuck by 1994 with the election of Nelson Mandela as South Africa's first post-apartheid president. With growing poverty replacing apartheid and colonialism as the common enemy, the OAU was forced to commit suicide in 2002 in the hope that another body— the African Union—could rise from its ashes like the Egyptian Phoenix, to invigorate the four-decade efforts to integrate the continent. Unlike the OAU Charter, the AU's Constitutive Act of 2000 allowed for interference in the internal affairs of its members in cases of unconstitutional changes of governments, egregious human rights abuses and genocide, and conflicts that threaten regional stability. This is potentially revolutionary in light of the OAU's rigid, noninterventionist posture in the first three decades of its existence. Learning from the difficulties of the OAU, the AU also sought to establish an African Standby Force, consisting of five subregional brigades, by 2010 (see chapter 2).

We next focus on the 'Grand Debate' on a 'United States of Africa' that took place at the African Union summit in Accra, Ghana, in July 2007. In the early nineteenth century, Mali's Timbuktu was a fabled city of gold in the grasping imagination of European explorers. The AU summit in Accra in July 2007 evoked images of a similar elusive quest for an African El Dorado. A 'Grand Debate' was staged between Africa's leaders that revived some of the early battles of African diplomacy in the 1960s. In Africa's contemporary battle, the gladiators had changed but the issues had not. Libya, under its mercurial leader Muammar Qaddafi, launched the vision of an African Union in 1999 that would be loosely modelled after the European Union. Tripoli called for a 'United States of Africa' with an appointed president and ministers, as well as a central bank. Senegal's Abdoulaye Wade came closest to backing this vision, continuing to advocate a limited continental government, with the AU serving as an embryonic federation with a common currency and appointing its own ministers of foreign affairs, infrastructure, health, and education. Uganda's Yoweri Museveni pushed for a sub-federalism that would eventually culminate in a political federation with Kenya, Tanzania, Burundi, and Rwanda under a revived East African Community.

This contemporary debate, however, seems ahistorical, quixotic, and impractical. The lessons of the divisions of the 1960s must be learned before progress can be made today. African leaders in Accra were presented with three options: first, to strengthen the AU and existing regional groupings; second, to create a 'Union Government' by 2015 with executive powers in specific areas as a transitory phase towards a 'United States of Africa'; and third, to proceed immediately towards a 'United States of Africa'. Nigeria, South Africa, and the majority of African states appeared to favour the second option. As in the days of Nkrumah, the more federalist vision of Africa (in particular, the third option) was rejected by African leaders. This is an idea whose time had not yet come. There appears to be a lack of priority, sequencing, or reality in these federalist schemes. Putting old wine in new bottles will clearly not integrate Africa. African leaders must revert to the first option and focus on the hard work of strengthening and funding fledgling institutions that they have created, and establishing one effective economic pillar in each African subregion (see chapter 2). They must get their domestic houses in order and build strong economies and stable democracies. After all, there has to be something to integrate for integration to succeed. Otherwise, this 'Grand Debate' could turn out to have been another 'Grand Distraction'. A 'Big Bang' approach to African unity by Africa's alchemists will clearly not turn lead into gold.[22]

From Paris to Maastricht: The European Economic Community

Charlemagne, the King of the Franks (a Germanic group), was one of the earliest visionaries of European integration. After a thirty-year military campaign, he united parts of modern-day Germany, Austria, France, Italy, Spain, Switzerland, Belgium, Luxembourg, and the Netherlands into the Holy Roman Empire. By C.E. 800, Charlemagne had established central government over much of Western Europe.[23] The modern roots of European integration, however, are often traced back to the Treaty of Westphalia in 1648, which ended thirty years of bloody religious conflicts and the delusions of the hegemony of the Holy Roman Empire, thus starting the long process of creating recognised sovereign states. 'Emperor' Napoleon Bonaparte had also sought to unite Europe through force of arms in the nineteenth century, while Germany's Adolf Hitler unsuccessfully attempted a similar forced integration of the continent in the twentieth century.

The real impetus for contemporary European integration came about as a result of the slaughter of the Second World War of 1939–1945, which left the continent in ruins. The European Coal and Steel Community (ECSC) was thus created in Paris in 1951 to integrate the coal and steel markets of its six founding members: France, Germany, Italy, Belgium, the Netherlands, and Luxembourg. The ECSC, however, did not succeed in integrating European coal and steel by preventing and promoting competition. National interests of members often prevailed over those of the Community. But this was an effort at supranationalism that laid the foundations for closer cooperation between 'the Six'. The basic strategy at the heart of this largely French initiative was to bring an end to the perpetual conflict between France and Germany by integrating their markets closer together. But America's need for strong allies and viable markets and its provision of a $100 billion (in today's currency) Marshall Plan of economic aid to Europe, as well as a nuclear umbrella to counter the threat of Soviet expansionism, were also key factors in the integration of Western Europe.[24]

In June 1955, the founding members of the ECSC met in the Italian city of Messina and agreed to establish a common market. The Treaty of Rome of 1957 established the European Economic Community and the European Atomic Energy Community (Euratom). Rome's preamble noted that the EEC sought to 'lay the foundations of an ever closer union among the peoples of Europe'. The basic bargain of the EEC was essentially a deal between French agriculture and German industry as a way of bringing peace to Europe. Where pan-Africanism was an ideology of liberation, pan-Europeanism was an ideology of peacemaking (though within the framework of the North Atlantic Treaty Organisation [NATO] and the Cold War).[25] The EEC saw immediate results: trade in industrial products doubled in four years and average growth within the Community in the 1960s was 5 to 6 per cent. The customs union was completed in July 1968, eighteen months ahead of schedule. The Common Agricultural Policy (CAP) was launched in 1962, which has now become a profligate $50 billion a year monstrosity of food mountains and corpulent farmers. In 1965, the ECSC, the EEC, and Euratom were merged into the European Community (EC). The *Trente Glorieuses* (Thirty Glorious Years) of sustained economic growth after 1945 delivered peace and prosperity to Europe.

The 1970s were however a dismal decade for European integration, with oil shocks in 1973 and 1979, and a global economic crisis that led to 'Eurosclerosis' in an era of stagflation. Even as Britain, Denmark, and Ireland joined the Community in 1973, member states seemed paralysed by indecision, and restricted supranational decisionmaking. Three of the few positive developments of the epoch were the first direct elections of the European Parliament in 1979, establishment of the European Monetary System in the same year, and the evolution of the European Court of Justice as a source of European law. But high inflation and low growth afflicted most European economies during the 1970s.[26] The gloomy mood of the EEC was captured in a cover of *The Economist*. After the first president of the European Commission, Walter Hallstein, a German professor of law and strong advocate of a federal Europe, died in March 1982, the influential but opinionated magazine—not renowned for its restraint and sense of proportion—depicted a front cover with a gravestone that read: 'EEC. Born March 25, 1957. Moribund March 25, 1982.'

The mid-1980s, however, saw a *relance* (relaunch) of European integration. The appointment of Frenchman Jacques Delors as Commission president in January 1985 started a period of dynamism for the European Community that saw the creation of a single market by 1992. The single market sought to promote freedom of goods, services, capital, and labour through the reduction of nontariff barriers and other measures. The ramparts of 'Fortress Europe' were finally being lifted. Qualified majority voting was increasingly used, and 297 pieces of Community legislation were identified to facilitate the creation of a single market. One of the big drivers of European integration during this period was European big business. Spain and Portugal joined the EC in 1986 (Greece had joined in 1981) and democracy-building appeared to be an additional goal of the Community.[27] The road to Maastricht appeared to be paved with gold.

From Maastricht to Lisbon: The European Union

The Maastricht Treaty was signed in December 1991. The treaty however soon suffered a setback by its rejection in a Danish referendum in 1992, and both Denmark and Britain won opt-outs from the European Monetary Union (Sweden would also win an opt-out after a failed referendum in 2003, having joined the EC with Austria and Finland in 1995). The Maastricht Treaty also enhanced the powers of the European Parliament. Two new 'pillars'—foreign and security policy, and freedom of movement and internal security—were established alongside the European Community, with the whole structure being renamed the European Union. A French referendum on Maastricht in 1992 only managed a wafer-thin 51 per cent majority. Despite the epoch-making achievements of the treaty, there were signs that Europe's leaders were not taking their populations with them on this integrationist journey without maps. The Yugoslav Wars of succession between 1992 and 1995 further exposed the EU as an economic giant and military dwarf. US diplomat Richard Holbrooke openly questioned Europe's inability to take care of security issues within its own neighbourhood. The conflict in Kosovo in 1999 would also require American military might to reach a conclusion.

The launch of a European currency—the euro—in 1999 (the bills and coins appeared in 2002) was the main achievement of European integration between 1999 and 2009. The prospect of German reunification accelerated the pace of monetary union, as France looked to tie the German Gulliver into a web of interdependence: a common thread in the whole project of European integration. The euro has proved to be a volatile currency. Its value fell 15 per cent in relation to the dollar in its first year. But by 2003, it had recovered ground. By 2008, the euro had yet to prove its worth in terms of creating economies of scale and lowering prices,[28] though it was widely viewed as a source of stability in the wake of the global financial crisis of 2007–2009.

By 2007, the EU had brought in twelve states largely from Central and Eastern Europe,[29] but the gloomy mood of the 1970s seemed to be returning. The divisions triggered by the US-led invasion of Iraq in 2003 led to divisions between 'Old Europe'—led by France, Germany, and Belgium—and a 'New Europe' led by Britain, Spain, Denmark, and several Eastern European countries like Poland and the Czech Republic. The events also embarrassingly exposed the failings of the EU's efforts to develop its Common Foreign and Security Policy. By 2008, the EU seemed to be suffering from indigestion, and was clearly having problems integrating the less wealthy countries as well as those, like Poland, having large agricultural sectors.

In February 2002, former French president Valéry Giscard d'Estaing was asked to chair a convention to draft a European constitution to build more effective and democratic institutions for the EU. But the constitution was rejected by large majorities in referendums in two founding and usually reliable EU supporters: France and the Netherlands.[30] Attempts to salvage the constitution by making amendments were agreed in October 2007, but ran into more trouble when Irish voters (whose Celtic Tiger economy had benefitted more than most from the EU) rejected the new treaty in a June 2008 referendum. Europe's elites seemed once again to be far ahead of their electorates, and the 'democratic deficit' at the heart of the EU was once again embarrassingly laid bare. There was, however, a paradox: needing to seek the support of citizens to approve technically dense and incomprehensible documents rendered leaders vulnerable to protest votes about parochial domestic issues that had nothing to do with the draft treaties. The political horse-trading that resulted in the election of Belgian, Herman Van Rompuy, and Briton, Catherine Ashton, as president of the EU Council and EU foreign policy chief respectively in November 2009, was also widely criticised.[31]

The Visionaries: Two Cassandras and Two Gauls

It was German playwright Bertolt Brecht who had noted in his play, first performed in 1943, *Galileo Galilei*: 'Pity the country that has no heroes.' We argue here that one should 'pity the *continent* that has no *prophets*.' Visionaries are dreamers and prophets who see further into the future than lesser mortals. They often wish to create utopias and a better future. Such prophets are even thought by some to be divinely inspired. In the African tradition, Wole Soyinka has shown in *The Jero Plays* of 1964 and 1973[32] that such prophets can be charlatans. Nostradamus, a prominent figure of the French Renaissance and sixteenth-century seer, is often viewed by most contemporary scholars as a false prophet of the Apocalypse. Greek mythology recalls Cassandra, a prophetess whom Apollo—the god of music and poetry—had granted the gift of prophecy due to her beauty. However, Apollo later invoked a curse to ensure that Cassandra's accurate prophesies would not be believed, after she did not requite his love. The four visionaries assessed here—Jean Monnet,

Adebayo Adedeji, Jacques Delors, and Alpha Konaré—will be examined with these prophetic typologies in mind.

Jean Monnet and Adebayo Adedeji

Jean Monnet is generally regarded as the 'Father of European Integration'. During the First World War of 1914–1918, Monnet coordinated the supplies of Allied merchant fleets, pushing them to charge the same freight rates to ensure more efficient delivery of priority supplies. He also led Anglo-French supply programmes during the Second World War. Though Monnet was keen to use cooperation to avoid war, he contributed to war efforts to achieve peace. He was always a pragmatic realist, and not just an idealistic pacifist. At the age of only thirty, Monnet became deputy secretary-general of the League of Nations—precursor to the United Nations—in 1919. He later went into private banking in Eastern Europe, New York, San Francisco, and Shanghai, learning about international cooperation through travel. Based on his experiences of playing a key role in fostering inter-Allied cooperation during Europe's two civil wars, one of Monnet's credos became that international cooperation could be used to overcome pernicious national rivalries.

Having headed the Commissariat du Plan, the commission for France's postwar reconstruction, Monnet became the architect of European integration, authoring the Schuman Plan of May 1950 (named after French foreign minister Robert Schuman). He became head of the High Authority of the Luxembourg-based European Coal and Steel Community from 1952 to 1955. Monnet was also the moving force of the Action Committee for a United States of Europe, a platform he used to push for the Treaty of Rome in 1957. He had an intuitive sense of what the political traffic could bear. As Monnet famously noted: 'Nothing is possible without men; nothing is lasting without institutions.'[33] He saw the Schuman Plan as chiefly a politico-economic means of dealing with strategic problems of peace and security.

Nigerian scholar-diplomat Adebayo Adedeji may well be Africa's most renowned visionary of African integration.[34] Having studied at the universities of Leicester, Harvard, and London, Adedeji became a full professor of economics and public administration at Nigeria's University of Ile-Ife (now Obafemi Awolowo University) at the age of thirty-six. By forty, he had become Nigeria's minister of economic reconstruction and development in 1972, overseeing the country's difficult post–civil war peacebuilding efforts. Adedeji is widely regarded as the 'Father of ECOWAS' (Economic Community of West African States). He had outlined a vision for integration in West Africa in an academic journal in 1970, before turning theory into practice, by 1975, in convincing subregional leaders to establish ECOWAS while serving as Nigeria's minister of economic development.[35] He has consistently argued that regional integration must be seen as an instrument for national survival and socioeconomic transformation.[36]

In 1975, Adedeji was head-hunted by the United Nations to lead its Addis Ababa–based Economic Commission for Africa (ECA). His sixteen-year tenure became one of the organisation's longest and most dynamic: he skilfully converted the ECA into a platform to continue his efforts to promote economic integration, leading the creation of the Common Market of Eastern and Southern Africa (COMESA) and the Economic Community of Central African States in 1981 and 1983, respectively. The dynamic Adedeji, who worked closely with successive OAU Secretaries-General in Addis Ababa, became a confidant and economic adviser to many African leaders. He established a particularly close relationship with Tanzania's Julius Nyerere after he had delivered a series of lectures in Tanzania in 1971 in which he indiscreetly declared not having met any socialists in the country! Having advised the Namibian government for six years, he was bestowed honorary citizenship of that country in 1997. At the ECA, he acquired a reputation for intellectual dynamism and boundless energy, but also for not suffering fools gladly, which some critics saw as arrogance. He famously instructed that one of the elevators in the ECA building in Addis Ababa be kept free for his use before his arrival at work each morning!

S.K.B. Asante, the renowned Ghanaian political economist who wrote a book on Adedeji's development strategies in 1991, described him as an 'African Cassandra': a visionary prophet who saw the future clearly, but whose prophesies often went unheeded until it was too late. After retiring from the ECA in 1991, Adedeji continued his integrationist efforts: he served on a committee to review the ECOWAS treaty in 1992; he was on another body to transform the OAU into the African Union in 2002; he was a member of the Eminent Panel of the African Peer Review Mechanism (APRM) from 2003[37]; and in 2007 he chaired the committee that audited the five-year integration efforts of the AU, becoming one of the continent's most accomplished intellectual public servants in the process.

Both Adedeji and Monnet were put in charge of reconstructing their countries after destructive conflicts: the Second World War and the Nigerian Civil War. Both were men of vision and grand ideas who enjoyed the trust of powerful actors on their continents. Both were pragmatists and realists who used the force of superior arguments and dynamic political manoeuvring to promote their goals. Both Adedeji and Monnet headed powerful international organisations through which they sought to promote their goals. Both were farsighted visionaries who saw the future more clearly than the leaders they sought to advise. But in the end, both proved to be Cassandras: Adedeji never saw his dream of an African Economic Market fulfilled, while Monnet's dream of a United States of Europe has yet to be born.

Jacques Delors and Alpha Konaré

Jacques Delors was undoubtedly the heir of Jean Monnet. With strong working-class roots, the former French finance minister and socialist was president of the European Commission from 1985 to 1994, overseeing a period of unparalleled success not witnessed since the halcyon integration days of the 1960s. The dynamism of the new Commission was evidenced by the fact that, in the first six months of 1988 alone, the EC took more decisions than it had between 1974 and 1984.[38] During Delors's tenure, the European Commission achieved a single market by 1992; created a single currency, the euro; promoted a common defence and foreign policy; and oversaw the birth of the European Union in November 1993. The Single European Act also gave the Community 'competences' in the areas of social policies, development, the environment, and technological research. This period significantly coincided with the reunification of Germany and the end of the Cold War: historic events that in many ways facilitated Delors's push for European integration.

Delors himself admitted that his leadership style was at first authoritarian, relying on a clandestine network of officials planted in strategic positions within a 17,000–strong Commission costing 2.3 billion ecu (£1.8 billion) a year to run. The Frenchman read and reflected a great deal during his tenure, interacted frequently with intellectuals,[39] and was a master of detail. European heads of state and foreign ministers often relied on his formidable knowledge of complex technical details to help stitch together political compromises.[40] Delors had always understood—from his time as finance minister in France—the importance of having powerful friends to get things done. As president of the Commission, he was close to many European leaders, particularly Germany's Helmut Kohl and his old boss François Mitterrand.[41] Not only could Delors deal well with leaders, but he was also able to popularise the idea of European integration and make it attractive to Europe's citizens.

Delors had a moral side that almost made him seem preachy, like a bureaucratic secular Pontiff of Brussels. The French dubbed him *grenouille de bénitier* (loosely meaning 'church hen'). A devout Catholic, Delors was visibly affected by what he described as the 'evil ethnic cleansing' of the Yugoslav Wars of succession between 1992 and 1995. He often drifted into depressive moods, carried a tortured cross of suffering, and felt guilty about treating his staff harshly. He also seemed sometimes to be suffering from a *folie de grandeur*, taking the tag of 'Mr. Europe' a tad too seriously. For all his strengths, Delors had a petty, petulant streak. He threatened to resign at least a dozen times a year if he did not get his way, throwing tantrums in front of leaders, ministers, and commissioners. But for all his flaws, by the time Delors left office in 1994, the European Union truly represented 'the House that Jacques built'.

Mali's Alpha Oumar Konaré, after retiring as the decade-long president of Mali in 2002, would go on to become the first chair of the African Union in July 2003, extending his federalist, visionary gaze from his own West African subregion to the entire continent. He was determined to change the negative perception of the OAU as an ineffectual 'club of dictators,' and often noted that his approach was to move the new organisation from a policy of 'nonintervention' to one of 'nonindifference'. As the chair of the AU Commission between 2003 and 2008, Konaré seemed to regain his idealism after a difficult end to his Malian presidency of 1992 to 2002, and energetically set about developing a five-year vision for the organisation. His vision and eloquence were impressive, but there was often a lack of focus and reality about Konaré's approach to integration. In a speech delivered to the University of South Africa (UNISA) in Tshwane, he called for 'political union', 'monetary and economic integration', and an end to Africa's conflicts; advocated increased intra-African trade, a rationalisation of Africa's regional economic groupings, and regional and continental infrastructure projects; and pushed for an end to Africa's 'brain drain' and the cancellation of its external debt of $290 billion.[42]

An AU audit report of December 2007, ironically chaired by Adebayo Adedeji—one of our four prophets—was however scathing about the administrative and management failings of the AU Commission under Konaré's leadership. The relationship between the chair, his deputy, and eight commissioners was described as 'dysfunctional', with infrequent meetings, a misunderstanding of mandates and authority levels, and a lack of coordination of overlapping mandates. Weak management systems and poor supervision were also identified between and within departments, as well as a lack of understanding and acceptance of a proper chain of command. In 2007, the Commission was operating with only 617 out of 912 approved staff (60 perc ent), relying heavily on short-term consultants.[43]

With member states failing regularly to pay annual dues of $40 million, Konaré incredibly proposed an increase of the Commission's budget to $600 million (later reduced to $158 million). His lack of prioritisation was evident, as he seemed with alarming regularity to propose, and sometimes implement, schemes of dubious utility: a conference of intellectuals, a 'Charter for Africa's Cultural Renaissance', and a Bob Marley memorial concert. Towards the end of his tenure, Konaré's frustration with his former colleagues was clear. After the AU's 'Grand Debate' on African integration in Accra in July 2007, the Malian noted: 'We shouldn't hide the fact that we ended up, after a difficult and sometimes painful debate, in a kind of confusion... I feel there is a crisis of leadership.'[44] Within a year, Konaré was out of office, visibly exhausted and frustrated. AU leaders had finally called his bluff after his constant threats to 'hand them back their Commission'.

Both Konaré and Delors were austere men who often stayed away from the ubiquitous *haute société* events in Addis Ababa and Brussels. Both threatened to resign if they did not get their way. Konaré, like Delors, often liked to avoid direct confrontation with his commissioners, and neither were rugged car mechanics prepared to get under the bonnets of their continental vehicles to get their hands dirty. Konaré's staff, however, did not seem to believe in nor share his integration vision in the way that Eurocrats shared Delors's vision. Even Delors's harshest critics offered grudging respect for his accomplishments. Konaré's critics, in contrast, often sounded like his domestic critics in Mali in ridiculing what they saw as his empty rhetoric and the lack of focus of an illusory dreamer.

In the African context, Cecil Rhodes, the great imperialist of the late nineteenth century, had sought to unite the continent from the Cape to Cairo through military conquest and economic exploitation under the patronage of the British crown (see chapter 10). Ghana's Kwame Nkrumah and his West African heirs like Adedeji and Konaré sought to unite Africa through more peaceful means than Rhodes's European *mission civilisatrice*. In the European context, French emperor Napoleon Bonaparte had similarly sought to unite Europe through military force of arms in the early nineteenth century. While

Rhodes was the precursor of apartheid,[45] Napoleon was arguably the precursor of fascism.[46] Two Gallic heirs of Napoleon—Jean Monnet and Jacques Delors—sought to unite Europe through more peaceful means, and both undoubtedly contributed more to European integration in the twentieth century than any other individuals. Both were creative thinkers who enjoyed ideas, but who also realised that they had to link thinking to practical action. While Adedeji and Konaré were both university professors, neither Monnet nor Delors had formal university education. While West Africans have dominated the quest for regional integration in Africa, French citizens have dominated the quest for European integration.

The Hegemons

We assess here the role of four hegemons in driving the integration processes of the African Union and the European Union: Nigeria and South Africa in Africa, and Germany and France in Europe. We wish to contrast and compare the leadership roles of the four actors on their own continent. It is important to note that while states in West and Southern Africa are often keen to tie down both African Gullivers in a web of interdependence to avoid aggressive unilateralism that could harm their interests, France and smaller Lilliputian neighbours have sought to do the same to the German Gulliver in Europe.[47] Between 1999 and 2007, Nigeria and South Africa were the axes around which the AU revolved, and both were the engines seeking to make the AU work,[48] in much the same way that Germany and France have kept the EU integration engine running.

Nigeria and South Africa: Prophets of Africa's Renaissance

Like Nigeria, which saw itself from its independence in 1960 as the 'Giant of Africa', apartheid South Africa was also suffused with a missionary zeal in its foreign policy, as its racist leaders talked patronisingly about their country having special responsibilities to spread Western values north of the Limpopo in a macabre *mission civilisatrice*.[49] Under the presidencies of Nigeria's Olusegun Obasanjo and South Africa's Thabo Mbeki between 1999 and 2007, both countries challenged the OAU's inflexible adherence to absolute sovereignty and noninterference in the internal affairs of its member states.[50] At the OAU summit in Algiers, Algeria, in 1999, Mbeki and Obasanjo, along with other leaders, pushed for the ostracism of regimes that engaged in unconstitutional changes of government. Both leaders successfully convinced their colleagues that the OAU must recognise the right of other states to intervene in the internal affairs of their members in egregious cases of gross human rights abuses and in order to stem regional instability. During the process to transform the OAU into the AU, Mbeki and Obasanjo ensured that the organisation adopted a gradualist approach to unity rather than the more federalist model being championed by Libya's maverick leader, Muammar Qaddafi. Both leaders also successfully pushed for Mali's president, Alpha Konaré, to become the first chairperson of the AU Commission between 2003 and 2008.[51] Both stressed the importance of strengthening the peacekeeping capacity of the African Union, and undertook peacemaking roles in Africa on its behalf during Mbeki's tenure as the AU chair in 2002–2003 and Obasanjo's term in 2004–2005 (see chapter 7).

Two incidents—at the AU and the UN—however, highlighted concerns about the leadership ambitions of Nigeria and South Africa, and the efforts of Lilliputian states to tie both African Gullivers into a web of interdependence. As the AU's security structures were being built between 2002 and 2004, the majority of African states declined to grant regional hegemons Nigeria and South Africa permanent seats and veto power on the AU's fifteen-member Peace and Security Council, similar to the UN's Security Council.[52] Nigeria and South Africa also unsuccessfully attempted—along with Egypt—during the UN reform process in 2005, to obtain a permanent seat on a reconstituted fifteen-member UN Security Council, which was to have been expanded to twenty-five members. Despite the support of Abuja and Tshwane (Pretoria) for this measure, it was reportedly defeated by an overwhelming forty-seven votes to five.[53] Neither country was able to carry its own subregion, West Africa and Southern Africa (a combined bloc of about thirty votes), to support an initiative that was of vital importance to Nigeria and South Africa, demonstrating the limits of regional hegemony in this instance.

Germany and France: Entente Cordiale?

As earlier noted, European integration was brought about as a result of the conflict between Germany and France. Both countries came to dominate the EU, and European integration has long revolved around the Berlin-Paris axis. Charles de Gaulle's view of the EEC was of an intergovernmental body. He famously noted in May 1962 that the only option for the continent was 'a Europe of countries ... for Dante, Goethe, Chateaubriand would not have served Europe well if they had been stateless, men thinking and writing some form of integrated Esperanto or Volapuk'.[54] Konrad Adenauer, West Germany's chancellor between 1949 and 1963, pursued an effective Westpolitik focused on the EEC and NATO, while Willy Brandt, chancellor between 1969 and 1974, promoted an Ostpolitik focused on peaceful cooperation with East Germany and the Soviet-led Socialist bloc. Adenauer and de Gaulle established a warm personal relationship that spilled over into bilateral diplomacy. Brandt helped raise Germany's profile in international affairs during the 1970s, earning himself a Nobel Peace Prize in 1971 in the process. The more sober French president, Georges Pompidou, established a pragmatic working relationship with Brandt. Pompidou was less obstructionist and confrontational towards the EC than was de Gaulle, though he was also wary of giving too much power to the European Parliament and Commission.

Valéry Giscard d'Estaing (French president between 1974 and 1981) had served as de Gaulle's finance minister, but was himself a typical Gaullist, with all the nationalist trappings entailed in this ideology. He pragmatically pursued an approach that stressed both the intergovernmental and the federal aspects of the European Community. Both former German finance minister and later chancellor Helmut Schmidt—with whom Giscard had forged a close ministerial relationship—and the French president, were hard-headed pragmatists who sought to use the development of a European monetary union to improve their domestic economies following the global down-turn of the 1970s.[55]

Helmut Kohl became German chancellor in 1983 and along with François Mitterrand, who had entered the Elysée palace two years earlier, led the political efforts to establish the single market and common currency. Kohl, of course, also became the 'Father of German Reunification'. The haughty Mitterrand is often credited with doing more to promote European integration than any other French president. He was able to establish a warm and constructive relationship with the earthy Kohl which both men used to drive forward the process of European integration. French president Jacques Chirac and German chancellor Gerhard Schröder, led the opposition to the US invasion of Iraq in 2003, and worked well together in Europe to complete the process of European monetary union. More recently, strains have been reported in Franco-German relations, with the hyperactive French president since 2007, Nicolas Sarkozy dubbed 'Monsieur Zorro' by a French parliamentarian—ruffling feathers in Berlin by failing to consult German chancellor Angela Merkel on plans for a Mediterranean union.

It is important to note the parallels in the roles of our four hegemons. Just as Germany's expansionist Nazi past forced it to tread carefully in playing a political and military role in Europe, South Africa's apartheid past and destabilisation of its neighbours forced Nelson Mandela and Thabo Mbeki to engage their neighbours with great caution (see chapter 5). Just as Berlin and Paris coordinate their policies at European summits through pre-summit bilateral meetings, Abuja and Tshwane also seek to coordinate their policies through their bilateral diplomacy before important African summits. Just as Germany often let France play a lead role in Europe, South Africa—particularly during the Mbeki presidency—often let Nigeria lead on sensitive issues within the AU. De Gaulle can, in a sense, also be compared to Mandela: both were towering figures who attained the presidencies of their countries in the twilight of their lives. De Gaulle was elected to save French democracy, Mandela to build South African democracy. Though the shadow of de Gaulle made Pompidou more cautious (even if more conciliatory) in Europe, Mbeki seemed to become bolder in Africa after he stepped out of Mandela's shadow.

The Spoilers

We assess here the roles of Libya and Britain, which are widely regarded as 'spoilers' to integration efforts by members of the African Union and the European Union respectively. We do not argue that Tripoli and London have acted out of similar motives: rather, not only have their motives differed, but the contexts in which they have acted, and the constraints they have faced, have also differed. But as Britain was regarded by its critics, like de Gaulle, as an American Trojan horse within the European Union, so too was Libya regarded by its critics in black Africa as an Arab Trojan horse within the African Union.

Libya and Britain: Splendid Isolation?

After seizing power in 1969, Libya's Colonel Muammar Qaddafi modelled his rule on that of Egypt's Gamal Abdel Nasser, the celebrated champion of pan-Arabism in his day (see chapter 14). Egyptian Nobel laureate Naguib Mahfouz confirmed this link in a fictional 1979 account called 'The Seventh Heaven'. In this tale, Abu the defence counsel, who meets all arrivals at the First Heaven, explains to a recently murdered Raouf that individuals are often sent back from that level to act as guides for individuals on earth before they can ascend to the Second Heaven. When Raoul asks what has happened to Nasser, Abu replies: 'He is now guiding al-Qaddafi.'[56] Overcome by emotion, the Libyan leader fainted twice during Nasser's funeral in Cairo in September 1970.[57]

Qaddafi did more than any leader to ensure the creation of the African Union, hosting an extraordinary meeting of OAU leaders in his hometown of Sirte in 1999 and forcing other countries like Nigeria and South Africa to respond to his frantic drive towards creating a federal body. It is thus paradoxical that the 'Father of the African Union' is at the same time portrayed here as its diabolical 'spoiler'. Angered by the lack of Arab support for Libya in contrast to strong black African backing after Western-inspired UN economic and travel sanctions were imposed on Libya in 1992 (the OAU summit of 1994 asked for the sanctions to be revoked), Qaddafi swapped his pan-Arab robes for pan-African garments. He walked out of the Arab League summit in Tunis in 2004 and called for the dismantling of the organisation, arguing that it cared more about governments than it did about people. His country's 'Voice of the Greater Arab Homeland' radio station (modelled on Nasser's 'Voice of the Arabs' programme on Radio Cairo) was rebaptised 'Voice of Africa'. Sanctions were eventually lifted on Tripoli in 1999 with the help of South African leader Nelson Mandela, who mediated with Washington and London.

In the 1980s, Qaddafi had sent troops to Chad in pursuit of his country's irredentist claims in the territory. The Libyan leader's isolation in African diplomacy was underlined by an OAU summit in Tripoli in 1982 that most states boycotted, leading to an embarrassing failure to achieve a quorum. In the 1990s, Qaddafi was also responsible for providing military training to the warlords of two of West Africa's most brutal rebel groups: Liberia's Charles Taylor and Sierra Leone's Foday Sankoh. The self-styled 'Brother Leader' also reportedly trained and armed Tuareg rebels who triggered a conflict in northern Mali in 1990. The support of dissident groups against 'neocolonial' regimes in Africa that had made Nkrumah so unpopular among his peers in the 1960s is another trait that the Libyan strongman shares with the Ghanaian leader. In the debate over the 'United States of Africa' in 2007, Qaddafi had been almost as isolated as Nkrumah had been at the birth of the OAU in 1963.

Significantly, despite his 'chequebook diplomacy' (using oil to pay the dues of indebted member states and hosting OAU meetings), Qaddafi never became chair of the OAU. He finally ascended the chair of the newer AU only in January 2009 after both Obasanjo and Mbeki had left the political stage, leaving leaders of lesser stature unable to obstruct the ascent of the 'Brother Leader' to the chair. Between 1979 and 1986, Libya had in fact become isolated within the OAU after Qaddafi's 1980 military intervention in Chad. The Libyan leader would eventually withdraw his troops from Chad after a ruling of the Hague-based International Court of Justice (ICJ) that went against him in 1994. The seven regional integration schemes that Qaddafi has attempted since 1969 have all failed.[58] In September and October 2000, widespread xenophobic attacks in the Libyan cities of Tripoli and Zawiyah against thousands of Nigerians, Cameroonians, Nigerois, Chadians, and Sudanese resulted in killings and a repatriation of the foreigners back home. This incident further created a serious credibility problem for a leader seeking to play a role as the 'Father of African Unity'.[59]

In Britain, war-time prime minister Winston Churchill had set the tone for his country's often tempestuous relationship with Europe in a 1946 speech in Zurich: 'We are with Europe but not of it. We are linked but not compromised.'[60] At a Labour Party conference in 1962, British scepticism of European integration was again underlined by Labour opposition leader Hugh Gaitskell's comment that the country joining the EEC would represent 'the end of a thousand years of history'.[61] The success of the Community, its importance as a market for British goods, and the country's poor economic performance in the two post-1945 decades finally convinced policymakers in Whitehall that the country should enter the EEC in 1973 (De Gaulle had vetoed British membership in 1963).

The 1979 British election saw both the Conservatives and Labour continuing to criticise an unfair European Community budget system that shortchanged Britain (the Labour Party actually campaigned for British withdrawal from the EC in 1983). London declined to join the European Monetary System in 1979. Margaret Thatcher came to power in 1979 and remained prime minister until 1990. Like Charles de Gaulle, she believed in a Europe of intergovernmentalism in which governments reigned supreme, rather than one of federal institutions in which unelected bureaucrats held sway. Unlike de Gaulle, however, Thatcher did not belong to a country that EC members felt was indispensable to the survival of the institution. Though the British case was justifiable and had sympathy among Community members, Thatcher's increasingly abrasive and trenchant style in demanding 'our money back' in sporadic fits of 'handbag diplomacy' irritated and eventually alienated her colleagues. Britain found itself isolated within the Community. The EC's Fontainebleau summit in June 1984 eventually settled the issue in favour of a British rebate, but Thatcher had squandered much political support in other key areas and was increasingly also alienating her cabinet ministers and back-benchers. Britain was often treated by the EC's founding members as a 'johnny-come-lately' who had arrogantly rejected joining the organisation at its birth. The country had joined the Community after much of its rules had already been set and a cosy culture of negotiations had been established. Britain was widely distrusted as an 'American Trojan horse' that appeared to value its 'special relationship' with its cousins across the Atlantic much more than it did its neighbours across the Channel.

Having uniquely secured an opt-out from the single currency and the social chapter of the Maastricht Treaty of 1992 during the negotiations on the European Monetary Union, British premier John Major's biggest success appeared to have been to expunge any references to 'federalism' from the text. The banning of British beef from the EU after the outbreak of 'mad cow disease' in the country further poisoned the waters between London and Brussels. Tony Blair, who had vowed to be at the 'heart of Europe', found himself, like his predecessors, at its edge. He signed up to the Social Chapter of the Amsterdam Treaty of June 1997, but opted out of the border controls of the Schengen Agreement (along with Denmark and Ireland). Blair was liked by his EU colleagues, but lost credibility for his strong support of George W. Bush's unpopular war in Iraq initiated in March 2003.[62] His relationship with Jacques Chirac notoriously deteriorated. The EU still remains more unpopular in Britain than in any other European country, and some have argued that the country's leaders have shied away from actively explaining to their citizens why Europe is pursuing supranationalism for the sake of peaceful coexistence and economic prosperity.[63]

Concluding Reflections: African Renaissance, European Renaissance?

The material for transforming visions into concrete realities often requires large funds and technical capacity. Europe—despite the destruction of the Second World War—had these resources in abundance in the form of America's $100 billion Marshall Plan of 1947. Europe already possessed highly trained citizens in countries with established education systems who could take advantage of this 'aid'. The two Frenchmen, Jean Monnet and Jacques Delors, were thus able to fulfil their visions in contributing to a 'more united Europe'. The two West Africans, Adebayo Adedeji and Alpha Konaré, were, in contrast, unable to match their words with deeds and realised that the stuff of which dreams are made were in short supply in Africa: a continent in which leaders often pull the levers of power only to discover no effect on the situation on the ground. Often small African economies emerging from the 'Curse of Berlin' remain largely dependent on external markets; the continent also continues to suffer from a $290 billion external debt and chronic internal corruption that have both drained Africa's scarce resources; and the continent's marginalisation from the globalisation process is underlined by Africa accounting for less than 2 per cent of world trade (see chapters 1 and 3).

European institutions like the Commission, the Council, the Parliament, and the Court of Justice evolved gradually over time and acquired increasing powers as they gained credibility and effectiveness. The AU's institutions, in contrast, do not appear to be evolving organically, and the appearance of a Commission, Peace and Security Council, and Pan-African Parliament all seem to be an unsynchronised process of a miraculous 'Big Bang'. The 'afro' has not followed the 'euro' as a pan-continental currency. Africa's new integrationists do not appear to have learned from past lessons of weak, poorly funded, moribund OAU institutions. European integration appears, in contrast, to have been more grounded in the politics, economics, and society of that continent than African integration. European integration was pushed by the concrete interests of politicians, bureaucrats, big business, and farmers who derived material benefits from the process, as did their populations. African integration was derailed by external Cold War rivalries and proxy wars, as well as by African political misrule and economic mismanagement (see chapters 1 and 8). Africa's integration thus became delinked from resources and concrete interests, often degenerating into meaningless declarations and empty pledges that governments apparently had no concrete interest in or real power to implement. The sole, noble exception was the consistent commitment to decolonisation and the anti–apartheid struggle in South Africa, which eventually bore fruit by 1994. While European integration is often compared to a bicycle in which all members have to keep pedalling to avoid falling off the contraption, African integration has often resembled a bumpy ride on the back of a rickety mammy-wagon on potholed roads with failing brakes and lights, and the memorable sign 'No condition is permanent' inscribed on the vehicle.

This chapter has covered the two Curses of Babel and Berlin, the prophecies of Du Bois and Cassandra, two Towers of Babel, four prophets, four hegemons, and two 'spoilers'. We conclude by returning briefly to five key issues with which we began: death, Paradise, God, Berlin, and Babel.

So, who uttered the paradoxically immortal words 'Death is an exercise in Pan-Africanism'? These were the words of Abiranja, one of Ali Mazrui's characters in the author's haunting 1971 novel *The Trial of Christopher Okigbo*. In the book, Christopher Okigbo, Nigeria's greatest poet, is tried for the 'crimes' of putting 'tribe' before nation, and for betraying his art by swapping the pen for the pistol. Mazrui's novel was set in a 'Herafter' called 'AfterAfrica' in the background of the traumatic, bloody disunity of the Nigerian civil war of 1967–1970.[64] Algerian freedom fighter and founding president Ben Bella—who was instrumental in creating the OAU's Liberation Committee at its inaugural summit in 1963—had similarly famously implored his fellow leaders in Addis Ababa: 'So let us agree to die a little or even completely so that the peoples still under colonial domination may be free and African unity may not be a vain word.'[65] Africa was the birthplace of humankind and the site of the Garden of Eden. As Ali Mazrui noted in 1986, this is now a Garden of Eden in Decay, and contemporary Africa may now represent a Miltonian example of 'Paradise Lost'. The challenge for this generation of pan-Africanists will be how to replicate the sacrifices of earlier generations in order to lift—at least partially—God's 'Curse of Babel', and—completely—Europe's 'Curse of Berlin', over Africa.

13

OBAMAMANIA

AFRICA, AFRICAN AMERICANS, AND THE AVUNCULAR SAM[1]

'I have the blood of Africa within me, and my family's own story encompasses both the tragedies and triumphs of the larger African story.'[2]

Barack Obama, president of the United States of America

The presidential campaign run by Barack Obama in 2008 to become the first black man in the White House was nothing short of phenomenal. This development may never happen again in our lifetime. With a father from Kenya and white mother from Kansas, this forty-seven-year-old Harvard-trained lawyer defied all expectations. In the South African context, Obama's win would have been as improbable as Helen Zille—the white leader of the opposition Democratic Alliance—becoming president of a black majority South Africa. Blacks constitute 12 per cent of the US population, and Obama—a first-term senator from Illinois—was only the fifth-ever black senator in US history. This is an America that has experienced slavery, lynching of black men, disenfranchisement of blacks, and continuing prejudice and social segregation, in a country in which some whites would never vote for a black candidate.[3]

After winning the first Democratic Party caucus in Iowa (a state with a 90 per cent white population) in January 2008, Obama won a majority of white votes in Virginia, New Mexico, Wisconsin, Illinois, Utah, and Wyoming. In a bitter and tough Democratic primary contest, Hillary Clinton—who was thirty points ahead in polls before voting began—won many of the big states, like California, New York, New Jersey, and Massachusetts, but was unable to overtake Obama's lead. A coalition of white women, white blue-collar workers, and Latinos backed Clinton, while Obama's coalition was built around white men, blacks, and young voters.[4] Several high-profile Democrats switched from Clinton to Obama, as polls correctly predicted that he would have a better chance than her of defeating Republican candidate John McCain in the November 2008 election. As president, Obama subsequently appointed Hillary Clinton as his secretary of state in a bid to heal the rifts of a bitter, protracted election campaign.

In his presidential campaign, Obama's grassroots-fuelled, Internet-savvy campaign raised more money than any other in history: over $600 billion. This will likely be recalled as a textbook campaign for years to come. Obama also garnered more white votes than had previous Democratic candidates John Kerry and Al Gore. Furthermore, 96 per cent of African Americans voted for him, 67 per cent of Latinos, 78 per cent of Jewish voters, and 67 per cent of young adults between the ages of eighteen to twenty-nine.[5] As David Mendell, Obama's insightful biographer and a Chicago journalist who has closely followed his rise, noted: 'Not since the days of Jack and Bobby Kennedy, and their luminous political Camelot, had a politician captured so quickly the imagination of such a broad array of Americans... Not since Ronald Reagan had a politician been so adept at sharing his own unwavering optimism with a disheartened electorate.'[6]

Dreams from Our Ancestors: Obama and Africa

When Barack ('blessed') Obama was elected as the first African American president of the United States in November 2008, a wave of 'Obamamania' swept across the African continent, its diaspora, and the world. Former South African president Nelson Mandela noted: 'Your victory has demonstrated that no person anywhere in the world should not dare to dream of wanting to change the world for a better place'; Kenyan president Mwai Kibaki said: 'The victory of Senator Obama is our own victory because of his roots here in Kenya. As a country, we are full of pride for his success'; the South African president at the time, Kgalema Motlanthe, opined: 'Your election ... carries with it hope for millions ... of people of ... African descent both in Africa and in the diaspora'; Nigerian president Umaru Yar'Adua noted: 'Obama's election has finally broken the greatest barrier of prejudice in human history. For us in

Nigeria, we have a great lesson to draw from this historic event'; and Ghana-ian former UN Secretary-General Kofi Annan observed: 'Obama's victory demonstrates America's extraordinary capacity to renew itself.'[7] Obama's father's homeland, Kenya, declared a public holiday to mark the occasion.

Six months into his tenure, Barack Obama's visit to Ghana in July 2009 was a twenty-four-hour sojourn that marked the first trip to sub-Saharan Africa by America's first black president.[8] This followed a brief stopover in Egypt a month earlier. In Accra, Obama delivered a major address to the Ghanaian parliament on development and democracy in which he stressed the interdependence of Africa with the rest of the world, declaring: 'The 21st century will be shaped by what happens not just in Rome or Moscow or Washington, but by what happens in Accra as well.' Obama also supported African 'agency' in resolving the continent's own problems, arguing that 'Africa's future is up to Africans'. But he also recognised the historical 'Curse of Berlin' in noting: 'yes, a colonial map that made little sense helped to breed conflict. The West has often approached Africa as a patron and source of resources rather than a partner'.

In his 2009 speech in Ghana, Obama further noted his own strong identi-fication with Africa by referring to his Kenyan father three times and observ-ing: 'I have the blood of Africa within me.' His message was one of 'good governance' (though his earlier praise of deceased tyrant of oil-rich Gabon, Omar Bongo, as a peacemaker in June 2009, and his embrace of autocratic oil-rich Arab sheikhs and Chinese communists, appear to contradict this), as well as increased opportunity, better health (announcing a vague $63 billion plan to combat AIDS and malaria), and conflict resolution. In his speech, Obama essentially noted that Africa needed 'strong institutions' rather than 'strong men'. He ended by reminding Africans that Martin Luther King Jr. had been inspired in his continued pursuit of the American civil rights struggle by attending Ghana's independence celebrations in 1957.[9]

In Ghana, Obama also visited the Cape Coast Castle: a major slave post with suffocating dungeons from which human cargo was transported to Europe and the Americas. The symbolism of the first African American US president at the site of a tragic and sordid historical monument to a trade in which an estimated 20 million Africans perished, was particularly poignant. However, this visit could also have revived feelings within sections of Ameri-ca's black community that Obama is not a 'real' African American, since his ancestors—his father—came by aeroplane from Kenya to study in America, and not on a slave-ship from Africa.

Some Africans complained that Obama's early presidential visits to Africa—Accra and Cairo—both resembled refuelling stops on the way to or from more strategic destinations. Kenyans and Nigerians were particularly peeved that he chose to go to Ghana before visiting them. Obama's aides, however, insisted that the Ghana trip was linked to the Group of Eight (G8) summit that the president attended in Italy in the same week, at which issues of critical importance to Africa—food security, climate change, world trade, and the global financial crisis—were discussed. The idea was to use Ghana—which held five multiparty elections between 1992 and 2008—as a role model of democratic governance and civil society in promoting development in Africa. The choice of Ghana was also not disinterested: the country is expected to become an important oil exporter. About two-thirds of recent US trade with Africa has been with oil-rich Nigeria, Angola, and Gabon.

Even before the Ghana trip in 2009, Obama had visited Kenya, South Africa, and Darfuri refugees in Chad as a US senator in 2006. In his ancestral homeland of Kenya on this earlier trip, he was enthusiastically received like a rock star and returning 'son of the soil'. His condemnation of human rights abuses and corruption in Africa was widely applauded.[10] As a student in the US, Barack had taken part in anti–apartheid demonstrations that had helped to raise his political consciousness. I went to listen to Obama speak in Cape Town on his senatorial safari in August 2006, during a visit in which he met one of his great heroes—former South African president Nelson Mandela, as well as former Cape Town archbishop Desmond Tutu—and criticised then-president Thabo Mbeki's AIDS policies. During his Cape Town speech in 2006, Obama noted the influence of Mahatma Gandhi and Martin Luther King Jr. on the anti–apartheid struggle, and called for South Africa and the US to assist poorer countries to 'build a vibrant civil society'.[11] I was somewhat disappointed, however, with Obama's performance. He seemed like a machine politician, and dodged difficult questions, sometimes giving vacuous responses.

David Mendell covered Obama's 2006 Africa visit, and confirmed that he was exhausted from jet-lag during the Cape Town speech.[12] I subsequently followed the continuing rise of Obama, and witnessed some of the most eloquent and inspirational performances given by any politician. His soaring, often biblical campaign oratory promising a vision of a better America espoused by prophets like Robert F. Kennedy and Martin Luther King Jr. who had preceded him, provided hope and succour to a pre-recession US that was desperately in need of both. Barack often appears to have a profound sense of justice and empathy, and has sought to speak for the voiceless and the power-less: people who are usually invisible to mainstream American politicians. As he himself put it, he wants to 'give voice to the voiceless, and power to the powerless'.[13]

In understanding the symbolism of Obama for the continent, it is essential to revisit his African heritage. His elegant 1995 memoir, *Dreams from My Father*,[14] describes a painful quest for identity and a vulnerability triggered by the death of an arrogant, impulsive, but determined Kenyan father (in a car crash in 1982) who left his family when Barack was only two years old. Obama met his father only one other time, when he was ten. Yet he still idol-ised his father, Barack Hussein Obama Sr. (a goat-herder as a boy), whose example inspired him to study at his father's alma mater, Harvard University. But Barack's father—a civil servant in Kenya—had died in penury, an alco-holic and abusive character who failed to fulfil either his personal ambitions or his family responsibilities. Obama was therefore determined to correct these flaws. His desire to become president of the US was born out of a deter-mination to fulfil the personal ambitions that his father had clearly failed to realize. The love and attention that Barack devotes to his two daughters, Malia and Sasha, appear to be a conscious attempt to make up for his own lack of paternal affection.

Obama clearly identifies with Africa, as is evident from his journey of self-discovery to Kenya as a twenty-six–year–old, as described in his 1995 memoir. As he puts it: 'The pain I felt was my father's pain. My questions were my brothers' questions. Their struggle, my birthright.'[15] But his father's legacy is also a heavy burden that the young, sensitive Barack is struggling to compre-hend. He is clearly caught in a cultural limbo, feeling neither completely American nor completely African, neither completely black nor completely white. As he prepares to fly to Africa for the first time, Obama describes him-self as a 'Westerner not entirely at home in the West, an African on his way to a land full of strangers'.[16] On his way to Africa, Barack tours historic sites in Europe and makes the startling observation: 'It wasn't that Europe wasn't beautiful... It just wasn't mine. I felt as if I were living out someone else's romance; the incompleteness of my own history stood between me and the sites I saw like a hard pane of glass.'[17] None of the previous forty-three Ameri-can presidents of European ancestry could have made such a statement. This is what makes Obama's ascent to the White House so phenomenal, and of such great interest to Africa.

But like many African Americans, Obama had a somewhat romanticised view of Africa before he arrived in his ancestral home, which, he notes, 'had become an idea more than an actual place, a new promised land, full of ancient traditions and sweeping vistas, noble struggles and talking drums'.[18] Once in Kenya, Barack feels his father's seemingly ubiquitous presence. He is nostalgic about Obama Sr.'s life and times, seeking to re-create—through this visit—a sometimes mythical past that he never knew but so badly needs to understand and feel a part of. It is with great trepidation and anxiety that Barack approaches this visit, as if fearing that his long quest for identity in America will once again be frustrated. Having struggled to become an African American in order to overcome his painful, fatherless childhood, it is as if he now wants to don the robes of an African identity in order to reconnect with his ancestral homeland. In Kenya, Obama meets, and enjoys the extravagant hospitality and warmth of, his large extended Kenyan family; he speaks a bit of his native Luo; he is exposed to the corruption and ethnic tensions of Kenyan politics; he rides in *matatus* (rickety taxis); he eats goat curry and *ugali;* he goes on safari, and discovers and appreciates the beauty of the historical site of the biblical Garden of Eden; he identifies with, and makes connections between, black Americans in Chicago ghettoes and Kenyans in dirt-poor Nairobi shantytowns (as well as identifying with poor Indonesians from his childhood in Jakarta); and he is appalled by the continuing, pernicious socio-economic impact of British colonialism on Kenya.

In a final moving scene in the ancestral rural hometown of Siaya (where Obama bathes in the open air and uses pit-latrines), Barack breaks down and cries by his father's grave. He is finally 'home', writing—perhaps a bit sentimentally—about no longer feeling watched, and not having awkward questions raised about his name or his hair. He had read about Dedan Kimathi, the great Kenyan liberation fighter during the Mau Mau struggle against British colonialism in the 1950s, and could now put a place to the legendary names he had learned about in America.

Kenyan scholar Ali Mazrui famously noted that Obama's parents' divorce could turn out historically to be 'one of the most significant matrimonial breakups in history'. If Obama's parents had stayed together, observed Mazrui, he would probably not have become US president. He would have grown up instead more African than American, and might have been 'another African sending remittances home to Kenya'.[19] His father may even have moved the family permanently back to Kenya, where Obama Sr. returned to live. The stability that sustained Barack's political ambitions appears to have been provided by three strong women: his Harvard-trained African American wife, Michelle; his white mother, Ann Dunham (who died of cancer in November

1995); and his white grandmother, Madelyn Dunham (who died at age eighty-six two days before her grandson's historic presidential victory in November 2008).

But despite his visits to Africa, Obama himself has sometimes been guilty of reinforcing stereotypes of the continent similar to those that he condemned in his 1995 memoir and 2009 Accra speech. In his 2006 book *The Audacity of Hope*, Obama talks about Africa in broad-brushed, Afro-pessimistic strokes: 'There are times when considering the plight of Africa—the millions racked by AIDS, the constant droughts and famines, the dictatorships, the pervasive corruption, the brutality of twelve-year-old guerrillas who know nothing but war wielding machetes or AK-47s—I find myself plunged into cynicism and despair.'[20]

Despite Obama's obvious identification with Africa, it must always be remembered that he is the president of America and not of Africa. Barack thus has other pressing policy priorities that will undoubtedly take precedence over the continent's problems: reviving America's economy and securing a viable healthcare plan; ending wars in Iraq and Afghanistan; making peace in the Middle East; repairing relations with European allies; fighting nuclear prolif-eration in North Korea and Iran; and engaging an increasingly wealthy China and erratically assertive Russia.

In spite of the great expectations unleashed by his historic election, in some African quarters, that Obama will act as a Messiah by increasing US support for Africa, even a black Gulliver will be held down by powerful Lilliputian legislators who control America's purse strings. The US still lacks a powerful, cohesive domestic constituency on Africa that can wield the influence of the Israel lobby. No American politician running for an important office can chal-lenge the unconditional American support for Israel, which scholars like John Mearsheimer and Stephen Walt have now begun to expose as damaging to America's foreign policy in the Middle East. By 2005, America had provided $154 billion in assistance to Israel, which still receives $3 billion a year, much of it in military assistance and high-tech weapons. Israel also obtains about $2 billion annually in private donations from US citizens. Egypt receives $2 bil-lion a year to remain friends with Israel.[21]

Israel disproportionately benefits from US support even though the Jewish American population of about 5.1 million (about 1.7 per cent of the total population) is much smaller than the African American population, which comprises 30 million people and 12 per cent of the country's total. In contrast to the large sums provided to Israel and Egypt, forty-eight sub-Saharan African countries, including some of the poorest in the world, share less than $1 billion annually: the clearest sign of the political nature of American aid (see chapter 8). In contrast to policy towards Israel, US policy towards Africa is not based on consistent congressional support and often involves seeking ad hoc coalitions in support of specific policies. In 2009, the Congressional Black Caucus had only 1 out of 100 members in the US Senate, and 43 out of 435 members in the House of Representatives. It is thus important that pro-Africa lobbyists work closely with progressive legislators and Washington-based interest groups to influence Obama's policies towards Africa, as they success-fully did in sanctioning apartheid South Africa in the 1980s.[22] The tens of thousands of highly educated Africans in America must also be mobilised in building a viable constituency for Africa. These groups must raise awareness among, and mobilise the support of, many of the 150 million black people in the diaspora, which the African Union (AU) has now defined as a sixth sub-region after Africa's five geographical ones (see chapter 12).[23]

The main outlines so far of Obama's early Africa policy, gleaned from his senatorial career and presidential campaign, include: support for the UN-AU peacekeeping mission in Sudan's Darfur region; advancing peacemaking efforts in South Sudan; increasing aid to the Democratic Republic of the Congo (DRC); supporting South Africa and Nigeria to play a leadership role in Africa; and pushing for reform of the UN, an institution that many Afri-cans see as vital to their security and economic development. US secretary of state Hillary Clinton made a one-week visit to Kenya, South Africa, Angola, the DRC, Nigeria, Liberia, and Cape Verde in August 2009 to reinforce Obama's message of mutually beneficial trade, conflict resolution, and demo-cratic governance.[24]

Johnnie Carson, an experienced African American former ambassador to Kenya, Zimbabwe, and Uganda, was appointed as Obama's assistant secretary of state for African affairs in 2009. This author encountered Carson at the African Studies Association meeting in New Orleans in November 2009, where he delivered a speech on US policy towards Africa. This address could easily have been delivered by a member of the George W. Bush administra-tion: it was disappointing in its disingenuous and ahistostical portrayal of US policy towards Africa, glossing over damaging American actions and exag-gerating apparent successes in areas like trade and security (see chapter 8 for a detailed assessment of US policy towards Africa). After the speech, Carson cowardly refused to take more than one question, which he answered patron-isingly: when asked about American agricultural subsidies ($108 billion in

2005) that were said to be harmful to African farmers, he talked belittlingly about the inadequacies of the latter. The assistant secretary of state also incredibly expressed surprise to the audience that Angola was not a breadbasket for Africa, conveniently forgetting that his own country had fuelled a civil war for three decades in which Washington supported a psychopathic warlord, Jonas Savimbi, as part of its ideological Cold War struggle with the Soviet Union. Carson then invited scholars in attendance to assist the US administration in its efforts on Africa. This was one of the worst sales pitches I had ever seen, and left me wondering whether more attention would better be given to exposing African American policymakers who peddle such destructive views about Africa. I also wondered whether such individuals were using a false solidarity with the continent, to the great detriment of Africa, in order to further their own professional careers.

Despite this disappointing experience, Obama must be encouraged, in building upon his Ghana trip, to support more strongly the role of UN peacekeeping in Africa, as well as the strengthening of African regional organisations and national health systems. Washington should play a greater role in annulling Africa's $290 billion debt. America must also eliminate its deleterious agricultural subsidies to its farmers, and allow free access to its markets for Africa's agricultural products. This must be done not just out of some altruistic feeling of charity, but also—as Obama himself noted in his 2009 speech in Accra—to take advantage of the potential of trade with an African market of nearly 1 billion consumers. It is these issues in which the first African American president must invest some political capital. Otherwise, these sporadic trips to Africa will become mere symbolic photo opportunities that feel the continent's pain but yield no concrete benefits for Obama's ancestral homeland. In the true spirit of our ancestors, Africans must always welcome Barack back home, but should continue to hold his feet to the communal fire.

The Audacity of Hope: Obama, America, and the World

Reflecting the 'Obamamania' in Africa following Barack's election as US president in November 2008, prominent individuals in the African diaspora added their voices to the global celebration. Tillman Thomas, prime minister of Grenada, noted: 'Your being the first African American to be elevated to this prestigious office fills us with additional pride and emotion', television mogul Oprah Winfrey gushed: 'It says that no longer will there be red states and blue states, it means that the colour purple rules.' Film director Spike Lee added: 'It's a new day, a big dawn, a new beginning not just for America but for the world over'; while world motor-racing champion Lewis Hamilton said: 'I'm very happy and proud to see Obama at the front. I think it's great for the world.' Civil rights leader Andrew Young—who had supported Hillary Clinton over Obama in the Democratic primary—noted: 'Thanks to Barack Obama, vision is replacing violence, faith is defeating fear, and grace is putting an end to greed.'[25] Jesse Jackson (publicly) and Colin Powell (privately) cried after Obama's victory, as did many Africans and African Americans. In a celebrity-obsessed America, Hollywood and its Tinsel Town stars, like Halle Berry, Will Smith, Bernie Mac, and George Clooney, rushed to embrace Obama—who won a Grammy for the spoken version of his memoir—like a rock star. After his victory, Barack was on the cover of almost every major magazine: *Ebony, Vogue, Time, Newsweek, The Economist, Foreign Policy*, and *New Statesman*.

Despite Obama's frequently expressed desire to support the voiceless and powerless, he has another side as a pragmatic, hard-headed politician who seems to want to please every group. Inevitably, Obama may lose his shine if he is unable to deliver on the incredible expectations that his inspirational campaign unleashed.[26] As Barack himself admitted, he is 'a blank screen on which people of vastly different political stripes project their own views'.[27] But it was inspirational performances that led the former Democratic governor of New York, Mario Cuomo—himself a formidable wordsmith—to declare Obama the best orator he has ever heard. The late Democratic senator Edward Kennedy declared Obama the inheritor of his brother John F. Kennedy's legacy. Former Democratic vice president Al Gore noted: 'Obama is rising because he is talking about politics in a way that feels fresh to people.'[28] Tom Daschle, the former Democratic majority leader and a mentor of Obama, noted: 'He's one of those rare individuals who has almost unlimited potential and seems to defy most of the laws of political gravity.'[29] Even Governor Bill Richardson of New Mexico—who served in former US president Bill Clinton's cabinet and was subsequently nominated as Obama's commerce secretary, before being forced to resign due to a prior ethical investigation—endorsed Obama for the presidency. Like the equally cerebral former South African president Thabo Mbeki (who sometimes wrote his own speeches, see chapter 11), Obama, the perfectionist orator, spends hours preparing and redrafting his own speeches.[30]

One of the most important aspects of Obama's 2008 presidential campaign was his ongoing attempt—evident in his 2006 book *The Audacity of Hope*—to try to educate Americans about their country's past sins. While praising his country's greatness, he also exposed its historical 'gunboat diplomacy' in Latin America and the Caribbean; its proxy wars that propped up corrupt autocrats throughout the Third World; its ill-conceived and illegal war in Iraq in 2003; and its 'extraordinary rendition' of terror suspects to countries in which they can be tortured (see chapter 8). As Obama noted:

[M]anifest destiny also meant bloody and violent conquest—of Native American tribes forcibly removed from their lands and of the Mexican army defending its territory. It was a conquest that, like slavery, contradicted America's founding principles and tended to be justified in explicitly racist terms, a conquest that American mythology has always had difficulty fully absorbing but that other countries recognized for what it was—an exercise in raw power.[31]

Having lived in the US for a decade, I believe that many Americans are instinctively generous and want to help people and countries in distress. But many people in Peoria (Middle America) are also spectacularly naive, parochial, and ill-informed. They are often ill-served by a compliant media, a parochial intellectual class, and a timid political class that seem to pander more to corporate interests than explain the world to its citizens. This highlights the importance of a politician like Obama—a Kenyan Kansan who was raised in Honolulu and Jakarta—who is perhaps the first truly global citizen who has run for, and won, the most powerful office on earth. One cannot imagine any of the forty-three white men who occupied the presidency before Obama listing radical Martiniquan scholar Frantz Fanon—author of *The Wretched of the Earth*[32]—as one of his formative intellectual influences.

In opposing the now widely discredited invasion of Iraq in 2003—which Obama described as a 'dumb war'—he showed an understanding of the need to address the root causes of poverty that allow terrorists to find fertile ground for recruiting followers. As president, he stopped using George W. Bush's unpopular 'War on Terror' slogan and restored his country's reputation across the globe. Barack has consistently sought to force America to live up to its founding ideals. But worryingly, however, he has reserved the right of the US to act unilaterally as a 'reluctant sheriff'; has described the UN Security Council as 'archaic'; and threatened, as a presidential candidate, to send American troops into Pakistan in 'hot pursuit' of terrorist suspects without the permission of its government.[33]

Obama has a self-deprecating sense of humour and, like his Democratic predecessor, Bill Clinton (1993–2000), is a policy wonk able to digest complicated detail and explain it to people in ways that are easy to understand.

But David Mendell notes that there are hidden flaws that the public often do not see, namely Obama's 'imperious, mercurial, self-righteous and sometimes prickly nature'.[34] The calm, unruffled, 'no drama' Obama is the picture often presented to the public, but in an uncharacteristic incident in the Illinois senate, Barack reportedly had to be physically restrained from coming to blows with Rickey Hendon, a black legislator with whom he had often clashed.[35] Like Bill Clinton, who had a legendary short-temper in private, Obama rarely loses his cool in public.

From the ages of twenty-four to twenty-seven, after graduating in political science from Columbia University in New York, Obama worked for three years as a community organiser in Chicago's rough South Side neighbourhoods: derelict, industrial areas with the largest concentration of black people in the US, over a million people. The idealistic, naive young man—nicknamed 'Baby Face' for his youthful looks—was somewhat of a loner who was keen to help improve the lives of the poor and destitute. He encouraged divided black churches to work together to improve their communities; lobbied the city council to open a job bank in destitute communities; and pushed for asbestos to be removed from housing projects. This was where Obama discovered the importance of black churches to local communities and he—whose mother had brought him up to be an agnostic, secular humanist—developed his strong faith and met the fire-breathing pastor he would later be forced to disown on the presidential campaign trail: Reverend Jeremiah Wright of the Trinity United Church of Christ. This is the same church that television host Oprah Winfrey and rapper Common have also attended. Obama had been spiritually attracted to Wright's church by an anti–apartheid 'Free Africa' message, as well as by Wright's cerebral, liberal (supporting gay rights), and radical social justice political message.[36] The title of Obama's second book, *The Audacity of Hope*, was in fact borrowed from a sermon by Wright, the fiery pastor who administered at Obama's wedding in 1992.

It was ironic that Obama had discovered the power of bottom-up approaches to uplifting black communities in Chicago, but ended up in a position as president to implement top-down approaches (though the federal government also provides funding for local communities through their state governments). Also ironic was the fact that the greatest electoral controversy faced by Obama was over a black Christian pastor. A large number of Americans—some estimates are about 15 per cent—still stubbornly continue to view Obama as a closet Muslim even after he has made his commitment to the Christian faith abundantly clear. Barack often carries around a Bible that he read on the campaign trail. In a deeply religious country like America, even an ethically challenged politician like Bill Clinton felt the need publicly to embrace religion and play the role of a good Southern Baptist, even in the midst of the Monica Lewinsky scandal in 1998. In Obama's case, religion was also a way of fitting into, and gaining acceptance of, the African American community. Barack's work in the black community, his attending of a black church, and his discovery of the black struggle in America all contributed to an intense identification with this group for a boy who had been raised in Hawaii and Jakarta by a white mother and white grandparents and abandoned by an African father. As Obama would later joke, New York cab drivers that refuse to stop to pick him up certainly failed to see the race of his maternal side![37] As conservative African American scholar Shelby Steele insightfully noted about Barack: 'His books show a man nothing less than driven by a determination to be black, as if blackness were more an achievement than a birthright.'[38]

Obama went to Harvard University in 1988 to obtain a law degree in order to be able to fight for the rights of poor black people in Chicago more effectively. As in Chicago, the brooding youngster was a bit of a loner. He took part in demonstrations against the dying apartheid regime in South Africa, was active in the Black Law Students Association, and famously became the first black editor of the prestigious *Harvard Law Review*. In a pattern that would be repeated in his future political career, Barack's election to the journal had been based on an ability to listen to conservative rivals as well as his liberal friends. He was, however, criticised by African American students at Harvard for not bringing more blacks into his seventy-five-member editorial team. This charge was equally true of Obama's US Senate office and is also true of his cabinet, which shows how incredible his achievement is when one sees him surrounded by mostly lily-white men. The failure to hire more blacks to one's inner circle has also hurt other prominent black figures, like Kofi Annan, the Ghanaian Secretary-General of the United Nations between 1997 and 2006 (see chapter 4).

Obama became a 'poor peoples' civil rights lawyer and worked for Project Vote, which registered 150,000 African American voters, before marrying fellow Harvard-trained African American lawyer and close confidante Michelle Robinson in 1992 at the age of thirty-one. As Ali Mazrui has observed, this choice was critical to Obama's political success. The Kenyan scholar noted that it is highly unlikely that Barack would have won the White House if he had married a white woman, since he would have alienated black women and white voters with such a combination.[39] Obama won a seat to the Illinois senate at the age of thirty-five, a job he did for eight years while also teaching constitutional law part-time at the University of Chicago and picking up golf and poker. As a state senator in the Illinois general assembly, Obama was seen as intelligent, but was not universally liked. Some black senators saw him as being 'not black enough', for talking like a white person, and for being an intellectual snob who mentioned his Harvard pedigree too often. Though the Democrats were the minority party for the first six of Obama's eight legislative years (as they would be when Obama first joined the US Senate in 2005), he won praise for being able to reach across the aisle to pass legislation with Republicans on issues he cared about: campaign finance reform, compensating crime victims, preventing early probation for gun-running felons, imposing harsher sentences for offenders using date-rape drugs on their victims, increasing state-funded screening programmes for prostate cancer, advocating more funding for children's after-school programmes, and improving funding to fight lead-abatement programmes. Many of these issues were of great concern to the black communities in which Obama had worked as a community organiser, and he developed a commitment to fighting poverty and promoting civil liberties. But Barack was somewhat frustrated by the slow, pork-ridden, populist grand-standing of the legislative process in the notoriously corruption-ridden, factionalised politics of Chicago, a city in which German playwright Bertolt Brecht had famously set his 1927 play on gangsters, *In the Jungle of Cities*.[40] But it was here that Obama honed his skills of political compromise and accepted that politics is the art of the possible, recognising that one needs both political power and effective alliances to get things done.[41]

One accusation that has often been levelled at Obama concerns his ruthless overambition and desire to run before he has learned how to walk. After barely three years in the Illinois state legislature, he had tried to win a seat in the US House of Representatives at the age of thirty-nine, a decision he later regretted after his heavy defeat by African American legislator Bobby Rush. Barack's decision to run for president of the US after only two years as a senator, however, was more successful. Despite his lofty rhetoric and grand visions, during his two years in the US Senate, Obama was a calculating and cautious politician. He was careful not to tackle any controversial issues, and returned frequently to Illinois to hold town hall meetings, ensuring that he did not forget his home base and be accused of having become a Beltway insider and creature of Washington. Senator Obama did, however, maintain his commitment to civil liberties, voting with thirty-three out of the other ninety-nine senators to oppose powers of special interrogation for so-called high-value detainees in Bush's 'war on terror'.[42] Barack was said to encourage debates among strong-willed aides in his office before taking his own decisions: a style of leadership that should help him in his presidential role. However, Obama coauthored just one substantial piece of legislation (with Republican senator Richard Lugar), to reduce stockpiles of conventional weapons. His two-year legislative record in the Senate was rather thin: mainly speaking out on 'soft' issues such as ethanol, avian flu, and funding for Illinois veterans.[43]

One controversial issue that Senator Obama seemed at first reluctant to speak out on was Hurricane Katrina in New Orleans in 2005. The storm had disproportionately affected African Americans, killing more than a thousand people and rendering tens of thousands as refugees in their own country. The displaced were carted into the Superdrome sports arena. This incident was a great source of national embarrassment, as a global audience saw the world's richest nation reduced to Third World status due largely to a slow, inept, insensitive response to the tragedy, which consequently lost George W. Bush much political support across the country. Hip-hop artist Kanye West famously complained that 'George Bush doesn't care about black people'.[44] Asked to comment on Katrina, Obama hesitated but eventually found his voice. He talked about the 'anger' and 'anguish' within the African American community, and criticised the 'historic indifference on the part of government towards the plight of those who are disproportionately African American'.[45] Obama was critical, but wanted as always to be a bridge-builder and voice of calm and reason. Other black voices were closer to Kanye West. Princeton academic Cornell West noted: 'From slave ships to Superdrome was not that big a journey', while veteran civil rights leader Reverend Jesse Jackson dubbed the Superdrome itself as akin to the 'hull of a slave ship'.[46]

One of Obama's earliest political influences was his reading of the first part of Taylor Branch's magisterial trilogy of Martin Luther King and the civil rights struggle, *Parting the Waters*, which appears to have had a decisive impact on a young Obama in his mid-twenties in search of a solid identity and life mission. As Barack noted after reading the book: 'This is my story.'[47] Obama echoed King as he accepted the Democratic Party nomination for president in August 2008: a symbolic passing of the torch from one black prophet of liberation to the current age's prophet of redemption. Both King and Obama represent charismatic speakers and leaders of grassroots movements; both were seen as moderate, eloquent prophets. But while King did not pursue public office and relied on Lyndon Johnson (a Southern president who had previously opposed anti–lynching legislation and the Civil Rights Act of 1957)[48] to implement the social changes he advocated, Obama is a consummate professional politician with the power to make changes directly. But his African American identity may paradoxically make it more difficult for him to prioritise the needs of his own community, since he was elected by overwhelmingly white voters to address the needs of the entire country. While Martin Luther King was a professional pastor who entered politics to end social injustices, Obama is a professional politician who has often entered the spiritual realm in a bid to end the moral degradation and social malaise of American society. Barack once—in an extravagant bout of messianic delusion—told an audience of evangelicals in South Carolina in October 2007 that he wanted to become 'an instrument of God' to create 'a Kingdom right here on Earth'.[49]

Obama can sound almost conservative at times in his message of self-reliance to the black community, urging black men to accept their personal responsibilities. During the 2008 presidential campaign, African American civil rights leader Jesse Jackson Sr.—who himself had unsuccessfully run for the Democratic Party nomination in 1984 and 1988—was unwittingly caught on a microphone whispering that he wanted to castrate Obama for 'talking down' to black people. But Obama's message was also deeply personal: having been abandoned by his own father and seen the devastation of broken homes in black communities in Chicago, he was determined not to absolve black fathers of their personal responsibilities.

Another early political influence on Obama was the first African American mayor of Chicago, Harold Washington, who held office between 1983 and 1987 (before dying unexpectedly of a heart attack shortly after his reelection). Washington stitched together a coalition of Chicago's 'dispossessed': blacks, Hispanics, Asians, and poor whites. It was not lost on Obama that the first black mayor of Chicago had been able to do the very things that the young community organiser would have sought but for lack of power: channelling city contracts, jobs, low-cost housing, and infrastructure projects to poor communities and nonprofit organisations.[50] Before becoming a community organiser, Barack had in fact written a letter to ask for a job in Washington's office—and got no reply. Washington's campaign showed Obama the power of grassroots organisation, and was the model that he himself would later successfully replicate in running for president in 2007–2008. Inspired by Washington's example, Barack undertook as his initial aspiration to become mayor of Chicago.

Obama has consciously cultivated an image of being an heir of Abraham Lincoln (1861–1865), America's most popular president (with the possible exception of the God-like 'Founding Father' George Washington [1789–1797], after whom the nation's capital is named). Like Lincoln, Obama was a lawyer from Illinois of humble origins with breathtaking inspirational eloquence who came out of relative obscurity to win the presidency from more fancied and better-known rivals; both had lost bids to enter the US Congress but emerged stronger from their failure; both men were tall and gangly; both had a deep commitment to social justice ingrained from their childhood; and both invited bitter rivals they had run against to enter their cabinet. Obama launched his election campaign outside the Illinois Old State Capitol, where Lincoln had served as a legislator and delivered his famous June 1858 speech in which he had noted: 'A house divided against itself cannot stand... I believe this government cannot endure, permanently half *slave* and half *free*.'[51] Obama keeps a portrait of Lincoln on his desk, installed a bust of the former president in the White House, and used Lincoln's Bible to swear his oath of office. He also invoked Lincoln at his victory speech and inaugural address. As Obama said in 2005: 'In Lincoln's rise from poverty, his ultimate mastery of language and law, his capacity to overcome personal loss and remain determined in the face of repeated defeat—in all this, he reminded me ... of my own struggles.'[52]

But Obama's infatuation with Lincoln could prove to be a fatal attraction. By immodestly setting himself up to meet such high standards, disappointment will be the most likely outcome. As we have noted earlier, Barack himself is an inspiration and role model for many black people around the world. Slavishly fawning over and idolising Lincoln therefore sometimes seems like star-struck imitation than the more sensible route of creating one's own path to success. One must also see Lincoln in perspective: his main priority during America's civil war of 1861–1865 was not to free black slaves but to preserve the union. He even offered in his inaugural address to guarantee the right to own slaves as part of the US constitution.[53] Despite his undoubtedly great war-time leadership, Lincoln promoted voluntary repatriation of black slaves to Africa (he supported the activities of the American Colonisation Society, which repatriated freed slaves to create the West African state of Liberia between 1822 and 1847), and was frequently attacked by African American political leader Frederick Douglass for his conservative views.[54]

While Obama has been compared to the charismatic John F. Kennedy, it must also be noted that 'Camelot' had its own dark side: it was, after all, JFK that launched the disastrous 'Bay of Pigs' invasion to topple Cuban leader Fidel Castro in April 1961. If Kennedy had succeeded, perhaps South Africa would still not be free today. Nelson Mandela and others have acknowledged the great debt they owe to Castro in shattering the myth of the invincibility of the white South African army in Angola in 1988: an incident critical to the liberation of both Namibia and South Africa (see chapter 5). Kennedy also sanctioned assassination plots against Congo's Patrice Lumumba and the Dominican Republic's Rafael Trujillo.[55] While JFK, like Obama, had undoubted charm and eloquence and did support the civil rights struggle in America and innovate programmes like the Peace Corps that sent young Americans to Africa, one must not get too caught up in the myths surrounding 'Camelot'. The comparison of Obama to Robert Kennedy, the martyred Democratic presidential candidate and brother of JFK who was killed at the Democratic Convention in 1968, may be more accurate, though RFK was his brother's attorney-general and undoubtedly took part in some of his foreign misdeeds. But domestically, like Obama, Robert Kennedy was committed to mobilising progressive forces to fight poverty in black urban ghettos, and both leaders represented eloquent defenders of the powerless and voiceless. RFK famously visited South Africa in 1966, where he publicly condemned apartheid in Soweto, a trip Barack repeated as a senator forty years later. Both leaders also represented handsome and youthful leadership, gaining them widespread support from America's younger population, while consistently championing a message of social change.[56]

Due to Obama's America experiencing its worst recession since the Great Depression of the 1930s, Barack has often been compared to Franklin Delano Roosevelt, another of the great American presidents. While FDR undoubtedly and skilfully led the US through economic crisis and the Second World War, one must also remember that even as he did the most to create a United Nations to promote global justice, Roosevelt denied the most fundamental civil rights to his own black population at home. It is also worth remembering that, for African Americans who could vote—mostly in Northern states— their loyalty to the Republican Lincoln for abolishing slavery was transferred to the Democrat FDR, who embarked on social programmes to fight the Great Depression.

Obama demonstrated his links to youth culture in noting at the Democratic Convention in Boston in July 2004, where he gave the soaring keynote address that launched him into nationwide prominence: 'I'm LeBron, baby. I can play on this level. I got some game.'[57] Barack—a keen basketball player himself—was of course referring to the phenomenally successful basketball superstar Le Bron James, who skipped college at age eighteen to join the highly competitive National Basketball Association (NBA) as the number one draft pick. Le Bron quickly established himself as a precocious wonderboy, leading his Cleveland Cavaliers to the NBA playoff finals against the San Antonio Spurs in 2007 (which they lost), and demonstrating maturity and skills far beyond his years.

Concluding Reflections: Africa and America in the Shadow of Obama

One of Barack Obama's most remarkable achievements is to have won the American presidency with the most liberal voting record in the Senate. 'Liberalism' itself has become a dirty word and term of abuse in American politics to such an extent that very few politicians are prepared openly to identify themselves with the cause. In the past four decades in American history, Republicans have held presidential power for a staggering twenty-eight years (from Richard Nixon to George W. Bush), while Democrats have occupied the White House for just twelve years (Jimmy Carter and Bill Clinton). The opportunity that Barack Obama now has is to use the annihilation of the Republicans in legislative and presidential elections in 2006 and 2008, respectively, to build a progressive coalition that can champion social justice and civil rights for African Americans and the poor, and to develop a more enlightened US policy towards Africa that can last for a generation. As Lebanese American former independent presidential candidate Ralph Nader memorably put it about Obama: 'The question is whether he's going to mobilize the people, or he's going to parade in front of the people.'[58] Obama must not merely dazzle the flock with his good looks and high-flowing rhetoric. He must build a coalition of progressives that can last after he has departed the political stage. He must be more Franklin Roosevelt than Michael Jackson. More 'Pied Piper' than 'Thriller'.

The lesson of one of Obama's mentors, Harold Washington, was that when the Chicago mayor died of a sudden heart attack in 1987, the grassroots coalition he had so arduously stitched together died with him. Can Obama's high-tech groupies avoid a fate similar to that of the dinosaur and the dodo? Former British prime minister Harold Macmillan had famously noted to a journalist when asked what could blow his government off course that it was 'Events dear boy, events.' Obama could well find himself overwhelmed by 'events' and reacting to financial, military, and political crises. It is unclear whether, by the time he lifts his gaze at the end of his presidency, the unful-filled and unrealistic 'great expectations' unleashed by his undoubtedly his-toric election will be dashed by the 'hard times' in America's Dickensian 'bleak house'.

Even early in his tenure, Obama had already acquired several 'progressive' critics on the political Left. Ricky L. Jones, chair of pan-African studies at the University of Louisville, complained about Obama: 'He offers light-hearted, non-confrontational rhetoric about change, but no clear vision or discernible commitment to it... [W]e do not know exactly who and what Barack Obama is.'[59] There is also much discomfort within the African American community that Obama is not a real African American. Cornell West—an admirer—noted that Obama was a 'voluntary immigrant' and thus lacked the 'rage' of 'involuntary immigrants'.[60] Ali Mazrui has defined this distinction as 'the Diaspora of Post-Enslavement' and 'the Diaspora of Post-Coloniality', and distinguished between 'African Americans' and 'American Africans'.[61] In con-trast, conservative African Americans have praised what some have described as the 'post-racial' era that Obama has ushered in by not adopting what they deem to be the unelectable 'angry black man' approach of leaders like Jesse Jackson Sr. and Al Sharpton to run against the system. For them, Obama is more of a 'bargainer' than a 'challenger'. As Shelby Steele, one of the apostles of this view, noted: 'Barack Obama ... is a living rebuke to both racism and racialism, to both segregation and identity politics—to any form of collective chauvinism.'[62] Obama is part of a growing crop of centrist black politicians like Deval Patrick, elected governor of Massachusetts in 2007, Harold Ford Jr., former Congressman and later chair of the Democratic Leadership Coun-cil, and Cory Booker, elected mayor of Newark in 2006. These are politicians who have been able to win elections based largely on white votes, and often talk more about class than race.[63]

Obama's first year in office was hyperactive, with plans announced to close down the Guantanamo prison camp within a year, end the use of torture in interrogation of terror suspects, deploy 30,000 more troops to Afghanistan, and withdraw American troops from Iraq. The signing of a $787 billion stimulus package in February 2009 represented an early success for Obama. His goal was to create 3.6 million jobs, revive the financial sector, build new infrastructure, and help the poor and unemployed. A historic healthcare bill was also passed by the US House and Senate by March 2010. But the date for closing Guantanamo was missed, and equally disturbing, reports continued of the 'rendition' of terror suspects to third countries where they might still be tortured.

As unemployment among African Americans reached 15.7 per cent (compared to a national unemployment rate of about 10 per cent) in November 2009, as underemployment among black Americans stood at 23.8 per cent, and as the poverty rate for black children reached an abysmal 35 per cent,[64] members of the Congressional Black Caucus started to become restless, with some accusing Obama of not focusing enough attention on addressing the problems within his own racial, ultra-loyal constituency (a charge the president predictably rejected). As Barack himself noted during his centenary celebration speech to the National Association for the Advancement of Coloured People (NAACP) in New York in July 2009: 'We know that...an African American child is roughly five times as likely as a white child to see the inside of a prison.'[65]

Some of Obama's early foreign policy actions unfortunately followed in the hawkish footsteps of his predecessor, George W. Bush: his first military action as president within days of taking office was to sanction two missile attacks in Pakistan, which killed twenty-two people, reportedly including women and children. Three more US missile strikes a month later, in February 2009, killed another fifty-five people, drawing the ire of Pakistani officials.[66] According to *The Economist*, in his first year in office, Barack ordered targeted assassinations of terror suspects through an average of one drone attack a week in the border area between Pakistan and Afghanistan, killing hundreds of innocent women and children,[67] and creating even greater resentment against Pax Americana. In September 2009, the *New York Times* reported the targeted assassination in Southern Somalia by American commandos of Saleh Ali Saleh Nabhan, the alleged ringleader of an Al-Qaeda cell in Kenya.[68] As a result of these actions, some were forced to ask whether Obama's foreign policy could come to represent 'Bush with a smile'.

As the first African American US president was preparing to send more troops to wage war in Afghanistan, word came through in September 2009 that Barack had won the Nobel Peace Prize. Obama—in office for barely nine months at the time—seemed to admit himself that the prize was more for aspirational rhetoric than for concrete accomplishments. The jury is still out on whether Barack can live up to the ideals of the prize.

In order to understand the significance of this award, we must place it in the context of the ten individuals of African descent who won it before Obama. Two African Americans won the Nobel Peace Prize before Barack. Ralph Bunche, an African American 'scholar-diplomat' with a doctorate from Harvard, was the first, in 1950, for his skilful mediation efforts in the Middle

East. Significantly, Bunche marched with Martin Luther King Jr. during America's civil rights struggle from the 1950s. King himself—a disciple of Mahatma Gandhi's nonviolence methods (see chapter 14) and one of Obama's heroes—was the youngest winner of the prize, at age thirty-five in 1964. The Baptist preacher was the most eloquent 'prophet of the civil rights movement', with his mythical status secured by his martyrdom four years later.[69]

Four South Africans have won the Nobel Peace Prize. President of the African National Congress and former lay preacher Albert Luthuli—'the Black Moses'—was the first African peace laureate, in 1960. Coming shortly after the Sharpeville massacre of 1960, the prize was an attempt to highlight apartheid's brutalities. In 1984, another 'Troublesome Priest', Cape Town archbishop Desmond Tutu, won the prize. Like Luthuli, Tutu used the Nobel platform in Oslo to protest against the repression of the racist apartheid regime. Nelson Mandela, another ANC chieftain and 'Avuncular Saint', won the prize after emerging from twenty-seven years in jail and preaching reconciliation with his former enemies (see chapter 10). Apartheid's last leader, F.W. De Klerk, was a 'Pragmatic Peacemaker', and controversially shared the Nobel Peace Prize with Mandela in 1993. De Klerk was a stalwart of the apartheid albinocracy and failed to see the policy as immoral, but deserves some credit for his role in South Africa's democratic transition.

Two non–South African black Africans have won the prize. Ghana's Kofi Annan served as UN Secretary-General between 1997 and 2006, and strongly advocated 'humanitarian interventions' to protect civilians caught in crises. He was crowned Nobel laureate in 2001 (see chapter 4). Kenyan environmental campaigner and 'Earth Mother' Wangari Maathai became the first African woman to be awarded the prize, in 2004. Maathai was the first East African woman to obtain a doctorate, and, from 1977, led the Green Belt Movement to plant 30 million trees across Africa. She also fought consistently for women's and human rights. The final two African Nobel peace laureates are distinguished Egyptians. The 'Peaceful Pharaoh', president Anwar Sadat, shared the prize with his Israeli counterpart, Menachem Begin, in 1978. Sadat's mother had been the daughter of a black African slave, and he remained true to his peasant values. His historic trip to Jerusalem in 1977 led to his assassination four years later, but in the true spirit of a villager, he saw it as important to break bread with the enemy and talk. Egypt's second peace laureate, in 2005, was Mohamed El-Baradei, the 'Rocket Man', who headed the UN's International Atomic Energy Agency (IAEA) between 1997 and 2009. El-Baradei consistently called for peaceful use of atomic energy and a nuclear-free world, worrying incessantly about nuclear weapons falling into the hands of terrorist groups. He famously stood up to bullying by Washington over Iraq's nonexistent nuclear weapons before the 2003 American-led invasion of the country.

Barack Obama thus follows in the footsteps of these ten illustrious laureates of African descent. His own achievements will be measured by how he builds on the legacy of those who came before him: from Bunche and King's civil rights struggle to the anti–apartheid struggle of Luthuli, Tutu, and Mandela; from Sadat and Annan's peacemaking to Maathai's environmental activism and El-Baradei's nuclear disarmament. None of Obama's ten Nobel ancestors of African descent were in a powerful enough position to secure world peace. The young Afro-Saxon president of the most powerful nation on earth is the first peace laureate of African descent who has a chance to leave an indelible mark on global peace.

Obama's Nobel acceptance speech in Oslo in December 2009, however, was somewhat disappointing, showing more of a pragmatic politician than an idealist prophet. He fittingly acknowledged the legacy of Martin Luther King: 'As someone who stands here as a direct consequence of Dr. King's life work, I am living testimony to the moral force of non-violence.' But much of the speech—delivered, as Obama himself acknowledged, in the shadow of two US wars in Afghanistan and Iraq—explained why force had to be used to bring about peace. A celebration of peace thus turned into a justification for war. Obama used the concept of 'just wars'[70] to explain why he could not be guided by Martin Luther King Jr.'s example alone, since nonviolence could not have halted tyrants like Adolf Hitler. In stark contrast to his earlier recognition of the historical imperial actions of the US, he glorified his country for having 'helped underwrite global security for more than six decades ... and enabled democracy to take hold in places like the Balkans'.[71] Obama went on, rather inappropriately in the context of a Nobel speech, to criticise Iran and North Korea's nuclear ambitions, while reserving his own country's right to act unilaterally in an echo of Bush's 'preemptive' use of force doctrine.

The African references in Obama's Nobel speech perpetuated negative stereotypes of the continent, with the Kenyan Kansan referring to Somalia as a failed state of terrorism, piracy, and famine, as well as talking of genocide in Darfur, rape in the Congo, and repression in Zimbabwe (though referring to the bravery of citizens in resisting it). This speech was unsurprisingly well received in the US, with Barack clearly trying to avoid charges that he was pandering to an international global audience that had no hand in his election. As Ghanaian journalist, Cameron Duodu exclaimed responding to the Nobel address: 'Out goes "the audacity of hope." That was an election ploy.'[72]

In the same Nobel speech, Obama also controversially referred to fellow Nobel peace laureate in 1952, Albert Shweitzer, as among the 'giants of history,' alongside previous peace laureates, Martin Luther King, Nelson Mandela, and American war hero, General George Marshall. Shweitzer was a German doctor who set up a mission hospital in Gabon in 1913 to help the local population cure diseases and to convert African 'pagans' to Christianity. He worked tirelessly in Gabon—with some spells in Europe—until his death in 1965. Shweitzer is, however, widely viewed as a racist who referred frequently to black Africans as 'primitives' and 'savages.' As he put it: 'I am of the opinion that a patriarchal establishment is in every way the best one to adopt in the colonies...The native moves under patriarchal authority. He does not understand dealing with an office, but dealing with a man....'[73] Schweitzer also despised Islam—a religion that Obama has sought to reach out to—dismissing it as having 'never produced any thinking about the world and mankind which penetrated to the depths.'[74] As Ali Mazrui—himself, paradoxically, the Albert Schweitzer Professor at the State University of New York!—noted about the German doctor: 'He could be accused of behaving as if the only good African was a sick one.'[75]

By January 2010, Obama's approval ratings hovered around an unimpressive 50 per cent, as Americans continued to worry about high unemployment, large debts, lingering fears of terror attacks, and the costs of two foreign wars, in Afghanistan and Iraq. Complaints also persisted that gluttonous bankers on Wall Street were bailed out to the detriment of honest workers on Main Street.[76] The sour mood in the country turned, in some cases, into one of frightening intolerance against America's first black president. Conservative Republican congressman from South Carolina, Joe Wilson (a supporter of the Confederate flag of the American Civil War's secessionist South) incredibly shouted out 'You lie!' at Obama as the president addressed both houses of Congress on healthcare reform in September 2009. Protesters at an anti–Obama rally in Washington, D.C., in the same month carried such offensive banners as: 'The Zoo has an African Lion and the White House has a Lyin' African', '"Cap" Congress and "Trade" Obama back to Kenya', and—menacingly—'We came unarmed (this time)'. As Jimmy Carter, president of the US between 1977 and 1980 and a Nobel peace laureate, observed: 'I think an overwhelming portion of the intensely demonstrated animosity toward President Barack Obama is based on the fact that he is a black man.'[77] A line in Obama's Nobel speech may unwittingly provide what could well become the epitaph of his own presidency: 'Even those of us with the best of intentions will at times fail to right the wrongs before us.'[78]

In concluding this chapter, it is worth reflecting briefly on a negative aspect of American political life. Colin Powell, chair of the US military joint chiefs of staff between 1989 and 1993 and secretary of state between 2001 and 2004, was the most popular politician in America in 1996, and could have mounted a strong challenge for the presidency. His African American wife, Alma, apparently dissuaded him from running for fear he would be assassinated—a fear that may well hold true for Obama. After all, America has a history of killing its prophets: from Abraham Lincoln, to John and Robert Kennedy, to Martin Luther King, to Malcolm X. The country almost seems to have a perverse need for sacrificial blood as if to appease the gods for the sins of a discredited past that began with a genocidal campaign against its original native inhabitants. Africa, African Americans, and the world should hope that history will not repeat itself with the most eloquent prophet of the current age.

14

THE HEIRS OF GANDHI

HOW AFRICA AND ASIA CHANGED THE WORLD[1]

'It is maybe through the Negroes that the unadulterated message of non-violence will be delivered to the world.'[2]

Mahatma Gandhi, Indian independence leader

The Making of a Politico-Religious Saint

I first encountered the legacy of Mohandas Mahatma ('the Great Soul') Gandhi as a young undergraduate at the University of Ibadan in my native Nigeria in 1985, when I watched Richard Attenborough's powerful 1982 film on India's most famous politico-religious figure. The first half of the film—unlike much of the literature—focused on Gandhi's formative twenty-one years in South Africa. At the time, I was deeply moved by the Jesus-like figure in a loincloth who had brought down the mighty British Empire through sheer willpower, incredible discipline, innovative strategy, and unbelievable mass mobilisation. The film galvanised many South African anti–apartheid and even South American freedom fighters.[3] A few years later during my study of international relations in England and the United States, I realised the impact of Gandhi's efforts in the successful decolonisation of Africa and Asia. It is doubtful that any other individual symbolises more powerfully the Afro-Asian 'Revolt Against the West' that culminated in the liberation of two continents.

The year 2006 marked the centenary of Gandhi's *satyagraha* ('soul force' or 'the firmness of force of truth') nonviolence methods that he developed to

313

fight the discrimination against the Indian community in South Africa, where he lived between 1893 and 1914.[4] As memories of arguably the greatest moral and political figure of the twentieth century fade, it is important that we—like the *griots* (storytellers) of ancient Africa—pass on this epic tale to future generations. The story that we tell here is of Gandhi's contribution to the liberation of Africa and Asia and the legacy of his contributions in the contemporary context of the Afro-Asian coalition in world politics.

Gandhi was descended from a Gujarati merchant class, with his father and grandfather—who both worked as chief administrators—instilling in him a sense of *noblesse oblige* (obligations of rank) and a devotion to public service. Gandhi left for England at the age of nineteen to train as a lawyer, promising his mother to avoid wine, women, and meat. He returned to India after his studies, but his shy personality constrained a successful legal career. Moving to South Africa at the age of twenty-four to spend a year, he ended up staying twenty-one years. The experience transformed Gandhi, and it was here that he 'experimented with the truth', eventually developing the philosophy and tactics he would use to bring independence to India. The Mahatma himself conceded that his real education had occurred in South Africa, and it was here that he saw clearly the links between socioeconomic, political, and religious issues and the need to match 'passive resistance' to constructive work.[5] As Judith Brown observed: 'Gandhi's fundamental spiritual vision was forged in Africa, and on this rested all his political, economic and social thought.'[6] The Mahatma also read Plato, Tolstoy, and John Ruskin, and lived an ascetic life in rural communes on Phoenix Farm in Natal and Tolstoy Farm outside Johannesburg. He believed political leaders must be morally pure, and took a vow of celibacy.

Gandhi was infamously thrown out of the first-class compartment of a train in Pietermaritzburg (an incident later immortalised by a statue of Gandhi at the railway station), and he was assaulted several times by South Africa's security forces. In 1894, Gandhi helped to establish the Natal Indian Congress, which fought for Indian voting and other civic rights, employing nonviolent resistance methods that involved provoking arrest and gracefully accepting punishment, while seeking to convert the oppressor to recognise the justness of their cause. The Mahatma and his supporters expressed unhappiness at being classified as 'Natives' in prison,[7] and this struggle has been criticised for championing parochially Indian rights and not black South African rights. However, inspired by Gandhi, black South African women used his methods to protest against pass laws in Bloemfontein in 1913; the African National

Congress (ANC) used the technique of non-violent resistance in Johannesburg in 1919, the Communist Party in Durban in 1930, and Indian South Africans in 1946; and 'nonviolence' protest was also used in the ANC-led Defiance Campaign against discriminatory apartheid laws in 1952. Gandhi returned to India in 1914, and there launched *satyagrahas*, strikes and mass demonstrations. The Amritsar massacre of 1919, in which the British general R.E.H. Dyer was exonerated after his soldiers killed 379 peaceful protesters and wounded 1,137, appeared to radicalise Gandhi against the British *Raj*. He launched his famous Non-Cooperation Movement a year later, employing an almost anarchic approach of urging Indians to desist from using colonial courts, schools, and other services; refusing to pay taxes and to serve in the army; and burning foreign cloth. The Mahatma's famous twenty-four-day 'Salt March' in 1930, to protest against British taxing of salt, internationalised India's independence struggle, and Gandhi adeptly used the media: another skill that had been honed in South Africa, where he had run his own newspaper. Imperialist warlord and British prime minister Winston Churchill had crudely and dismissively referred to Gandhi as a 'half-naked *fakir*'. But it would be this scantily clad Hindu mendicant who ensured that the sun finally set on the British Empire. Gandhi increasingly became disillusioned with the West from the 1930s, leading to his famous quip that Western civilisation would be a 'good idea'.[8]

The Mahatma was open to many religions, and flirted with the idea of converting to Christianity during his time in South Africa.[9] Gandhi developed a sophisticated synthesis that combined Hinduism, Christianity, and Buddhism, which led to some Hindu extremists depicting him as a closet Christian. He has often been compared to Jesus Christ, and believed strongly in the suffering love exemplified by the crucifixion. Gandhi wept when he saw a crucifix with an image of Christ at the Vatican in 1931, and also kept a crucifix in his modest hut in India. He sometimes compared his own suffering to the image of Christ on the cross.[10] As the Mahatma noted: 'Jesus possessed a great force, the love force, but Christianity became disfigured when it went to the West. It became the religion of kings.'[11] As Louis Fischer, a perceptive early Gandhi biographer observed, the Mahatma 'embraced Christ but rejected Christianity'.[12] Like Jesus, Gandhi was about thirty years old when he embarked on his mission. As Jesus had fasted as a form of self-sacrifice, so also did Gandhi frequently fast. Kenyan scholar Ali Mazrui argued that, while Jesus was like Karl Marx, Gandhi was like Lenin: one conceptualised the beliefs, while the other sought to implement them in institutional and organisational terms.[13] It was, remarkably, through a Hindu prophet that Jesus' teachings and love ethic were put into practice most effectively nearly two millennia after his death. Like Jesus, Gandhi became a martyr for his cause, killed by the bullet of a Hindu extremist in January 1948, five months after India's independence. Both Gandhi and Jesus died on a Friday.

Gandhi was also in many ways similar to South African president Nelson Mandela (see chapter 10). Both were among the greatest moral and political leaders of the twentieth century. Both were charismatic 'Fathers of the Nation' who led their countries to independence through prophetic, inspirational leadership. Both spent long spells in jail. Both were lawyers who practiced in Johannesburg and used their own subsequent trials as political platforms to expose the moral bankruptcy and illegitimacy of their oppressors. Both sought to turn their enemies into partners to overturn unjust systems. While Gandhi sought to unite Hindus and Muslims, Mandela attempted to reconcile blacks and whites. Both were septuagenarians by the time their countries achieved independence. Both had universities named after them. Both had biographies written about them by Indian South African scholar Fatima Meer. Both were teetotallers. Both cultivated rich businessmen to fund their activities. Both were anglophiles, with Mandela loving British institutions and reading William Shakespeare and Alfred Tennyson in a missionary education based on English traditions, while the English-educated Gandhi supported the British Empire during the First World War. Gandhi also lived like an English gentleman during his legal training, wearing a top hat and morning suit and carrying a silver-headed cane. Mandela hung a portrait of Gandhi in his first home in Johannesburg and kept a copy of Gandhi's biography with him in prison on Robben Island.[14] As Elleke Boehmer perceptively noted: 'Both were shrewd exploiters of their own myth, to the extent that even the inner, private spaces of their lives were turned outwards to the public in the service of the myth. Like Gandhi, Mandela delighted in using the language of dress to symbolize his politics.'[15]

But there were also differences between the two men. While Mandela became a political leader and assumed the presidency of his country from 1994 to 1999, Gandhi refused to play a formal political role, preferring to provide spiritual and moral leadership to India. Mandela was awarded the Nobel Peace Prize in 1993, while Gandhi was scandalously denied it. Mandela also eventually abandoned Gandhian 'nonviolence', arguing that such an approach could work only with a rational government like the British administration in India, but not apartheid's leaders,[16] a view that Gandhi himself later came to share about South Africa.[17]

But despite his saintly leadership and incredible political achievements, Gandhi also had his flaws. He was accused of parochially championing Indian causes in South Africa and not fighting for the rights of the oppressed black majority.[18] In India, Gandhi was said to have underestimated the depth of divisions between Hindus and Muslims, having united these trading communities in South Africa; his introduction of religious language into politics also alienated Muslim voters.[19] Critics, including Jawaharlal Nehru, accused Gandhi of being a faddist diverting attention from the urgency of politics.[20] Others have noted that even during Gandhi's time, the efficacy of his nonviolence methods varied widely and often depended on the situation and the nature of opponents.[21] Several critics have also observed contradictions in Gandhi's use of the spinning-wheel to discourage industrialisation, while being funded by the owners of the mechanised cotton factories in Ahmedabad. As one patroness reportedly noted: 'Ah, if Bapuji only knew what it costs to keep him in poverty!'[22] India's Nobel literature laureate, Rabindranath Tagore—who had conferred on his friend the honorific title of 'Mahatma' and fought alongside Gandhi to try to end discrimination against *dalits* ('untouchables')—was one of those who warned Gandhi against fuelling nationalism and xenophobia by urging his compatriots to burn foreign cloth. Tagore also criticised Gandhi's encouraging of the use of the spinning-wheel as uneconomic. The Mahatma offered a sharp riposte to his friend:

The poet lives for the morrow, and would have us do likewise... 'Why should I, who have no need to work for food, spin?' may be the question asked. Because I am eating what does not belong to me. I am living on the spoilation of my countrymen... Every one must spin. Let Tagore spin like the others. Let him burn his foreign clothes; that is the duty today. God will take care of the morrow.[23]

We continue this chapter by examining the Gandhi–inspired 'Revolt Against the West': the decolonisation of Africa and Asia that the 1955 Bandung conference was seeking to complete. A third section explores the goals, methods, and achievements of the Non-Aligned Movement (NAM), from Bandung in 1955 to Sharm El-Sheikh in 2009. The United Nations—a powerful forum for the NAM's political battles—was created in 1945, two years before Gandhi's death. He thus witnessed the creation of a body set up to promote global peace, but died eight years before the historic Bandung conference, and did not witness the decolonisation of Africa and Asia that he had done so much to bring about. We conclude the chapter by reflecting on the significance of the legacy of Gandhi and the Bandung conference for contemporary Africa and Asia, and also highlight the Africa policies of three Asian giants—Japan, China, and India.

The Afro-Asian Revolt Against the West

The year 2005 marked the fiftieth anniversary of the famous conference in Indonesia's Western Java town of Bandung, where a diplomatic banquet at which Egypt's Gamal Abdel Nasser and India's Jawaharlal Nehru made common cause to help spur the creation of the Non-Aligned Movement to challenge Western domination of the globe. This was the most symbolic event in the Afro-Asian 'Revolt Against the West', which unleashed the greatest change in the international system during the twentieth century and resulted in the eventual decolonisation of two continents. As British historian Geoffrey Barraclough noted: 'Never before in the whole of human history had so revolutionary a reversal occurred with such rapidity.'[24] Gandhi's 'Thirty Years War' against British imperialism in India had culminated in the country's independence in 1947, an event without which Bandung could not have taken place. The Afro-Asian leaders in Bandung were thus the inheritors of Gandhi's legacy. South Africa's port city of Durban hosted a meeting of the foreign ministers of the Non-Aligned Movement in August 2004. This was particularly appropriate since Gandhi lived for many years in Durban, and the city still hosts a large Asian community who have lived in South Africa for generations.

The legacy of Bandung is the independence of Africa and Asia, which culminated in the end of apartheid by 1994. Ironically, the country in which Gandhi had lit the fuse for the liberation of the Third World was itself the last to become free. These decolonisation struggles were waged through the Non-Aligned Movement, the United Nations, the Organisation of African Unity (OAU)—now the African Union (AU)—and the Arab League (see chapters 3 and 12). The Non-Aligned Movement can, in a sense, be regarded as a political strategy to ward off foreign intervention in Afro-Asia, while the UN was the legal instrument to protect the newly won sovereignty of these states. From the 1970s throughout the 1980s, Bandung's legacy moved from being purely political to being economic. Ghana's Kwame Nkrumah had famously urged his fellow leaders to 'Seek ye first the political kingdom and all things will be added to it'(see chapter 11). But Nkrumah's political kingdom would eventually be replaced by Malaysian leader Mahathir Mohammed's economic kingdom, as battles over unequal terms of trade, redistribution of wealth, exploitative multinational corporations, and neocolonial dependency took on a special urgency in the 1970s and 1980s. The Organisation of the Petroleum Exporting Countries (OPEC) challenged the international trading system in 1973, resulting in the tripling of global oil prices as Southern states flexed their economic muscle. Many of these battles were spearheaded by the NAM, but they were also waged through the UN, as marked particularly by the struggles in the UN Conference on Trade and Development (UNCTAD).[25]

As Gandhi and Nkrumah had been symbols of the Afro-Asian political struggle, Mahathir Mohammed became a symbol of the South's economic decolonisation. Mahathir was a respected leader of the Association of East Asian Nations (ASEAN)[26], the Organisation of the Islamic Conference (OIC), and the NAM (hosting the 2003 summit). Malaysia recovered from the bitter divorce with Singapore in 1965 and its own communal riots of 1969 to create a prosperous economy and a Malay economic class.[27] Mahathir was also a leading proponent of 'Asian values', celebrating Asian identity and dignity as a counter to Western cultural hegemony. He championed an East Asian economic bloc as a 'Caucus without the Caucasians' involving ASEAN, China, Japan, and Korea, but excluding the United States, Australia, and New Zealand; he was a fierce and fearless critic of American policies in the Middle East; and as host, gently chided Britain's Queen Elizabeth II at a Commonwealth summit in Kuala Lumpur in 1989 for presiding over a body in which 'the wealth was far from common'. During the Asian financial crisis of 1997–1998, Mahathir boldly and uniquely rejected the International Monetary Fund's (IMF) dictates, helping Malaysia to avoid some of the worst effects of the crisis.[28]

There are also parallels between Gandhi and former South African president Thabo Mbeki (see chapter 11). Both were visionary intellectuals who spent much of their lives in exile from their ancestral homes. Both seemed paradoxically to admire Western literature, even as they fought to restore the ancient glory of their own civilisations. Gandhi's Constructive Programme—a sort of Indian Renaissance project—sought to encourage the use of *khadi* (hand-spun cloth), to promote the use of indigenous languages, and to end discrimination against 'untouchables'—whom Gandhi called *Harijan*, meaning 'God's children'—and women. Mbeki's African Renaissance was a doctrine for Africa's political, economic, and social renewal and a call for political democratisation, economic growth, and the reintegration of Africa into the global economy.[29] Like Gandhi's quest for self-sufficiency, Mbeki's African Renaissance had as its central goal the right of people to determine their own future.

But there were also clear differences between Gandhi and Mbeki. Gandhi was more sceptical than Mbeki of Western technology and external economic forces (foreign capital and investment), believing strongly that development must occur from internal economic forces based on the rural economy, as exemplified by his spinning-wheel. One of Gandhi's first actions on returning to India was to travel around the country, discovering it for himself and talking to people. He sought to know the poor masses of India, living among them and even wearing clothes that identified with their poverty, and as a result was able to mobilise them for political action against their British oppressors. In contrast, Mbeki was often viewed as aloof, arrogant, and elitist, ruling over a country that he barely knew through skilful political manoeuvring within the ruling ANC party rather than through mass mobilisation. Many feel that these qualities contributed to his humiliating ousting from power by his own party in September 2008 (see chapter 11).

By the 1990s, Mahathir's economic kingdom would be replaced by Thabo Mbeki's security kingdom. South Africa became the leading peacemaker and Nigeria the leading peacekeeper during a decade of troubles in which the spillover of the Cold War's destructive support of autocratic regimes and fuelling of 'proxy wars' led to a new generation of conflicts in countries like Somalia, Liberia, Sierra Leone, Burundi, and the Democratic Republic of the Congo (DRC) (see chapters 5, 6, and 7). In Asia, conflicts in Sri Lanka, East Timor, and Kashmir remained intractable. African regional organisations like the Economic Community of West African States (ECOWAS) and the Southern African Development Community (SADC), originally established to promote economic integration and development, were forced to adapt new security roles. They sought—under the leadership of local hegemons like Nigeria and South Africa—to tackle these conflicts, before the UN eventually took over many of these peacekeeping missions (see chapter 2). In Asia, the end of the Cold War also enabled the UN to deploy peacekeepers to Cambodia and East Timor, and troops from ASEAN countries played a tentative and limited role in assisting these efforts. It was the North Atlantic Treaty Organisation (NATO) that deployed troops to Afghanistan to fight the Taliban. Asia thus has lessons to learn from African security cooperation efforts undertaken by ECOWAS and SADC, as well as the African Union. ASEAN, however, has been much more successful than Africa at promoting economic integration and development, and Africa has lessons to learn from the 'Asian tigers'—Singapore, Taiwan, Hong Kong, and South Korea—which have greatly stressed education, an activist government, domestic investment, and the promotion of 'national economic champions' in their industrialisation strategies.

As the father of pan-Africanism, William E.B. DuBois, had famously and correctly predicted in 1900: 'The problem of the twentieth century is the problem of the colour line—the relation of the darker to the lighter races of men in Asia and Africa, in America and the islands of the sea.'[30] DuBois had also graphically captured the common oppression of the 'darker races': 'Immediately in Africa a black back runs red with the blood of the lash; in India a brown girl is raped; in China a coolie starves; in Alabama seven darkies are more than lynched; while in London the white limbs of a prostitute are hung with jewels and silk.'[31]

By the end of the century, with the independence of apartheid South Africa in 1994, the decolonisation of Asia and Africa from foreign rule had been effectively completed. European imperialism had reached its apogee at the start of the twentieth century. Between 1945 and the *annus mirabilis* of 1960, forty African and Asian countries with populations of 800 million—over a quarter of the global population at the time—had won their independence. In Asia, Japan had shattered the myth of white invincibility through military victories over British, French, and Dutch armies during the Second World War of 1939–1945.[32] In 1954, Vietnamese freedom fighters famously defeated France at Dien Bien Phu (they would also later defeat the US), helping to blunt the prejudiced arrogance of Western powers.

These struggles, however, had earlier antecedents. The first Pan-African Conference was held in 1900, and called for the right of Africans to participate in their own governance. The Indian National Congress's struggles were spurred by Gandhi's return to the subcontinent from Africa in 1914, and inspired many West African nationalists such as Caseley Hayford, H.O. Davies, Kwame Nkrumah, and Obafemi Awolowo. Gandhi organised the successful 'civil disobedience' campaigns that eventually culminated in India's independence in 1947. The Mahatma had correctly, and somewhat patronizingly, predicted in 1924 that if Africans 'caught the spirit of the Indian movement their progress must be rapid'.[33] He had also opined in 1936 that it was 'maybe through the Negroes that the unadulterated message of non-violence will be delivered to the world'.[34] The Mahatma's beliefs were to inspire seven Africans and Americans who won the Nobel Peace Prize: Ralph Bunche (1950), Albert Luthuli (1960), Martin Luther King Jr. (1964), Anwar Sadat (1978), Desmond Tutu (1984), Nelson Mandela (1993), and Barack Obama (2009).[35]

Ralph Bunche greatly admired Martin Luther King's Gandhian methods of protest in waging the civil rights struggle in America, and after King was assassinated in April 1968, Bunche noted: 'The world's leading contemporary exponent of non-violence is now gone, all too ironically by an act of savage violence.'[36] ANC president Albert Luthuli came from Kwazulu-Natal, where Gandhi had honed his *satyagraha* techniques. Luthuli was also an apostle of nonviolence, though he was not a pacifist. He visited India in 1938, and Gandhi's influence on the devout Christian chief was unmistakable when Luthuli said: 'The white is hit harder by apartheid than we are. It narrows his life. In not regarding us as humans he becomes less than human.'[37] Further confirming Gandhi's influence, the former Anglican archbishop of Cape Town, Desmond Tutu, noted in New Delhi in January 2007: 'we legitimately lay a claim to a fairly significant part of Mahatma Gandhi. He was pivotal in the struggle against South African racism and honed his political skills in South Africa.'[38] Another Christian preacher, Martin Luther King—who considered Gandhi to be among the six most important figures in world history—was particularly influenced by the Mahatma's methods of nonviolence. As King noted: 'While the Montgomery boycott was going on, India's Gandhi was the guiding light of our technique of nonviolent change.'[39] Until he discovered Gandhi, King—a Baptist preacher—had been despairingly reflecting on the fact that Christian ethics of loving one's enemy and turning the other cheek could only work among individuals rather than racial groups. As King noted: 'Gandhi was probably the first person in history to lift the love ethic of Jesus above mere interaction between individuals to a powerful and effective social force on a large scale... I came to feel that this was the only morally and practically sound method open to oppressed people in their struggle for freedom.'[40]

During his Nobel prize speech in Oslo in December 2009, US president Barack Obama paid homage to both Martin Luther King and Mahatma Gandhi, noting: 'As someone who stands here as a direct consequence of Dr. King's life work, I am living testimony to the moral force of non-violence. I know there's nothing weak—nothing passive—nothing naïve—in the creed and lives of Gandhi and King.'[41]

Turning from a Nobel peace laureate of the African diaspora to a Gandhian laureate of the African continent; in his 1978 autobiography, Anwar Sadat amusingly describes his own early attempts at imitating Gandhi's ascetic lifestyle:

I was struck by his character and fell in love with his image. I began to imitate him. I took off my clothes, covered myself from the waist down with an apron, made myself a spindle, and withdrew to a solitary nook on the roof of our house in Cairo. I stayed there for a few days until my father persuaded me to give it up. What I was doing would not, he argued, benefit me or Egypt; on the contrary, it would certainly have given me pneumonia, especially since it was a bitterly cold winter.[42]

Other African leaders, like Zambia's Kenneth Kaunda and Tanzania's Julius Nyerere were also champions of Gandhi's approach (though both eventually supported armed struggle). Kaunda noted in New Delhi in January 2007: 'Mahatma Gandhi was our torch bearer without whose guidance the history of our struggle for freedom and national independence would have taken a different course.'[43]

The Non-Aligned Movement

Before assessing the Non-Aligned Movement, it should be noted that the Afro-Asian bloc in world politics is not monolithic. Countries like China, Singapore, South Korea and India are closer to joining the ranks of the international Brahmins of the rich world, while South Africa has some world-class manufacturers and multinational companies, though the majority of its population continue to live in stark poverty as a result of the inequities of colonialism and apartheid (see chapter 5). Many countries on both continents also belong to the group of international *dalits* whose impoverishment puts them in the ranks of the 'untouchables' in the international system of 'global apartheid' (see chapter 3). But Africa and Asia still have *enough* in common: both were colonised by European powers based on ideologies of racial supremacy; both have suffered from civil wars, famines, military strongmen, and autocrats; and both have struggled to evolve political and economic models based on those of the West, but adapted to suit local circumstances.

The 'Terrible Triplets'

The Bandung conference was held in April 1955 and expressed what Jawaharlal Nehru described as the 'new dynamism' of Asia and Africa. Bandung sought to promote economic and cultural cooperation, support the decolonisation of Africa and Asia, promote world peace, and end racial discrimination and domination.[44] Ending the 'politics of pigmentation'—in which arrogant white statesmen set themselves up as overlords over local 'natives' who were considered to be unable to stand on their own feet in the difficult conditions of Western civilisation—was very much the driving force during this conference. Three titanic figures towered over the Southern landscape in this 'Revolt Against the West': India's Jawaharlal Nehru was the intellectual father of the concept of 'non-alignment'; Egypt's Gamal Abdel Nasser was the leader of pan-Arabism, creating a political union with Syria between 1958 and 1961;

and Ghana's Kwame Nkrumah (who was prevented by the British colonial government from attending the Bandung conference) was the leader of pan-Africanism, creating between 1960 and 1961 a union with Mali and Guinea.

Gandhi described India's founding premier, Jawaharlal Nehru, as his 'political heir', and often gave the Cambridge-educated secular socialist advice, even supporting Nehru's deployment of troops to Kashmir in 1947. Nehru in turn referred to Gandhi as 'a man of God', and revered him. India's first post-independence prime minister appeared genuinely to identify with Africa. As Nehru noted in 1963: 'We think this awakening of Africa is of historic importance not only for Africa itself, but for the whole world.'[45] He pushed strongly for the NAM and the UN to support Africa's decolonisation efforts, and counselled African leaders against the dangers of one-party rule and military governments, though he remained firm friends with the autocratic Nasser, whose intellect he however did not greatly respect.[46] As Nkrumah was developing a personality cult in the 1960s, Nehru famously asked him: 'What the hell do you mean by putting your head on a stamp?'[47] This was a rebuke that Ghana's Osagyefo ('Redeemer') never forgave nor forgot. Nehru visited Nigeria, Sudan, and Egypt in the early 1960s, and sought to rally the Afro-Asian coalition at the UN to support the anti–apartheid struggle, settle the Arab-Israeli dispute, and establish an Indian Ocean zone of peace. He consistently warned Indian settlers in Africa that the interests of indigenous Africans must always be paramount.

Nehru's controversial military annexation of the former Portuguese colony of Goa in 1961 helped to legitimise the use of armed force to liberate colonial territories. India's flamboyant defence minister, Krishna Menon, eloquently argued the case at the UN, declaring colonialism to be 'permanent aggression.'[48] During the Suez crisis of 1956, Nehru helped to mobilise NAM support for Nasser, and the UN General Assembly rallied almost unanimously to condemn the Anglo-French-Israeli action. Like Gandhi, Nehru had a great influence on Nelson Mandela, sharing with him a support of the 'rationality of socialism' and state modernisation, and the need to respond to oppression through retaliation, in contradiction of Gandhian pacifism. On Robben Island, Mandela read Nehru's prison memoirs and quoted from the Indian brahmin's writings in his own work.[49] On receiving the Nehru Award, Mandela paid the Indian aristocrat a fitting tribute from Robben Island in August 1980: 'Truly, Jawaharlal Nehru was an outstanding man. A combination of many men into one—freedom fighter, politician, statesman, prison graduate, master of the English language, lawyer and historian. As one of the pioneers of the nonaligned movement, he has made a lasting contribution to world peace and the brotherhood of man.'[50] Other African leaders such as Uganda's Milton Obote and Kenya's Jomo Kenyatta also admired or retained contacts with Nehru. Nehruvian ideals of non-alignment, and embracing the Commonwealth without falling under the British crown, also won support among many African leaders.[51]

Egypt's Gamal Abdel Nasser was a close ally of Nehru and visited both Nehru's and Gandhi's tombs in New Delhi in 1965. The Egyptian colonel staged Africa's first military coup d'état, in 1952, and became the foremost champion of pan-Arabism, as well as a leading figure in the politics of the Third World.[52] Nasser strongly backed the Algerian independence struggle against France between 1954 and 1962. Like Nkrumah, the Egyptian leader championed 'positive neutrality': he bought arms and received assistance from both East and West. In his 1954 *Philosophy of the Revolution*, Nasser saw Egypt as being at the centre of three circles involving the Arab world, the Muslim world, and Africa. As he noted: 'we cannot in any way stand aside, even if we wish to, from the sanguinary and dreadful struggle now raging in the heart of the continent between five million whites and two hundred million Africans. We cannot do so for one principal and clear reason—we ourselves are in Africa.'[53] Nasser was even more immodest on his pan-Arab leadership role: 'For some reason it seems to me that within the Arab circle there is a role wandering aimlessly in search of a hero. And I do not know why it seems to me that this role, exhausted by its wanderings, has at last settled down, tired and weary, near the borders of our country and is beckoning us to move, to take up its lines, to put on its costume since no one else is qualified to play it.'[54]

Nasser stood at the intersection of the Non-Aligned Movement as the gatekeeper of North Africa as well as the political and cultural leader of the Arabian peninsula, which is classified in NAM terms as being part of Asia.[55] Egypt thus sought to be a bridge between Africa and Asia. Undoubtedly, the most significant historical event involving Nasser was the Suez crisis of 1956, when the Egyptian leader—shortly after buying arms from the Soviet bloc—nationalised the Suez Canal in July 1956 in response to Washington, London, and the World Bank reneging on an earlier promise to fund the building of the Aswan Dam. The British and French launched an invasion with Israel three months later, seeming to have forgotten that the Old European world of 'gunboat diplomacy' had been replaced by the bipolar superpower world of the nuclear age. Economic and political pressure by US president Dwight

Eisenhower, and his forceful secretary of state, John Foster Dulles, along with the Soviet Union and the UN General Assembly majority, forced a humiliating withdrawal that ended the Anglo-French-Israeli takeover of the canal.[56] Nasser had scored a famous political victory and added another sharp nail to the imperial coffin. By the time of his death on 28 September 1970—the same day as the Prophet Mohamed—Nasser bestrode the Arab world like a Colossus as the undisputed prophet of pan-Arabism. A biographer, Saïd K. Aburish, described Nasser as 'the most charismatic [Arab] leader since the Prophet Mohamed.'[57]

The third of our 'terrible triplets', Kwame Nkrumah, was a disciple of Gandhi, and his 'Positive Action' was clearly inspired by Gandhian methods of 'passive resistance'. The Ghanaian leader was sometimes referred to as 'Gandhi of Ghana', and he noted: 'We salute Mahatma Gandhi and we remember, in tribute to him, that it was in South Africa that his method of non-violence and non-cooperation was first practiced.'[58] Nkrumah helped to organise the fifth Pan-African Congress, in Manchester in 1945. He returned to Ghana from the West to champion a brand of 'populist nationalism' and, like Gandhi, used his great charisma and formidable organisational skills to win his country's independence.[59] After gaining independence for Ghana in 1957, Nkrumah sought to keep the torch of pan-Africanism alive by promoting the independence of the entire continent, backing liberation movements with training and other support, and proposing the idea of an African High Command as a common army to ward off external intervention and help support the continent's liberation struggles. Nkrumah was also a fierce champion of non-alignment, sending Ghanaian troops to the UN mission in the Congo in 1960 in a bid to prevent the country from becoming a Cold War theatre. When China invaded Indian territory in 1962, Nkrumah criticised Britain's provision of arms to Nehru as threatening the principle of non-alignment.[60]

The Birth of the Global South

The Non-Aligned Movement was born six years after Bandung in Belgrade, Yugoslavia, in 1961, under the chairmanship of the host Marshal Josip Broz Tito. Nehru, Nasser, and Tito are usually considered to be the NAM's 'Founding Fathers'. Twenty-five Arab, Asian, and African countries attended the conference (membership would later increase to 118). A highlight of the 1961 NAM summit was the condemnation of 'imperialism' in the Middle East and support for Arabs in Palestine. The NAM held further summits in Cairo

(1964) and Lusaka (1970), setting up a twenty-five-member New York–based coordinating bureau at the UN to oversee the movement's affairs between summits. By the time of the Algiers summit in 1973, there were widespread calls for a disengagement from the international capitalist system and attacks against exploitative Western multinational companies.[61] Preparatory meetings of NAM foreign ministers are held a year before summits, and Colombo (1976), Havana (1979), New Delhi (1983), Harare (1986), and Belgrade (1989) hosted further summits. The NAM, however, suffered from the problems of trying to maintain unity among such a large, diverse group. The Sino-Soviet split and the border war between China and India in 1962 shook the group's cohesion. Questions continued to be raised about the non-alignment of countries that hosted foreign military bases.

Other NAM summit highlights include the rejection of Cuba's unsuccessful bid to introduce a socialist, leftist tilt to the movement at the Havana summit in 1979, and an angry summit in Harare, Zimbabwe, in 1986 that revived many of the 'radical' slogans of the past. China has been a NAM 'observer' since 1992, preferring not to jeopardise key bilateral relations through full membership of the group, while using relations with Southern states to garner NAM support in forums such as the UN Human Rights Commission (now the Human Rights Council).[62] With the end of the Cold War and the collapse of the Soviet Union by 1991, many analysts started questioning the NAM's raison d'être. Critics wondered whether the movement had become a relic of the Cold War, and asked against what the organisation was claiming that it was not 'aligned' in a unipolar, American-dominated age. Like NATO, the NAM has had to define a new role for itself in a rapidly changing international system. By the time of its thirteenth summit, in Kuala Lumpur, Malaysia, in 2003, the NAM's members were focusing more on issues of peace, security, justice, democracy, and development. The organisation was also pushing for strengthening and democratising the UN, for stronger regional organisations, for Palestinian liberation, and for strategies to reverse the marginalisation of developing economies as a result of globalisation. Where foreign *intervention* had been opposed in the past, external *neglect* now seemed to be the greater concern. The NAM adopted a more pragmatic and less confrontational attitude towards the West, as its summits in Jakarta (1992), Cartegena (1995), and Durban (1998) demonstrated. The US is now invited as an observer to NAM summits. The fiftieth anniversary of Bandung was held in the historic Indonesian town in April 2005. The Asian-African Subregional Organisations Conference (AASROC) also took place in Bandung, co-hosted by Indonesia and South Africa. AASROC launched a 'new strategic partnership' between both continents. Further NAM summits were held in Cuba's Havana (2006) and Egypt's Sharm El-Sheikh (2009).

Concluding Reflections: Rekindling the Spirit of Gandhi and the Legacy of Bandung

It is important to identify ways of rekindling both Gandhian principles of 'nonviolence' and the 'spirit of Bandung' to foster a greater Afro-Asian role in world politics. Generally, Asia has done better economically than Africa in the first five post-independence decades, and several Asian states have joined the ranks of the *nouveaux riches*. The Asian financial crisis of 1997–1998, however, highlighted the continent's continuing vulnerability to Western financial actors and demonstrated the fragility of the 'Asian miracle'. Both Africa and Asia have adopted the Westphalian system of nation-states and largely accepted colonially imposed boundaries, with the African case described in this book as the 'Curse of Berlin' (see chapter 1). The few exceptions in which these borders have been changed include the creation of Singapore from Malaya in 1965, the creation of Bangladesh from East Pakistan in 1971 (which appeared to some to justify Gandhi's consistent opposition to the partition of India before 1947), the creation of Eritrea from Ethiopia in 1993, and the creation of East Timor from Indonesia in 2001. With the exception of Singapore, military intervention was required in all of these cases. But colonial borders in Africa and Asia have been remarkably durable, even though secessionist tendencies remain strong in parts of Indonesia, Sri Lanka, India, Pakistan, Sudan, Nigeria, and Ethiopia.

Culturally, Hollywood often demonstrates its lack of nuance and subtlety in depicting Africans and Asians negatively in such movies as *Coming to America, Barbershop*, and *Lost in Translation*. The Western media are often condescending in the way they report on events in both continents, continuing to reflect attitudes described as 'Orientalism' by the late Palestinian American intellectual Edward Said,[63] in which sometimes unconscious colonial attitudes and frameworks continue to guide how the West views its former 'possessions'. Unfortunately, several Asian scholars whom I have encountered at international seminars have also demonstrated these stereotypical views about Africa as a continent of disease and conflicts, preferring to wallow in a second-class, semi–developed status while looking to the West for acknowledgement of their progress.

Asia has, of course, had its own genocidal Khmer Rouge to rival Rwanda's *génocidaires*, while Indonesia's Suharto was as venal and corrupt an autocrat in his thirty-two years in power as Zaire's Mobutu Sese Seko during the latter's thirty-two-year grip on power. India, for all the hype about a dynamic tiger prowling the global stage, suffers higher levels of child malnutrition than sub-Saharan Africa.[64] Two brilliant recent Indian movies—*Monsoon Wedding* and *Slumdog Millionaire*—deliberately appealed to Western audiences, while trying to explain aspects of the country: one dealt with the wedding of a Westernised elite; the other with the travails of poverty-stricken slum children, one of whom makes a fortune from winning an imported Western game-show. *Slumdog Millionaire* undoubtedly better reflects the realities of Asian life for the majority of its population than does *Monsoon Wedding*. Many Africans have however often unconsciously adopted some Western-fuelled stereotypes of a paradise of wealthy, dynamic tigers, blissfully unaware of the widespread poverty and corruption that still bedevil much of Asia.

The 'New International Economic Order' (NIEO) promoted by Afro-Asian leaders in the 1970s proved in the end to be a tragic illusion. Instead, the global South found itself, after the Cold War, in an age of a neoliberal 'Washington Consensus' of free markets and a limited role for the state (though the global financial crisis of 2007–2009 forced a reassessment of this approach). In concluding this chapter, it is important that we assess Afro-Asian trade and the role of three Asian Gullivers—Japan, China, and India—in Africa.

In 2001, Africa's exports to Asia stood at $22.2 billion (out of $134 billion worth of global exports), based on Nigerian, Angolan, Congolese, and Sudanese oil; South African gold, platinum, and cars; Ugandan, Rwandese, and Mauritian seafood; Kenyan and Tanzanian tea; Ivorian and Malian cotton; and Botswanan diamonds. China, South Korea, India, and Taiwan were the largest importers of African crude oil; Pakistan of African tea; and Japan and Singapore of African garments. But while African exports to Asia represented 16 per cent of its total exports, only 2 per cent of total Asian imports came from Africa.[65] Africa increasingly supplies Asia with much of its oil (Asia was consuming 40 per cent of the world's total oil by 2008). South Africa has strong trade ties with East Asia. Japan, China, and India have formulated initiatives such as the Tokyo International Conference on Africa's Development (TICAD), the Forum on China-Africa Cooperation (FOCAC), and the India–New Partnership for Africa's Development (NEPAD) Cooperation.[66]

There is a pragmatic, if not utilitarian, side to Japan's Africa policy. Tokyo has used Africa's numerical strength of fifty-three UN members to lobby for support in the world body, particularly as it sought a permanent seat on the UN Security Council in 2005. But Japan's past relations with Africa were dogged by its controversial trade ties with apartheid South Africa (with Japanese citizens enjoying honourary status as 'whites'), and were characterised by its quest for strategic energy and raw materials, as well as by strategies to facilitate Japanese trade and investment that critics described as 'neo-mercantilist'.[67] By 1995, Tokyo was giving aid to forty-seven African states worth $1.33 billion.[68] TICAD summits were held in 1993, 1998, 2003, and 2008, though African governments have become increasingly disappointed with Japan's lack of consistent and concrete attention to Africa.

It is China's growing political, economic, and security ties in Africa that have attracted the most attention, as these ties represent one of the most important developments in the geostrategy of post–Cold War Africa. Former Chinese president Jiang Zemin visited Africa in 1996; Chinese president Hu Jintao visited the continent five times between 1999 and 2007; while over thirty African leaders have visited China since 1997. Beijing held a Forum on China-Africa Cooperation in October 2000 with forty-four African states, during which Western aid conditionalities were criticised, and after which Beijing announced the annulment of $1.2 billion of African debt to thirty-one countries. A second FOCAC was held in Addis Ababa, Ethiopia, in December 2003. By 2004, Africa's exports to China had reached $11.4 billion; Sino-African trade had grown from $2 billion in 1999 to $55.5 billion in 2006; Beijing offered the continent $5 billion in loans and credit; and China had become the third largest foreign investor on the continent—at an estimated $6.6 billion—behind the US and Europe. In November 2006, forty African leaders and ministers trekked to Beijing for a third FOCAC summit, where China promised to double aid to the continent, train 15,000 Africans, and provide 4,000 scholarships. A fourth FOCAC summit was held in Sharm El-Sheikh, Egypt, in November 2009 which agreed to provide $10 billion in concessional loans to African governments between 2010 and 2012. (See chapters 8 and 9.)

India is the third Asian country that is playing an important role in Africa. Though India still maintains a rhetorical commitment to reversing the inequities of the global economic system, it could in fact be transforming itself, like China, into a status quo power, as evidenced by its increasing nuclear cooperation with the United States. India's thirst for energy is similar to China's, and Africa appears to be a growing source to meet these seemingly insatiable needs. The Indian Oil and Natural Gas Company has signed agreements in

Nigeria, Sudan, Libya, and Gabon. Indian companies have clinched uranium exploration deals in Niger. Indian firms are also assisting in the power sector in Zambia, Tanzania, and Kenya, as well as in rail and road infrastructure in Sudan, Tanzania, Kenya, Uganda, Ethiopia, Nigeria, and Algeria. Trade between India and Africa increased from $967 million in 1991 to $9.5 billion in 2005, and reached $19.3 billion between April 2006 and January 2007. Despite these impressive advances, however, Africa accounted for only 7 per cent of India's global export market in 2006. Nigeria, South Africa, Egypt, Algeria, and Morocco are India's largest trading partners on the continent. In April 2008, the first India-Africa summit was held, in New Delhi, during which credit facilities to Africa were doubled to $5.4 billion, and a $500 million aid package was announced. But China's economy was three times larger than India's in 2008, and it is likely that Beijing will continue to increase its trade with Africa far quicker than New Delhi.[69]

In April 2005, African and Asian leaders met in Indonesia to commemorate the fiftieth anniversary of the Bandung conference and to launch the New Asian-African Strategic Partnership (NAASP). This body seeks to build a bridge between two continents across the Indian Ocean and envisages partnerships in the areas of political solidarity, economic cooperation, and socio-cultural relations. Countries like India, South Africa, and Brazil—under the auspices of the India, Brazil, and South Africa Trilateral Forum (IBSA)—have sought to coordinate their political and trade efforts to present a more powerful and united bloc that can more effectively defend their interests from the protectionist excesses of the profligate North. All three are part of a Group of Twenty countries that expanded the Group of Eight industrialised countries in 2009. The Afro-Asia bloc in world politics consists of 106 countries with 4.6 billion people (over 70 per cent of the world's population) and a combined economic strength of $9 trillion.[70] The last Bandung conference, in 1955, caused a political earthquake. With reports of earth tremors in Bandung as Afro-Asian leaders met there in April 2005, it was unclear whether the fiftieth anniversary conference could cause the same seismic shift in the global economic landscape that had given birth to 'the spirit of Bandung'.

Mahatma Gandhi started the chain-reaction that would lead to the liberation of Africa and Asia through his successful struggle for the liberation of India in 1947. The resistance of Algerian freedom fighters to France's savage colonial war from 1954 brought down the French Fourth Republic, and laid the foundation for Algerian independence in 1962.[71] The 1955 Bandung conference mobilised support for the decolonisation of Africa and Asia. The

Afro-Asians went on to humanise international diplomacy and to give birth to the concept of 'non-alignment' as a substitute to the destructive power politics that had lost Europe its global primacy and brought untold suffering to millions of people around the world during two world wars. As a result, the Western-dominated international system became a more truly international society. It is the torch of liberation that Gandhi handed to Martin Luther King Jr. to wage the successful civil rights movement in America that in turn made possible today for a black man, Barack Obama—a gifted Kenyan Kansan political prophet—to become the most powerful man on earth, after being elected president of the US in November 2008 (see chapter 13). For all these developments, the world largely has the Jesus-like man in a loincloth to thank. Nelson Mandela's 1992 tribute to Gandhi's legacy is particularly apt in this regard: 'Gandhiji was a South African and his memory deserves to be cherished now and in the post-apartheid era… Gandhian philosophy may be a key to human survival in the twenty-first century.'[72] *Satyagraha* was born in Africa, exported to Asia, and used to destroy European imperialism. Through Gandhi's inspiration and energy, Africa and Asia had changed the world.

NOTES

PREFACE: BLACK BERLIN AND THE CURSE OF FRAGMENTATION: FROM BISMARCK TO BARACK

1. This preface is partly indebted to my earlier writings on social conflict and the politics of identity.
2. Ralph H. Lutz, 'Bismarck', *Collier's Encyclopedia*, vol. 4 (New York: Macmillan, 1980), p. 224.
3. See the table in James F. Dunnigan and Austin Bay, *A Quick and Dirty Guide to War*, 3rd ed. (New York: Morrow, 1996), pp. 651–653.
4. Recent figures include the hundreds of thousands in Rwanda and Burundi, and the tens of thousands in Algeria and the Congo; see ibid., p. 387.
5. Not surprisingly, an article in *The Economist*, 25 January 1997, p. 17, argues that borders have not been the primary cause of conflict.
6. For an interesting article on this conflict, see Kjetil Tronvoll, 'Borders of Violence-Boundaries of Identity: Demarcating the Eritrean Nation-State', *Ethnic and Racial Studies* 22(6) (November 1999), pp. 1037–1060.
7. An overview of this conflict may be found in Robert A. Mortimer, 'Islamists, Soldiers, and Democrats: The Second Algerian War', *Middle East Journal* 50 (Winter 1996), pp. 18–39.
8. Hakim Darbouche, 'Algeria: Presidential 21st Century Vision of the Future,' *The Africa Report* no. 5, January 2007, pp. 72–74.
9. The struggle between religious groups in Egypt is analyzed in Hamied A. Ansari, 'Sectarian Conflict in Egypt and the Political Expediency of Religion', *Middle East Journal* 38 (Summer 1984), pp. 18–39. For an article on the conflict, see *The Economist*, 8 January 2000, p. 41.
10. Descriptions of the genocide may be found in Edward Nyakanvzi, *Genocide: Rwanda and Burundi* (Rochester, VT: Schenkman, 1998).
11. For one analysis of the identity conflicts that have bedeviled Sudan and brought war among the Sudanese, see Francis M. Deng, *War of Visions: Conflict of Identities in the Sudan* (Washington, DC: Brookings Institution, 1995).
12. The descent of Somalia is chronicled in Alice B. Hashim, *The Fallen State: Dissonance, Dictatorship, and Death in Somalia* (Lanham, MD: University Press of America, 1997).

13. These societies may also be termed as 'ethnically bipolar'; see R.S. Milne, *Politics in Ethnically Bipolar States: Guyana, Malaysia, and Fiji* (Vancouver: University of British Columbia Press, 1981).

14. For a positive assessment of the Belgian experience, see Michael O'Neill, 'Re-imagining Belgium: New Federalism and the Political Management of Cultural Diversity', *Parliamentary Affairs* 51(2) (April 1998), pp. 241–258.

15. An overview of the Cyprus situation may be found in Robert McDonald, *The Problem of Cyprus* (London: Brassey's, for the International Institute of Strategic Studies, 1989).

16. The split was peaceful; see Jiri Musil, *The End of Czechoslovakia* (Budapest: Central University Press, 1995).

17. The various kinds of violence bedeviling Sri Lanka are detailed in Jagath P. Senaratne, *Political Violence in Sri Lanka, 1977–1990: Riots, Insurrections, Counterinsurgencies, Foreign Intervention* (Amsterdam: VU University Press, 1997).

18. For an overview of the situation in the Great Lakes, consult the special issue of the *African Studies Review* 41(1) (April 1999), pp. 1–97. See also Georges Nzongola-Ntalaja, *The Congo: From Leopold to Kabila* (London: Zed, 2002); Gérard Prunier, *From Genocide to Continental War: The 'Congolese' Conflict and the Crisis of Contemporary Africa* (London: Hurst, 2009).

19. For an overview of the conflicts and peace efforts, see Ann M. Lesch, *The Sudan: Contested National Identities* (Bloomington: Indiana University Press, 1998). For more recent information, see the UN Secretary-General reports to the Security Council. (www.un.org).

20. For a guide to the Biafra war, consult Zdenek Cervenka, *The Nigerian War, 1967–70: History of The War—Selected Bibliography and Documents* (Frankfurt Am Main: Bernard and Graef, 1971).

21. The Westphalian compact also led to mores against international intervention in territories covered by a state's sovereignty, but internal excesses may be testing these mores; relatedly, see Gene M. Lyons and Michael Mastanutono (eds.), *Beyond Westphalia? State Sovereignty and International Intervention* (Baltimore: Johns Hopkins University Press, 1995).

22. For an overview of 'tolerance', see Susan Mendus (ed.), *Justifying Toleration: Conceptual and Historical Perspectives* (Cambridge: Cambridge University Press, 1988).

23. An interesting comparative analysis of the effect of type of electoral system on the number of political parties in regions where previously there was just one party is Robert G. Moser, 'Electoral Systems and the Number of Parties in Postcommunist States', *World Politics* 51(3) (April 1999), pp. 359–384.

24. The debate on the linkages between economic freedom and political freedom is historic and relevant; for an example, see Paul A. Cammack, *Capitalism and Democracy in the Third World: A Doctrine for Political Development* (London: Leicester University Press, 1997).

25. Consult Paul Q. Hirst, *From Statism to Pluralism: Democracy, Civil Society, and Global Politics* (London: University College London Press, 1998).

26. See Samuel P. Huntington, 'The Clash of Civilizations?' *Foreign Affairs* 72(3) (1993), pp. 22–49. Responses by Fouad Ajami, Kishore Mahbubani, Robert L.

Bartley, Liu Binyan, and Jeanne J. Kirkpatrick, among others, were published in the next issue of *Foreign Affairs*, 72(4) (1993), pp. 2–22.

27. An account of the Tanzanian intervention in Uganda may be found in Tony Avirgan and Martha Honey, *War in Uganda: The Legacy of Idi Amin* (Westport: L. Hill, 1982).

28. From having very bright prospects at independence, Uganda had lost its shine over the intervening decades due to ethnic and political rivalries and tyrannical governments; consult Thomas P. Ofcasky, *Uganda: Tarnished Pearl of Africa* (Boulder: Westview, 1996), pp. 59–61.

29. The new government included both Hutu and Tutsi; see *New York Times*, 20 July 1994, p. 6. For articles on the Rwanda crisis, see *Africa Today*, 45(1) (January 1998), pp. 3–61.

30. A guide to the parties who were involved and their rationales may be found in François Misser, 'Who Helped Kabila?' *New African* no. 354 (July–August 1997), pp. 9–10.

31. See Festus Aboagye and Alhaji M.S. Bah (eds.), *A Tortuous Road to Peace: The Dynamics of Regional, UN, and International Humanitarian Intervention in Liberia* (Tshwane: Institute for Security Studies, 2005); Adekeye Adebajo, *Liberia's Civil War: Nigeria, ECOMOG, and Regional Security in West Africa* (Boulder: Lynne Rienner, 2002); Karl Magyar and Earl Conteh-Morgan (eds.), *Peacekeeping in Africa: ECOMOG in Liberia* (Hampshire: Macmillan, 1998); Margaret Vogt (ed.), *The Liberian Crisis and ECOMOG: A Bold Attempt at Regional Peacekeeping* (Lagos: Gabumo, 1992).

32. See, for example, Adekeye Adebajo (ed.), *From Global Apartheid to Global Village: Africa and the United Nations* (Scottsville: University of Kwazulu-Natal Press, 2009).

33. See, for example, Wm. Roger Louis, 'The Suez Crisis and the British Dilemma at the United Nations,' in Vaughan Lowe, Adam Roberts, Jennifer Welsh and Dominik Zaum, eds., *The United Nations Security Council and War: The Evolution of Thought and Practice since 1945* (Oxford: Oxford University Press, 2008), pp. 280–297.

1. INTRODUCTION: BISMARCK'S SORCERY AND AFRICA'S THREE MAGIC KINGDOMS

1. I thank Devon Curtis, Maureen Isaacson, Christopher Clapham, and Chris Saunders for their useful comments on an earlier version of this introduction.

2. Quoted in H.L. Wesseling, *Divide and Rule: The Partition of Africa, 1880–1914* (Connecticut: Praeger, 1996), p. 110.

3. See Ali A. Mazrui, 'Africa Entrapped: Between the Protestant Ethic and the Legacy of Westphalia', in Hedley Bull and Adam Watson (eds.), *The Expansion of International Society* (Oxford: Clarendon, 1984), pp. 289–308.

4. Ali A. Mazrui, *The African Condition: A Political Diagnosis* (Cambridge: Cambridge University Press, 1980), p. 22.

5. See, for example, Pierre Barrot (ed.), *Nollywood: The Video Phenomenon in Nigeria* (Oxford: Currey, 2008); Trenton Daniel, 'Nollywood Confidential Part 2: A Con-

versation with Zeb Ejiro, Ajoke Jacobs, Tunde Kelani, and Aquila Njamah', *Transition* 13(1) (2004), pp. 110–128; John C. McCall, 'Nollywood Confidential: The Unlikely Rise of Nigeria's Video Film', *Transition* 13(1) (2004), pp. 98–109; Odia Ofeimum, 'In Defence of the Films We Have Made', in *Chimurenga* no. 8 (2006), pp. 44–54.

6. Ali A. Mazrui formulated the idea of Africa as 'pawn' and 'player' in his 1986 nine-part documentary *The Africans*.

7. Chinua Achebe, *Home and Exile* (Cape Town: Oxford University Press, 2000), p. 73.

8. See Niall Ferguson, *Empire: How Britain Made the Modern World* (London: Penguin, 2004, first published in 2003); Niall Ferguson, *Colossus: The Rise and Fall of the American Empire* (London: Penguin, 2004); Michael Ignatieff, *Empire Lite* (Toronto: Penguin, 2004). For an interesting critique of Ferguson and Ignatieff, see John S. Saul, *Decolonization and Empire: Contesting the Rhetoric and Reality of Resubordination in Southern Africa and Beyond* (Johannesburg: Wits University Press, 2008), pp. 83–113.

9. M.E. Chamberlain, *The Scramble for Africa*, 2nd ed. (London: Longman, 1999), p. 25.

10. Ali A. Mazrui, 'The Erosion of the State and the Decline of Race: Bismarck to Boutros; Othello to O.J. Simpson', inaugural address at the launch of the Foundation for Global Dialogue, Johannesburg, 10 August 1995.

11. See the 1917 pamphlet by V.I. Lenin, 'Imperialism: The Highest Stage of Capitalism' (Moscow: Foreign Languages Publishing House, n.d.).

12. A.J.P. Taylor, *Bismarck: The Man and the Statesman* (Gloucestershire: Sutton, 2003, first published in 1955), p. 111.

13. Wesseling, *Divide and Rule*, p. 107.

14. Quoted in Taylor, *Bismarck*, p. 115.

15. Quoted in Wesseling, *Divide and Rule*, p. 109.

16. Wm. Roger Louis, 'The Berlin Congo Conference and the (Non-) Partition of Africa, 1884–1885', in Wm. Roger Louis, *Ends of British Imperialism: The Scramble for Empire, Suez, and Decolonization* (London: Tauris, 2006), p. 120.

17. Quoted in Thomas Pakenham, *The Scramble for Africa: White Man's Conquest of the Dark Continent From 1876 to 1912* (New York: Avon, 1991), p. 248.

18. See A.J.P. Taylor, *Germany's First Bid for Colonies, 1884–1885: A Move in Bismarck's European Policy* (London: Macmillan, 1938); Pakenham, *The Scramble for Africa*, pp. 201–217.

19. Taylor, *Germany's First Bid for Colonies*, p. 6.

20. Cited in Louis, *Ends of British Imperialism*, p. 121.

21. See Wesseling, *Divide and Rule*, pp. 105–113.

22. Quoted in Pakenham, *The Scramble for Africa*, p. 213.

23. Taylor, *Germany's First Bid for Colonies*, p. 4.

24. Pakenham, *The Scramble for Africa*, p. 204.

25. Ibid., pp. 205–207.

26. Jan (previously James) Morris, *Pax Britannica: The Climax of An Empire* (New York: Harcourt Brace, 1968), p. 110.

27. Pakenham, *The Scramble for Africa*, p. 205.
28. Ibid.
29. Quoted in Wesseling, *Divide and Rule*, p. 110.
30. Quoted in Mazrui, *The African Condition*, p. 88.
31. See A. Adu Boahen, 'Africa and the Colonial Challenge', in A. Adu Boahen (ed.), *General History of Africa*, vol. 7, *Africa Under Colonial Domination, 1880–1935* (Berkeley: University of California Press, 1985), pp. 1–18.
32. See Louis, 'The Berlin Congo Conference', pp. 75–126.
33. Ibid., p. 95.
34. My summary of the Berlin conference in this section relies largely on the narratives in Pakenham, *The Scramble for Africa*, pp. 239–255; Louis, 'The Berlin Congo Conference', pp. 75–126; and G.N. Uzoigwe, 'The Results of the Berlin West Africa Conference: An Assessment', in Stig Förster, Wolfgang J. Mommsen, and Ronald Robinson (eds.), *Bismarck, Europe, and Africa: The British Africa Conference, 1884–1885, and the Onset of Partition* (Oxford: Oxford University Press, 1988), pp. 543–544.
35. Wesseling, *Divide and Rule*, p. 114.
36. Louis, 'The Berlin Congo Conference', p. 83.
37. Ibid., p. 101.
38. Mark Dummett, 'King Leopold's Legacy of DR Congo Violence', *BBC News*, 24 February 2004, http://news.bbc.co.uk/go/pr/fr/-/2/hi/africa/3516965.stm. For a more detailed study, see Adam Hochschild, *King Leopold's Ghost: A Story of Greed, Terror, and Heroism in Colonial Africa* (London: Pan Macmillan, 1998).
39. Quoted in Martin Meredith, *The State of Africa: A History of Fifty Years of Independence* (Johannesburg and Cape Town: Jonathan Ball, 2006), p. 2.
40. Quoted in J.F. Ade. Ajayi, 'Colonialism: An Episode in African History', in Toyin Falola (ed.), *Tradition and Change in Africa: The Essays of J.F. Ade. Ajayi* (Asmara: Africa World, 2000), p. 174, n. 12.
41. Quoted in Uzoigwe, 'The Results of the Berlin West Africa Conference', pp. 543–544.
42. See the pioneering study by Ronald Robinson and John Gallagher, *Africa and the Victorians: The Official Mind of Imperialism* (London: Macmillan, 1961). For critiques of this work, see Wm. Roger Louis (ed.), *The Robinson and Gallagher Controversy* (New York: New Viewpoints, 1976).
43. Morris, *Pax Britannica*, p. 107.
44. Eric Hobsbawn, *The Age of Empire, 1875–1914* (London: Abacus, 1994, first published by Weidenfeld and Nicolson in 1987), p. 69.
45. Ibid., pp. 61–62, 68. For further economic explanations of imperialism, see J.A. Hobson, *Imperialism: A Study* (London: Allen and Unwin, 1938); Walter Rodney, *How Europe Underdeveloped Africa*, rev. ed. (Washington, DC: Howard University Press, 1981, first published in 1972). For a critique of economic arguments of imperialism, see D.K. Fieldhouse, *Economics and Empire* (London: Weidenfeld and Nicolson, 1973).
46. Hobsbawn, *The Age of Empire*, pp. 63–66.

47. Quoted in Robinson and Gallagher, *Africa and the Victorians*, p. 5.

48. Morris, *Pax Britannica*, pp. 100–102.

49. See, for example, Rodney Davenport and Christopher Saunders, *South Africa: A Modern History*, 5th ed. (London: Macmillan, 2000), pp. 213–222.

50. Mazrui, 'Africa Entrapped', pp. 293–295.

51. Francis M. Deng, *Identity, Diversity, and Constitutionalism in Africa* (Washington, DC: US Institute of Peace, 2008), p. 3. See also Mahmood Mamdani, *Citizen and Subject: Contemporary Africa and the Legacy of Late Colonialism* (Kampala: Fountain, 1996).

52. Ajayi, 'Colonialism', p. 171. For a detailed case study, see Obaro Ikime (ed.), *Groundwork of Nigerian History* (Ibadan: Heinemann, 1980).

53. See A.H.M. Kirk-Greene, 'The Thin White Line: The Size of the British Colonial Service in Africa', *African Affairs* 79(314) (January 1980), pp. 25–44.

54. Meredith, *The State of Africa*, pp. 5–6.

55. John Iliffe, *Africans: The History of A Continent* (Cambridge: Cambridge University Press, 2007, Second Edition), p. 207.

56. See Lord Lugard, *The Dual Mandate in British Tropical Africa*, 5th ed. (London: Cass, 1965, first published in 1922).

57. A.H.M Kirk-Greene (ed.), 'Africa in the Colonial Period: The Transfer of Power—The Colonial Administrator in the Age of Decolonization', proceedings of a symposium held at St. Antony's College, Oxford University, 15–16 March 1978 (Oxford: University of Oxford Inter-Faculty Committee for African Studies, 1979), p. 12.

58. See Basil Davidson, *The Black Man's Burden: Africa and the Curse of the Nation State* (New York: Times Books, 1992), pp. 162–196.

59. Mahmood Mamdani, *When Victims Become Killers: Colonialism, Nativism, and the Genocide in Rwanda* (Princeton: Princeton University Press, 2001), p. 14 (original emphasis).

60. See, for example, J.F. Ade. Ajayi, *Christian Missions in Nigeria, 1841–1891: The Making of a New Elite* (Lagos: Longman, 1965); Horst Gründer, 'Christan Missionary Activities in the Age of Imperialism and the Berlin Conference of 1884–1885', in Förster, Mommsen and Robinson, *Bismarck, Europe, and Africa;* Holger Bernt Hansen and Michael Twaddle (eds.), *Christian Missionaries and the State in the Third World* (Oxford: Currey, 2002).

61. A. Adu Boahen, *African Perspectives on Colonialism* (Baltimore: The Johns Hopkins University Press, 1987), p. 106. Much of the analysis in this paragraph is also drawn from Boahen's work.

62. Boahen, *African Perspectives on Colonialism*, p. 109.

63. Edward W. Said, *Culture and Imperialism*,(New York: Vintage, 1994, first published in 1993), p. xi.

64. Chinua Achebe, 'An Image of Africa', in Achebe, *Home and Exile*, pp. 3, 17.

65. See Graham Greene, *Journey Without Maps* (London: Penguin, 1978, first published in 1936).

66. Cited in Chamberlain, *The Scramble for Africa*, p. 20.
67. See 'Sharks and Alligators', *The Economist*, 13 April 1996; Phillip van Niekerk, 'They Cooked My Brother's Heart and Ate It', *The Observer*, 14 April 1996.
68. See Robert Kaplan, 'The Coming Anarchy', *Atlantic Monthly*, February 1994.
69. Cited in A.I. Asiwaju, *Boundaries and African Integration: Essays in Comparative History and Policy Analysis* (Lagos: Panaf, 2003), p. 432.
70. Lecture by Ramtane Lamamra, AU Commissioner for Peace and Security, 13 March 2009, Cambridge University, England.
71. See Ali A. Mazrui, 'Conflict and the Bondage of Boundaries', in Ali A. Mazrui, *The Politics of War and the Culture of Violence: North-South Essays* (Asmara: Africa World, 2008), pp. 79–94; Ali A. Mazrui, 'The Bondage of Boundaries', *The Economist*, 11 September 1993, pp. 32–36.
72. Quoted in Asiwaju, *Boundaries and African Integration*, p. 433.
73. See ibid., pp. 432–447.
74. See Kofi Annan, *The Causes of Conflict and the Promotion of Durable Peace and Sustainable Development in Africa*, Report of the UN Secretary-General, 13 April 1998, UN Doc. S/1998/318.
75. See Christopher Clapham, *African Guerrillas* (Bloomington: Indiana University Press, 1998).
76. This paragraph and the two that follow are adapted from my contributions to the essay by Adekeye Adebajo and Chris Landsberg, 'Pax Africana in the Age of Extremes', *South African Journal of International Affairs* 7(1) (Summer 2000), pp. 11–26.
77. Davidson, *The Black Man's Burden*, p. 10.
78. See Mazrui, *Towards a Pax Africana*.
79. See, for example, Christopher Clapham, *Africa and the International System: The Politics of State Survival* (Cambridge: Cambridge University Press, 1996); Guy Martin, *Africa in World Politics: A Pan-African Perspective* (Asmara: Africa World, 2002); James Mayall, *Africa: The Cold War and After* (London: Elek, 1971); Ali A. Mazrui, *Africa's International Relations: The Diplomacy of Dependency and Change* (London: Heinemann, 1977).
80. See, for example, Sola Akinrinade and Amadu Sesay (eds.), *Africa in the Post–Cold War International System* (London: Pinter, 1998); John W. Harbeson and Donald Rothchild (eds.), *Africa in World Politics: Reforming Political Order*, 3rd ed. (Boulder: Westview,2008); Adebayo O. Oyebade and Abiodun Alao (eds.), *Africa After the Cold War: The Changing Perspectives on Security* (Asmara: Africa World, 1998); Ian Taylor and Paul Williams (eds.), *Africa in International Politics: External Involvement on the Continent* (London: Routledge, 2004).
81. See Adebayo Adedeji, 'NEPAD's African Peer Review Mechanism: Progress and Prospects', in John Akokpari, Angela Ndinga-Muvumba, and Tim Murithi (eds.), *The African Union and Its Institutions* (Johannesburg: Jacana, 2008) pp. 241–269.

2. PROPHETS OF PAX AFRICANA: AFRICA'S SECURITY ARCHITECTURE

1. This chapter builds on Adekeye Adebajo, 'The Peacekeeping Travails of the AU and the Regional Economic Communities (RECs)', in John Akokpari, Angela Ndinga-Muvumba, and Tim Murithi (eds.), *The African Union and Its Institutions* (Johannesburg: Jacana, 2008), pp. 131–161.

2. Quoted in Kubara Zamani, 'No Matter Where You Come From, So Long As You Are a Black Man, You Are an African', *New African*, October 2004.

3. Ali A. Mazrui, *Towards a Pax Africana: A Study of Ideology and Ambition* (Chicago: University of Chicago Press, 1967), p. 203.

4. Ibid.

5. Ali A. Mazrui, *The Africans: A Triple Heritage* (London: BBC Publications, 1986), p. 279.

6. Quoted in Tim Murithi, *The African Union: Pan-Africanism, Peacebuilding, and Development* (Hampshire: Ashgate, 2005), p. 109.

7. See African Union, 'Roadmap for the Operationalization of the African Standby Force', Experts' Meeting on the Relationship Between the AU and the Regional Mechanisms for Conflict Prevention, Management, and Resolution; Addis Ababa, 22–23 March 2005, EXP/AU-Recs/ASF/4(I); Jakkie Cilliers and Mark Malan, *Progress with the African Standby Force*, South Africa Paper no. 107 (Tshwane: Institute for Security Studies, May 2005); Musifiky Mwanasali, 'Emerging Security Architecture in Africa', *Policy: Issues and Actors 7(4)* (Johannesburg: Centre for Policy Studies, 2004).

8. African Union, *Audit of the African Union: Towards a People-Centred Political and Socio-Economic Integration and Transformation of Africa* (Addis Ababa, 2007).

9. Mwanasali, 'Emerging Security Architecture in Africa', p. 14.

10. See Adekeye Adebajo 'South Africa and Nigeria: An Axis of Virtue?' in Adekeye Adebajo, Adebayo Adedeji, and Chris Landsberg (eds.), *South Africa in Africa: The Post-Apartheid Era* (Scottsville: University of Kwazulu-Natal Press, 2007), pp. 213–235.

11. See *Protocol Relating to the Establishment of the Peace and Security Council of the African Union*, Durban, South Africa, 9 July 2002.

12. See Centre for Conflict Resolution and United Nations, 'United Nations Mediation Experience in Africa', Seminar Report, Cape Town, October 2006, http://www.ccr.org.za.

13. International Peace Academy, 'The AU in Sudan: Lessons for the African Standby Force', March 2007, p. 23.

14. African Union, *Audit of the African Union*, pp. 58–60.

15. See United Nations, *A More Secure World: Our Shared Responsibility*, Report of the UN Secretary-General's High-Level Panel on Threats, Challenges, and Change, UN Department of Public Information, December 2004, UN Doc. DPI/2367; Unites Nations, *In Larger Freedom: Towards Development, Security, and Human Rights for All*, Report of the UN Secretary-General, follow-up to the outcome of the Millennium Summit, 21 March 2005, UN Doc. A/59/2005.

16. See Seth Appiah-Mensah, 'The African Union Mission in Sudan: Darfur Dilemmas', *African Security Review* 15(1) (2006), pp. 2–19; Kristiana Powell, *The African Union's Emerging Peace and Security Regime: Opportunities and Challenges for Delivering on the Responsibility to Protect*, Monograph Series no. 119 (Tshwane: Institute for Security Studies, May 2005).

17. UN Security Council Resolution 1769, 31 July 2007.

18. Mahmood Mamdani, 'Darfur: the Politics of Naming', *Mail and Guardian*, 16–22 March 2007, pp. 23, 26. See also Mahmood Mamdani, *Saviours and Survivors: Darfur, Politics, and the War on Terror* (Cape Town: Human Sciences Research Council, 2009).

19. See Chris Alden and Guy Martin (eds.), *France and South Africa: Towards a New Engagement with Africa* (Pretoria: Protea, 2003); John Chipman, *French Power in Africa* (Oxford: Basil Blackwell, 1989); Anthony Kirk-Greene and Daniel Bach (eds.), *State and Society in Francophone Africa Since Independence* (Hampshire: Macmillan, 1995); Kaye Whiteman and Douglas Yates, 'France, Britain, and the United States', in Adekeye Adebajo and Ismail Rashid (eds.), *West Africa's Security Challenges: Building Peace in a Troubled Region* (Boulder: Lynne Rienner, 2004), pp. 349–379.

20. For accounts of these civil wars, see Adekeye Adebajo, *Building Peace in West Africa: Liberia, Sierra Leone, and Guinea-Bissau* (Boulder: Lynne Rienner, 2002); Adekeye Adebajo and David Keen, 'Sierra Leone', in Mats Berdal and Spyros Economides (eds.), *United Nations Interventionism, 1991–2004* (Cambridge: Cambridge University Press, 2007), pp. 246–273; Herbert Howe, 'Lessons of Liberia: ECOMOG and Regional Peacekeeping', *International Security* 21(3) (Winter 1996–1997), pp. 145–176; Robert Mortimer, 'From ECOMOG to ECOMOG II: Intervention in Sierra Leone', in John W. Harbeson and Donald Rothchild (eds.), *Africa in World Politics: The African State System in Flux*, 3rd ed. (Boulder: Westview, 2000), pp. 188–207.

21. The 15 ECOWAS states are: Benin, Burkina Faso, Cape Verde, Côte d'Ivoire, Gambia, Ghana, Guinea, Guinea-Bissau, Liberia, Mali, Niger, Nigeria, Sierra Leone, Senegal and Togo.

22. See Centre for Conflict Resolution (Cape Town), 'West Africa's Evolving Security Architecture', Seminar Report, Accra, 30–31 October 2006, http://www.ccr.org.za.

23. See Adekeye Adebajo, 'Mad Dogs and Glory: Nigeria's Interventions in Liberia and Sierra Leone', in Adekeye Adebajo and Raufu Mustapha (eds.), *Gulliver's Troubles: Nigeria's Foreign Policy After the Cold War* (Scottsville: University of Kwazulu-Natal Press, 2008), pp. 177–202.

24. See, for example, Adekeye Adebajo, 'The Security Council and Three Wars in West Africa', in Vaughan Lowe, Adam Roberts, Jennifer Welsh and Dominik Zaum, (eds.) *The United Nations Security Council and War: The Evolution of Thought and Practice since 1945* (Oxford: Oxford University Press, 2008), pp. 466–493; Comfort Ero, 'UN Peacekeeping in West Africa: Liberia, Sierra Leone and Côte d'Ivoire', in Adekeye Adebajo (ed.) *From Global Apartheid to Global Village: Africa and the United Nations* (Scottsville: University of Kwazulu-

Natal Press, 2009), pp. 283–304; and James O.C. Jonah, 'The United Nations', in Adebajo and Rashid, (eds.), *West Africa's Security Challenges*, pp. 319–347.

25. See Adebajo and Mustapha (eds.), *Gulliver's Troubles.*

26. Adebayo Adedeji, *South Africa in Africa: Within or Apart?* (London: Zed, 1996), p. 9.

27. See, for example, James Barber and John Barrett, *South Africa's Foreign Policy: The Search For Status and Security 1945-1988* (Cambridge: Cambridge University Press, 1990).

28. Other members of SADC include Angola, Botswana, the DRC, Lesotho, Madagascar, Malawi, Mauritius, Mozambique, Namibia, Seychelles, Swaziland, Tanzania, Zambia, and Zimbabwe.

29. See, for example, Anne Hammerstad, 'Defending the State or Protecting the People? SADC Security Integration at a Crossroads', Report no. 39 (Johannesburg: South African Institute of International Affairs, November 2003); Gabriel H. Oosthuizen, *The Southern African Development Community: The Organisation, Its Policies, and Prospects* (Midrand, South Africa: Institute for Global Dialogue, 2006); Rocklyn Williams, 'From Collective Security to Peacebuilding? The Challenges of Managing Regional Security in Southern Africa', in Christopher Clapham, Greg Mills, Anna Morner, and Elizabeth Sidiropoulos (eds.), *Regional Integration in Southern Africa: Comparative International Perspectives* (Johannesburg: South African Institute of International Affairs, 2001), pp. 105–113; Agostinho Zacarias, 'Redefining Security', in Mwesiga Baregu and Chris Landsberg (eds.), *From Cape to Congo: Southern Africa's Security Challenges* (Boulder: Lynne Rienner, 2003), pp. 31–51.

30. See Khabele Matlosa, 'The Lesotho Conflict: Major Causes and Management', in Kato Lambrechts (ed.), *Crisis in Lesotho: The Challenge of Managing Conflict in Southern Africa*, African Dialogue Series no. 2 (Braamfontein: Foundation for Global Dialogue, March 1999), pp. 6–10; Roger Southall, 'Is Lesotho South Africa's Tenth Province?' in Lambrechts, *Crisis in Lesotho*, pp. 19–25.

31. See Adebajo, Adedeji, and Landsberg (eds.), *South Africa in Africa;* Walter Carlsnaes and Philip Nel (eds.), *In Full Flight: South African Foreign Policy After Apartheid* (Midrand, South Africa: Institute for Global Dialogue, 2006); Elizabeth Sidiropoulos (ed.), *South Africa's Foreign Policy, 1994-2004: Apartheid Past, Renaissance Future* (Johannesburg: South African Institute of International Affairs, 2004).

32. See Adekeye Adebajo, 'The Pied Piper of Pretoria', *Global Dialogue* 10(1) (February 2005), pp. 1–3.

33. Elling N. Tjønneland, Jan Isaksen, and Garth Le Pere, *SADC's Restructuring and Emerging Policies: Options for Norwegian Support* (Bergen: Christian Michelsen Institute, May 2005), pp. 6–7.

34. Survey conducted by the University of Pennsylvania, published in *Foreign Policy*, January 2009.

35. Elling N. Tjønneland, *SADC and Donors: Ideals and Practices—From Gaborone to Paris and Back* (Gaborone: Botswana Institute for Development Policy Analysis, 2006), p. 1.

36. See René Lemarchand, *The Dynamics of Violence in Central Africa* (Philadelphia: University of Pennsylvania Press, 2009); Kankwenda Mbaya (ed.), *Zaire: What Destiny?* (Dakar: Council for the Development of Social Science Research in Africa, 1993); Georges Nzongola-Ntalaja, *The Congo: From Leopold to Kabila* (London: Zed, 2002); Gérard Prunier, *From Genocide to Continental War: The 'Congolese' Conflict and the Crisis of Contemporary Africa* (London: Hurst, 2009); Crawford Young and Thomas Turner, *The Rise and Decline of the Zairian State* (Madison: University of Wisconsin Press, 1985).

37. ECCAS's members are Angola, Burundi, Cameroon, the Central African Republic, Chad, Congo-Brazzaville, the DRC, Equatorial Guinea, Gabon, Rwanda, and São Tomé and Príncipe.

38. See Musifiky Mwanasali, 'Politics and Security in Central Africa', *African Journal of Political Science* 4(2) (1999), pp. 89–105.

39. See Centre for Conflict Resolution (Cape Town), 'The Peacebuilding Role of Civil Society in Central Africa', Seminar Report, Douala, Cameroon, 10–12 April 2006, http://www.ccr.org.za.

40. See Devon Curtis, 'South Africa: "Exporting Peace" to the Great Lakes Region?' in Adebajo, Adedeji, and Landsberg, *South Africa in Africa*, pp. 253–273; 'Report of the Chairperson of the Commission on Conflict Situations in Africa', Executive Council, 7th Ordinary Session, 28 June–2 July 2005, pp. 12–14.

41. See Abdelrahim A. Khalil, 'Africa's Peace and Security Architecture: The African Union and the Regional Economic Communities: The Case of CEWARN/ IGAD', paper presented at the conference 'Beyond the Year of Africa', Bradford University, England, 28–29 March 2006.

42. See Kasaija Phillip Apuuli, 'IGAD's Protocol on Conflict Early Warning and Response Mechanism (CEWARN): A Ray of Hope in Conflict Prevention', in Alfred G. Nhema (ed.), *The Quest for Peace in Africa: Transformations, Democracy, and Public Policy* (Addis Ababa: OSSREA, 2004), pp. 173–187; Kassu Gebremariam, 'Peacebuilding in the Horn of Africa', in Tom Keating and W. Andy Knight (eds.), *Building Sustainable Peace* (Alberta: The University of Alberta Press, and Tokyo: United Nations University Press, 2004), pp. 189–211; 'Strengthening the Role of IGAD in Regional Peace Initiatives and Post Conflict Reconstruction', report of a conference of the Intergovernmental Authority on Development, Nairobi, 1–3 December 2003.

43. See Medhane Tadesse, 'New Security Frontiers in the Horn of Africa', Friedrich Ebert Foundation Briefing Paper, June 2004.

44. See Abdi Ismail Samatar and Waqo Machaka, 'Conflict and Peace in the Horn of Africa: A Regional Approach', in *The Quest for a Culture of Peace in the IGAD Region: The Role of Intellectuals* (Nairobi: Heinrich Boll, 2006), pp. 26–55; Peter Woodward, *The Horn of Africa: State Politics and International Relations* (London: Tauris, 2003).

45. See Ruth Iyob, 'The Foreign Policies of the Horn: The Clash Between the Old and the New', in Gilbert M. Khadiagala and Terrence Lyons (eds.), *African Foreign Policies: Power and Process* (Boulder: Lynne Rienner, 2001), pp. 107–129.

46. See, for example, Francis Deng, *War of Visions: Conflict of Identities in the Sudan*, (Washington DC: The Brookings Institution, 1995); Dunstan M. Wai, *The African-Arab Conflict in the Sudan* (New York and London: Africana Publishing Company, 1981); Peter Woodward, *Sudan, 1898–1989: The Unstable State* (Boulder: Lynne Rienner, 1990).

47. See Roland Marchal, 'Horn of Africa: New War, Old Methods', *Africa Report* no. 8 (October–December 2007), pp. 47–50. See also Paul D. Williams, 'Into the Mogadishu Maelstrom: The African Union Mission in Somalia,' *International Peacekeeping*, volume 16 number 4 August 2009, pp. 514–530.

48. See Adekeye Adebajo, *Selling Out the Sahara: The Tragic Tale of the UN Referendum*, Occasional Paper (Ithaca: Cornell University, Institute for African Development, Spring 2002); William Durch, 'The United Nations Mission for the Referendum in Western Sahara', in William Durch (ed.), *The Evolution of UN Peacekeeping: Case Studies and Comparative Analysis* (New York: St. Martin's 1993), pp. 406–434; Erik Jensen, *Western Sahara: Anatomy of a Stalemate* (Boulder: Lynne Rienner, 2005).

49. See Benjamin Stora, *Algeria, 1830-2000: A Short History* (Ithaca: Cornell University Press, 2001); Hakim Darbouche, 'Algeria: Presidential 21st Century Vision of the Future', *Africa Report* no. 5 (January 2007), pp. 72–74.

50. See 'Steady but State', *The Economist*, 7–13 March 2009, p. 58.

51. Asteris Huliaras, 'Qadhafi's Comeback: Libya and Sub-Saharan Africa in the 1990s', *African Affairs* 100(398) (January 2001), p. 18. See also Yehudit Ronen, *Qaddafi's Libya in World Politics* (Boulder and London: Lynne Rienner, 2008); Dirk Vandewalle, *A History of Modern Libya* (Cambridge: Cambridge University Press, 2006).

52. Quoted in Pascale Harter, 'Icy Alliance', *BBC Focus on Africa*, April–June 2005, p. 18.

53. James Badcock, 'Wind of Change', *NewsAfrica*, 30 June 2005, pp. 20–22.

54. Wole Soyinka, 'Beyond the Berlin Wall', lecture delivered 1 September 1990 (Accra: Sedco, 1993), p. 63.

55. For a summary of the lively debates on this issue in Africa, see A.I. Asiwaju, *Boundaries and African Integration: Essays in Comparative History and Policy Analysis* (Lagos: Panaf, 2003), pp. 431–448.

3. FROM GLOBAL APARTHEID TO GLOBAL VILLAGE: AFRICA AND THE UNITED NATIONS

1. This chapter is adapted from Adekeye Adebajo, 'Ending Global Apartheid: Africa and the United Nations', in Adekeye Adebajo (ed.), *From Global Apartheid to Global Village: Africa and the United Nations* (Scottsville: University of Kwazulu-Natal Press, 2009). I thank Devon Curtis, David Malone, Tor Sellström, Mats Berdal, Dominik Zaum, and Sam Daws for their insightful comments on an earlier version of this chapter.

2. Ali A. Mazrui, 'Global Apartheid: Structural and Overt', *Alternatives* 19 (1994), p. 186.

3. Quoted in Patrick Bond, *Talk Left, Walk Right: South Africa's Frustrated Global Reforms* (Scottsville: University of Kwazulu-Natal Press, 2004), p. 3.

4. This memorable phrase was coined by an insightful observer of the UN, Conor Cruise O'Brien, in his book *The United Nations: Sacred Drama* (London: Simon and Schuster, 1968).

5. I am grateful to Ali Mazrui for the concept of 'Brahmins' and 'Dalits', as well as that of 'pawn' and 'player', in the international system.

6. See preamble to *Charter of the United Nations* (New York: United Nations, 1945).

7. Simeon Ola Adebo, *Our International Years* (Ibadan: Spectrum, 1988), p. 37.

8. See Ian Brownlie, 'The Expansion of International Society: The Consequences for the Law of Nations', in Hedley Bull and Adam Watson (eds.), *The Expansion of International Society* (Oxford: Clarendon, 1984), pp. 357–369; Nagendra Singh, 'The United Nations in the Development of International Law', in Adam Roberts and Benedict Kingsbury (eds.), *United Nations, Divided World: The UN's Role in International Relations*, 1st ed. (Oxford: Clarendon, 1989), pp. 159–191.

9. Singh, 'The United Nations in the Development of International Law', p. 179.

10. Ali. A. Mazrui, introduction to Ali A. Mazrui (ed.), *General History of Africa: Africa Since 1935*, vol. 8 (Oxford: Currey, 1993), p. 21.

11. Adebo, *Our International Years*, p. 85.

12. For an interesting account of these early struggles, see the memoirs of Nigerian permanent representative Simeon Adebo (1962–1967) and his Ghanaian counterpart Alex Quaison-Sackey (1959–1965) at the UN, in Adebo, *Our International Years*, and Quaison-Sackey, *Africa Unbound: Reflections of an African Statesman* (London: André Deutsch, 1963).

13. Quaison-Sackey, *Africa Unbound*, pp. 148–149.

14. See Ibrahim A. Gambari, 'Ending Apartheid in South Africa: The United Nations Strategy', in Ibraham A. Gambari, *Africa at the United Nations in a Changing World Order: Selected Speeches* (Atlanta: Chaneta International, 2006), pp. 183–191. Gambari was the last chair of the UN Special Committee Against Apartheid in 1994.

15. See Chris Landsberg, 'Exporting Peace? The UN and South Africa', *Policy: Issues and Actors* 7(2) (Johannesburg: Centre for Policy Studies, 1994). For eyewitness accounts, see Tunji Lardner, 'The True Meaning of Ubuntu', Adekeye Adebajo, 'Observing Apartheid's Funeral', and Ibrahim A. Gambari, 'To Pretoria and Back', all in *West Africa*, 23–29 May 1994, pp. 902–907.

16. United Nations, *A More Secure World: Our Shared Responsibility*, Report of the UN Secretary-General's High-Level Panel on Threats, Challenges, and Change, UN Department of Public Information, December 2004, UN Doc. DPI/2367.

17. See African Union, 'Draft Recommendations at the Ministerial Committee of Fifteen on the Report of the High-Level Panel on the Reform of the UN System', 20–22 February 2005, Mbabane, Swaziland, CTTE/15/Min/ReformUN/Draft/Recomm.(I).

18. See Edward C. Luck, 'Principal Organs', in Thomas G. Weiss and Sam Daws (eds.), *The Oxford Handbook on the United Nations* (Oxford: Oxford University

Press, 2007), pp. 653–674; Thomas G. Weiss, *What's Wrong with the United Nations and How to Fix It* (Cambridge and Massachusetts: Polity Press, 2009).

19. I am indebted for this summary to Kishore Mahbubani, Singapore's former permanent representative to the UN, for his chapter 'The Permanent and Elected Council Members', in David M. Malone (ed.), *The UN Security Council: From the Cold War to the 21st Century* (Boulder: Lynne Rienner, 2004), pp. 253–266.

20. Dumisani S. Kumalo, 'The UN: A Personal Appreciation', in Garth Le Pere and Nhamo Samasuwo (eds.), *The UN at 60: A New Spin on an Old Hub* (Midrand, South Africa: Institute for Global Dialogue, 2006), pp. 33–35.

21. See Adekeye Adebajo and Raufu Mustapha (eds.), *Gulliver's Troubles: Nigeria's Foreign Policy After the Cold War* (Scottsville: University of Kwazulu-Natal Press, 2008); Bola A. Akinterinwa (ed.), *Nigeria's New Foreign Policy Thrust: Essays in Honour of Ambassador Oluyemi Adeniji* (Ibadan: Vantage, 2004); U. Joy Ogwu (ed.), *New Horizons for Nigeria in World Affairs* (Lagos: Nigerian Institute of International Affairs, 2005).

22. See Kader Asmal, David Chidester, and Wilmot James (eds.), *South Africa's Nobel Laureates: Peace, Literature, and Science* (Johannesburg: Jonathan Ball, 2004).

23. See Adekeye Adebajo, Adebayo Adedeji, and Chris Landsberg (eds.), *South Africa in Africa: The Post-Apartheid Era* (Scottsville: University of Kwazulu-Natal Press, 2007); Walter Carlsnaes and Philip Nel (eds.), *In Full Flight: South African Foreign Policy After Apartheid* (Midrand, South Africa: Institute for Global Dialogue, 2006); Elizabeth Sidiropoulos (ed.), *South Africa's Foreign Policy, 1994–2004: Apartheid Past, Renaissance Future* (Johannesburg: South African Institute of International Affairs, 2004).

24. Quoted in Ali Mazrui, 'Africa and Egypt's Four Circles', in *On Heroes and Uhuru-Worship* (London: Longman), p. 111.

25. Thomas G. Weiss and Sam Daws, 'World Politics: Continuity and Change Since 1945', in Weiss and Daws, *The Oxford Handbook of the United Nations*, p. 13.

26. Ibid., p. 14.

27. See, for example, International Peace Academy and Center on International Cooperation, *Refashioning the Dialogue: Regional Perspectives on the Brahimi Report on UN Peace Operations*, Regional Meetings, February–March 2001, Johannesburg, Buenos Aires, Singapore, and London, pp. 6–11, http://www.cic.nyu.edu/projects/projects.html.

28. See United Nations, *Report of the Panel on United Nations Peace Operations* (Brahimi Report), 21 August 2000, UN Doc. S/2000/809.

29. See Harriet Martin, 'The Seasoned Powerbroker', in *Kings of Peace, Pawns of War* (London: Continuum, 2006), pp. 1–28.

30. Salim Ahmed Salim, 'The OAU Role in Conflict Management', in Olara Otunnu and Michael Doyle (eds.), *Peacemaking and Peacekeeping for the New Century* (Lanham: Rowman and Littlefield, 1998), pp. 245–253.

31. See David Hannay, *New World Disorder: The UN After the Cold War—An Insider's View* (London: Tauris, 2009).

32. See, for example, Georges Abi-Saab, *The United Nations Operation in the Congo, 1960–1964* (Oxford: Oxford University Press, 1978); Catherine Hoskyns, *The*

Congo Since Independence, January 1960–December 1961 (London: Oxford University Press, 1965); Alan James, 'The Congo Controversies', *International Peacekeeping* 1(1) (Spring 1994), pp. 44–58; Conor Cruise O'Brien, *To Katanga and Back: A UN Case History* (London: Hutchinson, 1962); Indar Jit Rikhye, *Military Adviser to the Secretary-General: UN Peacekeeping and the Congo Crisis* (London: Hurst, 1993).

33. For African perspectives on UN peacekeeping, see the chapters by Christopher Saunders, Comfort Ero, Gilbert Khadiagala, Medhane Tadesse, and Hakima Abbas in Adebajo, *From Global Apartheid to Global Village*. See also Adekeye Adebajo, 'From Congo to Congo: United Nations Peacekeeping in Africa After the Cold War', in Ian Taylor and Paul Williams (eds.), *Africa in International Politics: External Involvement on the Continent* (London: Routledge, 2004); Ibrahim Gambari, 'The United Nations', in Mwesiga Baregu and Christopher Landsberg (eds.), *From Cape to Congo: Southern Africa's Evolving Security Challenges* (Boulder: Lynne Rienner, 2003); James O.C. Jonah, 'The United Nations', in Adekeye Adebajo and Ismail Rashid (eds.), *West Africa's Security Challenges: Building Peace in a Troubled Region* (Boulder: Lynne Rienner, 2004); Agostinho Zacarias, *The United Nations and International Peacekeeping* (London: Tauris, 1996).

34. See, for example, Adekeye Adebajo, 'The Security Council and Three Wars in West Africa', in Vaughan Lowe, Adam Roberts, Jennifer Welsh, and Dominik Zaum (eds.), *The United Nations Security Council and War: The Evolution of Thought and Practice Since 1945* (Oxford: Oxford University Press, 2008), pp. 466–493; Jonah, 'The United Nations'.

35. See, for example, Margaret Vogt, 'The UN and Africa's Regional Organisations', in Adebajo, *From Global Apartheid to Global Village*, pp. 251–268; Fred Aja Agwu, *World Peace Through World Law: The Dilemma of the United Nations Security Council* (Ibadan: Ibadan University Press, 2007).

36. Salim, 'The OAU Role in Conflict Management', p. 246.

37. See Douglas Williams, 'The Specialised Agencies: Britain in Retreat', in Erik Jensen and Thomas Fisher (eds.), *The United Kingdom–The United Nations* (London: Macmillan, 1990), pp. 209–234.

38. See chapters 19–30 in Adebajo, *From Global Apartheid to Global Village*. See also Williams, 'The Specialised Agencies', p. 216.

39. See Tunde Zack-Williams, 'The UN Conference on Trade and Development', in Adebajo, *From Global Apartheid to Global Village*, pp. 417–436.

40. See Mbaya Kankwenda, 'The UN Development Programme', in Adebajo, *From Global Apartheid to Global Village*, pp. 399–416.

41. Williams, 'The Specialised Agencies', pp. 227–228.

42. See Frantz Fanon, *The Wretched of the Earth* (New York: Grove, 1963).

43. Stanley Meisler, *United Nations: The First Fifty Years* (New York: Atlantic Monthly, 1995), p. 226.

44. UN Conference on Trade and Development, *Economic Development in Africa: Debt Sustainability—Oasis or Mirage?* (New York: United Nations, 2004), p. 9.

45. See Alex De Waal, *AIDS and Power: Why There Is No Political Crisis—Yet* (Cape Town: David Philip, 2006); John Iliffe, *The African AIDS Epidemic* (Cape Town:

Double Storey, 2006); Angela Ndinga-Muvumba and Robyn Pharaoh (eds.), *HIV/AIDS and Society in South Africa* (Scottsville: University of Kwazulu-Natal Press, 2008); Centre for Conflict Resolution (Cape Town),'HIV/AIDS and Human Security: An Agenda for Africa', Seminar Report, Addis Ababa, September 2005.

46. Pratibha Thaker, 'Africa: Hope or Hype?' *The Economist*, 'The World in 2006', p. 82.

47. UN Development Programme, *Human Development Report* (Oxford: Oxford University Press, 2003), pp. 155–156.

48. See, for example, C. Hugueney, 'The G20: Passing Phenomenon or Here to Stay?' Friedrich Ebert Stiftung Briefing Paper, 2004.

49. See Bond, *Talk Left, Walk Right*, pp. 51–73.

50. See Dambisa Moyo, *Dead Aid: Why Aid Is Not Working and How There Is Another Way for Africa* (London: Allen Lane, 2009).

51. Dambisa Moyo, Richard Dowden, and Daniel Johnson, 'Dialogue: A Trillion Wasted Dollars?' *Standpoint* no. 10 (March 2009), p. 29.

52. For a fuller critique of this book, see Adekeye Adebajo, 'Economist's Self-Flagellating Aid Tract does Continent No Favours,'*BusinessDay*, 18 December 2009, p. 7.

53. Madeleine Bunting, 'The Road to Ruin', *Saturday Guardian* (London), 14 February 2009, p. 8.

54. Wangari Maathai, *The Challenge for Africa: A New Vision* (London: Heinemann, 2009), pp. 63–110.

55. Margaret Legum, 'Nyerere's Challenge: Deconstructing the Washington Consensus', in Adekeye Adebajo and Helen Scanlon (eds.), *A Dialogue of the Deaf: Essays on Africa and the United Nations* (Johannesburg: Jacana, 2006), pp. 167–181.

56. Maathai, *The Challenge for Africa*, p. 93.

57. Quaison-Sackey, *Africa Unbound*, p. 151.

58. Kenneth Dadzie, 'The United Nations and the Problem of Economic Development', in Roberts and Kingsbury, *United Nations, Divided World*, pp. 139–157.

59. Dadzie, 'The United Nations and the Problem of Economic Development', p. 153.

60. For different perspectives on the role of the Bretton Woods institutions in Africa, see Thomas M. Callaghy and John Ravenhill (eds.), *Hemmed In: Responses to Africa's Economic Decline* (New York: Columbia University Press, 1993); Charles C. Soludo and Thandika Mkandawire (eds.), *Our Continent, Our Future: African Perspectives on Structural Adjustment* (Trenton: Africa World Press, 1998); David Moore (ed.), *The World Bank: Development, Poverty, Hegemony* (Scottsville: University of Kwazulu-Natal Press, 2007); Bade Onimode, *The IMF, the World Bank, and African Debt* (London: Zed, 1989).

61. Adebayo Adedeji, 'The UN Economic Commission for Africa', in Adebajo, *From Global Apartheid to Global Village*, p. 394.

62. This information is gleaned from Dirk Messner, Simon Maxwell, Franz Nuscheler, and Joseph Siegle, *Governance Reform of the Bretton Woods Institutions and the UN Development System*, Occasional Paper no. 18 (Bonn: Friedrich Ebert Stif-

tung, 2005). See also Peter Draper, 'Pascal Lamy, Africa, and the WTO: Plus ça change ...?' in Le Pere and Samasuwo, *The UN at 60*, pp. 83–86.

63. Boutros Boutros-Ghali, foreword to Adebajo, *From Global Apartheid to Global Village*, p. xxiii.

64. Ibid., p. xxiv.

65. Patrick Bond and Ashraf Patel, 'International Financial Institutions in Africa: Is Reform on the Agenda?' *Openspace* 2(1) (2007), pp. 23–31.

66. This paragraph is summarized from Adekeye Adebajo, 'The G-20: Saying Farewell to the "Blue-Eyed Blond Men"'? *BusinessDay*, 14 April 2009, p. 11.

67. Adebayo Adedeji, 'Africa and the Crisis of Global Financial Governance', *New Agenda* (First Quarter 2009), p. 4.

68. Adedeji, 'Africa and the Crisis of Global Financial Governance', pp. 4–5.

69. Weiss and Daws, 'World Politics', p. 18.

70. Kwesi Armah, *Africa's Golden Road* (London: Heinemann, 1965), p. 209.

71. Quaison-Sackey, *Africa Unbound*, p. 155.

72. Kwame Nkrumah, *Africa Must Unite* (London: Panaf, 1963), p. 132.

73. Ali A. Mazrui, *The Africans: A Triple Heritage* (London: BBC Publications, 1986), p. 313.

74. Nelson Mandela, *From Freedom to the Future: Tributes and Speeches* (Johannesburg and Cape Town: Jonathan Ball, 2003), p. 524.

4. THE PHARAOH AND THE PROPHET: BOUTROS BOUTROS-GHALI AND KOFI ANNAN

1. This chapter builds on Adekeye Adebajo, 'Pope, Pharaoh, or Prophet? The Secretary-General After the Cold War', in Simon Chesterman (ed.), *Secretary or General? The UN Secretary-General in World Politics* (Cambridge: Cambridge University Press, 2007), pp. 139–157. I thank Simon Chesterman, James Jonah, and Elisabeth Lindenmayer for comments on the earlier chapter.

2. Boutros Boutros-Ghali, *Unvanquished: A US-UN Saga* (New York: Random, 1999), p.179.

3. See also James Cockayne and David M. Malone, 'Relations with the Security Council', in Chesterman, *Secretary or General?* pp. 69–85.

4. Chinmaya R. Gharekhan, *The Horseshoe Table: An Inside View of the UN Security Council* (New Delhi: Longman, 2006), p. 303.

5. David Hannay, *New World Disorder: The UN After the Cold War—An Insider's View* (London: Tauris, 2009), p. 76.

6. See generally Peter Wallensteen, *Dag Hammarskjöld* (Stockholm: Swedish Institute, 2004); Brian Urquhart, *Hammarskjöld* (New York: Knopf, 1972).

7. Cited in Urquhart, 'The Evolution of the Secretary-General', in Chesterman, *Secretary or General?* p. 27.

8. Marrack Goulding, 'The UN Secretary-General', in David M. Malone (ed.), *The UN Security Council: From the Cold War to the 21st Century* (Boulder: Lynne Rienner, 2004), p. 276.

9. See two informative biographies on Annan: Stanley Meisler, *Kofi Annan: A Man of Peace in a World of War* (Hoboken, New Jersey: Wiley, 2007); James Traub, *The Best Intentions: Kofi Annan and the UN in the Era of American World Power* (New York: Farrar, Straus, and Giroux, 2006).
10. See Traub, *The Best Intentions*.
11. See *Report of the Independent Inquiry into the actions of the United Nations during the 1994 genocide in Rwanda*, 16 December 1999, S/1999/1257; and UN document A/54/549, 15 November 1999 (Department of Peacekeeping Operations internal report on Srebrenica).
12. See, for example, Henry Anyidoho, *Guns over Kigali* (Accra: Woeli, 1999); Turid Laegreid, 'UN Peacekeeping in Rwanda', in Howard Adelman and Astri Suhrke (eds.), *The Path of a Genocide: The Rwanda Crisis, from Uganda to Zaire* (New Brunswick: Transaction, 1999), pp. 231–251; Linda Melvern, *A People Betrayed: The Role of the West in Rwanda's Genocide* (London: Zed, 2000); Gérard Prunier, *The Rwandan Crisis: History of a Genocide* (New York: Columbia University Press, 1995); Astri Suhrke, 'UN Peacekeeping in Rwanda', in Gunnar Sørbo and Peter Vale (eds.), *Out of Conflict: From War to Peace in Africa* (Uppsala: Nordiska Afrikainstitutet, 1997), pp. 97–113.
13. See, for example, Susan L. Woodward, 'The Security Council and the Wars in the Former Yugoslavia', and Rupert Smith, 'The Security Council and the Bosnian Conflict: A Practitioner's View', both in Vaughan Lowe, Adam Roberts, Jennifer Welsh, and Dominik Zaum (eds.), *The United Nations Security Council and War: The Evolution of Thought and Practice Since 1945* (Oxford: Oxford University Press, 2008), pp. 406–441 and pp. 442–451.
14. See, for example, Thomas M. Franck and Georg Nolte, 'The Good Offices Function of the UN Secretary-General', in Adam Roberts and Benedict Kingsbury (eds.), *United Nations, Divided World: The UN's Roles in International Relations*, 2nd ed. (Oxford: Clarendon, 1993); Kent J. Kille (ed.), *The UN Secretary-General and Moral Authority: Ethics and Religion in International Leadership* (Washington, DC: Georgetown University Press, 2007).
15. United Nations, *An Agenda for Peace: Preventive Diplomacy, Peacemaking, and Peace-Keeping*, Report of the Secretary-General (pursuant to the statement adopted by the Summit Meeting of the Security Council on 31 January 1992), 17 June 1992, UN Doc. A/47/277–S/24111, http://www.un.org/docs/sg/agpeace.html.
16. Marrick Goulding, *Peacemonger* (London: Murray, 2000), p. 18.
17. Quoted in Anthony F. Lang Jr., 'A Realist in the Utopian City: Boutros Boutros-Ghali's Ethical Framework and Its Impact', in Kille, *The UN Secretary-General and Moral Authority*, p. 265.
18. See Adekeye Adebajo (ed.), *From Global Apartheid to Global Village: Africa and the United Nations* (Scottsville: University of Kwazulu-Natal Press, 2009).
19. Quoted in Lang, 'A Realist in the Utopian City', p. 274.
20. This section is partly summarised from Lang, 'A Realist in the Utopian City', pp. 265–297. See United Nations, *An Agenda for Democratization* (New York, 1996).

21. Quoted in Ian Johnstone, 'The Role of the UN Secretary-General: The Power of Persuasion Based on Law', *Global Governance* 9 (2003), pp. 450–451.

22. Courtney B. Smith, 'Politics and Values at the United Nations: Kofi Annan's Balancing Act', in Kille, *The UN Secretary-General and Moral Authority*, p. 306.

23. Brian Urquhart, *A Life in Peace and War* (New York: Norton, 1987), p. 223.

24. See Cockayne and Malone, 'Relations with the Security Council', pp. 69–85.

25. Gharekhan, *The Horseshoe Table*, p. 25.

26. Stanley Meisler, 'Dateline UN: A New Hammarskjöld?' *Foreign Policy* 98 (Spring 1995), p. 186.

27. Ibid., p. 181.

28. Quoted in ibid.

29. Quoted in Ed Luck, 'The Secretary-General in a Unipolar World', in Chesterman, *Secretary or General?* p. 218.

30. Gharekhan, *The Horseshoe Table*, p. 293.

31. Madeleine Albright, *Madam Secretary* (New York: Miramax, 2003), p. 262.

32. Gharekhan, *The Horseshoe Table*, p. 224.

33. Quoted in Johnstone, 'The Role of the UN Secretary-General', p. 443.

34. Boutros-Ghali, *Unvanquished*.

35. Gharekhan, *The Horseshoe Table*, p. 248.

36. For an insightful account of this saga, see Douglas A. Yates, 'The UN Educational, Scientific, and Cultural Organisation,' in Adebajo, *From Global Apartheid to Global Village*, pp. 481–498.

37. Quoted in Gharekhan, *The Horseshoe Table*, p. 112.

38. Mats Berdal, 'Humanity's Mirror', review essay, *Survival* 50(5) (October–November 2008), p. 181.

39. Goulding, 'The UN Secretary-General', p. 272.

40. See Ali Alatas, 'Towards a New Strategic Partnership Between Asia and Africa', keynote address at the Institute of Defence and Strategic Studies conference 'Bandung Revisited: A Critical Appraisal of a Conference's Legacy', Singapore, 15 April 2005; David M. Malone and Lotta Hagman, 'The North-South Divide at the United Nations: Fading at Last?' *Security Dialogue* 33(4) (2002), pp. 399–414; Ali A. Mazrui, *Towards a Pax Africana: A Study of Ideology and Ambition* (Chicago: University of Chicago Press, 1967); Sally Morphet, 'Multilateralism and the Non-Aligned Movement: What Is the Global South Doing and Where Is It Going?' review essay, *Global Governance* 10 (2004), pp. 517–537.

41. See Mazrui, *Towards a Pax Africana*.

42. These observations are based on the author's five years at the International Peace Academy (now the International Peace Institute) in New York between 1999 and 2003 working closely with the UN.

43. See Boutros Boutros-Ghali, *Egypt's Road to Jerusalem: A Diplomat's Story of the Struggle for Peace in the Middle East* (New York: Random, 1997).

44. Goulding, 'The UN Secretary-General'.

45. Ali A. Mazrui, 'The Erosion of the State and the Decline of Race: Bismarck to Boutros; Othello to O.J. Simpson', inaugural address at the launch of the Foundation for Global Dialogue, Johannesburg, 10 August 1995, p. 9.

46. Interview with James Jonah, New York, 1999.

47. Interview with Ibrahim Gambari, New York, January 2000.

48. Confidential interviews.

49. Philip Gourevitch, 'The Optimist', *New Yorker*, 3 March 2003, p. 50.

50. Quoted in Henry Louis Gates Jr., 'Tricky Situation: A Conversation with Kofi Annan', *Transition* 10(2) (2001), p. 114.

51. Quoted in Gourevitch, 'The Optimist'.

52. Gharekhan, *The Horseshoe Table*, p. 245.

53. Linda Melvern, *A People Betrayed: The Role of the West in Rwanda's Genocide* (London: Zed, 2000), p. 93.

54. Cited in Lang, 'A Realist in the Utopian City', p. 291.

55. Quoted in William Shawcross, *Deliver Us from Evil: Peacekeepers, Warlords, and a World of Endless Conflict* (New York: Touchstone, 2000), p. 288.

56. Gourevitch, 'The Optimist'.

57. Quoted in Smith, 'Politics and Values at the United Nations', p. 300.

58. See Traub, *The Best Intentions*.

59. See James Traub, 'The Secretary-General's Political Space', in Chesterman, *Secretary or General?* pp. 185–201.

60. See United Nations *A More Secure World: Our Shared Responsibility*, Report of the High-Level Panel on Threats, Challenges, and Change, 1 December 2004, UN Doc. A/59/565, http://www.un.org/secureworld; United Nations, *In Larger Freedom: Towards Development, Security, and Human Rights for All*, 21 March 2005, UN Doc. A/59/2005, http://www.un.org/largerfreedom.

61. On UN reform, see in particular the contributions by Adekeye Adebajo, Simon Chesterman, Christopher Landsberg, and David M. Malone in the special edition of *Security Dialogue* 36(3) (2005). See also Mats Berdal, 'The UN's Unnecessary Crisis', *Survival* 47(3) (2005), pp. 7–32; Adekeye Adebajo and Helen Scanlon (eds.), *A Dialogue of the Deaf: Africa and the United Nations* (Johannesburg: Jacana, 2006).

62. See Traub, *The Best Intentions*; Meisler, *Kofi Annan*.

63. Traub, *The Best Intentions*.

64. Ian Williams, 'Oil for Food: A Hell of a Scandal', *Asia Times*, 1 April 2005.

65. John Bolton, *Surrender Is Not an Option: Defending America at the United Nations and Abroad* (New York: Threshold, 2007), p. 273.

66. Meryl Gordon, 'No Peace for Kofi: A Father's Burden', *New York Times*, 2 May 2005.

67. See Traub, *The Best Intentions*.

68. 'Nobel Peace Prize 2001' (Oslo: Norwegian Nobel Committee, 12 October 2001), http://nobelprize.org/peace/laureates/2001/press.html.

5. MESSIAH OR MERCANTILIST? SOUTH AFRICA IN AFRICA

1. An earlier version of this chapter appeared in *South African Journal of International Affairs* 14(1) (Summer–Autumn 2007). I thank Dianna Games, Chris Landsberg, Khabele Matlosa, Chris Saunders, and an anonymous reviewer for extremely useful comments on that earlier version.

2. James Barber and John Barrett, *South Africa's Foreign Policy: The Search For Status and Security 1945–1988* (Cambridge: Cambridge University Press, 1990).

3. See Adebayo Adedeji, 'Within or Apart?' in Adebayo Adedeji (ed .), *South Africa in Africa: Within or Apart?* (London: Zed, 1996), pp. 3–28.

4. For a general overview, see Adekeye Adebajo, Adebayo Adedeji, and Chris Landsberg (eds.), *South Africa in Africa: The Post-Apartheid Era* (Scottsville: University of Kwazulu-Natal Press, 2007); Chris Alden and Garth Le Pere, *South Africa's Post-Apartheid Foreign Policy: From Reconciliation to Revival?* Adelphi Paper no. 362 (London: Institute for Strategic Studies, 2003); Chris Landsberg, 'Promoting Democracy: The Mandela-Mbeki Doctrine', *Journal of Democracy* 11(3) (July 2000), pp. 107–121; Elizabeth Sidiropoulos (ed.), *South Africa's Foreign Policy, 1994–2004: Apartheid Past, Renaissance Future* (Johannesburg: South African Institute of International Affairs, 2004).

5. See James Barber, *Mandela's World: The International Dimension of South Africa's Political Revolution, 1990–99* (Cape Town: David Philip, 2004); Adam Habib and Nthakeng Selinyane, 'South Africa's Foreign Policy and a Realistic Vision of an African Century', and Jack Spence, 'South Africa's Foreign Policy: Vision and Reality', both in Sidiropoulos, *South Africa's Foreign Policy*, pp. 49–60 and 35–48; Maxi Schoeman, 'South Africa as an Emerging Middle Power, 1994–2003', in John Daniel, Adam Habib, and Roger Southall (eds.), *The State of the Nation: South Africa 2003–2004* (Cape Town: Human Sciences Research Council Press, 2003), pp. 349–367.

6. See, for example, Adekeye Adebajo and Chris Landsberg, 'South Africa and Nigeria as Regional Hegemons', in Mwesiga Baregu and Chris Landsberg(eds.), *From Cape to Congo: Southern Africa's Evolving Security Challenges* (Boulder: Lynne Rienner, 2003), pp. 171–203; Paul Kennedy, *The Rise and Fall of the Great Powers* (New York: Vintage, 1987), pp. 151–158; Ali A. Mazrui, 'Hegemony: From Semites to Anglo-Saxons', in *Cultural Forces in World Politics* (London: Currey, 1990), pp. 29–64.

7. Tony Smith, *The Pattern of Imperialism: The United States, Great Britain, and the Late Industrializing World Since 1815* (New York: Cambridge University Press, 1981), p. 6.

8. I owe this expression to Mazrui, 'Hegemony: From Semites to Anglo-Saxons', p. 30.

9. See, for example, Niall Ferguson, *Empire: How Britain Made the Modern World* (London: Penguin, 2003); Mazrui, *Cultural Forces in World Politics;* James Morris, *Pax Britannica* (London: Harvest, 1968).

10. Quoted in Wm. Roger Louis, *Ends of British Imperialism: The Scramble for Empire, Suez, and Decolonization* (London: Tauris, 2006), p. 964.

11. See Bernard Magubane, *The Making of a Racist State: British Imperialism and the Union of South Africa, 1875–1910* (Asmara: Africa World Press, 1996); Paul Maylam, *The Cult of Rhodes: Remembering an Imperialist in Africa* (Cape Town: David Philip, 2005); Robert Rotberg, *The Founders: Cecil Rhodes and the Pursuit of Power* (Johannesburg: Jonathan Ball, 2002); Stanlake Samkange, *On Trial for My Country* (London: Heinemann, 1967); Antony Thomas, *Rhodes: The Race for Africa* (Johannesburg: Jonathan Ball, 1996).

12. Quoted in Sam Nolutshungu, *South Africa in Africa: A Study in Ideology and Foreign Policy* (Manchester: Manchester University Press, 1975), p. 298.

13. Nolutshungu, *South Africa in Africa*, p. 51.

14. Barber and Barrett, *South Africa's Foreign Policy*, p. 6.

15. Quoted in ibid., p. 2.

16. Nolutshungu, *South Africa in Africa*, p. 127.

17. Barber and Barrett, *South Africa's Foreign Policy*, pp. 2–3.

18. See Nolutshungu, *South Africa in Africa*, pp. 60–77.

19. Adedeji, 'Within or Apart?' p. 21.

20. See Colin McCarthy, 'SACU and the Rand Zone', in Daniel C. Bach (ed.), *Regionalisation in Africa: Integration and Disintegration* (Oxford: Currey, 1999), pp. 159–168; Nolutshungu, *South Africa in Africa;* James Sidaway and Richard Gibb, 'SADC, COMESA, SACU: Contradictory Formats for Regional Integration in Southern Africa?' in David Simon (ed.), *South Africa in Southern Africa: Reconfiguring the Region* (Oxford: Currey, 1998), pp. 164–184.

21. Barber and Barrett, *South Africa's Foreign Policy*, p. 10.

22. Rodney Davenport and Christopher Saunders, *South Africa: A Modern History*, 5th ed. (London: Macmillan, 2000), p. 538.

23. See, for example, William Minter, *Apartheid's Contras: An Inquiry into the Roots of War in Angola and Mozambique* (London: Zed, 1994).

24. Adedeji, 'Within or Apart?' p. 9.

25. Quoted in Vladimir Shubin, *The Hot 'Cold War': The USSR in Southern Africa* (London: Pluto Press; and Scottsville: University of Kwazulu-Natal Press, 2008), p. 105.

26. Peter Vale, *Security and Politics in South Africa: The Regional Dimension* (Boulder: Lynne Rienner, 2003), p. 110.

27. See J.S. Crush and David A. McDonald, introduction to 'Special Issue: Evaluating South African Immigration Policy After Apartheid', *Africa Today* 48(1) (Fall 2001), pp. 1–13; Zimitri Erasmus, 'Race and Identity in the Nation', in John Daniel, Roger Southall, and Jessica Lutchman (eds.), *State of the Nation: South Africa 2004–2005* (Cape Town: Human Sciences Research Council, 2005), pp. 15–19; Audie Klotz, 'Migration After Apartheid: Deracialising South African Foreign Policy', *Third World Quarterly* 21(5) (2000), pp. 831–847; Sally Peberdy, *Selecting Immigrants:National Identity and South Africa's Immigration Policies, 1910–2008* (Johannesburg: Witwatersrand University Press, 2009).

28. Crush and McDonald, introduction to 'Special Issue', p. 6.

29. Cited in Erasmus, 'Race and Identity in the Nation', p. 18.

30. Barber, *Mandela's World*, p. 173.

31. Nelson Mandela, 'South Africa's Future Foreign Policy', *Foreign Affairs* 72(5) (1993), pp. 86–94.

32. Adebajo, Adedeji, and Landsberg, *South Africa in Africa*.

33. Ali A. Mazrui, *A Tale of Two Africas: Nigeria and South Africa as Contrasting Visions* (London: Adonis and Abbey, 2006), p. 190.

34. Barber, *Mandela's World*, p. 177. See also Len Le Roux, 'The Post-Apartheid South African Military: Transforming with the Nation', in Martin Rupiya (ed.),

Evolutions and Revolutions: A Contemporary History of Militaries in Southern Africa (Tshwane: Institute for Security Studies, 2005), pp. 235–266.

35. See Khabele Matlosa, 'The Lesotho Conflict: Major Causes and Management', and Roger Southall, 'Is Lesotho South Africa's Tenth Province?' both in Kato Lambrechts (ed.), *Crisis in Lesotho: The Challenge of Managing Conflict in Southern Africa*, African Dialogue Series no. 2 (Johannesburg: Foundation for Global Dialogue, March 1999), pp. 6–10 and 19–25.

36. Vale, *Security and Politics in South Africa*, p. 132.

37. Alden and Le Pere, *South Africa's Post-Apartheid Foreign Policy*, p. 32. See also Walter Carlsnaes and Philip Nel (eds.), *In Full Flight: South African Foreign Policy After Apartheid* (Midrand: Institute for Global Dialogue, 2006); Roger Southall (ed.), *South Africa's Role in Conflict Resolution and Peacemaking in Africa* (Cape Town: Human Sciences Research Council, 2006).

38. For a rich comparison of the foreign policy styles of Mandela and Mbeki, see Landsberg, 'Promoting Democracy'; Chris Landsberg, *The Quiet Diplomacy of Liberation: International Politics and South Africa's Transition* (Johannesburg: Jacana, 2004).

39. See Peter Kagwanja, 'Cry Sovereignty: South Africa in the UN Security Council, 2007/2008', in Peter Kagwanja and Kwandiwe Kondlo (eds.), *State of the Nation: South Africa 2008* (Cape Town: Human Sciences Research Council, 2009), pp. 275–302.

40. The preceding four paragraphs are based on Adekeye Adebajo, 'Time for SA Diplomats to Get Real', *Mail and Guardian*, 5–11 June 2009, p. 17.

41. See, for example, Mahmood Mamdani, 'There Can Be No African Renaissance Without an Africa-Focused Intelligentsia', in William Malegapuru Makgoba (ed.), *African Renaissance* (Cape Town: Mafube and Tafelberg, 1999), pp. 125–134.

42. See, for example, Annie E. Coombes, *History After Apartheid: Visual Culture and Public Memory in a Democratic South Africa* (Johannesburg: Wits University Press, 2004).

43. Rhoda Kadalie, 'Silence Around Murder of Somalis Speaks Volumes', *BusinessDay*, 7 September 2006, p. 13.

44. See *Report of the APRM Country Support Mission to South Africa, 9–11 November 2005* (Midrand, South Africa: APRM Secretariat, 2005).

45. See, for example, Shireen Hassim, Tawana Kupe, and Eric Worby (eds.), *Go Home or Die Here: Violence, Xenophobia, and the Reinvention of Difference in South Africa* (Johannesburg: Wits University Press, 2008).

46. Barber, *Mandela's World*, p. 179.

47. John Daniel, Varusha Naidoo, and Sanusha Naidu, '"The South Africans Have Arrived": Post Apartheid Corporate Expansion into Africa', in Daniel, Habib, and Southall, *The State of the Nation*, pp. 376–377.

48. John Daniel, Jessica Lutchman, and Sanusha Naidu, 'South Africa and Nigeria: Two Unequal Centres in a Periphery', in Daniel, Southall, and Lutchman, *State of the Nation*, pp. 544–568.

49. This is summarized from the insightful article by John Daniel and Nompumelelo Bhengu, 'South Africa in Africa: Still a Formidable Player', in Roger Southall

and Henning Melber (eds.), *A New Scramble for Africa? Imperialism, Investment, and Development* (Scottsville: University of Kwazulu-Natal Press, 2009), pp. 139–164.

50. Daniel, Naidoo, and Naidu, "'The South Africans Have Arrived'", p. 368.

51. South African Department of Foreign Affairs (Policy, Research, and Analysis Unit), 'A Strategic Appraisal of South Africa's Foreign Policy in Advancing the Agenda of Africa and the South', draft discussion paper compiled for the Heads of Mission Conference, Cape Town, 17–21 February 2005.

52. Barber and Barrett, *South Africa's Foreign Policy*, p. 124.

53. I thank Chris Landsberg for this important insight.

54. For an assessment of South African foreign policy after Mbeki, see Elizabeth Sidiropoulos, 'South African Foreign Policy in the Post-Mbeki Period', *South African Journal of International Affairs* 15(2) December 2008, pp. 107–120.

55. The two preceding paragraphs are summarized from Adekeye Adebajo, 'The G-20: Saying Farewell to the "Blue-Eyed Blond Men"'? *BusinessDay*, 14 April 2009, p. 11.

56. Maureen Isaacson, 'The Man with the President's Ear and the African Agenda', *Sunday Independent* (South Africa), 7 June 2009, p. 6.

57. Quoted in Moshoshoe Monare, 'Africa Will Top the Foreign Policy To-Do List', *Sunday Independent* (South Africa), 17 May 2009, p. 11.

58. Monare, 'Africa Will Top the Foreign Policy To-Do List', p. 11.

59. Isaacson, 'The Man with the President's Ear and the African Agenda', p. 6.

60. This section is a summary from Adekeye Adebajo, 'The Bicycle Strategy of South Africa's Bilateral Relations in Africa', *South African Journal of International Affairs* 15(2) (December 2008), pp. 121–136.

61. Sharath Srinivasan, 'A Marriage Less Convenient: China, Sudan, and Darfur', in Kweku Ampiah and Sanusha Naidu (eds.), *Crouching Tiger, Hidden Dragon? Africa and China* (Scottsville: University of Kwazulu-Natal Press, 2008), p. 61.

62. See Joseph Nye Jr., *Soft Power: The Means to Success in the World of Politics* (New York: PublicAffairs, 2004).

63. McCarthy, 'SACU and the Rand Zone', p. 161.

64. See the very informative article by Richard Gibb, 'The New Southern African Customs Union Agreement: Dependence with Democracy', *Journal of Southern African Studies* 32(3) (September 2006), pp. 583–603.

65. See the insightful article by two policy experts in South Africa's Department of Trade and Industry, Simon Qobo and Joseph Senona, 'Naïve and Unfair to Cast SA as Villain in EU/SACU Drama', *BusinessDay*, 11 June 2009, p. 9. See also Mathabo Le Roux, 'Threat of Regional Upheaval If SA Torpedoes Customs Union', *BusinessDay*, 8 June 2009, pp. 1–2.

66. Adedeji, 'Within or Apart?' p. 21.

67. See Adedeji, 'Within or Apart?'.

6. GULLIVER'S TROUBLES: NIGERIA IN AFRICA

1. An earlier version of this chapter appeared in Adekeye Adebajo and Raufu Mustapha (eds.), *Gulliver's Troubles: Nigeria's Foreign Policy After the Cold War* (Scotts-

ville: University of Kwazulu-Natal Press, 2008). I am immensely grateful to Martin Uhomoibhi, Darren Kew, and Kaye Whiteman for extremely useful comments on the earlier version of this chapter that greatly helped to sharpen my ideas and to avoid errors of fact and judgement.

2. Adebayo Adedeji, 'ECOWAS: A Retrospective Journey', in Adekeye Adebajo and Ismail Rashid (eds.), *West Africa's Security Challenges: Building Peace in a Troubled Region* (Boulder: Lynne Rienner, 2004), p. 46.

3. See 'Report of the Review Committee on Nigeria's External Relations', June 1976.

4. See Chinua Achebe, *Things Fall Apart* (Ibadan: Heinemann, 1958); Chinua Achebe, *No Longer at Ease* (Ibadan: Heinemann, 1960).

5. See Jonathan Swift, *Gulliver's Travels*, ed. Paul Turner (Oxford: Oxford University Press, 1986). The title of this chapter also borrows from Stanley Hoffman, *Gulliver's Troubles; Or, the Setting of American Foreign Policy* (New York: McGraw, 1968).

6. Ali A. Mazrui, *A Tale of Two Africas: Nigeria and South Africa as Contrasting Visions* (London: Adonis and Abbey, 2006), p. 154.

7. See, for example, Toyin Falola, and Matthew M. Heathon, *A History of Nigeria* (Cambridge: Cambridge University Press, 2008).

8. 'Big Men, Big Fraud, and Big Trouble', *The Economist*, 28 April 2007, p. 46.

9. Chukwuma C. Soludo, preface to Paul Collier, Chukwuma C. Soludo, and Catherine Pattillo (eds.), *Economic Policy Options for a Prosperous Nigeria* (Hampshire: Palgrave Macmillan, 2008), p. xiv.

10. 'Big Men, Big Fraud, and Big Trouble'.

11. Andrew Apter, *The Pan-African Nation: Oil and the Spectacle of Culture in Nigeria* (Chicago: University of Chicago Press, 2005), p. 247.

12. Figures cited in an insightful article by Adigun Agbaje, Adeolu Akande, and Jide Ojo, 'Nigeria's Ruling Party: A Complex Web of Power and Money', *South African Journal of International Affairs* 14(1) (Summer–Autumn 2007), p. 93.

13. Herman J. Cohen, 'Fooling People Some of the Time', *International Herald Tribune*, 15 February 2007, p. 6.

14. Prasad V.S.N. Tallapragada and B.S. Adebusuyi, 'Nigeria's Power Sector: Opportunities and Challenges', in Collier, Soludo, and Pattillo, *Economic Policy Options for a Prosperous Nigeria*, pp. 301–302.

15. Sola Odunfa, 'Time to Move Out', *BBC Focus on Africa*, April–June 2007, p. 24.

16. Agbaje, Akande, and Ojo, 'Nigeria's Ruling Party', p. 79.

17. Quoted in Patrick Laurence, 'Mbeki's Approval of Nigerian Poll Bodes Ill for Zimbabwe', *Sunday Independent* (South Africa), 6 May 2007, p. 8.

18. 'Democracy by Court Order', *The Economist*, 26 January 2008, p. 63.

19. See, for example, Oladapo Fafowora, 'The Unsung Player: The Nigerian Diplomat and the Foreign Service', in Adebajo and Mustapha, *Gulliver's Troubles*, pp. 81–95.

20. See Neil Ford, 'Economy in Best Shape for Years', *African Business*, October 2006, pp. 40–41; U. Joy Ogwu and W.O. Alli (eds.), *Debt Relief and Nigeria's Diplomacy* (Lagos: Nigerian Institute of International Affairs, 2006).

21. Paul Collier, Chukwuma C. Soludo, and Catherine Pattillo, 'Introduction: Towards Evidence-Based Policy', in Collier, Soludo, and Pattillo, *Economic Policy Options for a Prosperous Nigeria*, p. 6.

22. See Neil Ford, 'Will Bank Reforms Trigger Golden Era?' *African Business*, March 2006, pp. 44–45.

23. 'Big Men, Big Fraud, and Big Trouble'.

24. See, for example, Toye Olori and Paul Adams, 'Is Nigeria's Anti–Corruption Crusade for Real?' *eAfrica* (South African Institute of International Affairs), May 2005, http://www.saiia.org.za.

25. Dianna Games, 'Nigeria's Economy Can Fly Even As Democracy Limps', *Business-Day*, 7 May 2007, p. 9.

26. Dele Olojede, 'Nigeria's Best from a Bad Job', *Sunday Times* (South Africa), 13 May 2007, p. 29.

27. I thank Martin Uhomoibhi for this observation.

28. See Yemi Kolapo and John Alechenu, 'Nigerians Abroad Remit $8bn in Six Months', *The Punch* online, 18 July 2007, http://www.punchng.com/articl.aspx?theartic=art200707183245942. See also Ebere Onwudiwe, *The Question of Diaspora in Nigeria's International Relations*, Occasional Paper no. 2 (Lagos: Nigerian Institute of International Affairs, 2006).

29. See Sola Odunfa's insightful piece 'General Decline', *BBC Focus on Africa*, July–September 2006, p. 13; see also Cohen, 'Fooling People Some of the Time', p. 6.

30. Quoted in Odunfa, 'General Decline', p. 13.

31. See, for example, 'How Bribery Got Into the National Assembly, by Vice-President', *The Guardian* (Nigeria) online, 23 May 2007, pp. 1–3, http://www.guardiannewsngr.com.

32. See, for example, Larry Diamond, Anthony Kirk-Greene, and Oyeleye Oyediran (eds.) *Transition Without End: Nigerian Politics and Civil Society under Babangida* (Boulder: Lynne Rienner, 1997); Richard Joseph, *Democracy and Prebendal Politics in Nigeria: The Rise and Fall of the Second Republic* (Cambridge: Cambridge University Press, 1987); Eghosa E. Osaghae, *Nigeria Since Independence: Crippled Giant* (Bloomington: Indiana University Press, 1998); and Shehu Othman and Gavin Williams, 'Politics, Power and Democracy in Nigeria', in Jonathan Hyslop (ed.), *African Democracy in the Era of Globalisation*, (Johannesburg: Witwatersrand University Press, 1999), pp. 15–71.

33. See Karl Maier, *This House Has Fallen: Midnight in Nigeria* (New York: PublicAffairs, 2000).

34. See Benedict Anderson, *Imagined Communities* (London: Verso, 1983).

35. Patrick Utomi, 'Nigeria as an Economic Powerhouse: Can It Be Achieved?' in Robert Rotberg (ed.), *Crafting the New Nigeria: Confronting the Challenges* (Boulder: Lynne Rienner, 2004), p. 128.

36. See Ali A. Mazrui, 'Shari'ahcracy and Federal Models in the Era of Globalization: Nigeria in Comparative Perspective', in Alamin Mazrui and Willy Mutunga (eds.), *Governance and Leadership: Debating the African Condition, Mazrui, and His Critics*, vol. 2 (Asmara: Africa World Press, 2003), pp. 261–276; John N. Paden, *Muslim Civic Cultures and Conflict Resolution: The Challenges of Demo-*

cratic Federalism in Nigeria (Washington, DC: Brookings Institution, 2005), pp. 13–36.

37. I thank Ali Mazrui for this expression.

38. Wole Soyinka, *You Must Set Forth at Dawn: Memoirs* (Ibadan: Bookcraft, 2006), p. 219.

39. Cited in Raufu Mustapha, 'Nigeria After the April 2007 Elections: What Next?' paper presented to the Royal African Society, London, 31 May 2007.

40. Mohammed Haruna and Leonard Lawal, 'Family Wars', *Africa Report* no. 16 (April–May 2009), p. 20.

41. Quoted in Odunfa, 'General Decline', p. 13.

42. This summary is based largely on 'Nigeria's Economy: A Double Strike', *The Economist*, 14–20 March 2009, pp. 54–55.

43. This section is based partly on Adekeye Adebajo, *Liberia's Civil War: Nigeria, ECOMOG, and Regional Security in West Africa* (Boulder: Lynne Rienner, 2002), pp. 43–48.

44. See Bolaji Akinyemi, *Foreign Policy and Federalism* (Ibadan: Ibadan University Press, 1974).

45. Personal interviews with diplomatic and military officials on a research trip to Burkina Faso, Côte d'Ivoire, Guinea, Liberia, Nigeria, and Sierra Leone in July and August 1999.

46. Interview with Sule Lamido, 'I Will Surprise My Critics', *ThisDay*, 8 August 1999, p. 10.

47. See Charles Dokubo, 'Nigeria's International Peacekeeping and Peacebuilding Efforts in Africa, 1960–2005', and Julie Sanda, 'Nigeria's International Peacekeeping Efforts Outside of Africa, 1960–2005', both in Bola Akinterinwa (ed.), *Nigeria and the United Nations Security Council* (Ibadan: Vantage, 2005), pp. 251–269 and pp. 271–292.

48. See, for example, Paul Kennedy, *The Rise and Fall of the Great Powers* (New York: Vintage, 1987), pp. 151–158; Ali A. Mazrui, 'Hegemony: From Semites to Anglo-Saxons', in *Cultural Forces in World Politics* (New Hampshire and Nairobi: Heinemann; London: James Currey, 1990), pp. 29–64; Joseph Nye Jr., *Bound to Lead: The Changing Nature of American Power* (New York: Basic Books, 1990).

49. Quoted in Gabriel Olusanya and Raufu Akindele, 'The Fundamentals of Nigeria's Foreign Policy and External Economic Relations', in G.O. Olusanya and R.A. Akindele (eds.), *Nigeria's External Relations: The First Twenty-Five Years* (Ibadan: University Press, 1986), p. 7.

50. Dayo Oluyemi–Kusa, 'Refugees and Internally-Displaced Persons in Nigeria,' in Bola A. Akinterinwa (ed.), *Nigeria's New Foreign Policy Thrust: Essays in Honour of Ambassador Oluyemi Adeniji* (Ibadan: Vantage, 2004), p. 288.

51. See, for example, Ibrahim A. Gambari, 'From Balewa to Obasanjo: The Theory and Practice of Nigeria's Foreign Policy', in Adebajo and Mustapha, *Gulliver's Troubles*, pp. 58–80.

52. See, for example, Akinjide Osuntokun, 'Gulliver and the Lilliputians: Nigeria and Its Neighbours,' in Adebajo and Mustapha, *Gulliver's Troubles*, pp. 141–159.

53. See Ibrahim A. Gambari, *Theory and Reality in Foreign Policy Making: Nigeria After the Second Republic* (Atlantic Highlands, NJ: Humanities Press International, 1989), p. 21.

54. See, for example, Ike Okonta and Oronto Douglas, *Where Vultures Feast: Shell, Human Rights, and Oil* (London: Verso, 2003); Maier, *This House Has Fallen.*

55. Odunfa, 'Time to Move Out', p. 24.

56. See, for example, Kate Meagher, 'New Regionalism or Loose Cannon? Nigeria's Role in Informal Economic Networks and Integration in West Africa', in Adebajo and Mustapha, *Gulliver's Troubles*, pp. 160–176.

57. Collier, Soludo, and Pattillo, introduction to *Economic Policy Options for a Prosperous Nigeria*, p. 4.

58. William M. Gumede, Vincent Nwanma, and Patrick Smith, 'The Giants Tussle for Influence', *Africa Report* no. 3 (July 2006), p. 20.

59. See Adekeye Adebajo, 'Mad Dogs and Glory: Nigeria's Interventions in Liberia and Sierra Leone', Adebajo and Mustapha, *Gulliver's Troubles*, pp. 177–202.

60. See, for example, Adekeye Adebajo, *Building Peace in West Africa: Liberia, Sierra Leone, and Guinea-Bissau* (Boulder: Lynne Rienner, 2002).

61. I thank Raufu Mustapha for these observations.

62. On Olusegun Obasanjo's foreign policy, see Akinterinwa, *Nigeria's New Foreign Policy Thrust;* U. Joy Ogwu (ed.), *New Horizons for Nigeria in World Affairs* (Lagos: Nigerian Institute of International Affairs, 2005); U. Joy Ogwu and W.O. Alli (comps.), *Years of Reconstruction: Selected Foreign Policy Speeches of Olusegun Obasanjo* (Lagos: Nigerian Institute of International Affairs, 2007); Presidential Advisory Council on International Relations, *Foreign Policy in Nigeria's Democratic Transition* (Abuja, 2005).

63. See Ehiedu E.G. Iweriebor, and Martin I. Uhomoibhi, *UN Security Council: A Case for Nigeria's Membership* (New York: Times Books, 1999).

64. See Martin I. Uhomoibhi, 'A Triple Web of Interdependence: The UN, the Commonwealth, and the EU', in Adebajo and Mustapha, *Gulliver's Troubles*, pp. 223–254.

65. See, for example, John Chipman, *French Power in Africa* (Oxford: Blackwell, 1989); Guy Martin, 'Francophone Africa in the Context of Franco-African Relations'. in John Harbeson and Donald Rothchild (eds.), *Africa in World Politics: Post–Cold War Challenges*, 2nd ed. (Boulder: Westview, 1995), pp. 163–188; Kaye Whiteman and Douglas Yates, 'France, Britain, and the United States', in Adebajo and Rashid, *West Africa's Security Challenges*, pp. 349–379.

66. See Kaye Whiteman, 'The Switchback and the Fallback: Nigeria/Britain Relations', in Adebajo and Mustapha, *Gulliver's Troubles*, pp. 255–280.

67. See, for example, Wm. Roger Louis, 'The Suez Crisis and the British Dilemma at the United Nations', in Vaughan Lowe, Adam Roberts, Jennifer Welsh and Dominik Zaum, eds., *The United Nations Security Council and War: The Evolution of Thought and Practice since 1945* (Oxford: Oxford University Press, 2008), pp. 280–297.

68. See Gwendolyn Mikell, 'Players, Policies, and Prospects: Nigeria/US Relations', in Adebajo and Mustapha, *Gulliver's Troubles*, pp. 281–313; John N. Paden, *Faith*

and Politics in Nigeria: Nigeria as a Pivotal State in the Muslim World (Washington, DC: US Institute of Peace, 2008).

69. See Sharath Srinivasan, 'A Rising "Great Power" Embraces Africa: Nigeria/China Relations', in Adebajo and Mustapha, *Gulliver's Troubles*, pp. 334–366; Ndubisi Obiorah, Darren Kew, and Yusuf Tanko, '"Peaceful Rise" and Human Rights: China's Expanding Relations with Nigeria', in Robert I. Rotberg (ed.), *China Into Africa: Trade, Aid, and Influence* (Washington, DC: Brookings Institution, 2008), pp. 272–295.

70. See Joseph Nye Jr., *Soft Power: The Means to Success in the World of Politics* (New York: PublicAffairs, 2004).

71. Apter, *The Pan-African Nation*, p. 54.

72. See Adekeye Adebajo, 'Abuja', *Newswatch*, vol. 2 no. 23, 3 June 1996, pp. 8–9.

73. See Pierre Barrot (ed.), *Nollywood: The Video Phenomenon in Nigeria* (Oxford: Currey, 2008); Trenton Daniel, 'Nollywood Confidential Part 2: A Conversation with Zeb Ejiro, Ajoke Jacobs, Tunde Kelani, and Aquila Njamah', *Transition* 13(1) (2004), pp. 110–128; John C. McCall, 'Nollywood Confidential: The Unlikely Rise of Nigeria's Video Film', *Transition* 13(1) (2004), pp. pp. 98–109; Odia Ofeimum, 'In Defence of the Films We Have Made', *Chimurenga* no. 8 (2006), pp. 44–54.

74. 'Nollywood Dreams', *The Economist*, 29 July 2006, pp. 58–59.

75. See, for example, Ofeimum, 'In Defence of the Films We Have Made'.

76. See Adekeye Adebajo, 'Whither Nigeria's Foreign Policy?' *Tell*, 23 August 1999, pp. 48–49.

77. This memorable phrase was coined by Gabriel Olusanya, former director-general of the Nigerian Institute of International Affairs. 'Area boys' are thuggish local youths. See also Tunde Asaju and Dotun Oladipo, 'Ikimi's Jungle Diplomacy', *Newswatch*, 28 September 1998, pp. 8–16.

7. AN AXIS OF VIRTUE? SOUTH AFRICA AND NIGERIA IN AFRICA

1. This chapter builds on Adekeye Adebajo, 'South Africa and Nigeria: An Axis of Virtue?' in Adekeye Adebajo, Adebayo Adedeji, and Chris Landsberg (eds.), *South Africa in Africa: The Post-Apartheid Era* (Scottsville: University of Kwazulu-Natal Press, 2007), pp. 213–235. I thank Dianna Games for extremely useful comments on an earlier version of this chapter.

2. Quoted in Solomon O. Akinboye, 'From Confrontation to Strategic Partnership: Nigeria's Relations with South Africa, 1960–2000', in U. Joy Ogwu (ed.), *New Horizons for Nigeria in World Affairs* (Lagos: Nigerian Institute for International Affairs, 2005), p. 217.

3. Adekeye Adebajo, 'Tale of Two Giants', *Newswatch*, 11 September 1995, pp. 9–10. See also Adekeye Adebajo and Chris Landsberg, 'Trading Places: Nigeria and South Africa', *Indicator* 3(13) (Winter 1996), pp. 64–68.

4. See, for example, John Chipman, *French Power in Africa* (Oxford: Basil Blackwell, 1989). See also Guy Martin, 'Francophone Africa in the Context of Franco-African

Relations', in John Harbeson and Donald Rothchild (eds.), *Africa in World Politics: Post–Cold War Challenges*, 2nd ed. (Boulder: Westview, 1989), pp. 163–188; Kaye Whiteman and Douglas Yates, 'France, Britain, and the US', in Adekeye Adebajo and Ismail Rashid (eds.), *West Africa's Security Challenges: Building Peace in a Troubled Region* (Boulder: Lynne Rienner, 2004), pp. 349–379.

5. See, for example, Adebayo Adedeji, 'ECOWAS: A Retrospective Journey', and S.K.B. Asante, 'The Travails of Integration', both in Adebajo and Rashid, *West Africa's Security Challenges*, pp. 21–49 and 51–68.

6. The 15 ECOWAS states are: Benin, Burkina Faso, Cape Verde, Côte d'Ivoire, Gambia, Ghana, Guinea, Guinea-Bissau, Liberia, Mali, Niger, Nigeria, Sierra Leone, Senegal and Togo.

7. See, for example, James Barber and John Barrett, *South Africa's Foreign Policy: The Search For Status and Security 1945–1988* (Cambridge: Cambridge University Press, 1990). See also Deon Geldenhuys, *The Diplomacy of Isolation: South African Foreign Policy Making* (Johannesburg: Macmillan, 1994); Sam Nolutshungu, *South Africa in Africa: A Study in Ideology and Foreign Policy* (Manchester: Manchester University Press, 1975).

8. The nine founding members of SADCC were Angola, Botswana, Lesotho, Malawi, Mozambique, Swaziland, Tanzania, Zambia, and Zimbabwe.

9. Mark Gevisser, *Thabo Mbeki: The Dream Deferred* (Johannesburg: Jonathan Ball, 2007), p. 375.

10. Quoted in ibid., p. 376.

11. See, for example, Andrew Apter, *The Pan-African Nation: Oil and the Spectacle of Culture in Nigeria* (Chicago: University of Chicago Press, 2005).

12. Akinboye, 'From Confrontation to Strategic Partnership', p. 215.

13. James Barber, *Mandela's World: The International Dimension of South Africa's Political Revolution, 1990–99* (Cape Town: David Philip, 2004), p. 110.

14. Barber, *Mandela's World*, p. 64.

15. Wole Soyinka, *King Baabu* (London: Methuen, 2004).

16. See Ifeanyi Ezeugo, *Abacha: Another Evil Genius?* (Lagos: El-Rophekah International, 1998). See also Chuks Illoegbunam, 'A Stubborn Dictator', *The Guardian* (London), 9 June 1998, p. 16. See also Eghosa E. Osaghae, *Nigeria Since Independence: Crippled Giant* (Bloomington: Indiana University Press, 1998), pp. 273–310.

17. See Kader Asmal, David Chidester, and Wilmot James (eds.), *South Africa's Nobel Laureates: Peace, Literature, and Science* (Johannesburg: Jonathan Ball, 2004), pp. 74–100. See also Tom Lodge, *Mandela: A Critical Life* (Oxford: Oxford University Press, 2006); Nelson Mandela, *Long Walk to Freedom*, (New York: Little, Brown, 1994); Anthony Sampson, *Mandela: The Authorised Biography* (London: HarperCollins, 1999).

18. See Adewale 'Segun Banjo, 'South Africa's Policy Toward Nigeria: 1994–2004', unpublished paper (n.d.). See also Barber, *Mandela's World*, pp. 108–110; Paul-Henri Bischoff and Roger Southall, 'The Early Foreign Policy of the Democratic South Africa', in Stephen Wright (ed.), *African Foreign Policies*, (Boulder: Westview, 1999), pp. 172–173; Maxi van Aardt, 'A Foreign Policy to Die For:

South Africa's Response to the Nigerian Crisis', *Africa Insight* 2(26) (1996), pp. 107–117.

19. Banjo, 'South Africa's Policy Toward Nigeria', p. 8.

20. Emeka Anyaoku, *The Inside Story of the Modern Commonwealth* (London: Evans Brothers, 2004), p. 162.

21. Quoted in Banjo, 'South Africa's Policy Toward Nigeria', p. 14.

22. Cited in van Aardt, 'A Foreign Policy to Die For', p. 112.

23. Confidential interview.

24. Banjo, 'South Africa's Policy Toward Nigeria', p. 15.

25. Personal interview with Ambassador George Nene, former High Commissioner of South Africa to Nigeria, Pretoria, 22 July 2004.

26. Osaghae, *Nigeria Since Independence*, p. 309.

27. Quoted in Barber, *Mandela's World*, p. 110.

28. Ibid.

29. See, for example, Chris Alden and Garth Le Pere, *South Africa's Post-Apartheid Foreign Policy: From Reconciliation to Revival?* Adelphi Paper no. 362 (London: Institute for Strategic Studies, 2003). See also Chris Landsberg, *The Quiet Diplomacy of Liberation: International Politics and South Africa's Transition* (Johannesburg: Jacana, 2004); Lloyd Sachikonye, 'South Africa's Quiet Diplomacy: The Case of Zimbabwe', in John Daniel, Roger Southall, and Jessica Lutchman (eds.), *State of the Nation: South Africa 2004–2005* (Cape Town: Human Sciences Research Council, 2005), pp. 569–585.

30. I thank Chris Landsberg for this insight.

31. See Mark Gevisser, *Thabo Mbeki: The Dream Deferred* (Johannesburg: Jonathan Ball, 2007); William Mervin Gumede, *Thabo Mbeki and the Battle for the Soul of the ANC* (Cape Town: Zebra, 2005); Adrian Hadland and Jovial Rantao, *The Life and Times of Thabo Mbeki* (Rivonia: Zebra, 1999). See also Sean Jacobs and Richard Calland (eds.), *Thabo Mbeki's World: The Politics and Ideology of the South African President* (Pietermaritzburg: University of Natal Press, 2002); Lucy Mathebe, *Bound by Tradition: The World of Thabo Mbeki* (Tshwane: UNISA Press, 2001); Mukanda Mulemfo, *Thabo Mbeki and the African Renaissance* (Pretoria: Actua, 2000); Thabo Mbeki, *The Time Has Come: Selected Speeches* (Cape Town: Tafelberg, 1998); Thabo Mbeki, *Mahube: The Dawning of the Dawn: Speeches, Lectures and Tributes* (Braamfontein, South Africa: Skotaville Media, 2001); Brian Pottinger, *The Mbeki Legacy* (Cape Town: Zebra, 2008); Ronald Suresh Roberts, *Fit to Govern: The Native Intelligence of Thabo Mbeki* (Johannesburg: STE, 2007).

32. See Reuben Abati, 'Obasanjo: A Psychoanalysis', *The Guardian* (Lagos), 8 July 2001, p. 57. See also Olusegun Obasanjo, *My Command* (London: Heinemann, 1980); Olusegun Obasanjo, *Not My Will* (Ibadan: Ibadan University Press, 1990); Olusegun Obasanjo, *This Animal Called Man* (Abeokuta, Nigeria: Africa Leadership Forum, 1999); Oluremi Obasanjo, *Bitter-Sweet: My Life with Obasanjo* (Lagos: Diamond, 2008); Onukaba Adinoyi Ojo, *Olusegun Obasanjo: In the Eyes of Time* (Lagos: Africana Legacy, 1997).

33. Gevisser, *Thabo Mbeki*, pp. 377–388.

34. Ibid., p. 374.
35. Ibid., pp. 370–388.
36. See Obasanjo, *Not My Will*, pp. 123–148.
37. See Chris Landsberg, 'South Africa and the Making of the African Union and NEPAD: Mbeki's "Progressive African Agenda"', in Adebajo, Adedeji, and Landsberg (eds.), *South Africa in Africa*, pp. 195–212.
38. Adekeye Adebajo and Chris Landsberg, 'The Heirs of Nkrumah: Africa's New Interventionists', *Pugwash Occasional Paper* 1(2) (January 2000), pp. 65–90.
39. See Ali A. Mazrui, *Towards a Pax Africana: A Study of Ideology and Ambition* (Chicago: University of Chicago Press, 1967).
40. Personal interview with Ambassador Tunji Olagunju, High Commissioner of Nigeria to South Africa, Tshwane, 22 July 2004.
41. See 'Progress Report of the Chair, Olusegun Obasanjo, to the Third Ordinary Session of the Assembly of Heads of State and Government of the African Union', Addis Ababa, 6–8 July 2004, NEPAD/HSGIC/07–2004/Doc.4, pp. 4–5.
42. Personal interview with Ambassador Welile Nhlapo, head of South Africa's Presidential Support Unit, Tshwane, 22 July 2004.
43. Department of Foreign Affairs of South Africa, 'South Africa and Nigeria Bi-National Commission Communiqué', Pretoria, 6 October 1999.
44. 'Agreed Minutes of the 6th Session of the Binational Commission Between the Republic of South Africa and the Federal Republic of Nigeria', Durban, South Africa, 6–10 September 2004.
45. Confidential interview.
46. I am indebted for these points to Dianna Games 'An Oil Giant Reforms: The Experience of South African Firms Doing Business in Nigeria', *Business in Africa Report* no. 3 (Johannesburg: South African Institute of International Affairs, 2004).
47. Confidential interviews.
48. Olu Adeniji, *Essays on Nigerian Foreign Policy, Governance and International Security* (Ibadan: Dokun Publishing House, 2000), p. 84.
49. See interview with Bangumzi Sifingo, South Africa's High Commissioner to Nigeria, in *Traders* 13 (February–May 2003), pp. 18–19.
50. See James Lamont, 'Mobile Phone Network Opens in Nigeria', *Financial Times*, 10 August 2001, p. 7.
51. Games, 'An Oil Giant Reforms', p. 57.
52. John Daniel, Jessica Lutchman, and Sanusha Naidu, 'South Africa and Nigeria: Two Unequal Centres in a Periphery', in Daniel, Southall, and Lutchman, *State of the Nation*, pp. 559–560.
53. John Daniel and Nompumelelo Bhengu, 'South Africa in Africa: Still a Formidable Player', in Roger Southall and Henning Melber (eds.), *A New Scramble for Africa? Imperialism, Investment, and Development* (Scottsville: University of Kwazulu-Natal Press, 2009), p. 148.
54. Games, 'An Oil Giant Reforms', p. 66.
55. Cited in Dianna Games, 'Decade of Success and Missed Chances Between SA and Nigeria', *BusinessDay*, 23 November 2009, p. 11.

56. Daniel and Bhengu, 'South Africa in Africa', pp. 149–150, 158.

57. Ibid., p. 149. See also William M. Gumede, Vincent Nwanma, and Patrick Smith, 'South Africa/Nigeria: The Giants Tussle for Influence', *Africa Report* no. 3 (July 2006), p. 16.

58. Cited in Games, 'Decade of Success and Missed Chances Between SA and Nigeria', p. 11.

59. Daniel and Bhengu, 'South Africa in Africa', p. 149.

60. Ibid., p. 156.

61. Ibid., p. 157.

62. See Apter, *The Pan-African Nation*. See also Eboe Hutchful and Kwesi Aning, 'The Political Economy of Conflict', in Adebajo and Rashid, *West Africa's Security Challenges;* Karl Maier, *This House Has Fallen: Midnight in Nigeria* (New York: PublicAffairs, 2000); Ali A. Mazrui, 'Shari'ahcracy and Federal Models in the Era of Globalisation: Nigeria in Comparative Perspective', in Alamin Mazrui and Willy Mutunga (eds.), *Governance and Leadership: Debating the African Condition, Mazrui, and His Critics*, volume 2 (Trenton: Africa World Press, 2003), pp. 261–276; John N. Paden, *Muslim Civic Cultures and Conflict Resolution: The Challenges of Democratic Federalism in Nigeria* (Washington, DC: Brookings Institution, 2005).

63. Patrick Bond, *Talk Left, Walk Right: South Africa's Frustrated Global Reforms* (Scottsville: University of Kwazulu-Natal Press, 2004), pp. 112–113.

64. This information on Côte d'Ivoire draws upon United Nations, *Fifth Progress Report* and *Sixth Progress Report of the UN Secretary-General on UN Operations in Côte d'Ivoire*, 17 June 2005, UN Doc. S/2005/398, and 26 September 2005, UN Doc. S/2005/604,.

65. Confidential interview.

66. Confidential interview.

67. Government of South African, 'Toast Remarks of the President of South Africa, Thabo Mbeki, in Honour of the President of the Federal Republic of Nigeria, H.E. Alhaji Umaru Musa Yar'Adua', Tuynhuys, Cape Town, 3 June 2008.

68. I thank an anonymous external reviewer for bolstering the information in this sentence.

69. I thank Chris Landsberg for this insight.

70. Musifiky Mwanasali, 'Emerging Security Architecture in Africa', *Policy: Issues and Actors* 4(7) (February 2004), p. 14.

8. AN AXIS OF EVIL? CHINA, THE UNITED STATES, AND FRANCE IN AFRICA

1. This chapter builds on Adekeye Adebajo, 'An Axis of Evil? China, the US, and France in Africa', in Kweku Ampiah and Sanusha Naidu (eds.), *Crouching Tiger, Hidden Dragon? Africa and China* (Scottsville: University of Kwazulu-Natal Press, 2008). I thank Kweku Ampiah and Sally Hines for editorial comments on the earlier version.

2. Quoted in *The Guardian* (Lagos), 23 March 2003, p. 58.

3. See Sally Morphet, 'Multilateralism and the Non-Aligned Movement: What Is the Global South Doing and Where Is It Going?' review essay, *Global Governance* 10 (2004), pp. 517–537.

4. Ali A. Mazrui, 'Africa and Asia', in *Africa's International Relations: The Diplomacy of Dependency and Change* (London: Heinemann, 1977), p. 126.

5. I am indebted for the information in this paragraph to Garth le Pere and Garth Shelton, *China, Africa, and South Africa: South–South Cooperation in a Global Era* (Johannesburg: Institute for Global Dialogue, 2007), pp. 41–63.

6. See the informative article by Sanusha Naidu and Martyn Davies, 'China Fuels Its Future with Africa's Riches', *South African Journal of International Affairs* 13(2) (2006), pp. 69–83.

7. Quoted in ibid., p. 69.

8. Garth Le Pere, 'The Geo-Strategic Dimensions of the Sino-African Relationship,' in Ampiah and Naidu, *Crouching Tiger, Hidden Dragon?* p. 27.

9. Ngozi Okonjo-Iweala, 'Viewpoint: China Becomes Africa's Suitor', *BBC News*, 24 October 2006, http://www.news.bbc.co.uk/1/hi/business/607938.stm.

10. See Garth Shelton and Farhana Paruk, *The Forum on China-Africa Cooperation: A Strategic Opportunity*, Monograph no. 156 (Tshwane: Institute for Security Studies, December 2008).

11. See Garth Shelton, 'FOCAC IV—New Opportunities for Africa,' *The China Monitor* (Stellenbosch: Centre for Chinese Studies) Issue 46 November 2009, pp. 4–6. See also Centre for Conflict Resolution, Cape Town, 'Taming the Dragon? Defining Africa's Interests at the Forum on China-Africa Co-operation,' report of a policy seminar held in Tshwane on 13 and 14 July 2009 (Available at www.ccr.org.za).

12. See Ian Taylor, 'The "All-Weather" Friend? Sino-African Interaction in the Twenty-First Century', in Ian Taylor and Paul Williams (eds.), *Africa in International Politics: External Involvement on the Continent* (London: Routledge, 2004), pp. 83–101. See also Garth le Pere, *China Through the Third Eye: South African Perspectives* (Johannesburg: Institute for Global Dialogue, 2004).

13. See Chris Alden, *China in Africa* (London: Zed, 2007); Chris Alden, Daniel Large, and Ricardo Soares De Oliveira (eds.), *China Returns to Africa: A Rising Power and a Continent Embrace* (London: Hurst, 2008); Ampiah and Naidu, *Crouching Tiger, Hidden Dragon?;* Garth le Pere (ed.), *China in Africa: Mercantilist Predator or Partner in Development?* (Johannesburg: Institute for Global Dialogue and SAIIA, 2006); Robert I. Rotberg (ed.), *China Into Africa: Trade, Aid, and Influence* (Washington, DC: Brookings Institution, 2008); Ian Taylor, *China's New Role in Africa* (Boulder: Lynne Rienner, 2009); Drew Thompson, 'China's Emerging Interests in Africa: Opportunities and Challenges for Africa and the United States', *African Renaissance* 2(4) (2005), pp. 20–29; Anver Versi, 'China and Africa: A Meeting of Minds—and Needs', *African Business*, July 2006, pp. 16–21; Neil Ford, 'Economic War for Africa's Loyalties Begins', *African Business*, July 2006, pp. 16–21.

14. Council on Foreign Relations, *More Than Humanitarianism: A Strategic US Approach Toward Africa*, Independent Task Force Report no. 56 (New York, 2006), p. 49.

15. See Richard Dowden, 'China's Healing Power', *Time*, August 2007; James Miles, 'China's Coming-Out Party', *The Economist*, 'Special Issue: The World in 2007', p. 46.

16. This section builds on Adekeye Adebajo, 'Africa and America in an Age of Terror,' *Journal of Asian and African Studies*, volume 38, issue 2–3, August 2003, pp. 175–191.

17. See Salih Booker, 'US Foreign Policy and National Interests in Africa', *South African Journal of International Affairs* 8(1) (2001), pp. 1–14; Michael Clough, *Free at Last? US Policy Toward Africa and the End of the Cold War* (New York: Council on Foreign Relations, 1992); Jeffrey Herbst, *US Economic Policy Toward Africa* (New York: Council on Foreign Relations, 1992); Peter Schraeder, 'Removing the Shackles? US Foreign Policy Toward Africa after the End of the Cold War', in Edmond J. Keller and Donald Rothchild (eds.), *Africa in the New International Order: Rethinking State Sovereignty and Regional Security* (Boulder: Lynne Rienner, 1996).

18. On Clinton's Africa policy, see Jendayi E. Frazer, 'The United States', in Mwesiga Baregu and Chris Landsberg (eds.), *From Cape to Congo: Southern Africa's Evolving Security Challenges* (Boulder: Lynne Rienner, 2003), pp. 275–99; Gilbert M. Khadiagala, 'The United States and Africa: Beyond the Clinton Administration', *SAIS Review* 21(1) (2001), pp. 259–273; Chris Landsberg, 'The United States and Africa: Malign Neglect', in David M. Malone and Yuen Foong Khong (eds.), *Unilateralism and US Foreign Policy: International Perspectives* (Boulder: Lynne Rienner, 2003); Marina Ottaway, *Africa's New Leaders: Democracy or State Reconstruction?* (Washington, DC: Carnegie Endowment for International Peace, 1999); John Stremlau, 'Ending Africa's Wars', *Foreign Affairs*, July 2000, pp. 117–132.

19. See Hussein Adam, 'Somalia: A Terrible Beauty Being Born?' in I.William Zartman (ed.), *Collapsed States: The Disintegration and Restoration of Legitimate Authority* (Boulder: Lynne Rienner, 1995), pp. 69–78; Boutros Boutros-Ghali, *Unvanquished: A US-UN Saga* (London: Tauris, 1999); Walter Clarke and Jeffrey Herbst (eds.), *Learning from Somalia: The Lessons of Armed Humanitarian Intervention* (Boulder: Westview, 1997); John L. Hirsch and Robert B. Oakley, *Somalia and Operation Restore Hope: Reflections on Peacemaking and Peacekeeping* (Washington, DC: US Institute of Peace, 1995); Terrence Lyons and Ahmed I. Samatar, *Somalia: State Collapse, Multilateral Intervention, and Strategies for Political Reconstruction* (Washington, DC: Brookings Institution, 1995); Mohamed Sahnoun, *Somalia: The Missed Opportunities* (Washington, DC: US Institute of Peace, 1994).

20. See Roméo Dallaire, *Shake Hands with the Devil: The Failure of Humanity in Rwanda* (London: Arrow, 2004).

21. Anver Versi, 'At Last, a Win-Win Formula for African Business', *African Business*, March 2003, pp. 12–15.

22. See, for example, Randall Robinson, *The Debt: What America Owes to Blacks* (New York: Plume, 2000), pp. 182–187.

23. Raymond W. Copson, *The United States in Africa* (London: Zed, 2007), pp. 34–36.

24. Henning Melber, 'Global Trade Regimes and Multi–Polarity: The US and Chinese Scramble for African Resources and Markets', in Roger Southall and Henning Melber (eds.), *A New Scramble for Africa? Imperialism, Investment, and Development* (Scottsville: University of Kwazulu-Natal Press, 2009), pp. 65–67.

25. Quoted in *New York Times*, 1 February 2003, p. A11.

26. Quoted in *The Guardian* (Lagos), 23 March 2003, p. 58.

27. Z. Pallo Jordan, 'A Global Regime Built on Force?' *New Agenda* no. 9 (First Quarter 2003), p. 17.

28. 'African Leaders Condemn War', *The Guardian* (Lagos), 22 March 2003, pp. 1–2.

29. See, for example, Adebajo, 'Africa and America in an Age of Terror'; Mwesiga Baregu, 'Terrorism and Counter-terrorism: Dialogue or Confrontation?' in Adekeye Adebajo and Helen Scanlon (eds.), *A Dialogue of the Deaf: Essays on Africa and the United Nations* (Johannesburg: Jacana, 2006), pp. 261–274; and Princeton N. Lyman, 'The War on Terrorism in Africa,' in John W. Harbeson and Donald Rothchild (eds.), *Africa in World Politics: Reforming Political Order*, 4th ed. (Boulder: Westview Press, 2009), pp. 276–304.

30. See Economist Intelligence Unit, 'Country Report: Morocco', February 2003, p. 15.

31. See Aboubakr Jamai, 'Morocco's Choice: Openness or Terror', *New York Times*, 31 May 2003, p. A25.

32. Elaine Sciolino, 'At a Traumatic Moment, Morocco's King Is Mute', *New York Times*, 27 May 2003, p. A3.

33. Quoted in Frank Bruni, 'Deep US-Europe Split Casts Long Shadow on Bush Tour', *New York Times*, 15 June 2001, p. A6.

34. Copson, *The United States in Africa*, p. 28.

35. See ibid., pp. 17–41.

36. See Council on Foreign Relations, *More Than Humanitarianism*.

37. Copson, *The United States in Africa*, pp. 42–65.

38. Ali A. Mazrui, 'A Danger of Mushrooming Religious Enthusiasms', interview by Patrick Smith, *Africa Report* no. 6 (2007), p. 44.

39. See Michele Ruiters, 'AFRICOM Bodes Ill for Africa', *Global Dialogue* 12(1) (2007), pp. 4–5, 38; Theresa Whelan, 'Why AFRICOM?' *Global Dialogue* 12(2) (2007), pp. 31–36.

40. This section builds on Adekeye Adebajo, 'Folie de Grandeur', *The World Today* 53(6) (1997), pp. 147–150.

41. See John Chipman, *French Power in Africa* (Oxford: Blackwell, 1989); Paul Gifford and W.R. Lewis (eds.), *The Transfer of Power in Africa: Decolonization 1940–1960* (New Haven: Yale University Press, 1982); Guy Martin, *Africa in World Politics: A Pan-African Perspective* (Asmara: Africa World, 2002); Victor T. Le Vine, *Politics in Francophone Africa* (Boulder: Lynne Rienner, 2007).

42. Quoted in Christopher M. Andrew, 'France: Adjustment to Change', in Hedley Bull (ed.), *The Expansion of International Society* (Oxford: Clarendon, 1984), p. 337.

43. Quoted in Douglas A. Yates, *The French Oil Industry and the Corps Des Mines in Africa* (Asmara: Africa World, 2009), p. 206.

44. For a review of France's Africa policy, see Chipman, *French Power in Africa*.
45. Ali A. Mazrui, *Africa's International Relations: The Diplomacy of Dependency and Change* (Boulder: Westview, 1977), p. 55.
46. See Jean-François Médard, 'Crisis, Change, and Continuity: Nigeria/France Relations', in Adekeye Adebajo and Raufu Mustapha (eds.), *Gulliver's Troubles: Nigeria's Foreign Policy After the Cold War* (Pietermaritzburg: University of Kwazulu-Natal Press, 2008); pp. 314–333.
47. See, for example, Guy Martin, 'Continuity and Change in Franco-African Relations', *Journal of Modern African Studies*, vol. 33 no. 1, March 1995, pp. 1–20.
48. Quoted in Chipman, *French Power in Africa*, p. 134.
49. Martin, 'Continuity and Change in Franco-African Relations', pp. 9–10.
50. See Douglas Yates, *The Rentier State in Africa: Oil-Rent Dependency and Neo-Colonialism in the Republic of Gabon* (Asmara: Africa World, 1996).
51. See, for example, Yates, *The French Oil Industry*, pp. 204–207.
52. For two recent detailed studies on French complicity in Rwanda's genocide, see Daniela Kroslak, *The Role of France in the Rwandan Genocide* (London: Hurst, 2007); Andrew Wallis, *Silent Accomplice: The Untold Story of France's Role in the Rwandan Genocide* (London: Tauris, 2006).
53. See Henry Kwami Anyidoho, *Guns over Kigali* (Accra: Woeli, 1999); Turid Laegreid, 'UN Peacekeeping in Rwanda', in Howard Adelman and Astri Suhrke (eds.), *The Path of a Genocide: The Rwanda Crisis from Uganda to Zaire* (New Brunswick: Transaction, 1999), pp. 231–251; Linda Melvern, *A People Betrayed: The Role of the West in Rwanda's Genocide* (London: Zed, 2000); Gérard Prunier, *The Rwandan Crisis: History of a Genocide* (New York: Columbia University Press, 1995); Astri Suhrke, 'UN Peacekeeping in Rwanda', in Gunnar Sørbo and Peter Vale (eds.), *Out of Conflict: From War to Peace in Africa* (Uppsala: Nordiska Afrikainstitutet, 1997), pp. 97–113.
54. See François Soudain, 'La Coopération dans le Sang', *Jeune Afrique*, 8–14 January 1997, p. 7.
55. See Guy Martin, 'France's African Policy in Transition: Disengagement and Redeployment', in Chris Alden and Guy Martin (eds.), *France and South Africa: Towards a New Engagement with Africa* (Pretoria: Protea, 2003), p. 105.
56. Cited in Le Vine, *Politics in Francophone Africa*, p. 345.
57. Nicholas Atkin, *The Fifth French Republic* (Hampshire: Palgrave Macmillan, 2005), pp. 163–172.
58. Theodore Zeldin, *The French* (New York: Kodansha International, 1996), p. 509.
59. See Adekeye Adebajo, 'Pretoria, Paris, and the Crisis in Côte d'Ivoire', *Global Dialogue* 11(2) (2006), pp. 20–22, 36; Abdul Rahman Lamin, *The Conflict in Côte d'Ivoire: South Africa's Diplomacy and Prospects for Peace*, Occasional Paper no. 49 (Johannesburg: Institute for Global Dialogue, 2005); Kaye Whiteman, 'Côte d'Ivoire: The Three Deaths of Houphouet-Boigny', in African Centre for Development and Strategic Studies, *African Conflict, Peace, and Governance Monitor* (Ibadan: Dokun, 2005), pp. 43–59.
60. Alexander Parker, 'Sarkozy's Balancing Act', *The Weekender*, 28–29 April 2007, p. 7.

61. The quotes in this paragraph are all from Achille Mbembe, '*Sacré Bleu!* Mbeki and Sarkozy?' *Mail and Guardian*, 24–30 August 2007, p. 24.

62. Ibid. p. 24.

63. 'Central Africa: On the Brink', *Africa Confidential*, 12 January 2007, p. 6.

64. See, for example, 'The New Colonialists', *The Economist*, 15–21 March 2008, p. 13.

65. Alden, *China in Africa*, p. 104.

66. The expression 'Afro-Saxon' is borrowed from Ali Mazrui.

9. THE SPRINGBOK AND THE DRAGON: SOUTH AFRICA VS. CHINA IN AFRICA

1. I thank Garth Le Pere and Daniel Large for their useful comments on an earlier version of this chapter.

2. Quoted in Devon Curtis, 'Partner or Predator in the Heart of Africa? Chinese Engagement with the DRC', in Kweku Ampiah and Sanusha Naidu (eds.), *Crouching Tiger, Hidden Dragon? Africa and China* (Scottsville: University of Kwazulu-Natal Press, 2008), p. 68.

3. Ronald Hyam and Peter Henshaw, *The Lion and the Springbok: Britain and South Africa Since the Boer War* (Cambridge: Cambridge University Press, 2003), pp. 15–16.

4. The nine founding members of SADCC were Angola, Botswana, Lesotho, Malawi, Mozambique, Swaziland, Tanzania, Zambia, and Zimbabwe.

5. Members include Indonesia, Malaysia, Singapore, Brunei, Vietnam, Burma, Thailand, Laos, and the Philippines.

6. This term was coined by Ali Mazrui.

7. I thank Daniel Large for refining this point.

8. John Daniel and Nompumelelo Bhengu, 'South Africa in Africa: Still a Formidable Player', in Roger Southall and Henning Melber (eds.), *A New Scramble for Africa? Imperialism, Investment, and Development* (Scottsville: University of Kwazulu-Natal Press, 2009), pp. 146–148.

9. See George Orwell, *Animal Farm* (London: Penguin, 1945).

10. I thank Daniel Large for this point.

11. See Garth Le Pere and Garth Shelton, *China, Africa, and South Africa: South-South Co-operation in a Global Era* (Midrand: Institute for Global Dialogue, 2007), pp. 160–181; Garth Shelton, 'South Africa and China: A Strategic Partnership?' in Chris Alden, Daniel Large, and Ricardo Soares De Oliveira (eds.), *China Returns to Africa: A Rising Power and A Continent Embrace* (London: Hurst, 2008), pp. 275–294.

12. I thank Garth Le Pere for this observation.

13. These figures are from China's Ministry of Commerce and are cited in a short report by a policy analyst with the United Kingdom's Department for International Development in China, Mark George, 'China Africa Two-Way Trade: Recent Developments', 30 January 2009, pp. 1–2.

14. Le Pere and Shelton, *China, Africa, and South Africa*, p. 171.

15. I have relied in the preceding two paragraphs on Sanusha Naidu, 'Balancing a Strategic Partnership? South Africa-China Relations', in Ampiah and Naidu, *Crouching Tiger, Hidden Dragon?* pp. 167–191.

16. Cited in Garth Shelton and Farhana Paruk, *The Forum on China-Africa Cooperation: A Strategic Opportunity*, Monograph no. 156 (Tshwane: Institute for Security Studies, December 2008), p. 180.

17. Sharath Srinivasan, 'A "Rising Great Power" Embraces Africa', in Adekeye Adebajo and Raufu Mustapha (eds.), *Gulliver's Troubles: Nigeria's Foreign Policy After the Cold War* (Scottsville: University of Kwazulu-Natal Press, 2008), p. 349.

18. Lucy Corkin, 'Competition or Collaboration? Chinese and South African Transnational Companies in Africa', *Review of African Political Economy* 35(115) (March 2008), pp. 129–131.

19. Daniel and Bhengu, 'South Africa in Africa', pp. 159–160.

20. The case studies in this section and the next draw on Adekeye Adebajo, 'The Bicycle Strategy of South Africa's Bilateral Relations in Africa', *South African Journal of International Affairs* 15(2) (December 2008), pp. 121–136.

21. Daniel and Bhengu, 'South Africa in Africa', pp. 145–154.

22. This paragraph is summarised from Augusta Conchiglia, 'South Africa and Its Lusophone Neighbours: Angola and Mozambique', in Adekeye Adebajo, Adebayo Adedeji, and Chris Landsberg (eds.), *South Africa in Africa: The Post-Apartheid Era* (Scottsville: University of Kwazulu-Natal Press, 2007), pp. 237–247.

23. George, 'China Africa Two-Way Trade', pp. 1–2.

24. Information in this paragraph is derived from Lucy Corkin, 'All's Fair in Loans and War: The Development of China-Angola Relations', in Ampiah and Naidu, *Crouching Tiger, Hidden Dragon?* pp. 108–123 .

25. Henry Lee and Dan Shalom, 'Searching for Oil: China's Oil Strategies in Africa', in Robert I. Rotberg (ed.), *China Into Africa: Trade, Aid, and Influence* (Washington, DC: Brookings Institution, 2008), p. 134, n. 23.

26. Ibid., p. 122.

27. Peter Vale and Sipho Maseko, 'Thabo Mbeki, South Africa, and the Idea of an African Renaissance', in Sean Jacobs and Richard Calland (eds.), *Thabo Mbeki's World: The Politics and Ideology of the South African President* (Pietermaritzburg: University of Natal Press, 2002), p. 132.

28. Martin Rupiya, 'Zimbabwe in South Africa's Foreign Policy: A Zimbabwean View', in *South African Yearbook of International Affairs 2002/2003* (Johannesburg: South African Institute of International Affairs, 2003), p. 164.

29. Patrick Bond, 'Zimbabwe, South Africa, and the IMF', *South African Yearbook of International Affairs 2005/2006* (Johannesburg: South African Institute of International Affairs, 2006), p. 58.

30. Ibid., p. 59.

31. Daniel and Bhengu, 'South Africa in Africa', p. 153.

32. Ibid., p. 154.

33. Quoted in John Blessing Karumbidza, 'Win-Win Economic Cooperation: Can China Save Zimbabwe's Economy?' in Firoze Manji and Stephen Marks (eds.),

African Perspectives on China in Africa (Cape Town, Nairobi and Oxford: Fahamu, 2007), p. 87.

34. Cited in Henning Melber, 'Global Trade Regimes and Multi–Polarity: The US and Chinese Scramble for African Resources and Markets', in Southall and Melber, *A New Scramble for Africa?* p. 73. Daniel and Bhengu, 'South Africa in Africa', p. 74.

35. The information in this paragraph is from Lloyd Sachikonye, 'Crouching Tiger, Hidden Agenda? Zimbabwe-China Relations', in Ampiah and Naidu, *Crouching Tiger, Hidden Dragon?* pp. 124–137.

36. John Daniel, Jessica Lutchman, and Alex Comninos, 'South Africa in Africa: Trends and Forecasts in a Changing African Political Economy', in Sakhela Buhlungu, John Daniel, Roger Southall and Jessica Lutchman (eds.), *State of the Nation 2007* (Cape Town: Human Sciences Research Council, 2007), p. 526.

37. Daniel and Bhengu, 'South Africa in Africa', p. 154.

38. See Judi Hudson, 'South Africa's Economic Expansion into Africa: Neo-Colonialism or Development?' in Adebajo, Adedeji, and Landsberg, *South Africa in Africa*, p. 137.

39. See Martyn Davies, 'China's Developmental Model Comes to Africa', *Review of African Political Economy* 35(115) (March 2008), pp. 134–137.

40. Martyn Davies, 'Special Economic Zones: China's Developmental Model Comes to Africa', in Rotberg, *China Into Africa*, pp. 143–144.

41. I thank Daniel Large for this point.

42. This information is gleaned from Muna Ndulo, 'Chinese Investments in Africa: A Case Study of Zambia', in Ampiah and Naidu, *Crouching Tiger, Hidden Dragon?* pp. 138–151.

43. Melber, 'Global Trade Regimes and Multi–Polarity', p. 73.

44. See, for example, Adekeye Adebajo, 'The United Nations', in Gilbert M. Khadiagala (ed.), *Security Dynamics in Africa's Great Lakes Region* (Boulder: Lynne Rienner, 2006), pp. 141–161.

45. Daniel and Bhengu, 'South Africa in Africa', p. 154.

46. Hudson, 'South Africa's Economic Expansion into Africa', p. 138.

47. Jenni Evans, 'Anglo "Messed Up" in the DRC', *Mail and Guardian* online, 2 June 2005, http://www.mg.co.za/printformat/single/2005–06–02–anglo-messed-up-in-the-drc.

48. Daniel and Bhengu, 'South Africa in Africa', p. 151.

49. Much of the information in this paragraph is gleaned from Claude Kabemba, 'South Africa in the DRC: Renaissance or Neo-Imperialism?' in Buhlungu et al., *State of the Nation 2007*, pp. 533–551. See also Devon Curtis, 'South Africa: "Exporting Peace" to the Great Lakes Region?' in Adebajo, Adedeji, and Landsberg (eds.), *South Africa in Africa*, pp. 253–273.

50. Quoted in Curtis, 'Partner or Predator in the Heart of Africa?' p. 86.

51. This information is derived from ibid., pp. 86–107.

52. See interview with Bangumzi Sifingo, South Africa's High Commissioner to Nigeria, in *Traders* no. 13 (February—May 2003), pp. 18–19.

53. See James Lamont, 'Mobile Phone Network Opens in Nigeria', *Financial Times*, 10 August 2001, p. 7.

54. Dianna Games, *'The Oil Giant Reforms': The Experience of South African Firms Doing Business in Nigeria*, Business in Africa Report no. 3 (Johannesburg: South African Institute of International Affairs, 2004), p. 57.

55. John Daniel, Jessica Lutchman, and Sanusha Naidu, 'South Africa and Nigeria: Two Unequal Centres in a Periphery', in John Daniel, Roger Southall, and Jessica Lutchman (eds.), *State of the Nation: South Africa 2004–2005* (Cape Town: Human Sciences Research Council, 2005), pp. 559–560.

56. Cited in Dianna Games, 'Decade of Success and Missed Chances Between SA and Nigeria', *BusinessDay*, 23 November 2009, p. 11.

57. Daniel and Bhengu, 'South Africa in Africa', p. 149.

58. George, 'China Africa Two-Way Trade', p. 2.

59. Quoted in Srinivasan, 'A "Rising Great Power" Embraces Africa', p. 334.

60. Ndubisi Obiorah, Darren Kew, and Yusuf Tanko, '"Peaceful Rise" and Human Rights: China's Expanding Relations with Nigeria', in Rotberg, *China Into Africa*, p. 274.

61. Obiorah, Kew, and Tanko, '"Peaceful Rise" and Human Rights', p. 281.

62. Davies, 'Special Economic Zones', p. 148.

63. Obiorah, Kew, and Tanko, '"Peaceful Rise" and Human Rights', pp. 279–280.

64. This paragraph is also partly based on information from Alaba Ogunsanwo, 'A Tale of Two Giants: Nigeria and China', in Ampiah and Naidu, *Crouching Tiger, Hidden Dragon?* pp. 192–207.

65. See, for example, Francis Deng, *War of Visions: Conflict of Identities in the Sudan*, (Washington DC: The Brookings Institution, 1995); Dunstan M. Wai, *The African-Arab Conflict in the Sudan* (New York and London: Africana Publishing Company, 1981); Peter Woodward, *Sudan, 1898–1989: The Unstable State* (Boulder, Colorado: Lynne Rienner, 1990).

66. See Iqbal Jhazbhay, 'South Africa's Relations with North Africa and the Horn: Bridging a Continent', in Adebajo, Adedeji, and Landsberg, *South Africa in Africa*, pp. 274–292.

67. George, 'China Africa Two-Way Trade', p. 2.

68. Daniel Large, 'China and the Contradictions of "Non-Interference" in Sudan', *Review of African Political Economy* 35(115) (March 2008), p. 94.

69. This information is partly drawn from Sharath Srinivasan, 'A Marriage Less Convenient: China, Sudan, and Darfur', in Ampiah and Naidu, *Crouching Tiger, Hidden Dragon?* pp. 55–85.

70. See Richard Dowden, 'China's Healing Power', *Time*, vol. 170 no. 6, 13 August 2007; James Miles, 'China's Coming-Out Party', *The Economist*, 'Special Issue: The World in 2007', p. 46.

71. Lee and Shalom, 'Searching for Oil', p. 135, n. 32.

72. See Ali Askouri, 'China's Investment in Sudan: Displacing Villages and Destroying Communities', in Manji and Marks (eds.), *African Perspectives on China in Africa*, pp. 71–86; Large, 'China and the Contradictions of "Non-Interference" in Sudan', pp. 95–97.

73. Large, 'China and the Contradictions of "Non-Interference" in Sudan', pp. 99–100.

74. Daniel and Bhengu, 'South Africa in Africa', p. 154.

75. Ibid., p. 158.

76. John Daniel, Jessica Lutchman, and Alex Comninos, 'South Africa in Africa: Trends and Forecasts in a Changing African Political Economy', in Buhlungu et al., *State of the Nation 2007*, p. 526.

77. Davies, 'Special Economic Zones', p. 147.

78. This paragraph is partly based on Mwesiga Baregu, 'The Three Faces of the Dragon: Tanzania-China Relations in Historical Perspective', in Ampiah and Naidu, *Crouching Tiger, Hidden Dragon?* pp. 152–166.

79. See Chris McGreal, 'UK's \$1 Billion Transport Network Across Africa', *The Guardian*, 20 February 2009, p. 26.

80. See Bertolt Brecht, *The Good Person of Szechuan*, Collected Plays vol. 6 (New York: Random, 1976).

10. MANDELA AND RHODES: A MONSTROUS MARRIAGE

1. An earlier version of this chapter appeared in Sarah Rowland Jones (ed.), *Faith in Action: Njongonkulu Ndungane Archbishop for the Church and the World* (Epping, South Africa: ABC, 2008). I thank Sarah Rowland-Jones, Paul Maylam, Chris Saunders, and Bill Nasson for extremely useful comments on that earlier version.

2. John Daniel, 'Soldiering On: The Post-Presidential Years of Nelson Mandela, 1999–2005', in Roger Southall and Henning Melber (eds.), *Legacies of Power: Leadership Change and Former Presidents in African Politics* (Cape Town: Human Sciences Research Council, 2006), p. 44.

3. Robert H. Jackson and Carl G. Rosberg, *Personal Rule in Black Africa: Prince, Autocrat, Prophet, Tyrant* (Berkeley: University of California Press, 1982), pp. 182–188.

4. Maylam, *The Cult of Rhodes: Remembering an Imperialist in Africa* (Cape Town: David Philip, 2005), p. 134.

5. I thank Ali A. Mazrui for this insight in his 1986 documentary *The Africans*.

6. See Desmond Tutu, *The Rainbow People of God: The Making of a Peaceful Revolution* (New York: Image, 1994).

7. See Gerald L'Ange, *The White Africans: From Colonisation to Liberation* (Johannesburg: Jonathan Ball, 2005); John Flint, *Cecil Rhodes* (Boston: Little, Brown, 1974); Bernard Magubane, *The Making of a Racist State* (Asmara: Africa World Press, 1996); Maylam, *The Cult of Rhodes;* Martin Meredith, *Diamonds, Gold, and War: The Making of South Africa* (Johannesburg: Jonathan Ball, 2008); Robert Rotberg, *The Founder: Cecil Rhodes and the Pursuit of Power* (Johannesburg: Jonathan Ball, 2002); Stanlake Samkange, *On Trial for My Country* (London: Heinemann, 1967); Antony Thomas, *Rhodes: The Race for Africa* (Johannesburg: Jonathan Ball, 1996).

8. Maylam, *The Cult of Rhodes*, pp. 67–70.

9. See Magubane, *The Making of a Racist State*.

10. Maylam, *The Cult of Rhodes*, p. 14.

11. See Rotberg, *The Founder*, p. xxxiv; Thomas, *Rhodes*, p. 268.
12. Quoted in Thomas, *Rhodes*, p. 9.
13. See ibid., pp. 12, 172.
14. Maylam, *The Cult of Rhodes*, p. 140.
15. Ibid., p. 131.
16. Quoted in Thomas, *Rhodes*, p. 4.
17. I thank Ali Mazrui for this insight from his 1986 documentary *The Africans*.
18. See Thomas, *Rhodes*, pp. 210, 261–272.
19. Olive Shreiner, *Trooper Peter Halket of Mashonaland* (London: T. Fisher Unwin, 1897).
20. See, for example, Bill Nasson, *Abraham Esau's War: A Black South African War in the Cape, 1899–1902* (Cambridge and New York: Cambridge University Press, 1991); Thomas Pakenham, *The Boer War* (London: Weidenfeld and Nicholson, 1979).
21. Magubane, *The Making of a Racist State*, p. 106.
22. Maylam, *The Cult of Rhodes*, p. 159.
23. Rotberg, *The Founder*, p. xxv.
24. Quoted in Maylam, *The Cult of Rhodes*, p. 101.
25. See the impressive volume by the former Warden of the Rhodes House, Anthony Kenny (ed.), *The History of the Rhodes Trust* (Oxford: Oxford University Press, 2001), pp. 251–314. See also A.H.M. Kirk-Greene, 'Doubly Elite: African Rhodes Scholars, 1960–1990', *Immigrants and Minorities* vol. 12 no. 3 (November 1993), pp. 230–236; Philip Ziegler, *Legacy: Cecil Rhodes, the Rhodes Trust, and Rhodes Scholarships* (New Haven: Yale University Press, 2008).
26. See the informative chapter by Tim Nuttall, 'A Century of South African Rhodes Scholarship', in Kenny, *The History of the Rhodes Trust*, pp. 251–314.
27. See Kader Asmal, David Chidester, and Wilmot James (eds.), *South Africa's Nobel Laureates: Peace, Literature, and Science* (Johannesburg: Jonathan Ball, 2004), pp. 74–100; Mary Benson, *Nelson Mandela: The Man and the Movement* (London: Penguin, 1986); Elleke Boehmer, *Nelson Mandela: A Very Short Introduction* (Oxford: Oxford University Press, 2008); Nelson Mandela, *From Freedom to the Future: Tributes and Speeches* (Johannesburg: Jonathan Ball, 2003); Tom Lodge, *Mandela: A Critical Life* (Oxford: Oxford University Press, 2006); Anthony Sampson, *Mandela: The Authorised Biography* (London: HarperCollins, 1999).
28. I thank Leon Levy for this insight.
29. Quoted in Boehmer, *Nelson Mandela*, p. 103.
30. See Nelson Mandela, *Long Walk to Freedom* (New York: Little, Brown, 1994).
31. Quoted in Lodge, *Mandela*, p. 157.
32. See ibid., p. 204.
33. See F.W. De Klerk, *The Last Trek—A New Beginning* (London: Pan Books, 2000, first published in 1999), pp. 293–301; and pp. 342–368.
34. Lodge, *Mandela*, p. 205.
35. Ali A. Mazrui, *A Tale of Two Africas: Nigeria and South Africa as Contrasting Visions* (London: Adonis and Abbey, 2006), p. 266.
36. Kofi Annan, foreword to *Mandela: The Authorised Portrait* (London: Bloomsbury, 2006), p. 5.

37. Xolela Mangcu (ed.), *The Meaning of Mandela: A Literary and Intellectual Celebration* (Cape Town: Human Sciences Research Council, 2006).

38. This term is used in reference to a group of South Africa's new black middle-class who have a proclivity for conspicuous consumption, epitomized in the acquisition of Mercedes-Benzes as a status symbol.

39. See Cornel West, 'Nelson Mandela: Great Exemplar of the Grand Democratic Tradition', in Mangcu, *The Meaning of Mandela*, pp. 13–23.

40. See Wole Soyinka, 'Views from a Palette of the Cultural Rainbow', in Mangcu, *The Meaning of Mandela*, pp. 24–40.

41. Wole Soyinka, *Selected Poems* (London: Methuen, 2001), p. 197.

42. Soyinka, 'Views from a Palette of the Cultural Rainbow', p. 33.

43. Desmond Tutu, 'Religious Freedom', in Mandela, *From Freedom to the Future*, p. 315.

44. See the informative chapter by Daniel, 'Soldiering On', pp. 26–50.

45. See Adekeye Adebajo, Adebayo Adedeji, and Chris Landsberg (eds.), *South Africa in Africa: The Post-Apartheid Era* (Scottsville: University of Kwazulu-Natal Press, 2007).

46. Matthew 5:9.

47. See Kristina Bentley and Roger Southall, *An African Peace Process: Mandela, South Africa, and Burundi* (Cape Town: Human Sciences Research Council, 2005). See also Chris Alden and Garth Le Pere, *South Africa's Post-Apartheid Foreign Policy: From Reconciliation to Revival?* Adelphi Paper no. 362 (London: International Institute for Strategic Studies, 2003); James Barber *Mandela's World: The International Dimension of South Africa's Political Revolution, 1990–99* (Cape Town: David Philip, 2004); Chris Landsberg, 'Promoting Democracy: The Mandela-Mbeki Doctrine', *Journal of Democracy* 11(3) (July 2000), pp. 107–121.

48. Adebayo Adedeji (ed.), *South Africa and Africa: Within or Apart?* (London: Zed, 1996), p. 9.

49. Quoted in Eboe Hutchful, 'Understanding the African Security Crisis', in Abdel-Fatau Musah and J. Kayode Fayemi (eds.), *Mercenaries: An African Security Dilemma* (London: Pluto, 2000), p. 218.

50. Quoted in *New York Times*, 1 February 2003, p. A11.

51. Mandela, *From Freedom to the Future*, p. 524.

52. Ahmed Kathrada, 'A Self-Effacing Hero', in Mandela, *From Freedom to the Future*, p. 443.

53. Sampson, *Mandela*, p. xxvi.

54. Quoted in ibid., p. 417.

55. Ziegler, *Legacy*, pp. 321–328.

56. 'A Speech by President Mbeki', University of Cape Town, November 2004, quoted in *The Mandela Rhodes Foundation Yearbook 2003–2005*, p. 15.

57. Quoted in Maylam, *The Cult of Rhodes*, p. 137.

58. Ibid.

59. Ibid., p. 138.

60. 'A Message from the Chairman', *The Mandela Rhodes Foundation Yearbook 2003–2005*, p. 16.

11. THABO MBEKI: A NKRUMAHIST RENAISSANCE?

1. I thank Ben Turok, Kweku Ampiah, Ricardo Soares De Oliveira, Gavin Williams, and Raufu Mustapha for their useful comments on an earlier version of this chapter.

2. Thabo Mbeki, *Mahube: The Dawning of the Dawn, Speeches, Lectures, and Tributes* (Braamfontein, South Africa: Skotaville Media, 2001), pp. 194–195.

3. For accounts on Kwame Nkrumah's leadership and thinking, see Tawia Adamafio, *By Nkrumah's Side: The Labour and the Wounds* (Accra: Westcoast, 1982); Colonel A.A. Afrifa, *The Ghana Coup* (London: Cass, 1966); Major-General H.T. Alexander, *African Tightrope: My Two Years As Nkrumah's Chief of Staff* (London: Pall Mall, 1965); David Apter, *Ghana in Transition* (Princeton: Princeton University Press, 1972); Dennis Austin, *Politics in Ghana, 1946–1960* (Oxford: Oxford University Press, 1964); Geoffrey Bing, *Reap the Whirlwind: An Account of Kwame Nkrumah's Ghana from 1950 to 1966* (London: MacGibbon and Lee, 1968); David Birmingham, *Kwame Nkrumah* (London: Cardinal, 1990); Henry L. Bretton, *The Rise and Fall of Kwame Nkrumah: A Study of Personal Rule in Africa* (London: Pall Mall, 1967); Basil Davidson, *Black Star: A View of the Life and Times of Kwame Nkrumah* (London: Allen Lane, 1973); Trevor Jones, *Ghana's First Republic, 1960–1966: The Pursuit of the Political Kingdom* (London: Methuen, 1976); Ali A. Mazrui, 'Nkrumah: The Leninist Czar', in *On Heroes and Uhuru-Worship* (London: Longman, 1967), pp. 113–134; June Milne, *Kwame Nkrumah: A Biography* (London: Panaf, 2006); T. Peter Omari, *Kwame Nkrumah: The Anatomy of an African Dictatorship* (London: Hurst, 1970); Erica Powell, *Private Secretary (Female) Gold Coast* (London: Hurst, 1984); David Rooney, *Kwame Nkrumah: The Political Kingdom in the Third World* (London: Tauris, 1988); Bankole Timothy, *Kwame Nkrumah: His Rise to Power* (London: Allen and Unwin, 1963); Alfred Babatunde Zach-Williams, 'Kwame Francis Nkrumah', in David Simon (ed.), *Fifty Key Thinkers on Development* (Oxford: Routledge, 2006), pp. 187–192.

4. For accounts on Thabo Mbeki's leadership and thinking, see Mark Gevisser, *Thabo Mbeki: The Dream Deferred* (Johannesburg: Jonathan Ball, 2007) (South African edition unless specified); William Mervin Gumede, *Thabo Mbeki and the Battle for the Soul of the ANC* (Cape Town: Zebra, 2005); Adrian Hadland and Jovial Rantao, *The Life and Times of Thabo Mbeki* (Rivonia: Zebra, 1999); Sean Jacobs and Richard Calland (eds.), *Thabo Mbeki's World: The Politics and Ideology of the South African President* (Pietermaritzburg: University of Natal Press, 2002); Lucy Mathebe, *Bound by Tradition: The World of Thabo Mbeki* (Tshwane: University of South Africa Press, 2001); Mukanda Mulemfo, *Thabo Mbeki and the African Renaissance* (Pretoria: Actua, 2000); Brian Pottinger, *The Mbeki Legacy* (Cape Town: Zebra, 2008); Ronald Suresh Roberts, *Fit to Govern: The Native Intelligence of Thabo Mbeki* (Johannesburg: STE, 2007).

5. I thank Kweku Ampiah for this point.

6. See Kwame Nkrumah: *Ghana: The Autobiography of Kwame Nkrumah* (London: Panaf, 1957); *I Speak of Freedom* (London: Panaf, 1958); *Towards Colonial Free-*

dom (London: Heinemann, 1962); *Africa Must Unite* (London: Panaf, 1963); *Consciencism: Philosophy and Ideology for Decolonization* (London: Panaf, 1964); *Neo-Colonialism: The Last Stage of Imperialism* (London: Panaf, 1965); *Axioms of Kwame Nkrumah* (London: Panaf, 1967); *Challenge of the Congo* (London: Panaf, 1967); *Voice from Conakry* (London: Panaf, 1967); *Dark Days in Ghana* (London: Lawrence and Wishart, 1968); *Handbook of Revolutionary Warfare* (London: Panaf, 1968); *Class Struggle in Africa* (London: Panaf, 1970); *The Struggle Continues* (London: Panaf, 1968); *Revolutionary Path* (London: Panaf, 1973); *Rhodesia File* (London: Panaf, 1976) . See also Thabo Mbeki, *Africa: The Time Has Come—Selected Speeches* (Cape Town: Tafelberg and Mafube, 1998); Mbeki, *Mahube;* Thabo Mbeki, *Africa: Define Yourself* (Cape Town: Tafelburg and Mafube, 2002).

7. Ali A. Mazrui, 'The Monarchical Tendency in African Political Culture', in *Violence and Thought* (London: Longmans, 1969), p. 230.
8. Ibid.
9. David E. Apter, 'Ghana's Independence: Triumph and Paradox,' in *Transition*, Issue 98 2008, p. 17.
10. Hadland and Rantao, *The Life and Times of Thabo Mbeki*, p. 109.
11. Mazrui, 'Nkrumah', pp. 113–134.
12. Ibid., p. 113.
13. Omari, *Kwame Nkrumah*, p. 153.
14. Robert H. Jackson and Carl L. Rosberg, *Personal Rule in Black Africa* (Los Angeles: University of California Press, 1982), p. 182.
15. Timothy, *Kwame Nkrumah*, p. 172.
16. Rob Smith (ed.), *Julius Caesar: Cambridge School Shakespeare* (Cambridge: Cambridge University Press, 2008).
17. Austin, *Politics in Ghana*, p. 383.
18. Rex Gibson, *Coriolanus: Cambridge Student Guide* (Cambridge: Cambridge University Press, 2004, p. 4).
19. These expressions are Mark Gevisser's.
20. Cited in Gevisser, *Thabo Mbeki*, p. xxxix. The paragraph is also based largely on this source.
21. Quoted in Mazrui, 'Nkrumah', p. 121.
22. See the pioneering study by Austin, *Politics in Ghana*.
23. Richard Rathbone, 'Ghana', in John Dunn (ed.), *West African States: Failure and Promise* (Cambridge: Cambridge University Press, 1978), p. 22.
24. A.H.M. Kirk-Greene, 'West Africa: Nigeria and Ghana,' in Peter Duignan and Robert H. Jackson (eds.), *Politics and Government in African States 1960–1985* (Stanford, California: Hoover Institution Press, 1986), p. 36.
25. See, for example, A.H.M. Kirk-Greene, 'His Eternity, His Eccentricity, or His Exemplarity? A Further Contribution to the Study of H.E. the African Head of State,' *African Affairs*, vol. 90 no. 359 April 1991, p. 178; W. Scott Thompson, *Ghana's Foreign Policy, 1957–1966* (Princeton: Princeton University Press, 1969), p. 419.
26. The summary of the play and Soyinka's views are from the excellent, James Gibbs, *Wole Soyinka* (New York: Grove Press Inc, 1986), pp. 87–98. See also Wole

Soyinka, *Kongi's Harvest*, in Collected Plays 2, (Oxford, New York and Cape Town: Oxford University Press, 1974).

27. Nkrumah, *Consciencism*.
28. Apter, *Ghana in Transition*, p. 386.
29. Davidson, *Black Star*, pp. 189–190.
30. See Ama Biney, 'The Development of Kwame Nkrumah's Political Thought in Exile', *Journal of African History* 50 (2009), pp. 81–100.
31. Milne, *Kwame Nkrumah*.
32. See Tom Lodge, *Mandela: A Critical Life* (Oxford: Oxford University Press, 2006); Nelson Mandela, *Long Walk to Freedom* (New York: Little, Brown, 1994); Nelson Mandela, *From Freedom to the Future: Tributes and Speeches* (Johannesburg: Jonathan Ball, 2003); Anthony Sampson, *Mandela: The Authorised Biography* (London: HarperCollins, 1999).
33. These included Essop and Aziz Pahad, Joel Netshitenzhe, Sydney Mufamadi, Joe Modise, Charles Nqakula, Sam Shilowa, Jabu Moleketi, Geraldine Fraser-Moleketi, Nkosazana Dlamini–Zuma, Phumzile Mlambo-Ngcuka, Smuts Ngonyama, Frank Chikane, Trevor Manuel, Tito Mboweni, and Alec Erwin.
34. Thabo Mbeki, prologue to Malegapuru William Makgoba (ed.), *African Renaissance* (Cape Town: Tafelberg and Mafube, 1999), p. xv.
35. Peter Vale and Sipho Maseko, 'Thabo Mbeki, South Africa, and the Idea of an African Renaissance', in Jacobs and Calland, *Thabo Mbeki's World*, p. 124.
36. Gevisser, *Thabo Mbeki*, p. xxvi.
37. Ibid., p. xxix.
38. Ibid., p. 387.
39. Mbeki, *Mahube*, pp. 4–5.
40. Mbeki, *Africa: The Time Has Come*, pp. 31–32.
41. Quoted in Gumede, *Thabo Mbeki*, p. 64.
42. Quoted in Gevisser, *Thabo Mbeki*, (2009 updated international edition), p. 261.
43. Gevisser, *Thabo Mbeki*, p. xxiii.
44. Ibid. (2009 updated international edition), p. 167.
45. See, for example, Roberts, *Fit to Govern*; and Christine Qunta's articles in *BusinessDay* and other South African media .
46. See Andrew Feinstein, *After the Party: A Personal and Political Journey Inside the ANC* (Johannesburg: Jonathan Ball, 2007); Pottinger, *The Mbeki Legacy*, pp. 50–58.
47. Cited in Pottinger, *The Mbeki Legacy*, p. 60.
48. For an example of this sort of writing, see Xolela Mangcu, *To the Brink: The State of Democracy in South Africa* (Scottsville: University of Kwazulu-Natal Press, 2008), pp. 131–152.
49. See Angela Ndinga-Muvumba and Robyn Pharoah, *HIV/AIDS and Society in South Africa* (Scottsville: University of Kwazulu-Natal Press, 2008); Angela Ndinga-Muvumbna and Shauna Mottiar, 'HIV/AIDS and the African Renaissance: South Africa's Achilles Heel?' in Adekeye Adebajo, Adebayo Adedeji, and Chris Landsberg (eds.), *South Africa in Africa: The Post-Apartheid Era* (Scottsville: University of Kwazulu-Natal Press, 2007), pp. 177–194; Nicoli Nattrass,

Mortal Combat: AIDS Denialism and the Struggle for Antiretrovirals in South Africa (Scottsville: University of Kwazulu-Natal Press, 2007).

50. For sympathetic, and sometimes sycophantic, accounts of Ghana's pan-African foreign policy by two of Nkrumah's most senior diplomats, see Kwesi Armah, *Africa's Golden Road* (London: Heinemann, 1965); Alex Quaison-Sackey, *Africa Unbound: Reflections of An African Statesman* (London: André Deutsch, 1963).

51. See Ali A. Mazrui, *Nkrumah's Legacy and Africa's Triple Heritage Between Globalization and Counter-Terrorism* (Accra: Ghana Universities Press, 2004).

52. See 'Your 100 Greatest Africans of All Time', *New African*, August–September 2004, pp. 12–23.

53. Quoted in Mazrui, 'Nkrumah', p. 124.

54. See Nkrumah, *Africa Must Unite*.

55. See, for example, Ali A. Mazrui, *Towards a Pax Africana: A Study of Ideology and Ambition* (Chicago: University of Chicago Press, 1967); Thompson, *Ghana's Foreign Policy;* and Immanuel Wallerstein, *Africa: The Politics of Unity* (New York: Vintage, 1967).

56. On the rivalry between Ghana and Nigeria, see Olajide Aluko, *Ghana and Nigeria, 1957–70: A Study of Inter-African Discord* (London: Collings, 1976).

57. Thompson, *Ghana's Foreign Policy*, p. 428.

58. Elleke Boehmer, *Nelson Mandela: A Very Short Introduction* (Oxford: Oxford University Press, 2008), pp. 105–106.

59. See Nkrumah, *Africa Must Unite*, pp. 132–140.

60. See Mazrui, *Towards a Pax Africana*.

61. Quoted in Gevisser, *Thabo Mbeki* (2009 updated international edition), p. 221.

62. Ibid., p. 264.

63. See, for example, Adebajo, Adedeji, and Landsberg, *South Africa in Africa;* Chris Alden and Garth Le Pere, *South Africa's Post-Apartheid Foreign Policy: From Reconciliation to Revival?* Adelphi Paper no. 362 (London: International Institute for Strategic Studies, 2003); Chris Landsberg, *The Quiet Diplomacy of Liberation: International Politics and South Africa's Transition* (Johannesburg: Jacana, 2004); Elizabeth Sidiropoulos (ed.), *South Africa's Foreign Policy, 1994–2004: Apartheid Past, Renaissance Future* (Johannesburg: South African Institute of International Affairs, 2004).

64. Ali A. Mazrui, *A Tale of Two Africas: Nigeria and South Africa as Contrasting Visions* (London: Adonis and Abbey, 2006), p. 206.

65. Nkrumah, *Ghana*, p. x.

66. Rathbone, 'Ghana', pp. 31–32.

67. Kirk-Greene, 'West Africa', p. 41.

68. Martin Kilson, 'African Autocracy', *Africa Today* (April 1966), pp.???–???.

69. This summary is from Birmingham, *Kwame Nkrumah*, pp. 64–72.

70. Bing, *Reap the Whirlwind*, p. 445.

71. Austin, *Politics in Ghana*, p. 411.

72. Ibid., p. 105.

73. See, for example, Maxwell Owusu, *Uses and Abuses of Political Power: A Case Study of Continuity and Change in the Politics of Ghana* (Chicago: University of Chicago University Press, 1970); Afrifa, *The Ghana Coup*, p. 89.

74. Birmingham, *Kwame Nkrumah*, p. 92.

75. Cited in Mazrui, 'Nkrumah', pp. 122–123.

76. Gevisser, *Thabo Mbeki*, p. xxxi.

77. Quoted in ibid.

78. Gumede, *Thabo Mbeki*.

79. Quoted in Vishwas Satgar, 'Thabo Mbeki and the South African Communist Party', in Jacobs and Calland, *Thabo Mbeki's World*, p. 164.

80. Patrick Bond, 'Thabo Mbeki and NEPAD: Breaking or Shining the Chains of Global Apartheid?' in Jacobs and Calland, *Thabo Mbeki's World*, pp. 68–69.

81. See J.O. Adesina, Yao Graham, and A. Olukoshi (eds.), *Africa and Development Challenges in the New Millennium: The NEPAD Debate* (Dakar: CODESRIA, 2006); Patrick Bond (ed.), *Fanon's Warning: A Civil Society Reader on the New Partnership for Africa's Development*, 2nd ed. (Asmara: Africa World Press, 2005); Patrick Bond, *Talk Left, Walk Right: South Africa's Frustrated Global Reforms* (Scottsville: University of Kwazulu-Natal Press, 2004).

82. Gevisser, *Thabo Mbeki*, p. xxxiv.

83. The analysis in this section has benefitted from Gumede, *Thabo Mbeki*, pp. 67–95.

84. These are South African government figures cited in Mark Gevisser, 'Time of Reckoning', *BBC Focus on Africa Magazine* 20(2) (April–June 2009), p. 18.

85. Gumede, *Thabo Mbeki*, p. 224.

86. See, for example, Khehla Shubane, 'Black Economic Empowerment: Myths and Realities', in Adebajo, Adedeji, and Landsberg, *South Africa in Africa*, pp. 63–77.

87. This summary is largely based on Roger Southall, 'The ANC and Black Capitalism in South Africa', *Review of African Political Economy* 31(100) (June 2004), pp. 313–328. See also Ben Turok, *From the Freedom Charter to Polokwane: The Evolution of ANC Economic Policy* (Cape Town: New Agenda, 2008).

88. Pottinger, *The Mbeki Legacy*, p. 5.

89. Andile Mngxitama, 'Zuma and Mbeki Are Two Sides of the Same Coin', *Sunday Independent*, 17 May 2009, p. 10.

90. Quoted in Jackson and Rosberg, *Personal Rule in Black Africa*, p. 203.

91. Davidson, *Black Star*, p. 60.

92. Nkrumah, *Dark Days in Ghana*, p. 26.

93. Birmingham, *Kwame Nkrumah*, p. 88.

94. Davidson, *Black Star*, p. 186.

95. This expression is borrowed from Wole Soyinka's 1971 play *Madmen and Specialists*, Collected Plays vol. 2 (Oxford: Oxford University Press, 1974).

96. Rathbone, 'Ghana', p. 35.

97. See Wole Soyinka, *The Lion and the Jewel*, Collected Plays vol. 2. I am also grateful for the summary in this paragraph to Gibbs, *Wole Soyinka*, pp. 45–53.

98. Achille Mbembe, 'South Africa's Second Coming: The Nongqawuse Syndrome', *Open Democracy News Analysis*, 14 June 2006, pp. 2–3, http://www.opendemocracy.net.

99. Jones, *Ghana's First Republic*, p. 24.

100. Cited in Richard Calland, *Anatomy of South Africa: Who Holds the Power?* (Cape Town: Zebra, 2006), p. 45.

12. TOWERS OF BABEL? THE AFRICAN UNION AND THE EUROPEAN UNION

1. I thank Chris Hill, Mette Eilstrop-Sangiovanni, and Kaye Whiteman for their extremely useful comments on an earlier version of this chapter.
2. Muammar Qaddafi, 'They Want to Dominate Us, We Shouldn't Fall Into the Trap Again', *NewAfrican* no. 460 (March 2007), p. 13.
3. See John Leonard, introduction to John Milton, *Paradise Lost* (Johannesburg: Penguin, 2000). The book was first published in 1667.
4. I thank Chris Hill for reminding me to make more explicit this important fact.
5. See, for example, Francis Kornegay, 'The AU and Africa's Three Diasporas', in John Akokpari, Angela Ndinga-Muvumba, and Tim Murithi (eds.), *The African Union and Its Institutions* (Johannesburg: Jacana, 2008), pp. 333–352.
6. See Ali A. Mazrui and Alamin M. Mazrui, *The Power of Babel: Language and Governance in the African Experience* (Cape Town: David Philip, 1998), pp. 23–25.
7. This section builds on Adekeye Adebajo, 'Towards a New *Pax Africana:* Three decades of the OAU', *Praxis*, Spring 1993, pp. 59–71.
8. Quoted in Geoffrey Barraclough, 'The Revolt Against the West', in Prasenjit Duara (ed.), *Decolonization: Perspectives from Now and Then* (London: Routledge, 2004), p. 118.
9. See, for example, Kwame Nkrumah, *Africa Must Unite* (London: Panaf, 1963).
10. See Tajudeen Abdul-Raheem, 'Introduction: Reclaiming Africa for Africans— Pan-Africanism, 1900–1994', in Tajudeen Abdul-Raheem (ed.), *Pan-Africanism: Politics, Economy, and Social Change in the Twenty-First Century* (London: Pluto, 1996), pp. 1–30.
11. Immanuel Wallerstein, *Africa: The Politics of Unity* (New York: Vintage, 1967), p. 15.
12. See, for example, Wole Soyinka, *The Burden of Memory: The Muse of Forgiveness* (Cape Town: Oxford University Press, 1999), pp. 93–194.
13. Quoted in Ali Mazrui, 'Africa Entrapped: Between the Protestant Ethic and the Legacy of Westphalia', in Hedley Bull and Adam Watson (eds.), *The Expansion of International Society* (Oxford: Clarendon, 1984), p. 296.
14. Quoted in Ubang P. Ugor, 'Reparation, Reconciliation, and Negritude Poetics in Soyinka's *The Burden of Memory, the Muse of Forgiveness*', in Onookome Okome (ed.), *Ogun's Children: The Literature and Politics of Wole Soyinka Since the Nobel* (Asmara: Africa World Press, 2004), p. 273.
15. The Brazzaville group consisted of 12 francophone African states: Benin, Burkina Faso, Cameroon, Central African Republic, Chad, Congo-Brazzaville, Côte d'Ivoire, Gabon, Mauritania, Madagascar, Niger and Senegal. The Monrovia group consisted of Liberia, Togo, Ethiopia, Libya, Nigeria, Sierra Leone and Somalia. Members of the Casablanca Group included Ghana, Guinea, Mali, Morocco, Egypt and the Algerian provisional government.
16. See Georges Abi–Saab, *The United Nations Operation in the Congo 1960–1964* (Oxford: Oxford University Press, 1978); Catherine Hoskyns, *The Congo since*

Independence, January 1960–December 1961, (London: Oxford University Press, 1965); Conor Cruise O'Brien, *To Katanga and Back: a UN Case History* (London: Hutchinson, 1962).

17. Ali A. Mazrui, *Towards a Pax Africana: A Study of Ideology and Ambition* (Chicago: University of Chicago Press, 1967).

18. I am grateful for my analysis to Zdenek Cervenka, *The Unfinished Quest for Unity: Africa and the OAU* (London: Friedmann, 1977); Domenico Mazzeo (ed.), *African Regional Organizations* (Cambidge: Cambridge University Press, 1984); Gino Naldi, *The Organization of African Unity* (London: Mansell, 1989); Wallerstein, *Africa: The Politics of Unity*.

19. See Dominique Jacquin-Berdal and Aida Mengistu, 'Nationalism and Identity in Ethiopia and Eritrea: Building Multiethnic States', in Dorina A. Bekoe (ed.), *East Africa and the Horn: Confronting Challenges to Good Governance* (Boulder: Lynne Rienner, 2006), pp. 81–100; Tekeste Negash and Kjetil Tronvoll, *Brothers at War: Making Sense of the Eritrean-Ethiopian War* (Oxford: Currey, 2000); David Pool, 'The Eritrean People's Liberation Front', in Christopher Clapham, *African Guerrillas* (Bloomington: Indiana University Press, 1998), pp. 19–35; Peter Woodward, *The Horn of Africa: Politics and International Relations* (London: Tauris, 2003); John Young, 'The Tigray People's Liberation Front', in Clapham, *African Guerrillas*, pp. 36–52.

20. See Yassin El-Ayouty (ed.), *The Organization of African Unity After Thirty Years* (New York: Praeger, 1994); Solomon Gomes, 'The Peacemaking Role of the OAU and the AU: A Comparative Analysis', in Akokpari, Ndinga-Muvumba, and Murithi, *The African Union and Its Institutions*, pp. 113–130; Salim Ahmed Salim, 'The OAU Role in Conflict Management', in Olara Otunnu and Michael Doyle (eds.), *Peacemaking and Peacekeeping for the New Century* (Lanham: Rowman and Littlefield, 1998), pp. 245–253; Amadu Sesay, Olusola Ojo, and Orobola Fasehun, *The OAU After Twenty Years* (Boulder: Westview, 1984).

21. Naldi, *The Organization of African Unity*, p. 123.

22. See Adekeye Adebajo, 'Africa's Quest for El Dorado', *Mail and Guardian*, 29 June 2007. For another perspective, see Kwesi Kwaa Prah, 'Without Unity There Is No Future for Africa', *Mail and Guardian*, 29 June 2007.

23. Gordon Kerr, *A Short History of Europe: From Charlemagne to the Treaty of Lisbon* (Harpenden: Pocket Essentials, 2009), pp. 13–16; Lucidcafé Library, 'Charlemagne,' http://www.lucidcafe.com/library/96apr/charlemagne.html.

24. For a background, see Anne Deighton, 'The Remaking of Europe', in Michael Howard and Wm. Roger Louis (eds.), *The Oxford History of the Twentieth Century* (Oxford: Oxford University Press, 1998), pp. 190–202; Chris Hill and Michael Smith, *International Relations and the European Union* (Oxford: Oxford University Press, 2005); Anand Menon, *Europe: The State of the Union* (London: Atlantic, 2008); Brent F. Nelsen and Alexander Stubb (eds.), *The European Union: Readings on the Theory and Practice of European Integration*, 3rd ed. (Boulder and London: Lynne Rienner, 2003); Loukas Tsoukalis, *What Kind of Europe?* (Oxford: Oxford University Press, 2005).

25. I thank Chris Hill for this nuance.

26. Richard T. Griffiths, 'A Dismal Decade? European Integration in the 1970s', in Desmond Dinan (ed.), *Origins and Evolution of the European Union* (Oxford: Oxford University Press, 2006), pp. 169–190.

27. I have relied here on the excellent chapter by N. Piers Ludlow, 'From Deadlock to Dynamism: The EC in the 1980s', in Dinan, *Origins and Evolution of the European Union*, pp. 218–232.

28. I have relied in this section on Dorothee Heisenberg, 'From Single Market to the Single Currency', in Dinan, *Origins and Evolution of the European Union*, pp. 233–252.

29. Bulgaria, Romania, Poland, the Czech Republic, Hungary, Estonia, Latvia, Lithuania, Slovenia, Slovakia, Cyprus, and Malta.

30. The information from this paragraph and on the Amsterdam and Nice treaties is gleaned from John Pinder and Simon Usherwood, *The European Union: A Very Short Introduction* (Oxford: Oxford University Press, 2007), pp. 9–35.

31. See, for example, Charlemagne, 'We are All Belgians Now', *The Economist*, 28 November 2009, p. 39; Peter H.Koepf, 'This is Europe Speaking', *The African Times*, December 2009, vol. 2 no. 12, p. 1 and p. 4.

32. Wole Soyinka, *The Jero Plays: The Trials of Brother Jero and Jero's Metamorphosis* (Ibadan: Spectrum, 1988).

33. Quoted in Michael Maclay, *The European Union* (Gloucestershire: Sutton, 1998), p. 28.

34. This section on Adebayo Adedeji is based on Adekeye Adebajo, '"African Cassandra" Adedeji Comes Full Circle on NEPAD', *BusinessDay*, 1 September 2006.

35. See Adebayo Adedeji, 'ECOWAS: A Retrospective Journey', in Adekeye Adebajo and Ismail Rashid (eds.), *West Africa's Security Challenges: Building Peace in a Troubled Region* (Boulder: Lynne Rienner, 2004), pp. 21–49; Adebayo Adedeji, 'The ECA: Forging a Future for Africa', in Yves Berthelot, *Unity and Diversity in Development Ideas: Perspectives from the UN Regional Commissions* (Bloomington: Indiana University Press, 2004), pp. 233–306.

36. See Adebayo Adedeji, *Africa Within the World: Beyond Depression and Dependence* (London: Zed, 1994); S.K.B. Asante, *African Development: Adebayo Adedeji's Alternative Strategies* (Ibadan: Spectrum, 1991); Reginald Cline-Cole, 'Adebayo Adedeji', in David Simon (ed.), *Fifty Key Thinkers on Development* (Oxford: Routledge, 2006), pp. 3–9; Bade Onimode and Richard Synge (eds.), *Issues in African Development: Essays in Honour of Adebayo Adedeji at 65* (Ibadan: Heinemann, 1995); Bade Onimode et al., *African Development and Governance Strategies in the 21st Century: Looking Back to Move Forward—Essays in Honour of Adebayo Adedeji at Seventy* (London: Zed, 2004); Temilolu Sanmi–Ajiki, *Adebayo Adedeji: A Rainbow in the Sky of Time* (Lagos: Newswatch, 2000).

37. See Adebayo Adedeji, 'NEPAD's African Peer Review Mechanism: Progress and Prospects', in Akokpari, Ndinga-Muvumba, and Murithi, *The African Union and Its Institutions*, pp. 241–269.

38. Cited in Charles Grant, *Delors: The House That Jacques Built* (London: Nicholas Brealey, 1994), p. 88.

39. I thank Chris Hill for this observation.

40. See the excellent biography by Charles Grant, *Delors*, pp. 91–115.

41. I am grateful for these insightful observations to Grant, *Delors*, pp. 139–142.

42. Address by Alpha Oumar Konaré, chair of the AU Commission, at the University of South Africa, 24 June 2006, http://www.dfa.gov.za/docs/speeches/2006/konare0624.htm.

43. See African Union, *Audit of the African Union: Towards a People-Centred Political and Socio-Economic Integration and Transformation of Africa* (Addis Ababa, 2007), pp. 42–77.

44. 'Hurdles to Africa's Integration, by Konare', http://www.guardiannewsngr.com/news/article04/100707.

45. See, for example, Paul Maylam, *The Cult of Rhodes: Remembering an Imperialist in Africa* (Cape Town: David Philip, 2005).

46. See, for example, A.J.P. Taylor, *Europe: Grandeur and Decline* (Middlesex: Pelican, 1967), pp. 11–21.

47. I thank Mette Eilstrop-Sangiovanni for the point on France and Germany here.

48. See Adekeye Adebajo, 'South Africa and Nigeria in Africa: An Axis of Virtue?' in Adekeye Adebajo, Adebayo Adedeji, and Chris Landsberg (eds.), *South Africa in Africa: The Post-Apartheid Era* (Scottsville: University of Kwazulu-Natal Press, 2007), pp. 213–235; Chris Landsberg, 'An African "Concert of Powers"? Nigeria and South Africa's Construction of the AU and NEPAD', in Adekeye Adebajo and Raufu Mustapha (eds.), *Gulliver's Troubles: Nigeria's Foreign Policy After the Cold War* (Scottsville: University of Kwazulu-Natal Press, 2008), pp. 203–219.

49. See Adekeye Adebajo, 'Tale of Two Giants', *Newswatch*, 11 September 1995, pp. 9–10; Adekeye Adebajo and Chris Landsberg, 'Trading Places: Nigeria and South Africa', *Indicator* 13(3) (Winter 1996), pp. 64–68.

50. Adekeye Adebajo and Chris Landsberg, 'The Heirs of Nkrumah: Africa's New Interventionists', *Pugwash Occasional Paper* 2(1) (January 2000), pp. 65–90.

51. Personal interview with Ambassador Welile Nhlapo, head of South Africa's Presidential Support Unit, Tshwane, 22 July 2004.

52. Musifiky Mwanasali, 'Emerging Security Architecture in Africa', *Policy: Issues and Actors* 7(4) (February 2004) (Johannesburg: Centre for Policy Studies), p. 14.

53. Alaba Ogunsanwo, 'A Tale of Two Giants: Nigeria and China', in Kweku Ampiah and Sanusha Naidu, *Crouching Tiger, Hidden Dragon? Africa and China* (Scottsville: University of Kwazulu-Natal Press, 2008), p. 203.

54. Quoted in Nicholas Atkin, *The Fifth French Republic* (Hampshire: Palgrave Macmillan, 2005), p. 90.

55. Pinder and Usherwood, *The European Union*, pp. 21–22.

56. Naguib Mahfouz, *The Seventh Heaven: Stories of the Supernatural* (Cairo: American University in Cairo Press, 2005), p. 17.

57. Saïd K. Aburish, *Nasser: The Last Arab* (London: Gerald Duckworth & Co., 2005), p 316

58. See, for example, Yehudit Ronen, *Qaddafi's Libya in World Politics* (Boulder and London: Lynne Rienner, 2008); Dirk Vandewalle, *A History of Modern Libya* (Cambridge: Cambridge University Press, 2006).

59. Victor T. Le Vine, *Politics in Francophone Africa* (Boulder: Lynne Rienner, 2007), p. 350.

60. Quoted in Maclay, *The European Union*, p. 5.

61. Ibid., p. 33.

62. I thank Chris Hill for reminding me of this point.

63. Stephen Wall, *A Stranger in Europe: Britain and the EU From Thatcher to Blair* (Oxford and New York: Oxford University Press, 2008), p. 205. See also Alistair Jones, *Britain and the European Union* (Edinburgh: Edinburgh University Press, 2007); Hugo Young, *This Blessed Plot: Britain and Europe from Churchill to Blair* (New York: Overlook Press, 1998).

64. Ali A. Mazrui, *The Trial of Christopher Okigbo* (New York: Third Press, 1971).

65. Quoted in Wallerstein, *The Politics of Unity*, p. 67.

13. OBAMAMANIA: AFRICA, AFRICAN AMERICANS, AND THE AVUNCULAR SAM

1. I thank John Hirsch, Francis Kornegay, and Douglas Yates for useful comments on an earlier version of this chapter.

2. Barack Obama's speech to the Ghanaian parliament, 11 July 2009, http://www.americ.gov.

3. This introductory section builds on Adekeye Adebajo, 'The Phenomenal Appeal of Barack Obama', *BusinessDay*, 21 April 2008.

4. See, for example, two insightful articles by Martin Kilson, 'Crisis and Revitalization Dynamics in the Obama Campaign', and 'What Obama's Democratic Party Nomination Victory Means', both in *The Black Commentator*, 8 May and 5 June 2008 respectively.

5. Manning Marable, 'The Four Legged Stool That Won the Us Presidential Election', *Socialist Review*, 31 December 2008, p. 16.

6. David Mendell, *Obama: From Promise to Power* (New York: HarperCollins, 2007), p. 9.

7. The preceding quotes are from 'The World Rejoices', *New African*, December 2008, pp. 22–23.

8. See Cameron Duodu, 'Obama Do Something Before You Go', *New African*, August–September 2009, pp. 10–17.

9. Barack Obama's speech to the Ghanaian parliament, 11 July 2009.

10. See Mendell, *Obama*, pp. 338–354.

11. See ibid., pp. 330–331.

12. Ibid., p. 331.

13. Quoted in ibid., p. 6.

14. Barack Obama, *Dreams from My Father: A Story of Race and Inheritance* (New York: Three Rivers, 1995).

15. Ibid., p. 430.

16. Ibid., p. 301.

17. Ibid., p. 301.

18. Ibid., p. 302.

19. Ali A. Mazrui, 'Barack Obama: Brain Drain or Brain Gain?' presentation at the quarterly luncheon of the Kenya Alliance of Resident Association (KARA), Nairobi, 17 July 2008, pp. 2–3. See also Ali A. Mazrui 'The Black Atlantic from Othello to Obama: In Search of a Post-Racial Society', paper presented at the Centre for Conflict Resolution seminar 'From Eurafrique to Afro-Europa: Africa and Europe in a New Century', Cape Town, 11–13 September 2008.

20. Barack Obama, *The Audacity of Hope: Thoughts on Reclaiming the American Dream* (New York: Crown, 2006), p. 319.

21. See John J. Mearsheimer and Stephen M. Walt, *The Israel Lobby and US Foreign Policy* (London: Penguin, 2007), pp. 1–48.

22. See Raymond W. Copson, *The United States in Africa* (London and Cape Town: Zed and David Philip, 2007),

23. See, for example, Francis Kornegay, 'The AU and Africa's Three Diasporas', in John Akokpari, Angela Ndinga-Muvumba, and Tim Murithi (eds.), *The African Union and Its Institutions* (Johannesburg: Jacana, 2008), pp. 333–352.

24. See Honore Banda, 'Who Will Be Best for Africa?' *Africa Report* no. 10 (April–May 2008), p. 48.

25. The preceding quotes are from 'The World Rejoices', *New African*, December 2008, pp. 22–23.

26. See, for example, Ricky L. Jones, *What's Wrong with Obamamania? Black America, Black Leadership, and the Death of Political Imagination* (Albany: State University of New York Press, 2008); John Pilger, 'Don't Believe the Hype', *New Statesman*, 17 November 2008, p. 22.

27. Mendell, *Obama*, p. 12.

28. John K. Wilson, *Barack Obama: The Improbable Quest* (Boulder: Paradigm, 2008), p. 165.

29. Quoted in Wilson, introduction to *Barack Obama*, p. v.

30. Mendell, *Obama*, p. 315.

31. Obama, *The Audacity of Hope*, p. 281.

32. See Frantz Fanon, *The Wretched of the Earth* (New York: Grove, 1963).

33. Obama, *The Audacity of Hope*, p. 309.

34. Mendell, *Obama*, p. 7.

35. Ibid., p. 126.

36. Ibid., p. 176.

37. Ibid., p. 73.

38. Shelby Steele, *A Bound Man: Why We Are Excited About Obama and Why He Can't Win* (New York: Free Press, 2008), p. 18.

39. Mazrui, 'Barack Obama', p. 3.

40. Bertolt Brecht, *In the Jungle of Cities*, trans. Gerhard Nellhaus, in *Bertolt Brecht: Plays, Poetry, and Prose*, Collected Plays vol. 1, ed. John Willett and Ralph Manheim (London: Methuen, 1970).

41. I have relied for this summary on Mendell, *Obama*, pp. 121–139

42. Mendell, *Obama*, p. 311.

43. Ibid., pp. 303–312.

44. Quoted in ibid., p. 316.

45. Ibid., p. 317.
46. Ibid., p. 318.
47. Ibid., p. 74.
48. Quoted in Anthony Painter, *Barack Obama: The Movement for Change* (London: Arcadia, 2008), p. 9.
49. Crisina Corbin, 'As Obama Talks Religion, Questions Surround His Controversial Pastor', *Fox News*, 8 October 2007, http://www.foxnews.com.
50. For more details of Washington's legacy, see Manning Marable, 'Harold Washington's Chicago: Race, Class Conflict, and Political Change', in *Black Leadership: Four Great American Leaders and the Struggle for Civil Rights* (London: Penguin, 1999), pp. 127–146.
51. Quoted in Doris Kearns Goodwin, *Team of Rivals: The Political Genius of Abraham Lincoln* (London: Penguin, 2005), p. 198.
52. Quoted in Lexington, 'The War over Lincoln', *The Economist*, 14 February 2009, p. 58.
53. Trevor MacDonald, 'The Great Emancipator', *The Independent on Sunday*, special supplement, p. 13.
54. See Goodwin, *Team of Rivals*.
55. See, for example, Seymour Hersch, *The Dark Side of Camelot* (London: HarperCollins, 1997); Larry Devlin, *Chief of Station, Congo: Fighting the Cold War in a Hot Zone* (New York: PublicAffairs, 2007).
56. Painter, *Barack Obama*, p. 11.
57. Mendell, *Obama*, p. 2.
58. Quoted in Wilson, *Barack Obama*, p. 166.
59. Jones, *What's Wrong with Obamamania?* p. 19.
60. Quoted in ibid., p. 23.
61. Mazrui, 'Barack Obama,' pp. 4–5.
62. Steele, *A Bound Man*, p. 8.
63. Marable, 'The Four Legged Stool', p. 17.
64. Bob Herbert, 'A Recovery for Some', *New York Times*, 14 November 2009, p. A23.
65. Speech reproduced as 'Obama Answers His Critics,' in *New African*, no. 491 January 2010, p. 20.
66. See Ewen MacAskill and Saeed Shah, 'US Casualties in Afghanistan to Rise, Says Biden', *The Guardian*, 26 January 2009, p. 17; 'Saeed Shah, 'US Missiles Strike on Taliban Stronghold in Pakistan Tribal Area Kills 30', *The Guardian*, 17 February 2009, p. 23.
67. Lexington, 'One Year of the One', *The Economist* online, 29 October 2009, http://www.economist.com.
68. Jeffrey Gettleman and Eric Scmitt, 'American Raid in Somalia Kills Qaeda Militant', *New York Times*, 15 September 2009, pp. A1, A11.
69. This and the three successive paragraphs are summarized from Adekeye Adebajo, 'Obama's Nobel Ancestry', *Mail and Guardian*, 16–22 October 2009, p. 23.
70. See, for example, Michael Walzer, *Just and Unjust Wars: A Moral Argument With Historical Illustrations* 2nd ed., (New York: Basic Books, 1992).

71. The quotes in this paragraph are from Barack Obama's Nobel Peace Prize speech delivered in Oslo on 10 December 2009, http://nobelprize.org.

72. Cameron Duodu, 'So, this is the Obama We've got,' in *New African*, no. 491 January 2010, p. 26.

73. Quoted in Ali A. Mazrui, 'Dr. Shweitzer's Racism,' *Transition*, no. 53 1991, p. 101.

74. Quoted in ibid., p. 99.

75. Quoted in ibid., p. 101.

76. For an assessment of Obama's first year in office, see *The Economist*, 'Barack Obama's First Year: Reality Bites,' 16–22 January 2010, pp. 24–26.

77. Quoted in Maureen Dowd, 'Rapping Joe's Knuckles', *New York Times*, 16 September 2009, p. A31. The information in this paragraph is also gleaned from Dowd's insightful article.

78. The quotes are from Barack Obama's Nobel Peace Prize speech delivered in Oslo on 10 December 2009, http://nobelprize.org.

14. THE HEIRS OF GANDHI: HOW AFRICA AND ASIA CHANGED THE WORLD

1. This unpublished article was delivered as the Gandhi memorial lecture at the Phoenix settlement in Durban, South Africa, on 5 October 2008. Parts of it also build on Adekeye Adebajo, 'From Bandung to Durban: Whither the Afro-Asian Coalition?' in See Seng Tan and Amitav Acharya (eds.), *Bandung Revisited: The Legacy of the 1955 Asian-African Conference for International Order* (Singapore: National University of Singapore Press, 2008), pp. 105–131.

2. Quoted in Ali A. Mazrui, 'Africa and Other Civilizations: Conquest and Counter-Conquest', in John W. Harbeson and Donald Rothchild (eds.), *Africa in World Politics: The African State System in Flux*, 3rd ed. (Boulder: Westview, 2000), p. 127.

3. Salman Rushdie, *Step Across This Line: Collected Non-Fiction, 1992–2002* (London: Vintage, 2003), pp. 181–182.

4. See M.K. Gandhi, *An Autobiography, Or, the Story of My Experiments with the Truth* (London: Penguin, 2001); Judith M. Brown, *Gandhi:Prisoner of Hope* (New Haven and London: Yale University Press, 1989).

5. This is summarised from Margaret Chatterjee, 'Reviewing the Gandhian Heritage', in Judith M. Brown and Martin Prozesky (eds.), *Gandhi and South Africa: Principles and Politics* (Pietermaritzburg: University of Natal Press, 1996), pp. 95–110.

6. Brown and Prozesky, *Gandhi and South Africa*, p. 4.

7. Elleke Boehmer, *Nelson Mandela: A Very Short Introduction* (Oxford: Oxford University Press, 2008), p. 96.

8. I have extracted much of the information in the preceding two paragraphs from the excellent study by Bhikhu Parekh, *Gandhi: A Very Short Introduction* (Oxford: Oxford University Press, 1997).

9. Louis Fischer, *Gandhi: His Life and Message for the World* (New York: Mentor, 1954), p. 131.

10. Parekh, *Gandhi*, p. 8.

11. Quoted in Fischer, *Gandhi*, p. 131.

12. Ibid.

13. Ali A. Mazrui, 'Black Nationalism and Mahatma Gandhi', in Ali A. Mazrui, *The Politics of War and the Culture of Violence: North-South Essays* (Asmara: Africa World, 2008), p. 304.

14. Boehmer, *Nelson Mandela*, pp. 92–94.

15. Ibid., p. 101. For an interesting comparison of Gandhi and another Nobel peace laureate, Aung San Suu Kyi, see Penny Edwards, 'Gandhiji in Burma, and Burma in Gandhiji,' in Debjani Ganguly and John Docker (eds.), *Rethinking Gandhi and Nonviolent Rationality* (London and New York: Routledge, 2007), pp. 163–182.

16. Nelson Mandela, *Long Walk to Freedom* (New York: Little, Brown, 1994), p. 137.

17. Parekh, *Gandhi*, p. 121; Rushdie, *Step Across This Line*, pp. 183–184.

18. See James D. Hunt, 'Gandhi in South Africa', in John Hick and Lamont C. Humpel (eds.), *Gandhi's Significance for Today* (London: Macmillan, 1989), pp. 61–81; David Hardiman, *Gandhi in His Time and Ours* (Scottsville: University of Natal Press, 2003), pp. 277–284.

19. See Parekh, *Gandhi*.

20. Brown and Prozesky, *Gandhi and South Africa*, p. 26.

21. See, for example, Judith M. Brown, 'The Vision of Non-Violence and the Reality', in Brown and Prozesky, *Gandhi and South Africa*, pp. 111–128.

22. Quoted in Eric Hobsbawn, *The Age of Empire, 1875–1914* (London: Abacus, 1994, first published by Weidenfeld and Nicolson in 1987), p. 77.

23. Quoted in Amartya Sen, *The Argumentative Indian: Writings on Indian Culture, History, and Identity* (London: Penguin, 2005), p. 101.

24. Geoffrey Barraclough, *An Introduction to Contemporary History* (Middlesex: Penguin, 1964), p. 153.

25. See Tunde Zack-Williams, 'The UN Conference on Trade and Development,' in Adekeye Adebajo (ed.), *From Global Apartheid to Global Village: Africa and the United Nations* (Scottsville: University of Kwazulu-Natal Press, 2009), pp. 417–436.

26. Members include Indonesia, Malaysia, Singapore, Brunei, Vietnam, Burma, Thailand, Laos, and the Philippines.

27. See, for example, Frank-Jürgen Richter and Thang D. Nguyen, *The Malaysian Journey: Progress in Diversity* (Singapore: Times Editions, 2003).

28. See, for example, Joseph Stiglitz, *Globalization and Its Discontents* (London: Penguin, 2002), pp. 89–132.

29. Thabo Mbeki, prologue to Malegapuru William Makgoba (ed.), *African Renaissance* (Cape Town: Mafube and Tafelberg, 1999), p. xv.

30. Quoted in Geoffrey Barraclough, 'The Revolt Against the West', in Prasenjit Duara (ed.), *Decolonization: Perspectives from Now and Then* (London: Routledge, 2004), p. 118.

31. Quoted in Ali A. Mazrui, 'Africa and Asia', in *Africa's International Relations: The Diplomacy of Dependency and Change* (London: Heinemann, 1977), p. 121.

32. Barraclough, 'The Revolt Against the West', p. 118. See also Rupert Emerson, *From Empire to Nation: The Rise to Self-Assertion of Asian and African Peoples* (Boston: Beacon, 1960); Hedley Bull, 'The Revolt Against the West', in Hedley Bull and Adam Watson (eds.), *The Expansion of International Society* (Oxford: Clarendon, 1985), pp. 117–126; D.A. Low, 'The Asian Mirror to Tropical Africa's Independence', in Prosser Gifford and Wm. Roger Louis (eds.), *The Transfer of Power in Africa: Decolonization, 1940–1960* (New Haven: Yale University Press, 1982), pp. 1–29.

33. Quoted in Mazrui, 'Africa and Other Civilizations', p. 126.

34. Ibid., p. 127.

35. See ibid., p. 130.

36. Quoted in Brian Urquhart, *Ralph Bunche: An American Odyssey* (New York: Norton, 1993), p. 450.

37. Quoted in Kader Asmal, 'Albert Luthuli: Introduction', in Kader Asmal, David Chidester, and Wilmot James (eds.), *South Africa's Nobel Laureates: Peace, Literature, and Science* (Johannesburg: Jonathan Ball, 2004), p. 9.

38. Desmond Tutu, 'The Spirit of Togetherness', in Anand Sharma (ed.), *Gandhian Way: Peace, Non-Violence, and Empowerment* (New Delhi: Academic Foundation, 2007), pp. 43–44.

39. Clayborne Carson (ed.), *The Autobiography of Martin Luther King Jr.* (London: Abacus, 2000), p. 121. See also Thomas Kilgore Jr., 'The Influence of Gandhi on Martin Luther King, Jr.', in Hick and Humpel, *Gandhi's Significance for Today*, pp. 236–243.

40. Quoted in Mazrui, 'Black Nationalism and Mahatma Gandhi', p. 304.

41. Barack Obama's Nobel Peace Prize speech delivered in Oslo on 10 December 2009, http://nobelprize.org.

42. Anwar el-Sadat, *In Search of Identity* (London: Collins, 1978), pp. 12–13.

43. Kenneth Kaunda, 'Re-launching the Satyagraha Movement', in Sharma, *Gandhian Way*, p. 51.

44. See Kweku Ampiah, *The Political and Moral Imperatives of the Bandung Conference of 1955* (London: Global Oriental, 2007); Tan and Acharya, *Bandung Revisited*.

45. Quoted in Hari Sharan Chhabra, *Nehru and Resurgent Africa* (New Delhi: Africa Publications, 1989), p. 121. For a more recent perspective, see Chris Landsberg, *Beyond the 'Cargo Cult': Learning from India's Principle-Based Foreign Policy*, Research Report no. 65 (Johannesburg: Centre for Policy Studies, October 1998), pp. 35–51.

46. Wm. Roger Louis and Roger Owen, 'Introduction,' in Wm. Roger Louis and Roger Owen (eds.) *Suez 1956: The Crisis and its Consequences* (Oxford, New York and Cape Town: Oxford University Press, 1989), p. 6.

47. Quoted in Chhabra, *Nehru and Resurgent Africa*, p. 123.

48. See Michael Brecher, *India and World Politics: Krishna Menon's View of the World* (New York: Praeger, 1968).

49. Boehmer, *Nelson Mandela*, pp. 93–94.

50. Quoted in Chhabra, *Nehru and Resurgent Africa*, pp. 151–152.

51. Mazrui, 'Africa and Asia', pp. 117–121.

52. See, for example, Saïd K. Aburish, *Nasser: The Last Arab*, (London: Gerald Duckworth & Co., 2005); Anne Alexander, *Nasser: His Life and Times* (Cairo: The American University in Cairo Press, 2005).

53. Quoted in Ali Mazrui, 'Africa and Egypt's Four Circles', in *On Heroes and Uhuru-Worship: Essays on Independent Africa* (London: Longman, 1967), p. 96.

54. Quoted in Stanley Meisler, *United Nations: The First Fifty Years* (New York: The Atlantic Monthly Press, 1995), p. 96.

55. See ibid., p. 99.

56. See, for example, JD Hargreaves, *Decolonization in Africa* (London: Longman, 1988), pp. 156–158; Keith Kyle, *Suez: Britain's End of Empire in the Middle East*, 2nd ed. (London: Tauris, 2003); Wm. Roger Louis, *Ends of British Imperialism: The Scramble for Empire, Suez, and Decolonization* (London: Tauris, 2006).

57. Aburish, *Nasser*, p. 4.

58. Quoted in Mazrui, 'Black Nationalism and Mahatma Gandhi', p. 304.

59. See Hargreaves, *Decolonization in Africa*, pp. 114–121; Ali A. Mazrui, 'Nkrumah: The Leninist Czar' in Mazrui, *On Heroes and Uhuru-Worship*, (London: Longman Group, 1967), pp. 113–134; Kwame Nkrumah, *Ghana: The Autobiography of Kwame Nkrumah* (London: Panaf, 1973).

60. See Ali A. Mazrui, *Towards a Pax Africana: A Study of Ideology and Ambition* (Chicago: University of Chicago Press, 1967), pp. 150–151.

61. Mazrui, 'Africa and Asia', p. 121.

62. Sally Morphet, 'Multilateralism and the Non-Aligned Movement: What Is the Global South Doing and Where Is It Going?' review essay, *Global Governance* 10 (2004), pp. 529–530.

63. See Edward W. Said, 'Orientalism Reconsidered', in *Reflections on Exile and Other Essays* (Cambridge: Harvard University Press, 2002), pp. 187–197.

64. See David M. Malone, 'India: Challenges in Agriculture', *The Hindu* online, 7 February 2009, http://epaper.thehindu.com.

65. See World Bank Group, *Patterns of Africa-Asia Trade and Investment: Potential of Ownership and Partnership* (Washington D.C.: October 2004).

66. See Francis A. Kornegay, Pax *AfroAsiatica? Revisiting Bandung amid a Changing World Order*, Occasional Paper no. 46 (Midrand, South Africa: Institute for Global Dialogue, October 2004).

67. See Kweku Ampiah, *The Dynamics of Japan's Relations with Africa: South Africa, Tanzania, and Nigeria* (London: Routledge, 1997).

68. See Scarlett Cornelissen, 'Japan-Africa Relations: Patterns and Prospects', in Ian Taylor and Paul Williams (ed.), *Africa in International Politics: External Involvement on the Continent* (London: Routledge, 2004), pp. 116–135.

69. This information is gleaned from Sanusha Naidu, 'India's Growing African Strategy', *Review of African Political Economy* 35(115) (March 2008), pp. 116–128; Adam Habib, 'Western Hegemony, Asian Ascendancy, and the New Scramble for Africa', in Kweku Ampiah and Sanusha Naidu (eds.), *Crouching Tiger, Hidden Dragon? Africa and China* (Scottsville: University of Kwazulu-Natal Press, 2008), pp. 259–277.

70. See Ali Alatas, 'Towards a New Strategic Partnership Between Asia and Africa', keynote address at the Institute of Defence and Strategic Studies conference 'Bandung Revisited: A Critical Appraisal of a Conference's Legacy', Singapore, 15 April 2005.

71. See, for example, Alistair Horne, *A Savage War of Peace: Algeria, 1954–1962* (New York: New York Review Books, 2006).

72. Nelson Mandela, *From Freedom to the Future: Tributes and Speeches* (Johannesburg: Jonathan Ball, 2003), p. 344.

INDEX

Abacha, General Sani, 147; and
Babangida, General Ibrahim, 147;
conflict with Mandela, Nelson,
149–51; death of, (1998) 125, 148,
151; EU sanctions against, 137;
hanging of Saro-Wiwa, Ken (1995),
109, 148–9, 205, 228; Provisional
Ruling Council (PRC), 148; regime
of, 109, 137, 141, 144, 148, 205; rise
to power, 147; return of looted
money, 125

Abubakar, General Abdulsalaam: and
Mbeki, Thabo, 151; invitation to
Mandela, Nelson, 151; regime of,
143, 151; temperament of, 151

Addis Ababa: AU and IGAD early
warning systems, 34; ECA headquarters, 55

Adebo, Simeon: former executive
director of UN Training and
Research Institute, 60

Adedeji, Adebayo: chair of South
Africa's peer review process, 101;
former executive secretary of
UNECA, 60, 123; Nigerian minister
of economic development and
reconstruction, 123

African Caribbean and Pacific Group
(ACP): negotiations of, 67

African National Congress (ANC),
119, 192, 224, 253, 308, 322; and

Mandela, Nelson, 57, 101, 150, 216,
230; and Mbeki, Thabo, 150, 158,
244–5, 320; and Obasanjo, General
Olusegun, 152; and Tutu, Desmond,
229; and Zuma, Jacob, 115–16;
Congress of the People (COPE),
255; corruption allegations, 246;
invited to participate in UN debates,
57; non-violent protests of, 315;
opposition to in Mozambique and
Zimbabwe, 112; Youth League, 224

African Peace Support Facility (APSF):
created by EU (2003), 36

African Peer Review Mechanism
(APRM), 113; established (2003),
27

African Standby Force (ASF): and
AUPSC, 33, 266; and EASBRIG, 47

African Union (AU), 6, 27, 110, 153,
159, 318; African Economic
Community Project (AEC), 262;
and Algeria, 50, 118; and Burundi,
36–7, 63, 153; and Comoros, 37;
and EASBRIG, 47; and ECOWAS,
39; and Egypt, 50, 118; and
Ethiopia, 48; and EU, 28, 33; and
Libya, 118, 280; and Mbeki, Thabo,
233, 235; and Nigeria, 118, 277; and
Nkrumah, Kwame, 233, 235; and
SADC, 43; and Pretoria, 211; and
Sudan, 51, 63, 136–7; and South

395

lent elections of, 181; French military presence, 178, 180; future French interests in, 186; pro-democracy protests, 180; provision of French oil and uranium, 179, 181

Gambari, Ibrahim: Nigerian foreign minister, 133; Nigerian permanent representative to UN, 90; UN Special Representative to Darfur, 60, 136; Undersecretary-General for Political Affairs, 60–1, 91

Gambia: and MCA funding, 174

Gandhi, Mahatma, 7, 323, 328, 331; and Mandela, Nelson, 316, 332; and Mbeki, Thabo, 319–20; and Nehru, Jawaharal, 324; and Nkrumah, Kwame, 326; and South Africa, 314; Amristar Massacre (1919), 315; assassination of (1948), 316–17; background of, 313–14, 322; contributions of, 5, 314: criticisms of, 316; Indian independence movement, 17, 318, 320; religious views of, 315–16

General Act of Berlin (1885), 16

Germany: Cold War division of, ix, Diet, 12; xvi; fall of Berlin Wall (1989), xxix, 32, 52; Holocaust reparations, 121; Nazism, 280; unification of, ix, x, 2, 274

Ghana, 26, 117, 290, 295; and China, 165; and Nkrumah, Kwame, 23, 37, 165; and Nigeria, 140; and TSCTI, 174; and US European Command, 173; Convention People's Party (CPP), 234, 239–40, 251–2; economy of, 251; independence of (1957), 7, 257; Industrial Relations Act (1958), 251; National Libera-tion Movement (NLM), 239–40

Gharekhan, Chinmaya: appointed as personal representative by Boutros-Ghali, Boutros, 84

Group of 20 (G20): and Motlanthe, Kgalema, 115; and Obama, Barack, 72; London Meeting (2009), 72, 115; members of, 194

Group of 20+ (G20+); Doha negotiation efforts of member nations, 67

Group of 4 (G4): relationship with African foreign ministers, 58

Group of 7 (G7): correspondence from Boutros-Ghali, Boutros, 89; expansion into G8, 89

Group of 77 (G77), 266; and UN General Assembly, 88; established (1964), 88; led by South Africa, 111, 250; members of, 88, 164, 186, 194

Group of 8 (G8), 110; and Mbeki, Thabo, 254; Obama, Barack, 290; donations of member nations, 64; expansion to G20, 72; formerly G7, 89; Gleneagles Accord (2005), 68

Guinea, 26; provision of French bauxite, 179

Guinea-Bissau: and ECOWAS, 37; and France, 39; arrears to OAU, 50; failures of ECOMOG, 38; UN role in, 55

Hammarskjöld, Dag: manner of, 79; posthumous Nobel Peace Prize (1961), 83; UN Secretary-General, 74, 78, 84

Hitler, Adolf, 268, 309; appeasement of, 93; blitzkrieg, 176; defeat of, xi, 4; theories of, 11

HIV/AIDS, xviii, 289, 293; and South Africa, 246–7; policies, 153, 188, 246; treatment of, 58, 68, 83, 136, 188, 228

Holbrooke, Richard: and Annan, Kofi, 92–3, 96; former USA ambassador to UN, 91–2, 270

Houphouet-Boigny, Félix: significance of death, 181

144, 148, 195, 218–19; Black
Economic Empowerment (BEE),
193; chair of AU Committee on
Post-Conflict Reconstruction in
Sudan, 207; Communist Party of
(CPSA/SACP), 224, 245, 315;
Congress of South African Trade
Union (COSATU), 253; denial of
visa to Dalai Lama (2009), 115;
Department of International
Relations and Cooperation, 117;
Department of Trade and Industry,
117, 120; Development Bank of
Southern Africa, 117; economic
investments of, 113–14, 156–7,
195–6, 202–3; economic conflict
with Namibia and Zimbabwe,
120–1; economy of, 61, 102, 106–7,
109, 114, 145, 195; end of apartheid
(1994), xii, xiv, xxx–xxxi, 24, 57,
108, 117–18, 225, 253, 266, 284;
Federated Chamber of Industries,
104, 221; financial contributions to
AMIB, 46; foreign policy of, 102,
105–7, 114, 145, 147, 150; Foreign
Trade Organisation, 104, 221;
goldmines of, 18; Highlands Water
Project Incident, 41, 103; Growth,
Employment and Redistribution
Programme (GEAR), 253; immigration to, 108; Industrial Development
Corporation (IDC), 106, 117, 203;
influence over SACU, 106; joined
SADC (1994), 109; interest in
permanent seat on AUPSC, 161;
member of G20, 194; member of
G77, 194, 250; member of NAM,
194; member of UN Security
Council (2007–8), 35, 61, 111, 250;
member of WTO, 194; military of,
61, 101; Mobile Telephone
Networks (MTN), 119, 156, 196,
204; nuclear capabilities, 145;

Olympic Games bid (2004), 161;
peacekeeping efforts of, 109;
president of G77, 111; recognition
of Taiwan, 195; Reconstruction and
Development Programme (RDP),
253; Sharpeville Killings (1960),
105, 145, 308; suspended from UN
General Assembly (1974), 57; UN
Security Council embargo (1977),
57, 146; UN World Summit on
Sustainable Development, 53;
universities of, 118; xenophobia of,
111–13, 155–6, 160, 210, 255;
World Cup 2010, 192
South African Broadcasting Corporation (SABC), 118; allegations about
Obasanjo, General Olusegun, 156;
and Mbeki, Thabo, 246
South Africa-China Business Association (SACBA): establishment of,
195
South African Defence Force (SADF):
Cuito Cuanavale defeat, 107
South African Human Rights
Commission (SAHRC): condemnation of Operation Crackdown
(2000), 112
South West African People's Organisation (SWAPO), xii; guerrilla
campaign of, 107
Southern African Customs Union
(SACU): and EU, 120; conspiracy
theories regarding, 102; established
(1910), 106; external EU trade
agreements controversy, 120;
headquarters of, 120; members of,
106, 155, 195; restructuring of, 120;
trade agreement with China, 195
Southern African Defence and Security
Management (SADSEM); aims of,
43; and SADC, 43; members of, 43
Southern African Development
Community (SADC), 6, 27, 32, 63,